MW00897676

THE PRIDE OF MAGEE

Magee Trojan Football: 1926-2000

"Well, as far as I'm concerned, Magee is the most powerful football team that I have ever seen. I was impressed by their quietness when they arrived and after the game. Old Chinese proverb say, 'he who walks softly carries a big stick'. I wonder what they carried? In fact, I was happy to see them miss a few extra point conversions. It proved they were human".

Lawrence County Press; October 21, 1965

"...they grow boys mean and tough in Simpson County."

The Clinton News; September, 1979

A NOTE TO ALL WHO PLAYED

Being a former high school player at Saint Aloysius in the mid-1980s, I understand that the following account will be filled with inaccuracies. Even when the right players are identified for their accomplishments (depending on which source you trust), names will be omitted or misspelled. And most who fought to give the glory to the one with the newspaper ink aren't mentioned at all.

All efforts were undertaken to get it right. Player rosters are perhaps the most frustrating part of the project. Even yearbooks fail to mention every person who donned the jersey, put in the practices, and more. If you missed a team picture, for example, it could be that your name was lost forever. Efforts were high to garner old programs so that those mentioned would get their rightful acknowledgement. But even that, while nearly impossible over this many years, may be missing certain individuals.

This is especially true of the early years of Magee football. It was common that many young men enrolled in a football program would be late additions or leave school at a moment's notice. A great number of students did not graduate. Once a job opportunity arose, many would drop out of school to begin working and building their life and families.

In the case of managers, that part is highly incomplete. It was rare that those who gave their time and talents to help the squad gained any notoriety. I found as many as I could and have included since it would inappropriate to leave them out. The same could be said, though in a lesser degree, to the assistant coaches, cheerleaders and mascots.

As for statistics, well ... that is for entertainment purposes only. If you compared reports from two sources, it's doubtful that you would find the same numbers. Add in another source such as The Clarion-Ledger (Jackson, MS) or The Hattiesburg American and it gets even more confusing.

Please understand that the best efforts were invested to get it as accurate as possible. Regardless, this is for you. It's my sincere hope that it brings back fond memories, helps to create more conversation and comradery among you and your brothers about your time together, and brings back the tradition of Magee Football. Anyone is welcome to add to this project and continue it for future years. As an aside, I know there will by typos in this book. It's a one-man project, so my apologies if it does not come out to be as perfect as I hope!

ACKNOWLEDGEMENTS

Perhaps the most amazing thing I discovered during this year-long project is the unmatched love that so many have for this football program. Everyone with whom I spoke was more than anxious to assist in providing as much information as they had to ensure that the Magee High School football story was saved and told. It is almost a disservice to mention any one person, but there are exceptions.

Lee West was the very first person I called when I had gotten sufficiently far enough to know that I was going to be able to reach the finish line. It was because of him that I was able to gain valuable insight and speak with others to fill in many of the pieces. A great deal of gratitude is owed to Lee by not only me, but also those who enjoy what you read herein.

Joyce Barnes and her family welcomed me into their home to go over their collection. And, that proved more invaluable than most of the things I found in other sources. They also put me in contact with others who pitched in to provide what they had. My most sincere thanks go to them.

Pete Russell and Otto Walker were gracious enough to spend time to fill in as much of the missing information for the 1930s and 1940s as they could. They are among the previous few who now stand as a representation of their now-deceased teammates who gave their all for the program.

The staff of the Mississippi Department of Archives and History played a vital role in this venture. It's a vast undertaking to try and find every mention of Magee football in other newspapers so that a complete picture can develop. I've been blessed to get to know all of those fine folks and have gained new friends along the way. To name just one person is not fair. They know who they are!

Finally, this book would be impossible were it not for the fine people at The Magee Courier and The Simpson County News. Had it not been for their commitment to reporting on Burrhead and Trojan football, almost every bit of the history would not exist aside from the memories of those who played. Starting in it's infancy, those institutions recorded the activities of your team for almost every contest. There are few newspapers who can claim that honor, and it's important that any who love the Trojans share with them your deepest gratitude.

For all of the young men who left high school halls to fight, and sometimes die, on foreign soil for a cause that they believed in, your service is still appreciated.

To all who put on the Magee jersey to represent your school in every year, share your love with those who came before and those who will come afterwards. In the end, you are all part of one amazing "fraternity".

And, as always, my thanks to Lee, Haley and Ty.

1926-1929

1926 (0-4)

School opened on September 6th under Professor Samuels, but very little was noted about the fact that the Magee High Tigers now had their very first organized school football team. An article covering the 75th annual contest between Mendenhall and Magee noted the following:

"Uniforms were purchased without numbers on the jerseys and the players had to purchase their own shoes (high top brogans) and carry them to the shoe shop to have leather cleats made and installed. Magee was a different school district in those days. The field was located across from what was the Thames Boarding House, later the old Magee Hospital. There was no grass, no lights, no seating, no public address system. The players marked the field with lime prior to each game".

GAME 1: MAGEE (0-0) @ RANKIN COUNTY AHS (0-0)
MAGEE 0 RANKIN COUNTY AHS 6
October 1, 1926

The Aggies under Professor Luther Allen had started their football program the year before as their opponent was entering their inaugural season. Graduation had hurt AHS *"but the new men who are coming in will more than over-balance the loss sustained at that time"*. Rankin County AHS was presumably in the Johns community; a neighbor of Brandon in Rankin County.

Magee gave a good first-appearance in the game called *"clean (and) sportsmanlike"*. Game details were not noted, but The Rankin County News said that *"Much interest was manifested in this game by the large crowd (and) boosters for both teams. Both teams are to be congratulated for their sportsmanship. Each played his part exceedingly well, considering the fact that most of the boys were inexperienced players with only two weeks' practice"*.

GAME 2: MAGEE (0-1) @/vs FOREST (0-0)
MAGEE 0 FOREST 12
October 8, 1926

The Clarion-Ledger provided the few details found. They reported on October 10th that *"The heavy team from Forest defeated the fast Magee Tigers in a hard-fought game. Featuring for Magee was McNair at quarterback, (Joe) Field at full(back) and Watkins at right tackle"*.

GAME 3: MAGEE (0-2) @ COLLINS (UNREPORTED)
MAGEE 0 COLLINS 12
October 15, 1926

This game was called *"the best battle that has ever been waged on the local field"*. Collins, at least in their 4th season of football, took their opening drive to paydirt thanks to a McIntosh run. In the 2nd quarter, Terrell escaped for an 82-yard score behind the *"perfect interference of J. Myatt"*. McIntosh was a substantial piece of the Collins victory, with interceptions to go along with his scoring run.

GAME 4: MAGEE (0-3) @/vs WAYNESBORO (UNREPORTED)
LOSS – SCORE UNREPORTED
October 22, 1926 (estimated)

Before the contest, the paper said, *"The Magee football team expected (a) matchup with the Waynesboro team on the home ground Friday. Our boys have been beaten two or three times, but they are game and we are proud of them as this is their first year. Magee has never had a bona-fide football team and in every game so far they have been far out-matched in size; though not in 'pep"*. No report of the activity is found aside from notations printed before memories were unrecorded and lost. Another indication found in another publication notes a possible loss.

1927 (2-2)

Pre-season information on the Tigers was not found. For the first time, a coach (reportedly with the last name Carr) was in charge of the team.

GAME 1: MAGEE (0-0) vs MORTON (UNREPORTED)
MAGEE 55 MORTON 6
September 16, 1927

Morton was coached by a *"popular Magee boy"* named Claude Mangum. The Clarion-Ledger pointed to *"local players who distinguished themselves"* as Puckett, Magee, Walters and Stroud. As a historical side note, another source put the Magee win at 45-7.

Wylie Kees, ex-player in this era, noted in 1978 that *"Clifton (Clip) Myers was reportedly the first man to score a touchdown for Magee. One source said he heard Myers talk about the event which occurred on a football field which ran in just the opposite direction from the present (1978) Trojan field"*. If accurate, then Clip scored that first tally in the opener against Morton; thus marking his as the first Magee football player to cross the goal in what would be a successful future for the program.

GAME 2: MAGEE (1-0) vs D'LO (UNREPORTED)
MAGEE 0 D'LO 50
October 13, 1927

In an October 6th portion of The Simpson County News, Magee was noted as facing D'Lo at The Simpson County Fair at 3:30pm. For historical purposes, it's possible that the games could have been played in the interim after the Morton win. One report had D'Lo embarrassing the Tigers 50-0.

GAME 3: MAGEE (1-1) @ RANKIN COUNTY AHS (UNREPORTED)
MAGEE LOSS
Unknown, 1927

The Rankin County News reported that Aggies Coach Kersh was *"fast rounding his football team into shape"* before the season started. They had 17 players with some holding valuable playing experience. We know that they beat Magee on their way to a 2-4 season thanks to a December 8th Rankin County News article. Their other victory had been the Morton team that Magee had destroyed.

GAME 4: MAGEE (1-2) @/vs MOUNT OLIVE (UNREPORTED)
MAGEE 9 MOUNT OLIVE 0
Unknown, 1927

According to one source, Magee also faced Mount Olive on the season; taking a 9-0 victory. No reporting was found of the details.

1928 (2-3-1)

Reporting on Coach R.T. Walker's two-year old squad now found more newspaper ink. However, games noted here may be incomplete. The ones below are the only games found. There are other games that were alluded to have occurred in this season, and while possible, it may have been practice scrimmages. For historical purposes, they are noted as a footnote at the end of the season.

GAME 1: MAGEE (0-0) @ CRYSTAL SPRINGS (UNREPORTED)
MAGEE 7 CRYSTAL SPRINGS 18
September 28, 1928

Crystal Springs Consolidated School was led by Professor McCormick and was optimistic about his chances on the gridiron. It was reported that he was *"working up an ambitious squad and prospects for a successful season look good"*. Unfortunately, we know only that Crystal Springs took the contest by a final of 18-7.

GAME 2: MAGEE (0-1) vs D'LO (2-0)
MAGEE 0 D'LO 31
October 12, 1928

Once again the Magee team was a Friday feature at The Simpson County Fair. While D'Lo football today is not thought of as being a particularly prominent opponent, the teams of the early century in that town were powerful. They showed it on this day in front of a reported 1,000 fans. Captain Pete Dennis was the star for D'Lo after a catch and long run for a touchdown followed by another later. Leslie O'Steen pointed a pair of scores and Cassibry notched another in the drumming of the local eleven. A later article said afterwards that *"so far no team has even scored on the D'Lo team"*. They had shut out Rankin 20-0 and also Canton 13-0.

GAME 3: MAGEE (0-2) @ RANKIN COUNTY A.H.S. (1-2-1)
MAGEE 6 RANKIN COUNTY A.H.S. 13
October 26, 1928

Magee's next opponent, barring any missing reports, would be the Rankin Aggies to be played in Johns. As a side note for future reference, the team name would later be changed to Johns High. If the game took place, it would have been with a common opponent as D'Lo had beaten RCAHS 20-0 before September 21st.

The Brandon newspapers said that *"Coach Kersh's Tigers bared their fangs with blood in their eyes and gnashed the Magee eleven to a 13-6 score"*. D. Lowery had the opening tally via an 8-yard run *"through the Magee line"* while Kersh ran in from the 7 shortly afterwards. Captain Simms added the final extra point. Magee scored in the final quarter on a QB end-run.

GAME 4: MAGEE (0-3) vs PRENTISS (UNREPORTED)
MAGEE 0 PRENTISS 0
November 2, 1928

Coach John Sproles was getting *"his material into tip-top shape"* for the season. We know that they probably had at least a pair of games beforehand with Meadville and Lumberton, but no report of their record is known. As for the scoreless affair, the paper said that it was *"hard fought all the way"*. They added that Magee got as far as the Prentiss 5-yard line after recovering a Bozeman fumble but could not score. Each team completed two passes and had two intercepted. Prentiss counted eight first downs while Magee had only six. *"The game was clean and fast all the way through and honors were pretty evenly divided"*.

GAME 5: MAGEE (0-3-1) @ COLLINS (UNREPORTED)
MAGEE 24 COLLINS 12
November 1928

Though the date of the report was November 20th, the game must have occurred much earlier. Regardless, Collins was first to the scoreboard in the road tilt when a fumble put them at the 20 and resulted in a J. Stubbs touchdown pass to G. Stubbs. After receiving the kick, Magee drove to answer behind the running of Luper Cole and the 6-yard Bobby Thames touchdown escape. Magee notched two more touchdowns before halftime. Thames and C.J. Kees connected for the first from the 30-yard line while Thames provided the next. In the 3rd, J. Stubbs put Collins back in points but Magee had one more left in them. Robert Magee *"charged the line on continuous line bucks for twenty yards and, with :05 left to play, (Wiley) Kees slipped over the right tackle for the tally"*.

The Clarion-Ledger said that *"Tullos, star tackle for Magee, played his usual splendid game; tackling on both sides of the line. C. Kees, diminutive end, attended to all plays in his direction while Thames, Cole and Magee dealt the Collins line plenty of misery"*.

GAME 6: MAGEE (1-3-1) vs SUMRALL (UNREPORTED)
MAGEE 24 SUMRALL 0
November 1928

A report from November 21st puts Magee (Independent) pitted against Sumrall in a home contest. If accurate, it was a great way to finish the season. The Clarion-Ledger said that *"it was evident from the beginning ... that the teams were unevenly matched. So, after scoring three touchdowns in the first quarter, the second string men were put in"*. Sumrall was held to just a pair of first downs while Magee notched fourteen. *"The entire Magee team, both first and second string men, played stellar ball (being better on defense than on offense). (Luper) Cole and R.T. Walker did the scoring with two touchdowns each to their credit"*.

In early December, a banquet was given for the team at Harrison's Café. Professor Arrington praised the team, saying that their "*success in football should inspire them to greater efforts throughout the year*". Thames, Captain of the team, presented Coach Walker with "*a handsome gift as manifestation of their appreciation of his services throughout the season*". Robert May Tullos was rewarded as MVP while Austin Jones was named an Alternate Captain.

Another source on Simpson County football history mentions other games (12-0 victory) against Prentiss, a 7-0 win over Collins, and a loss to Simpson County AHS. No other validation is found.

1929 (8-3)

It appears that there may have been "*about 25 or 30 boys on the Squad*" though most never saw newspaper ink. Notations throughout the season put the team anywhere between a 148-pound average to a 180-pound average. A Vicksburg Evening Post snippet from October said that the Magee "*team boasts of no stars and is well-balanced from end to end... The backfield moves with clock-like precision and is capable of passing as well as running*".

This is the first time that Magee would be called the "Burrheads" instead of Tigers. The article noted above on the history of Magee football said that "*with the heat from the basement they used as a storage and field house, the players got so hot they went to the barber shop and had their hair cut off. When they returned to practice the next day, the coach (not happy with their decision) referred to them as 'burrheads'. The name stuck*".

GAME 1: MAGEE (0-0) vs PUCKETT (0-0)
MAGEE 7 PUCKETT 0
September 6, 1929

The lid-lifter of the 1929 season was noted as "*an interesting game*" against Puckett. Only a notation from The Simpson County News on September 12th lets us know that the winning touchdown came from "*efficient quarterback*" Bobby Thames. "*Magee feels proud of her ball squad this year and has one of the best ever in this school. They have many more hard teams to face; namely Crystal Springs and Central High (Jackson)*". The date of the contest is a guess since the report made the paper on September 12th. Additionally, another report put the score to be 6-0.

GAME 2: MAGEE (1-0) vs MENDENHALL A.H.S. (UNREPORTED)
MAGEE 24 MENDENHALL 0
September 13, 1929

The Mendenhall team reportedly hadn't "*had as much practice as Magee boys; however, they played good ball*" in this matchup. The touchdowns in the tilt came from Thames, C.J. Kees, Earl Walters and "Ferd" Puckett. The Clarion-Ledger on the 20th erroneously reported the final to be 18-0.

GAME 3: MAGEE (2-0) @ JACKSON CENTRAL HIGH (0-0)
MAGEE 0 JACKSON CENTRAL 24
September 20, 1929

The orange and black Tigers from the capital city had been playing organized football for quite some time. Coach Frank Broyles' "*courageous eleven*" had just finished intensive practices and were ready to finally get the season started. Their team numbered not only transfer players from past championship teams, but also an "*amateur bantamweight boxer*". Meanwhile, Magee's relatively new squad would count only 18 players and a manager making the trip to Central's practice field. But, "*about 20 cars of rooters (were) expected to accompany the team*".

In a "*ragged and somewhat disorganized brand of football*", Magee threatened to draw first blood after an interception. But forced to punt, Central's Davis cashed in with a touchdown and 6-0 lead. Marvin Thompson added the next before halftime to increase the advantage to 12-0. They added more to the board in the 3rd quarter on a Ferguson run. Now in the 4th quarter with "*the visitors ... hurling about promiscuously in a desperate attempt to score*", Emmett Simpson picked off a Magee throw. He took the errant ball 37 yards to the end zone for what would be the final points.

The Clarion-Ledger said that "*C.J. Kees at right end was a little stick of dynamite, while Captain Tullos was a consistent tackler besides getting off good kicks behind a leaking line*".

GAME 4: MAGEE (2-1) vs PRENTISS (0-1)
MAGEE 19 PRENTISS 0
September 27, 1929

Coach John Sproles was "*driving his men hard for the rather strenuous schedule*" before the season. They had opened the campaign with a loss to Crystal Springs but it had "*not dampened the spirits of the local boys*" before October rolled around. The matchup between the two schools in 1928 had produced a scoreless tie, but when this contest was over, the paper said that "*The Magee Burrheads paraded over the Prentiss Hi team in a very decisive* manner" to give their opponent at least two losses on the early season.

Behind the running of Thames and his interception, Cole turned the potent plays into the game's first touchdown; that a 10-yard run. Cole also provided the second tally on a 15-yard reception. The next touchdown was the result of "*straight line plays*" by Walters, Puckett and Luper Cole. Walters added the only extra point of the affair. Magee racked up 14 first downs while holding Prentiss to just 4.

GAME 5: MAGEE (3-1) vs D'LO (UNREPORTED)
MAGEE 7 D'LO 0
October 4, 1929

The revenge game against D'Lo was at hand with Magee hoping to avenge the 31-0 shutout put on them in 1928. The Clarion-Ledger said that in the end, "*it was too much Burrheads for the strong D'Lo team. Magee was stronger on offense and pushed through the D'Lo line time and time again for twelve first downs; holding D'Lo to five*".

Magee notched the only score of the defensive battle in the first three minutes of play. A long kick return by Walters was followed by positive runs by Cole to put Thames into a position to cross the goal "*over the center*". Walters provided the extra point "*over left tackle with very little opposition*". D'Lo came close to tying with a drive to the Magee 3, but the defense held on four-straight runs. "*During the rest of the game, the ball see-sawed up and down the field with Magee having the advantage in every department except passing and twice threatening the D'Lo goal line*".

GAME 6: MAGEE (4-1) vs COLUMBIA (UNREPORTED)
MAGEE 14 COLUMBIA 6
October 11, 1929

After a home game against McComb, Columbia was scheduled to play Magnolia on October 11th. However, a December 12th article from The Simpson County News noted that the Wildcats faced Magee instead. This is in question as the report of the Saint Aloysius game a few weeks later had Magee's record as 5-1 instead of 6-1. It's unlikely that they played each other after the last game of the season, and with a two-week portion of the Magee schedule missing, it's probable that it did occur and within that two-week frame. It is counted as such here.

GAME 7: MAGEE (5-1) @ MORTON (UNREPORTED)
MAGEE 19 MORTON 12
October 25, 1929

It was apparent that this would not be the same Morton squad that Magee whipped 55-6 back in 1927. They had recently turned heads with wins over "*strong*" Newton High and Scott County teams. For the Burrheads, injuries would keep some starters out. "*In Morton, Magee met the fastest set of backs it has encountered this season. Without the aid of Kees, lightning end, and Puckett, plunging fullback, Magee went into the game with a dogged determination...*"

Magee was first on the board in the 2nd quarter of the conference fight when Thames found Puckett from the 30 and Cole drop-kicked the point-after. Then after blocking a Morton punt, Cole found daylight again to make it 13-0. The home team managed to cut into the lead just before halftime when Lindsey crossed the goal. That put intermission 13-6. As play resumed, it took Morton just 3:00 to notch their last points on a Gaddis dash. They threatened to take the lead with a pair of drives to just inches of the goal but Magee's defense stood tall. Now with just :10 on the clock, Thames went through the middle from the 8-yard line for the game-winner.

The Clarion-Ledger said that *"The entire Magee line held extremely well in critical moments, with Jones, Taylor and Tullos bearing the brunt of the defense. The backfield worked with machine-like precision with occasional flashes by Walters and Cole over tackles and Thames over center. Smith, a new man at full(back), performed well"*.

GAME 8: MAGEE (6-1) @ SAINT ALOYSIUS (1-1-1)
MAGEE 6 SAINT ALOYSIUS 0
October 30, 1929

The Flashes from Vicksburg were led by ex-player Jack Roberts and expectations were good for the season. With some returning veteran players, The Vicksburg Evening Post thought them *"one of the best teams in the history of the school"*. Saint Al had been playing organized football since at least 1912, and perhaps a year or two earlier, and had posted a 5-1-1 record in 1927. For this game, however, they would be missing at least three starters.

The paper reported that *"the gridiron battle was waged in a field ankle-deep in mud"*. Not only had it rained before the contest, it rained during the contest. *"Once or twice players were heavily tackled and had their faces buried in the mud"*. After numerous goal line stands by both teams, it appeared that the tilt would end in a scoreless tie. But with :40 remaining, a Wright punt was blocked by Magee at midfield. After a number of runs and passes, Cole swam over for the last-second game-winner. The extra point was understandably unsuccessful.

"In the line for Magee there was Captain Tullos at tackle and Jones at center that prevented gains, and Smith and Allen at the wing positions frustrated any attempts at end runs. Cole was outstanding in the backfield, but no less creditable was the work of Puckett and Walters, who opened holes consistently. Thames at quarter ran his teammates like a veteran, often breaking over tackle or center for considerable gains". Magee dominated 11-1 in first downs.

GAME 9: MAGEE (7-1) vs LUMBERTON (UNREPORTED)
MAGEE 38 LUMBERTON 0
November 8, 1929

The 7-1 Magee team now faced a Lumberton team in a game that was *"replete with thrills and long runs"*. It was the defense providing the first couple of touchdowns for Magee. A blocked kick led to Cole's 25-yard scamper while a blocked punt led to Walters *"carrying the ball over"*. Still in the opening frame, Walters picked off a pass and raced 60 yards to paydirt *"behind perfect interference"*. Now in the 2nd quarter, Cole added to the board with a 55-yard pick-six.

In the second half, *"Old King"* Cole took the kickoff and dashed 60 yards to the end zone. Tullos began carrying and throwing the pigskin; his last to Allen to set up a Smith scoring run. Lumberton threatened afterwards when Lenoir broke away for an 80-yard pickup only to have the Magee defense hold. *"The Burrheads showed greater offense in this game than in any other, with the entire line functioning well. Tullos, Thames and Puckett furnished the interference that made possible the long runs. Every Magee Hi squad member had an opportunity to see action in this game"*.

While Lumberton's record wasn't reported, they had peeled off two-straight wins earlier in the season; the last over Sumrall.

GAME 10: MAGEE (8-1) @ CLINTON (1-2-2)
MAGEE 6 CLINTON 7
November 16, 1929

Clinton's only win came in mid-October against Canton 13-0, but they had played tough D'Lo to a scoreless draw. Originally, this contest was scheduled for November 22nd, but obviously moved up on the calendar. With such a record against Magee's 8-1 mark, it was no wonder the paper said afterwards that *"the fighting Clinton High School football team upset the dope"* with a win.

Robert Johnson provided both the touchdown *"off tackle"* and the point-after thanks to *"neat interference"*. Cole notched the Magee score *"breaking away around end for 50 yards and a touchdown after the entire Clinton team had failed to hurl the fleeting back earthward. He was ably assisted by Tullos; whose defensive work was exceptional"*. The crucial point-after failed and gave Magee their second loss.

GAME 11: MAGEE (8-2) @ SIMPSON COUNTY AHS (UNREPORTED)
MAGEE 0 SIMPSON COUNTY 13
November 21, 1929

On apparent short rest, Magee was trying to get back into their winning form while Simpson County (Mendenhall) AHS was coming off of a 37-0 win over Morton. However, AHS showed *"the effects (of the previous game) ... getting under way. They showed little offensive power during the first half"*. The game was scoreless through three quarters before Holland *"drove over left tackle for five yards and a marker"* to make it 6-0. Before the final whistle, Whitten *"broke loose on a wide end run to check off double figure yardage..."* for the last score. He also notched the conversion.

At season-end, Cole stood out as scoring leader with 11 touchdowns with one college coach saying of him *"That is the toughest, (most) scrapping sixteen-year old football player I have ever seen"*. Before the season, newspaper reports had Magee facing off against Crystal Springs and Hattiesburg. However, it appears that those games never materialized.

1930-1939

1937 Magee Burrheads

1930 (8-3)

Coach R.T. Walker and assistant "Mossy" Traylor faced "*the hard task of rounding out a squad of almost entirely new material this season*" as "*only three of last year's crew are back in uniform this time. Although the material is green, Coach Walker is not discouraged in the least and will put his men through their paces with daily practice in preparation for the opening game...*" The student body was ready and chanted: "*Ray (hooray) for Coach Walker; Ray for Coach Walker; the coach of them all; we can only say, 'ray for Coach Walker; Until the end of football*".

His squad consisted of 22 players, including "*scrubs*" who were being "*trained, too*". They would participate again in the Middle Mississippi Conference alongside at least Saint Aloysius, D'Lo, Vicksburg and Forest.

GAME 1: MAGEE (0-0) @ PRENTISS (0-0)
MAGEE 0 PRENTISS 7
September 19, 1930

The Prentiss Headlight said that the Bulldogs, under the leadership of Coach Frank Kelly, "*completely outclassed Magee in every department of play; far better than the score dictates. Magee never advanced into the Bulldogs territory farther than the 30-yard line. Magee played well but could not penetrate the stonewall line of the local eleven*". That was despite having one touchdown called back for penalty.

Scoring apparently came from Berry ("*fleet-footed halfback*") on a "*crisscross*" touchdown in the 2nd quarter while Prentiss' "*Two Tom*" Terrell "*bucked in for the extra point*". The Clarion-Ledger said that "*Prentiss was on the aggressive all the way. In the fourth quarter, Magee attempted to gain by passes but could not get through McDaniel and Livingston, who intercepted pass after pass*". The Simpson County News said that "*Prentiss' victory was just luck and not because of having such a big team*". The Clarion-Ledger added that "*the Simpson County boys put up a tough fight*".

GAME 2: MAGEE (0-1) vs GEORGETOWN (UNREPORTED)
MAGEE 47 GEORGETOWN 0
October 3, 1930

As was prominent in this day due to scarcity and inaccuracies of reporting, this game was questionable. However, that was not unusual. Originally, Magee was slated to play Simpson County AHS. But since it's noted that they played later in the season, it's possible that the contest was rescheduled and Georgetown took their place. An October 4th notation from The Clarion-Ledger shows Magee with an overwhelming 47-0 whitewash over Georgetown. That same score and opponent was mentioned in another source.

GAME 3: MAGEE (1-1) @ SAINT ALOYSIUS (1-0)
MAGEE 18 SAINT ALOYSIUS 0
October 10, 1930

The victory in 1929 against the Vicksburg purple and gold was a nail-biter until the last :40. Coach Walton Shannon was working his Flashes hard before the season to get into "*first class condition*" with a team consisting of "*green timber*". This marked the first home contest for Saint Aloysius; a Catholic team headed by the priests, or "Brothers", that would go on to enjoy numerous successful years in the 1930s. They would, however, be without star players Bill Jacquith and Marion DiRago for this tilt. Still, The Vicksburg Evening Post thought it would be "*one of the liveliest football battles of the season*" between "*two well-matched teams*".

Bobby Thames scored the first Magee touchdown in the opening frame and added another in the next behind a balanced Magee attack of running and passing by himself, Jones and Myers. The point-after again failed. An interception by Magee late in the half almost gave them another score, but the whistle sounded beforehand. Magee's dagger came in the 3rd quarter; this time on a run by Jones.

GAME 4: MAGEE (2-1) vs D'LO (UNREPORTED)
MAGEE 6 D'LO 0
October 16, 1930

Coach Morgan was putting his "*green group*" of D'Lo players through "*strenuous practice*" in preparation for the contest. They appeared strong, having just beaten Pelahatchie 47-0, but would not match that effort on this Thursday. Still, it was called "*one of the best exhibitions of high school football ever witnessed in this section*". The Clarion-Ledger went on to say that "*neither side (was) able to get away with anything spectacular*".

The only score of the tilt came in the 2nd quarter after Thames runs, Myers passes and Keyes receptions put the ball at the 12-yard line. Thames gained 10 of those afterwards and added the final 2 yards for the touchdown. D'Lo threatened with a Cassibry pass to Baker that got them to within three inches of the goal. But, Magee held to preserve the win. Magee pointed more first downs (13-7) in the end. The paper said that "*Magee's touchdown was a result of line perfection and the glory of the day rests with the linemen as they often opened up gaping holes for the backs and many times broke through to stop the opposition for losses*".

GAME 5: MAGEE (3-1) vs PELAHATCHIE (UNREPORTED)
MAGEE 40 PELAHATCHIE 0
October 24, 1930

It was apparent that Pelahatchie was not enjoying the most successful campaign thus far; though records of their overall performance aren't known. In this game, Magee "*ran rough shod*" over them with five touchdowns coming via the air. Kees was the recipient of three touchdown hauls with two coming from 30- and 50-yards away. Jones added a pair of interceptions that were "*converted ... into scores*". The 6th touchdown came from Allen from the 5-yard line after runs by him and Thames. Magee "*used practically two teams during the game*".

Pelahatchie's only threat came in the last frame when they got as far as the 1-yard line, "*but the Magee line tightened and the visitors were unable to advance the ball*". With the win, and victories over Saint Aloysius and D'Lo, Magee would now share regional honors with Forest.

GAME 6: MAGEE (4-1) @ FOREST (3-0)
MAGEE 0 FOREST 19
October 28, 1930

It appeared that the muddy game against Forest would be held only four days later. The Bearcats were strong this season; so much so that D'Lo had just cancelled a game against them. Expectedly, Forest was dominant in the contest and could have made it worse had not "*fumbles at critical moments*" (apparently inside the 10-yard line) not lost scoring opportunities. Anderson had the first touchdown from the 5 in the opening frame to make halftime a slim 6-0 affair. He added the next from the same yardage in the 3rd quarter while he notched his third in the last frame. Farmer provided the last point from the middle of the line on the conversion. The game ended on Ormond's interception of a Magee pass.

Magee went 2-8 in the air with a pair of picks. Forest was 1-3 passing and (according to The News Register) amassed 16 first downs while Magee "*failed to get the ball in their possession in Forest territory the entire game*". Another paper said that "*Straight line plays were used continuously by the (Forest) team which accounted for 16 first downs to (Magee's) 2. Farmer and Anderson made steady gains for the Bearcats*". The loss put Magee out of the of regional championship hopes, with Forest and Vicksburg High representing the conference for title honors.

GAME 7: MAGEE (4-2) @ COLLINS (UNREPORTED)
MAGEE 38 COLLINS 0
November 7, 1930

In a Clarion-Ledger article from October 5th, it was noted that Mississippi School for the Deaf would face Magee on November 7th at Magee. Unfortunately, no reporting of the affair was found in newspaper ink. It has been included here for historical purposes but conflicts with the September 26th report having Magee face Collins on this day. A later source shows a 38-0 victory over Collins and that has been included for the official history.

GAME 8: MAGEE (5-2) @/vs D'LO (UNREPORTED)
MAGEE 7 D'LO 0
November 14, 1930

The same September 26th article on the Magee football schedule pointed to a match with Coach Dykes' Seminary squad on November 14th. Unfortunately, nothing else was found as to whether the game was played. Another report had Magee once again going against D'Lo and winning 7-0. Since it was common for teams to add and drop contests at any time without reporting, I have included the D'Lo score for historical purposes.

GAME 9: MAGEE (6-2) @ JACKSON CENTRAL B-TEAM (UNREPORTED)
MAGEE 25 JACKSON CENTRAL B 0
November 18, 1930

After losing 24-0 to the varsity the season before, Magee now faced the Jackson JV squad. The paper called them the "*Baby Tigers*". The report of the game said "*Coach (Norval) Willis' protégés were completely outplayed throughout the contest; the locals making 12 first downs to Jackson's 3 and completing 7 passes for 75 yards compared with 3 passes for 35 yards for the visitors*". Magee put up one touchdown in the cold 2nd quarter and another two in the 3rd quarter. Finally, late in the last frame, "*the visitors succeeded in pushing over another marker*".

GAME 10: MAGEE (7-2) @ SIMPSON COUNTY AHS (UNREPORTED)
MAGEE 0 SIMPSON COUNTY AHS 7
November 20, 1930

Again, and not unusual for the day, Magee appeared to be playing two games in three days. This time it was against Coach Sollie Crain's Simpson County Aggies. What is in question is a November 22nd notation in The Clarion-Ledger that said it was Magee's "*first defeat of the season*". We know that it was the same Magee team from the lineup of players that were mentioned as the starters. Aside from that, it noted only that "*The play see-sawed over the field until the last quarter when the Aggies managed to push over a touchdown. The game was the hardest-fought of the season in the section and brought out a big crowd despite the inclement weather*".

GAME 11: MAGEE (7-3) @ JACKSON CENTRAL B-TEAM (UNREPORTED)
MAGEE 25 JACKSON CENTRAL B 0
November 20, 1930

Magee would finish the 1930 season with a rematch against the B-Team from Jackson Central. The visitors scored in the 2nd and 3rd quarters via "*a series of line plays mixed with a few end runs which completely swamped the Baby Orange. Those tactics counted one touchdown in the 2nd period and two in the 3rd section. Late in the final period, the visitors succeeded in pushing over another marker…*"

An article published at the end of season said "*The Burrheads played eleven games during the season, winning eight of them and losing three; amassing 225 points against 39 scored by the opposition*". Clinton was also on the schedule as of September 26th, but that game did not come to fruition. The final 8-3 mark posted here is reflective of the year-end report of the Burrhead record.

1931 (4-5)

New coach Heber Ladner, formerly of Millsaps, was now "*rapidly whipping his Magee High Burrheads into condition for the fall games*". The only other notation of what the team could expect for the season was that a new rule was in place for 1931 that Middle Mississippi state championships would not be held in football due to "*disruption of the school schedules and the cancellation of the many games to make way for championship tilts*".

GAME 1: MAGEE (0-0) @ MOUNT OLIVE (UNREPORTED)
MAGEE 12 MOUNT OLIVE 0
October 9, 1931

The opening contest was to be against Coach Sollie Crain's Crystal Springs Tigers. Fans were in high spirits for the 1931 campaign as "*only one of that great 1930 machine (was) not reporting*", causing the paper to say that "*the Tigers this year will doubtless have one of the most versatile teams in the circuit*". Unfortunately, probably due to a month-long delay in rebuilding of the new school building, Magee cancelled the mid-September game and Crystal Springs went on to beat replacement Mississippi Industrial Training School by a 19-0 final.

Magee, meanwhile, opened with Mount Olive on the road almost a month later. Though practicing for three weeks, The Simpson County News said that the *"game brought out many defects which Coach Ladner is trying to iron out this week before tackling the Hazlehurst Indians..."* No other reports of the action were found in newspaper ink.

GAME 2: MAGEE (1-0) @ HAZLEHURST (5-0)
MAGEE 0 HAZLEHURST 18
October 16, 1931

Hazlehurst, under Coach Bobby Therrill, had surprised fans in 1930 with a *"remarkable record in view of the fact that he lost practically his entire team the previous graduation"*. His team averaged 145 pounds and were *"said to be the fastest bunch of Indians seen in the history of the Hazlehurst* school". By game day, they had defeated opponents by a total 179-0.

It was called *"the most exciting game of the season thus far"* by their paper. *"At all times, both teams had eleven men fighting; neither was a one-man show. Both teams came upon the field smiling and both left smiling. There were a few worthy line gains but both teams relied mostly on punt defense"*. Ainsworth had one of the two touchdowns before halftime to make it 12-0. Now in the 4th quarter, Hazlehurst tallied once more. The two other Indian scores came from Aldridge and Young.

GAME 3: MAGEE (1-1) vs PRENTISS (UNREPORTED)
MAGEE 14 PRENTISS 13
October 23, 1931

Prentiss had been a mainstay on the Magee schedule since at least 1928. If records were correct, each team stood 1-1-1 against one-another. In this tilt, it was Magee breaking the tie behind the two touchdowns of *"plunging fullback"* Captain Bobby Thames. His first came in the opening quarter. Prentiss tallied scores in the 2nd and 3rd quarters, but could not convert the point-after on their first touchdown; thus giving Magee the eventual win. The first score for Prentiss came via the air from Berry while he also pulled off a 70-yard scamper for the last.

The Prentiss Headlight called it *"an uphill fight"*. They added that *"Captain Berry of Prentiss was outstanding on both offense and defense, continuously smearing Magee plays as well as scoring all the points for Prentiss. The local boys, playing their best game of the season, outfought their rivals but Magee got the breaks. Time after time, Prentiss threatened to score but bad or intercepted passes would stop the rally"*. They continued by saying that Prentiss *"kept the ball within scoring distance all during the last quarter, twice the ball was within the 10-yard line, but offside penalties and other misplays kept the boys from winning the game"*.

GAME 4: MAGEE (2-1) @ D'LO (UNREPORTED)
MAGEE 12 D'LO 6
October 30, 1931

Originally, Magee was slated to play Mendenhall (Simpson AHS) but The Simpson County News showed a win on the road in D'Lo instead. It was called *"one of the cleanest games ever witnessed on the D'Lo field; there being only one five-yard penalty inflicted during the entire game"*. The paper reported that *"The D'Lo boys were outweighed several pounds to the man but the accurate passing and sweeping end-runs by Douglas Baker made up for the charging line of Magee"*.

Thames appeared to take control of the offense with plunges through the line *"during the latter part of the fourth quarter"*. D'Lo put up their only points on an intercepted pass. The crowd was called *"one of the largest ... for the past three years"*. Magee did their part with *"almost one hundred percent to back the Burrheads"*.

GAME 5: MAGEE (3-1) @ CRYSTAL SPRINGS (UNREPORTED)
MAGEE 0 CRYSTAL SPRINGS 32
November 6, 1931

After at least two rescheduled affairs, the contest against Crystal Springs was now ready to kick off. The Simpson County News said afterwards that Crystal Springs *"fought fury with fury"* against the stubborn Burrheads. Unfortunately, an opening Magee fumble put the Tigers just 40 yards from the goal to start the game and they converted for their first score. Now in the 3rd,

Thurman's 25-yard dash and Bill Mize's pass to McBride made it 13-0. Their next was via a long Mize pass to McBride who ran *"quickly across for the third touchdown"*.

The next came in the 4th quarter on a 65-yard dash to paydirt with Mize hitting his receiver for the conversion. Late in the frame, and after a Doss fumble recovery, Finley pulled in a McBride toss for a score. McBride picked off a Burrhead pass that led to another touchdown, but a penalty brought it back to keep it 32-0.

GAME 6: MAGEE (3-2) vs FOREST (5-1)
MAGEE 0 FOREST 41
November 13, 1931

The game was, according to the Forest newspaper, *"a surprise to many because of the one-sided score. It was not that Magee played bad ball but that Forest played much better ball than usual…"*. The Bearcats held the ground while Magee managed a few first downs, *"mostly by forward passes"*.

GAME 7: MAGEE (3-3) vs MENDENHALL – SIMPSON AHS (UNREPORTED)
MAGEE 12 MENDENHALL 0
November 20, 1931

If records are correct, Magee as 2-1 thus far in their early tilts with Coach Howard Selman's Mendenhall's Simpson AHS. The score from the contest came from a December 11th report of Mendenhall records that point to the Burrhead win. A later notation points to the victory when the two teams faced each other for the second time of the 1931 campaign. The source on Simpson County football history notes it a 13-12 Simpson AHS win, but that could not have been accurate.

GAME 8: MAGEE (4-3) @ MENDENHALL – SIMPSON AHS (6-3)
MAGEE 6 MENDENHALL 13
November 27, 1931

It is apparent that Magee played more games between their first head-to-head match and this one; presumably two or three weeks later. However, no reports of the results of those contests are found. In this particular battle, Mendy was looking for *"revenge for a defeat that Magee had given the Aggies earlier"*. Early in the tilt, Strait blocked a Thames punt and Vinson recovered in the end zone for a touchdown. Miley's conversion made it 7-0. In the next half, Thames cut into the lead with a 37-yard scoring run to make it 7-6, but Mendenhall inserted the dagger in the last quarter via *"a variety of line plays and passes"*.

GAME 9: MAGEE (4-4) vs PUCKETT (UNREPORTED)
MAGEE 6 PUCKETT 14
December 4, 1931: MENDENHALL, MS

The Burrheads now had a chance to play once more against the winner of the Forest/Morton game to see who would claim the Middle Mississippi regional championship. Their road would be close to home in Mendenhall against the Puckett squad. *"The game was played deep into the Magee territory most all the time"*. Puckett threatened 5 times inside the Burrhead 20 but lost the chances to fumbles and penalties. *"Magee was never able to withstand the strong plunges of the Puckett line"*.

Puckett apparently had one touchdown called back; that on a 98-yard Walters breakaway that was nullified by motion. Magee was actually first to the scoreboard as the result of *"several completed passes and with gains from Puckett penalties and fumbles"*. Puckett responded with a pair of touchdowns in the final frame to give them the Southern Half Middle Mississippi district honor. They would now meet Forest for the title. They said *"Thames was the only real player from the Magee team and he really showed good tactics for a high school player"*.

In December, Magee held its annual football banquet at the high school under the support of Magee Drug Company. Sixteen letters were awarded in the ceremonies. James Everett was elected captain for the upcoming 1932 season with Robert Kees chosen as Alternate Captain. Nine of the players would be lost for the next campaign due to graduation. Puckett defeated Forest for bragging rights of the division. In their region, Hazlehurst went 10-0-1 and claimed their championship due to Crystal Springs deciding not to play.

As a side note about the season, it's entirely possible other games were played. The Simpson County News noted the day before Christmas that it had been *"one of the best football teams this year in the history of the school"*. Considering that the 1929 and 1930 squads both went a reported 8-3, the accolade was either gracious or other wins were recorded.

1932 (8-2-1)

School opened on September 5th for Magee High School with over 390 students. That was called the *"largest enrollment on opening day in the history of the school"*. On the gridiron, new Coach Claude Mangum held the whistle. He had run his Burrheads through *"two full weeks of practice ... with long scrimmages each afternoon..."*. The Clarion-Ledger added that *"With the possible exception of one or two places in the backfield, all positions have been filled"*.

GAME 1: MAGEE (0-0) vs JOHNS HIGH (0-0)
MAGEE 33 JOHNS HIGH 0
September 16, 1932

First up for Magee was the school formerly known as the Rankin AHS Aggies. The final score is somewhat in doubt. One source had the final 33-0. An October 6th Newton Record article said that Magee had outscored opponents 90-0 by their tilt. It could have been 99-0, or the reporting from either source is inaccurate by a few points. Regardless, Magee had opened the season with a convincing win.

GAME 2: MAGEE (1-0) @/vs JACKSON CENTRAL B-TEAM (UNREPORTED)
MAGEE 26 JACKSON CENTRAL B-TEAM 0
September 16, 1932

No reporting was found. Only a historical source points to a 26-0 win for Magee.

GAME 3: MAGEE (2-0) vs BRANDON (1-0)
MAGEE 40 BRANDON 0
September 30, 1932

Another record enrollment (300) awaited Brandon Consolidated School when it opened on September 5th. Coach W.C. Mills had the same number of players for Brandon's second season of organized football, including numerous returners from the inaugural squad. The team continued work on fundamentals through mid-September with The Clarion-Ledger saying that, *"Prospects for this year are much more encouraging than they were a year ago... With the added experience of one year, and several transfer pupils, a much more successful season is anticipated."*

They opened with a win over Georgetown but it would eventually be their only victory of the season. The only report of the contest came from the October 13th Clarion-Ledger after a Brandon loss to Union gave us the outcome.

GAME 4: MAGEE (3-0) @ NEWTON (2-1)
MAGEE 0 NEWTON 20
October 7, 1932

Coach E.L. Morgan's Tigers were expected to be very strong for 1932 as they lost only a pair of lettermen and had *"plenty of good reserve material"*. Though opening with only slight wins over Lake (6-0) and Pelahatchie (23-19) before losing to Quitman (7-6), and despite the Burrheads being undefeated and outscoring opponents 90-0, The Newton Record said that *"the Newton gridders are rated to win. The Magee aggregation has been scouted and a great deal of work is being done on the defense plays so that they can become adjusted to hold the fast Magee team back"*.

Though Magee blocked a Tiger kick, Newton managed their first touchdown via a Payne run and a PAT by Stone. They added another before halftime after Magee fumbled and the home team *"marched down the field for another score and the extra point"*. In the last quarter, Coach Morgan sent in the reserves, but they also scored. Newton recorded 13 first downs while Magee bragged of only two.

GAME 5: MAGEE (3-1) @ SAINT ALOYSIUS (0-2)
MAGEE 20 SAINT ALOYSIUS 0
October 12, 1932

First-year Coach Jack Roberts was trying to improve on a 1-7 campaign in 1931 for his Flashes. Things seemed no better in their first tilt at Tallulah, LA when they were embarrassed 69-0. The game the following weeks against Simpson County AHS was closer (13-0) but still a loss. It was enough improvement that the paper called it an "*impressive showing*". Strenuous practices were underway with new "*deceptive*" plays and position changes.

Saint Al looked good in the opening half of play but neither team could cross the goal. In the 3rd, Kees hit Winstead for a 55-yard touchdown and 6-0 lead. The two hooked up again from 75 yards on the next drive and Winstead converted the extra point. In the last quarter, Bill Jacquith's pass was picked off by Brister and he converted that into a touchdown on his second carry afterwards. Burnham converted the PAT. Saint Al got close to the Burrhead goal twice but the defense stiffened to preserve the shutout.

GAME 6: MAGEE (4-1) @/vs SEMINARY 0
MAGEE 8 SEMINARY 0
October 19, 1932

The historical source on Simpson County football noted a game against Seminary in this time period. It makes sense as there was a sixteen-day gap in dates. The game is noted as an 8-0 Magee win but the date noted here is an estimation.

GAME 7: MAGEE (5-1) vs GEORGETOWN (UNREPORTED)
MAGEE 6 GEORGETOWN 0
October 28, 1932

The Simpson County News said that "*Suffering from a case of too much over-confidence, (Magee was) hard-pushed to eke out a 6-0 victory over a fighting Georgetown team. Doped to win by three touchdowns and somewhat surprised by an alert offensive drive by the visitors in the early stages of the game, the Burrheads fought with their backs to the wall throughout the last half; desperately trying to protect the 6-point lead they had gained early in the second quarter*".

GAME 8: MAGEE (6-1) @/vs COLLINS (UNREPORTED)
MAGEE 0 COLLINS 0
November 6, 1932

The Clarion-Ledger reported that Magee would face a Florence squad about this time of the season. But no source indicated that any such tilt occurred. However, another report showed a 0-0 tie with Collins in this spot. Taking a November 21st Clarion-Ledger report on Magee's record as of that day, and taking the D'Lo and Mendenhall games into consideration, it would make perfect sense.

GAME 9: MAGEE (6-1-1) vs D'LO (UNREPORTED)
MAGEE 7 D'LO 0
November 13, 1932

After dropping the 1928 contest, Magee had gone on to win three games in a row. The only tally of the day came in the second quarter "*on a series of passes and off-tackle plays which carried the ball from the 50-yard line. Kees drop-kicked the extra point*". D'Lo came very close to tying the game in the third quarter, marching 60 yards to the three-inch line. However, the Burrhead defense stood tall and captured the win. "*One of the prettiest punting duels of the season was witnessed during the game as Kees of Magee and Baker of D'Lo gained ground consistently by their punting*".

GAME 10: MAGEE (7-1-1) @ MENDENHALL/SIMPSON AHS (5-2-1)
MAGEE 0 MENDENHALL/SIMPSON AHS 33
November 18, 1932

While Magee had taken the victory in 1930, the two teams traded wins and losses in both 1929 and 1931. This one would never be in doubt in a game touted as "*one of the biggest and best football games played in this territory this season"*. The Clarion-Ledger said that Robert Strait scored three times while Earl Walters and Walter Dilmore each added another.

GAME 11: MAGEE (7-2-1) @/vs PRENTISS (UNREPORTED)
MAGEE 13 PRENTISS 0
November 25, 1932

An early report indicated that Magee actually finished the season with a game against Prentiss with a 13-0 victory.

1933 (8-3)

Unfortunately, there was no write-up about Coach Hobart Stowers' prospects for the 1933 campaign.

GAME 1: MAGEE (0-0) vs BRANCH (0-0)
MAGEE 20 BRANCH 0
September 15, 1933

It was apparent from the reporter that Magee was expected to put up a much-more impressive lid-lifter than they did. In fact, after three quarters, the tilt sat 0-0. But during the last 5:00 of the game, Magee *"ran wild"*. The first pair of touchdowns came *"in rapid succession by short passes with Kees and (Otho) Winstead alternating on the receiving end"*. Winstead had the first reception for a score and made the PAT while Kees had the next to make it 13-0. Winstead geared the last tally with two runs of 10 yards before hitting Kees for the touchdown.

The paper said that *"Both teams were evenly matched until the last quarter. (Branch) lost a chance to score in the second as a pass rolled incomplete into the end zone"*. Also this week, the JV team of *"Junior Burrheads"* drew even 0-0 with Mount Olive.

GAME 2: MAGEE (1-0) @ FLORA (UNREPORTED)
MAGEE 14 FLORA 0
September 22, 1933

The only notation of the contest came in the September 24th Clarion-Ledger where it noted the final score. Sometime between this game and the varsity match against Johns High, the *"little boys"* (junior varsity) played the *"Rinkey-Dinks"* of Mount Olive on the road. Mount Olive's youngsters won the *"exciting game"* by a 12-0 score.

GAME 3: MAGEE (2-0) vs JOHNS HIGH (UNREPORTED)
MAGEE 33 JOHNS HIGH 0
October 6, 1933

A report from September 20th showed Clarkburg as the next Burrhead opponent on September 29th. However, just before the matchup, the game was cancelled; presumably by Clarkburg. That was confirmed in numerous articles later. The Baby Burrheads got their revenge on Mount Olive during the week by a 19-16 score. Everett Walker was called *"the mainstay in the Burrhead line, with Thornton gaining most of the ground on end runs"*.

The first of two consecutive games against teams from Rankin County started with a *"strong Johns team"*. Despite the 33-0 whitewash, The Clarion-Ledger called it a *"slow, listless game"*. Scoring came in the first and third quarters with Kees scoring twice, while (Lincoln) Stubbs, (Buford) Neely and Winstead each pitched in a lone score. Magee was 1-6 in the air while Johns was 0-3. Magee led 9-5 in first downs.

GAME 4: MAGEE (3-0) vs BRANDON (3-0)
MAGEE 50 BRANDON 0
October 13, 1933

Coach W.C. Mills had 30 men reporting for football as of September 14th. The official tally by year-end was 24, so it was apparent that not all who came out finished the season. However, the boys that did report managed to set a benchmark for future teams. Though Magee had beaten Brandon 40-0 in 1932, the Bulldog 6-0 *"upset"* over Union had caused what The

Clarion-Ledger called a *"quiet chill to fall on Magee players"*. The Burrheads were getting back a key player by the name of May whose presence would *"add more power to the Magee team than they have shown this season"*. Unexplainably, the score would be worse than the 1932 tally for those in Rankin County.

The Clarion-Ledger thought the Magee win to be *"one of the biggest upsets in football circles this season"* based on *"past performances this season"*. Brandon had only one first down and was *"never able to complete a pass, although they were fighting from the opening of the game until the final whistle."* Magee's play was highlighted by blocking, according to the paper. Winstead and Allen ended up the scoring leaders with 18 points each. As a side note, an October 21, 1935 Clarion-Ledger article called the score 54-0.

GAME 5: MAGEE (4-0) vs GEORGETOWN (UNREPORTED)
MAGEE 43 GEORGETOWN 0
October 20, 1933

Magee had destroyed Georgetown back in 1930 by a 47-0 score. This one would be almost as bad. *"The game was featured by long runs by the Burrheads backfield, especially Winstead, who tore off ten to twenty yards repeatedly and on one occasion ran a punt back 55 yards for a touchdown"*. Winstead notched 24 points, Kees had 13 and Stubbs chipped in 6 more. *"Every substitute available saw action before the game was over"*.

GAME 6: MAGEE (5-0) vs MENDENHALL/SIMPSON AHS (UNREPORTED)
MAGEE 18 MENDENHALL/SIMPSON AHS 0
October 27, 1933

This game had become a big attraction of local football fans. With the all-time series sitting 3-3, this one would pit the undefeated and unscored-upon Burrheads against *"a strong Mendenhall eleven"*. Scoring began in the second quarter when Magee blocked a kick for a safety and 2-0 lead. Kees followed that with a touchdown pass to Allen while Winstead notched the last touchdown in the third *"on a line play"*. Kees drop-kicked the extra point and added a 25-yard FG in the third quarter.

"The Burrheads displayed brilliant football, with the backfield slicing off-tackle for nice gains almost at will and the line blocking nicely. The defeat of Mendenhall makes the Burrheads strong contenders for district honors as well as adding the county championship; an honor Mendenhall held from last season".

GAME 7: MAGEE (6-0) vs MISS SCHOOL FOR THE DEAF (UNREPORTED)
MAGEE 34 MISSISSIPPI SCHOOL FOR THE DEAF 0
November 3, 1933

The Burrheads were undergoing *"extensive drilling along points of weakness shown in the Mendenhall game of last week"*. The Clarion-Ledger went on to say that *"The Burrheads have displayed marked ability thus far in the season and bid fair to being in the fight for football honors in this section. The victory Friday has them the championship of the county and are now in a strong position to be favorites in the district honors"*.

When it was over, it proved to be yet another easy win. The action was described as *"slow, neither team playing up to the football ability they have shown this season. The Burrheads had considerable trouble penetrating the visitors' line and three of the touchdowns scored against the Jackson crew came by way of the aerial route. Allen scored 18 points from his position at end for the Burrheads and also played a good defensive game"*.

GAME 8: MAGEE (7-0) @ LAKE (UNREPORTED)
MAGEE 13 LAKE 39
November 17, 1933

Originally, Magee was to have faced the Hattiesburg JV, but like Clarkburg, they had cancelled. That meant that yet another two-week delay was in store for the Burrheads with a strong Lake team up next on the road. All sources pointed to Lake being the *"hardest game of the season"*. This marked the first out-of-conference game of the year. A report from The Newton Record on November 23rd reported that the Hornets had drummed undefeated Magee 39-13.

GAME 9: MAGEE (7-1) @ SEMINARY (UNREPORTED)
MAGEE 0 SEMINARY 14
November 24, 1933

After a shocking loss to Lake, the Magee team was "*turning their attention ... toward Seminary. The strength of the Seminary team has been manifested in games throughout their schedule this season and the Burrheads are expecting the hardest game of the year from them*". Seminary was also coming off a 6-0 loss to Brooklyn in regional play.

The Collins newspaper said of the non-conference game that "*Six men, led by Coot Moore (diminutive QB) and playing their last game before the home folks and in a high school uniform, successfully withstood repeated attacks by (Magee) and in turn penetrated their territory twice for touchdowns. Both scores were counted by Elfert after the ball had been advanced into scoring position by Moore, Johnston and Lott*". It was noted afterwards that one player, Floyd, was in the hospital with a leg ailment as the result of the contest.

GAME 10: MAGEE (7-2) vs PUCKETT (UNREPORTED)
MAGEE 7 PUCKETT 6
November 29, 1933

Magee was to square off with Prentiss to close the season. But, with a 7-0 mark in their region, Magee was chosen to play Puckett on the road to regional honors. The winner would face Forest and then the winner of that game would meet Morton. The Burrheads would redeem themselves on this night to win the championship of the southern half of the Middle Mississippi conference.

The home team was first on the scoreboard in the second quarter on a 40-yard scoring pass from Kees to Sanders. Kees then hit Winstead for the extra point in what would be the deciding factor in the contest. In the final frame, Puckett came to life to avoid being eliminated. They moved inside the Magee 5-yard line from where Patrick "*slipped off tackle for the touchdown*". On their PAT, Sanders blocked the attempt and sealed the win. "*Winstead and Bradford in the backfield, and Sanders and May in the line were outstanding for the Burrheads*".

GAME 11: MAGEE (8-2) @ MORTON (UNREPORTED)
MAGEE 13 MORTON 24
December 8, 1933

Unbelievably, Forest forfeited their chance at the championship game and set Magee up to play for the honors. The Clarion-Ledger said that "*Magee had made a strong bid this season in Middle Mississippi football circles, climbing to a new position much higher than they formerly occupied. Coach Hobart Stowers has brought the Burrheads along very smartly and has them ready for their supreme test in the championship tilt with Morton*". While Morton was favored, "*Magee is expected to put up one of the stiffest battles of the entire season*".

A later article noted that the Burrs were "*trying to perfect a defense that will stop Morton passes. The Panthers have improved on their passing game considerably in the last three games. The Burrheads have a fine offense that will do plenty of damage to the Panthers if it ever starts clicking in the right way*". Morton featured a player named Glenn Walker, one of the best in the state.

Unfortunately for the visitors, "*the Panthers outplayed the Burrheads and came through in the pinches with scoring punches*". No further details of scoring activity were found to date.

An end-of-season all-star list named Winstead as a member and Floyd as an Honorable Mention.

1934 (6-3)

The Burrheads opened practices with 35 "*aspirants*". Eight lettermen, including Captain Truman Allen, returned "*with a fight beginning (in the second week of September) for the vacant places on the squad...*" The Clarion-Ledger said that with the returners and "*a number of promising reserves*", Magee fans had "*high hopes for another successful team*". That changed before the first game as it was reported that "*Lack of experienced reserves has been tending to make life miserable for the local mentor, but the showing of the entire squad for the past week has somewhat improved the situation. The team will probably be lighter in weight than has been the case for the past few years but will be one of the fastest".*

It is probable that the team was once-again coached by Hobart Stowers as his name was listed as a sponsor of certain youth groups at Magee High School.

GAME 1: MAGEE (0-0) @ CRYSTAL SPRINGS (1-0)
MAGEE 0 CRYSTAL SPRINGS 39
September 21, 1934

Heavy Crystal Springs opened the season impressively with a 30-0 win over Puckett. Against the Copiah County team, Magee had lost at least in 1928 and 1931; the last their worst defeat of the season (32-0). The Clarion-Ledger said that Magee *"flashed a dangerous offense at times, but never seriously threatened the Tiger goal line. Magee's pass work was successful in midfield, but a tightened defense destroyed it in scoring territory"*. The Tigers would go on to lose at least four games and be held to just six points in those contests.

GAME 2: MAGEE (0-1) vs PINOLA (UNREPORTED)
MAGEE 40 PINOLA 0
September 28, 1934

Originally Magee was slated to play the 36-man roster under Lake's Coach C.H. Stuart. But somewhere between the last few weeks of the month, it became apparent that Pinola would take their place. The Simpson County News said Pinola's *"boys conducted themselves in such a manner on the field that we know that they will enjoy a successful year even though they have not played before"*.

GAME 3: MAGEE (1-1) @ FOREST (1-?)
MAGEE 0 FOREST 20
October 5, 1934

The Clarion-Ledger noted three days before kickoff that *"the Burrheads can present a quartet of backs sufficient to give most any team trouble, and the Bearcats are no exception"*. Turnovers, namely a fumble, gave Forest the most heartache when they moved steadily to five first downs with the ball at the 10-yard line before coughing up the football. On their next possession, however, they ran steadily through the Magee line with Jones doing the honors on a *"six-yard off-tackle play"*. King's PAT put it 7-0.

They added to the scoreboard in the second quarter on a Buster Seales fumble recovery and later dive, but Gibson's PAT run failed. The 13-0 lead held until the 3rd quarter when Seales capped a 50-yard march with a one-yard (or ten-yard) plunge. Magee then started hitting passes in the final frame, but their final one was picked off by Logan and returned 75 yards for their final tally. Details for the Burrheads was not reported, but statistics showed Forest 1-5 in the air while Magee was 9-18 with 3 intercepted. Forest tallied 22 first downs in all with Seales accounting for 210 yards out of the total Forest 336 yards.

One report said that C. Allen was the *"outstanding player"* on offense and defense while F. Allen *"carried the brunt of the play in Magee's backfield"*. As a side note, this game was reported as a Magee loss of 19-12 (Clarion-Ledger 10-5-34), 25-0 (Clarion-Ledger 10-7-34) and finally 20-0 (News Register 10-11-34). For this instance, I accept the Forest newspaper account as it is local and much more detailed.

GAME 4: MAGEE (1-2) vs JOHNS HIGH (UNREPORTED)
MAGEE 13 JOHNS HIGH 0
October 11, 1934

The second loss meant *"strenuous training for the remainder of the games, most of which will be played at Magee"*. The Clarion-Ledger predicted a Magee win of 38-0 *"in lightning time"*. While the accuracy of the predicted victory was true, the margin was not. A later report that week noted that the Burrheads barely took the 13-0 margin over the Rankin County School.

GAME 5: MAGEE (2-2) @ MENDENHALL (4-1)
MAGEE 14 MENDENHALL 0
October 26, 1934

Magee had a week of rest to prepare for the rival Tigers. The paper said that *"this is by far the most important game on the schedule of either team, as a friendly rivalry has existed for years in an athletic way"*. Mendenhall opened with a 7-0 loss to Puckett before running off wins against Mount Olive (13-0), Jackson Central JV (7-6), Prentiss (12-0) and New Hebron (13-0).

The Clarion-Ledger said that *"the Tigers are not under-estimating the ability of the Magee boys to make touchdowns and they realize that only with their best will they be able to acquire the much-wanted victory"*. The event would be highly-attended as a carnival would follow the 3:00pm contest. In the end, it was reported only that after such *"a poor showing"*, Mendenhall was now shifting players around to strengthen their club.

GAME 6: MAGEE (3-2) @ MISS SCHOOL FOR THE DEAF (UNREPORTED)
MAGEE 0 MISSISSIPPI SCHOOL FOR THE DEAF 33
October 2, 1934

While no final score was reported, The Clarion-Ledger did say that *"The Burrheads let the strong School for the Deaf team of Jackson slip up on them last week and were decisively defeated by them in Jackson"*. A later source indicates that the game ended in a 33-0 thrashing.

GAME 7: MAGEE (3-3) vs SEMINARY (UNREPORTED)
MAGEE 7 SEMINARY 6
November 9, 1934

A few things were providing incentive for the Burrs to get back on the winning track. First, Seminary had provided Magee with only their second loss in 1933. Second, Magee was trying to protect a home winning streak that stretched back to October of 1928 when D'Lo proved to be the last team to win on the home field. As time went along, the reports changed to saying that Magee had never lost on their home turf, though a five-year span was impressive enough.

Coach A.I. Rexinger's Seminary team was considered this week to be *"the best team in that district"*, but The Clarion-Ledger's Harrison Saunders still predicted that Magee would win 21-6. *"A determined bunch of Burrheads will keep their home field slate clean"*. After it was over, the same paper would call it *"one of the hardest-fought games ever witnessed on the local field"*.

The game was every bit of a *"nail biter"*. Seminary held a 6-0 lead thanks to a Johnson 3-yard touchdown in the third quarter. Magee had driven to *"the shadow of the goal"* in the final quarter, but turned the ball over on downs. With one chance left and just :30 on the clock, they took to the air. C. Allen caught 15 passes, but his biggest was the one that gave them the touchdown. The critical extra point was good to snatch the come-from-behind win. Allen also threw 13 passes while F. Allen *"also made the game very profitable to the Burrhead claims"*.

As a side note, it's possible that this game was played on Saturday, November 10th.

GAME 8: MAGEE (4-3) vs MOUNT OLIVE (UNREPORTED)
MAGEE 14 MOUNT OLIVE 6
November 16, 1934

While Magee *"upset all predictions"* by beating Seminary, they were now *"favored decisively to lick the visitors this week"*. Mount Olive was apparently *"boasting one of the best teams it has ever had"* but the Burrheads were playing tough football. *"The local squad will be fighting again to hold their home record of victories perfect against all opposition"*.

The matchup was called *"listless"* as Magee put up their pair of touchdowns and PATs early and were then *"satisfied to take matters easy for the remainder of the game"*. Those scores came on a Bradford run and a blocked punt that was recovered in the end zone by Cyril Allen. Mount Olive's only response came in the final frame when McNair found Courtney.

GAME 9: MAGEE (5-3) @ NEW HEBRON (UNREPORTED)
MAGEE 6 NEW HEBRON 0
November 23, 1934

The Clarion-Ledger thought that Magee would wrap up the 1934 season with an 18-0 shutout over New Hebron. *"In their final of the season, the Burrheads are the choice of this department with little or no trouble"*. It would not be that easy, as it was called a *"hard fight"*. But, Magee wrapped up yet another season with a win, had a winning season, and ended still undefeated in six years on the home turf.

1935 (1-6-3)

At least six starters from the 1934 team were now lost to graduation. The team would now have *"a number of new players in the lineup"* by the first tilt accordingly. In addition, they had a new coach. A.D. Lott was a graduate of the State Teachers College (later USM) and played football there in 1933. By September 17th, Magee had continued *"their drive for the honors of being one of the best football teams in his district with strenuous workouts each afternoon with approximately 30 candidates..."* After three weeks of practice with *"game length scrimmages"*, the paper said that *"the prospects for a winning combination is inevitable"*.

As for the individual positions, The Clarion-Ledger noted many players but said that *"The line will probably be one of the heaviest that ever represented a Burrhead eleven, with the backfield remaining an unknown quality"*.

GAME 1: MAGEE (0-0) vs FLORENCE (0-0)
MAGEE 7 FLORENCE 0
September 20, 1935

The Clarion-Ledger reported that Florence would *"again have a strong team"*. That proved accurate as the lid-lifter of the 1935 season featured two defenses determined to hold each other out of the end zone. That played out until the final quarter when Terry *"went off tackle from the three-yard stripe"* and plucked the extra point on a pass from S. Allen. Florence came back in the closing minutes to *"cause alarm among the followers of the local team"* but could not get across the goal before time expired. Magee led in first downs 10-3.

Little did Magee fans or players know that the Terry touchdown and Allen point-after would be the only points scored in 1935.

GAME 2: MAGEE (1-0) @ LAKE (1-0)
MAGEE 0 LAKE 32
September 27, 1935

The Burrheads were now on the road to face perennially powerful Lake; a team that had just beaten Brandon 6-0 and destroyed Magee 39-13 back in 1933. Unfortunately, when over, it would be about the same for this season. The only notation came from The Newton Record and showed only the final score.

GAME 3: MAGEE (1-1) @ COLLINS (UNREPORTED)
MAGEE 0 COLLINS 6
October 4, 1935

The week of the game, the paper reported on *"long scrimmages each afternoon ... to iron out the inexperienced spots in the squad"*. One report said that Magee outweighed Collins *"fifteen pounds to the man"*. The Covington County News called the *"first three periods"* a *"kicking duel between Stubbs for the locals and the Magee QB"*. It was late in the final quarter before Stubbs passes to Davis, Johnson and Bullock put the ball at the 3-yard line. From there, Broome *"hit the line twice to go over"*.

GAME 4: MAGEE (1-2) vs PINOLA (UNREPORTED)
MAGEE 0 PINOLA 0
October 11, 1935

The season began with the Burrheads scheduled to hit the road to face Newton. However, that changed before the actual game and now Pinola would be the opponent. The game would be remembered more for the touchdown-killing fumbles than the fact that Magee kept their spotless home streak alive. An early Pinola fumble was recovered by Magee, but the Burrs turned it right back over at the 6-yard line. Magee moved as far as the 25-yard line in the second quarter but again fumbled.

Magee took to the air in the 3rd quarter but Pinola alertly picked off the errant throw. Now in the final frame, the home team started marching toward paydirt in hopes of a dramatic game winning touchdown. But, a fumble at the 20-yard line was recovered by Pinola and that effectively sealed play for the evening. Pinola *"gained most of their ground on reverse plays ... while Magee gained their ground on plays over the center and tackle"*. Magee managed only a pair of first downs. Pinola garnered on a single first down.

GAME 5: MAGEE (1-2-1) @ BRANDON (2-3)
MAGEE 0 BRANDON 7
October 18, 1935

It was reported that, *"... the Magee lads will have to hustle this week to hold that record (no losses to Brandon) clean as the boys from Rankin are stronger this year than ever before."* Playing without an injured Brandon starter, this slugfest came down to just a few highlights. Coach Bill Jacobs' Bulldogs put up the game's only points in the opening quarter. Cox blocked a Magee punt and it was recovered by Joe Bullock. Gordon Worthington found Sidney Ragland and then Cox with aerials that moved the ball to the 10. From there, it was Frances Myers with the only touchdown of the game with Bill Dan Maxey adding the extra point via a run *"around his own left end"*.

Brandon got inside the 10-yard line three times but lost on fumbles and downs. Magee, meanwhile, got to the Bulldog 15 in the 3rd but couldn't get any further. The Rankin County News said that *"The visitors combined their skill with Brandon's bad breaks which had the game looking dangerous before the end."*

GAME 6: MAGEE (1-3-1) vs NEW HEBRON (UNREPORTED)
MAGEE 0 NEW HEBRON 0
October 25, 1935

Despite the not-so-stellar record, Magee fans were encouraged to show up on the home field for the game against New Hebron. *"This is to be one of our best games, so come on out and see it. The boys need your help!"* Eerily similar to the Pinola game, the Burrheads managed to avoid a loss on the home turf, but again could not score offensively.

The Clarion-Ledger reported that *"neither team seriously (threatened) to score. The game was played on equal terms throughout, with the defensive work of the Burrheads the feature work of the tilt"*. New Hebron's only real opportunity came in the final quarter when *"Schmaltz, New Hebron quarter, ran straight through the Burrhead line of thirty yards to place the ball on the twenty-yard line"*. Magee managed to hold on downs thereafter. Bradford copied the 30-yard dash later, but to no avail.

GAME 7: MAGEE (1-3-2) @ PETAL (UNREPORTED)
MAGEE 0 PETAL 14
November 1, 1935

Instead of a road game at Pelahatchie, Magee now boarded the bus for Hattiesburg and the State Teachers College to take on Petal High. Coach Ott and Petal's Coach Vernon Clay "Goofus" Boyd were teammates at the college back in 1933; probably lending itself to the rationale behind the match. Magee's team would be *"intact, with injuries and ineligibles being ready for the game"*. Petal was coming off of a *"disputed"* 12-6 loss the week before to Waynesboro.

The only notation came from November 5th saying, *"Grinding away monotonously at the Magee line, the Petal Panthers of Forrest County whipped the Burrheads 14-0"*.

GAME 8: MAGEE (1-4-2) @ MOUNT OLIVE (UNREPORTED)
MAGEE 0 MOUNT OLIVE 19
November 11, 1935

With ten days of rest, Magee and Coach Ott were working to get the offense to match the efforts of the defense. They had beaten Mount Olive in 1931 and again in 1933 but neither win had been blowouts. The paper called the tilt *"the most important, as well as the most strenuous, of the year"*.

The Armistice Day game against the Red Devils was played in horrid conditions. *"There was water two or three inches deep. If we could have seen how Van dived on the ball when it was in the deepest part of the water, we would have thought it was a diving contest. Now boys, don't let the loss of all these games discourage you. You know we have our greatest rivals to play yet and we sure want to beat them*". A local report noted that "*The Pirate offense clicked easily, though handicapped by a muddy field, and their defense smothered all attempts of the invaders to cross the last, counting white stripe*".

GAME 9: MAGEE (1-5-2) @ CRYSTAL SPRINGS (9th GAME)
MAGEE 0 CRYSTAL SPRINGS 52
November 15, 1935

Not only was it a quick turnaround for the team, but they would be facing traditionally powerful Crystal Springs on the road. Coaches Bishop and Miller had "*a nucleus of both linemen and backs now available to build around*" following graduation of some starters. If other reports were right, Crystal Springs had been on somewhat of a downturn the past two seasons. This year, they appear to have already dropped games to Brookhaven and Columbia while tying McComb. Once again the offense failed to materialize, but to the surprise of all, the solid defense proved to be no match against such an explosive opponent.

GAME 10: MAGEE (1-6-2) vs MENDENHALL (UNREPORTED)
MAGEE 0 MENDENHALL 0
November 27, 1935

The Burrheads would close the season against rival Mendenhall in their 9th meeting since 1929. A win would somewhat ease the pain of a campaign that had produced only a single touchdown back in September. In the end, it was described as "*a hard-fought game throughout the entire four quarters*".

The opening quarter was simply an exchange of punts while the next saw both teams ending drives on downs. Shows broke away for 35 yards for the visitors before Magee drove as far as the 20-yard line unsuccessfully. Before halftime, Magee had made it to the Mendy 8 before time ran out. Peck Allen thwarted at least two Mendenhall drives with interceptions, "*nearly getting away once for a touchdown*". Lewis Bradford gave Magee fans hopes in the last frame when he escaped for 30 yards, but again the drive came up empty. For historical purposes, it was reported some decades later to be a 6-6 contest.

1936 (1-4-2)

Magee High School opened with 631 students in September of 1936. As for the young men on the gridiron, they started workouts on September 8th under second-year mentor A.D. Lott. Lott had a reported 17 returning lettermen from a 1-6-3 team. Ironically, the paper noted that, "*the team this year should be equally as good as that of last, but a number of vacancies caused by graduation in the spring will be difficult to fill*".

GAME 1: MAGEE (0-0) vs PRENTISS (0-1)
MAGEE 6 PRENTISS 0
October 2, 1936

A quick note from the October 1st Simpson County News said that "*Our boys won the fast football game over Prentiss here last Friday. The Burrheads came through in fine style. The teams were about evenly matched. Coach Ott promises an A-1 football team this season. The boys haven't lost on the home field in 10 years. Surely Mr. Ott won't let them fail to keep this record for another year at least*".

Prentiss had opened with a loss to Columbia "*by a large score after only one week of practice*". For this tilt, The Prentiss Headlight said that "*The lads looked rather well in this game and it was to a much heavier team that they finally gave way (in) the closing minutes of the contest*".

GAME 2: MAGEE (1-0) vs/@ MIZE (UNREPORTED)
MAGEE 6 MIZE 6
October 9, 1936

Mize High was originally scheduled for November 13th. The Burrheads were scheduled to face New Hebron on the road this day, but apparently schedules changed along the way. The

Simpson County News said that *"The Magee Burrheads failed to beat Mize last Friday. Yet, they did not lose. Score 6-6. They'll have to try that again and do a better job of it next time"*.

GAME 3: MAGEE (1-0-1) vs/@ JACKSON CENTRAL (UNREPORTED)
UNREPORTED
October 16, 1936

When the Magee football schedule was announced for 1936, the list included a home game against Jackson; presumably Jackson Central's B-Team. No report of the final has been found.

GAME 4: MAGEE (1-0-1) vs MOUNT OLIVE (UNREPORTED)
MAGEE 0 MOUNT OLIVE 33
October 22, 1936

The Pirates had roughly 26 players under new Coach R.C. Shows. The previous year they were reported to have had the best season in their history. For historical records, the Collins newspaper reported this as a 33-0 final. They added that Mount Olive eclipsed *"the Burrhead boast of not having been defeated on their home field in 10 years. The Pirate backs overcame the Magee resistance to score five times while their forwards stemmed every Burrhead drive"*.

A report from The Simpson County News on October 29th said that *"Our boys were just outclassed (against Mount Olive). With odds painfully against them, they stayed in there and fought like Tigers even though they are Burrheads"*. It could be that Mount Olive felt bad about running the score up on their opponent, as a November 12th article said, *"Mount Olive has requested the Magee football team (and) Coach Ott to be their guests at a game Wednesday between (them) and Seminary. It is thought that Mount Olive feels somewhat sorry for the treatment they gave the Magee team recently"*.

GAME 5: MAGEE (1-1-1) vs BRANDON (4-0-1)
MAGEE 0 BRANDON 0
October 30, 1936

With the departure of Bill Jacobs to be Superintendent of Leakesville High School, the Bulldogs were now under the tutelage of their 3rd head coach. Also serving as Athletic Director, Southwestern of Memphis graduate Z.L. "Sheriff" Knight led a group of roughly 27 players forming the 6th edition of Brandon football. Knight had coached at Seminary in 1934 and 1935, winning the Southeast Regional Championship the first time and losing by a point in the last. Assisting the team would be Millsaps alum Tom "Tite" Ross.

It was noted that *"The team lost several first string players off last year's team and the coaches are building an entirely new team with the material they have. The line will average around 155 pounds and the backfield around 140."* That didn't mean that prospects were dismal. The Brandon News reported on September 3rd that, *"Brandon should produce one of the best high school football teams anywhere in this section of the state this fall"*. That was due to the leftover *"well-trained players, both backfield and linemen, who expect to participate in every grid battle this year"*.

This contest was a *"punting duel"* resulting in a scoreless affair. The most exciting play for Brandon was consecutive Billy Swilley runs of 21 and 11 yards while Magee faked a punt for 15 yards and their only first down. *"Brandon out-played Magee throughout the game but were unable to score over the stubborn Magee line. Brandon threatened to score twice but was unable to do so. Magee lost their chance to score when they fumbled on the Bulldogs' 20-yard line. The last quarter found Brandon continuously pushing Magee deep into her own territory"*.

First downs (4-1) went to Brandon. The Bulldogs went 1-4 passing while Magee went 0-2 with an interception.

GAME 6: MAGEE (1-1-2) @ FOREST (3-?)
MAGEE 0 FOREST 19
November 6, 1936

A Bearcat player named Craig would be the workhorse for this affair, scoring all three touchdowns in route to the shutout. His first came in the opening quarter on a 3-yard dive and the PAT was notched by Simmons. His next came on the receiving end of a long Simmons pass. Magee had a couple of good opportunities, but the last was intercepted by Simmons at midfield. That would eventually lead to Craig's third and last score.

It could have been a bit bigger margin as W.J. Waldrop escaped Magee defenders in the final quarter for a breakaway touchdown. But at midfield, with nobody near him, the ball slipped from his grasp and was recovered by a Burrhead player. Forest had 10 first downs and went 6-22 in the air. Forest was 5-12 passing.

GAME 7: MAGEE (1-2-2) @/vs NEW HEBRON (UNREPORTED)
MAGEE 0 NEW HEBRON 14
November 13, 1936

There are reports of a 14-0 loss to New Hebron from earlier in the season. But unless Magee played three times in short order, it's more likely that it occurred this week. While there are no confirmations or details elsewhere, it's included here.

GAME 8: MAGEE (1-3-2) @ MENDENHALL (UNREPORTED)
MAGEE 0 MENDENHALL 7
November 20, 1936

The season-ender was somewhat welcome relief. Still, it was Mendenhall and pride was on the line. The small margin of loss could be considered somewhat of a moral victory. Said The Simpson County News of the affair, *"The line plays of Magee didn't work as well as they were supposed to. They were stopped before they could get to the line of scrimmage. Penalties kept Mendenhall from scoring at least three other touchdowns and the whistle for the half kept them from scoring another"*. First downs went to Mendenhall 9-2. The Burrheads obtained their only pair via a penalty and the last on a pass in the game's last minute.

Somewhat strangely, they added the same day the following; a compliment to neither team! *"From the noise (Mendenhall) created about our streets that afternoon, we wondered if it was their first victory. If so, we don't blame them for such merriment. We believe our boys are about to become used to defeat and that such kiddin' doesn't bother them"*.

The year-end banquet was held in early December at a nearby hotel. Coach Ott, serving as toastmaster, was *"in good form and kept those present scared and laughing. Much fun, good music and clever speeches were enjoyed"*. As a historical note, one source had a second game with Mize played on the season. No score was reported for the affair if, indeed, it was played.

1937 (5-2-3)

Scant details are found about the beginning of the gridiron season in Magee. It is known, however, that the team was now lead by first-year Coach Brad White. The former Ole Miss football star would begin pulling together a Burrhead team *"largely composed of first-year players"*.

GAME 1: MAGEE (0-0) vs GEORGETOWN (0-0)
MAGEE 13 GEORGETOWN 0
September 17, 1937

The Eagles under Coach H.H. Gambrell were wary as, even though their players seemed bigger this season, the team would be led by only two returning lettermen. As for the game, it was said that *"The Eagles found a very strong team, but ... played a very fine game"*. An interesting note about their next game included *"With exception of minor mishaps and the loss of practice due to cotton picking, our boys will be in fair condition for the Mount Olive game..."*

GAME 2: MAGEE (1-0) vs/@ NEW HEBRON (UNREPORTED)
MAGEE 33 NEW HEBRON 0
October 1, 1937

Apparently the Burrs opened the campaign with a win and then immediately took an off-week as the Mount Olive contest would be played later in the season. It was either that or an unreported loss on September 24th. The Simpson County News reported that the *"Magee Burrheads won over New Hebron Wildcats last Friday 33-0. With two victories to their credit, the boys of the football team are in high spirits for meeting (the) Clinton eleven there Friday. Our band members and many others will accompany them"*.

GAME 3: MAGEE (2-0) @ CLINTON (1-0)
MAGEE 0 CLINTON 13
October 8, 1937

Indications point to a match in Clinton against the Arrows led by Coach Stute Allen did take place. While doing research on the history of Clinton football (See "ARROW NATION"), I found a note that Clinton won the contest 13-0. There was no further reporting by any source on the contest, but Clinton had no other opponent that week. So it appears very likely that it did occur.

GAME 4: MAGEE (2-1) @ BRANDON (3-1)
MAGEE 6 BRANDON 25
October 14, 1937

After just one season as assistant under Z.L. Knight, Tommy "Tite" Ross now took the reins of the Bulldog football program. Of the 23 players out by September 15th, Ross described them as *"green and light, but scrappy"*. The squad had lost 14 lettermen from a wonderful 1936 team and would add starting QB Allen Harvill to the list before the first game. His *"severe sprain"* would apparently keep him out of at least the first five or six weeks of play.

Practices started on August 30th with *"the athletic prospects of the Brandon High School ... such as to warrant much anticipation as the opening of the pigskin season approaches. If reserve strength is developed, Brandon is headed up the ladder of football fame. A fine spirit of cooperation and plenty of pep signify the mental readiness of the Brandon Bulldogs. We are behind you men to take the last step. Come on! Let's take them as they come"*.

Brandon was first on the board early when Woodrow Swilley capped a long drive with a 3-yard run. Magee answered in the 2nd on what was called a *"freak play"*. Apparently the Magee runner was stopped by Charlie Cox, but then continued to run to the end zone for a touchdown. The score stood and halftime was 7-6 in favor of Brandon. After a scoreless 3rd, *"the Bulldogs' pent up fury was released and they scored three times"*. Bob Busick picked off one pass for a 38-yard touchdown, Swilley dove in from the 3, and Busick added another later.

The Brandon News said that *"Magee had several brilliant players. Two brothers stood out. B. (Ben) Allen and V. (Van) Allen playing halfback and left end respectively. These are especially brilliant. Another outstanding man was (Paul) Hughes, diminutive QB. It was his brilliant playing that led to Magee's touchdown"*. The Bulldogs were enjoying a tremendous string of successes during this period. From October 25th, 1935 until November of 1938, they lost only one contest; that coming against Canton this season by a score of 13-0. They finished 8-1 on the 1937 campaign.

GAME 5: MAGEE (2-2) vs/@ MOUNT OLIVE (UNREPORTED)
MAGEE 0 MOUNT OLIVE 0
October 22, 1937

It's assumed that the game was played as a normal Friday affair, though the date is never mentioned. What is found stated that the out-weighed Mount Olive eleven *"gleaned a 0-0 tie with the strong Magee Burrheads. After neither team was able to score in the initial half, the local gridders came into the eight-yard line early in the 3rd quarter"*. Said Coach White afterwards, *"There were no individual stars on the Magee team because they all work as a unit"*.

GAME 6: MAGEE (2-2-1) vs JACKSON B TEAM (3rd GAME)
MAGEE 6 JACKSON B TEAM 6
October 29, 1937

For weeks, Magee had been thinking that they would journey to Bay Saint Louis on the 29th to take on their local team. The team was to leave on Thursday and return on Saturday, with all expenses paid for the players. Even The Sea Coast Echo published the schedule to include the tilt. However, it appears that instead of the long road trip, they stayed home to take on Coach Scrap Crawley's Jackson Central B Team. Only a notation of the final score exists.

GAME 7: MAGEE (2-2-2) @ FOREST (UNREPORTED)
MAGEE 13 FOREST 0
November 5, 1937

In the four all-time games reported since 1926, Magee had lost by a combined 70-0 score. The Simpson County News reported that *"Forest had been on their defeat list for some time"*.

Forest was without key players in Weems, Simmons and Sparks due to either injury or discipline. The News Register noted that *"The Magee team played heads-up football from the start of the game to the finish, making the final score of the game 13-0 in their favor"*. The Simpson County News said, *"Several of our boys have been seen watching the daily papers mighty closely since. Think they expect to see their pictures on front page for accomplishing such a feat"*.

GAME 8: MAGEE (3-2-2) @ UTICA (2-5)
MAGEE 13 UTICA 6
November 12, 1937

Due to several minor injuries, Coach White put the Burrs only through a light scrimmage on practice week. At Utica, they bragged only of wins over Chamberlain Hunt (7-0) and Port Gibson (35-0). The Port Gibson contest would be the only one this year where Utica scored more than 7 points.

Magee opened the initial quarter with a short Preston Gordon scoring run and followed with Ben Allen's extra point. Going to the air in the second quarter to gain yardage, Utica gained their only tally on a sprint by Price. The try for the point-after was fumbled. Hughes provided the last score in the 4th quarter via the ground.

Apparently, there was as much action after the whistles as there was between. In the 3rd quarter, *"an altercation between Canterbury, captain for Utica, and a Magee player, took them both to the benches for unsportsmanlike conduct"*. Meanwhile, *"Utica and Magee spectators staged a free-for-all scrimmage on the sidelines that proved to be just about as interesting as the football game. It seems that Utica bunch still needs much schooling in the art of How To Take It"*.

GAME 9: MAGEE (4-2-2) vs PRENTISS (2-5?)
MAGEE 25 PRENTISS 0
November 19, 1937

With only two more games on the calendar, Coach White *"made it plain to the boys: no smokes, no sweets, and no sweeties until after the Mendenhall game"*. The only notation comes from The Simpson County News on November 25th, wherein they said *"(The team) claims they could have made a better job of it but were saving a good dose for Mendenhall, which will be measured out to them Wednesday afternoon. The Magee Burrheads say "Shoot Mendenhall! We've got you covered!"*

GAME 10: MAGEE (5-2-2) vs MENDENHALL (UNREPORTED)
MAGEE 0 MENDENHALL 0
November 24, 1937

For such an important and hyped meeting, it's unfortunate that more reporting was not enjoyed on the details. One pro-Magee article said *"We had really expected our boys to take Mendenhall to the cleaners, but they found them so good that it was all they could do to keep them from scoring"*. A pro-Tiger writer, presumably a student, published a lengthy poem to brag that Mendenhall was clearly the best team on the field. One excerpt says *"We lacked one yard in making a touchdown; Ask anybody in ye ole' home town!"*

It was apparently a rough affair. A notation for 1938 said that Olis Herrington *"received injuries that almost ended his playing days. It was after several months of care and treatment that he was declared sufficiently recovered to enter activity"* in the 1938 season. As an aside, Magee apparently brought a casket on the field at halftime while a student held a *"ceremony"*.

1938 (5-4-1)

Magee High opened on September 5th with 800 students. Two days before, the football team and 35 *"prospective players"* were already at work under second-year Coach Brad White.

Prospects seems good since "*Only 3 positions were left vacant by graduation: center and both halfbacks. The remainder of the team (is) intact. A lively battle is expected for the open places since the squad has a number of capable reserves and a number of new faces will be on hand for the opening workout*".

Before the week was over, previously injured star guard Olis Herrington broke his ankle in a scrimmage and was predicted to be out for the majority of the season. Preston Gordon was elected captain of the squad.

GAME 1: MAGEE (0-0) vs TAYLORSVILLE (0-0)
MAGEE 12 TAYLORSVILLE 0
September 16, 1938

Magee was scheduled to kick off the 1938 campaign against Georgetown but the schedule took a turn with Taylorsville providing the competition. It was a successful lid-lifter as Magee hit the board early on "*short end runs and passes*". (Preston) Gordon provided both touchdowns for the Burrheads via the air. Maurice Ward was "*on the receiving end of nearly every pass and was one hundred percent in his efforts*". A later report noted that "*The Burrheads displayed good football. Gordon and (Paul) Hughes in the backfield gives the Burrheads plenty of power in that department and should be able to win several ball games for Magee this season*".

GAME 2: MAGEE (1-0) vs RALEIGH (SECOND GAME)
MAGEE 32 RALEIGH 0
September 23, 1938

Much like the week before, the schedule changed. This time, it was Raleigh substituting for scheduled Prentiss High. The paper said that "*the tilt promised to be one of the best of the year. Reports for the Smith County school state that Raleigh has one of the best teams in the history of its football*". In the end, Magee would continue their shutouts on the 1938 season while getting their offense going nicely.

The opening touchdown came from Sodon on a five-yard run. Hughes provided the next "*on an off-tackle play*". That 12-0 advantage carried all the way to the final quarter. Hughes pointed for the first, and added the PAT. "*Diminutive*" Lloyd Brooks then "*stole the show from his more experienced teammates by galloping 15 yards in the closing minutes of the game for his second touchdown of the day*" and Belton Hester converted. The Smith County Reporter noted the score and only that the Raleigh "*boys played a good game*".

GAME 3: MAGEE (2-0) vs CLINTON (1-0)
MAGEE 0 CLINTON 0
September 30, 1938

The Arrows opened the season with a 40-0 thrashing of Georgetown and were now on the road to Magee to face the Burrs. Unfortunately, details of the scoreless affair are non-existent. It was said, however, that "*Clinton displayed one of the best running attacks seen here in the three games the Burrheads have played but was always held for downs before they could register a touchdown. The Burrheads, not having the offensive drive they have shown in previous games, were better on the defense than they usually are. Gordon and Hughes were the offensive threats for the Burrheads while (Theron) Blackwell and (Durwood) Myers were outstanding in the Magee line*".

GAME 4: MAGEE (2-0-1) @ NEW HEBRON (UNREPORTED)
MAGEE 13 NEW HEBRON 7
October 7, 1938

On game week, a report said that "*the Magee team was badly off its usual offensive power (the previous week). However, the defense ...was somewhat above that of past games and Coach White is working overtime this week in developing his scoring threat the Burrheads displayed in the opening game*". Magee went on to win the contest with the paper saying "*An undefeated season seems to be the spark that keeps the Magee High school Burrheads going at full speed down the tough schedule ...*"

GAME 5: MAGEE (3-0-1) @ MOUNT OLIVE (UNREPORTED)
MAGEE 13 MOUNT OLIVE 7
October 13, 1938

It was time for a regular face in the Mount Olive Pirates on a Thursday tilt. *"Intensive preparations are the order this week as Coach White irons out flaws developed in the game last week"*. Only the final score was reported on October 15th.

GAME 6: MAGEE (4-0-1) @ BAY SAINT LOUIS (UNREPORTED)
MAGEE 12 BAY SAINT LOUIS 13
October 29, 1938

Originally schedule for mid-November, the Burrs were now headed to the Mississippi Gulf Coast to take on Bay Saint Louis. White was again practicing his team hard to *"iron out flaws"* and now it appeared that Herrington may be able to return to the team. Magee appeared to be on their way to keeping the undefeated dream alive, holding a 12-0 lead through three quarters. But, they eventually *"weakened to the extent that they were defeated 13-12"* in the final minutes.

Magee started strongly with a drive to the Bay High 20 but couldn't advance. But they used a *"series of running and passing plays"* on their next possession that set up a 35-yard Hughes pass to Ward to make it 6-0. That score held through halftime despite Tiger drives to the Magee 8 and 11 yard lines. In the 3rd, a Wigham pass attempt was partially blocked by Clifton Duckworth and into the arms of Clyde Benton who *"raced over the goal for a touchdown"*.

Back came Bay High. After driving to their 30, it was the Tigers' McDonald who then picked off a Magee pass. Now at the 35-yard line, Wigham found Osbourne for the score to make it 12-7. In the last 3:00 of the contest, the Tigers marched to the visitors' 20-yard line. Wigham and Osborne connected for 18 yards and Thomas went over from there on the next play to insert the dagger. Magee drove to the BSL 20 with :15 left, but threw four incomplete passes to give the game away.

GAME 7: MAGEE (4-1-1) @ FOREST (UNREPORTED)
MAGEE 0 FOREST 16
November 4, 1938

To avoid a repeat of the Bay Saint Louis game, White was *"putting the squad through strenuous workouts in preparation for the game this week. Much stress has been given to defensive work and is expected that the team to meet Forest Friday night will be in the best of condition for the game"*. The Simpson County News noted that *"An usual large crowd accompanied our boys to Forest to witness the interesting game"*.

Magee gave Forest all they wanted in the first half. The only score of the first half came early in the game when a Burr punt blocked by Lott and Weems was eventually recovered for a safety. The News Register said that *"The Bearcats were outplayed in the first half, but spurred by a two-point lead came back in the last half to rhythmically jog eleven first downs over the Magee boys and to convert those first downs into two touchdowns with extra points"*.

Standout on the Forest team was Wee Willie Weems, who *"continuously rushed the passer"*. Hughes appeared to be the key offensive sparkplug for Magee on this day. Forest led in first downs 13-11 and went 2-7 in the air with one intercepted. Hughes went 5-18 with an interception.

GAME 8: MAGEE (4-2-1) vs COLLINS (UNREPORTED)
MAGEE 0 COLLINS 53
November 11, 1938

The report of this week's game is in doubt. Originally Magee was to play Mize. Then on game day, they were scheduled to play Collins. However, a report afterwards said that Utica drummed the Burrs 53-0. Another source offered a bit of clarity by pointing out a Collins tilt in 1938; thus making the notation of Utica a probable misprint.

GAME 9: MAGEE (4-3-1) vs RAYMOND (UNDEFEATED)
MAGEE 14 RAYMOND 0
November 18, 1938

The game against Raymond would play *"a strong Raymond High School team"* that marked *"the initial athletic meeting of the two schools"*. This being the last home game of the season, it was important to keep their good record at home in tact. *"The entire Burrhead team will be in condition for the game and although they are aware of the fact that Raymond will give them one of the toughest games of the year, the entire squad of Magee players is keeping their eyes on the game next week with Mendenhall"*.

In a *"sea of mud and water"*, fumbles and a lack of ability to pass kept the score low. Hughes had several nice runs and contributed to both Magee touchdowns. His first was a pass to Maurice Ward while the next was a 30-yard run.

GAME 10: MAGEE (5-3-1) @ MENDENHALL (UNREPORTED)
MAGEE 0 MENDENHALL 6
November 23, 1938

Rival Mendenhall came to the Raymond game to scout their upcoming opponent but could gauge very little due to conditions. Coach Obie Brown had been very excited about his chances for 1938 *"due to the excellent material being put out and the strenuous efforts the boys"* had been putting forth. They had lost 12 players to graduation but had 8 lettermen back in uniform.

This game would have *"considerable bearing on who shall represent this half of the district in the elimination playoffs"*. Additionally, it would *"settle for the year the football supremacy of these two rival teams"*. Magee was predicted as the favorite *"with every member of the team in good condition"*. Local businesses decided to close early in order to allow participants to see the game.

The only score came in the opening minutes of play when Bud May raced 91 yards to paydirt to provide all the points that Mendenhall would eventually need. The Simpson County News said that *"The third and fourth quarters were very exciting for the spectators with the Tigers threatening to score two more touchdowns. The Magee Burrheads soon found out that the Tigers were their complete masters"*.

1939 (8-3)

Enrollment at Magee High grew another 100 students to over 900. Brad White, back for his third year as head of the Burrheads, once again had experience on his side. The paper said that having *"an entire team of veterans around which to mold this year's team, Coach Brad White will probably have one of the best teams in the history of football in the Magee school..."*. White could claim not only a few transfer students, but also *"an entire backfield with men of two-or-more years' experience"*. Paul Hughes was chosen as Captain of the team.

A report from The Vicksburg Evening Post on December 5th described the Magee line with a 169-pound average; *"well-balanced in that the lightest man on the line is 160 and the heaviest 180"*.

GAME 1: MAGEE (0-0) @ CANTON (0-0)
MAGEE 7 CANTON 0
September 22, 1939

Coach Mark Wentz, first-year man for the Panthers, lost only 5 men to graduation. But, with 45 players out for football, there were many capable replacements. They were indeed prepared with a strong team and came very close to opening the season with a home win over Magee. In fact, though they were outweighed *"by fifteen pounds to the man"*, Canton came close to scoring on more than one occasion.

They were able to tear *"the heavier Magee line to shreds throughout the game"* at Ben Roberts Field, but could not get the ball over the goal when it counted. Early drives got inside the 9-yard line twice before turning over on downs. One Magee pass was picked off by James Shepherd but again they couldn't make it count. Finally, late in the game, *"a swivel-hipped substitute halfback (Allen) intercepted a Canton pass on the Panthers' 38-yard line ... and ran down the sidelines behind four-player interference"*. Hughes notched the point-after.

The game was marred by *"fisticuff ambitions"* that saw players from both teams ejected. Canton led in first downs 9-7 (or 8-5). Canton led on the ground 129-44 while Magee led in the air 59-30.

GAME 2: MAGEE (1-0) vs ACKERMAN (4-1)
MAGEE 25 ACKERMAN 0
September 29, 1939

Magee was originally scheduled to play New Hebron, but apparently the win over Canton caused them to cancel the Burrhead tilt. First-time opponent Ackerman was quickly added to the schedule. *"Very little is known of the comparative strength of the two teams, but an interesting game is expected by local fans and Coach Brad has been working overtime in expectation of a hard-fought game"*.

For this contest, the Robinson brothers were instrumental in spelling defeat. Leon Robinson accounted for 19 points; mainly set up by brother Kenneth Robinson's carrying the ball *"in scoring distance"*. Hughes notched the other touchdown *"after a thirty-yard run through the entire Ackerman line. The passing combination of Hughes to Ward, elongated end, was working at its best in the game and the line play of Blackwell and Herrington was outstanding"*. Ackerman nearly tied the game in the final frame, but turned the ball over on downs at the Magee 10-yard line.

GAME 3: MAGEE (2-0) vs MADISON (0-0-1)
MAGEE 39 MADISON 6
October 6, 1939

Little would change in the lineup for the contest against first-time opponent Madison. As for Magee's visitor, they were geared (at least on this night) by a 185-pound QB named Yendel. *"He did everything to the Burrheads that was possible for one to do. His forty-yard pass to Bell was good for a touchdown in the second period with his running and passing a continuous threat to Magee"*.

In fact, Magee didn't get going until *"the fading minutes of the third period"* and continued the scoring flood until the final whistle. *"The entire Magee team played good ball, with the offensive work of Hughes, Lloyd Brooks and Keith Robinson bordering on spectacular. Keith Robinson also played a great defensive game. In the line, the Burrheads were almost invincible with most of the gaining done by Madison being in the air. Blackwell, Ward, Herrington and Benton were outstanding for the Burrheads"*.

The Simpson County News reported the final as 38-6.

GAME 4: MAGEE (3-0) vs MOUNT OLIVE (UNDEFEATED)
MAGEE 13 MOUNT OLIVE 0
October 12, 1939

The paper said of the upcoming opponent, *"Mount Olive is always one of the hardest opponents on the Burrhead schedule and the game this year will be no exception. Since Friday is a holiday at both schools, the game has been advanced one day as is the usual custom here, and a large crowd is expected on this occasion"*.

Magee jumped out to a 6-0 lead on Coach R.C. Shows' team via Keith Robinson's running. In the second quarter, Hughes found Ward with a pass at the five-yard line and Ward *"stepped over for a touchdown"*. Hughes' PAT marked the final points. *"Keith Robinson (was) by far the outstanding offensive player in the game... The consistent end runs of Hughes and Keith Robinson and the stellar work of Blackwell and Benton in the line proved a continuous threat to the undefeated Mount Olive team. Their best effort fell short of the Burrhead twenty-yard line with most of the offensive work being done by Knight, fullback"*.

The (Collins) News-Commercial said that *"The Burrheads were probably the strongest team the Pirates have faced this season. They kept the ball in Mount Olive territory most of the afternoon. Mount Olive stopped several Magee thrusts within their twenty-yard line"*. One scare in the contest came in the final frame when Hughes was injured and had to be removed from the game. *"From then until the close of the game, the Magee team appeared to be lost and at no time threatened to do anything with the visitors. This is bringing quite a bit of attention from Coach White as he prepares for the invasion of Quitman Friday"*.

As a side note for historical records, The Simpson County News incorrectly reported the score to be 12-6 in one edition before correcting it the next week.

GAME 5: MAGEE (4-0) @ QUITMAN (UNREPORTED)
MAGEE 0 QUITMAN 6
October 20, 1939

This was originally to be an open week for the Burrs, but it was filled later by Pachuta. For unknown reasons, that changed to the non-conference Quitman squad on the road. The Clarke County Tribune said that the Magee team ..." *has played a number of the leading high school teams in the state so far this season and remains undefeated*".

When it was over, the same publication said that "*The Panthers gave a splendid account of themselves in last Friday's game with Magee...*" As for game specifics, it was noted elsewhere only that the home team beat Magee by a slight 6-0 margin and that Hughes and Blackwell both suffered injuries in the game and could be lost against upcoming Bay Saint Louis.

GAME 6: MAGEE (4-1) @ BAY SAINT LOUIS (UNREPORTED)
MAGEE 18 BAY SAINT LOUIS 0
October 27, 1939

It was noted in November that "*... the Burrheads defeated Bay St. Louis last week 18-0 without much trouble and will be in the best of condition for the game this (coming) week. The Burrheads were handicapped with injuries and ineligibility ...*" So, it appears that Magee's road win may have come without the services of Hughes and Blackwell.

GAME 7: MAGEE (5-1) @ FOREST (UNDEFEATED)
MAGEE 19 FOREST 7
November 3, 1939

The undefeated Bearcats under Coach Hollingsworth would pose perhaps the strongest competition of the season. And as a conference matchup, "*A victory for either team will make them strong contenders for conference honors this year. Last season, the Bearcats defeated Magee 16-0 to spoil a good season for the Burrheads, and it is with a sense of revenge that the local squad settled down to hard training here today for this particular tilt*".

Info on the game came from a November 8th snippet that said if you're going to face Magee, "*you had better be sure about your anti-aircraft defenses, for Magee completed 34 of 37 passes against Forest Hi in winning 19-7 last week*". A later part of The Simpson County News called it "*a most excellent game. A large crowd of Magee fans witnessed the game. Many of the Forest citizens are loud in their praise of the fine playing and good sportsmanship of the Magee players*".

GAME 8: MAGEE (6-1) vs CLINTON (2-3-1)
MAGEE 19 CLINTON 0
November 10, 1939

The paper opined that the success of the passing game the week before caused Poplarville to cancel their game against Magee on the 18th. But the tilt with Clinton was still due for kickoff this week. The game was originally scheduled to be in Clinton, but "*by mutual consent*" would now be on the Burrhead field.

Hughes notched the first Burrhead score in the 2nd quarter and added the point-after. That score held until the 3rd quarter when Leon Robinson got into the end zone "*on a short play through the line*" and Hughes counted his second score and the game's last in the final frame. The Clarion-Ledger said that Clinton "*had considerable difficulty penetrating the Burrhead line and never seriously threatened to score at any time*". The Simpson County News said "*Magee's football team chalked up another win Friday. Say, Coach White, what are you feeding your boys, huh?*"

GAME 9: MAGEE (7-1) @ WIGGINS (ONE LOSS)
MAGEE 6 WIGGINS 12
November 18, 1939

One last non-conference matchup was in store in a game to be played at Perkinston Junior College against a "*strong Wiggins football team*". Like Magee, they had lost only one game thus far while "*meeting some of the strongest teams of that section*" and were expected to "*outweigh the Burrheads and have a fast backfield which has been a threat to every opponent they have* met".

The Stone County Enterprise called it a *"rip-roaring clash"*. The Tomcats notched touchdowns in the second and fourth quarters, with Blaylock gaining the first on a 26-yard dash and Blaylock finding Batson from the 19-yard line for the last. Both PATs failed. Magee's lone tally came in the final frame. Rainey picked off a Wiggins pass at the 1-yard line and returned it to the Wiggins 27 *"before he was hit down by Wiggins' Yeager"*. A few plays later, Ward squeezed in from the 8 after picking up a Hughes fumble. A notation from a few days later was puzzling as the paper called this game a *"B-team"* contest. Only so many varsity players could play in a B-team match or else they could not play for a championship. Thus, it is a possibility.

GAME 10: MAGEE (7-2) vs MENDENHALL (UNREPORTED)
MAGEE 39 MENDENHALL 7
November 22, 1939

This game was circled on the calendar every year, but this edition of the rivalry carried a bit more importance. A loss to Mendenhall would *"deprive the Burrheads of an opportunity of entering the playoff for championship honors later"*. Magee came through with flying colors to post an undefeated conference record before *"one of the largest crowds to ever witness a football game in Magee"*.

The Burrheads were *"handicapped"* with injuries to both Rainey and Leon Robinson serious enough to keep them out. Apparently, Magee was up 19-7 at the end of three quarters; the lone Mendy score coming in the 3rd via a *"series of passes and a penalty"*. Hughes was credited with four TDs *"and his passing and end runs were a constant threat"*. Keith Robinson tacked on a score and notched a pair of extra points. *"In the line, Blackwell, Herrington, Ward, Duckworth and Calhoun were outstanding"*. Decades later, it was reported erroneously that Mendy had not scored in the game.

GAME 11: MAGEE (8-2) @ SAINT ALOYSIUS (10-0)
MAGEE 7 SAINT ALOYSIUS 13
December 8, 1939

Magee now had a chance to grab the Class A Middle Mississippi regional championship. They had ended the season with a tie alongside Saint Aloysius; a Vicksburg team they had faced at least in 1929, 1930 and 1932. The week delay in playing was good for the Burrheads as they had at least three starters out with injuries; not from the Mendenhall scrap but rather against Wiggins. The paper said that Magee *"was at considerable loss throughout the first half (of Mendenhall) without them"*.

Light workouts were in place for the first off-week while practices resumed at full-strength the next. As game day approached, all three players (Leon Robinson, Rainey and Womack) appeared to still be out of commission. *"The Burrheads will be greatly handicapped unless capable reserves can be found to fill their places immediately"*.

In Vicksburg, legendary Coach Joe Balzli was looking to secure his second-straight undefeated season. His last loss had come in November of 1937. His prospects were good as the game would be played at Johnson Field thanks to efforts of The Vicksburg Chamber of Commerce. Things started roughly for the Flashes, however, as on the opening kick, Hughes lateraled to Kenneth Robinson and he took it 75 yards for the touchdown. Hughes also added the extra point. The game was delayed briefly thereafter as a blown fuse on the main transformer had to be quickly repaired.

Saint Al responded before the quarter ended after a bad snap caused a fumble at the Magee 5. Miller Evans recovered and, two plays later, Joe Booth plunged in. Harry Hude converted the game-tying point-after. That would be all of the scoring until the final frame. Evans blocked a Magee punt at the Burrhead 20, Van Stewart picked it up and then raced across the goal for what would be the game-winner. Saint Al bested Magee in first downs 6-3 while Magee held the advantage in penalty yards 30-0.

A football banquet to honor the team was held in mid-December. Fifteen letters were awarded by Coach White with Duckworth and Blackwell called *"outstanding me on this years' football team"*.

1940-1949

1946 Team (9-2-1): MIDDLE MISSISSIPPI CHAMPIONS

1940 (5-5-1)

New coaches David Holland and Irie Wilson initially welcomed 9 lettermen back to the practice field. The paper said that *"Only a few places were left vacant by graduation last spring. Only one vacancy occurs in the line which will be practically intact with lettermen at every position"*. That disposition changed by early September when The Clarion-Ledger reported that *"Injuries in scrimmages ... since the opening of school have continued to dim the hopes of the most ardent fans of the Burrheads to a very successful season"*.

GAME 1: MAGEE (0-0) @ McCOMB (0-0)
MAGEE 0 McCOMB 55
September 13, 1940

Coach C.C. Moore and Assistant Coach Cuthbert Ishee welcomed the Burrheads to their field that now had new *"modern"* lighting for a night tilt. Their roster had at least 55 players with 6 letter-winners back on the field. They may have anticipated a different Magee team as The Enterprise Journal claimed that the Burrs were undefeated the previous year and Middle Mississippi Class A champions.

The first McComb score came in the opening quarter on a 1-yard dive and Alfred Hodges conversion. Vernon Rushing captured the next touchdown in the 2nd quarter via a 13-yard escape and Hodges made it 14-0. Magee could have cut into the lead before halftime but fumbled the ball away inside the 10-yard line. To make it worse, Robinson later threw an interception to Gerald Smith before the whistle. The 3rd quarter would see the game slip away. Bill Carpenter had the first score on a 42-yard dash to make it 21-0.

Magee drove to the McComb 15-yard line to open the 4th quarter but could not convert. Hodges made it count with a 41-yard scoring response, Jack Eddy pulled off a 60-yard pick-six for a score, Aubrey Magee raced 40 yards and, with Hodges conversions, it was 42-0. Both teams then traded fumbles, but Magee threw an interception to Hodges who took it 45 yards to paydirt. Proby Smith had the final tally after he took an interception 75 yards for the touchdown.

The Enterprise Journal said that *"From the first, Magee found little hospitality on the local grid ... hardly permitting the visitors to get within shouting distance of a face-saving tally"*. Including the games where the scores were reported, this one served as the worst defeat of a Magee team since they started playing in 1926. McComb would finish their undefeated season by outscoring opponents 286-33.

GAME 2: MAGEE (0-1) @ CANTON (0-0)
MAGEE 7 CANTON 0
September 20, 1940

Coach Wentz and Coach Bledsoe had nine spots to fill for his opener against Magee. The paper said that *"The competition is keen and there are some promising players showing up"*. It was probable that more injuries than previously alluded were in play in Magee. The paper said that the Burrheads suffered from *"an entire team shot full of reserves from last season and with men never-before having played football. (Coach Holland) faces a real situation in trying to work out a winning combination from the material he had on hand. The game with Canton this week should prove equally as tough as the game with McComb and plenty of hard work has been the order for this week's preparation"*.

Perhaps the biggest upset to date, Magee rode to Hinds County and did what others may have thought impossible. The only tally came early in the 2nd quarter via a 3-yard pass from Robinson to Maurice Ward. Each squad counted 6 first downs when it was over. Interestingly, The Madison County Herald noted in November that Canton had lost only to Benoit, tied Boyce, and defeated Culkin Academy, Belzoni, Tchula and Lexington.

GAME 3: MAGEE (1-1) vs NEW HEBRON (UNREPORTED)
MAGEE 12 NEW HEBRON 6
September 27, 1940

The coaches were *"working overtime in an attempt to have the team at the best possible condition"*. However, with an injury situation taking the team to dire straits, it was unwelcome news that *"star performer"* W.C. Jones broke his leg in a practice scrimmage during the week. He was easily predicted to be lost for the season.

At kickoff, Magee found themselves also without the services of Ward and Robinson. So, they relied on *"short end runs and passing"* to pull out the victory. Earl Holmes had the initial score in the 2nd quarter on a 15-yard reverse while Hobart Brooks tallied the last Magee score in the final frame from the 10-yard line. New Hebron had tied things in the 3rd when Buckley picked off an errant throw and took it 60-yards to the 5-yard line from where Garner found his way for the touchdown. The paper said that *"Gill, Blackwell and Herrington in the line and Holmes and Brooks in the backfield were best for Magee"*.

GAME 4: MAGEE (2-1) vs QUITMAN (UNREPORTED)
MAGEE 0 QUITMAN 0
October 4, 1940

The two teams had faced each other in 1939 with Quitman pulling off a slim 6-0 win. This rematch would show the teams still almost exactly equal in strength as the contest ended in a scoreless tie. Magee did have a chance to snatch the last-minute victory on a *"drive that had all the appearances of a scoring punch, only to bog down on a series of line plays in the visitors' territory"*. They went on to say that *"the defensive work of Blackwell, Ward and Herrington ... was equally as good at opportune times"*.

It was noted on the 7th that Magee apparently played the game *"with only two men in the entire lineup unfettered by hurts"*. Said the writer about Coach Holland's inaugural season, *"Football coaching will make you gray-haired before your time, folks!"*

GAME 5: MAGEE (2-1-1) @ MOUNT OLIVE (UNREPORTED)
MAGEE 26 MOUNT OLIVE 7
October 10, 1940

Since Friday was a school holiday, the two teams agreed to meet for a Thursday tilt. For this week, it appeared that some of the Burrhead players would return from injury. Brooks, however, was injured in the Quitman game and was expected to miss. Magee had Red Robinson in the lineup and that would make the difference on this night.

The Burrs scored while holding the home team *"on the defensive practically the entire game"*. Robinson notched the first touchdown early in the game *"through the center of the Mount Olive line"* from the 11-yard line and added the PAT. In the 3rd quarter, Robinson ran in from the 15 and followed that with a Brooks (now back in the game) lateral for 60 yards. Brooks had the final tally from the 4-yard line and then hit Ward for the PAT. Mount Olive's lone score came late on a J. King pass to Jerry Guess. McLeod found Guess for the final conversion point.

"The Burrheads deserved to win the game. They played steadier football and took advantage of scoring chances. Duckworth's punting was a real defensive weapon. In the Magee line, Duckworth, Herrington, Ward, Blackwell and Shivers were outstanding, with B. Stubbs, Robinson and Brooks playing good ball in the backfield".

GAME 6: MAGEE (3-1-1) @ HAZLEHURST (UNREPORTED)
MAGEE 0 HAZLEHURST 26
October 18, 1940

Magee was originally scheduled to play a tough Puckett teams this week. However, it was announced on the 15th that Puckett cancelled the contest. In their place, Hazlehurst offered to provide the competition on their home field.

Their local paper said that *"The Magee team has a reputation throughout the state as being a hard team to defeat, but the Indians succeeded in winning by making long runs, by fine passing, and with a spirit of cooperation shown by all. H.A. Smith and John Magee made the touchdowns and Truett Smith and W.L. Stampley the extra points. All the teams played a good game and the results of this (is) shown by the score. Sidney Thompson was injured in the beginning of the game and was unable to play anymore"*.

GAME 7: MAGEE (3-2-1) @ FOREST (UNREPORTED)
MAGEE 6 FOREST 12
October 25, 1940

Coach John Rich's Bearcats were predicted to give Magee *"probably their hardest game this year"*. Robinson was expected to miss due to a leg that was re-injured against Hazlehurst.

"Minor injuries to several members of the squad has held scrimmages to very little more than drills and Burrhead hopes for a victory over the strong Bearcat aggregation are very dim".

The game ended much closer than anyone expected with Magee up 6-0 at halftime. But *"after limping through the first half, the Forest Bear Cats woke up and fought to a victory…"*. Both Forest scores came in the second half. Lester Smith crossed the goal in the 3rd quarter *"through the line"* while Britt Sparks added the last in the final frame *"standing up"*. Said the paper, *"Magee's passing was weak, but the Burrheads have a brick wall line defense to make up for it"*.

The Scott County Times was impressed with the Magee play. *"When the half ended, believe me that there was never a more surprised and outplayed team than ye olde Bearcats. The score was then 6-0 chiefly because of a one-man whirlwind who went through the Bearcats line like sand through an hour glass, which is running"*. Afterwards, the Forest paper said *"None of the Bearcats were seriously hurt, but as for Magee, yours truly does not know. They carried two off the playing field. Here's hoping that they were not hurt badly for they played a clean, hard game"*.

GAME 8: MAGEE (3-3-1) @ KOSCIUSKO (UNREPORTED)
MAGEE 12 KOSCIUSKO 47
November 1, 1940

The Whippets, under Coach Walter "Juicy" Scales, had won the Big Black district championship the previous year. They were no joke this season, outscoring opponents thus far 152-6. Their most recent victim had been Philadelphia, over whom they won 32-0.

After the lopsided win, the paper said that Kosciusko *"showed versatility both on the ground and through the air last week. (Numerous players) looked impressive in carrying the pigskin for sizeable yardage through a scrappy but over-powered Burrhead outfit. The Attalans unraveled a pair of excellent pass receivers and each did his share of ground gaining during the tilt. The Kosciusko forward wall repeatedly forced the visitors to punt and although the Simpson aggregation appeared to be moving at times, it was unable to drive consistently through an aggressive line"*.

GAME 9: MAGEE (3-4-1) vs BAY SAINT LOUIS (UNREPORTED)
MAGEE 13 BAY SAINT LOUIS 0
November 8, 1940

Coach George Westerfield's Mississippi Gulf Coast squad had been bitten by the injury bug. But Magee was also suffering heavily with that problem, giving *"the visitors a pre-game advantage in this seasons tilt"*.

Bay Saint Louis came close to a pair of scores thanks to the running of Capdepon and McDonald *"only to lose the ball in the shadow of the Magee goal line"*. Brooks opened scoring in the 1st quarter via his 1-yard dive. Now in the final minute, Robinson escaped from the 30 *"on an end-around play after a series of line plays had failed to penetrate the visitors' line"*. Robinson found Ward for the only extra point.

GAME 10: MAGEE (4-4-1) @ SAINT ALOYSIUS (3-3)
MAGEE 0 SAINT ALOYSIUS 7
November 22, 1940

The rematch of the Middle Mississippi championship teams from 1939 was now at hand. Coach Joe Balzli's Flashes had bested the Burrheads in Vicksburg for the title the previous year in a close contest. He now had his purple and gold going through *"their hardest practice week of the season"* in anticipation. He felt confident in his preparation and predicted *"that his charges would take Magee and roll on to a second Class A championship"*. Saint Al chose to wear gold jerseys; the same as they had worn in the aforementioned contest. The Vicksburg Evening Post said that *"Fans … will see some real straight football with a sprinkling here and there of razzle dazzle"*.

A muddy field made *"passes … conspicuously dangerous"*. It was, however, a pass that allowed Saint Al to go on to that championship game against Forest (which they won 39-0). On the first play of the 2nd quarter, Bob King hit Edwin Evans for a 48-yard score and King converted the PAT. Saint Al reached the Burrhead 1 at least once and got close two other times. When the game ended, the Flashes were at the Magee 10. The crowd was small and both teams *"came out looking as though they had been through the traditional hog wallow"*.

GAME 11: MAGEE (4-5-1) @ MENDENHALL (4-4-1)
MAGEE 33 MENDENHALL 6
November 29, 1940

Coach Rudolph Whitten began the 1940 season with *"a squad of practically no experienced men. Only two regulars had ever played before. Nine of the starters put on uniforms for the first time this fall"*. They fared pretty well considering and had an off-week to prepare for a winning season.

The Saint Al game had apparently re-injured both Robinson and Duckworth for this rivalry week. It wouldn't matter as the Burrheads scored three times in the opening quarter before Mendenhall got on the board thanks to a fumble recovered at the Magee 20. Robinson's pass to Gill opened scoring and his pass to Ward ended things in the final quarter. In between, Gill notched a pair of touchdowns while Blackwell and C. Robinson each counted a score.

At the end-of-year banquet held on December 12th, 18 players were awarded letters for their efforts. They included, Duckworth, Ward, Gill, McAlpin, Shivers, Herrington, Rainey, Holmes, Carr, Blackwell, Garner, R. Robinson, C. Robinson, B. Stubbs, R. Stubbs, Brooks, A. Garner and C. Carr.

1941 (5-5-1)

The 1941 Burrheads were called *"one of the lightest and most inexperienced teams in its history"*. For the third time in three years, they would have a new mentor in Coach Ira Wilson. He had 28 men out for his Middle Mississippi Region team *"of which only two are experienced players"*.

GAME 1: MAGEE (0-0) vs NEW HEBRON (0-0)
MAGEE 13 NEW HEBRON 0
September 12, 1941

Excluding unreported contests, Magee had put up a 4-0-1 record against New Hebron with the tie coming in the 1935 season. The Burrs were understandably expected to be the underdog to the "strong" New Hebron team, but pulled off the shocker in the lid-lifter. Magee was outweighed a reported *"12 pounds per member"*.

Hobart Brooks was the hero of the night with both touchdowns *"after the Magee line pounded the opponents unmercifully. Their fighting spirit and team work was described as the winning factor by Coach Wilson"*. After the upset, Sanatorium Theatre manager Mr. Kyle treated the team to a picture show that night.

GAME 2: MAGEE (1-0) @ GULF COAST MILITARY ACADEMY (0-0)
MAGEE 0 GULF COAST MILITARY ACADEMY 27
September 20, 1941

If Magee thought they were outweighed against New Hebron, they had a new reality against first-time opponent GCMA. The Academy outweighed them a reported *"40 pounds to a man"* but Magee still *"put up a stiff fight"*. The gulf coast paper called Magee *"outweighed but scrappy"*.

Despite the weight disadvantage, *"the Magee boys put up a gallant fight and displayed a never-say-die spirit right up to the very end"*. Thanks to numerous GCMA fumbles, the first half sat only 6-0. Early in the opening quarter, Charley Black finished a long drive with a 5-yard plunge. In the 3rd quarter, a blocked punt by Mooty set up a 3-yard Starnes run and Kelly point-after. Magee nearly pulled off a quick response when Stubbs *"snatched a Cadet pass out of the ozone and dashed 21 yards before he was hauled down from behind by Black two yards short of the goal line"*. Four straight runs failed to get the Burrheads into paydirt.

In the final frame, the Cadets notched a pair of touchdowns. Black *"cut away on an off-tackle jaunt and propelled 81 yards, easily outstepping his opponents"* for the first. Shortly after, Doran crossed from the 7. Thomas added the first PAT; Doran the last. The local paper said that *"Our Burrheads are to be commended for the fine work they did in this game"*.

GAME 3: MAGEE (1-1) @ GULFPORT (1-0)
MAGEE 0 GULFPORT 37
September 26, 1941

Coach Nick Duncan was changing his Commodore lineup *"in order that they might present a strong offensive team of the Middle Mississippi Region"*. They were coming off of a 12-7 win against Brookhaven. This one would never be in doubt as most starters played less than one half. Gulfport tacked on 12 first quarter points with Charles Gaudria's 21-yard dash on a reverse while Richard Streiff added the next from the 8. Leroy "Jiggs" James capped a 57-yard drive in the 2nd quarter on a 12-yard pass from Kenneth Murphy. The 18-0 score stood until the 3rd quarter when Gulfport tallied again.

That score came as the result of a Magee fumble that Gaudria later turned into a 4-yard dive. The last frame saw the Commodores put up two touchdowns. James Edwards counted the first from the 13-yard line while James added a 37-yard pick-six for the last. Whitney Carvin had the PAT on the Edwards tally.

With blown fuses putting the field in semi-darkness for most of the last quarter, Magee still *"waged a hard fight all the way, with Holmes (right guard) the standout in the forward wall"*. The Magee Courier said that Magee *"made a very creditable showing against one of the strongest teams of the state. The excellent punting by the Magee team was one of the outstanding features of the game"*. The Burrheads enjoyed their time at the Edgewater Gulf Hotel over the weekend.

GAME 4: MAGEE (1-2) @ QUITMAN (UNREPORTED)
MAGEE 19 QUITMAN 6
October 3, 1941

With two straight road losses by a combined 64-0, Magee was expected to be an underdog on the road for the third-straight week. But they pulled off the stunner in fine fashion. Billie Stubbs *"ripped the Quitman line for 35 yards with beautiful blocking"* in the 2nd quarter to set up a 1-yard Brooks dive. Quitman responded in the 3rd but Magee didn't quit. Not long after, *"and with the good running of Brooks and the good blocking of the rest of the team"*, they tacked on another score. In the final frame, they moved steadily downfield for their last touchdown and added the point-after.

GAME 5: MAGEE (2-2) vs FOREST (2-1)
MAGEE 0 FOREST 0
October 10, 1941

Amazingly, while Magee had faced Forest at least seven times, all games had apparently been at Forest. Now, the Bearcats would pay a visit to Simpson County in the first conference tilt. The paper said that *"The Burrheads are expecting a lot of trouble from the Forest team"*. In the game, *"neither side showed much offense"*. Forest got inside the Magee 25 but fumbled away the opportunity. Forest edged Magee in total yardage while the Burrheads' Bell *"repeatedly kicked the locals out of tight spots"*.

GAME 6: MAGEE (2-2-1) vs MOUNT OLIVE (UNREPORTED)
MAGEE 0 MOUNT OLIVE 7
October 17, 1941

Magee held the edge in all-time games but there were no guarantees on the outcome of this contest. The Pirates were called *"larger and more experienced"* and were able to pull out a one-score victory. Late in the 3rd quarter, Brooks fumbled to Mount Olive at the 18-yard line. They used just one play to have McLeon hit Slawson for the touchdown. McNair added the point-after. The paper gave credit to the Pirates *"demonstrating a tricky running attack to run up six first downs"*.

Apparently the Burrheads could have scored in the 2nd quarter with Carr open for a touchdown on a run play. The paper said that *"this was the first defeat of a Magee team on the local gridiron in five years, and the second in the history of Magee football. Both defeats were handed down by Mount Olive"*. It was possible that they lost in 1928 and once more later; but those results are up for debate.

Mount Olive led in first downs (6-2), completed passes (5-0) and interceptions (2-1). Magee's 8 punts averaged 45 yards while Mount Olive's 8 punts averaged 34 yards. Magee had 4 penalties for 20 yards while the Pirates had 4 penalties for 30 yards.

GAME 7: MAGEE (2-3-1) vs CANTON (UNREPORTED)
MAGEE 6 CANTON 7
October 24, 1941

In the afternoon game with the Panthers, Canton *"mixed brute strength with speed and deception to score on a sustained drive in the 3rd quarter"*. The Canton team was led by ex-Magee mentor David Holland. Magee had put up their points in the 2nd quarter when Carr *"pulled one of the oldest tricks in football"* from the 48-yard line by *"laying out"*. Billie Stubbs then hit him to put the ball at the 1-yard line. Earl Homes then dove off-tackle for the score. Canton's winning response was on an 80-yard drive with Coleman providing the eventual game-winning extra point.

GAME 8: MAGEE (2-4-1) vs BYRAM (UNREPORTED)
MAGEE 47 BYRAM 0
October 31, 1941

This should have been the inaugural game against a *"very inexperienced"* Byram eleven. The starters didn't stay long, scoring twice in the first quarter. The Magee Courier said that *"The game was played from start to finish in a steady downpour of rain; therefore, with a wet ball, neither team showed much in trick plays, punting or passing"*. Byram had only one first down; that coming on a pass. Not once did they cross midfield. Before the next game, the JV team would face Star on the road. They came out with a 14-7 win.

GAME 9: MAGEE (3-4-1) @ SAINT ALOYSIUS (1-5)
MAGEE 12 SAINT ALOYSIUS 6
November 14, 1941

Coach Joe Balzli had taken his Flashes to undefeated seasons in 1938 and 1939 but also won the Class A championship in 1940. This year, he had only 7 lettermen back and was doing his best to figure a way to keep the success going. He changed the offensive playbook to a "T-formation" to best use his personnel. The Vicksburg Evening Post said that *"A fighting team is hard to beat; and from all indications, Balzli's men will be scrapping bunch"*.

Despite their record, Magee was called *"one of the strongest teams in the Middle Mississippi Conference"*. The game was up for grabs late. In the 2nd, Saint Al was driving and sat at the Magee 37. But William Stewart's pass was picked off by Holmes and taken the distance for a touchdown. Bell joined the pickoff parade afterward but the Burrheads got only to the Flash 6 before halftime. Now 6-0 midway through the 4th quarter, a bad punt put Saint Al at the Magee 10. Shelby Flowers got in four plays later to tie the game.

Coming back, Magee put together a couple of long runs to set up a Brooks dash of 32 yards for the game-winning touchdown. Carr had actually picked off another Flash pass in the opening quarter but the Burrheads could get no closer than the Flash 9. Saint Al also dodged bullets in the 2nd (a Brooks run of 36 for a score was called back for holding) and twice in the final frame (getting to the Flash 5 and Flash 10) before the defense held. One came on a Garner interception.

Out of respect for Joe Balzli, it should be noted that it was his last year as coach until 1945 as he entered the Marine Corp to serve in the Pacific. On his return, he continued his coaching until 1960.

GAME 10: MAGEE (4-4-1) vs MENDENHALL (8-2)
MAGEE 0 MENDENHALL 6
November 19, 1941

Rivalry week was at hand for this Wednesday game. Impressive Mendenhall, with losses only to Forest Hill and Raymond, would be a bit hampered by the loss of Dan Smith with an injured ankle. As was customary, Magee merchants closed shop early to allow people to witness the game. Unfortunately for Magee, it marked the end of a short streak of wins against Mendenhall.

The visitors had numerous chances to score in the first half, but *"each time they would get a bad break and miss scoring"*. Mendy's touchdown came in the 3rd on a 60-yard pass play from Johnnie Toland to Howard Cook. Magee's best chance came on a drive starting at their 20 that made it to the 25 thanks to running by Holmes and McAlpin. "*The game was played with very few penalties on either side. Mendenhall had 25 yards marked up against them and the Burrheads received only 5 yards. This seems to be a new low between these two teams*".

GAME 11: MAGEE (4-5-1) vs/@ FOREST (UNREPORTED)
MAGEE 13 FOREST 0
November 28, 1941

Though not playing in the playoffs, the Burrheads did manage a rematch with Forest to end the season. The Magee Courier said that "*The Burrheads were complete masters of the game Friday*". Holmes started the scoring in the 2nd quarter with a 65-yard burst "*unmolested*". Holmes found Charles Carr for the extra point and 7-0 lead. In the 3rd, Jake McAlpin went through the middle of the line for a 75-yard escape to finish scoring for Magee football in 1941.

The paper said that "*Coach Wilson used men he expected to play next year and the results look very promising. This was the final game of the season and left the standing at 5-5-1*".

1942 (2-8-1)

After a pair of one-year coaches, Magee now had their tenth mentor in B.L. Kisner. He had started working the boys in two-daily sessions in early September but warned that "*the public should not expect too much of the team until midseason. This is the smallest squad in respect to weight and number than Magee High has had in the past six years of competition*".

There is one thing to keep in mind when reading what little is found about each contest. Magee, and the world, now found themselves in war. For many, the football programs disbanded for as many as three years due to the numbers of young men who enlisted for service. On the home front, newspapers understandably devoted much of their efforts to keeping readers up-to-date on events as they unfolded. Additionally, with rationing in play, it was almost impossible for reporters to follow the team around to so many away contests. High school sports reports were thereby scant; if ever mentioned at all.

GAME 1: MAGEE (0-0) @ CRYSTAL SPRINGS (0-0)
MAGEE 0 CRYSTAL SPRINGS 19
September 11, 1942

Unfortunately, we know only from a recap of the season's results that Magee opened the 1942 campaign with a 19-0 road loss.

GAME 2: MAGEE (0-1) @ GULFPORT (UNREPORTED)
MAGEE 0 GULFPORT 6
September 18, 1942

Kisner's team found themselves on the road for the second-straight week; this time to the Mississippi Gulf Coast. The result was probably a surprise to spectators and fans alike. It was reported that "*the Commodores were having a tough time disposing of a surprisingly defensive-minded Magee club. The Magees, though unable to get an attack of their own underway, also managed to hold Gulfport scoreless during the first half. Not until Jimmy Edwards hit Baxter Hotio with an (11-yard) runt pass did the Commodores break through*".

GAME 3: MAGEE (0-2) @ MOUNT OLIVE (UNREPORTED)
MAGEE 0 MOUNT OLIVE 6
September 25, 1942

When the season began, this contest had not been scheduled and the Magee squad was to enjoy an open date. But, Mount Olive would sign on to play one of two tilts against Magee on the season. That is probably the result of a lack of opponents due to the aforementioned events of the day. Two notations from different sources indicate the final outcome.

GAME 4: MAGEE (0-3) @ MORTON (UNREPORTED)
MAGEE 0 MORTON 0
October 2, 1942

The week's opponent was scheduled to be Quitman, but changes were again in store for the Burrs. Instead, they faced Morton and came away with a scoreless tie.

GAME 5: MAGEE (0-3-1) @ FOREST (4TH GAME)
MAGEE 12 FOREST 6
October 9, 1942

Forest held roughly a 6-3-1 all-time advantage over Magee, with the majority of those games played in Scott County. Magee had pulled the upset back in 1937 and 1941 against the Bearcats and were hoping to repeat history. One report had Magee outweighing their hosts by *"ten pounds to a man"*.

It was the Cats with an opening period score courtesy of Charlie Brueck's dive through right tackle from inside the 1-yard line. That had been set up by a bad Magee punt recovered by Tony Austin. That 6-0 score held until the 3rd quarter when Earl Holmes took a punt back 53 yards to paydirt. The PAT pass was knocked down by Sidney Cooper. In the final frame, an errant pass was picked off by Edward Lee to kill a drive. But then runs by Holmes, Odell Stubbs and Phillip Bell got the ball to the 2-yard line from where Holmes *"bucked over the pay-off stripe"*.

Magee nearly scored again after Cooper picked off another pass but it was given right back via a fumble. A penalty pushed them to the 17-yard line from where Holmes ran in. But, as he was diving into the end zone, the ball came loose and was recovered by Cotton Robinson. Forest didn't have enough time to at least tie the game and ended at the 40-yard line.

GAME 6: MAGEE (1-3-1) vs MOUNT OLIVE (UNREPORTED)
MAGEE 0 MOUNT OLIVE 6
October 15, 1942

The upset win at Forest put spirits high on the team. With a rematch against Mount Olive at hand, a *"large crowd (was) expected to turn out"*. Unfortunately, despite a *"hard-fought game from start to finish"*, the Pirates were able to take another game from the Burrs.

Mount Olive hit the board in the 2nd quarter thanks to a King pass to Sullivan. Magee came close to giving them another score after fumbling near midfield, but the defense held on to keep halftime 6-0. Magee began in earnest to come back in the final quarter thank to good play by Holmes, Hudson McNair, Bobby Mangum, Earl Stubbs and Odell Stubbs. But, they could not manage to get the ball across to the goal line.

GAME 7: MAGEE (1-4-1) @ CANTON (UNREPORTED)
MAGEE 6 CANTON 14
October 23, 1942

Originally the team was to play Tylertown on the 23rd, but the schedule changed somewhat to afford a contest against Canton. Apparently the Tylertown contest was not cancelled, but instead moved back to November. No reports on the Canton details other than the final score have been found.

GAME 8: MAGEE (1-5-1) @ HATTIESBURG (UNREPORTED)
MAGEE 0 HATTIESBURG 45
October 30, 1942

Unbelievably, Magee was now on the road for their seventh time out of eight games. This time they faced Coach Elwyn Ward's powerful Hattiesburg Tigers on Hawkins Field. Idle the week before, they *"expected to show Magee a spectacular brand of football"* while Kisner was *"confident they will make a good showing"*. It turned out to be the most lop-sided Burrhead game since the opening tilt of 1930 against McComb.

The Hattiesburg American said that *"The Tigers had the snap and crackle of championship teams of yore as they scored almost at will"*. The first score came so fast that *"even the fans were caught flatfooted"*. A Mangum fumble at the 21 was recovered by Maizie Street and, two plays later, Benny Ray Nobles hit Billy Copeland from the 16. Nobles' PAT made it 7-0. The score sat 20-0 at halftime. Magee's only serious shot at a score came in the 3rd quarter where they got as far as the 4-yard line before being held. Other Tigers crossing the goal included Watkins, Berry, Stone, Reed and Nobles; all coming in the final quarter.

Hattiesburg led in passing (8-11 vs 2-7) and first downs (13-5). Magee fumbled twice while the Tigers never did. For Magee, it was said that "*Phillip Bell deserves mention for his kicking. He arched long spiraling kicks down the field consistently. And Magee's Holmes was an effective runner, penetrating the tight Tiger defense several times during the night*".

GAME 9: MAGEE (1-6-1) vs TYLERTOWN (UNREPORTED)
MAGEE 13 TYLERTOWN 6
November 6, 1942

This was probably the first meeting between the two teams on the gridiron, and it proved to be the second win for the Burrs. Magee was the first to the scoreboard in the 2nd quarter "*on a long drive due to beautiful teamship of both the line and the backfield*". Holmes added the point-after. They scored again in the frame due to a Tylertown fumble at the 28. That made halftime 13-6 in favor of Magee.

The Blue Devils had their only other score of the contest in the 3rd quarter thanks to a 27-yard dash. The visitors threatened in the final frame on a drive from their 30-yard line to the Burrhead 20-yard line "*but were unable to score*". The Tylertown Times had the final score at 13-7.

GAME 10: MAGEE (2-6-1) @ COLUMBIA (UNREPORTED)
MAGEE 0 COLUMBIA 19
November 13, 1942

The Wildcats were coming off of a 39-0 shutout of Big Eight Conference Brookhaven. This week's tilt marked their final home tilt and money raised from the contest was used for the purchase of team letter jackets. All of Columbia's points came in the last half. The initial touchdown was set up by J.B. Knight, while Watts hit Oswalt for another and Howard pulled in a 25-yard Oswalt pass for the last.

GAME 11: MAGEE (2-7-1) @ SAINT ALOYSIUS (5-2)
MAGEE 6 SAINT ALOYSIUS 14
November 26, 1942

On Friday the 20th, presumably due to an open date, an inter-squad scrimmage was held with the teams consisting of Seniors and Freshmen taking on Juniors and Sophomores. They held the event to raise funds to purchase football letter jackets.

In Vicksburg, the Flashes had lost their head coach (Joe Balzli) to the Marines. As an all-male Catholic school, the team was led by Brothers Roderick and John. The paper originally thought Saint Al "*not as heavy as it had been in previous years. The line's average weight is 150 pounds. The backfield, which is exceptionally light, averages 130 pounds in weight. However, what the team lacks in weight, it hopes to compensate for in spirit and deception*". The brothers had led them to a 5-2 record thus far with losses only to Lake Providence, LA and Natchez.

This would be the only home game for Saint Al this season. With reporting at such a minimum, they had no idea of what type of team was in store. The Vicksburg Evening Post said that Magee was "*rated as having one of the best teams in this section of the state and promise to give the Vicksburgers a hard fight from start to finish. The Flashes are out to chalk up a win over the Magee team, but are firmly convinced it will be rather a tough task*".

Saint Al started quickly, with a 75-yard drive ending in a David Theobald touchdown and PAT. That held until the final quarter. Magee picked up a loose Flash football at the 32. Six plays later, Holmes hit Everett from the 19-yard line for the TD. Holmes' PAT was blocked "*by a half dozen or more Flashes*". During this drive, Magee had a scare when Hilton Stuard was carried from the field on a stretcher with an apparent back injury. Saint Al answered on the ensuing drive. Charles Kette "*on a spinner*" cracked the Burrhead goal from the 4-yard line and "*(Earl) Evans on a run around end crossed the coveted line standing up*".

1943 (1-7)

B.L. Kisner was back for his second year but didn't expect things to be a whole lot better. His squad was called "*small*" with a number of newcomers to the field. An October report from Hattiesburg noted the team to be "*light and fast with the line averaging 147 pounds and the backfield also averaging 147*". Much like the previous year, and at least one more to follow, many details are missing regarding the condition and preparation of the squad. Odell Stubbs would serve as Captain while Bobby Buffington was Alternate Captain.

GAME 1: MAGEE (0-0) @ CRYSTAL SPRINGS (0-0)
MAGEE 0 CRYSTAL SPRINGS 20
September 17, 1943

If information is accurate, the two teams had not faced one-another since 1935. In the four all-time games, Crystal Springs had taken the victory. Reporting on this tilt give only the fact that Magee dropped it 20-0.

GAME 2: MAGEE (0-1) vs BAY SPRINGS (UNREPORTED)
MAGEE LOSS BAY SPRINGS WIN
September 24, 1943

The inaugural game against Bay Springs is a mystery. A report from The Magee Courier mentions the matchup beforehand, but no source gives us the outcome. It is noted as a loss since a report from the same paper on October 21st indicates that the best the Burrheads had played to that point had come in a 14-0 loss to Hazlehurst. However, the book written about Simpson County football notes it as a win. Either way; a mystery.

GAME 3: MAGEE (0-2) @ BRANDON (0-1)
MAGEE 7 BRANDON 19
October 8, 1943

For the fourth-straight season, the Bulldogs would be under new leadership on the gridiron. Now in the hands of Mississippi State alum T.S. Myers, the team faced a shortened season. The reason is unmentioned except for the cryptic notation on August 21st saying, "*Pending unforeseen developments, the Brandon Consolidated School plans to play a six-game football schedule this fall*". If history is a judge, many schools had abandoned football programs since many young men were entering the armed services at their earliest possible signing date.

As practices started on August 23rd, prospects seemed good for Myers' team. "*Many of last year's squad will not be here this season, yet it is believed that the Bulldogs will develop into a formidable team relatively speaking, and that the spectators will get their money's worth from seeing the games. Brandon boasts one of the neatest passers in high school football circles in Billy Joe Campbell. This is the last year of high school football for some of these boys. No one can say where they will be next year*".

Magee's opening fumble led immediately to a Bulldog touchdown and 6-0 lead. After failing on their next drive, they allowed Brandon to notch yet another score. The extra point was good this time for a 13-0 advantage through halftime. Brandon opened the 3rd quarter with their last touchdown. The Burrheads' only score came in the final quarter when Roland Dale picked off a Dog pass to set up a score. Orell Pendergrass provided the PAT.

The report of the game from The Brandon News stated that "*Billy Joe Campbell, Dan Campbell and Red Storey carried the ball over the goal line for 18 points of the score, and their teammates, playing an offensive game, allowed only one touchdown to be scored by the Magee boys*".

GAME 4: MAGEE (0-3) @ HAZLEHURST (UNREPORTED)
MAGEE 0 HAZLEHURST 14
October 14, 1943

Despite yet another loss on the season, The Magee Courier said that they "*proved to their faithful followers that they were capable of playing real football. This game was undoubtedly the best the Burrheads have played this season and if they continue to as well next Friday, Hattiesburg will have a good scrap coming*".

The first quarter was scoreless thanks to a Magee interception at the 5-yard line to stop a drive. Hazlehurst did find paydirt in the 2nd quarter on a 45-yard march and PAT. Buddy Tanner was credited with the score. A Burrhead fumble did no damage immediately afterwards and they nearly scored before halftime on a 40-yard James Bell run and Bobby Buffington reception. In the 3rd quarter, the Indians picked off an errant pass but Magee's defense held. Now late in the final period of play, and with Bell out due to injury, Hazlehurst marked one more Tanner touchdown and extra point.

The Simpson County News said that *"The game was well-played by both sides, but the Indians proved too fast and powerful for their opponents to handle"*.

GAME 5: MAGEE (0-4) @ HATTIESBURG (UNREPORTED)
MAGEE 0 HATTIESBURG 33
October 22, 1943

A rematch with Coach Murphree's purple and gold Tigers was once again on the road at Hawkins Field. The previous season's game had been a 45-0 disaster for Magee and this one, while closer, would not be any better for the visitors that snaked their way down Highway 49. The Hattiesburg American said that *"Magee was completely outclassed and never really threatened"*.

The Tigers opened with a 70-yard march capped by Bill Reed's 1-yard dive to make it 7-0. In the 2nd, they added another on a 71-yard drive and Sonny Stone *"end run"* from inside the 1-yard line. Halftime, however, stood only 13-0. But they would add three touchdowns in the 3rd quarter alone. Reed added the first, Magee fumbled deep to set up Bob Kleeb's 15-yarder on a reverse and Kleeb did the same on the next drive from the 5 on the same play. With Robert Cleveland extra points, it was 33-0.

Hattiesburg dominated in first downs (17-6), yardage (344-85), and passing (8-10 for 144 yards versus 4-8 for 31 yards). The Magee Courier noted that Odell Stubbs and Travis Hughes were taken out of the contest due to injuries along the way.

GAME 6: MAGEE (0-5) @ TYLERTOWN (UNREPORTED)
MAGEE 0 TYLERTOWN 7
October 29, 1943

Much like the Bay Springs game, it was noted that the boys were headed to Tylertown to see if they could make it two years in a row of victories. Unfortunately, and despite a narrow score, Magee was again on the wrong side of the scoreboard. Byrd notched Tylertown's lone score on a 40-yard punt return while Robert May added the PAT with a plunge over right tackle.

GAME 7: MAGEE (0-6) vs CANTON (UNREPORTED)
MAGEE 0 CANTON 41
November 5, 1943

In what possibly may have been the worst Magee performance since the 1942 Hattiesburg game, The Madison County Herald still called it *"a very interesting contest"*. The Panthers counted touchdowns in each quarter, with the final frame seeing them cross three times.

Canton scored quickly in the game on a short run by Ring and Tisdale PAT. In the second quarter, and after a Panther interception, Pevey rushed in from the 6 to make intermission 13-0. After halftime, Pevey hit Alford from 60 yards and Tisdale again converted. In the fourth quarter, Tisdale hit Pevey from the 6, Skulley added a 45-yard pick-six and Wesley plunged in from the 4. The last was set up by Johnny Killiam's 49-yard interception and return. Tisdale added extra points on the first two attempts.

"Buffington, Bell and Pendergrass were Magee's outstanding players, making nice gains and very deceptive plays". Magee actually led in first downs (9-1) and committed fewer penalties (65-56 yards). But Canton out-rushed Magee 167-76 and picked off a total of 4 passes. The Burrheads had one theft via the air.

GAME 8: MAGEE (0-7) @ COLUMBIA (UNREPORTED)
MAGEE 14 COLUMBIA 13
November 12, 1943

The game the previous week had been a tough one from an injury standpoint, keeping Travis Hughes from the playing field. When this one was over, others would also find themselves on the sidelines. That included Lavelle Tullos (hip) and Bobby Buffington (leg). Regardless, Magee had pulled out a precious victory in *"undoubtedly the most thrilling game of the season and the boys out-played the opposing team throughout the entire game"*.

Columbia was first to the scoreboard when, after Red Rawls pounced on a loose Magee football, Jackie Lowe *"drove off left tackle, cut his field and sprinted for a touchdown"*. Joe Rankin's pass to Bill Gray added the extra point. Buffington came back in the 2nd quarter with a running score and notched the extra point. The Columbian Progress actually gave credit for the score to Pendergrass via a 55-yard kick return and Buffington conversion to Bell.

In the 2nd quarter, Columbia re-took the lead on a Jackie Lowe run. But *"the failure of the of the pass for point gave the game to Magee at the end"*. The Wildcats ended the half on a Joe Rankin interception of Pendergrass. Bobby Mangum opened the 3rd quarter with a toss to Buffington *"who outraced the Columbia back 25 yards for the needed 6 points"*. Mangum then hit Buffington for the eventual game-winning point. Again, the Columbia paper disagreed. They called it a Bell touchdown *"on a trick pass and lateral"* while Buffington notched the game-winning PAT. Columbia drove to the Burrhead 15-yard line in the last period but the defense stood tall.

Credit was given to a large number of players for their performances. The paper also noted that *"One of the largest crowds of the year accompanied the team to Columbia and gave their support to the cheering section"*.

GAME 9: MAGEE (1-7) vs MORTON (UNDEFEATED)
UNREPORTED
November 19, 1943

Morton had apparently stayed undefeated (according to The Magee Courier) despite a mid-season coaching change. G.C. Magers' departure from the team left new man Ance Blakney in charge. It was said that Morton was contenders for a Lion's Bowl bid, *"but the Magee boys hope to shatter their chances"*. The Magee seniors would treat the team to *"a picture show, party and picnic"* that night. No result has been found.

On November 3rd, the football team held an intra-squad game to again raise money for letter jackets. The teams were divided into the Maroons and the Whites. That included a number of younger players from the B Team. As late as mid-December, reports from The Simpson County News said that Magee would be playing Mendenhall on Christmas Eve. It apparently did not happen as a report from much later said that the two teams hadn't faced one-another in a string of seasons.

The team was honored at The Magee Community House on December 11th with a banquet. Letters were given out and individuals recognized for their contribution to the season. Roland Dale (Captain) and James Bell (Co-Captain) were selected for the 1944 season.

1944 (4-6-2)

If reporting is accurate, Magee and Coach B.L. Kisner would continue their streak of playing the majority of their contests on the road. In this particular season, they played every game away from the Simpson County home field.

GAME 1: MAGEE (0-0) @ COLUMBIA (0-0)
MAGEE 0 COLUMBIA 0
September 8, 1944

Despite the shutout tie game, it was called by The Magee Courier to be *"one of the best games ever played in the history of the school"*. Both tried valiantly to cross the opponent goal but all efforts were denied. *"The Burrheads did some spectacular playing on the offensive and the defensive and proved themselves the better team by making 15 first downs to Columbia's 1 first down"*. The Columbian Progress said that *"Neither team was able to penetrate far into its opponent's territory, but Columbia's defensive play was good"*.

GAME 2: MAGEE (0-0-1) @ CRYSTAL SPRINGS (UNREPORTED)
MAGEE 0 CRYSTAL SPRINGS 6
September 15, 1944

It was yet another *"hard-fought and well-played football game"* for the Magee squad, but this time it resulted in defeat. Magee had moved to the Crystal Springs 15-yard line early in the game but fumbled the opportunity away. Late in the 3rd quarter, Crystal Springs *"smashed"* in for the only tally of the evening. *"The Burrheads came back fighting only to have a pass intercepted that ended all hopes of a winning score"*.

GAME 3: MAGEE (0-1-1) @ HAZLEHURST (UNREPORTED)
MAGEE 7 HAZLEHURST 12
September 22, 1944

Another week and another loss; though "*The Burrheads played an exceptional game in spite of many obstacles*". Hazlehurst began the scoring early in the 2nd quarter but the PAT was blocked by Buck Odom. The action really began afterwards.

James Bell returned the ensuing kickoff to near midfield, but the ball was taken back to the 25-yard line "*due to roughness and quarreling among the players*". The two teams exchanged fumbles, but Hazlehurst was awarded the last to disapproval. They moved to the 1-yard line where Tommy Everett was disqualified. This stirred the Burrs to push their hosts back and regain possession of the football. Magee was held to a punt and then Buddy Walters sealed any further scoring in the half with an interception.

Controversy arose again in the 3rd quarter when Roland Dale picked off an Indian pass. However, an "*offside whistle blew and the referee brought the ball back to the 25-yard line, penalized Magee 5 yards and gave the ball to Hazlehurst*". Magee still forced a punt which was blocked by Cecil Herrington and recovered by Dale. After an exchange of possessions, Hazlehurst put up their last touchdown. The Burrheads managed their lone score in the 4th quarter on a triple-pass from Buddy Winstead to Dale to Bell for a 25-yard touchdown. The kicked PAT was true.

GAME 4: MAGEE (0-2-1) @ NATCHEZ (UNREPORTED)
MAGEE 0 NATCHEZ 19
September 29, 1944

This marked the inaugural game against the Adams County squad. Natchez had apparently not done too well the week before against Tylertown, and The Natchez Democrat called the Rebel performance "*vastly better*" in front of 1,200 fans. Despite a strong first-drive by the blue and white, Magee "*mustered its strength in the neck of time and stopped scoring*".

However, Natchez would put up a pair of touchdowns before halftime. The first was a Williams pass to Wise while Foster "*took the pigskin through center for the other*". One PAT was successful on a Wise reception. Magee threatened in the 3rd quarter but came up short. In the final quarter, Stoney Rowbotham "*carried the ball across the goal line through a hole opened by the excellent Rebel interference*".

The Natchez Democrat noted that "*Both squads ... fought til the end in a scrappy, exciting scrimmage*". They also gave credit to Dale, Everett, Bell and Walters for "*doing some fast, though futile, work on the offense*". The Magee Courier noted that "*the game was much more interesting than the score indicates*" against a team they called "*strong*".

GAME 5: MAGEE (0-3-1) @ FOREST HILL (2-0)
MAGEE 0 FOREST HILL 7
October 6, 1944

Coach T. Pears' Rebels were reported to have played only two games. That included a 35-0 win over Taylorsville and a 13-0 win over Yazoo City. Their last against Forest had been cancelled. Now, Magee traveled to Alumni Field at Millsaps College to face another Middle Mississippi opponent.

The only score of the night came on Forest Hill's second possession, where they drove 60 yards and capped the effort with a Cowan run over left tackle and a "*line plunge*" for the extra point. Magee played a sounder brand of football in the second half and kept "*the ball the greater part of the time in the Rebel's territory but were never able to reach paydirt*". Their last-ditch effort in the 4th quarter ended on an interception. A later report notes that one Magee touchdown may have been called back on a penalty.

GAME 6: MAGEE (0-4-1) @ FOREST (UNREPORTED)
MAGEE 6 FOREST 6
October 12, 1944

Though the two teams started playing in Magee's very first year of organized football, the games had been fairly even since 1936. Still, the Burrheads had not yet tasted victory there and would be hard-pressed to do so this time. The Bearcats started strong with a first-drive touchdown by Singleton but Magee blocked their conversion attempt. Back came the visitors with a drive to the Forest 1, but they turned over the opportunity at that point.

As the 2nd opened, they had driven to the Forest half-yard line but again came up empty. Finally, on their next opportunity, Winstead threw to Dale who turned on the jets for a 20-yard score. The PAT was fumbled; thus making halftime 6-6. Forest actually opened the door with a kickoff fumble, but time ran out. After that, it was simply a series of punts and turnovers to keep both elevens out of the end zone. Forest did reach the Magee 10-yard line but *"they were held for four downs"*. The Magee Courier reported that *"Both teams were fighting to the end"*. Magee held serve in first downs 16-8.

GAME 7: MAGEE (0-4-2) @ LAUREL B-TEAM (UNREPORTED)
MAGEE 7 LAUREL B-TEAM 0
October 21, 1944

Another new team was now on the Magee schedule as the Burrs traveled to Laurel's Watkins Stadium to meet the JV Tornadoes. With two strong performances in the last two weeks, the visitors were crossing fingers that things were finally coming together. This time was a charm as their opening possession moved steadily to the end zone thanks to the running of Walters and Bell, and Dale's passes to Tullos. The 1-yard score, accompanied by Dale's PAT, would be the final score of the night.

Laurel fumbled in the 2nd to give hope but Magee could not advance. Dale passes continuously got the ball deep and as the halftime whistle blew, Magee sat on the 18-yard line. The only highlight of the 3rd quarter was an interception by Dale while Walters matched the effort in the final frame at the 10-yard line to keep Laurel from reaching paydirt. Also notable was a last-quarter penalty on the Tornadoes *"for slugging"*.

The paper said that *"Throughout the four quarters, the Burrheads did better playing than the Tornadoes. However, the two teams had excellent plays and teamwork to make the game very interesting. The Burrheads made more first downs and most of the playing was done in Laurel's territory by the Burrheads"*.

GAME 8: MAGEE (1-4-2) @ GULFPORT (UNREPORTED)
MAGEE 6 GULFPORT 27
October 27, 1944

Another road game against a Big Eight team awaited with their opponent consisting of *"more and heavier men"*. However, *"the Burrheads made a name for themselves by preventing the unusually high score which was expected"*.

Gulfport quickly hit the end zone on a 50-yard drive capped by Jimmy Edwards to make it 6-0. Magee got as far as the Gulfport 20 at the 2nd quarter started but could get no further. A later Burrhead pass was picked off by the coast team but an Odom tackle killed any chances for them to increase the lead. The home team took only 3 plays to open the second half with an Edwards touchdown and Leonard Papania converted the extra point. Magee responded with a drive kept alive by a roughing-the-punter call and eventual 21-yard Everett reception. But, the touchdown was called back and then Gulfport picked off a Magee pass to set up the third Edwards touchdown and PAT.

Unfortunately, the hosts picked off yet another throw and Murray scored on the drive. Papania was true on the kick. Early in the 4th quarter, *"perfect teamwork on the part of a powerful line and fast-moving backfield carried Magee over for their first touchdown made by Everett"*. The Magee Courier noted that *"Outstanding players in Magee's line were Brewer, Tindall, C. Herrington, Tullos and Odom"*.

GAME 9: MAGEE (1-5-2) @ MOUNT OLIVE (UNREPORTED)
MAGEE 32 MOUNT OLIVE 13
November 3, 1944

This matchup was about even since their first meeting in 1931. The second victory of the late season came as the result of *"excellent teamwork and sportsmanship which made the town and school of Magee proud of them. They proved that each one has what it takes for a good ball club"*.

It took only two plays before Bell escaped the Pirate defense for a 90-yard dash to daylight. Dale's extra point put them quickly up 7-0. On their next drive, the now-potent offense pulled off another touchdown thanks to Dale's pass to James Brewer *"who ran 66 yards for a second touchdown"* to make it 13-0. A Mount Olive punt block led to an early 2nd quarter touchdown. Then, after some deep drives by both teams, Bell did it again. *"With excellent blocking by his line"*, be dashed 97 yards for the score and Everett added the 20-6 extra point.

Mount Olive opened the 3rd quarter with their last touchdown; that a 9-yard McLeod run and subsequent Pirate extra point. Magee answered immediately in the form of a Dale pass to

Everett, lateral to Brewer and 40-yard scamper for points. But it was called back due to off-sides. Starting at the Mount Olive 35-yard line in the final quarter, Magee pushed forward with Dale hitting Walters for the touchdown. An exchange of interceptions followed (one by Bell for Magee) though the Burrs were nearing their fifth touchdown when the game was finished.

"The outstanding men on the Magee line-up were Tullos, Brewer, C. Herrington, Stubbs, Sanders, Odom and Tindall".

GAME 10: MAGEE (2-5-2) @ QUITMAN (UNREPORTED)
MAGEE 44 QUITMAN 0
November 10, 1944

Two wins in three weeks gave plenty of hope for Magee players and fans. But little did they know that they would nearly match the output in the 1941 game against Byram where they won 47-0. It was reported that *"only once did the Panthers invade Magee's territory, and that was in the last half of the ball game"*.

The opening frame consisted of good Magee drives that didn't pay off. One ended in a fumble that was recovered by Quitman. But, the next quarter opened with a 25-yard Winstead pass to Dale for the score and PAT. They reached the 1-yard line on the next drive before giving the ball over, but after holding, Dale hit Winstead for a 30-yard touchdown to make it 13-0. Dale then intercepted a pass, leading to Bell's escape for a 50-yard tally and 20-0 advantage.

Everett provided the next score in the 3rd quarter on a 3-yard run to cap a 60-yard march. Up 26-0, Dale picked off another pass and took it the distance for the score to put it 32-0. Walters notched the next tally on a run from inside the 5-yard line in the final frame, but they weren't done. Walters was able to hit Everett *"behind the goal line"* for the last TD of the night. First downs went to Magee 15-2.

GAME 11: MAGEE (3-5-2) @ CANTON (UNREPORTED)
MAGEE 6 CANTON 20
November 17, 1944

The score in this contest apparently doesn't show the closeness of the game. The Magee Courier said that at the end that first downs (16-12) and completed passes (15-5) favored the Burrheads.

The first quarter was a good display of defense on both sides. In the 2nd, Canton finally captured the first score when they took over the ball at the Magee 23 and drove to paydirt *"in a series of plays"*. The point-after made it 7-0. An unfortunate punt attempt fumble gave Canton the ball at the Magee 25 and, again, they drove in for a score to make it 13-0 at halftime. The 3rd quarter started no better with another Magee fumble that put the hosts at the Magee 20. But they got only to the 4-yard line before giving up on downs.

Canton applied the pressure with another touchdown via the air and added their final point. In the 4th quarter, Dale, Everett, Bell and Winstead combined to move the ball steadily downfield until Winstead hit Dale for the touchdown. The PAT was blocked. The paper noted afterwards, perhaps incorrectly as we don't know the record of Canton, that *"This was the second time during the season that the Canton Tigers had been scored on"*.

GAME 12: MAGEE (3-6-2) @ MENDENHALL (UNREPORTED)
MAGEE 44 MENDENHALL 0
November 22, 1944

The Simpson County News said that *"The Magee team has been successfully coached throughout the season and has made a favorable record in the face of many heavier teams"*. On the Mendy sideline, they had lost Coach Shorty May to the Navy and apparently had no official head man. But, *"their determination to win will aid materially in making the game a hard-fought one"*.

For a 44-0 score, one would think that it was a murderous affair with scoring coming on almost each possession. But that wasn't the case as it was scoreless going into the 2nd quarter. Magee had gotten as far as the Mendy 4 in the 1st quarter but pushed through in the next after a Walters interception allowed Bell a 4-yard run for a 6-0 lead. Bell matched that with another inside the 11-yard line after to make it 12-0 at halftime.

An opening-kick fumble put Magee at the Mendy 45. It took 2 plays before they were at the 4-yard line and 2 more plays before they scored. Magee then crossed again with Winstead's pass to Everett and it was 24-0. Walters then picked off a Mendenhall pass to set up Bell's lateral to Everett for a 31-yard tally. In the 4th quarter, Mendy fumbled at their 25-yard line and Everett topped the effort with a 1-yard run and his PAT to make it 37-0. Bell's next score came on a 7-yard run and Winstead provided what would be the last point of the contest.

The Magee Courier said that *"This was one of the most important games of the season to both teams involved. There were several casualties in the game, but a spirit of friendly rivalry prevailed. Both teams are to be commended for their sportsmanship"*. One of those injured was Mendenhall's Carol Thomas May, who was taken to Jackson for a broken collar bone.

Forest Hill ended up with the Class A championship of the Middle Mississippi Literary and Athletic Association. They were to have played Canton for the bragging rights, but Canton lost to Greenwood in the Lions Bowl and decided to relinquish the right to attend the playoff game.

1945 (6-4)

The Burrheads, under Coach B.L. Kisner, had *"been following a schedule of rigid practice and (were) in tip-top condition. We are certain that our boys will be able to tame (their first opponent)"*. James Bell (Captain) and Billy Earl Stubbs (Co-Captain) would lead the squad.

GAME 1: MAGEE (0-0) @ COLUMBIA (1-0)
MAGEE 6 COLUMBIA 20
September 14, 1945

The Wildcats opened their season with a 14-7 win over Varnado, LA thanks to Douglas Dedeaux touchdowns. They would chalk up their second win of the year at home against the Burrheads *"after four hard-fought quarters"*. About five minutes in, they capped a 70-yard drive with a Daniels run and Millard Van toss to Cook to make it 7-0. In the next quarter, Magee *"drove hard to move down the field and make their first touchdown"* to cut the advantage to 7-6 at halftime. That came from Buck Odom on a 1-yard plunge.

Columbia piled on the points in the 3rd quarter with a pair of scores and an extra point. Van had the first on a 65-yard escape. The last, a Van pass to Ratcliff, was set up by a Burrhead fumble. *"The playing in the final quarter led to no scoring. However, the Burrheads reached Columbia's 4-yard line before the end of the game"*. The Columbian Progress noted that Magee *"kept the ball during most of the last quarter (but) they were unable to produce another point"*.

The Magee Courier was still upbeat about the season, saying *"You'll see a marked improvement in the coming scores of the season"*.

GAME 2: MAGEE (0-1) vs BAY SPRINGS (UNREPORTED)
MAGEE 6 BAY SPRINGS 0
September 21, 1945

This time, six points was good enough for Magee to capture their first win of the season in front a large crowd of home fans. The first quarter was scoreless, but Magee put on a fine display of football in the next, moving *"deep into the Bulldog territory by overcoming a strong line and several penalties. Excellent running and driving on the part of Bell, Mangum, (Buck) Odom and Stubbs and excellent backing by the line kept the Burrheads well-into the Bulldogs' half of the field throughout..."*

The 3rd quarter was the same *"give and take playing (with) neither team (succeeding) in making a score"*. The Burrs came alive in the last period. With 5:00 left, they *"outmaneuvered the Bulldogs and, in a final plunge, Bell was over for a touchdown"*. The Magee Courier said that *"The Burrheads played top-notch ball ... and they'll do ever better (for the next game)"*.

GAME 3: MAGEE (1-1) @ NATCHEZ (UNREPORTED)
MAGEE 6 NATCHEZ 0
September 28, 1945

The blue and white under A.I. Rexinger had *"lost every one of last season's regular starters with only six lettermen returning out of 49 boys on the squad. Coach Rexinger, too, says that the average weight of the team is the lightest for some time"*. Again on the road, and in front of a reported 1,600 fans, Magee once again put up a grand total of 6 points. Like the previous week, it would be enough.

Magee got going on their first drive, moving 70 yards behind *"runs and drives by Bell, Odom and Mangum"* to reach paydirt. Bell had the honors from 35 yards away. The point-after run was short of the mark. Though Stubbs recovered a fumble in the 2nd quarter, penalties killed any chances of increasing the lead. Joe McNair had an interception called back in the 3rd quarter while the last frame saw the game tighten. Natchez got to the Magee 15-yard line but Mangum intercepted a pass and took it to midfield *"just as the game ended"*.

The paper said that *"Natchez suffered heavy penalties and good tackling and blocking by the Magee team during the final quarter"*. The Natchez Democrat said that *"Both clubs turned in excellent games with Bell sparking the visitors' ball-handling"*. Natchez led in first downs 13-11; and went 6-14 passing while the Burrs were 0-4.

GAME 4: MAGEE (2-1) @ GULFPORT (UNREPORTED)
MAGEE 7 GULFPORT 13
October 5, 1945

Headed back to the Gulf Coast, prospects of a win over Big Eight conference Gulfport would be a tall task. Gulfport was in the top 10 of highest-ranked schools at the time according to The Clarion-Ledger. The Enterprise Journal predicted the hosts to win, albeit slightly, by a unique 11-0 score. That prediction would not be too far off, with the Burrheads proving *"that they could play football – rain or shine"*. The reference was to the fact that the game was played in a *"downpour of rain"*.

After holding Magee on their first march, Gulfport took the ball and drove from the 40-yard line to paydirt with Alren Neihart making it 6-0. A fumble set the Commodores up for their second touchdown (Jack Bobo) and his point-after made it 13-0 going into the 2nd quarter. Magee was able to respond after Stubbs picked up a Burrhead fumble at the 1-yard line an *"went through the Gulfport line"*. Odom found Kelly Herrington for the point-after.

Despite a 3rd quarter fumble recovery, the Burrs did not tally. They did, however, move to the Commodore 10-yard line thanks to a 70-yard Bell run. That put Gulfport *"into extremely wide-awake defensive action"*. The drive faltered as did their last chance at the Gulfport 30-yard line when the final whistle blew.

The Magee Courier said that *"The Burrheads were greatly outweighed by the Big Eight team but they had the necessary fighting spirit to be stiff competition"*. It was clear that the defense was doing a remarkable job in the 1945 campaign. If the offense could get established, things could be bright quickly.

GAME 5: MAGEE (2-2) @ HAZLEHURST (UNDEFEATED)
MAGEE 7 HAZLEHURST 13
October 12, 1945

The Enterprise-Journal predicted a Hazlehurst win of 7-0 at home. Indeed, they were a good team that year if reports are accurate as Hazlehurst was reported to have gone undefeated in their classification at the close of the season. The Hazlehurst Courier said that *"in the first few minutes of the game, our contesters (Magee) got the pigskin and managed to run the score up to 7-0"*. Buddy Tanner answered for the home team with a 55-yard escape. Magee *"fought hard"* to score again, but the Hazlehurst defense held.

Hazlehurst added the go-ahead touchdown in the 2nd quarter on a 1-yard Karl Hansen plunge and Tanner provided the point-after. *"The remainder of the game was nip-and-tuck with each team fighting hard, fumbling a lot and getting plenty of penalties, but the game ended with the score remaining 13-7 in favor of the Indians"*.

GAME 6: MAGEE (2-3) vs JACKSON CENTRAL JV (UNREPORTED)
MAGEE 52 JACKSON CENTRAL JV 0
October 19, 1945

This week could have marked a rarity in Magee football as rival Mendenhall would have faced the Burrheads mid-season instead of the last-game-for-bragging-rights finale. However, the Tigers cancelled and Magee was able to reschedule the Jackson Central JV (B-Team) as their opponent. The varsity squad was a perineal power, but if the B-Team thought they were competition for Magee, the Burrs proved them wrong.

Scoring came early and often, with a Mangum pass to Odom and lateral to Bell for the first score. Bell counted the next from 61 yards (McNair PAT), McNair picked off a pass to set up Mangum's *"unmolested"* score from the 12-yard line, and Bell dashed 80 yards for another (McNair

PAT) to make halftime 26-0. Stubbs opened the 3rd with a 70-yarder and added another from the 1 (McNair).

Second-string players entered for the final frame but Odom still played and ran in from the 9-yard line. Scott Buffington got his first Burrhead touchdown afterwards from the 23-yard line and Cecil Herrington *"drove through the line to make the extra point"*. The paper said that *"The Burrheads merit applause and cheers from every student and patron of Magee H.S. They played an excellent and a clear football game"*. Only in 1927 (with known reports) did a Magee team score more points. In their second year of football, Magee defeated Morton 55-6.

GAME 7: MAGEE (3-3) @ MORTON (UNREPORTED)
MAGEE 53 MORTON 0
October 26, 1945

The 1927 scoring record against Morton was in serious jeopardy in Scott County on this Friday night. The Clarion-Ledger said that *"Magee unleased a power attack here that spelled defeat .... Morton was completely outclassed both offensively and defensively"*. The offense under Bell, Mangum, Odom and Stubbs *"behind a forward wall which starred May, McNair, Harrington and Layton, with Layton showing exceptionally well on defense"* finally seemed to finally be catching up with their defense.

GAME 8: MAGEE (4-3) vs MOUNT OLIVE (UNREPORTED)
MAGEE 25 MOUNT OLIVE 0
November 2, 1945

The Pirates and Burrheads had played at least 12 times since 1926 with the series favoring Magee only slightly. Fans at home were anxious to see if the offense that had been so potent the last two weeks could continue to match the effort of a defense that had allowed precious few points. *"Great rivalry exists between the two teams and school spirit was high among the large crowd on both sides"*.

On their second possession of the contest, Magee marked the scoreboard with a run by Bell. The extra point was blocked. Next, a Stubbs 55-yard run sparked a drive to the Pirate goal but they couldn't cross. After holding, the Burrs drove 50 yards with a Mangum pass to Kelly Herrington capping the march. Mount Olive's effort to respond before halftime was thwarted by Odom's interception to keep it a 12-0 affair.

It took little time for Magee to rack up their third score when Odom *"drove through the center"* for a 60-yard tally. Mangum hit May for the point-after. The last score came early in the final frame, despite a Pirate interception, after a blocked punt was recovered by Kelly Herrington on the 1-yard line. Bell did the work from there for the final points. *"Every Magee player displayed excellent defensive and offensive playing and good sportsmanship during the game. We should all be proud of their victory..."*

GAME 9: MAGEE (5-3) vs FOREST (4-3)
MAGEE 26 FOREST 7
November 9, 1945

Magee had now exploded out to a 130-0 record in points in just three weeks. Their next opponent, although in the confines of the home field, had never been an easy team to beat. The Bearcats were looking to gain their fifth win on the 1945 season at the expense of the Burrs. But it took only three plays before Stubbs *"took the ball and ran 65 yards"* for the touchdown with Mangum hitting Odom for the point-after.

Stubbs tallied again in the frame from inside the 11-yard line to make it 13-0. Their next march was killed by a lost fumble and Forest used the gift to move to the Burrhead 10-yard line. However, the stout defense stood tall and kept them out. That defense came through again on the Cats' next possession that moved to the half-yard line. After holding, the halftime whistle sounded. Odom opened the 3rd quarter with a touchdown and 19-0 advantage.

Uncharacteristically, a fumble recovered by Forest on the Magee 38 resulted in a 7-play drive that reached paydirt when Kelly hit Guy Henderson. Their point-after was converted by Thurman Weems and it was now 19-7. But Magee's offense returned the scoring favor shortly after. A sustained drive that ended with Odom going in from the 6 was called back. With penalties, they now started again from the 18-yard line, but Forest picked off a pass. After stopping the Bearcats, Magee ended scoring on a 7-yard Mangum run and his point-after pass to Kelly Herrington.

Kisner *"praised his boys for their blocking and ball-handling, with special honors going to (Buster) May for his excellent defensive play"*. The game was pretty rugged as J.B. Kelley, Jimmie Lackey and Thurman Weems *"sustained injuries in the rough affair with Magee. These three boys will probably be out for the rest of the season"*.

GAME 10: MAGEE (6-3) @ CANTON (7-1)
MAGEE 0 CANTON 13
November 16, 1945

Coach G.B. Edgar's Panthers lost their initial game and then proceeded to win the next seven tilts. They had just been invited to play in The Lions Bowl on December 7th in Greenwood and did not want to lose the opportunity with a loss to Magee. The Clarion-Ledger said that *"The team has progressed steadily during the season and is just now reaching its peak"*.

The Magee Courier said *"The Magee Burrheads played one of the hardest-fought games of the season"* though coming out on the losing end. After a nice Magee gain was called back on penalty, the Burrs punted to Canton and they marched for their initial touchdown by George along with Mustin's PAT. Penalties raised their heads again for Magee and forced a punt. Then after the Tigers fumbled back to Stubbs at midfield, Magee moved to the Canton 15-yard line. But another penalty erased the gains and forced a punt. The half ended just 7-0.

Magee fumbled the opening kickoff but the defense once again held. After moving forward, another penalty was called against Magee and forced a punt. That was fumbled by Canton to McNair at the 22-yard line, but Magee returned the favor via fumble. The teams then exchanged punts for a few possessions. The Tigers got a good break when Mustin *"made a break-through"* in the last 5:00 on the Burr 47 and raced to the 1 before Kelly Herrington tackled him. Farrish managed to cross *"through center"* on the next play, however, for what would be the final score. Magee's last gasp ended on an interception at the Canton 30-yard line to end the season.

Canton led in first downs (11-5) and went 1-4 in the air for 14 yards. Magee was also 1-4 passing. Amazingly, Canton had more penalties (60-43 yards) than Magee.

The football team held their banquet in early December with 14 individuals honored with letters. The guest speaker for the event was Coach Reed Green of Mississippi Southern.

1946 (9-2-1): MIDDLE MISSISSIPPI CHAMPIONS

Perhaps a partial reason for the number of road games over the war years was given by The Simpson County News on September 12th when they said that *"During the past summer, the new athletic field was constructed on the site of the old football field. The field is to be lighted in the near future. We feel that these improvements should generate a higher school interest and also a more cooperative spirit by the citizens of the town and surrounding territory that has been exhibited in the past"*.

GAME 1: MAGEE (0-0) vs MORTON (0-0)
MAGEE 36 MORTON 0
September 13, 1946

While Magee had played Morton in 1927 and 1929 before losing in 1942, this Scott County opponent was still a new face to the players. But, Magee *"started off the football season in proper style"* with a shutout.

Morton's best player, Scotty Hughes, *"was lost on the opening kickoff"* due to a concussion. After attending to the injured Hughes, the game restarted. It didn't take long before Magee scored via a Joe McNair run *"standing up"* thanks to *"good blocking"* by Buddy Walters and Buck Odom. Odom tallied again in the 2nd quarter to make it 12-0 at halftime. Taking the ball on the kickoff for the next half, McNair hit *"Tynimte"* (Billy) Smith for the touchdown.

The Burrheads kept up the pressure on the next drive with another Smith touchdown to make it 24-0. In the final frame, after a number exchanges that left both clubs near midfield, McNair hit Odom for a score and then tallied the final touchdown himself. The paper said that *"From the abilities shows by the players, we are expecting a successful season. Before (it's) over, the team will meet a few members of the Big Eight conference, and we are 'a thinkin' that these teams are going to be slightly surprised when they come up against our boys"*.

GAME 2: MAGEE (1-0) @ GULFPORT (UNREPORTED)
MAGEE 12 GULFPORT 19
September 20, 1946

The Commodores under Coach James H. Landrum were *"reshaping very well"* to start the Big Eight season. The Hattiesburg American said that they were *"possibly a little heavier over last fall's outfit"* but the coach noted that *"he cannot say anything about the squad until he sees them under pressure"*. Magee seemed always to play the Commodores on the road; thus lending itself to having no victories to date. For this tilt, The Simpson County News said that Gulfport *"outweighed the Magee team with a goodly margin per man"*.

A Magee fumble to Gulfport early did no damage, but the hosts were first on the board with Lester Padgett's 1-yard dive *"over tackle"* in the 2nd quarter to complete a 44-yard march. Tommy Compton kicked the PAT for a 7-0 lead. In the 3rd, Padgett again scored via a 55-yard escape before Magee's Odom dove in from the 2-yard line in the final frame. Then, Jesse Harrison hit Roy Anderson from the 18 to re-pad the lead. Finally, with 1:00 remaining, McNair hit Odom from 60-yards out with 1:00 left to make it more respectable before the whistle blew.

Of the schedule of Big Eight games this week, Magee *"was the only non-conference team to score on one of the Big Eight elevens"*. The Simpson County News said that *"most of Magee"* went to watch the game and that *"our boys gave a good account of themselves and the issue was in doubt until the last play. The team had improved considerably over the week before and we believe that they will reach their top-playing form this week..."*

GAME 3: MAGEE (1-1) @ NATCHEZ (1-0)
MAGEE 7 NATCHEZ 13
September 27, 1946

Coach A.I. Rexinger had been *"losing some weight with worry"* before the season as his Rebels were *"faced with the toughest grid schedule in local history"*. By the time they faced Magee, they had already steamrolled Rolling Fork 75-0. In light of this, The Hattiesburg American predicted a *"run-away"* loss for Magee on their journey to Natchez by a 10-0 score; which is not so much of a *"run-away"*.

It was called *"a heartbreaker"* since the Burrheads *"put up quite a battle"*. The opening half ended 7-7 with Natchez gaining on a 4-yard Bernard Callendar run and Bill O'Malley PAT. That had been set up by a Natchez fumble recovery and quick-hit pass later from Ray Boyd to Callender and capped a 40-yard march. A long Odom kick return put Magee at the 38-yard line. They drove to the 4 with Walters (or Odom) getting in from there along with McNair's PAT.

Natchez notched their last in the 3rd quarter after a bad punt snap to McNair put the ball at the 28-yard line. Callendar escaped defenders from the 20-yard line for the final tally. *"Magee unleashed a desperation pass attack in the final period, but was held to no completions on five attempts"*. Natchez sat on the Magee 10 when the game ended. First downs went to the home team 13-8.

GAME 4: MAGEE (1-2) vs BRANDON (1-1)
MAGEE 33 BRANDON 6
October 4, 1946

Brandon had gone 3-10-1 over the past two seasons. Probably as a result, Coach Collier Jordan was now the 9th head coach on the Rankin County gridiron. His purple and gold squad would field at least eight games in which to compete. The Brandon News that *"there is a feeling already evident that the Brandon Bulldogs of 1946 will be tougher foes than has been the case in recent seasons"*. Jordan readied his squad for the season opener, with Captain Watson Purvis and Alternate Captain Buddy Farish leading the team, with rigid night scrimmages.

By the week of kickoff, the coach reported that *"the Bulldog team shows promise of having a very strong line and that there is plenty of backfield material that will probably work into some winning combinations before the season is very far advanced"*.

Though Brandon held a 3-2-1 record against the Burrheads since their first game in 1932, this contest would be in Magee. The home team was known to be nearly invincible in Simpson County and that would hold true this season. The contest was moved from a night game to a 2:30 kickoff due to trouble with the field lighting. Brandon now added Anderson Busick after a return from a stint in the Navy.

According to The Simpson County News, Magee's Odom scored first early in the game via *"steady runs"* and a McNair extra point. McNair then picked off a Bulldog pass and *"wormed and twisted his way for a 65-yard run back"* to put them in scoring position. Three plays later, Scott Buffington crossed to make it 13-0 at halftime. Odom got in again in the 3rd and added the PAT. *"After the kick, Magee found Brandon trying hard to reach paydirt and shortly they pulled an old lay-out pass which brought them the only tally of the game"*. Magee would add at least one more via a McNair *"perfect spiral"* to Buffington.

The Brandon News added, *"Outweighed man-for-man and considerably more experienced, the Magee squad kept the Bulldogs on the defensive throughout most of the game. However, a neat pass (Vernon Campbell to Gird Warren) accounted for Brandon's touchdown"*.

GAME 5: MAGEE (2-2) vs PETAL (UNREPORTED)
MAGEE 41 PETAL 7
October 18, 1946

Magee made up for the 14-0 loss in 1935 against Petal when they *"ran, passed, trotted, (and) walked across the goal line to defeat the Petal High School eleven"*. Scoring came early and often, with McNair providing the first by *"winding and weaving down the field"*. In the 2nd, McNair added another while *"Buffington and Smith blocked the runner"* to yet another. After that, Kisner began substituting. Still, Buffington tallied again before halftime.

Herrington notched another in the 3rd quarter on a reverse and Kisner began bringing in yet more reserves; called the *"pee-wee team"*. They still played well before giving up a James Hollingsworth touchdown to the visitors. *"Even though the Petal team was no match for the crashing Burrhead eleven, the game was hard-fought and a lot of good football was exhibited by both teams"*. The Hattiesburg American said that *"The Panthers were outplayed from start to finish, coming to life enough to score once early in the fourth quarter. McNair monopolized the show. The big 185-pounder turned in a nice defensive game despite the fact that he was doing most of the ground gaining for the Burrheads"*.

GAME 6: MAGEE (3-2) vs JACKSON B TEAM (UNREPORTED)
MAGEE 41 JACKSON B TEAM 0
October 25, 1946

Not much is reported about the contest against the reserves of Jackson. What is reported, aside from a different score (43-0), is that Magee may have played some starters in the game. The Clarion-Ledger noted that *"is it possible that some of the Magee varsity stars twinkled a bit in that encounter?"* Local papers did not cover or print details of the tilt. A few days before, Kisner and *"several of his football players"* went to the Mississippi Southern vs LSU game in Hattiesburg. The score taken as the final is the result of numerous end-of-year reports on the season.

GAME 7: MAGEE (4-2) @ BAY SPRINGS (UNREPORTED)
MAGEE 0 BAY SPRINGS 0
November 1, 1946

Bay Springs must have had a decent team in 1946. The Simpson County News called them *"goodly matched"* against Magee and the final score proves it. There weren't a lot of penalties, except for *"only one holding penalty imposed on either team"* and several off-sides flags.

Magee made several first downs in the opening half while Bay Springs made none. Odom scored on an 80-yard run in the 3rd quarter but it was called back on a penalty (or due to the quarter ending). Bay Springs' best chance came on a *"desperate effort to score"* but a *"long spiral down midfield away from the secondary to an open receiver"* was dropped by an *"over-anxious"* player. It *"slipped beautifully through his arms, thus ending the Bay Springs threat"*.

The Burrs committed too many turnovers to have a chance. Charlie Fail picked off passes in their first two drives while they threw another interception later. Again, they fumbled deep in Bay Springs territory before halftime. The contest was well-attended well by locals in Jasper County, and they proclaimed it to be *"the hardest-fought game, yet the cleanest sportsmanship ever witnessed by sideliners. That is certainly a flower in the hat of all participants of both teams and an asset to both communities as well as a reputable remark favoring the coaching staffs of the two* schools".

GAME 8: MAGEE (4-2-1) @ CRYSTAL SPRINGS (UNREPORTED)
MAGEE 25 CRYSTAL SPRINGS 0
November 8, 1946

In seven attempts since 1928, Magee had never bested Crystal Springs. But on this night, the "*Burrheads were all over the field*". Magee started quickly with McNair's first-drive touchdown and 6-0 lead. They tallied again before the quarter was over with Smith making it 12-0. "*The Burrhead line, playing a fast-charging game, made it impossible for the Crystallies to pick up yardage through or around the line*". Still, Crystal Springs' defense held in the 2nd quarter and halftime sat 12-0.

The 3rd quarter held a "*fast, hard-charging game resuming with the blowing of the whistle*". But Magee with McNair's legs scored again early to make it 18-0. In the final frame, McNair hit Buster May, who lateraled to Odom to put the ball deep into Crystal Springs territory. Running plays put them at the 5 from where Odom burst through for the last touchdown. McNair converted the PAT for the last point.

GAME 9: MAGEE (5-2-1) vs COLUMBIA (6-2)
MAGEE 14 COLUMBIA 0
November 15, 1946: HOMECOMING

In Magee, the field lighting was finally done as of the end of October and ready to go for the Burrheads next home tilt. The Simpson County News said that "*The Columbia team has a splendid record and no doubt they will prove to be the strongest opponent since Natchez. Columbia is reported to have one of the best high school lines in the state and one of the best line-plunging backs*".

While there may have been Homecoming games beforehand, this was the first reported official Homecoming game found. Mary Joyce Stephens, a cheerleader for the Burrheads, would serve as Queen for the occasion and be officially crowned at halftime with the Copiah-Lincoln Junior College Bank present. As for the contest, Odom started in the first quarter with a touchdown when he "*smashed his way over from the five-yard line*" and McNair converted. Now 7-0 in the 3rd quarter, Magee partially blocked a Dedeaux pass and McNair made it count from 30 yards and added the PAT.

"*Outstanding in the Magee backfield were Odom, McNair, K. Herrington, Smith and Buffington...*" Magee also led in first downs by a 19-5 tally.

GAME 10: MAGEE (6-2-1) vs MENDENHALL (UNREPORTED)
MAGEE 38 MENDENHALL 0
November 22, 1946

Long-time rival Mendenhall, in a series that barely favored the Burrheads, would make their way south to Magee for the grudge match. The Simpson County News said that they "*ran into an impregnable force of opposition where they met and were defeated... While Mendenhall played what was considered one of the best games of the season, they were no match for the powerhouse attack thrust at them by the Magee team. Mendenhall played a game that was something to see in the line of amateur contests, and while their best efforts were unavailing against the superior weight and strategy of the Burrheads, all attending gave the Tiger eleven loud plaudits over their performance*".

As for scoring, we know that Odom was responsible for three of the touchdowns for Magee "*while McNair and Herrington capably turned in their usual stellar performances*". Billy Allen picked off one pass and took it 60 yards to paydirt while Kelly Herrington and McNair tallied the other scores.

GAME 11: MAGEE (7-2-1) @ FOREST HILL (7-0-2)
MAGEE 12 FOREST HILL 6
November 30, 1946: PROVINE FIELD; CLINTON, MS

This contest was huge for the Simpson County eleven and their fans. Their beloved Burrheads had gone numerous years with mediocre or losing records; some years scoring almost no points in a given season. Now revived, they met a Forest Hill team that had yet to lose and had been scored upon only twice. This would be the semi-final game of the regionals with the winner meeting the victor of Yazoo City and Canton for bragging rights.

Early in the opening quarter, Kelly Herrington put Magee up on a 35-yard scamper. McNair's point-after attempt was blocked. The rest of the half consisted of both teams exhibiting "*concrete defense*" to keep halftime 6-0. In the 3rd, Forest Hill went to the air and was successful in evening up the scoreboard. But in the same frame, McNair put the Burrheads back up on "*a nice drive over the center of the line*". Forest Hill, in a desperate final-minute march, went back to the air. But Billy Smith "*rushed under a long coffin corner pass and intercepted it to freeze the last chance (they) would have to stage an offensive movement*". Kudos went to most of the Burrhead team for their play.

GAME 12: MAGEE (8-2-1) @ YAZOO CITY (UNREPORTED)
MAGEE 13 YAZOO CITY 0
December 5, 1946: PROVINE FIELD; CLINTON, MS

The title of Middle Mississippi Champions was up for grabs. Magee, now traveling back to Clinton, would face a Yazoo City team that had apparently handled Canton with ease. "*These two teams have been showing bruising strength throughout the season and they are planning on 'shooting the works'... The Yazoo City line has been plenty strong this year with opponents scoring only three touchdowns all season*".

A steady aerial attack moved Yazoo City deep into Magee territory early, but the Burr defense stiffened. Odom and Kelly Herrington then began a series of runs deep into Indian territory from where Herrington "*took a spinner from McNair and crashed through the left side of his line standing up*". McNair's toe made it 7-0; a score that stood through halftime.

Yazoo City opened the 3rd quarter with several strong drives into scoring position but could not convert them into points. Magee's last points came courtesy of a Tullos and Pete Russell sack of the QB that caused a fumble. The ball "*rolled across the goal line to be covered by Pete Russell, counting for the second touchdown*".

The team was honored after the new year with a banquet at the Community House. In attendance was the Homecoming Queen (Mary Joyce Stephens) and Coach Weaver of Mississippi State University. Fourteen "M Club" members were honored and selections for 1947 Captain (Billy Smith) and Co-Captain (Kelly Herrington) were announced.

1947 (4-5-1)

Coach Kisner, by far the longest-serving head man in Magee football history, now entered his sixth season. Coach A.L. Walker would once again serve as assistant.

GAME 1: MAGEE (0-0) vs CRYSTAL SPRINGS (0-0)
MAGEE 25 CRYSTAL SPRINGS 0
September 12, 1947

The Burrheads were definitely looking to improve on the all-time 1-7 record against the Copiah County team. Last year, they had snapped the streak with a 25-0 win. For this lid-lifter, an overflow crowd of 2,500 stuffed the stands and fences to see the defending Middle Mississippi champions do just that.

Bill Smith got Magee going with a 7-yard run through "*the middle of the Tiger's line*" to make it 6-0. Joe McNair added the next in the 2nd quarter when he "*romped off on a nice jaunt*" over the left side. That made halftime 12-0. Despite a 3rd quarter touchdown nullified by a penalty, Kelly Harrington still put a score on the board with a 30-yard (or 55-yard) dash and McNair converted. In the waning minutes of the game, Smith pulled in a long McNair toss for the last tally.

The coaches were "*well-pleased with their club in its initial contest, but noticed mistakes which must be ironed out before the next contest*". The Simpson County News gave credit specifically to Cecil Herrington and Robert Yates for their play. Unfortunately, McNair "*and other backs*" were injured in the tilt to the extent that they would not see action until at least November.

GAME 2: MAGEE (1-0) @ NATCHEZ (1-0)
MAGEE 0 NATCHEZ 12
September 19, 1947

The two teams traded wins each of the past three years on the gridiron. This season, Natchez was called "*strong*" and The Enterprise Journal predicted a runaway win for the Rebels 34-7. They had opened their season the week before with a 33-0 shutout win.

Natchez set up the opening score in the 1st quarter with a Fred Foster pass to Claude Porter. From the 3-yard line, Buzz Ratcliffe dove in and it was 6-0. In the 2nd quarter, Foster hit Porter from the 20-yard line to cap a 50-yard drive set up by a partially-blocked punt. "*The Rebs outplayed Magee one-sidedly in the first half, scoring 10 first downs to the invaders' 1. But the Burrheads tightened up in the last two scoreless quarters and held a 5-4 edge in first downs".*

The highlight of Magee play came when Scott Buffington picked up a fumble and raced 75 yards to paydirt. However, it was called back to the point of the fumble "*as the ruling declared that you can't pick up a fumble and run with it*". The Burrheads suffered several injuries in the contest, but was hoping to be healed for the next contest.

GAME 3: MAGEE (1-1) @ BRANDON (1-1-1)
MAGEE 0 BRANDON 0
September 23, 1947

Coach Collier Jordan had been attending summer school at The University of Alabama but returned to Brandon by practice week to start his second season at the Bulldog helm. His ten-game schedule was called "*probably the toughest in several seasons, though the squad for this year will be much better than usual*". By the beginning of September, he had been putting "*his charges through strenuous workouts...*" and had the advantage of being able to field two full teams with numerous experienced players. "*Some of the newcomers are showing plenty of ability and fight*".

The Bulldogs, "*fighting against huge odds*", came close to a final quarter win. Though they had first down at the half-yard line, the Burrhead defense held Brandon out of the end zone. Leland Harrison's attempted field goal missed its mark and kept the game scoreless. "*Coming back in the last half of the game ... the Bulldogs shoved the Burrheads around unmercifully, though failing to score*".

The Simpson County News appeared to dislike the quality of officiating. "*Last Friday night the Magee Burrheads didn't break the three-year long tradition of Brandon High School not being defeated on their home field. Neither did the refereeing staff break the three-year long tradition of not permitting Brandon to be defeated on their home field. Many times the Burrheads beat their way to the pay dirt stripe but each time they would suffer long penalties that would put them out of scoring position...*" Apparently the writer was unaware of the fact that Brandon had no such three-year long home field winning advantage, having lost 3 times at home in 1945.

Magee outpaced Brandon in first downs 7-6, though the Bulldogs went 3-5 passing against only one successful Magee toss. Bulldog passes came from Vernon Campbell to John Campbell. Ralph Moore, "*one of the Bulldog stalwarts*", would be out the remainder of the season after fracturing his collarbone in the game.

GAME 4: MAGEE (1-1-1) @ BROOKLYN (UNREPORTED)
MAGEE 8 BROOKLYN 12
October 3, 1947

Originally the Burrs were to have an off-week to prepare for Hazlehurst, but a last-minute opportunity arose and found the team on the road to Forrest County. The Simpson County News noted that "*There weren't many Magee boosters in attendance ... due to the fact that the date was filled only a few days before Friday and not many folks had time to make plans to go*". The high school was also having "school day" at the State Fair; thus lightening the crowd. The same paper reported that "*our boys played a mighty fine game even though we lost by a few points*". Cecil Herrington would miss this game and many to follow as the result of a broken ankle against Natchez. He joined a number of still-missing and injured Burrhead players on the sidelines.

GAME 5: MAGEE (1-2-1) vs HAZLEHURST (5-0)
MAGEE 0 HAZLEHURST 13
October 17, 1947

Again the schedule seemed to change and Magee now got their off-week as originally planned the week before. Hazlehurst was dominant in the series, holding a 5-0 margin. To top it off, their backfield was called "*one of the best ... in the state which has gained wide publicity throughout the season*". The good news was that they had their opponents at home.

The Indians scored on their first possession via a 55-yard drive capped by a 3-yard Jimmy Spitchley run. Magee made it to the Hazlehurst 2-yard line "*with 200-pound QB Joe McNair giving a good display of fancy ball-handling and faking*". They could not make it count, however. Their last score came in the 2nd quarter when Leroy Bullock "*vaulted into the open with good blocking and proceeded to outrun the Magee secondary for 83 yards and a touchdown*".

Hazlehurst got to the Magee 9 and 12-yard lines but fumbled away each opportunity. Magee, desperately trying to get back in the game, had a pass picked off by Bryan Simmons near the end.

GAME 6: MAGEE (1-3-1) @ MORTON (UNREPORTED)
MAGEE 0 MORTON 6
October 24, 1947

The Panthers were noted as being *"undefeated in the Choctaw Conference (2-0) and the Middle Mississippi region"*. The Burrheads were still trying to find their offense that had been missing since the first game against Crystal Springs.

Both Morton touchdowns came in the initial quarter of play. Scottie Hughes notched the first on a 65-yard dash. The Burrheads had actually crossed the goal first, but it was nullified by a penalty. Magee was able to threaten many times in the last half of play *"only to be halted by their opponents before they could break across the paydirt line"*. Apparently the running game of the Panthers lived up to the hype, with The Simpson County News calling it *"one of the best exhibitions of high school blocking the public has been privileged to witness"*.

GAME 7: MAGEE (1-4-1) vs ELLISVILLE (UNREPORTED)
MAGEE 34 ELLISVILLE 0
October 31, 1947

Very little was written about first-time opponent Ellisville. The Simpson County News noted that they *"enjoyed"* the contest and that *"Our boys scored in every quarter... We like that scoring; when it's in our favor, that is"*. Ellisville would be later known as South Jones.

GAME 8: MAGEE (2-4-1) vs CANTON (UNREPORTED)
MAGEE 14 CANTON 7
November 7, 1947: HOMECOMING

Coach G.B. Edgar started work on August 15th with 36 players. They came to Magee trying to break a short losing streak to the Burrs, but apparently this one did not go their way. Only a report from the week of the Mendenhall contest gives us the final outcome. The Madison County Herald, also, gave only the final score.

GAME 9: MAGEE (3-4-1) vs COLUMBIA (UNREPORTED)
NOT COMPLETED
November 14, 1947

Columbia, under Coach R.G. Weems, had been on the road at least 3 weeks in a row before heading to Magee. The Columbian Progress said *"Magee is best remembered by the local gridsters for having defeated them last year by one touchdown as they go into this game with a successful season behind them"*. Apparently the reporters in Columbia thought their opponent to have only 2 losses.

Due to widespread and heavy storms, this contest got only through three quarters before being officially called off. Apparently the deciding factor came when the lights went off during the game. The Columbian Progress reported that their local squad played Crosby on that day and won 19-6. So, there is some discrepancy on actual details as to when the game was cancelled and when Columbia was able to schedule another opponent.

GAME 10: MAGEE (3-4-1) @ MENDENHALL (5-4)
MAGEE 13 MENDENHALL 6
November 21, 1947

Once again, rival Mendenhall would bring down the curtain on the regular season. The Simpson County News said that *"Mendenhall is favored with games won, although Magee has played stronger opposition in their won and lost column. Going back to the beginning of the history of football of Mendenhall and Magee schools, it has been annually accepted that the football classic between the two teams would be the grudge battle of the season"*. Ironically, after the loss, the same paper said that Mendenhall was speculated before the game as *"several touchdowns under the Magee eleven"*.

After holding Coach Henry Stienriede's Tigers on their initial drive, Magee drove steadily downfield with McNair going in for the initial score. The point-after made it a quick 7-0. The home team could have potentially tied things in the 2nd quarter when "*McNeill broke through the Magee line, swerved towards the left sideline, dodging several tacklers, broke into the clear, and slipped on the muddy field when headed towards the goal*". Both teams had good 3rd quarter drives killed by penalties, but the Burrs still managed to score on a 9-yard Buffington run.

The contest would be hard-hitting. In the final frame, Buffington "*picked up speed and drove at the Tiger line, hitting a solid brick wall named Keen with a loud resounding crash. The small back bounced back and hit the rain soaked field with such force that he was almost buried in the mud*". However, Mendy had the last score afterwards on an 80-yard drive capped by Knight's 1-yard plunge. They nearly scored again as the clock expired, but McNeill's run came just short as the whistle sounded.

Mendenhall led in first downs (13-10) and went 1-3 passing. Magee was 1-1 in the air. "*The Tigers were headed towards paydirt (several times) but were stopped by penalties. The Tigers had no strength in reserves while the Magee coach substituted freely throughout the entire game*". A later report put this at 20-6.

GAME 11: MAGEE (4-4-1) @/vs NEWTON (?-2)
MAGEE 6 NEWTON 14
December 4, 1947

The November 27th paper noted that Magee would end the season against a strong Newton squad in the Veterans Bowl. A later source pointed to a 14-6 defeat. That notation is included here.

1948 (7-3-1)

B.L. Kisner's seventh season would also be his last. No other details about the health or conditioning of the team returning from a 4-4-1 record have been found. This would also serve to be one of the more under-reported years for Magee football from all sources; including opponents.

GAME 1: MAGEE (0-0) vs BILOXI (0-0)
MAGEE 6 BILOXI 40
September 17, 1948

The inaugural game between Magee and the Indians would never be in doubt. As a historical side note, this was probably the second tilt for the Indians before their first Big Eight encounter the next week. In this game, their local paper said that "*The Redskins took advantage of numerous fumbles by the opponents, turning them into scores*".

An opening Magee fumble on the 22 (recovered by Charles Boone) was turned quickly into a 5-yard Elizey Burch pass to Boone for the touchdown. John Radich recovered the ensuing kickoff in the end zone for "*an automatic touchdown*" and Norman Broussard converted for a fast 13-0 lead. James Pope fell on a later Radich fumble at the Biloxi 25. Then W.E. Bishop hit Harold Winborne on a pass that put them at the 10-yard line. "*Winborne, who carried the brunt of the losers' running attack, knocked three would-be Biloxi tacklers to the turn during this jaunt with his stiff-arm tactics*". He went in "*through center*" on the next play for the score.

A Magee fumble in the 2nd, recovered by Broussard at the 40, allowed Norman Duplain an eventual 10-yard tally and his conversion. Just before halftime, a Tom Ferrill interception set up Burch's sneak "*around right end after a fake handoff*" for their next tally. Broussard sent the team to the lockers 27-6. Radich tallied again in the 3rd on a run and set up his next in the final frame when he recovered a Burr fumble at the 6-yard line. He scored, Broussard converted, and the game was over. Magee made it to the 30-yard as the whistle sounded.

Biloxi led in first downs (7-5) and passing (4-12 vs 1-3).

GAME 2: MAGEE (0-1) vs BRANDON (0-1)
MAGEE 38 BRANDON 0
September 24, 1948

Coach Collier Jordan started August practices hoping to round out a strong Bulldog team. "*Admitting that the Brandon eleven will probably be outweighed by the (first opponent) Gulfport squad, Brandon football fanciers still are certain that the intensive workouts Coach Jordan has been giving his boys will make them a match for the coast team. A bitter battle, with plenty of thrills, is anticipated"*. Newell Holyfield served as Captain while Billy Sowell was Co-Captain.

In that opener, Brandon was throttled 38-0. This would be a rebound game for Magee while Brandon would suffer yet another tremendous loss. *"The Burrheads seemed to run around, through and over the Bulldogs at will, with the locals having put on only one concerted goal-ward drive and that in the closing minutes of the third period. Individually, several of the Brandon boys played a good game, but they failed to clock as a scoring unit"*.

GAME 3: MAGEE (1-1) @ WAYNESBORO (UNREPORTED)
MAGEE 6 WAYNESBORO 0
October 1, 1948

The only record we have of the encounter came from The Hattiesburg American on October 2nd noting the final score.

GAME 4: MAGEE (2-1) vs/@ FORREST COUNTY AHS (UNREPORTED)
MAGEE 8 FCAHS 0
October 8, 1948

The only notation for the Brooklyn, MS-based team was in The Clarion-Ledger on October 9th.

GAME 5: MAGEE (3-1) @ HAZLEHURST (0-3)
MAGEE 13 HAZLEHURST 7
October 14, 1948

Due to the upcoming state fair, both teams agreed to move the contest to Thursday night. Coach Carroll Shows started the season by *"sending his squad through some good, hard workouts in an effort to have them in top condition"*. They were winless in three encounters; their last a 7-0 loss to (Vicksburg) Culkin Academy. Hazlehurst hit the board first on a Leroy Bullock 45-yard run and his PAT. Winborne came back with a score but the failed point-after kept it 7-6.

In the second half, it was Magee with *"sweeping end-runs behind nice interference that was good for 7- and 8-yards per try and this eventually (led to) two touchdowns"*. Otto Walker notched the last tally *"on a wide end run of 30 yards and converted"*. They also got as far as the 5-yard line before the game neared the end, *"but the Indians' line held very strongly"*.

GAME 6: MAGEE (4-1) vs MORTON (UNREPORTED)
MAGEE 6 MORTON 13
October 22, 1948

Morton was very-likely a dominant team. Coach Ira Wilson's overall record at the end of the year was 46-6-2. That report came from a December 15, 1948 snippet. The final score for this game was ported by The Clarion-Ledger on October 23rd.

GAME 7: MAGEE (4-2) @ ELLISVILLE (UNREPORTED)
MAGEE 19 ELLISVILLE 6
October 29, 1948

The only notation of this tilt was found in the final score, reported by The Clarion-Ledger on October 29th.

GAME 8: MAGEE (5-2) @ CANTON (UNREPORTED)
MAGEE 13 CANTON 7
November 5, 1948

Canton was reported to be 0-5-1 in conference play and had been outscored 128-6. This tilt looked as though it would not occur due to horrid weather. But, the rain cleared and the game was on.

Magee hit the board in the opening frame after recovering a Panther fumble at the 35-yard line. Winborne made it count *"standing up"* and Bishop nailed the PAT. Canton came back with a *"succession of passes, line-plunges and a double-reverse play"* which got them to the Magee

13-yard line, "*but lost the ball on downs*". Winborne scored again before halftime but the extra point, thought good at the time, was later ruled "*not legally made*".

The home team cut into the lead in the final frame on "*successive line drives and passes*" when Pevey "*went across*" from the 8-yard line. Montgomery added the final point-after. Winborne took the kickoff back to paydirt but it was ruled that he stepped out of bounds on his run. "*Both teams played an unusually good game, taking into consideration the wet, slippery field*".

GAME 9: MAGEE (6-2) vs COLUMBIA (UNREPORTED)
MAGEE 7 COLUMBIA 7
November 12, 1948

It is unusual that The Columbian Progress did not recap the road game for their Wildcats against Magee. Only The Clarion-Ledger noted the final tally on November 13th.

GAME 10: MAGEE (6-2-1) vs MENDENHALL (UNREPORTED)
MAGEE 13 MENDENHALL 0
November 19, 1948

This would yet another Thursday game "*due to the fact that the Regional playoffs will begin Tuesday (23rd)*". The Clarion-Ledger noted the score on November 19th. It was also reported that Mendenhall got a "*good walloping from the Magee eleven. As we were leaving the game, we heard someone say that what Mendenhall needed with a HAD-A-COL. Perhaps that's true, for there's no need denying that lots of Mendenhall folks were disappointed*".

GAME 11: MAGEE (7-2-1) vs CLINTON (8-1)
MAGEE 6 CLINTON 26
November 24, 1948

The Arrow football season started with a bit of turmoil. First, the school year would be pushed back a week as the school was taking new enrollment. A new cafeteria, gymnasium, vocational shop, class rooms and music rooms were still under construction and not expected to be finished until late October or November. On the football field, long-time coach James "Stute" Allen was now Athletic Director at Clinton. In his place, the school had hired Wendell Webb as new mentor. By mid-August, however, Webb had decided to take the job at Crystal Springs. On August 17th, The Clarion-Ledger ran a "**Coaches Wanted**" article for both Clinton and Bentonia. With no hires imminent, Allen stepped back into the role as head man alongside assistant Carlos Langston.

The Arrows, with their win over Magee, would be playing Yazoo City for the Class A Championship of District 6. The only report found (the November 8th Clarion-Ledger) noted that "*Clinton qualified for the district finals by decisively defeating Magee 26-6 on November 24th.*" It was also reported as a 27-7 win. Yazoo City would go on to beat Clinton for the title.

Coach Kisner would leave in July of 1949 to take the Athletic Director role for Jones County Junior College and Agricultural High School. It seemed a perfect fit as he was a 1933 graduate of JCJC where he was a "*star performer*".

1949 (2-7-2)

Surprisingly, the 1949 Magee football team was one of the more under-reported seasons in their now twenty-four-year history. There were a couple of "firsts" occurring for the team. They had a new head man in Coach Jim Carballo. He would be the 11th in program history. Also, this was the very first year that reporting services referred to the team as Trojans; replacing the long-held nickname of Burrheads.

A 1978 article from The Magee Courier included an interview with Wiley Kees, an ex-player from the late 1920s. "*We felt like we needed to come up with a more suitable name, so we conducted a contest among the touchdown club members and someone submitted the name 'Trojans', symbolic of great victories in Greek mythology and history. That name won...*"

GAME 1: MAGEE (0-0) vs SEMINARY (1-0)
MAGEE 6 SEMINARY 6
September 9, 1949

The two teams had played sporadically since at least 1930. Magee opened their season at home and was looking to get off to a good start before very rough competition followed. Seminary had already played against Purvis and won 7-0. Unfortunately, they got a bit more than the coaches expected.

Magee went up just a minute into the game when Bob Myers *"returned the short kickoff (70 yards) to the Seminary nine-yard line"*. It took three plays before Billie DeJong went in from the 2 for the touchdown. The Bulldogs came back in the next frame on a 61-yard march *"paced by Newton and his throwing arm"*. Foots Sanford capped the drive with the score but, like Magee, their PAT was unsuccessful. That 6-6 score would go unchanged for the rest of the contest.

GAME 2: MAGEE (0-0-1) at BILOXI (0-0)
MAGEE 0 BILOXI 26
September 16, 1949

The Hattiesburg American said that *"Biloxi High will have to depend largely on weight in the coming football season. The Indians, with only four regulars and five lettermen from last year's squad, will have to hustle to equal the below-average record of (5-6) in 1948. But more beef in the line and backfield may offset the lack of experience some. To add to the problem, the team will have a new coach (E.A. "Oscar" Wright) and operate from a new formation"*.

Over 3,000 fans attended a game called a *"listless affair"*. Biloxi tacked on three touchdowns in the first half while Magee *"stood up in the second half and time-and-again threw back the Indians offense"*. Shannon Suarez counted the first score on a 13-yard run in the 1st quarter. In the 2nd, John Radich *"broke off-tackle, feinted two would-be tacklers and scampered the remaining distance"* (56 yards) for the next. Norman Broussard converted for the 13-0 lead. With 2:00 left before intermission, Billy Hollis sprinted to the right for a 20-yard score and it was 20-0.

Radich notched the last points in the 4th quarter from 57 yards on a pitchout that he *"cut back to the middle of the field"*. Magee made it as far as the Biloxi 25-yard line as the game ended. *"Otto Walker, left half, was the sparkplug for the visitors as he led Magee's late-game drive with a 34-yard run; the longest game of the night for the Burrheads (now Trojans). J. White also reeled off sizeable gains in the drive"*. Biloxi led in first downs (5-4) and picked off 3 Magee throws. Biloxi, however, led in fumbles 6-3.

GAME 3: MAGEE (0-1-1) @ BRANDON (0-0-1)
MAGEE 19 BRANDON 19
September 23, 1949

Coach Collier Jordan was back for his fourth year as leader of Bulldog football. However, Jordan wouldn't be coaching until September as he was in school at The University of Alabama. In the interim, Superintendent Gycelle Tynes stepped in to direct activities on the field. Prospects for the squad were unknown as they lost six lettermen from the previous year. Added to that, *"Several other lettermen will not attend school at Brandon this year"*.

Brandon would be the beneficiary of a new stadium in 1949. First used against Magee on this night, the field had lights for night football and 1,060 concrete seats. Since the work was done in large part by students and teachers, the total costs was kept under $5,000. Dedication of the new stadium was the highlight of the evening. Much like the previous week, the Bulldogs would find themselves in a battle with no winner.

Bill Sims provided the game's first points in the 2nd. Picking a fumble out of the air at the Magee 5, he returned it 95 yards for a touchdown. Frank Hemphill's extra point attempt failed and kept it 6-0. Magee tied it shortly after on a 3-yard Bennie Garner run. A last-second Brandon attempt for another first half score was halted by a Mize pickoff of Hemphill. In the 3rd, Garner scored again; this time from the 2. Mize's PAT made it 13-6. Hemphill provided Brandon's response on a run from the 2 but his extra point to tie the game did not work.

Now 13-12 in the last quarter, Garner appeared to insert the dagger via a 47-yard escape for a touchdown. However, the extra point failed and gave Brandon life. They capitalized after a Tommy Norsworthy 36-yard connection with Bill Sims, a 19-yard hook up with Bob Sims, a Jack Taylor run to the 5 and then his touchdown. Hemphill managed to convert to tie it. Though the scoring was done, both teams had chances. Brandon got as far as the 2 while Magee marched as far as the 10.

GAME 4: MAGEE (0-1-2) vs WAYNESBORO (3-0)
MAGEE 0 WAYNESBORO 38
September 30, 1949

Waynesboro was reported by their paper to have *"made hamburger out of the beefy Magee line"* as the *"Magee fans sat in amazed and stunned silence"*. To paint the picture, Magee was clad in white pants, red jerseys with white numerals and white helmets.

The visitors' first score came on their initial drive thanks to the running of Slay, Clark and Holland. They crossed the goal on their next march via a 65-yard play. As the 2nd quarter opened, it was now 19-0. But, Waynesboro pushed that lead to 31-0 before halftime. *"In the second half, most of the (Panther) first string team was taken out and the second team played"*. Still, they managed one more score. Magee got as far as the Panther 8-yard line as the game neared ending before the starters came back in to stop the advance.

GAME 5: MAGEE (0-2-2) @ FORREST COUNTY AHS (2-2)
MAGEE 0 FCAHS 13
October 7, 1949

This week featured a trip to Brooklyn, MS to take on the Class 8 Aggies. Coach Roland Loper said that his team had *"shown up well in practice this week in spite of the fact that several of them are still nursing bruises incurred in the Purvis game last Thursday"*. Two starters were definitely out; one due to an injury in practice during game week.

The Hattiesburg American noted that *"The Aggies outplayed the Burrheads most of the game (note Burrheads for this article). Neither team threatened in the first quarter, but the Aggies' first touchdown drive started four plays before the end of the quarter"*. That score came in the 2nd quarter on an 11-yard Mapp pass to McMichael and Mapp point-after. Magee attempted to even the score before intermission with a drive to the Aggie 9 but were held on downs due to a stubborn defense.

There was no scoring in the 3rd quarter thanks to *"a series of interceptions and fumbles"*. But in the final period, Herbert Jackson picked off a Magee throw and took it 34 yards to the Trojan 1. From there, Mapp snuck in for the final tally. They threatened to increase the lead afterwards but lost the opportunity due to a fumble.

GAME 6: MAGEE (0-3-2) @/vs HAZLEHURST (UNREPORTED)
MAGEE 7 HAZLEHURST 20
October 14, 1949

Numerous reports point to a 20-7 loss against Hazlehurst during the week. Unfortunately, the details were not reported.

GAME 7: MAGEE (0-4-2) @ MORTON (0-?)
MAGEE 12 MORTON 13
October 21, 1949

Two winless teams had pride on the line in Scott County, but it was the home team *"nosing out"* the visitors. The final winning touchdown came from Morton on a 60-yard Lee aerial to Lester.

GAME 8: MAGEE (0-5-2) vs FOREST HILL (UNREPORTED)
MAGEE 6 FOREST HILL 7
October 28, 1949

Forest Hill was coming off a 27-0 win over Magee rival Mendenhall. Unfortunately, details for such a tight contest are unavailable. Only the final score remains.

GAME 9: MAGEE (0-6-2) vs/@ COLUMBIA (1-?)
MAGEE 0 COLUMBIA 21
November 4, 1949

Once-injured star Eagle Day came back into the contest long enough in the 2nd quarter to spear a Wildcat drive. A 40-yard connection with Richard Ball set up a 15-yard Wallace run and Day extra point. It didn't take long before Max Thornhill *"broke into the clear and weaved through the secondary, shaking off three tacklers on the way into the end zone"* J.C. James' PAT was true to make halftime 14-0.

Columbia nearly scored to open the 3rd quarter but fumbled to Jim Henry White at the 22-yard long. However, a DeJong fumble on the ensuing march was recovered by Jody Piner. That drive got to the Magee 12 but fizzled. Columbia, meanwhile, had one more score in them thanks to Day's re-entry and pass to Richard Ball for a 58-yard tally. James' PAT marked the end of scoring. It could have been different since a Garner kick was blocked by Hugh White, but they got only to the 14-yard line before Sammy Anderson recovered a Cat fumble.

GAME 10: MAGEE (0-7-2) vs/@ PUCKETT (UNREPORTED)
MAGEE 51 PUCKETT 0
November 11, 1949

Like the Hazlehurst game, Magee also had an under-reported game against Puckett. The 51-point output for a team thus far winless must have been a welcome relief with one more contest to go.

GAME 11: MAGEE (1-7-2) @ MENDENHALL (UNREPORTED)
MAGEE 13 MENDENHALL 7
November 18, 1949

The Simpson County News said that *"According to football fans, the teams this year are about equal in performance. Both teams lost several good players at graduation time last year. The prediction is that there will be the largest crowd in football's history... For the past several years, Magee has been the victor in the annual classics of these rival schools, but there is SOME speculation this year as Mendenhall feels more equal to the occasion than she has in some time"*.

The Clarion-Ledger reported the final score on November 19th. The Simpson County News said that Mendenhall *"certainly played a good game all right, and the coaches of both representative teams are to be congratulated on the good training exemplified. The referees were as impartial as could be and not one word of criticism has been heard about that; which has not always been the case history when these two teams played. We congratulate all concerned: team members, coaches, referees, student rivals and fans"*.

1950-1959

1951 Team (9-3): Class A Champions

1950 (8-3)

Second-year mentor Jim Carballo, assisted again by Emmett Gordon, had some thirty players out that included 11 lettermen. Both felt that the team would "*be stronger than last year*". In the backfield, they averaged 148 pounds while pushing up to roughly 165 on the line.

During hot practices in preparation for the season, the team (and the town) received word that former Burrhead standout Otho Winstead was missing in Korea. Playing both football and baseball from 1935 to 1938, Winstead was considered "*one of the best athletes to ever attend (Mississippi College). He was also one of the best athletes to attend Magee High School and his deeds on the gridiron will long be remembered by the Magee fans*". His death was confirmed a month later.

GAME 1: MAGEE (0-0) @ MENDENHALL (0-0)
MAGEE 0 MENDENHALL 20
September 1, 1950

For those who want the final record of 1950 to be technically accurate, there is an argument that this tilt should not count towards the final tally. Indeed, it's mentioned as a "*pre-season*" game on September 2nd by The Clarion-Ledger. However, other times during the season, the matchup is counted against the Magee overall record. For clarification purposes, and to avoid confusion in years to come, it is noted as an official game. Each side has a legitimate point of debate, but that is best left to the reader.

The reason it was eventually counted as an official contest had a lot to do with Magee's report of their upcoming 1951 season. In that, they note that "*Last year the Trojans won eight and lost three games. The eleven scored 288 points while the opponents were scoring only 89*".

GAME 2: MAGEE (0-1) @ FOREST (0-0)
MAGEE 46 FOREST 7
September 8, 1950

Coach Red Mangum's Bearcats had 8 returning letter-winners and averaged 130 pounds; "*believed to be the lightest in Bearcat history*". Though the game was played "*in a quarter mile of mud and water*", the Trojans "*showed a vast improvement over their last outing. Especially did their line play, blocking and running attack show improvement*". The score is alternately shown as 46-7 and 39-7.

GAME 3: MAGEE (1-1) @ NEW HEBRON (0-0)
MAGEE 21 NEW HEBRON 0
September 15, 1950

The Golden Bears were getting a late start compared to Magee as this was their 1950 lid-lifter. They were working "*hard trying to find the right combination*" with six returning letter-winners in camp. Only the score remains.

GAME 4: MAGEE (2-1) vs BRANDON (2-0)
MAGEE 14 BRANDON 19
September 22, 1950

Brandon had a new coach in Jack "Pop" Warner and assistant Joe Stewart. Warner was a Louisville native who played QB at Ole Miss while Stewart was a first-year coach from Millsaps. Warner kept expectations low, saying "*We can't promise a winning team for every game, but there will always be eleven men on the field and every one of them will be giving the best that they have*". They opened practices in August with The Brandon News noting that "*A tough schedule has been arranged but a good team is expected this year*".

Coach Warner, unhappy with Brandon's passing attack against Forest despite a win, was putting the team "*through rough workouts this week*". As for this game, the cliff-hanger wouldn't be settled until the last minute. Brandon opened scoring in the 1st after Bob Sims picked up a loose Trojan football and returned it 80 yards to paydirt to make it 6-0. Magee responded in the 2nd with a 45-yard Dick Welch scoring run. Mize's PAT gave them the 7-6 advantage. Before halftime, Brandon answered when Prince found Jerry Baker for a 60-yard touchdown and Baker added the extra point.

In the 3rd, numerous Kelly Bishop runs put Magee at the 1 where Mize found the end zone. Jim Henry White's toe put it at 14-13. But with just a minute left in the game, and after successful Prince passes to Bill and Bob Sims, he found Bill for the game-winning points. The extra point failed. Statistically, Brandon led in first downs 19-18 and had no penalty yardage. The Trojans racked up 40 yards in flags. The score is alternately shown by one source as 19-13.

GAME 5: MAGEE (2-2) vs FORREST COUNTY AHS (1-?)
MAGEE 16 FORREST COUNTY AHS 0
October 6, 1950

The B Team played Coach Bill Shirley's Pinola squad the day before but no final score was announced. As for the big brothers, they were facing a Brooklyn team that had scored their first touchdown of the season the previous week in a 6-0 win over Purvis. Despite that, one report thought that FCAHS would win by less than six points. *"Brooklyn's faster backfield may be the deciding factor"*. Only the report from the October 7th Clarion-Ledger gives us the outcome.

GAME 6: MAGEE (3-2) @ HAZLEHURST (7th game)
MAGEE 34 HAZLEHURST 6
October 12, 1950

Coach Shows thought his team to be *"progressing nicely"* as the season opened despite losses due to injuries, operations, graduation and enlistment in the armed forces. The week before they hosted Magee, they played to a 13-13 draw with Magnolia High on the Hazlehurst field. That had been seen as an upset of the *"dope bucket"*. More important than the score was the fact that numerous key players were *"somewhat crippled"*. Shows had seen Magee play and said that the Indians *"will have to go their top speed if they intend to taste victory"*.

The Copiah County News thought that the Indian loss was due to being overweighed *"20 pounds per man"* and a *"bit of over-confidence"*. Magee's first score was set up by a fumble that was later turned into a Welch touchdown and Anderson PAT for the 7-0 lead. Hazlehurst responded with their only tally on a 50-yard Buckshot Prine run. Halftime sat 14-6 and Magee started the next half with numerous scores. Anderson had the first with a White conversion and at least one other later *"on a long run"*. The CCN said *"White was at his best for the Trojans as he converted successfully twice and was very accurate in both his kickoffs and punting"*.

GAME 7: MAGEE (4-2) vs MORTON (UNREPORTED)
MAGEE 26 MORTON 0
October 20, 1950

The Panthers were humiliated the week before in a 54-13 stomping by Enterprise. This caused one sports prognosticator to say that *"Magee's surprising Trojans will walk all over Morton, another whirlwind win this week"*. The final score was reported in the October 21st Clarion-Ledger.

GAME 8: MAGEE (5-2) @ FOREST HILL (1-5)
MAGEE 47 FOREST HILL 6
October 27, 1950

Coach J.C. McDonald had 3 returning lettermen for his Jackson-area team. By game day, they hadn't fared well overall, with just a lone victory (if reports area accurate). The Clarion-Ledger though Magee looked *"14 points better"* than McDonald's squad in this matchup. That same paper reported only the final score in their October 28th edition.

GAME 9: MAGEE (6-2) vs COLUMBIA (UNREPORTED)
MAGEE 6 COLUMBIA 20
November 3, 1950

The conditions were not what fans and players had hoped for. The Columbian Progress said that there was *"cold wind and (a) muddy field"* while a Clarion-Ledger recap said that *"The Trojans suffered their third defeat on a slippery and boggy field against the strong Columbia eleven"*.

Charles Mize and Dick Welch runs put the ball at the Columbia 7 early in the 2nd quarter, but they could get no further. The two did the same on the next drive but a fumble gave the ball back to the Cats. That led to an 11-yard Joe Cook run and Richard Ball extra point. Another Magee fumble put them at the 45-yard line to allow Eagle Day a run *"through a hole in the line"* from where he *"fought across the Trojan secondary"* into the end zone. That put halftime 13-0.

A 3rd quarter interception by Frank Geiger did no harm but their following march ended when Geiger *"went through the line ... and out into the clear and ... into the end zone standing up"*. Ball's conversion finished Cat scoring. White managed Magee's only tally in the same quarter on a 1-yard run. A last-minute threat to cut into the lead was thwarted when Geiger picked off another pass.

Columbia led in first downs (13-11) and rushing (225-167). Magee "controlled" the air going 2-7 while Columbia was 0-1.

GAME 10: MAGEE (6-3) vs ELLISVILLE (UNREPORTED)
MAGEE 20 ELLISVILLE 0
November 10, 1950: HOMECOMING

This was called by The Clarion-Ledger *"one of the top games in the district... it should be a real humdinger with Magee winning by a touchdown"*. In Magee, it was Homecoming week with the Co-Lin offering halftime music for the coronation of the Queen. This game proved to be a mystery for the book. One notation had Magee against Ellisville, though their paper doesn't report any news about the affair. Later, it was reported to be a win over Puckett. One source noting a 20-0 win over Ellisville on this week somewhat cleared the doubt.

GAME 11: MAGEE (7-3) @ MENDENHALL (UNREPORTED)
MAGEE 40 MENDENHALL 12
November 17, 1950

In late October, Mendenhall sat undefeated thus far on the season. They had opened with the win over Magee that had broken at least a string of 5 straight defeats. For this game, the Trojans and Coach Henry Stienriede's Tigers met in what the paper called *"the top class A contest of the week. Mendenhall played Puckett and won last week. This week, they (Magee) look to take their revenge for the 20-6 opening defeat at the hands of the Tigers"*.

This score is up for debate. The Clarion-Ledger reported it on November 18th at 42-7. The Simpson County News reported decades later that it was actually 40-12. For this report, we are taking the word of the local paper.

The Mississippi State University publication (The Reflector) released the first composite All-State High School Football Team in mid-December. On the list for Magee was Jim Tuggle.

1951 (9-3) CLASS A CHAMPIONS

Jim Carballo was *"faced with the task of replacing several outstanding players who graduated last year"*. The Trojans started practices on August 16th *"working overtime in an effort to be ready for"* the opener against Mendenhall. The previous year, Mendy had shocked the eventual 8-3 Magee squad with a win in a stellar year for the rival Simpson County team. But, Magee had gotten revenge in spades at year's end.

Among the departed Trojans were All-State player James Tuggle and Ralph Everett.

GAME 1: MAGEE (0-0) vs MENDENHALL (0-0)
MAGEE 6 MENDENHALL 0
August 31, 1951

The Clarion-Ledger noted that *"Magee's Trojans will play host to the Mendenhall Tigers and this annual grudge battle is setting the pace for the pair of Simpson County schools"*. The original scheduled date of August 31st was postponed due to a *"flash flood of rain here early in the evening"*. The only report of the outcome came on September 12th, saying *"The Tigers were previously defeated by Magee 6-0"* after their win against Pinola.

GAME 2: MAGEE (1-0) @/vs PINOLA (UNREPORTED)
MAGEE 6 PINOLA 0
September 7, 1951

A notation from a source on the history of Simpson County football noted a contest against Pinola on this open day. The 6-0 score, if accurate, mirrored the opener against Mendenhall the week before.

GAME 3: MAGEE (2-0) @ NEW HEBRON (0-1)
MAGEE 25 NEW HEBRON 6
September 14, 1951

New Hebron was coming off of a 9-6 loss to Crystal Springs and now made the trip to Magee. The only notation we have is found in the September 15th Clarion-Ledger that showed the final tally.

GAME 4: MAGEE (3-0) @ BRANDON (1-1)
MAGEE 35 BRANDON 0
September 21, 1951

Jack "Pop" Warner was back for his second stint as Bulldog mentor, but he would be facing low expectations this year versus that of the 6-4-1 season from 1950. The Clarion-Ledger predicted a dismal campaign by saying that they would *"be in the lower brackets this season and look forward to anything but successful seasons. Brandon lost key men ... and it looks anything but good there"*. Jerry Baker would serve as team Captain while Tommy Sumrall was Co-Captain.

In 1950, Brandon had come back to beat Magee by a 19-14 tally. After two road games, it was time for the Bulldogs to get a home contest. The Brandon News said that if Brandon *"opened up in the first quarter like they did the last half Friday night, they should be able to give the Trojans a rough night, although it can be expected to be a close fight"*. It would not be as they had hoped.

The Clarion-Ledger said that *"Magee's Trojans did not show the vaunted power they are supposed to have, and without covering nine Brandon fumbles, three of which led mainly to touchdowns, would have won only by the hardest effort"*. Magee scoring came twice in the 1st, twice in the 3rd and once in the 4th. Four of the five scores came as a result of either fumbles or interceptions. Like Jerry Lott's performance against Philadelphia, Sammy Anderson would be almost unstoppable. His first was a 40-yard run, the second a 66-yard fumble return off of a Jerry Baker drop, and the last a 35-yard dash to paydirt. Additional scores came from Dick Welch and Grafton Grubbs while Jim White booted 4 PATs and ran in another.

The paper also erroneously reported the game to be 36-0. Magee racked up a 233-65 advantage in total yardage and had one more interception (2-1). Brandon led in first downs 4-3.

GAME 5: MAGEE (4-0) @ CLINTON (2-1)
MAGEE 33 CLINTON 0
September 28, 1951

A power-rating index of District 6 teams now had Magee 4th behind Canton, Clinton and (ironically) Mendenhall. Only two of the Trojan wins had been in conference; thus perhaps giving a somewhat skewed rating.

Meanwhile, the Arrows opened practice under new Head Coach C.G. "Bubba" Muse on August 15th hoping to improve over the dismal recording of 1950. Their eleven game District 6 schedule would feature seven of the contests on the road. The former MC Choctaw star *"said that the squad had been looking good in workouts despite the fact that the Arrows, long a short punt formation team, would this year employ the Split T (offense)."* They featured at least 10 returning lettermen and had *"newcomers"* (and future stars) fighting for spots.

The Clinton News said that *"Plenty of knock, work on fundamentals and deception, and a possible two drill a day routine will be the order of the day. From here, it looks as if Clinton will field a spirited group of hustlers ready to give battle their best."*

The reports noted that Magee combined *"a powerful line and lightning-fast backs"* in the domination. The Magee Courier said that the Trojans entered *"the game as underdogs according to Jackson newspaper predictions (but) proved early in the game that they were much the Clinton's boy's superiors."* Halftime sat 14-0 after touchdowns from Anderson and Bishop. The PATs were added by Jim Henry Mangum. Other scorers in the second half included Welch, Anderson, White and Gordon Shoemaker. Shoemaker's points came off of *"a 40-yard run on a hidden ball play"*. The Magee Courier said that he *"stole the show"* on an *"old Vanderbilt play"* where the guard silently takes the ball while the offense moves the other way. Jimmy Mangum added one PAT.

GAME 6: MAGEE (5-0) vs FOREST (0-3)
MAGEE 13 FOREST 0
October 5, 1951

The Clarion-Ledger noted that Magee should *"have a breather"* and *"win as it pleases"* against the Bearcats. It wasn't as easy as they had predicted as Magee got all of their points in the first half against the Choctaw Conference opponent. Anderson had the opening score with a 30-yard run while Welch provided the last. The lone extra point was provided by Anderson. The Welch touchdown was set up by a fumbled handoff by Jimmy Trammel. Welch also had an 80-yard scoring dash called back due to clipping.

It was said that *"Forest gave Magee the scare of their lives and actually had a few touchdowns called back. Had a foul not been committed on these runs, Forest would have won the game. Magee scored touchdowns in the first and second ..."* The Scott County Times noted that *"Twice the Forest boys dug in and stopped Magee threats which penetrated inside the Forest 10-yard line, and as the game ended, Magee had churned up to the Forest 5"*.

GAME 7: MAGEE (6-0) vs HAZLEHURST (?-1)
MAGEE 0 HAZLEHURST 6
October 11, 1951

After the Forest game, The Clarion-Ledger noted for the tilt against Coach Carroll Shows' Indians that, *"Magee will have possibly the toughest battle of the year when the once-defeated Hazlehurst team invades the Trojan field. Magee will be a one touchdown underdog in the battle to a team that has lost only to Brookhaven"*.

A report on the 18th said that *"Magee's Trojans had their necks out a bit too far and nearly got their heads shaved when Hazlehurst's Indians invaded and won a hard-fought game by 6-0... The game saw many good gains with both team threatening on several occasions. The defeat dropped Magee just a fraction (in strength polls) but still enough to place them Number 2 in the week's rating"*.

GAME 8: MAGEE (6-1) @ MORTON (UNREPORTED)
MAGEE 40 MORTON 6
October 19, 1951

This game, *"paced by hard-charging fullback Dick Welch, who ran for three touchdowns"*, the contest was put away early for the visiting Trojans. Grubbs and Anderson *"played sterling ball on the offense and the Magee line did fine defensively"*.

The (Kosciusko) Star-Herald said that Morton's *"young but heavy team ran into a squad with more experience Friday night and lost to invading Magee 39-6 (see reported score). Only Panther touchdown was made when Ray Neal intercepted a Magee pass. Fullback Dick Welch led the Magee scoring with three touchdowns. Also scoring were Sammy Anderson, J.H. White and John McAlpin. Two extra points were added by White and McAlpin converted one"*.

GAME 9: MAGEE (7-1) vs FOREST HILL (UNREPORTED)
MAGEE 27 FOREST HILL 0
October 26, 1951

Before the game, a Clarion-Ledger article said that *"Magee will have to play a good brand of ball to whip the crippled Rebels from Forest Hill who still have plenty of fight and know full well a win could lead to bigger and better things. In a top game, Magee is picked only on its past record to win a close one"*. The Rebels were *"working hard"* in preparation, *"stressing defensive play and polishing of the offensive attack"*. The game against Pearl the previous week caused a few injuries and could make the difference.

In the end, Magee would have few problems with the visitors. White led with a pair of touchdowns, Anderson *"scored another on a 37-yard romp over right guard (possibly the longest run of the game)"* while Welch notched the other. White also went 3-4 in extra points. In all, Magee led in rushing (228-30) while their hosts went 6-20 in the air for 62 yards. Magee was a woeful 0-6 passing.

For those keeping track of historical records, The Clarion-Ledger reported numerous Magee scores wrong on their October 31st update on the race for playoff berths. It wasn't a slight towards any team. Simply, reporting of the day was not electronic in the sense that any score or overall record was immediately available; even if that publication had reported it beforehand.

GAME 10: MAGEE (8-1) @ COLUMBIA (UNREPORTED)
MAGEE 13 COLUMBIA 31
November 2, 1951

Yazoo City had won 26-0 over Kosciusko the week before. That's important because Magee was second to the Indians in the rankings; *"closer than a flea on a dog's back"*. The bigger problem for Magee this week was a player for Columbia named Eagle Day. After high school, he would play for Ole Miss, the NFL and the Canadian Football League.

By game day, Day had 119 points scored; his last against Crystal Springs where he tallied 20 points in a 26-20 win. Had scored all 25 points against Vicksburg and was already called *"one of Mississippi's most spectacular football stars"*. By comparison, Dick Welch had reportedly notched 148 points in the 1950 season.

The Columbian Progress said that *"A big factor in the game for the players and fans alike was the north wind which whipped through the stadium, blocking punts and freezing ears and noses"*. One punt was pushed back to the punter during the contest. A short Magee punt early in the game set up an eventual 10-yard Day run. His pass later in the frame to Jerry Taylor gave Day a next-play 20-yard dash and 12-0 lead. Day opened the 2nd with another touchdown but the PAT was blocked by Tullos. The Trojans cut into the lead before halftime on a Welch run and White point-after. An onside kick was successful, but produced no points.

Frank Robertson got his turn at crossing the goal in the 3rd when he dashed 48 yards. Day's conversion was true. A few minutes later, and after Arnold blocked a White punt at the 14, Day found the end zone again from there. Grafton Grubb's interception afterwards stalled a solid Cat drive and led to a 24-yard Bishop strike to Welch for the final points. Columbia gained to the 1-yard line as the game closed, but the Trojan defense held.

GAME 11: MAGEE (8-2) vs/@ ELLISVILLE (UNREPORTED)
MAGEE 0 ELLISVILLE 25
November 9, 1951

Due to playoff rules, Magee could play only 10 games during a regular season. They still had two teams left to go: Ellisville and Mendenhall. So, if they wanted to eliminate themselves from post-season play, they could play the starters in both contests. The Trojans elected to send in their B Team in order to preserve a chance at a title. The second-string ended up losing to Ellisville. Though the starters did not play, it still counted as a regular season game.

GAME 12: MAGEE (8-3) @ MENDENHALL (UNREPORTED)
MAGEE 20 MENDHENHALL 14
November 15, 1951

This matchup was called by The Clarion-Ledger *"one of the top rival games of the state"*. Magee was 6-1 since 1944; that loss coming on the opening day of 1950 in what may have been similar to a scrimmage. With extra importance for the week, Magee was *"still very much in the picture for the Class A championship playoff"*. They had elected to play substitutes against Ellisville, but a loss to Mendenhall may have made that useless.

Mendy opened with a 20-yard Marshall Magee touchdown in the first few minutes of the game. That had been set up by a pass from Gerald Morgan to Elton Smith. Marshall Magee almost gave them a second one, but Welch made a touchdown-saving tackle after a 40-yard reception. Welch tied the contest before halftime when he took a pitchout from Mangum to the end zone. Mendy actually matched that accomplishment, but it was brought back on a penalty.

In the 3rd quarter, Welch gave Magee all they would need on touchdown runs of 20 and 60 yards. Mendenhall got their final tally on a 45-yard connection between Morgan and Smith. Morgan and Smith hooked up 9 times on the night.

It was now a wait-and-see period for the Trojans. As it turned out, Canton (Northern Division Winner) was now Magee's opponent for the Class A title. That was decided somewhere around the end of November, meaning that Magee had been idle for a couple of weeks. On November 28th, it was announced by Otis Bufkin, chairman of MHSAA District 6 that Canton decided not to enter the playoffs. Thus, Magee was awarded the Class A title.

1952 (3-8)

Coach Jim Carballo entered his fourth season with a *"great drought"* as he had *"lost his entire starting line and three-fourths of the backfield which carried the team to the 1951 championship. In all, ten of the starting regular offensive players have left the Magee campus"*. The Clarion-Ledger noted that *"This year, Magee will field a light, scrappy team but will be too slow for the eleven game schedule. She keeps to be a consistent winner. But the more seasoned teams had not better take them too lightly, else they want to find themselves on the short end of the score"*.

GAME 1: MAGEE (0-0) @ MENDENHALL (0-0)
MAGEE 0 MENDENHALL 12
August 29, 1952

Rival Mendenhall, now led by Coach Red Mangum, had 13 lettermen back in camp. That put them substantially better than Magee on paper. The game was called a *"bitterly contested ground duel before 3,000 paying fans"*. Mendy got their first score early when Van Peacock capped a 65-yard march with a QB sneak. In the final quarter, Gerald Morgan did the same on a sneak for the last tally. Mendy had a 15-1 lead in first downs. They were 8-12 in the air while the Trojans didn't complete a pass. To make it worse, Magee only rushed for 45 total yards while Mendenhall ran for 158.

The local paper said that *"We have got a team that we can be proud of, even though it is inexperienced and light. The more experience they pack under their belts and the more seasoned they become, the better their plays will click, the more furious their blocking will be and the more tactful their strategy will become..."*

GAME 2: MAGEE (0-1) vs PRENTISS (0-0)
MAGEE 7 PRENTISS 26
September 5, 1952

The Prentiss team, led by legendary Coach Orville Foshee, had a number of new opponents this season. Still, *"and despite the rugged schedule, we predict that the Bulldogs will give a good account of themselves and bring credit to the local school"*. Prentiss, too, had lost a lot to graduation but were still called *"stronger"* than Magee. Carballo was *"giving the boys the works this week and has tended to iron out the wrinkles of inexperience and will no doubt have the Trojans in tip-top shape..."*

Prentiss started quickly when Alton Dagle took the opening kick back 65 yards for a 6-0 lead. They quickly increased the lead when Son Speights, 140-pound halfback, romped in and added the PAT to give them *"a sizeable lead over the Trojans"*. Magee tallied their only score in the 2nd quarter after recovering a Bulldog fumble at the 15-yard line. Sammy Anderson provided the points and the successful PAT followed. Speights had a few more tallies later for Prentiss on double-handoff plays, each over 50 yards in distance.

"At several points in Friday night's ball game, it looked like the Trojans were going to get things going their way, but because of lack of experience, they were unable to make their efforts pay off... Regardless of the score, the game brought about many thrills, which was caused by the fine passing of Bill Caughman who made contact on several occasions with Mitchell and Ware for nice gains. Beautiful kicking by Tullos and nice gains by Anderson and Andrews brought about more activity than the score reveals".

GAME 3: MAGEE (0-2) @ NEW HEBRON (UNREPORTED)
MAGEE 7 NEW HEBRON 0
September 12, 1952

New Hebron was defending BB champions of District 7 and obviously favorites in the home tilt. For this game, they would use *"a shifted six-man line"*. Carballo would offset this with *"fast backs scouting the weak side of the line which proved successful throughout the playing period"*.

Magee was dominant in the game, nearly scoring a pair of times at the New Hebron goal before fumbles killed the threats. However, they did convert on one of the 2nd quarter drives when newcomer Elden Puckett *"carried the pigskin to the 3-yard line on a beautiful end-run which set up the touchdown which was bucked over on a quick opening play"* by Anderson. Anderson's PAT was true and would mark the end of scoring.

Larry Mitchell pulled in 3 passes from Caughman while *"running on the part of Puckett, Anderson, Grubbs and Dan Tullos gave the Trojans nice gains all night"*. It was also noted that *"Even through inexperience cropped up frequently in the ball game, the Trojans are showing remarkable strides of shaping into a veteran ball club and developing the techniques and precision that will carry them on to victory against other foes this season"*. Magee led in first downs 16-2 and allowed New Hebron over the midfield stripe just once.

GAME 4: MAGEE (1-2) vs BRANDON (1-0)
MAGEE 13 BRANDON 14
September 19, 1952

Coach Jack Warner was back for his third year. Though still *"putting the final punch polish on a backfield..."* the coach remained *"non-committal as to the strength and stamina, the speed and skill of the 1952 men. Local fans, however, are as usual, raring for the kickoff and their hopes are high"*. The Clarion-Ledger, though, thought that *"a strong team is expected in Brandon"* with Jerry Baker in the lineup. In late August, Warner thought things were *"looking up since some of his new material is fitting in so well with his veterans"*. By the day before kickoff, he expected *"to field the strongest team he has had in the three years he has been with Brandon"*.

By kickoff, the prediction was in favor of Brandon 12-7. Warner noted that *"over-confidence of the Bulldogs has been his greatest problem this week. He expects his charges to 'take' Magee but he warns them that it'll be no easy job"*. The Trojans were first on the board late in the 1st when Caughman found Grafton Grubbs from the 30. Anderson's extra point run made it 7-0. Brandon responded with a long drive, 2-yard Frank Hemphill dive and a fake-kick PAT from Tommy Swilley to Beasley to make halftime 7-7. *"It was apparent that they intended to kick. However, the ball went to the man in the back position who passed across complete for the extra point and tying the ball game"*.

The 3rd started with an exchange of fumbles. Brandon had the last one and it led to Joe Campbell's (or Jerry Baker's) 50-yard escape for a touchdown. Baker's reception for the extra point made it 14-7. Magee staged a comeback in the 4th via a 50-yard Caughman connection with Jimmy Ware. This time, Anderson's extra point attempt was stuffed by Jones and Baker to seal the win. The Magee Courier noted that rushing was the same while penalties, passes completed and yardage were *"rather evenly distributed"*.

GAME 5: MAGEE (1-3) vs CLINTON (3-0)
MAGEE 6 CLINTON 20
September 26, 1952

Coach "Bubber" Muses' Arrow team had only three veterans on it: Bob Bell, Alvin Hudson and Gene Norman. The rest were called by The Clarion-Ledger *"new boys"*. The Clinton News said there actually 5 returning starters, adding Buck Carl and Cliff Rushing while also mentioning Jimmy Hammond. Practices began August 15th. The team would feature new uniforms of navy blue with white stripes down the pants, white letters and gleaming white helmets. If true, it would be a departure momentarily from the traditional red and white.

It was reported that the *"Magee Trojans will be going all-out to stop the Clinton Arrows ... The Trojans, playing on their home field, are favored by one touchdown over the Arrows, whom they thoroughly trounced last year 33-0"*. The prediction would be inaccurate, though Magee did hold a 6-0 halftime lead. That was set up by a Tullos pickoff of an errant Arrow pass brought back to the Clinton 35. They hit the end zone from there on a 30-yard pass from Caughman to Grubbs.

In the 3rd, the Trojans took the opening kickoff back 50 yards to the Arrow 20. But the defense held and the Arrows drove steadily to the Magee 10. This led to a Hudson break from there to make it a 6-6 game. The PAT was blocked by Magee's Charles Ray Pope. In the 4th, Rushing scored twice to steal the victory. He pushed the ball 43 yards to the Trojan 17 and then got into the end zone from the 2. Norman converted the PAT. His last would be from the 1-yard line accompanied by another Norman PAT.

The Magee paper said *"Good kickoff and punt returns were made all during the game. The Trojan blocking was improved and the entire team played a jam up ball game, especially in the first half."*

GAME 6: MAGEE (1-4) @ HAZLEHURST (0-5)
MAGEE 14 HAZLEHURST 0
October 10, 1952

Daily workouts were underway in August for Coach J.R. McPhearson and his team that featured 7 returning letter-winners. In a game that featured one-win Magee against winless Hazlehurst, one prognosticator called it for the Trojans by a single point. Another said *"in a close, hard scuffle, looks like the Trojans will win"*.

Reports from The Magee Courier noted that touchdowns were tallied by James Andrews and Sammy Anderson. Andrews was also credited with a pair of PATs. They said *"According to the reports, the Trojans played almost a letter-perfect ball game. Bill Caughman hit them four for five tries with his spot passes, interference was paving the way for the running backs and the defense was airtight throughout the playing period."*

GAME 7: MAGEE (2-4) vs MORTON (2-3-1)
MAGEE 25 MORTON 0
October 17, 1952

Morton was *"strengthened by the return of about 14 lettermen"* from the 1951 team. Coach Clyde Benton thus had experience with which to make a first-rate squad, but by game day his team sat under .500. Their last game had been against Clinton where they had been beaten 32-14. To make matters worse for the Panthers, two starters were now out for the year with back injuries, making the paper say that *"Magee, who traditionally plays inspired ball at home looks 2 TDs better"*. Another reporter said that since both were *"out of the championships"*, it would be a *"thriller"* with Morton winning by six points. Only a report from The Clarion-Ledger gives us the final score.

GAME 8: MAGEE (3-4) @ FOREST HILL (3-3-1)
MAGEE 0 FOREST HILL 13
October 24, 1952

It was a rebuilding year in the Jackson area for ex-Millsaps star athlete Coach Ray Bell. Thirteen *"top men"* graduated but they still had *"around 14 lettermen"* coming back. They sat about where expected at game day, just pulling off a 14-7 upset of Pearl the week before. Due to that game, The Clarion-Ledger through them a 12-point favorite against Carballo's team. The report of the final score came amazingly from The Delta Democrat Times on October 26th.

GAME 9: MAGEE (3-5) vs COLUMBIA (5-1)
MAGEE 6 COLUMBIA 26
October 31, 1952

Columbia was now under the leadership of new head man Leonard McCullough; an ex-Mississippi State athlete. The Clarion-Ledger noted that *"Columbia will face a complete rebuilding job with only five lettermen back"*. Columbia still had 5 wins on the season by kickoff and McCullough thought his team *"in good shape for the encounter"*.

Magee was first on the board with a 2nd quarter drive consisting of a Jimmy Ware reception, runs by Anderson and Grubbs, and finally a 3-yard Andrews dive. But the Cats would take control of the tilt from there on. They took the lead in the frame on a 50-yard pass from McDonald to Lloyd Earl Regan and Jerry Taylor's PAT. Then, Monkey Jones picked off a Caughman pass to set up 7-yard Regan scoring run and 13-6 halftime lead.

They added to the total in dramatic fashion in the 3rd quarter when Al Brooks dashed 75 yards to paydirt. In the final frame, another Jones interception led to Al Brooks' 60-yard reception from McDonald for a score. Taylor's kick was good to insert the dagger.

GAME 10: MAGEE (3-6) @ FOREST (3-4-1)
MAGEE 0 FOREST 25
November 7, 1952

Coach Audie Gill's Bearcats were not enjoying a great year, but Magee actually had more losses than Forest. Still, the paper expected a Magee win in a *"close, hard game"* while saying that the Cats *"are capable of uncorking at any time, so expect a tight game"*. The score came only from a November 8th Clarion-Ledger recap of Mississippi games.

GAME 11: MAGEE (3-7) vs MENDENHALL (8-2)
MAGEE 19 MENDENHALL 21
November 14, 1952

Though records this season were decidedly in favor of the visitors, the Magee Courier noted that *"in this annual game of tug-of-war, dog-eat-dog, and what have you, you can throw your statistics away because they don't amount to a hill of beans"*. Coach Magnum had taken his Tigers to an 8-2 record; just 2nd behind Brandon in The Little Dixie. They had already shut out the Trojans on opening day 12-0 and Carballo was *"training the boys to stay a claw's distance from the Tigers and schooling them instead on using their noodle instead of the hands (in order to keep down holding and pushing penalties)"*.

Though the game was predicted to be either an 18- or 20-point affair, it was nothing like that. Magee hit the board in the 2nd quarter via Caughman's pass *"into the waiting arms"* of Mitchell, but the *"attempt to buck the point was unsuccessful"*. Mendy took the 7-6 lead seconds before halftime when Marshall Magee crossed the goal and Munn converted. The Tigers added another in the 3rd quarter and Munn made it 14-6. Magee responded with a QB sneak by Caughman and Anderson crossed to cut it to 14-13.

Both clubs *"turned on the coal"* in the final frame and each scored. Midway through the quarter, Grubbs crossed from the 2-yard line to make it 19-14. But Mendy returned the favor with a 40-yard pass *"into the waiting receiver who managed to get behind the pass defense and race across standing up"*. Munn converted again for what would be the final point of the final game for Magee's 1952 campaign.

Undefeated in conference play, the Columbia Wildcats would wind up the unofficial winner of the Little Dixie by a unanimous vote. It was a bit unique, but the Little Dixie mandated that you could not play more than 11 games before a championship. Mendenhall had done just that, and instead of giving Brandon the chance to vie for the title, they relied on the protocol that stated it would be only the number 1 team against the number 2 team.

1953 (2-8-1)

Jim Carballo, assisted by Coach Raymond Everett, was back for his fifth session as head Trojan. He started with an unexpected loss of numerous starters and players due to ineligible status (two had played for the max four years), two entries into the US armed forces; one player 8-days too old to play; and two (appendectomy and broken leg) sidelined to injuries. Said Carballo, *"Regardless of our losses, the former Burrheads will give a good account of themselves in all games played"*. They were reported with only three *"veteran first-stringers in the lineup"* and ten lettermen to start the season.

GAME 1: MAGEE (0-0) vs MENDENHALL (0-0)
MAGEE 13 MENDENHALL 18
August 28, 1953

Losing both games of 1952 was tough to swallow, but there was not much hope for this year. The Magee Courier said that *"Even though the Trojans are confronted with a veteran shortage and the Tigers are fortunate to have an almost complete eleven returning this season, everyone is in high spirits... Carballo has given his men an intensive period of training, readying them for the clash and the progress he has made with the newcomers will surprise everyone"*.

The first ball game of the season against Coach A.J. Mangum's Tigers was actually held before school opened. Like most of the rivalry games, it was not an easy fight. In fact, it came down to the last two minutes of play. Magee started quickly on their first drive via Grafton Grubbs' 2-yard run *"standing up"* to make it 6-0. Mendy threatened in the 2nd, but halftime still stood 6-0. *"Mendenhall opened the second half like a different team"*. Marshall Magee tied things by capping a 50-yard drive with a 10-yard escape.

The second half differs on which report you follow. The Clarion-Ledger said that following that touchdown, they drove 67 yards with Marshall Magee going in from the 6. Another said that he went in from the 18-yard line. The Magee Courier said that the Trojans responded in the 4th quarter when 7th grader Joe Mangum took *"a handoff from (Bill) Caughman, took to the right side of the line and went across standing up after a brilliant run to tie the score. Caughman then was successful in carrying across for the point which put the Trojans out in front 13-12"*.

The Clarion-Ledger said that *"Magee, never giving up quickly, retaliated..."* by noting that Grubbs *"swept wide for the score"*. As the game was nearing the end, Dan Peacock hit Williamson for a 40-yard gain. Williamson would fumble at the 3-yard line but Peacock picked it up in the end zone for the game-winner. Marshall Magee converted the PAT. Another report failed to mention the fumble, but rather said that Peacock just ran in from the 1-yard line. Mendy had more yardage than Magee (213-143) and held rushing (132-79) and passing (81-64).

GAME 2: MAGEE (0-1) @ PRENTISS (0-0)
MAGEE 0 PRENTISS 20
September 4, 1953

The scarlet and white under Coach Orville Foshee finished 7-3 the previous season. Magee hit the road for Legion Field with hopes that the admirable effort put forth against Mendenhall would carry over to Prentiss.

Fumbles caused both teams problems on their first drives. Prentiss fumbled to Charles Ray Pope on the 38-yard line, but a Caughman handoff to Bennie Prince was fumbled to give the ball back. On Magee's next drive, a hit on Caughman gave the ball away on the Prentiss 45. That drive would result in a 2nd quarter touchdown when *"(Jimmy) McGee, snappy Prentiss end, took a double handoff and traipsed around right end"*. McGee converted and halftime sat 7-0.

The 3rd was notable in that Caughman sustained a *"severe right knee injury"* on a tackle and would be done for the night. The Magee Courier said that *"His absence from the lineup badly crippled the Trojans from both the air and in team management and they were unable to click throughout the rest of the playing period"*. Prentiss was driving for a score on that series but gave the ball away at the 4-yard line. Magee got another gift via a Prince interception, but then Magee fumbled the pigskin away to the Bulldogs.

That led to McGee's 10-yard scoring run and a Son Speights toss to Buck Terrell for the point-after. They would add another tally on their next march when Speights found Brinson *"in the flat who carried across for the score"*. Prentiss led in first downs (13-8). They went 6-13 in the air while Magee was 2-5.

GAME 3: MAGEE (0-2) vs NEW HEBRON (0-0)
MAGEE 6 NEW HEBRON 12
September 10, 1953

Coach James Jones' Golden Bears had 10 returning lettermen from a 5-5 team. Magee enjoyed a good run of success against New Hebron over the past years, but that would not be so easy on this night. It was said that *"two main stringers"* had *"turned in their uniforms"* during the week. The reason was not revealed. As for the game, it was moved up to a Thursday tilt due to the fact that so many were anxious to attend the Mendenhall/Prentiss contest on Friday.

A 2nd quarter fumble by Mangum, along with a personal foul penalty, put the ball at the goal from where Newsome crashed through for a 6-0 lead at halftime. After intermission, New Hebron put together a string of nice ground gains to set up Newsome's plunge into the end zone. Now 12-0, Magee rallied with a 9-yard Mangum scoring dash. Their point-after failed. Andrews later picked off a Golden Bear pass, but the Trojans could not turn it into points. They got inside the NH 30-yard line before the game ended, but to no avail.

GAME 4: MAGEE (0-3) @ BRANDON (1-1)
MAGEE 0 BRANDON 13
September 18, 1953

The departure of the successful Pop Warner led to the hiring of ex-Inverness coach and former Ole Miss Rebel Erm Smith. The Clarion-Ledger noted in early September that *"Chances are good that the Bulldogs will post another winning season, though not quite as powerful a unit as the 1952 contingent, they even it up somewhat with a less powerful schedule. About four of their opponents are in the rebuilding category"*. On October 15th, the paper said that *"This definitely was not Brandon's year, according to the books. The Bulldogs, BB champions of District 6 last year and one of the LDC leaders, lost eight men from that club in addition to the coaching staff"*. Eight seniors would suit up for Brandon.

The Dogs' first score came on the opening drive. Alternating runs by Joe Campbell, Roy Lee Worthy and Sonny Hutchinson ended in a 15-yard Hutchinson scamper. Freddie Dungan converted the extra point. A Trojan fumble in the 2nd led to the next touchdown: a long Billy Beasley pass from the Trojan 16 to Campbell *"who weaved his way past grabbing hands and scored standing up"*. Magee got as far as the Bulldog 3 late in the game but lost the opportunity on a fumble.

The Magee Courier noted that that the *"holding (of) Brandon to 13 points is not a bad showing and they are to be commended for the fine fight they are showing in each game. Any team that is crippled by the loss of any player or the injury of any man is putting a lot into the game when they allow only two touchdowns"*. Mangum and Prince were noted on the 22nd for their Outstanding Performance by The Clarion-Ledger.

GAME 5: MAGEE (0-4) @ CLINTON (1-1)
MAGEE 0 CLINTON 13
September 25, 1953

Clinton had a new coach in Glynn Kitchens. He had dire circumstances with only 3 returning lettermen. By kickoff of the first game, one of them (Byrd Allen) would be out with a separated shoulder. The Arrows welcomed Magee to Clinton with a win over Pinola and a one-point loss to Forest Hill. The Clarion-Ledger reported on October 1st that the two Arrow touchdowns had come from Cliff Rushing and Jerry Ivy. But the worst news for Clinton was that Rushing had suffered a knee injury that would keep him sidelined for an unknown amount of time.

GAME 6: MAGEE (0-5) vs HAZLEHURT (0-5)
MAGEE 7 HAZLEHURST 0
October 9, 1953

Something had to give in a battle of winless teams. Magee now at least had Caughman back to give the Trojans a better chance of winning. The only score came in the final frame when Magee went on a 50-yard drive with *"various backs alternating in the ball-carrying duties"*. From the 10-yard line, Andrews scampered over for the score and Caughman hit Jimmy Way for the point-after. The Magee Courier said that *"Both teams were evenly matched... Infractions were many in the night's play, with both teams receiving their share of the penalties and likewise both teams did their share of fumbling"*.

Said Carballo, *"We finally won and I am not surprised. Despite all the bad luck and the fact that many of the boys on the first string have never played football before this, they are playing good ball. They have scrapped all the way in each one of our games and I know that they will continue to have this spirit and determination for the rest of the season."*

GAME 7: MAGEE (1-5) @ MORTON (UNREPORTED)
MAGEE 12 MORTON 0
October 16, 1953

Coach Clyde Benton had 9 letter-winners on his squad of 28 players for the 1953 campaign. Amazingly, this game has almost no reporting. Only a notation from the November 23rd Scott County Times. Recapping the year for Morton, they point to a 12-0 loss to Magee.

GAME 8: MAGEE (2-5) vs FOREST HILL (5-2)
MAGEE 6 FOREST HILL 31
October 23, 1953

Coach Ray Bell's Rebels were *"at full strength for the first time since the Prentiss encounter a month ago"*. Like Magee, injuries had made an impact on the squad along the campaign. Forest Hill was working hard during game week *"on blocking and tackling fundamentals"*. They had just beaten Pearl and were looking to continue a good season. Unfortunately, only the final score was reported in the October 24th Clarion-Ledger.

GAME 9: MAGEE (2-6) vs PETAL (5-3)
MAGEE 0 PETAL 12
October 30, 1953

Much like other contests during the season, only the final score of the Trojan game against the Panthers is found. That came from The Clarion-Ledger on October 31st.

AME 10: MAGEE (2-7) vs FOREST (4-3-1)
MAGEE 6 FOREST 6
November 6, 1953

Coach Audis Gill had started his Bearcats in twice-a-day practice on August 17th. By game day, they were coming off of a disappointing loss to Newton by a 14-13 score. For their trip to Magee, the paper encouraged everyone *"to be present and lead the Trojans support"* in a game which *"promises to be a good one"*.

The opening frame saw a trade of fumbles. Magee was first on their first drive while Forest gave the ball away as the 1st quarter ended. Magee then fumbled back but Forest threw an interception to Caughman. That march went as far as the Cat 15 but to no avail. Magee promptly fumbled their next possession but the defense managed to hold. The Trojans then unbelievably threw an interception but Forest could get only to the 6-yard line as the half expired.

A blocked punt by Wilkerson in the 3rd allowed him to run in for the touchdown and 6-0 lead. In the final quarter, Magee moved all the way to the Bearcat 5 but yet again put the ball on the ground. However, before the whistle, John Spencer escaped defenders for a 23-yard game-tying tally. The critical point-after failed. *"In the closing minutes, both teams tried in vain to score but were unsuccessful and the game ended in a 6-6 tie"*.

GAME 11: MAGEE (2-7-1) @ MENDEHNALL (10-0)
MAGEE 0 MENDENHALL 24
November 13, 1953

If Magee were ever an underdog in this rivalry, it was this year. And, it was Homecoming up the road. *"However, be this as it may, the game Friday night promises to be one of fireworks as is always the case when the Trojans and the Tigers lock horns. Statistics don't mean anything ... with several of the Trojans playing their last game under the Trojan banner, the local boys are going to Mendenhall with a desire to win and are going to pull everything in the book to set back their rival"*.

Perhaps the score shows the intensity and the desire to win on behalf of Magee as it seemingly would be a larger victory on paper. Halftime sat only 6-0 thanks to Dan Peacock's 4-yard plunge to cap a 76-yard drive. They opened the 3rd with an 81-yard advance and topped it with a Weathersby 1-yard plunge. Their next was a 65-yard march with Weathersby doing the honors from the 15-yard line. With 2:00 on the clock, they blocked a Trojan punt to set up Peacock's 8-yard scoring run.

The Magee Courier summed up Carballo's fifth season by saying *"though lacking in material many times, he has demonstrated his know-how in setting up an excellent defense against the strongest teams, which completely baffled their offense. This is a tribute to his football intuition"*. For historical purposes, an ancillary report from September 9th reported that Port Gibson had placed Magee on their schedule for November 13th. It's obvious that it was incorrect as that was the date of the Mendenhall contest.

In late November, the team accompanied the Pee-Wee football team on a trip to Jackson to see the USM-Georgia football game.

1954 (0-11)

Perhaps owing to a pair of straight two-win seasons, Jim Carballo had now departed Magee and made way for ex-Mississippi State player Prentiss Irving. He would be assisted by Raymond Everett. The Clarion-Ledger said that *"the coaches face a huge rebuilding job, but prospects look brighter than they have in the past few years. Twice-a-day workouts will be held until the opening of school on September 2nd"*. With 46 participants out for practices, The Magee Courier though that *"with continued interest from each candidate, backed with determination to play football for Magee High, the Trojans should turn out one of the best teams in this section of the country this year"*.

In reality, it could not have been further from the truth. Two starters, Joe Mangum (FB) and Billy Smith (QB), were in the 8th and 9th grades respectively. Other starters had never played and would see action in key roles with just two weeks of practices. Additionally, with unexpected injuries along the way, the results were predictable.

GAME 1: MAGEE (0-0) vs MOUNT OLIVE (0-0)
MAGEE 7 MOUNT OLIVE 19
August 27, 1954

After just two weeks of practice, Irving put his Trojans on the field against first-year coach David Lingle. The Magee Courier said that *"The Trojans have been coming along but could use several more weeks to get ready for an opening contest. The game will be a test for many of the boys as they are seeing action for the first time".* Roughly 4,000 fans were expected to watch *"these long-time rival squads, both green and eager, lock horns for their campaign opener".*

Unfortunately, the game would begin without Captain Jerry Sullivan (broken hand) and Billy Smith (injury). Mount Olive, reportedly with just one loss in three years, was able to score all of their points in just the first quarter of play. They blocked two Trojan punts to set up scores, the first putting the ball at the Trojan 2 from where Bernard Harvey *"bucked across"* for the score. Their next was blocked by Bob Gardner and was *"scooped up"* by John Gatewood for a 30-yard score. They added a 25-yard Harvey pass to Walter Lee Hollingsworth for their last.

"A different Trojan eleven returned to the field the second half, after having received valuable instruction from Coaches Irving and Everett". Mangum was able to put Magee on the board in the 3rd quarter with a 20-yard escape and the conversion made it 19-7. They nearly cut into the deficit on the last play of the contest when Mangum snagged an errant pass and raced 90 yards. But, he was tackled by Harvey at the 5-yard line to end the game.

GAME 2: MAGEE (0-1) vs PRENTISS (0-0)
MAGEE 6 PRENTISS 39
September 3, 1954

During game week, it was said that *"Many of the Trojan players received their baptism of fire and looked fairly good as the game progressed. Five starters had only two weeks of football experience and seemed a little lost the first quarter…"* They went on to say that *"Prentiss will be the heavy favorite as they have a heavy, experienced team".* That included a 225-pound fullback named Pope. The Bulldogs, under the leadership of Orville Foshee, ended the previous season with a 7-6 win over New Hebron in The Gas Bowl.

Only the score is found, along with a Magee Courier notation that *"In last week's loss to Prentiss, the Trojans' offense showed signs of life. Joe Mangum, crack fullback, played great ball on offense and defense. Hollis Shoemaker, tackle, and Jerry Sullivan, center, played well in the line. The inexperience is gradually rubbing off the Trojans and with a few more games under their belt they should post a better record".* The B-team fared worse in their game against Jackson on the road, coming back with a 41-0 loss.

GAME 3: MAGEE (0-2) @ NEW HEBRON (0-0)
MAGEE 7 NEW HEBRON 40
September 10, 1954

Things would only get worse for Magee. In the last game, Marion Munn and John Barr (dislocated shoulder) were injured and now out of commission. Taking their place was at least one eighth-grader (John D. Jones). New Hebron was called *"heavily favored"* as a result. Expectedly, the scoreboard showed the results of such big losses.

New Hebron *"ran and passed over a determined, but outnumbered Trojan eleven"* who was *"woefully lacking at times against the stalwart wall of the New Hebron boys and the offense was apparently non-existent…"* New Hebron divided their scoring into two halves while Mangum chalked up Magee's only score in the last few minutes *"as he raced around his end".* The Magee Courier said that *"the Trojans scrapped all the way and with such spirit and determination their results will be victorious in the next few ball games".*

The B team was scheduled for an away game with Mendenhall on the 14th.

GAME 4: MAGEE (0-3) vs BRANDON (1-1)
MAGEE 7 BRANDON 34
September 17, 1954

Another week and more missing starters. Now John Barr (dislocated knee) and James Harold Kennedy (severe lime burns) would be absent from games. Still, *"Trojan morale is high and if they can stop the powerful full-backing of All-Dixie Joe Campbell and the dashes of Beasley, they have an outside chance at an upset".*

The defending Little Dixie District 6 Class BB champion Bulldogs would be helmed by yet another new coach. Future Brandon legend Louis Strickland was the 12th head coach of the Bulldogs and assisted by former Byram coach Wade Bass. They had the services of seven lettermen; two of which were LDC All-Stars and one Honorable Mention. Strickland, *"putting emphasis on speed and ground attacks"*, noted that *"We are an untested ball club, but don't count us out until the final whistle".*

Brandon pushed out early on a 1st quarter 42-yard drive of 4 plays with Travis Leach scoring from the 4. Dan Boyce tacked on the conversion. Just before halftime, Boyce "*uncannily sensing the next play, intercepted a pass on the Brandon 5 and scored on a 95-yard run and Rose Thames ... extra point*". In the 3rd, Billy Beasley took a punt back 75 yards to paydirt "*like a wild deer*" and Boyce kicked the PAT to make it 21-0. In the 4th, Beasley completed 5 passes to the 8-yard line where Boyce "*packed right end for the tally*". Magee managed their score in the last frame on a 5-yard Gilbert Winborne run and John Spencer PAT, but Joe Campbell managed another for Brandon with 4:00 left on a 30-yarder.

Brandon "*used reserves the greater part of the last half with every squad member seeing action*". First downs went to the Dogs (12-10) and, in passing, they went 9-11 while Magee was 9-20.

GAME 5: MAGEE (0-4) vs CLINTON (0-3)
MAGEE 13 CLINTON 21
September 24, 1954

It was announced in March that Glynn Kitchens had resigned as head man of the Arrows. Superintendent S.M. Crain promoted Assistant Coach Johnny McDaniel to the top spot and added Bobby Hannah to join him on the staff. Hannah was a former Arrow and Mississippi College athlete. With both teams winless, The Magee Courier said "*We are making a prediction for the first time this season. Friday night is Trojan night and they are going to chalk up their first win against Clinton*".

Magee opened in spectacular fashion when Mangum took the kickoff 70 yards for a touchdown. Clinton responded immediately with a Gerald Miles touchdown and extra point. With just :15 on the 2nd quarter clock, Charles Gilmore picked off a Charles Turner pass and raced for another Arrow touchdown to make intermission 14-6. Gilmore opened the 3rd with a 5-yard scoring run to widen the lead, but Mangum once again brought fans to their feet with a 40-yard dash. In the last quarter, and down by one score, Mangum did it again. But, his 75-yard breakaway for a touchdown was called back for "*an infraction of the rules.*"

In a conflicting report, The Clinton News said that three Arrows would see the end zone on the night. Those players included Charlie Gilmore with a touchdown and three extra points while Jerry Ivy and Jimmy Anderson each contributed a score. The B team was scheduled for a game against Brandon on the 30th.

GAME 6: MAGEE (0-5) vs MONTICELLO (UNREPORTED)
MAGEE 7 MONTICELLO 31
October 1, 1954

The Red Devils, under Coach Doug Colston, lost six starting lettermen from the previous team. Only four players with experience in a starting role returned. "*The team is light and inexperienced as a whole and the loss of the experienced men will be keenly felt*". It would still be enough to take advantage of the under-manned Trojans.

The Magee Courier said that Magee "*made a game of it until the closing moments of the ball game*". Monticello was first on the board with a 65-yard drive capped by Robert Lea. Magee came back with an 80-yard drive with Mangum racing the last 12 yards for the touchdown. Smith hit Wayne Wallace for the PAT and 7-6 lead. In the 2nd, Wayne Stephens "*raced 40 yards*" for the next Devil tally. Magee punched back with a 60-yard Barr scoring dash only to have it called back. In the second half of play, Gerald Little "*broke loose for three long touchdown jaunts. One of those came on the last play of the game*".

A local report from Monticello said that Gerald Little tallied four touchdowns while it was Wayne Stephens with the other. Stephens also notched the lone PAT. Monticello led in first downs (7-5) and was 3-6 in the air. The Trojans were a miserable 2-13 passing. "*Hollis Shoemaker and Jerry Sullivan led a Trojan line that, at times, looked improved on defense. Pat Barr and L.J. Runnels were also outstanding on defense*". The B-team got a win the upcoming Thursday when they destroyed Mize 32-0.

GAME 7: MAGEE (0-6) @ HAZLEHURST (UNREPORTED)
MAGEE 7 HAZLEHURST 35
October 8, 1954

Coach Shag Pyron had 8 returning lettermen "*plus several very good players*". They were called "*strong*" by the paper but their record may not have been that solid. They had won the week before and tied Monticello, but were still trying to "*get a winning streak going*". Hazlehurst put up three touchdowns in the first half. Eddie Beach tallied twice in the game, Herbert Hugh Johnson had a TD and 5 PATs, while Shelby Henley and Leon Boone each had a score.

The Copiah County Courier said that "*The line made it possible for the hard-charging backs to gain huge chunks of yardage and rip the slow Magee line to shreds*". The Magee Courier noted on the 14th that "*Magee's defense had been sieve-like all year, yielding no fewer than 3 touchdowns*". The B-team had a game scheduled on the 7th this week against Clinton.

GAME 8: MAGEE (0-7) vs MORTON (UNREPORTED)
MAGEE LOSS
October 14, 1954

The game against Coach Clyde Benton's team was moved from Friday to Thursday "*due to Friday being Fair Day for Simpson County schools*". Morton was, like others, a heavy favorite. No score was reported from any source, but due to the winless season, we know that it went down as a Morton win. Magee did, however, score three times on Morton. Mangum tallied twice with James Kennedy added the third. The Magee Courier noted that Mangum had "*scored in every single game he has played in*". The B-team took on Mendenhall at home the day before the Forest Hill game.

GAME 9: MAGEE (0-8) @ FOREST HILL (7-0)
MAGEE 14 FOREST HILL 27
October 22, 1954

Forest Hill was predicted to be a strong Little Dixie contender for 1954 and were proving prognosticators right by kickoff. Coach Ray Bell lost only 4 lettermen from a 7-3-1 squad and had 16 coming back. Expectations weren't high in Magee, with the paper saying that "*Although no match for the Rebels, the Trojans are still improving and they are building for the future*".

Details of the loss were not found, but interesting is a Simpson County News snippet from November 4th. In it, it was announced that "*The Magee gridders*" were now "*under the tutorage of former Mississippi Southern great Bucky McElroy*". He had come on board weeks before to provide assistance in the team's development. His records at USM still stand among some of the best to this day. The details of Irving's departure were not discussed. Either way, it would be only for three games as there was a coaching change for the 1955 season forthcoming.

The B-team was originally scheduled to take on Clinton later in the week, but apparently changed that to Mize. They moved their record to 4-1-1 with a 20-7 win.

GAME 10: MAGEE (0-9) @ FOREST (UNREPORTED)
MAGEE 0 FOREST 38
November 5, 1954

Coach Audis Gill was "*fielding an older and heavier team for the 1954 season*". He had "*confidence of a good showing against possibly the most formidable area of opponents in the history of (the) school*". While their official record wasn't available at print, their performance would show his expectations to be accurate; especially against a young and inexperienced team.

The Scott County Times called it a "*bench cleaning bonanza*". It was said that Gibbs hit Sawyer from 50 yards while going 7-13 with a pair of TDs. Mills had two; one on a pass and another on a "*blocked kick pick-up*". Weger, Goodwin and Chambers also got into the scoring column for Forest.

GAME 11: MAGEE (0-10) vs MENDENHALL (5-4)
MAGEE 2 MENDENHALL 18
November 12, 1954

Yet another new head coach was in Mendenhall. Wally Beach was a former Mississippi State grid star and would now wear the whistle. His Tigers had only 2 starters back and 7 lettermen in all from the Little Dixie championship team. By game day, they sported "*a much better record and have played more consistent ball than the Trojans...*" For the last tilt, James Harold Kennedy would be out with a broken arm suffered against Forest Hill; James Earl Little had an injured knee; Cecil Walker had an infected leg; Leon Canoy was also "*on the ailing list*; John Mac Mitchell had an appendectomy; John Spencer was dealing with a pulled muscle; and Winborne was out due to a "*back injury*".

The Clarion-Ledger said that *"Spirit, however, is still high and the Trojans will put up their traditional fight against the invaders"*. Mendy marched 50-yards on their opening drive and topped it in 10 plays with a 4-yard Bynum run. In the 2nd, Magee got to the Tiger 37 but lost the ball. With :30 left in the half, Sullivan sacked Bennie Monk for a safety to make it 6-2. Late in the 3rd, a fumbled punt led to a 25-yard Dykes scoring run.

Early in the 4th quarter, a fumble to Burkett Neely led to a march to the Magee 5, but penalties followed by a fumble gave the Trojans the ball back. Being forced to punt, Mendenhall went on a 50-yard drive that ended with a 5-yard Dykes plunge for the final score. The Tigers had 183 rushing and 51 passing on the night. *"The Trojans played their best ball of the season as the line fought it out with a much heavier and experienced Tiger fore wall"*. Forest Hill went on to capture the Little Dixie crown for the season.

1955 (5-5-1)

For the third time in three years, Magee was led by a new coach. The new mentor was ex-Delta State player Jack Bailey with ex-Mississippi College player Bobby Clark stepping to assist. Twice-a-day practices started August 15th with *"prospects much brighter than last year's victor-less squad..."* That was not without setbacks as at least a pair of starters enlisted in the armed forces. Two others had moved out of state, but despite the *"loss of these experienced boys, enthusiasm does seem high"*. Over 48 players showed up for preparations with some still absent for duty in the National Guard. *"Several newcomers have good possibilities of breaking into the lineup as drills have been spirited"*. Many were *"composed of 8th, 9th and 10th graders"*.

GAME 1: MAGEE (0-0) vs MOUNT OLIVE (0-0)
MAGEE 33 MOUNT OLIVE 0
August 26, 1955

Magee opened with Coach David Lingle's purple and white in a non-conference tilt. They were called *"large and powerful"* with *"several 200lb linemen"* from a 2-4-3 season. Yet another report said that there were *"six boys in the lineup who had never played a football game."* New lights had been added to the Trojan home field to make the game much better for everyone. But the game was even better for fans when Jimmy Tindall took the opening kickoff 65 yards to the end zone with Joe Mangum converting. The Hattiesburg American said it was an 80-yard return, another put it 82 yards and the Mount Olive Tribune attributed 65 yards to the effort.

Pat Barr grabbed a 62-yard punt return later to set up now-9th grader Joe Mangum's 1-yard touchdown. One recap from Mount Olive gave the score to Jackie Stubbs. The first half ended when a punt snap went out of the end zone for a Trojan safety and 15-0 intermission lead. Mangum scored twice more in the 3rd quarter. His first was set up by Stubbs' gallop of 50 yards to the 5-yard line. The last score came from Stubbs from 15 yards in the final frame. Mount Olive got to the Magee 3-yard line before time ran out. The Magee Courier praised too many Trojans to mention for their efforts.

GAME 2: MAGEE (1-0) @ PRENTISS (0-0)
MAGEE 13 PRENTISS 40
September 2, 1955

The scarlet & white Bulldogs under ex-USM alum Coach Orville Foshee, 9-2 the previous season, were called *"a formidable foe. Prentiss has one of the largest teams in the conference and is loaded with returning vets."* Foshee had 9 starters back on the field and outweighed Magee by *"as much as 40 pounds per man."*

Mangum opened scoring early on his blocked Dog punt. Billy Lee tied things with a 55-yard dash while Jack Magee got in from the 7 to make it 14-6 at halftime. James Roberts pulled in a Buster Lee throw in the 3rd from the 22-yard line and did the same later on a pass from Frank Holloway. In the final period, Lee hit Frank Holloway from the 25 and then returned a kickoff 80 yards for another. The Hattiesburg American noted that both Magee touchdowns came from Mangum while Barr had the lone PAT. *"Richard Edmonson and Jerry Magee led the Magee defense and Jimmy Swords was a pillar of strength in the Prentiss line"*.

When over, The Magee Courier said that *"their defeat was no thermometer of the gallant battle they put up against their superior foe. Prentiss is a wonderful team which is well-balanced with a lot of manpower on the line and plenty of spark and coordination in the backfield.*

The Trojans played superior ball throughout the entire game and, even though they realized early they were outclassed, their 'never-say-die' spirit led them to two TDs against the strong eleven."

GAME 3: MAGEE (1-1) vs NEW HEBRON (0-1)
MAGEE 34 NEW HEBRON 0
September 9, 1955

The week-after came with another loss to the Trojans when starting QB Billy Smith, called *"one of the mainstays of Coach Jack Bailey's Split-T offense"*, transferred to Clinton. Gilbert WInborne would now move into his spot. Magee had been blasted by New Hebron 40-7 the previous year and were looking for revenge against a team *"seeking their first Little Dixie win in over two years"*. Their opener had been dismal, losing 39-0.

A Winborne handoff to Joe Magee in the opening frame produced a 19-yard TD with Winborne converting. Early in the next quarter, Winborne picked off a pass and turned it into an 80-yard pick-six. Mangum *"scampered 49-yards"* for another tally with Barr converting. That made halftime 21-0. Mangum *"raced 70 yards on a clear field except for one Golden Bear"* without scoring while a New Hebron drive was lost via a fumble. But in the final quarter, Barr capped a 66-yard drive with a 30-yard dash. Barr added a pair of extra points.

Magee out-rushed New Hebron 374-131. Leading rushers for Magee were Mangum (154), Winborne (114), Barr (44) and Stubbs (42). *"Linemen who started were Hollis Shoemaker, Cecil Walker, John Jones and Richard Edmonson"*. The Golden Bears were paced by Fred Newsom, Charles Hard and Larry Little. This marked the first Trojan conference win since 1953. *"Coach Jack Bailey stated that his entire defense played an outstanding game"*.

The night after the game, Mr. & Mrs. Curtis Switzer *"honored the Magee football boys, the cheerleaders and several friends with a barbecue... All reported a wonderful time"*. The B-team was preparing for a game at home against Mendenhall on the 15th that would end 6-6. Later that week, it was announced that Mangum was now in the running for conference scoring honors. His 7 touchdowns and 2 point-after successes had him at 44 points while Crystal Springs' Don Purvis close behind (41 points).

GAME 4: MAGEE (2-1) @ CLINTON (2-0-1)
MAGEE 0 CLINTON 0
September 23, 1955

New head man Stan Martin opened practices on August 15th *"in an effort to find a winning combination"*. They had 10 returning lettermen on the squad and a couple of new additions (one of which was ex-Trojan Billy Smith). Martin sized up the squad by saying *"We have some very fine prospects and a great deal of potential. The boys want to play ball and, although we have a tough schedule, I expect us to be a top contender for the Little Dixie title."* Jimmy "Hoss" Anderson and Gary Harmon would co-captain the squad.

Magee had the honor of being Clinton's only win in 1954 and the Trojans *"do not plan for the Arrows to send them back down the road of defeat."* Before a large Clinton crowd, the Arrows would play their second straight scoreless game. And like the last game, fumbles were a key contributor to the result. Penalties on both teams also played a role in the killing of drives. Clinton did get to the Trojan 2 in the first half, but were held out of the end zone by a stubborn defense. Magee fumbled to Clinton in the 3rd at their 45 but Clinton would return the favor. A Trojan threat late in the 4th was killed by their fumble.

A later report noted the Joe Mangum *"led Magee on offense"* while Jerry Mangum *"stood out on defense"*. The Magee Courier called it *"a battle royal"*, and said that it was *"a true measuring stick of the Trojans' ability this season..."* On the 27th, the B-team were defeated by Mize 20-0; though numerous Trojans were praised as *"outstanding"*.

GAME 5: MAGEE (2-1-1) @ MONTICELLO (1-2)
MAGEE 14 MONTICELLO 19
September 30, 1955

The Red Devils under Coach Cadman Porter were a respectable 7-2-1 the previous season. In what was probably their first-ever meeting in 1954, Monticello had beaten Magee 31-7. Now Magee went to Will C. Cannon Field to see if they could redeem themselves and win their third game of the early season.

It was the Trojans on the board first when Barr tallied to make it 7-0. Monticello fumbled the kickoff and Joe Mangum made it count later to make it 14-0. In the 2nd, Jimmy Wilson answered for Monticello with Brinson Foster notching the PAT. That kept halftime 14-7. Now in the final frame, Wayne Stephens scored but the Devils failed to convert the extra point. It looked as though Magee would hold on for the road win, but with :40 on the clock, Charles Davis got into the end zone to kill hopes for visiting fans.

GAME 6: MAGEE (2-2-1) @ HAZLEHURST (2-2-1)
MAGEE 18 HAZLEHURST 21
October 7, 1955

Another week and another road game. The Trojans were called underdogs since *"four regulars will miss action Friday night"*. John D. Jones (broken leg) joined three suspended linemen for *"breaking training"*. The game would, however, come down to extra points.

Joe Mangum raced 88 yards *"on a fake kick"* with *"split-second blocking from the right side of the Trojan line"* for the first TD. Hazlehurst, however, was up to the challenge by scoring three times. Johnson, Carroll Davis and Bob Freeman all made their touchdowns on runs. In the 3rd, Mangum ran for 7 yards for the next score while, in the last quarter, he *"twisted and separated"* for 50 yards for the last. Herbert Johnson's three extra points would spell defeat for Magee for the second straight Friday night.

It was alluded by The Mage Courier later that Magee almost pulled out the win. *"Joe Mangum brought the football fans to their feet in what came near to being a photo finish ... as he almost outmaneuvered the entire Hazlehurst team to take a winning touchdown in the closing seconds of the game. Reversing his field from the sideline to another ... several times, with every member of the Hazlehurst team attempting to stop him, he almost took himself loose ... Had he been able to evade one more tackler, he would have accomplished this almost impossible feat"*.

The Clarion-Ledger said *"Richard Edmonson and Hollis Shoemaker led the Magee defense"*.

GAME 7: MAGEE (2-3-1) vs MORTON (4-2)
MAGEE 25 MORTON 6
October 14, 1955

The navy and blue Panthers under Charlie Callaway may have lost 6 lettermen, but 7 returned from a 7-3 squad. *"Although the Panthers are favored, the Trojans aren't beaten until the final whistle blows"*. The Magee Courier would later say it was a *"wallop"* in a *"thrilling battle from start to finish"*.

An early fumble by Morton led to Mangum's 55-yard run *"through the left side of the line"* while evading *"three Panthers ... down the sideline for the first Magee score"*. Ted Herrington's PAT made it 7-0. In the same quarter, a bad-luck fumble on a punt was recovered by Morton at the Trojan 1 from where Robert Lewis plunged in for their only touchdown. Mangum erased it quickly with a 60-yard run for a score. In the next frame, runs by Winborne and Jerry Mangum set up a Winborne score. His PAT put halftime 19-6.

In the 3rd quarter, Oscar Stephens fell on a loose Panther football at the Morton 31. That led to a final-frame run by Joe Mangum *"around end"* for a touchdown. Winborne picked off a Morton pass later at the Magee 1-yard line to kill another Panther threat. Cecil Walker and Pat Barr *"missed action due to injuries"*.

GAME 8: MAGEE (3-3-1) vs FOREST HILL (1-4-1)
MAGEE 19 FOREST HILL 7
October 21, 1955: HOMECOMING

The game against Coach Ray Bell's blue and white Rebels, 9-0-2 the previous season, would be in Magee for Homecoming. Expectations were probably small against such a previously powerful team when the schedule was printed; not to mention having beaten a winless Magee team 27-14 that season. But at kickoff, Forest Hill was a lowly 1-4-1.

Magee struck quickly on a Jerry Mangum throw to Cecil Walker *"behind two Rebels on the 30 for a 62-yard completion on the first play of the game"*. In the 2nd, an Edmonson block recovered at the Rebel 31 produced no points, as did an interception by Forest Hill to keep intermission 6-0. Back came Forest Hill in the 3rd quarter with a 5-yard *"end sweep"* by Wimpy Martin and PAT by Norman Pearson *"bare-footed"*. But on the next kick, Winborne *"scooped up the ball on the Magee 1-yard line and carried to the 20"*. On the first play in the final quarter, Joe Mangum *"brushed off several Rebel tacklers and galloped 35 yards for a score"*. Edmonson converted for the Trojans.

Forest Hill's M.J. Harrison would intercept a Magee pass later, but on the play he fumbled to Jerry Mangum. *"Seconds later, (he) kept and started off the right side, cut back and key blocked by Oscar Stephens clearing him a path square between the goals for 29-yard play and score"*. Late come-back tries by the Rebs *"were halted by two pass interceptions by Jerry Mangum and Jimmy Tindall"*. Magee led in yardage 299-185 with both teams gaining 7 first downs.

The B team, defeated by Pinola the week before 33-0 due to fumbles and penalties, took on that team again during the coming week.

GAME 9: MAGEE (4-3-1) vs CRYSTAL SPRINGS (7-0)
MAGEE 13 CRYSTAL SPRINGS 33
October 28, 1955

Undefeated Crystal Springs was a co-leader in the Little Dixie, and though Bailey had *"improved the Trojan team noticeably within the last couple of weeks"*, expectations could not have been very high in Magee. The visitors shut the door fairly easily behind the two touchdowns (and three conversions) by Don Purvis. Gerald Dungan also crossed the goal twice while Larry Dell added the other touchdown. For Magee, Joe Mangum had one of the Trojans' scores while Stephens had the other and a conversion.

Amazingly, it was Magee with the lead in total yardage 230-222. Purvis put a stranglehold on LDC scoring with 133 total points, 19 touchdowns and 19 extra points. Mangum was in second place with 98 points.

GAME 10: MAGEE (4-4-1) vs FOREST (3-4-2)
MAGEE 7 FOREST 34
November 4, 1955

Magee now found themselves against a Bearcat team with a new coach. Bennie Ray Nobles' squad had seven returning starters but lost a lot of weight on the front lines from their 7-4 red and blue 1954 team. In this tilt, it was Forest with the only opening quarter score via a 60-yard drive capped by Albert Elmore's 4-yard plunge.

In the 2nd, and after a multitude of penalties had put Magee back at their half-yard line, Jerry Mangum and Pat Barr found themselves *"thrown out of the game"*; presumably from *"sudden and strong language"*. Clyde Mills took advantage of the opportunity with a touchdown reception from 15 yards away. Before halftime, Gerald Saxon got in from the 2-yard line. After the break, a Trojan fumble allowed Forest to again put up points; this via a 5-yard Saxon run and Shelton PAT. On that play, Winborne was injured and taken to the hospital.

Mangum avoided the shutout soon after when he *"romped around end after the line failed to open and left Bearcats biting 70 yards of dust"*. Forest punctuated the night with one more touchdown before the final whistle. That came on an 80-yard Elmore run *"through the center"* and Shelton PAT. An incorrect report from The Simpson County News gave credit for three touchdowns to Durwood Shirley.

GAME 11: MAGEE (4-5-1) @ MENDENHALL (6-3-1)
MAGEE 13 MENDENHALL 7
November 11, 1955

Coach Wally Beach had 5 lettermen among his initial 25 player squad. The paper said that *"Both teams will go on the field with an even break. Both teams have received similar defeats from the same opponents during the season and this fact should bring to the spectators"* a good game. Mendenhall was expecting a fully-recovered team from the injuries sustained during their Homecoming affair.

Mendenhall hit the board late in the opening stanza when George Berry dove in from the 1 and the Tigers converted. Despite a fumble, the Magee defense held to give the offense the ball. Joe Mangum then capitalized with a 42-yard dash to make it 7-6. After a series of fumbles, Barr gave Magee the lead on a 75-yard punt return reverse. Winborne's point-after would mark the end of scoring. The home team actually got to the Magee 7 before halftime but could not make it count.

With just 2:00 left in the last game of the season, Mendenhall moved to the Trojan 4-yard line. *"A true test was given to the Trojan line and it proved to be everything it was built to be by holding the Tigers to four downs on the Trojan one-foot line. The Trojans took over with the ball barely off the goal line. Thirty seconds later when the ball game ended, the Trojans had moved out of the end zone to safety"*.

First downs (16-4), rushing (182-120) and passing (81-0) were all dominated by Mendenhall. Mendy was 4-8 in the air while Magee attempted no passes. One report said that *"Mendenhall halfback Ira Coates seemingly went over the goal line on two occasions, but head linesman Bill Thames ruled the ball dead each time one foot away"*.

All Little Dixie Conference awards were announced in mid-November. Richard Edmonson was named "Most Valuable Lineman". Ted Herrington, Jerry Mangum, Pat Barr and Gilbert Winborne were added to the Honorable Mention list.

1956 (3-7)

Coach Jack Bailey and assistant Bobby Clark were back for their second season in the Little Dixie Conference and called two-a-day practices on August 15th. *"The ever-looking-upward Trojans will field a more experienced club than they have the past few years; although they will still be young and light"*. The blight on the season was that *"The Trojans' eleven will be composed mostly of ninth, tenth and eleventh graders"*. Equally as much of a hindrance was the fact that *"Not a man on the entire squad will weigh as much as 190 lbs. Even though the Trojans aren't picked to rate very high in the conference, they will field the best team Magee has had in several years"*.

Bailey was betting that his 13 veterans would produce *"a better record than last year's (team) when the Maroon and White eleven (went) 5-5-1"*.

GAME 1: MAGEE (0-0) @ NEW HEBRON (1-0)
MAGEE 31 NEW HEBRON 12
September 7, 1956

Coach David Letteri's Golden Bears opened the 1956 campaign with a 7-6 win over Tylertown. For this game, the paper said that *"the team plans to put up a spirited fight against Magee for a conference win"*. After the 34-0 whitewash of 1955, The Magee Courier said that *"The Golden Bears may prove tough to handle..."*

Jerry Mangum got things going the right way in the opening quarter of play when he *"ripped 48 yards off right guard and into the end zone"* for the first touchdown. New Hebron tied the game on an Ausbin Barnett pass to Douglas Dickerson while Bobby Joe Sutton notched the PAT. Joe Mangum put Magee back in front with a 2-yard romp while Jimmie Riley *"stepped into the end zone"* from the 8 for New Hebron in response. That meant that halftime stood 12-12.

Leon Canoy fell on an early 3rd quarter fumble to set up Joe Mangum's 9-yard blast. The Bears moved to the Magee 1-yard line, but the Trojan defense *"tightened up and held the Bears to four downs when Jerry Butler picked a Bear pass out of the air on the one and was stopped instantly"*. After fumbling back to New Hebron, Butler did it again with an interception. This time he took it 50 yards to the 15-yard line, but again Magee fumbled away the gift.

On their next possession, Joe Barnes crossed the goal and added the extra point. Butler then came through with his third theft and he took it the entire 24 yards to paydirt.

GAME 2: MAGEE (1-0) vs PRENTISS (0-1)
MAGEE 6 PRENTISS 7
September 14, 1956

Prentiss had already faced favorite Mendenhall and were stomped 45-0. That meant that any hope for the LDC South for either team would hinge on winning this game. Coach Bailey worked his Trojans *"hard during the last week even though practice has been hampered the past week because of injuries to several players"*. Manley Holbrook, Daniel McAlpin and Johnny Green would be on the disabled list.

It appeared that Magee caught a break when Prentiss fumbled a punt to Ted Herrington. But their defense stiffened to kill the threat. Magee surprised their visitors on the next possession when Joe Mangum took a fake 4th down punt 89 yards *"with two Bulldogs hanging onto him and minus his jersey"*. After trades of fumbles in the 2nd quarter, Prentiss finally capitalized on a mistake and drove 55 yards with Billy Lee providing the last foot to score. Henry Taylor's PAT was *"squarely through the uprights"* to make halftime 7-6.

Magee fumbled in the 3rd, but Prentiss copied the error. A trade of punts ensued and, now in the final quarter, Lee carried *"8 out of 11 times"* to move the ball to the Trojan 18 but they fumbled once again. The final whistle blew shortly after and the game was over.

GAME 3: MAGEE (1-1) vs CLINTON (1-1)
MAGEE 7 CLINTON 13
September 21, 1956

The Roy Burkett era was officially beginning in Clinton. Former Mississippi College quarterback and later head coach at Columbia High School, he also worked at Skipper Chevrolet for a year. Practices started on August 15th with eight returning lettermen. Burkett summed up his squad on August 18th by saying that they were "*relatively inexperienced and lack both speed and depth. But, I am greatly impressed with the spirit and determination shown by the squad in the first few workouts. This is a pretty scrappy squad and the boys want to play football. We should have a good starting unit. With eight returning lettermen in the lineup, we should be able to hold our own against most of the teams we play.*"

The paper predicted that the Arrows "*really ragged against Forest Hill, probably will run smack into more trouble at Magee.*" On the 20th, they went further by saying that "*the climate will not be healthy for the visiting Arrows ... Clinton, however, could be improved by Coach Roy Burkett's promised personnel changes after that sad showing against Forest Hill.*" Forest Hill had only beaten them 12-0. In Magee, Bailey and Clark expected "*definite improvement from the line due to the fact that the material on the Trojan forward wall is much better than the Friday night game with Prentiss showed*".

Clinton would shock disbelievers on their opening possession when Jimmy Anderson found the end zone from the 5. That capped a 71-yard march in 18 plays. Dan Gore's PAT made it 7-0; a lead that would remain until halftime. In the 3rd, Anderson added his second touchdown from the 7-yard line after Clinton recovered a Trojan fumble. Magee avoided the shutout in the 4th on a 10-yard run by Joe Mangum followed by Jerry Mangum's extra point run. Anderson rushed 27 times for 129 yards in the game. The Clinton yearbook reported the score as 14-7.

GAME 4: MAGEE (1-2) vs MONTICELLO (2-2)
MAGEE 7 MONTICELLO 14
September 28, 1956

Coach Cadman Porter's Red Devils lost 8 lettermen from an 8-2-1 season but returned 10. They had beaten Magee in both 1954 and 1955; the last tilt being a very close contest. For this one, Magee was their own worst enemy; fumbling numerous times to give the game away at home.

One fumble was in the 2nd quarter at their own 17-yard line. Four plays later, Brinson Foster ran in from the 6 and Charles Davis converted. Magee came back in the 3rd when Joe Mangum topped a 72-yard drive with his 14-yard "*excursion*". Joe Barnes' PAT run through the center tied the game. They made it back to the Monticello 9 in the same frame only to fumble the football. Getting the ball back the same way, they went four-and-out. Davis came back out for the next possession and ran 68 yards to paydirt. Foster notched the point-after.

The Trojans fumbled 9 times in all. Monticello coughed up the football only twice.

GAME 5: MAGEE (1-3) @ HAZLEHURST (UNREPORTED)
MAGEE 0 HAZLEHURST 45
October 5, 1956

Former MSU player Mercer Miller returned 9 lettermen from the 5-5-1 Indian team. The Magee Courier called them "*highly-rated*". Like the 1955 game against Monticello, they dropped a heartbreaker in the last encounter to Hazlehurst. "*Coach Jack Bailey and Bobby Clark will be pounding their heads together in an effort to revenge the loss last year and put an end to the Trojans' losing streak...*"

No detailed reporting of the affair was found. But, it appeared to be a strenuous time in Magee. First, John D. Jones broke his leg in the scrap and was lost for the season. As important, he was now joined by "*several names that have dropped out due to injuries and others that are off the squad*". It's very likely that this was the cause of the worst loss since the 1942 Hattiesburg road contest.

GAME 6: MAGEE (1-4) vs MORTON (3-1-1)
MAGEE 7 MORTON 9
October 12, 1956: HOMECOMING

The Panthers were looking "*good in practice*" during game week and Coach Charlie Callaway "*states that the squad will all be in full swing when the whistle sounds*". Their lone loss had come the week before against Brandon. Meanwhile, Magee was looking to break a four-game streak of losses in front of alumni, and it came :50 from happening.

Laurence Beasley's 49-yard escape in the 2nd quarter was stopped by Ted Herrington at the 6-yard line. The Trojan defense stepped up and eventually got the ball back at the 2-yard line. That would unfortunately lead to a safety when Jerry Butler mistakenly stepped out of the end zone when punting. The 2-0 score held until the 3rd quarter when Jerry Mangum "*blasted across the final yards for the tally*" and Jack Davis provided the PAT.

Another deep Panther drive to the 11-yard line was again foiled by the defense. Now with just :50 left in the game, Dick Livingston heaved a 40-yard strike to Beasley "*who stepped 10 yards into the end zone for a 50-yard play*". Johnny Jolly's extra point finished the night.

GAME 7: MAGEE (1-5) @ FOREST HILL (UNREPORTED)
MAGEE 21 FOREST HILL 2
October 19, 1956

New coach Lawrence Matulich had 14 lettermen but was "*not expecting to field any world-beating squad in his first season at the helm*". They went a paltry 1-7-2 the previous year but had 30 players from which to develop talent. "*We should be able to field a pretty good first team and all the boys are showing a lot of spirit and* hustle". The Magee Courier said that the Trojans, despite their loss the week before, did "*show signs of improvement and may prove to be a surprise to the Rebel squad*".

Like the previous week, Magee gave up the first points of a game when they suffered an early safety. A bad snap ended with Jerry Mangum "*mass-tackled in the end zone for the Rebels' lone 2 points of the night*". Also like the week before, the Trojans came back; this time when Joe Mangum ran "*through the right side of the line and, after shaking off several would-be tacklers, raced 54 yards for the tally*". Jerry Mangum's PAT made it 7-2.

Forest Hill seemed to re-take the lead on a 79-yard kick return, but the runner stepped out of bounds at the Magee 44. Now in the 2nd quarter, Jerry Mangum ran around the end and, just before being tackled, pitched to Jerry Butler "*who sped the rest of the 55-yard scoring play*". Jerry Mangum's extra point put intermission 14-2. Magee fumbled twice in the 3rd, committed three 15-yard penalties, and had Herrington ejected. But they still "*dominated play in the final stanza*".

Joe Mangum dove in from the 3-yard line to cap a 75-yard march thanks to numerous carries by Jack Davis. "*The best efforts of the season were demonstrated against the Rebels and the score could have been much more had the Trojans not fumbled and been penalized excessively. Leon Canoy, Ted Herrington and Dan Tullos were the main objectives in the Trojans' forward wall.*"

GAME 8: MAGEE (2-5) @ CRYSTAL SPRINGS (5-1)
MAGEE 0 CRYSTAL SPRINGS 7
October 26, 1956

Crystal Springs entered the season as the one team given any realistic hopes of taking the LDC title aside from Mendenhall. Magee may have been on the road, but they did have momentum with a solid game against Forest Hill. They held strong in this tilt with a good chance to build on the success, but it slipped away late in the cold weather.

They had two great drives in the opening quarter, getting as far as the one-foot line, but were stopped; the last on a fumble. In the final quarter, Crystal Springs finally broke the deadlock when Gerald Dungan capped a 63-yard drive with a 1-yard plunge and Larry Dell extra point. Magee tried passing thereafter to come back, but the Tigers picked off one throw. Magee returned the favor to begin their last-chance march but Crystal Springs' E.J. Mason picked off a pass deep into Tiger territory to kill any final hopes.

GAME 9: MAGEE (2-6) @ FOREST (1-5-2)
MAGEE 14 FOREST 13
November 2, 1956

A Forest team that once beat Magee regularly now held a record worse than that of the Trojans. The Magee Courier said that "*The Bearcats from Forest High School had better be on their toes when they host the Magee Trojans Friday night. In their last three contests, the Trojans have made rousing improvements and with only two games left this season, they are going to be hard to handle by any team".*

On the first play of the game, Joe Barnes raced 80 yards to paydirt. Ironically, "*ace kicker*" Tony Broussard was injured on that play and would not return. Larry Johnson retaliated shortly after with a scoring run, but the PAT failed. Forest put up their last touchdown in the 2nd quarter when Bill Herron dodged in from the 8-yard line. Tommy Cottrell ran in the point-after and halftime was 13-7. Despite Mangum runs that got to the 7-yard line, each team traded two fumbles each. Magee had the last on the 24-yard line, Freddie Akers ran to the 3 and then capped it from there on the next play. Mangum's PAT was true.

As the game ended, Forest desperately tried to snatch the win. Runs and passes put them at the Trojan 3-yard line when the whistle blew. Forest held serve in first downs 11-6.

GAME 10: MAGEE (3-6) vs MENDENHALL (9-0)
MAGEE 6 MENDENHALL 13
November 9, 1956

Wally Beach lost 6 lettermen but had 13 back. They received the "*proverbial kiss of death*" by the LDC, naming them as favorite to win the championship. That would be their first since 1953. "*However, the team faces a tough schedule and almost any team to be faced is quite capable of downing the Tigers*". The Magee Courier said of this game, "*statistics (don't) play a leading role in the outcome of this rival tilt because it is in the game that all orthodox football tactics are tossed out the window and both coaches send their teams into the ball game to win by out-guessing, out-playing and out-thinking their opponent*".

Magee students and fans were getting ready by hanging posters and holding a parade with "*hundreds of students*". However, they knew that their opponent had scored 352 points this year while allowing only 25 to be recorded against them. At stake was the McBroom Trophy; a new trophy for the first team to win two of the first three games.

An opening-play fumble on the "*frosty field*" by Mendenhall fell into the hands of Jack Davis, but they could get no further than the 9-yard line. A trade of fumbles followed, but Mendy still managed the first tally on an 8-yard Tommy Dykes run. That score would be the only of the half. Now 6-0, and after more fumbles, Dykes "*ripped open the Magee line for 44 yards and crossed the goal line, but the play was nullified by an offside penalty against Mendenhall*".

They still moved as far as the Trojan 16 but a fumble to Canoy killed the opportunity. However, Mendy did manage one more tally when Charlie Furlow "*rifled a pass to Ira Coats who was all alone on the Magee 30 and traveled the remaining distance unmolested. Bailey converted from placement*". Magee got the ball back with :57 left and Joe Mangum hit paydirt on the game's final play. The whistle had blown during the run. Then, things got ugly.

The Magee Courier said that "*the play ... started the fireworks on the field and the center of the gridiron was filled with spectators from both sides for what turned out to be a near-riot*". The Simpson County News published an editorial on November 15th entitled "**SHAME! SHAME! SHAME!**" and called for the ending of the rivalry. Apparently there were "*fisticuffs*" on the field and the referees had no part in assisting in breaking up the unfortunate incident. That same article noted the fact that "*three people were shot and killed and several others wounded at a Magee-Mize game a number of years ago...*" That probably alluded to a basketball contest against Mize numerous years before where there were two people killed in a shooting over a game.

Another report by that publication said that it began "*on the line of scrimmage and (was) completely ignored by game officials. Players of both teams jumped into the melee and were joined by a huge throng of spectators. One Mendenhall player received deep facial wounds when struck with a flashlight held by an adult and another was almost struck when a Mendenhall man stepped in to assist in halting the proceedings*". No verification of fault on either side was reported otherwise.

Mangum led Magee rushers with 153 yards. Mendenhall led in first downs (14-9) and passing (153-1) while Magee led in overall rushing (179-155). "*For Magee, Tackle Leon Canoy, Guard Ted Herrington and End Billy Henry Stephens were standouts in the line*".

Mendenhall went on to win the Little Dixie championship with a victory over Morton. All-Little Dixie honors at year-end included Second Team selections Dan Tullos and Joe Mangum. Others noted as award winners included Oscar Stephens, Leon Canoy and Jerry Mangum.

1957 (7-3-1) GAS BOWL CHAMPIONS

Coach Jack Bailey started two-a-day practices on August 15th with *"at least one letterman at every position"*. For that reason, the maroon and white were picked as favorites in the Little Dixie South. That would be amazing considering that they were coming off of a 3-7 season. At least 60 potential candidates were in camp trying to find positions. For historical purposes, football programs were reported to have begun this year. But, due to the late beginning of the effort, they would put only pics and rosters of the 1956 team inside.

GAME 1: MAGEE (0-0) vs NEW HEBRON (0-0)
MAGEE 46 NEW HEBRON 7
September 6, 1957

The Golden Bears under Coach Bobby Joe Barton were picked dead-last in the Little Dixie North and were trying to better a 4-5 campaign. Ironically, that was a better record than the Trojans but they had dropped that season's opener 31-12 to Magee. The blue and gold did not start as hoped in Magee for their 1957 lid-lifter, and the game was even worse though Bailey used a reported 59 players in the contest.

Joe Mangum recorded the first TD on the opening drive and Jerry Mangum made it 7-0. He did it again when he went over from the 2-yard line on the next possession. Freddie Akers notched the third on a punt return to end the opening quarter, but Magee kept it going with another (presumably by Curtis Switzer). Jerry Mangum then hit Switzer for a score and, with extra points, it was 33-0. After halftime, the Bears fumbled to Magee, it was picked up by Ted Herrington, and he raced 70 yards to paydirt.

The B-team allowed the only Golden Bear score of the game in the 4th quarter, but Ted Allen *"raced 50 yards"* and Amie Green converted the opportunity for a 46-7 tally. *"Several spectators commented on the fact that Coach Bailey was very lenient with the opposing team, in that he allowed them to score on the second and third string players"*.

GAME 2: MAGEE (1-0) @ PRENTISS (0-1)
MAGEE 0 PRENTISS 0
September 13, 1957

Coach Orville Foshee was doing a *"tremendous building job as 10 regulars ... have departed and only 6 boys returning have had any game experience"*. The red and white were picked 6th in the LDC South but coming off of a 7-4 mark. <u>The Hattiesburg American</u> said that *"The Bulldogs are light and inexperienced but have plenty of determination"*. Their last affair had been a 34-19 thumping by Mendenhall. *"Now all eyes will be on Magee, rated as the top team to oust Mendenhall in the South title chase, can better that effort"*.

It was called a *"vain battle"* on a *"rain-soaked field which rendered all passing useless and, seemingly, the scoring, too"*. Add to that the fact that the power was out for 45 minutes. The first half went without a Trojan score despite a fumble recovery. Appropriately, they recovered another fumble as the game ended. The Trojans had efforts to the 6- and the 12-yard lines but each were repelled with *"the rest of the game ... a see-saw affair almost in the middle of the field"*.

First downs went to Magee 6-4. Neither team completed a pass though Magee tried 6 times. Total yardage favored Magee 126-81 while the visitors suffered more penalty yardage (60-15) and fumbled 6 times.

GAME 3: MAGEE (1-0-1) @ MONTICELLO (4-0)
MAGEE 0 MONTICELLO 7
September 28, 1957

Magee was to play Clinton, but an outbreak of flu forced a cancellation of the affair. The Trojans had a reported 28 *"key players knocked down"*. Said Bailey, *"It would be impossible to play a game with that kind of team"*. They initially had no decision on whether it would be picked back up, but they did eventually meet at the end of the regular season.

The next opponent had been picked 4th in the South division of the LDC but was undefeated and co-leader with Mendenhall in conference play. <u>The Magee Courier</u> said that *"the Trojans will be weak physically (but) they are expected to put up a good fight. All of the boys have not returned to school but are expected back (before the game)"*. Injuries from the Prentiss game had, too, dimmed hopes. Both Mangums were at a point that they were not expected to be back still after two weeks of rest. So, many thought Monticello a three-touchdown favorite.

Playing conditions on Saturday at Will C. Cannon Field were called a rain-soaked *"thick mass of mud, but the lime spread upon it severely burned many of our players. They were given treatment at Magee General Hospital..."* The game had been mutually-agreed upon to be reset for Saturday due to conditions.

The first couple of possessions for both teams resulted in fumbles near midfield. But Magee's last led to Brinson Foster's run *"through the Trojan wall"* for a 50-yard tally. The PAT by Charles Davis would be the final score. The remainder of the action, thanks to more Magee fumbles, *"hovered about the middle of the field; occasionally more from one end to the other"*. Magee picked off a 4th quarter pass, but fumbled the game-tying possibility away.

GAME 4: MAGEE (1-1-1) vs HAZLEHURST (2-4)
MAGEE 7 HAZLEHURST 0
October 4, 1957

Magee was to take on Pinola this evening but apparently the schedule went through a late change. Thus, 3rd-place pre-season Hazlehurst was now on the local field. This time it was the Trojans' turn to win a close contest.

A Jerry Magnum interception late in the opening quarter gave Magee the ball but also hampered him with a nose injury. Guy Barr *"paced the team to the Indian 41... Several powerful drives brought the Trojans to the 1-yard line and a charge by Joe Mangum across the goal line added to an extra point..."*. The Trojans got to the Indian 5 in the 3rd frame but missed a FG attempt. Likewise, Hazlehurst drove late and moved to the 6-yard line but *"were a couple of yards short of getting the needed first down"*. Time expired three plays later.

GAME 5: MAGEE (2-1-1) vs BRANDON (3-1)
MAGEE 34 BRANDON 19
October 10, 1957: HOMECOMING

Wade Bass, assistant coach under Louis Strickland from 1954-1956, now held the Bulldog whistle. He would have as many as 35 players from which to choose. They had lost 10 lettermen from the previous 4-4-1 season but did count 7 returning key players. Brandon was picked 4th in a tie with Clinton in pre-season expectations.

The Trojans were celebrating Homecoming but were missing at least *"three first-teamers"*. Magee opened with a 49-yard drive capped by a Joe Mangum 1-yard run and Jerry Mangum extra point. Brandon answered with a 4-yard G.T. Thames touchdown and extra point by Henry Watson. The Bulldogs added another *"paced by G.T. Thames"* from the 1 for the 13-7 halftime lead. The Magee Courier said that *"Magee fans began to fret as the Trojans milled around till halftime... However, in the second half, it was almost all Magee"*.

A 3rd quarter Brandon fumble at the 40-yard line led 6 plays later to a Joe Mangum 2-yard touchdown. Jerry Mangum's toe made it 14-13. Jerry then took an ensuing drive handoff 46 yards to paydirt, but Brandon answered with a 6-play drive and (Paul or Robert) Breazeale 10-yard score. Joe Mangum took the kickoff and returned it 70 yards for a quick response. In the last minute of the contest, he picked off a Brandon ball leading later to a Jerry's 21-yard touchdown. Dennon May's kick ended scoring.

GAME 6: MAGEE (3-1-1) @ MORTON (6-0)
MAGEE 7 MORTON 32
October 18, 1957

Coach Hollis Rutter's 11 returning letter-winners gave his Panthers the nod as favorite for the LDC North. The Magee Courier called Morton *"favored by at least three touchdowns"*. They would live up to expectations in Scott County.

Edgar Simpson was the hero of the home team while Lawrence Beasley was close behind. Beasley pulled a 40-yard pick-six on the first drive. Gaines Massey fell on a loose Trojan ball to set up Simpson's first TD when he *"slashed off-tackle, shook off several would-be tacklers and ran 36 yards"*. Dick Livingston's PAT put it 13-0. Beasley finished the first half with a 1-yard dive to cap a 36-yard march and Livingston converted. Magee's only points came in the 3rd when James Barnard picked up a fumble and scampered 82 yards to paydirt. Jerry Mangum notched the PAT.

A Beasley run of 61 yards then allowed Simpson a 1-yard effort. With 3:00 remaining, Jerry Fortenberry fell on another fumble and Simpson turned it into a 9-yard TD. *"The game ended with Magee threatening deep in Morton territory"*. Morton dominated rushing (346-91) and passing (41-0). Magee lost 3 fumbles in all.

GAME 7: MAGEE (3-2-1) vs CRYSTAL SPRINGS (3-3)
MAGEE 25 CRYSTAL SPRINGS 6
October 25, 1957

In an effort to change things around against the team picked 5th in the LDC South, Bailey went to several B-team players. It worked, despite an opening drive that got to the 1-yard line before a fumble. However, Jerry Mangum picked off a Tiger pass a few plays later and took it 35 yards to the 1-yard line from where Joe Mangum dove in. Freddie Akers then picked off an errant throw and Joe capitalized from the 15-yard line to make it 12-0.

Crystal Springs had a concerted 3rd quarter effort, with Grantham hitting Nichols from the 11 for their only score. Magee eventually came back with a Joe Mangum scoring run and copied it in the final quarter with an 88-yard dash. Jerry converted to end scoring. Numerous Trojans were complimented for their play.

GAME 8: MAGEE (4-2-1) vs FOREST (4-4)
MAGEE 20 FOREST 13
November 1, 1957

The big news of the week was that Magee had accepted a bid to play in The Gas Bowl; held on Thanksgiving. The bowl was organized shortly after the discovery of the Gwinville Oil Field. Prentiss had taken on the role as opponent; making the game appear to be exciting as they had played to a scoreless tie in the second game of the season.

As for their upcoming opponent, Forest was picked a dismal 6th in the LDC under Coach Ken Bramlett. They had 45 *"hopefuls"* on the team but had finished only 1-8-1 the year before. Magee hit the scoreboard first on a consistent drive with a key reception by Barnard capped by an 8-yard tally by Joe Mangum. A bad pitch by Forest allowed Budgie Wallace to snatch *"a Forest fumble and (sprint) 50 yards for a touchdown"*. Jerry Mangum's PAT put it 13-0.

In the 2nd, Jack Davis lugged the pigskin to the Cat 5 before Joe rushed in and Jerry converted. Down 20-0 in the 3rd, Forest began their comeback attempt. Jimmie Underwood made it into the end zone from the 4 and Johnson converted on a run. Magee then fumbled at their 9, leading to a Johnson run and 20-13 deficit. Forest was trying to pull out the tie but fumbled late to run out the clock. Rushing went to Magee (164-117) while passing (45-17) went to Forest. Both teams had 10 first down but Forest lost two fumbles.

GAME 9: MAGEE (5-2-1) @ MENDENHALL (7-1)
MAGEE 6 MENDENHALL 13
November 8, 1957

Mendenhall was picked 2nd in the division behind Magee. On game day, they sat 2nd but Magee was positioned in the 3rd place spot. The paper said that Bailey's Trojans had *"intensive workouts ... through this week as the Trojans prepare themselves for the annual thriller which will feature two teams very evenly-matched as their records will indicate"*. Mendenhall featured prolific player Charlie Furlow and LDC leading scorer (104 points) Ira Coates.

"Both teams played good, clean football" in front of an estimated 3,500 fans. A Mendy first-quarter drive got to the 1-yard line before they gave it away on a fumble. They hit the board in the 2nd quarter, however, on a 51-yard drive topped by a 31-yard Coates run. That 6-0 lead held until the 3rd quarter. A Tiger fumble was recovered by Magee and Joe Mangum *"carried three successive times"* for the eventual score and 6-6 tie. Mendenhall got what they needed with just under a minute gone in the final frame when Furlow snuck in from the 1. They ended any hopes as the game ended by intercepting a Trojan football at the Magee 13-yard line.

Coates ran for 170 yards while Joe Mangum led Magee rushers with 23 yards. Mendy led in first downs (19-5) and rushing (312-54) while Magee led in the air (52-15).

GAME 10: MAGEE (5-3-1) @ CLINTON (2-7)
MAGEE 20 CLINTON 7
November 15, 1957

Coach Roy Burkett was hoping to replicate or improve upon the past season's record of 8-2 and stressed conditioning to the team. Burkett's squad was inexperienced and had only 5 returning lettermen. As early practices continued, the coach was optimistic of a good performance, saying that they were the *"best-conditioned team I ever had. This is a hustling, self-disciplined squad that wants to play football and is co-operating in practice as expected."*

The Clinton News noted that *"Our football team ought to be in swell shape after having two workouts a day for two weeks. Coach Burkett is not making any predictions as even the line-up is undecided but says a lot of work needs to be done. 'We will take each game as it comes and are determined to hold our own against all competition in or out of the Little Dixie Conference North Division this year', the head man said."* This night would be special in that Clinton would dedicate their new athletic field (Crain Field) in the honor of School Superintendent S.M. Crain.

The Trojans would play without Joe Mangum and *"other first stringers"*. Clinton's initial drive got to the Arrow 26 but a fumble was recovered by John Mangum. Four plays later, Barr escaped for a 55-yard touchdown to make it 6-0. The Simpson County News says that afterwards, *"Clinton's workhorse Wayne Post received (the kickoff) and repeatedly banged away at a Trojan wall until the Arrows got to the 30. The Trojans grabbed another fumble but a penalty and a pass intercepted on the next play by Post put the Arrows even 6-6."* The PAT gave Clinton a 7-6 halftime lead.

Magee opened the 3rd with an Akers touchdown run of 58 yards. Jerry Mangum's catch made it 13-7. Clinton fumbled yet again, this time at the 50, but the defense was able to hold. On their ensuing possession, Barr crossed the goal from the 5 and Edwin Pearson's PAT finished scoring. Another Arrow fumble in the 4th killed an attempted comeback drive. Post, however, ended the night with two interceptions of his own.

Magee out-rushed Clinton 300-180 and held the Arrows to no passing yards.

GAME 11: MAGEE (6-3-1) @ PRENTISS (LOSING RECORD)
MAGEE 16 PRENTISS 13
November 28, 1957: 10TH ANNUAL GAS BOWL

Organizers of the bowl, including The Prentiss Lions Club, had arranged for a big parade on game day (Thanksgiving) complete with bands, homecoming queens, floats and more. Magee would *"rate the favorites role … boasting of a heavier and more-experienced club and having compiled an outstanding record in the LDC. Prentiss, although not a winning club this season, has made a commendable record…"* Prentiss was called *"light and scrappy"*.

On their home turf, Prentiss was first on the board with a Phillip Douglas 2-yard reception. But Ted Allen took the ensuring kick and, *"with blocking assistance by his teammates"*, dashed 90 yards to tie the game. Akers converted the point-after and Magee led 7-6. That was the score at halftime before Prentiss went to the air three straight times; scoring on the last toss (Eddie Dale to Jeppie Rush) to make it 13-7. Now in the 4th, Toby Fortenberry picked off a Bulldog pass at the 20-yard line.

Joe Mangum made the effort count with a long 65-yard gallop to the end zone to tie things 13-13. As time was nearing expiration, Magee sat at the Prentiss 10-yard line. However, the officials penalized the Trojans because *"some spectators were standing on the edge of the field"*. Now with just second left, Dennon May kicked a FG *"over 20 yards out"* and gave fans *"perhaps the most enjoyable game of the season"*. For clarity, The Clarion-Ledger called it a 25-yard FG with :05 remaining while The Hattiesburg American said it was a 20-yarder with :12 left by Kenneth Bishop.

Magee led in total yardage (340-170) with rushing (278-90) on their side. Magee lost 2 of their 4 fumbles while Prentiss lost 1 of 2. Magee had one interception to their credit.

At the end of the year, the Little Dixie All-Conference Honors were released. Daniel McAlpin was the lone First Team player while Second Teamers included Leon Canoy, Ted Herrington and Jerry Mangum. Honorable Mention nods went to James Barnard, Freddie Akers, Joe Barnes and Joe Mangum.

1958 (5-5)

Coach Charlie Callaway had his Trojans finishing practices the end of August in preparation for their first-ever meeting with Pearl High. That tilt would also mark his first game as new Magee mentor.

GAME 1: MAGEE (0-0) @ PEARL (0-0)
MAGEE 19 PEARL 0
September 5, 1958

Like Magee, the Pirates had a new coach. Corwin "Bubber" Muse entered his first season as leader with an unfortunate mess. Since the Mississippi Accrediting Commission had removed the Pirates from contests prior to the season, it caused many teams to re-shuffle their schedules in anticipation of filling an open date previously penciled in for Pearl. Fortunately, the issue was resolved on a probationary period prior to kickoff.

Since Pearl was unable to schedule Forest and Forest Hill, the MHSAA designated Hazlehurst and Magee as Little Dixie North opponents in order to make things work out for standing purposes. Twenty-eight players were suited up tentatively for the Pirates with prospects said *"to be on the gloomy side with only four or five seniors on the squad"*. In this tilt, Guy Barr, George Earl Fortenberry and Clifton Reed served as team captains.

The Magee Courier reported that a 49-yard drive, spurred by Ray Walters and Jack Davis runs, set the table for Dennon May's opening quarter first touchdown of the young season. Just before halftime on a 51-yard march, Barr found Daniel McAlpin for 25 yards to set up a 6 yard *"quickie"* by Barr for another score. In the 4th, Walters dodged Pirate defenders from the 9 for the final score that topped a 79-yard march. The Brandon News claimed that the touchdown came from Larry Roberts. The drive covered 79 yards. May (or Barr) was successful on the PAT.

Said Callaway, *"I was real proud of our defensive work as our boys held Pearl to only 40 yards rushing the second half. All-in-all, I think our first outing (was) successful"*.

GAME 2: MAGEE (1-0) vs PRENTISS (2nd GAME)
MAGEE 0 PRENTISS 27
September 12, 1958

The Prentiss squad was led by legendary coach Orville Foshee. Said Callaway, *"I believe that we will be ready for them. Our boys have been working hard this week and I, as coach, could not ask for any more hustle on the part of our boys. They have been giving all and I believe that if this type of spirit keeps up, we will have something to say about who wears the South Division crown"*.

The Bulldogs began scoring in the 2nd quarter when Jeppy Rush went in from the 16-yard line and Paul Farr notched the PAT. B.G. Loftin increased the lead in the 3rd quarter with touchdowns from the 1-yard line and the 3-yard line. Rush and Henry Taylor provided the points-after. Eddie Speights pulled a QB sneak that was good for a 65-yard tally in the last frame. Magee led in first downs (12-9) and passing (14-0) but lost the ground game 297-120.

Prentiss came away with at least two players inured. Paul Farr and Emmitt Smith both had *"shoulder injuries that will keep them out indefinitely"*. One was reported to be hospitalized. Callaway wrote an article on September 18th about the weaknesses he found in the contest and promised to fix them.

GAME 3: MAGEE (1-1) vs CLINTON (0-2)
MAGEE 21 CLINTON 12
September 22, 1958

Roy Burkett's first practice, two-a-days until the start of school, was held on August 17th. Afterwards, he said *"We looked pretty good for the first day of practice. We will have between 30 and 35 out by Monday and we will have several new players who I hope will come through. On the whole, we are inexperienced and untried. We still need a lot of polish on both offense and defense, but if everyone has the same spirit we've had the last two weeks, we should be able to take them."* The Arrows would still be playing in the Little Dixie Conference with *"a trio of letterman backs: Russell Williams, Jack Walker and Lloyd Daniel."*

By the week before the kickoff of the season, Burkett was *"well pleased with the progress the Clinton squad has been making. The team is in good condition and we have had plenty of contact work although the backfield needs quite a bit of drilling on their timing. I have never seen as much team spirit, which is credited to the fact that we have so much competition at every position. We scrimmaged the latter part of last week and yesterday afternoon and the boys are looking pretty good."*

The game scheduled for Friday the 19th was postponed due to a state-wide rain storm. Still, Callaway said, *"I believe our boys will come back fighting and striving to learn from this defeat we suffered"*. When the two teams played on Monday, the fields were still muddy and slippery.

Magee played through the conditions and put up two first half touchdowns. The first drive of 60 yards was capped by Barr from the 1 and May provided the extra point. A 2nd quarter Arrow fumble set up a 21-yard drive with Robert Barnes hitting John Maddox from the 9. Davis converted for Magee.

In the 3rd, John Quisenberry found George McMullan from the 5 but the Jimmy Dukes PAT failed. Magee responded with a 60-yard drive wrapped up by a 1-yard Davis plunge. Barr's extra point was successful. Clinton tried to cut the lead in the 4th with a Jerry Rankin fumble recovery at the Trojan 40. Dukes ran in from the 3 but again the PAT failed.

After the game, the players were treated to a steak supper at the Green Derby Restaurant. Mr. Slaughter, manager of the establishment, *"said that this was the best-behaved group they had ever served. The Trojans are to be commended not only upon their football victory, but also upon their fine conduct"*.

GAME 4: MAGEE (2-1) vs MONTICELLO (3-0)
MAGEE 0 MONTICELLO 19
September 26, 1958

Magee now faced undefeated Monticello on just a few days of rest and preparation. The game was important as Prentiss was 3-0 and this game would probably put the loser out of the race barring any big upsets.

The Trojan defense did their job for *"nearly three periods"* before the Red Devils broke loose before the final frame. Ray Funnels' (or Roy Russell's) recovery and 38-yard return of a Barnes fumble counted for their first score near the end of the 3rd quarter. Charles Davis picked off a Magee pass in the 4th quarter which led to his 2-yard plunge later. Buddy Ward blocked a Magee punt at the 2-yard line late and Davis dove in as the horn sounded. Miller Reed added a PAT after the second touchdown.

First downs were even (11-11) as was passing (0-0). Rushing went to Magee 170-143. Monticello picked off 2 passes while Magee lost a fumble.

GAME 5: MAGEE (2-2) vs/@ HAZLEHURST (0-4)
MAGEE 32 HAZLEHURST 0
October 3, 1958

It took little time before May *"threw a (12-yard) pass which hit the helmet of Hazlehurst's Kenneth Bishop and fell into the arms of (McAlpin) for the touchdown"*. In the 2nd, Davis added a 34-yard score and Barr converted. An Indian fumble at their own 18-yard line then led to a Barnes run two plays later for a score to make halftime 19-0.

Third quarter runs by May, Barnes and Barr put the ball at the 1-yard line from where May dove in. Barr converted on the point-after. In the final quarter, Larry Roberts ran for 13 yards to allow Barr a 1-yarder for the final tally. Numerous Magee players were commended for their play. Magee led in first downs (17-5) and rushing (352-56) while passing was in favor of Hazlehurst (15-12).

"Our kids have not lost their morale even though we have suffered two defeats; one of which was a real heartbreaker, for I feel that our boys gave all but the breaks weren't to be ours. It takes eleven boys fighting all the way to have that outstanding team..."

GAME 6: MAGEE (3-2) vs MORTON (UNREPORTED)
MAGEE 13 MORTON 27
October 10, 1958

Superintendent G.L. Tutor tried in vain to move this contest to Thursday due to the State Fair in Jackson. Still, Magee was intent on honoring the team mothers and fathers before the game. Callaway had once been a part of the coaching staff at Morton; thus making this game interesting on many fronts.

An early Magee fumble at the 1-yard line allowed Freddie Roberts a later run from there to make it 6-0. In the next period, Morton coughed up the pigskin. May took it to the 5-yard line and Barr did the honors while May gave Magee a 7-6 lead. A surprise onside kick was recovered by the Trojans at the 41-yard line. May would hit John Cullen Maddox from the 14-yard line to increase it to 13-6. With just :30 left, Bill Richardson *"heaved"* to Nick Nichols at the 15 and then hit Reed Davis for the score to make halftime 13-13.

It took 10 plays before Morton tallied in the 3rd quarter on a 62-yard drive capped by an 8-yard Roberts escape. In the last frame, Richardson picked off a Trojan throw. That led to an 88-yard march to the 4-yard line from where Buddy Lewis got in. Jerry McNeese notched the PAT.

GAME 7: MAGEE (3-3) @ CRYSTAL SPRINGS (1-4)
MAGEE 34 CRYSTAL SPRINGS 2
October 17, 1958

A 1-4 team was just the medicine that the Trojans needed to run *"roughshod"* to their fourth win. A multitude of Crystal Springs fumbles allowed Magee to sit 34-0 at intermission and substitute *"freely through the last two periods"*.

Just into the game, Barr picked up a Glen Nichols fumble and raced 30 yards for the TD. The Tigers fumbled the kick and Davis raced 32 yards to the 3-yard line from where Barr ran in for the TD and PAT. Arch Long then fumbled to allow Davis a later 40-yard scoring run. Barr notched the PAT. In the 2nd, Barr added a touchdown and PAT to top a 58-yard drive while May accentuated a 42-yard Davis run from the 5-yard line. Barr was again good on the point-after.

The Tigers avoided the shutout in the 3rd when Ray Reed fell on a loose Trojan football in the end zone. First downs (10-3), rushing (273-39) and overall yardage (284-39) favored Magee. Crystal Springs picked off 2 passes but fumbled 4 times to Magee.

GAME 8: MAGEE (4-3) vs PINOLA (0-3 CONFERENCE)
MAGEE 49 PINOLA 0
October 24, 1958

Magee had faced Pinola in 1934 and 1935; the first a win and the next a tie. This game would better their 40-0 mark in 1934 by nine points. Scoring came early and often. Barr had scoring runs of 1, 85 and 60 yards and added a pair of PATs. May ran in from 58 yards, Davis from 60 yards, Charles Holbrook from the 33, and May found Barnes for a 24-yard strike. May and Davis notched point-after runs while Barnes counted twice in that category. Magee also picked off a football to set up the pass completion for a touchdown.

Pinola led in first downs (10-8) but Magee held the ground (473-111) and passing (52-29). Magee picked off 3 passes but lost a fumble. Pinola picked off one pass but lost 2 fumbles.

GAME 9: MAGEE (5-3) @ FOREST (6-1-1)
MAGEE 0 FOREST 14
October 31, 1958

Magee had broken a four-game losing streak with back-to-back victories over the Bearcats. But that would change on this Friday night in Forest. The Scott County Times said that *"The game was played on a sloppy field and under intermittent rains that brought out the umbrellas among the smallest crowds of the season"*.

Forest scoring started on their very first possession when Stanley Douglas took advantage of numerous Ronnie Mitchell runs to scamper in from the 9-yard line. An attempt to increase the 6-0 lead failed when James Harvey's FG attempt from the 28-yard line fell short. Late in the 3rd quarter, a Trojan fumble at the 21 recovered by Jimmy Stokes led to a 19-yard Mitchell dash and finally a 2-yard plunge from Douglas. Like the first PAT, it was blocked by Magee. They did, however, get a late safety thanks to a Joe Hunt sack of May.

Magee lost 2 of their 5 fumble while recovering a pair of Cat fumbles. Forest dominated in first downs (13-3).

GAME 10: MAGEE (5-4) vs MENDENHALL (8-1)
MAGEE 0 MENDENHALL 18
November 14, 1958

Magee enjoyed a needed off-week to prepare for the rival Tigers under Coach Wally Beach. Mendenhall was, by anybody's definition, a dominant squad. They held Little Dixie championships in both 1956 and 1957 and would play for their third-straight against Morton in the coming weeks. The Magee Courier said that *"Past performances have proven that statistics mean nothing when these two arch rivals clash. From the opening whistle, the game becomes a hair-raising affair as quarterbacks for both elevens attempt to pull every trick out of the bag to get an early period lead"*.

After holding the first Mendy assault, Magee fumbled two plays into their drive to E.C. Mullins. That led to a 1-yard Truett Powell sneak and 6-0 lead. A Clifton Reed turnover in the 2nd could not be converted but Fortenberry recovered a Tiger punt fumble at the 32-yard line. Solid runs moved the ball inside the 20, but to no avail. To make matters worse, Magee then fumbled on their ensuing drive to Dudley Nichols. It took only a couple of plays before Powell "*went around left end on the bootleg play, cut back to the right, side-stepped tacklers as he ran, and went over on the 27-yard run.*"

The final Mendenhall dagger began with a 49-yard connection between Powell and Wesley Sullivan. Numerous runs moved the ball to the 11-yard line from where the two players hooked up for the touchdown. First downs (9-5), rushing (109-38) and passing (81-34) all favored Mendenhall. Each team picked off an errant throw while Magee lost one more fumble (2-1) than the Tigers.

1959 (6-2-2)

Magee had 15 returning lettermen under 2nd year Coach Charlie Callaway and assistant Jerry Taylor. Only four letter-winners had departed due to graduation; thus making prospects bright for the maroon and white Trojans. Little Dixie Conference voters still picked three-time champion Mendenhall to repeat, but Magee was only 3 votes behind in the South.

GAME 1: MAGEE (0-0) vs PEARL (0-0)
MAGEE 55 PEARL 6
September 4, 1959

After only one season, "Bubber" Muse had moved on from Pearl and his whistle was now in the hands of Fred Foster. Foster had earned All-Big Eight honors at Natchez High in 1949 while playing at least once against Magee, played freshman football at Ole Miss and ended his career with Delta State. Foster was trying to improve on the Pirate's 3-7 record but with only 6 lettermen. His biggest problem was a lack of depth. "*The trouble lies in our reserves. We don't have but 18 men and if anything happens to our first eleven, we are in bad shape*". By September 3rd, the coaches noted that "*Their team has worked real hard and has rounded into good condition...*"

According to The Magee Courier, both Callaway and assistant Jerry Taylor met with the Magee Lions Club during game week and reported that, with 15 lettermen back, they "*have been putting the boys through the paces and that prospects are good for a good season*".

Magee held only a 7-0 lead after the 1st thanks to a Ray Reed 20-yard pass to James Robert Magee. Guy Barr added the PAT. Scoring erupted in the 2nd, however. After recovering a Pirate fumble, Barr hit John Maddox to the 1 where Barr plunged in and added the extra point. A Pirate fumble on the kickoff put the ball at the 10. Amie Green got in and Reed found Magee for the PAT. Another fumble on the 20 set up a 35-yard Carrol Horn run and Larry Roberts extra point. Pearl's only score came afterwards on an 85-yard Bobby Stribling kick return, but Green would add another for Magee from the 1-yard line with Barr providing the point-after.

Another fumble in the 3rd was grabbed by John Mangum and taken 61 yards to paydirt. Reed's toss to Daniel McAlpin made it 42-6. On the kickoff, Pearl fumbled again where the Trojans managed a drive to the 6. From there Reed hit Horn and Fred Womack crossed for the extra point. The last score came in the 4th on a 10-yard Reed toss to Maddox.

The Clarion-Ledger reported afterwards that "*Magee sent shivers through the South by crushing Pearl 55-6 in the only inter-division tangle. Just about everyone got a chance to score... Amie Green and Carrol Horne had two touchdowns each while Robert Magee, Guy Barr, John Mangum and John Maddox got one apiece*".

GAME 2: MAGEE (1-0) @ PRENTISS (1-0)
MAGEE 13 PRENTISSS 0
September 11, 1959

Orville Foshee's Bulldogs went 9-2 last season, but now they had to "*replace 8 starters and 3 alternate starters*" for the season. Though they were picked 4th in the Little Dixie South, they still held a 6-1-1 record against Magee since 1952 and were playing at home.

It was called a "*hard-fought contest*". In the opening frame, Reed's connection with James Robert Magee moved the ball to the 9-yard line while runs by Reed and Green moved it to the 1-yard line. From there, Barr dove in and then notched the point-after. Strong defensive play on both sides kept the 7-0 score intact until the final frame. Punting from their end zone, Green took the ball to the 29. Horn and Green drove to the 1-yard line and Barr snuck in with less than 2:00 remaining for the dagger.

First downs (12-3) and rushing (214-14) were in favor of Magee while Prentiss edged them in the air (36-33). Prentiss had an interception while neither team fumbled. Magee allowed Prentiss their initial first down in the 3rd quarter.

GAME 3: MAGEE (2-0) @ MONTICELLO (2-1)
MAGEE 27 MONTICELLO 6
September 25, 1959

Though it was their first of two open dates, Callaway and Taylor were *"going to devote this period toward ironing out a bunch of wrinkles detected in the Prentiss game"*. The Red Devils had a wonderful 8-2 record the previous year, but Cadman Porter's team was now slotted 5th in the Little Dixie South. The Tuesday before the contest, both coaches *"revealed to the Magee Touchdown Club ... that many rough places ... had been ironed out and that they expected the Trojans to render a splendid performance..."*

This game was dedicated to Harold Barnes, Jr; a *"fellow member of our student body who is a leukemia victim"*. It was Monticello first on the board in the opening frame on a Paul Johnson 1-yard plunge. Green hit paydirt shortly after on a 60-yard escape and Barr nailed the PAT to give them a lead they would not relinquish. Green then picked off a 2nd quarter pass and took it 31 yards to the end zone. Horn's extra point put Magee up 14-6 at halftime.

Reed increased the advantage in the 3rd on a 21-yard run and threw a 25-yard TD strike to Maddox in the final quarter. Barr was true on the first extra point, but the damage was already done. The Magee Courier said of the final score, *"Reed tossed a pass to John Cullen Maddox, who turned around to make the catch. Maddox found two Monticello boys hot on him and, in the same action, he began to stiff-arm them as he began marching backward. This activity continued until (he) crossed the goal line backing up..."*

"Outstanding linemen were John Mangum, John Maddox, Daniel McAlpin, Edwin Pearson, Robert May, Ray Walters, Robert Lang, Charles Meadows, George Robinson and James Magee". First downs were even 9-9, rushing (302-78) went to Magee while Monticello led in passing 94-39. Magee had a pair of fumbles on the night.

GAME 4: MAGEE (3-0) vs HAZLEHURST (0-4)
MAGEE 46 HAZLEHURST 0
October 2, 1959

Ronald Bennett's Indians were 2-8 the previous season, winless on this campaign, and picked last in the Little Dixie South. That caused
The Clarion-Ledger to say that Magee was *"safe enough from any Hazlehurst threat"*. Indeed, scoring came early and often with Barr providing the first tally in the opening frame from the 2-yard line. Green tacked on more in the 2nd from the 11-yard line and Magee recovered a fumble to allow Barr another score and another point-after.

Reed notched the third while Green provided the PAT. With the reserves in play, Fred Womack got in from 2 yards out and Clifton Reed pulled a 39-yard pick-six. In the 4th quarter, Reed hit Milton Griffith for a touchdown while Womack capped the point-after.

GAME 5: MAGEE (4-0) @ MORTON (4-0)
MAGEE 0 MORTON 20
October 9, 1959

This week would not be like the past four. Hollis Rutter's Panthers were 8-2 the previous year, but had twice won the Little Dixie North title. The blue and gold were picked first in that division again this season. The Magee Courier thought it would be tough, saying *"we are realistic enough to believe that the Trojans are going to know they have been in a real contest"*. Magee had lost all but one game (1955) since 1953.

The Clarion-Ledger though this may be a preview of the end-of-year battle for the Little Dixie title. *"This spotlight attraction pits the hottest LDC offense against the toughest defense. Morton has rolled up 147 points in four games while Magee has given up only 12 in four outings. Morton, meanwhile, has a rugged defense of its own, having given up only 39 points..."*

An overflow crowd was in store for a great game; though not one that Magee fans loved after the final whistle. Midway through the 2nd quarter, Reed Davis fell on a loose Trojan football at the 18-yard line. Freddy Roberts went in from the 7 only two plays later. Near the end of the 3rd quarter, Roberts did it again and Victor Purvis' PAT made it 13-0. Purvis added the third and final score on a 3-yard run while Roberts hit Davis for the point-after.

GAME 6: MAGEE (4-1) @ CRYSTAL SPRINGS (WINNING RECORD)
MAGEE 7 CRYSTAL SPRINGS 7
October 15, 1959

Wade Alexander's blue and gold Tigers were only 1-9 the past campaign. Picked 3rd in the LDC South, they now held a reported fantastic record (5-1-2) the week after Magee's open date. Their record at kickoff is not reported.

Late in the 1st, White Graves recovered a fumble and raced 15 yards for a score while Beasley added the PAT. Now in the final quarter, Magee drove 68 yards in 21 plays to the 9-yard line. But, a fourth-down play was unsuccessful. Holding to a punt, the Trojans began again at the 21-yard line. Reed eventually hit Roberts for 34 yards to the 2-yard line. Barr "*slanted off tackle for the score and also added the game-tying extra point*".

GAME 7: MAGEE (4-1-1) @ PINOLA (UNREPORTED)
MAGEE 56 PINOLA 0
October 23, 1959

Almost nothing was reported about the Pinola team leading up to the contest. In fact, the only notation came from a Clarion-Ledger recap of scores noting the final.

GAME 8: MAGEE (5-1-1) vs TYLERTOWN (3-4-2)
MAGEE 33 TYLERTOWN 6
November 6, 1959: HOMECOMING

Another open date awaited the Trojans (in order that they could play in two possible bowl games) as they prepped for Coach E.L. Perritt's Blue Devils. The blue and gold had gone 5-5-1 the previous year and were now picked second-to-last (6th) in the LDC South. During the week, the team had accepted a bid to play in the newly-organized Oil Bowl on Thanksgiving day. The event was sponsored by their own Touchdown Club.

In the cold, Reed hit Maddox (21 yards) and Magee (5 yards) for a pair of first half touchdowns. Reed notched the first point-after but failed on the next. Horn added a 66-yard score later to make things easier. Tylertown provided their only points in the 2nd quarter on Bobby Boyd's 3-yard plunge. In the final quarter, Green raced in twice on runs of 3 yards and 20 yards. Green added the first PAT while Reed did the honors on the last.

Magee now knew that their opponent would be a very tough Petal squad of the DeSoto Conference for the Oil Bowl. As for the Homecoming game just played, the team and fans honored the 1946 Burrheads under B.L. Kisner.

GAME 9: MAGEE (6-1-1) @ MENDENHALL (9-0)
MAGEE 0 MENDENHALL 20
November 13, 1959

The winner of this rivalry game would have more than bragging rights as they would also hold the LDC South title and a chance to play for the overall championship. It would be no easy task. Coach Wally Beach was 10-1 the previous season (39-2 in the last four years) with three-straight rings and returned 11 gold and black letter-winners. On a beautiful night in front of 3,500 fans, Mendenhall responded to the Trojan threat "*by outplaying the visiting eleven both in rushing and passing*".

A Magee fumble near midfield led to James Sullivan's first-of-three touchdowns; this from the 8-yard line. They did it again shortly after when Sullivan "*went the distance*" to make them pay and Brunt notched the point-after. Numerous exchanges of the football via interception came afterwards. Horn found an errant Mendy throw, May picked off a Reed pass, and Green added his own in response. But Sullivan put up the Tigers' final points when he took a Trojan punt at the 38 and proceeded to weave his way to paydirt behind excellent blocking. Brunt's PAT marked the end of scoring.

First downs (15-5), rushing (248-93) and passing (69-65) favored the home team. They were also the beneficiary of 3 Magee fumbles though the Trojans recorded thefts of three Tiger passes.

GAME 10: MAGEE (6-2-1) vs PETAL (9-1)
MAGEE 21 PETAL 21
November 26, 1959: THE OIL BOWL

Like Magee, Coach Lewis McKissack's Panthers were also runners-up in their division. But, they had suffered only a lone loss and were thought to be a tough opponent. Thus far, they had rushed for 2,494 yards and passed for another 771. They had picked off 11 passes and outscored opponents 290-53. Their only defeat had come against Poplarville 20-13.

The Trojan coaches went to a Touchdown Club meeting on Tuesday in mid-November and told attendees that "*Intensive workouts have put the Trojans in tip-top physical condition and they are ready to go*". The California Oil Company would present a trophy to the winner.

Petal reached paydirt first on Mackie McKissack's 15-yard pass to Tommy Walters "*with defenders hanging on him*". Jerry Myrick provided the 7-0 point-after. They made it 14-0 in the 2nd quarter when McKissack hit Ray Perkins and Myrick converted. Just before halftime, Reed hit brother Clifton Reed for a score and Womack provided the PAT. Petal seemed to have iced things in the 3rd quarter when Tommy Sellers crossed the goal and Phil Gatwood's catch made it 21-7. That came on a 72-yard punt return many thought should have been blown dead by a Magee player touching the football.

But in the final frame, Magee stormed back. They took the ensuing kick back on a long drive to the 8-yard line from where Horn scampered in with just :14 left in the 3rd quarter. Green notched the PAT. Now with 2:45 on the clock, the Trojans began driving again. Reed hit Horn for 27 yards and Clifton Reed rammed it to the 1-yard line. Womack dove in from there and Ray Reed's PAT tied the game.

Since it was a tie, the trophy was to be split with each team holding it for six months. But, Petal agreed to allow Magee to take the trophy for keeps. Magee led in first downs (11-6) and rushing (189-139). Green led Trojan ball-carriers with 87 yards. Petal held the air 115-55. Magee lost the only fumble of the night.

The 1959 All-Little Dixie team consisted of John Maddox, John Mangum, Daniel McAlpin and Guy Barr as First Team vote-getters. Robert Lang garnered an Honorable Mention.

1960-1969

1960 Team (11-0): State Champions

1960 (11-0) LITTLE DIXIE CHAMPIONS

Coach Charlie Callaway and assistant Jerry Taylor were back to lead the Trojans. Callaway entered his third season as head man with 14 returning lettermen and predicted to be the front-runner in the Little Dixie South conference. According to The Clarion-Ledger, "*his team averages 189 pounds per man for the starting eleven, so it looks as though the Magee team will do right well*". His players, and all of the students, now had a new 10-classroom high school, complete with a cafeteria and offices. Of the 600 students, approximately 375 were in grades 10-12.

In mid-August, parents were honored at the first meeting of the Magee Touchdown Club. Roland Dale, assistant head coach at Ole Miss and former Burrhead, served as the guest speaker. Callaway also went back to the club's September 1st meeting to "*give a rundown on this year's Magee Trojan squad*". Reports had to be positive, considering how his team performed this season.

GAME 1: MAGEE (0-0) @ PEARL (0-0)
MAGEE 21 PEARL 0
September 2, 1960

Fred Foster returned for his second stint as Pirate head man with hopes of improving on the lackluster 1-9 campaign of 1959. By first practices on August 15th, he had reason for optimism as the team had "*an encouraging spring training session*". Additionally, he had 10 returning lettermen that included a "*prospective all-conference player*". The Brandon News added that "*In addition to these veterans, the coaches have a new, large crop of recruits who are expected to be close on the heels of the lettermen for positions*".

Pre-season voting from the Little Dixie coaches put Pearl next-to-last in the North Division; only a handful of votes ahead of Brandon. However, The Clarion-Ledger did say that the Pirates "*could be in the North title running with just a little twist of luck...*" Foster's Pirates would provide stiffer competition this season than the 55-6 shellacking in 1959, but the game was still chalked up as an opening loss.

In the initial frame, Mickey Medlock dove in from the 1-yard line and added the extra point to make it a slim 7-0 halftime lead. The September 3rd Clarion-Ledger featured a perfect picture of his score. In the next half, and after "*short jabs in the middle of Pearl's line*", they added two more scores. Fred Womack dodged in from the 4 while Ray Reed provided the extra point. Larry Roberts "*added the clincher*" from the 7 after the Trojans blocked a Pearl punt. Womack tacked on the PAT.

The Magee Courier noted that two touchdowns came from Womack. They also reported that "*the Pirates were never able to cross the Trojan 40-yard line at any time of the game*". Rushing was dominated by the visitors 325-50.

GAME 2: MAGEE (1-0) vs PICAYUNE (0-0)
MAGEE 20 PICAYUNE 0
September 9, 1960

Coach Frank Branch had 13 lettermen back from a 1-9 team called "*short-handed*" the previous season. Of those, 6 were starters. Unfortunately, we know only that Womack notched a pair of touchdowns (and an extra point) while the last Trojan score came on a 10-yard pass from Reed to Bobby Myers. Clifton Reed was credited with the other point-after.

First downs favored the home team 13-9. Picayune threw for 40 yards and rushed for 78 more. They gave up four of their seven fumbles and had two passes picked off. On Thursday, the B-team made the trip to Puckett to take on Coach Durwood Graham's Wolves.

GAME 3: MAGEE (2-0) vs PRENTISS (UNREPORTED)
MAGEE 52 PRENTISS 0
September 16, 1960

The scarlet and white of Coach Leslie Smith went a break-even 5-5 in 1959 and were predicted to be near the cellar (6th) in the Little Dixie South. The Magee Courier said that, for the home tilt, reports "*reveal that a large crowd will follow their Bulldogs to Magee, which means that a capacity crowd in anticipated in Trojan Stadium*".

Things got out of hand early with Magee notching three touchdowns within the first five minutes. A Clifton Reed toss to Womack counted for the opening score, Reed recovered a Rippy fumble to give Billy Medlock a 43-yard gallop (Reed PAT), and Roberts picked off a pass and raced 59 yards for the third tally. Milton Griffith added the PAT to make it 20-0. After solid runs, Womack dove in from the 1 for the first score of the 2nd quarter.

Another fumble at the 25-yard line recovered by Clifton Reed was turned into a Roberts toss to Ronnie Brooks for the 14-yard touchdown. Roberts would find Myers for the next with Roberts' PAT making halftime a whopping 39-0. Roberts kept up the pressure by taking a Dog punt 90 yards to paydirt. Now in the final quarter, Prentiss amassed their best drive to the Trojan 9 but were turned back. Brooks then ran for a 54-yard TD only to have it called back. That drive ended on an interception by Shotts.

Womack added another tally with a 46-yard dash to end scoring; though he recovered a fumble on Prentiss' last drive to set the Trojans up at the 10-yard line as the game ended.

GAME 4: MAGEE (3-0) vs MONTICELLO (0-3)
MAGEE 49 MONTICELLO 0
September 23, 1960

This game was not predicted to be much of a contest as Coach Butler Tucker's Red Devils were picked last in the LDC South. To their credit, they had gone 7-3-1 the previous year.

Medlock started with a 65-yard dash to give Magee the early advantage and Womack converted. Ray Reed then fell on a fumble at the 41-yard line to set up Clifton Reed's ensuing 60-yard race to paydirt, "*worming his way into the secondary and then taking to the right sideline*". Medlock's 20-yard run, capped by Lee West's conversion, made it 21-0 going into the 2nd quarter. Brooks added a 35-yard TD to send the teams to the lockers with the scoreboard reading 28-0.

After Medlock opened the 3rd with an interception, Ray Reed hit John Maddox for a 40-yard score. Monticello got as far as the Trojan 10-yard line but were held. On the first play afterwards, Womack brought fans to their feet with an 86-yard race to the end zone. Maddox pulled in the PAT for a 42-0 lead. Womack took advantage of a Jimmy Wells fumble recovery in the 4th quarter to set up a 20-yard Womack run.

GAME 5: MAGEE (4-0) @ HAZLEHURST (4-0)
MAGEE 34 HAZLEHURST 7
September 30, 1960

The Indians under Coach Ronald Bennett had a new athletic field for the game. They were also "new" in the sense that they had gone 2-8 the previous season and were picked 5th in the Little Dixie South to start the season. But at kickoff, they had beaten Prentiss, Chamberlain Hunt, Monticello and Wesson while amassing a 132-7 advantage over all of them. "*Magee is favored to win, but the Indians are determined to make it a battle all the way in a game that should draw an overflow attendance*"

Magee entered the game with only Coach Herbert Stowers' 1933 team having started with four-straight shutout wins; though the 1960 team had scored well-more points that that fantastic squad. In this one, Maddox started things with a blocked punt and Womack made it count from the 3 with his TD and PAT. They increased the lead to 13-0 with a 15-yard Womack run and then, in the 2nd quarter, added a pair of scores.

A Maddox-forced fumble was returned the same way shortly after. But Womack would cap their ensuing drive with a plunge from the 5-yard line. "*Going to the air in a desperate attempt to move the ball up field*", Maddox picked off an Indian throw to eventually allow Ray Reed to hit him for the 25-yard tally. That made halftime 27-0. They quickly moved the scoreboard when Womack notched another score and Wells pulled in a throw for the PAT and final Magee points. Unfortunately, Clifton Reed was injured enough at that time to be carried away on a stretcher.

In the final frame, Myers recovered a Hazlehurst fumble but Magee gave it right back to Don Harrison. Don Raggio broke the defense's record of having not allowed a score when he hit Tommy Sanderson at the "*back of the goal line*" and, with Hunter Kergosien's PAT, finished the night. Magee had moved to the Indian 5-yard line as the game ended.

GAME 6: MAGEE (5-0) vs MORTON (4-1)
MAGEE 34 MORTON 0
October 7, 1960: HOMECOMING

All bets were off for the game against Morton; a team that had beaten Magee the last four meetings on their way to Little Dixie North championships. Bill Shirley's blue and gold Panthers were 8-1 the last season but had, once again, lost in the title game to Mendenhall. The

Clarion-Ledger said that the Morton eleven was *"formidable"* They also complimented Magee by saying that the Trojans possessed *"a line that might be the biggest in Mississippi prep circles..."* Not only was it Homecoming, the night also honored the parents of the senior class.

Late in the opening quarter, Womack *"kept alternating through the gaping holes opened by tackles John Mangum and Robert May, clipping off 10 to 15 yards at a clip until he crossed paydirt for 6 points, to follow with the extra point"*. Medlock captured the next score from the yard line in the following frame and, with the PAT, it was 14-0. As halftime neared, Clifton Reed hit Maddox at the 35, *"with the big end shifting gears as he roared into the secondary to go all the way"*. That made it 20-0.

After a scoreless 3rd quarter, Ray Reed hit Myers for the next score and the Wells PAT made it 27-0. As the crowd yelled *"more points"*, Medlock gave them their wish with a 1-yard plunge. Clifton Reed hit Maddox for the point-after to finish things. Ray Reed picked off a Panther pass as the game ended to seal the shutout win.

The Clarion-Ledger featured a Q&A in their October 11th edition. The question was *"Just how strong is this Magee football team in the Little Dixie?"*. The response was, *"The Trojans are possibly the biggest ball club in Mississippi and are definitely the largest in the LDC. They have a huge end that is 6'2" or more and weighs about 225. He can run with good speed and is tough. Besides that, they have one of the highest scoring backs in the conference in their fullback. They are strong both offensively and defensively."*

GAME 7: MAGEE (6-0) @ CRYSTAL SPRINGS (4-0-1)
MAGEE 7 CRYSTAL SPRINGS 0
October 14, 1960

This would also be no easy win. The Trojans were on the road to face the blue and gold Tigers coached by Wade Alexander. That team had gone 7-2-2 in 1959 and were picked second to Magee in the LDC South by only 5 votes. Their only blemish had come against Magnolia in a scoreless tie but had outscored opponents 79-12 thus far. The Clarion-Ledger said that *"this game should be one that the fans will talk about for many weeks"*. It would almost assuredly make the winner the South Little Dixie champs.

A first half interception at Graves-Myers Stadium by Tiger Tommy Blaylock did no damage; nor did the Trojan drive to the CS 14-yard line before halftime. Now in the final quarter and scoreless, Ray Reed hit Maddox from midfield *"without breaking his stride"* for the game's only touchdown. Womack's PAT put icing on the cake. Magee recovered a Tiger fumble from where they got as far as the 6-yard line.

"Magee played all of the second half and part of the first without the services of ace signal caller Kelly Roberts who suffered from a swallowed tongue early in the second period. Roberts circled right end and was upended by a host of Crystal Springs tacklers to suffer the injury that could have been fatal to the Trojan offense".

First downs (13-6), rushing (171-75) and passing (94-29) favored Magee. Crystal Springs lost two fumbles while Magee gave up only one. Both teams threw interceptions on the evening. Womack sat 2nd in LDC scoring (78 points) behind Clinton's Jimmy Dukes.

GAME 8: MAGEE (7-0) @ COLUMBIA (UNREPORTED)
MAGEE 40 COLUMBIA 7
October 28, 1960

Coach Charlie Martin faced a *"major rebuilding problem"* with his Big Eight Conference Wildcats. Martin was serving his first term as Columbia coach after the resignation of Ben Rascoe to *"take a similar post at Pascagoula"*. Said Martin in late August, *"It's too early to make any predictions ... just yet, but I will know who I can count on after the first game..."* The Hattiesburg American said that there was *"just one way ...to go ... And that's up!"* They had gone 0-10-1 but had 11 lettermen back on their Homecoming affair.

Said Martin, *"They're big up front and boast a good backfield"*. The Columbian Progress said that *"As to who is the visitors' big gun, there was little doubt that Fred Womack, strapping 200-pound fullback, was the hammer for the Magee team. Womack is a tough and powerful runner"*. Though hanging a Magee *"effigy"* before the game, the Wildcats generously offered up their recreation hall to the Trojan students afterwards.

The week of rest did not hurt the Trojans. Though a late opening-quarter drive got to the Trojan 15-yard line, it was still Magee scoring first in the 2nd quarter after recovering a Wildcat fumble. Womack capped the Trojan march with a run from inside the 4-yard line and added the PAT. Ray Reed's toss to Maddox put them at the 5-yard line from where Clifton Reed found paydirt. Womack's PAT made it 14-0 at halftime. The ensuing frame was a disaster for Columbia, with Magee claiming three TDs.

Womack was first with Clifton Reed's PAT; a Tuggle hit caused a fumble to Jerry Garner and Ray Reed hit Maddox for the next score. A Wildcat kick fumble found Walter McCallum on the ball to allow an eventual Donald Womack 2-yard plunge and 35-0 lead. Medlock recovered yet another Columbia fumble as the 3rd ended to allow Ray Reed's 2-yard score. He hit Wells for the point-after. Columbia avoided the shutout with just 2:00 left when Tommy McNeese passed to Jerrell McDaniel and McNeese snuck in for the point-after.

GAME 9: MAGEE (8-0) @ TYLERTOWN (4-4-1)
MAGEE 20 TYLERTOWN 6
November 4, 1960

Believe it or not, Magee was not the most prolific team thus far. Big Black Conference Weir had outscored opponents 246-6 in their undefeated season thus far while Magee had given up a grand total of 14 points. Meanwhile, Coach E.L. Perritt's Blue Devils were a dismal 3-5-2 the previous season and picked 4th in the Little Dixie South this campaign.

Mangum would be out for the game against Tylertown. With 3:00 left in the 2nd quarter, Womack ran to the 2-yard line and then later in for the first score. Clifton Reed hit Maddox to make it 7-0. Tylertown cut into the lead on their next drive behind Henry Fortinberry's 2-yard plunge. That was set up by a Trojan fumble. A long Brooks kick-return took the ball to the 3-yard line from where Womack *"crashed it across with only :45 remaining"*. His PAT made it 14-6.

Both teams fumbled away scoring opportunities in the 3rd quarter, but Womack gave a bit of cushion in the final quarter with a 5-yard dive. After recovering another Magee fumble with 1:42 left, the Devils went to the air but *"the big line crashed through ... with each attempt..."* to hold the game to 20-6. The win assured Magee of a date in the LDC title game. Only Crystal Springs could have challenged, but with a win over the Tigers, it was all settled.

GAME 10: MAGEE (9-0) vs MENDENHALL (4-3-1)
MAGEE 43 MENDENHALL 0
November 11, 1960

Coach A.J. Mangum's black and gold Tigers had been the best team in the Little Dixie for years. They were 10-0 the previous year, had 14 lettermen coming back and were picked 3rd in the Little Dixie South. Their four-time LDC titles spoke for themselves. But by kickoff, they were 4-3-1 and called *"bruised and battered"* by The Simpson County News. Magee had won only once (1955) in the last 10 games going back to 1952.

A crowd estimated at 3,000 sat in *"abnormal temperatures"* to watch this annual rivalry game. It was called a *"nerve-tingler ... hard-fought and highly-aggressive ... from beginning to end with only four penalties for a total of 30 yards"*. Womack hit the end zone in the 1st quarter and added the 7-0 point-after. In the 2nd quarter, he added another touchdown and PAT before Clifton Reed hit Maddox. Maddox took the pass *"professional style"* at the 40 and raced to paydirt. The two then hooked up to make it 21-0.

Mendenhall appeared to have an advantage late in the 3rd when a bad punt snap pinned Maddox deep with rushers all around. But he got off a 65-yard boot from where Milton Griffith smothered the receiver in the end zone for a safety. Womack notched another score before the quarter was over and Clifton Reed *"then executed his famous bootleg play to go across standing up for the point to put the Trojans out from 30-0"*. Clifton Reed's final-frame 1-yard plunge and Medlock's fade pass to Ray Reed accounted for the final two tallies. Womack's PAT came with just :45 left.

GAME 11: MAGEE (10-0) v CLINTON (7-1-1)
MAGEE 47 CLINTON 0
November 17, 1960: NEWELL FIELD; JACKSON, MS

Roy Burkett, alongside assistants Billy Ray Smith and Albert Brooks, had been working the Arrows heavily with two-a-days since August 15th. The head man was optimistic about the squad. *"We have more depth and more weight than usual."* He also had the picks of all six opposing North Division LDC coaches (36 votes) as season-ending champion.

A Little Dixie Championship was on the line at Newell Field, but so also could be the title of scoring leader. Womack and Jimmy Dukes would face off with blazing guns to see which would boast of the honor after the final whistle. The Clarion-Ledger called the teams *"a couple of prep powerhouses*" while The Magee Courier said that "*both teams have their work cut out for them.*" On paper, 10-0 Magee looked like a clear favorite.

The game wouldn't be close, with The Clarion-Ledger saying "*Magee's giant-like Trojan Warriors shattered Clinton's Arrows into a billion pieces.*" Magee started their first scoring drive from the Arrow 33 and finished it with Medlock's 7-yard run. Womack added the second touchdown from the 3 and Clifton Reed's PAT pass to Ray Reed made it 13-0. Magee's third came as the 2nd quarter opened; a 32-yard strike from Clifton Reed to Maddox. Reed added the 20-0 PAT. Still in the 2nd, Medlock picked off a Robert Williams pass at the Clinton 49. Eight plays later, Maddox scored from the 20 and Reed made halftime a 27-0 affair.

Maddox opened the 3rd with a 75-yard gallop to the 1 setting up a Womack touchdown and Reed PAT. In the 4th, and after Clinton gained their only first down of the evening, Ray Reed picked off an Ottis Horne pass and brought it back to the Arrow 8-yard line. Womack scored again and the Reeds connected with one-another to make it 41-0. Clinton finished the game appropriately with a fumble that was picked up Wells and taken 13 yards for the touchdown.

Statistics were ever-so-much in favor of Magee. First downs (12-1), offensive yards (307-15), passing (4-13 vs 2-10), fumbles (0-3) and penalty yards (5-45) all favored the Trojans.

The Mississippi Sportscasters Association All-State team included John Maddox on the First Team while John Mangum and Fred Womack earned Honorable Mentions. All-LDC awards differed.. Charlie Callaway was named Coach of the Year, Maddox was "Most Outstanding Lineman", and Womack "Most Outstanding Back". Mangum, Jerry Hall, and Clifton Reed also made First Team news. Honorable Mention LDC went to Robert May, Charles Meadows, Jerry Garner, Ray Reed, and Billy Medlock.

In 1981, National Football Foundation and Hall of Fame Executive Director Jimmy McDowell called the 1960 Magee team "*the best high school football team he had ever seen*". For the first time in history, a non-Big Eight team was declared State Champion by the Big Eight Writers Association.

1961 (9-1-1) MISSISSIPPI BOWL CHAMPIONS

Fourth-year Coach Charlie Callaway opened two-a-day practices in mid-August with a plethora of potential players. He would be assisted by Jerry Hutchinson. While 15 letter-winners from the undefeated 1960 squad were gone, he did have 12 back. The Clarion-Ledger called the Trojans "*a top-heavy favorite*" for the LDC South title. The Simpson County News called Magee "*heavily favored to win this year*" and "*formidable opposition*".

GAME 1: MAGEE (0-0) vs PEARL (0-0)
MAGEE 31 PEARL 7
September 1, 1961

Fred Foster was no longer at Pearl and his whistle was now held by Coach Bob Parker. The good news was that Parker had 14 returning players The Clarion-Ledger said "*Any coach in the Little Dixie Conference would be glad to have …*" They also said that Pearl was "*highly regarded*" pre-season in terms of North LDC chances and, as such, voters put them 2nd behind Forest Hill. Trying to turn around a 3-7 season, it would not help that key player Bobby Stribling had a knee injury that The Brandon News said "*may possibly keep him out of action all season*".

An opener on the road against a dominant team wasn't the best-case scenario. Once over, it was reported that Magee "*showed no signs of letting up … as they ushered in the … season by blasting Pearl's Pirates … before an overflow home crowd*". Their first possession led to a 76-yard drive capped by a 14-yard run by Ray Reed. They added another on a Donald Womack 3-yarder and finished the half with a 6-yard Reed pass to Womack and Fred Womack PAT.

The Simpson County News noted that "*Magee pushed Pearl all over the stadium in the second half and even liberal substituting by Coach Callaway failed to halt the rampaging Trojans*". Reed and Womack hooked up for the next score while both Reed (11 yards) and Bill Medlock (2 yards) crossed the goal. Pearl's only tally came from a Danny Neely 2-yarder and Billy Clay's PAT pass to Glenn Rhoads.

The Trojans rushed for 254 yards, held first downs (12-3) and passing (106-42). Johnny Wells and Womack both succeeded in picking off Pirate throws.

GAME 2: MAGEE (1-0) @ PICAYUNE (0-0)
MAGEE 13 PICAYUNE 13
September 8, 1961

The Maroon Tide of the Big Eight Conference were a break-even 5-5 in 1960. Coach Twig Branch had 9 returners and figured to *"field a stronger club this year"*. The previous year's matchup had been their first, with Magee shutting out Picayune 20-0. But this time, on a field in a *"boggy condition"* due to a *"late afternoon flood"*, it would not be so easy.

The Tide moved 75 yards on their opening possession and capped things on a 1-yard Joel Pigott dive. That score held only until Donald Womack could take the ensuing Kent Smith kickoff 90 yards to paydirt. Just minutes before halftime, Granville Stockstill faded back and hit Richard Dossett from the 20-yard line. With the PAT, halftime sat 13-6. Though Magee recovered a Tide fumble in the 3rd, they gave it back when a punt snap was fumbled.

Picayune went to the air midway through the 4th quarter, but Lee West picked off an errant pass. They moved to the 15-yard line thanks to Reed runs and Picayune penalties. Reed later found Wells for the score and Donald Womack *"on a layout"* for the crucial point-after. The Tide, after picking off a Trojan pass with :30 left, decided to simply allow the clock to run out.

Picayune had 175 rushing and 20 passing yards while Magee had 136 total markers. First downs favored Picayune 7-6 while each team recovered a fumble and intercepted a pass.

GAME 3: MAGEE (1-0-1) @ PRENTISS (0-2)
MAGEE 25 PRENTISS 0
September 15, 1961

The Bulldogs of Coach Leslie Smith provided the first Little Dixie competition of the season. They were coming off of a 3-7 season but had 12 returning letter-winners. As such, they were slotted 3rd in the LDC South pre-season.

Magee got it going on their first drive when two Reed throws set up his 17-yard keeper. Their next march was halted by a fumble but Fred Womack got it back later via interception. He actually took it 90 yards to the end zone but a penalty brought it back. He would eventually plunge in from the 5-yard line to make it 12-0 at halftime.

Lee West got into the end zone in the 3rd and Jerry Garner pulled a 45-yard pick-six in the final frame for the dagger. The PAT came from Fred Womack on a run through the middle.

GAME 4: MAGEE (2-0-1) @ MONTICELLO (0-3)
MAGEE 59 MONTICELLO 0
September 22, 1961

The only good news Coach George Arendale had in 1961 was that 12 lettermen were back in Monticello. But, the Red Devils had gone an abysmal 0-10 the previous season and Little Dixie voters picked the Red Devils to again end up last in the South division. Predictably, it would be what one report called a *"slaughter"*.

The Medlock 42-yard touchdown just under 2:00 into the game set the tone for scoring that came often. A West interception set up a Reed QB sneak and 12-0 lead. In the 2nd, Magee tallied five times. Fred Womack's interception allowed Reed a 24-yarder, Medlock a 30-yarder, Reed passed to Kelly Roberts for the third (Donald Womack PAT), a fumbled kickoff in the end zone was recovered by Larry Brewer (Fred Womack PAT), and Medlock picked off a Devil throw to allow Reed to hit Roberts from the 45-yard line. That gave Magee three TDs in the last 1:46 of the half.

Brewer opened the 3rd with a 97-yard escape and 52-0 lead. Finally, in the final frame, a desperation throw toward the end zone was picked off by Garner and taken the necessary 90 yards for the final score. If there was bad news, it was that Magee suffered 93 yards in penalties. However, the 59 points was the most recorded for a Magee football team. The total eclipsed the 56 points put up by the 1927 (Morton) and 1959 (Pearl) teams. By the end of the decade, it still sat as the fourth-largest amount of points in a game and the second-largest margin of victory (1997).

GAME 5: MAGEE (3-0-1) vs HAZLEHURST (4-0)
MAGEE 40 HAZLEHURST 0
September 29, 1961

Coach Ronald Bennett's Indians were a surprise thus far into the year. They only had 8 lettermen back from a 6-3-1 squad and were picked 4th in the Little Dixie South division. But by kickoff, they were undefeated.

Just 4:00 into the contest, Magee moved 80 yards with Fred Womack "*doing the honors*" from the 9 and Donald Womack (sock-footed kicker) notching the PAT. He added another PAT after Jerry Hall pulled a 45-yard pick-six to make it 14-0. Reed had the next score in the 2nd quarter on an 18-yard dart and Donald made it 21-0. It was West's turn to pick off a pass to set up Donald Womack's touchdown and 27-0 halftime lead.

Fred Womack, minus a shoe lost along the way, tallied in the 3rd from 39 yards away while Donald Womack "*crashed right tackle and into the secondary*" for the next score. Medlock's point-after made it 40-0. For this game, Magee had cut their penalty yards down to just 30 yards.

GAME 6: MAGEE (4-0-1) @ MORTON (4-1-1)
MAGEE 20 MORTON 6
October 6, 1961

The Panthers were just 5-5-1 the previous year after many seasons of competing for Little Dixie titles. There were 13 lettermen back in blue and gold looking to get on the right track. The 1960 Trojan team had broken a four-game losing streak to the Scott County eleven and this edition was looking to extend the bragging rights.

Morton dominated the opening frame, though it ended scoreless. In the 2nd quarter, "*fleet-footed*" John Richardson broke the tie with a 56-yard dash. As the quarter neared ending, Medlock's long run set up a Fred Womack plunge from short distance and then "*rammed across*" to make it 7-6 at intermission. The Magee Courier said that "*What went on in the dressing room, nobody knows except the Magee coaching staff and the Magee Trojans. But whatever it was worked because the Trojans came back ... all fired up...*"

Reed was first into the end zone from the 9-yard line and added the PAT. In the final quarter, "*the Trojans put the cream on the pie after a pass interference gave the Trojans the ball on the Panther 38*". One play later, Donald Womack "*hit the left side of his line*" for the final touchdown. Magee led in yardage (319-191) and first downs (15-8).

The Clarion-Ledger said that "*Magee's Trojans passed their biggest test of the 1961 football season ... and today must be regarded as the 'team to beat' for this season's championship*". Reed was now 4th in LDC scoring (44 points) while Donald Womack (7th) and Fred Womack (9th) were also in the conversation.

GAME 7: MAGEE (5-0-1) vs CRYSTAL SPRINGS (4-1)
MAGEE 13 CRYSTAL SPRINGS 0
October 13, 1961

Callaway's team were to have their "*strongest test*" of the year this week with sportswriters picking "*this game as the most outstanding and decisive one to be played this week...*" Wade Alexander only had 6 letter-winners back from an 8-1-1 team, but it was still good enough for the Tigers to be ranked 2nd in the division.

Over 4,000 fans were on hand for the big event. It was a slugfest until just :02 before the half when Reed hit Wells from the 5-yard line to cap a 70-yard march. Crystal Springs got to the Trojan 9 in the 3rd but could not make it count. Magee engineered a 77-yard drive in the last frame, keeping "*possession of the pigskin for practically the entire period*". Reed capped it with a 29-yard line when he "*rolled out to the right with deft deception and went across standing up for a second score and the insurance that the Trojans needed...*"

Magee led in yardage (337-214) and first downs (15-7). For the third game in a row, penalties on Magee were held at a minimum. Any threat Crystal Springs could have had at challenging Magee for the South Little Dixie title were put to bed the next week when Prentiss upset them 19-13.

GAME 8: MAGEE (6-0-1) vs COLUMBIA (1-?)
MAGEE 54 COLUMBIA 12
October 27, 1961: HOMECOMING

Columbia was called "*light but fast*" for the coming season under second-year Coach Charlie Martin. Of his 14 lettermen out of 42 total players, only two of the Cats were over 200 pounds. They had put up only a 2-8 record in their previous campaign and garnered their first victory the week before by beating Monticello 25-15. The Trojans, after enjoying a week off to prepare for the Big Eight team, dedicated this Homecoming affair to Dr. Wayne Cockrell.

In such a lop-sided game, it was actually Columbia with the first score when Bill Pachmyr hit Shelby Sharp from 59 yards to make it 6-0. Reed answered quickly with a 15-yard TD and Fred Womack tacked on a 6-yard TD in the 2nd quarter to make it 13-6 after his point-after. With :01 left, Reed hit Roberts from the 31 for the TD and Fred Womack converted for the 20-6 lead at intermission. Columbia did not go away as Sharp took advantage of a Barnes interception with a 2-yard dive.

Up 20-12, Magee turned on the offensive thrusters. Roberts returned a kick 70 yards for one tally while Fred Womack added another and converted both PATs. In the final frame, Medlock charged in from the 2-yard line, Columbia fumbled to set up an 11-yard West run *"standing up"*, and Terry Lee McMillan's 1-yard QB sneak ended scoring.

GAME 9: MAGEE (7-0-1) vs TYLERTOWN (3-6)
MAGEE 61 TYLERTOWN 7
November 3, 1961

The field efforts of the Blue Devils must have been pretty bad. Jack Poole's team was slotted 6th in the LDC South with 9 lettermen back from a 6-5-1 campaign. The Magee Courier predicted that week that *"the Trojans should score just about as many points as they want to in this one. Let's make it Magee 48-6"*. The record of most points scored in a game, set back in the fourth week against Monticello, was again to fall as *"a rapier-sharp hand ... applied the hot knife to a buttery Tylertown..."*.

After a fumble only seconds into the game at the 25-yard line, Fred Womack got in from the 5-yard line and converted. The Devils fumbled again and Reed hit Roberts *"who rambled unmolested into the end zone"*. Reed made it 14-0. A third fumble led to Reed hitting Medlock and the two also converted. Donald Womack *"skipped gaily down the sidelines"* from the 45 for the next and Reed made it 28-0. Before long, Reed hit Donald Womack from the 30-yard line.

Reports for the next series of scoring is convoluted. Tylertown *"dented the Magee goal"* on a Moore pass to Prescott and their conversion. But Magee still had more in them. Fred Womack (12 yards) and Donald Womack (65 yards), a McMillan 15-yarder to Wells, and finally a 60-yarder from Reed to West finally brought a merciful end. At decade's end, it was the third-largest amount of points scored by a Magee team.

GAME 10: MAGEE (8-0-1) @ MENDENHALL (8-1)
MAGEE 6 MENDENHALL 13
November 10, 1961

The biggest game of the year, despite any records or honors on the line, was now at hand. Coach A.J. Mangum's Tigers had not done very well the previous year, and despite 10 returning lettermen, he was slotted 5th in the South division. By kickoff, they had lost only to Crystal Springs in the second game of the year. Magee, meanwhile, had a better record of points-scored (316-263) and points-allowed (45-71) than their rivals. On the other hand, Magee had only beaten Mendy twice in the last 11 years.

The winner of this one would represent the Little Dixie South in the title game; though a Magee loss would still have them as co-champs of the division. Said Mangum, *"Just tell the people in Magee that Mendenhall expects to be on the field when the whistle blows Friday night. I know what kind of a team they have in Magee and it should be a fine ball game"*. Added Callaway, *"We expect a tough ball game, as all Magee-Mendenhall games are. With so much at stake, we look for this to be a real struggle. Mendenhall has a well-balanced club and we look for the breaks to make the difference"*. The Clarion-Ledger stated that *"Any way you look at this game it shapes up as the top game in high school football this year"*.

The game was played *"before the largest crowd, some say 6,000, ever to see a high school grid game in Simpson County"*. In a *"tough, bruising"* game of *"line play"*, it was the Tigers that would break the 21-game streak of undefeated Trojan football. Two of the Tiger touchdowns came directly as the result of a pair of the four Trojan fumbles on the night.

Magee's first drive ended in a fumble, as did many others. The Magee Courier said *"that was the story of the first half. Mendenhall kicking and Magee fumbles kept the Trojans back in their own territory and the first half ended in a scoreless tie"*. As the 3rd quarter ended, a Magee fumble was scooped up by Cecil Puckett and taken 40 yards to paydirt. H.N. Shows' PAT made it 7-0. The Trojans awoke the home fans soon after when, near their end zone, they *"faded back ... and hit Johnny Wells at the midfield marker, and Wells, aided by a key block thrown by Jerry Gray, rambled for a touchdown"*. Magee tried for two points (Reed to Medlock) but it went for naught.

In the final frame, Truett Benton took advantage of a *"partially fumbled Reed pass at the Magee 20-yard line"*. It took 3 plays before Shows *"blasted through a big hole in the line and exploded into the end zone for a six-pointer"*. Desperation passes by Reed to save the game *"were unable to click"*.

GAME 11: MAGEE (8-1-1) vs NEWTON COUNTY (8-0-1)
MAGEE 34 NEWTON COUNTY 6
November 24, 1961: FIRST ANNUAL MISSISSIPPI BOWL

Now that Mendenhall represented the Little Dixie South in the title game, Magee was free to play in a bowl contest. They had wanted to play Provine as both teams were battling for undefeated/unscored-upon seasons up until a certain point in the year. Callaway had confidently stated beforehand that *"he would play anybody in the state"*. They were eventually matched with Choctaw Conference Newton County in the inaugural Mississippi Bowl at Newell Field. *"In Newton County, the Trojans face formidable opposition"*.

Coach W.R. Lindsey's Tigers had gone 17-3 in their last 20 contests. Morton was the only common opponent during the season. NCHS had beaten them 27-7 while Magee had posted a 20-6 tally. Both teams were even in weight, with Magee holding a slight overall 181-180 advantage. Magee had a chance to "scout" Newton County in the Choctaw Conference playoff game against Macon. The Clarion-Ledger said that *"Both teams are well-drilled on knocking and both are considered among the best hard-nosed teams in the state"*. They also called the contest *"a genuine toss-up"*.

"A horde of galloping backs behind a powerfully blocking line" put any doubts to mind that night in front of a 4,000-person crowd. Magee started quickly with a 68-yard march in 10 plays with Reed's 7-yard throw to Roberts. Fred Womack's PAT run made it 7-0. Brewer then recovered a Newton County fumble at midfield. Several plays later, Fred Womack plunged in from the 2-yard line and Reed added the point-after. Another Tiger fumble was picked up by Garner at the 32-yard line. Fred Womack did the honors again and Reed found Donald Womack for the extra point.

In the 3rd quarter, Magee went 48 yards with Reed capping from the 4 on a run. Donald Womack notched the PAT. Newton's only score came late in the frame when Buddy Lindsey hit Bill Freeman on a 70-yard surprise. Magee had one more in them and made a 75-yard drive count in ten plays when Fred Womack *"plowed over"* from the 3-yard line. Magee dominated in first downs (22-4), rushing (262-17) and passing (146-121). Both teams suffered a myriad of interceptions.

The Magee Courier said that *"The Trojans' effort ... was nothing short of magnificent. They played an inspired brand of football and completely overwhelmed a good Newton team. Every member of the football team is to be congratulated on this victory"*. Bobby Ray Baucum (Newton County) was Most Outstanding Lineman while Reed was named Most Outstanding Back.

When All-State honors were announced, Magee had only one more player than did Newton County. First Team members included Jerry Hall and Fred Womack. Honorable Mentions went to Kelly Roberts and Ray Reed. On the All-Little Dixie list, Hall, Womack, Kelly Roberts and Ray Reed garnered First Team awards. Honorable Mentions included Johnny Wells, Billy Womack, Thomas Tuggle, Willis May, Jerry Garner and Billy Medlock.

1962 (11-0) LITTLE DIXIE CHAMPIONS

Despite a 20-1-1 mark over two seasons, Charlie Callaway was now replaced by former East Tallahatchie (Charleston) coach John Williams. Expectations were high for the new mentor as he took his team to Copiah-Lincoln Junior College in mid-August for twice-a-day workouts over a week span. *"During these days ahead, we intend to do nothing but eat, sleep and think football. Another interesting feature of the camp will be that all the Trojans will be eating on the same training table with the college athletes. A great deal can be accomplished by such a camp. Because we will all be living and sleeping together for a week, such a camp has definite advantages to both coaches and players"*.

Over 50 young men had signed up to represent the Trojan banner for 1962. Williams told the Touchdown Club that *"We've got a 203-pound line average, a 174-pound backfield average, and a team average of 180 pounds. (The camp gave) me a chance to live with the boys and get to know them and observe them every minute of the day, and now I know better what to expect out of every man*". The UPI Poll had Magee tied for 10th place in overall voting to start the season while Little Dixie voters had them winning the LDC South.

GAME 1: MAGEE (0-0) @ TALLULAH, LA (0-1)
MAGEE 32 TALLULAH 0
September 14, 1962

The Trojan opener would come against a "*highly-touted*" Louisiana team that had started with a disappointing loss to Vicksburg 34-0. "*They are extremely strong on defense and the score doesn't indicate the true ability of the team*". Tallulah had been Louisiana Class A champs for straight seasons and held the title five of the last seven years. The only casualty to start the season was Mickey Hughes, but it was still enough for the win. The Clarion-Ledger said that Magee "*blasted the daylights*" out of their opponent.

Magee took a 6-0 lead in the opening frame when Ray Reed capped an 80-yard drive with a 5-yard run. A bad snap gave Magee the ball back later at the 32-yard line. Reed hit Donald Womack from there and, with :40 left in the quarter, he hit Kelly Roberts for a 64-yard tally. That made halftime 18-0. Roberts then picked off a pass in the 3rd quarter and raced 55-yards to paydirt. Womack's PAT was true. In the final frame, Womack did the honors on a dash and ended scoring.

The Magee Touchdown Club was treated to a film of the contest at their next meeting with Coaches Williams and Malcolm Nesmith providing commentary.

GAME 2: MAGEE (0-1) @ PEARL (1-1)
MAGEE 27 PEARL 0
September 21, 1962

Bob Parker was back for year-two as head Pirate. Practices began mid-August with "*a large group of returning lettermen who will form a nucleus of what should be a record-setting 1962 team. In addition, several outstanding prospects showed up for practice as the workouts began*". The Clarion-Ledger and Coach Parker weren't as optimistic as The Rankin County News as the Pirates had lost dominant players.

They returned 7 lettermen and the paper called the outlook "*dim*". "*The team will be as good as the boys want it to be. We have some good young prospects moving up who can help us if they come through. It looks like it will be a rebuilding year*", noted Parker. Voters agreed and put them in the "*last three*" of the LDC North.

Pearl opened with a 6-0 loss to Thibodeaux, LA but came back strong to beat Prentiss 25-13. Though The Magee Courier thought that the Trojans would be "*confronted with one of their tougher battles of this year's schedule*", The Simpson County News though that Magee would "*take on Pearl and take them with ease*". It wouldn't be as easy as thought.

Magee appeared to be about to blow away the Pirates as they opened the contest with a 75-yard drive capped by a 15-yard Reed toss to Womack. The PAT failed, but it appeared to be inconsequential. That's when The Magee Courier said they were "*taken to task by the stubborn Pearl defense and aggressive offense and held for naught until the last and final period*". That was when Williams gave the Trojans "*a halftime dressing-down*".

Pearl nearly tied the game in the 3rd before a Danny Neely pass was picked off at the 12-yard line by Johnny Wells. That led to an opening 4th quarter score when Womack raced from the 15. His PAT made it 13-0. They had time in the frame for two more scores. A long drive put Hughes in from the 4-yard line (PAT good). A late fumble by Pearl was recovered by Larry Tolbert at the Trojan 36. With seconds left, Reed hit Roberts who ran the entire 65 yards for the last score. Womack converted for the win "*over the unusually strong Pearl Pirates.*"

GAME 3: MAGEE (2-0) @ CRYSTAL SPRINGS (1-2)
MAGEE 27 CRYSTAL SPRINGS 0
September 28, 1962

Coach Wade Alexander's blue and gold Tigers had gone 6-3 the previous campaign, but Magee was expected to top their hosts "*without too much trouble*". By kickoff, Womack was the leading LDC scorer with 29 points. A defensive battle complete with numerous punts continued into the 2nd quarter. With 4:00 left, Womack broke the ice when he "*crashed into the center of the line, did a sharp cutback to the left side and went racing 40 yards against the entire Tiger secondary for the first score of the ball game*".

The 6-0 halftime score could have been different as Crystal Springs fell on a loose ball at the Trojan 5, but were held on four-straight downs. Brewer opened the 3rd with a fumble recovery at the Tiger 27 but gave it back the same way at the 5-yard line. Two plays later, however, Reed got it back via a Tiger fumble and Hughes made it count from the 6-yard line. Womack's PAT made it 13-0. In the final frame, Reed hit Womack from the 3 and Brewer from inside the 10-yard line. Womack notched both extra points.

Magee led in first downs (12-2) and was 8-10 passing. Crystal Springs was a reported 1-4 in the air and were dominated in total yardage 271-18. The (Crystal Springs) Meteor said that *"Womack was perhaps the finest halfback to perform on the Tiger field in the past couple of seasons."*

GAME 4: MAGEE (3-0) vs PRENTISS (0-4)
MAGEE 32 PRENTISS 14
October 5, 1962: HOMECOMING

The red and white Bulldog squad was focused on improving on their 1961 break-even 5-5 season and it wouldn't be easy. Coach Leslie Smith's team was reported to be playing *"probably their toughest schedule in history as they meet nine Little Dixie foes"*. With All-LDC halfback Glynn Stephens returning, voters put them 3rd and expected them to be *"a contender this season for the first time in several years"*.

Hughes hit paydirt first from the 5-yard line while Reed followed with a 20-yarder. Womack converted the last to make it 13-0. Prentiss became the first team to score on Magee when Carl Taylor pulled a 10-yard pick-six off of Reed, but Hughes responded with a 43-yard escape. Womack's kick was good. In the 4th quarter, a Kelly Roberts hit on McNease forced a fumble to set up an eventual 21-yard Womack run. Back came Prentiss with a 70-yard kick return by Stephens. James Cole provided the PAT. Finally, however, Womack *"became twinkle-toed as he crashed over center and broke into the clear for a 40-yard TD"*.

The Prentiss Headlight gave credit for the first Bulldog TD to Carey Bennett on a run of 25 yards followed by a McNease PAT.

GAME 5: MAGEE (4-0) @ HAZLEHURST (3-1)
MAGEE 18 HAZLEHURST 6
October 11, 1962

Coach Ronald Bennett's Indians were break-even (5-5) the season before but were now at the top of LDCS standings. The Simpson County News said that *"Magee's huge line should stop Hazlehurst's offense, but can Hazlehurst stop the Magee offense? This is the question to be answered and I don't think Hazlehurst has enough to stop them. Magee to ease by Hazlehurst."*

In a tight contest, it was Hughes *"ramming it over"* for the first score and Reed *"rolling out"* for the point-after. *"Both teams seemed to catch on fire periodically (in the 2nd quarter) but to no avail"*. Magee did move to the 5-yard line but fumbled away the opportunity. In the 3rd, Womack gave Magee some breathing room while Reed *"rolled out like a freight train around right end leaving three Indians on the ground"* for the last touchdown. Hazlehurst put up their only score with :10 remaining when Bass hit Ronnie Woods.

GAME 6: MAGEE (5-0) vs MONTICELLO (3-3)
MAGEE 47 MONTICELLO 0
October 19, 1962

The Red Devils under Coach George Arendale had 52 players; *"the largest in the history of the school"*. Though just 3-3, one reporter thought *"Monticello could give Magee an interesting evening if its top-flight youngsters ... get back in condition"*. Though Womack was leading LDC scoring with 64 points, it was disappointing that Magee was only 10th in the UPI poll. There were three teams in front of them with losses and 8 of them had tie ball games.

Williams was confident enough before kickoff to keep some of his *"main hosses"* on the sidelines and let some second- and third-string players start. It was still a bloodbath despite losing one opportunity at the 5-yard line. A march of 99 yards ended with a Larry Roberts TD, but it came at the cost of an injured Womack. In the 3rd, Reed pulled off a 25-yard *"gallop"* and Mike Carmichael notched the PAT. Then Reed picked up a loose Devil ball and raced 15 yards for another.

Brewer then ran for 45 yards and a score and Billy Womack recovered a fumble to set up Roberts' 15-yarder. Donald Womack, back in the game, added the extra point. Jack McAlpin then intercepted a Miller throw and took it 35-yards to daylight. Donald Womack did the same for a 20-yard touchdown.

GAME 7: MAGEE (6-0) @ COLUMBIA (0-3 CONFERENCE)
MAGEE 28 COLUMBIA 6
October 26, 1962

The Cats were expected to *"face another challenging season"* under new mentor Bobby Joe Oswalt. The team *"consisted of 34 boys, barring injuries and drop-outs"* and lacked *"size, depth and experience"*. No returners could be found from tackle-to-tackle. Still, a report said that *"Magee will find its roughest going so far against Big Eight member Columbia, but should win"*. Womack still led LDC scorers with 73 points and Magee had inched up to 9th in the UPI.

The opening frame was scoreless thanks to a Magee fumble at the Cat 2. But Terry Runnels' fumble recovery in the 2nd quarter set up Donald Womack's 15-yard scamper and his PAT. A Trojan fumble at midfield led to Bill Packmayr hitting Craig Jones from the 8-yard line with no time on the clock. Two *"completely different teams"* came back for the second half. Reed crossed the goal from the 11-yard line and Womack converted. The teams exchanged fumbles later while Magee also picked off a pass.

Early in the final quarter, Womack ran in from the 11-yard line and added the PAT. Hughes then raced 70 yards for a touchdown and Womack converted. *"The still-determined Wildcats fought back and were threating for another last-minute score when Johnnie Wells latched on to a Wildcat pass on the Trojan 30 to end the threat and the ball game"*.

Magee led in first downs (9-6) and rushing (409-58) but lost the air (86-25). Both teams lost 2 balls via interception. Magee lost 4 fumbles in all while Columbia lost only 2. The Lawrence County Press said that *"The Devil line was out-sized but they fought Magee tit-for-tat. In the third quarter, the bubble broke"*.

GAME 8: MAGEE (7-0) @ TYLERTOWN (1-6-1)
MAGEE 19 TYLERTOWN 0
November 2, 1962

The Trojans boarded the bus for an 80-mile trip to visit Coach Jack Poole's blue and gold Blue Devils. They were 3-7 the previous year, including a 61-7 thrashing by Magee, and were worse this season. Tylertown had beaten Magee only in 1943 (7-0). The stormy night probably kept the score from looking somewhat similar to the year-before.

The reports of the game are not complete due to the *"rain torrents which fell from beginning to end"*, causing spectators to be reportedly *"chased from the bleachers"*. Tylertown threatened on a drive to the Magee 5 early in the game, but the defense held. Late in the 2nd quarter Magee recovered a fumble at the 18-yard line. Hughes went in from the 2 with 1:24 remaining and Womack converted. After missing a 3rd quarter FG, they still came back with a 10-yard Reed touchdown strike to Zeno Cone. Late in the 4th, and after a Womack interception, Reed rolled in from the 7-yard line.

One of the strangest reports in Magee football history occurred during the game. The Magee Courier reports that, in the last quarter, *"Johnnie Wells ... sustained a serious knee injury when a Tylertown player charged from the bench and tackled Wells who was racing downfield near the Tylertown sideline (after an intercepted pass). Wells underwent knee surgery Monday and, because of the accident, will be out of the lineup the remainder of the season"*. There is no mention of the event in The Tylertown Times.

GAME 9: MAGEE (8-0) @ MORTON (6-2)
MAGEE 20 MORTON 6
November 9, 1962

Though coming off of a 6-3 season, the blue and gold Panthers under Coach Dale Brasher were strangely picked among the bottom of the LDC North. Now, they were in first place in that section. The Simpson County News said that *"Morton will be tough, but I don't think they have enough to stop Magee"*.

Magee scored in each of the first three quarters. Womack was in from the 3 and later from the 11. The PAT made halftime 13-0. In the 3rd, Womack took *"a pitchout from Reed on the 16"* and raced to paydirt. Morton added their only tally in the 3rd when McCrory escaped from the 14-yard line. Reed and Brewer pitched in with interceptions in the second frame while Runnels did the same in the 3rd quarter.

GAME 10: MAGEE (9-0) vs MENDENHALL (9-0)
MAGEE 14 MENDENHALL 0
November 16, 1962

Coach A.J. Mangum's black and gold rival Tigers were a fierce opponent. They had gone 10-1 the last year (beating Magee) and were undefeated this season; bragging of 18-straight wins. This was agreed to be *"the top high school football classic of the week"* as both teams were looking to claim the Little Dixie bragging rights. The Magee Courier said that *"standing room will be crowded and seating room will be unheard of"*. Mendenhall was 255-37 on the scoreboard this year while Magee was 251-32. Said Williams, *"This is a case of two good teams getting together and, with favorable weather, spectators will see the best brand of football they have seen in many years"*. Womack was still running away with scoring honors (110 points). Magee was still only 7th in the UPI despite what others' records showed, while Mendenhall could claim a 10th spot.

Brewer broke a defensive battle in the 2nd quarter by picking off a Tiger throw. Magee went 79 yards, all on the ground, and capped it with a 1-yard Hughes plunge with 1:20 left. Womack's successful kick was all the Trojans would eventually need. Magee put it away in the 3rd by going 69 yards with Hughes providing the last 5 yards. Womack's point-after ended scoring. Magee scored again with :10 left via Reed's 38-yard connection with Roberts, but it was called back for off-sides. Mendy's only real threat came late in the 1st quarter after Frank Lang recovered a Magee fumble at the 27-yard line.

Hughes led Magee rushers with 127 yards. Magee dominated first downs (15-2), rushing (236-47) and passing (23-0). Each had an interception while Magee lost the lone fumble. Unlike past years where the animosity was altogether too high, that had changed by 1962. Said The Magee Courier, *"In every engagement, the boys and men from Simpson County have done nothing short of bringing honor back home to their respective schools and their county and, in so doing, have caused the public's eye to become focused upon Simpson County with admiration"*.

GAME 11: MAGEE (10-0) vs FOREST HILL (8-2)
MAGEE 26 FOREST HILL 6
November 22, 1962: LITTLE DIXIE CHAMPIONSHIP

The Rebels had a new face in the leadership position. Tom Cheney, ex-Louisville native and former assistant coach at Louisiana College, now made his debut season at Forest Hill. He would have only 2 starters and 12 lettermen back and noted that *"My biggest disappointment ... is the lack of depth. That is our main problem"*. It didn't stop LDC coaches from having them only 1 point out of first place North predictions. That had held true as they now faced the Trojans for LDC honors.

The Simpson County News said that *"Forest Hill has a good team and should make a game out of it, but Magee with its massive line and swift backfield should win this one with ease"*. Williams was not so bold. *"After our superb effort against Mendenhall last week, I am afraid of a letdown. They (Forest Hill) haven't allowed over three touchdowns to any club except Canton and they have a few halfbacks who can hurt you if they get loose"*. Magee felt better, however, as the game was to be played on the home field.

It took the Trojans no time to get going as Brewer took the kickoff 67 yards to set up Womack's 27-yard run to the 3-yard line and Reed's rollout from there. Forest Hill came right back behind solid Robinson passes that put them near the Magee goal. But his last pass was just off the fingertips of Lee that would have tied things. In the 2nd, Hughes *"crashed left tackle standing up from 10 yards out"* while Womack notched the 13-0 point-after. The visitors, however, put up their only points before halftime on Tommy Vinson's 8-yard rush.

Vinson nearly scored in the 3rd on a long run but it was called back on penalty. Magee later drove to the 5-yard line before giving up the ball but Forest Hill then fumbled to Larry Tolbert at the 9-yard line. It took Hughes three plays to get in from the 4-yard line and Womack finished scoring with the kick. A late fumble recovery by Terreal Garner allowed Magee one last touchdown when Womack escaped from inside the 17-yard line.

"Line play was outstanding by offensive thrusts and defensive defiance of a highly-aggressive Rebel team. The Trojan backs moved with deception as they had done throughout the season and ... threw their weight around ... to bring home another Little Dixie Championship". Hughes again led rushers with 134 yards. Magee led in first downs (13-9) and rushing (218-39) while the Rebs held the air (93-22). Forest Hill had an intercepted pass and lost four fumbles.

Ray Reed was awarded a UPI All-State Back of the Year honor while he and Donald Womack garnered Mississippi Sportscasters' Association All-State honors. Larry Roberts picked up an Honorable Mention. Magee ended tied with 8-1-1 Columbus for 6th place in the UPI poll. Three teams above them (Gulfport, Meridian and Greenville) had at least one loss. Columbus, too had a loss. And, each of the teams ranked higher had a tie ball game on the season.

1963 (11-0) LITTLE DIXIE CHAMPIONS

Second-year Coach John Williams had taken his Trojans to an undefeated season and Little Dixie Championship in 1962. It was no surprise that they were picked unanimously to repeat as title-holders in the LDC South. The UPI had them 6th in the state of Mississippi. The team hit the road to Copiah-Lincoln Junior College for a week in early August to practice and have team-bonding. Like the previous season, they opened with a bye-week to allow more practices and faced a Louisiana team for the opener.

GAME 1: MAGEE (0-0) @ TALLULAH, LA (UNREPORTED)
MAGEE 32 TALLULAH 0
September 13, 1963

With the *"entire population of Magee"* making the 120-mile journey, the Trojans made it worthwhile by *"out-passing, out-kicking, out-blocking, and in general, out-playing the boys from Louisiana"*.

The first quarter was scoreless, thanks in part to a Jack McAlpin pick-six that was called back. In the 2nd, Mickey Hughes got things started with a rushing TD behind the blocking of Ted Mangum. Then Terry McMillan hit Johnny Wells for a 20-yard score and Mike Carmichael toed the PAT. In the 3rd, Wells picked off a Tallulah throw at midfield. Hughes finished the drive with an 8-yard score and Carmichael converted. Hughes would evade tacklers before the end of the frame with a 10-yard escape.

Substitutes took the field for Magee but still the Trojans held and scored. This time it was Earnest McAlpin finding Carmichael for *"the final score of the game"*. Magee led in rushing (375-89), passing (120-15) and first downs (11-2). Kelly Roberts was credited with fine punts averaging 42 yards. The line held Tallulah to no first downs against the varsity starters.

GAME 2: MAGEE (1-0) vs PEARL (1-1)
MAGEE 48 PEARL 6
September 20, 1963

Bob Parker wasn't overly-enthusiastic about his chances in 1963. He had 10 returning lettermen, but lost key players such as All-Little Dixie stars Danny Neely and Glenn Rhoads. On top of that, they played a traditionally-tough schedule. *"Each game will be a rough one ... and even though we have 10 boys back, we will be green at QB and the end positions"*. The two teams had started playing against one-another since 1958 but the Pirates had never been successful. The Simpson County News predicted that *"Magee should take Pearl by a nice score"*.

Parker knew what was in front of his Pirates. *"We'll really have to scrap to say on the field with Magee tonight. The Trojans remind me all too much of Thibodaux (Louisiana), what with all their depth, speed and weight"*. On Thursday night, Williams attended the Magee Touchdown Club meeting at Windham's Café to show film of the Tallulah contest and preview the upcoming scrap with the Pirates.

Scoring was only recapped in a general manner, due to the overwhelming offensive attack of the Trojans. They put up two touchdowns in the 1st, 2nd and 4th quarters while adding a lone score in the 3rd. Hughes (2), Roberts, Wells, Lamar Carter, and McAlpin crossed for Magee; McMillan threw for 3 TDs; Carter had a 96-yard pick-six; and Carmichael converted 6 of 7 extra points. Dennis Neely provided the only Pirate score in the 2nd via a 54-yard reception from Holder. Magee outpaced Pearl via the ground (397-140), the air (181-64), and first downs (13-3).

GAME 3: MAGEE (2-0) vs CRYSTAL SPRINGS (UNREPORTED)
MAGEE 32 CRYSTAL SPRINGS 6
September 27, 1963

Ten returning letter-winners were on hand for Coach Wade Alexander's blue and gold. Picked 3rd in the LDC South, they were called a *"dark horse"*. By game day, The Magee Courier said that they would be *"considered one of the tougher opponents of the South Little Dixie loop"*.

Williams told the student body at the pep rally that Crystal Springs should be *"our toughest game for the next five games"*. Despite a 2-0 record, Magee was now 8th in the UPI.

The coach was right, as Crystal Springs was still very-much in the game until the last quarter. A scoreless opening frame saw a Carter touchdown called back and Terreal Garner block a Tiger FG. Wells picked off a ball at the 30 in the next quarter and Carter made it count with a 15-yard escape. After Carmichael's PAT, Big Crystal responded with a 42-yard George Thornton scoring toss to Tommy Henry with :02 left. But Garner's second kick-block kept it 7-6 at halftime.

McMillan was next with an interception and Hughes capitalized with a 1-yard plunge. Now in the last quarter, Magee put the game out of reach. McMillan and Carter hooked up for the first TD and Robert Landrum dove in from the 1-yard line (Carmichael PAT) for the next. Thomas McAlpin's interception later allowed McMillan to find Carmichael from midfield for the last touchdown. Magee led in first downs (17-4), rushing (267-60) and passing (109-70). On the negative side, Magee was once again around the 100-yard mark in penalties.

GAME 4: MAGEE (3-0) @ PRENTISS (UNREPORTED)
MAGEE 25 PRENTISS 0
October 4, 1963

Former Clinton assistant and Forest Head Coach Ken Bramlett was now in Prentiss. The red and white Bulldogs had gone 2-9 the previous year and were tied for 4th in the pre-season LDC South. Hughes (36) and Carmichael (22) were ranked 3rd and 6th in Little Dixie scoring for Magee and the team was now up to 7th in the UPI.

Unlike other games where Magee was slow to get rolling, this one saw the Trojans put up all of their points in the first half of play. Roberts was first to the end zone on a 50-yard dash though McMillan had a 40-yarder called back. In the next frame, McMillan found Donald Cowart for a 30-yard tally, Jack McAlpin blocked a punt and Larry Tolbert recovered for a score, and Carter *"rammed it over"* from the 1-yard line for the last.

GAME 5: MAGEE (4-0) vs HAZLEHURST (3-1)
MAGEE 41 HAZLEHURST 0
October 10, 1963: HOMECOMING

This contest against the pre-season 4th-ranked Indians was notable in that they were now led by Charlie Callaway. Callaway had done such a wonderful job in Magee before departing and now was back to see if he could get his maroon and white squad competitive with the Trojans. Thus far they were tied in conference wins for the top spot in the LDCS. Magee had moved up to their highest UPI ranking (6th) after the win over Prentiss.

An Indian punt fumble early in the 2nd quarter led to the first score; that a Wells recovery of a Roberts fumble in the end zone. They then drove 80 yards with 40 yards of it being a McMillan strike to Wells. Before halftime, McMillan found Jack McAlpin for a 60-yard connection and Carmichael's two PATs made it 20-0 at halftime. Carter provided a 1-yard TD run in the 3rd and Carmichael converted. In the final frame, McMillan plunged in from the 1-yard line while Hughes raced in from the 35-yard line for another. Carmichael was true on one kick. The game ended with a Tolbert pickoff followed by one from Hazlehurst by Woods.

Hazlehurst was drowned in first downs 17-1. *"Defensively, the Trojans were great. The big line from end-to-end just wouldn't permit much to come their way..."* Said Williams afterwards, *"Those Indians hit harder than any group of little players I have seen"*.

GAME 6: MAGEE (5-0) @ MONTICELLO (3-3)
MAGEE 55 MONTICELLO 0
October 18, 1963

The Red Devils were picked 6th in the LDCS after a 5-5 campaign. Coach Rex Dawsey was *"working to build a team around a number of valuable returnees, while feeling keenly the loss by graduation"* of key personnel. The Clarion-Ledger said of the upcoming tilt that Magee was *"expected to have little trouble ... where the fast-starting Red Devils had cooled off somewhat in the last few games..."* Hughes (42), Wells and Carter (30) were sitting 3rd and 8th in Little Dixie scoring.

Unfortunately, and probably just as good, the recap of the action is scant. Roberts notched a pair of touchdowns while Carmichael, Wells, Hughes, Carter, Earnest McAlpin and Tom McAlpin each got into the books with a score. Carmichael converted on six of eight extra points. Magee held a 21-0 halftime lead with at least one interception in the half. Confusingly, the UPI poll dropped Magee to 7th despite the undefeated season and blowout win.

GAME 7: MAGEE (6-0) vs COLUMBIA (1-4)
MAGEE 28 COLUMBIA 0
October 25, 1963

The Big Eight Wildcats under Coach Bobby Joe Oswalt had enjoyed a bye week and prepped for Magee during the interim. The scoring began in the 2nd quarter with a Hughes 10-yard gallop. Before halftime, Carter added two more touchdowns and Carmichael was true on all extra points for a 21-0 lead at intermission. The second Trojan score came as the result of a Tolbert-forced fumble recovered by Thomas McAlpin. In the final frame, Carter dove in from the 2-yard line for the last touchdown.

Columbia played better than expected, but their lone threat moved only as far as the 19-yard line before DeMartinos fumbled to Wayne Garner. McAlpin also picked off an errant throw. Magee led in first downs (12-3).

GAME 8: MAGEE (7-0) vs TYLERTOWN (1-?)
MAGEE 33 TYLERTOWN 0
November 1, 1963

It was time for another home game, but this time it would be against a blue and gold squad that was picked last in the Little Dixie South. Coach Earl Marshall's boys had gone 2-8-1 the previous year and this night would not improve upon things. As for the road to the LDC title, Mendenhall's 13-13 tie with Crystal Springs made it easier for Magee. Now, finishing out even with a loss against Mendy would still give the title to the Trojans.

Conditions were not prime as *"a slippery ball (and) a damp field"* awaited both teams. There were 3 fumbles in the opening frame alone. One forced by Jack McAlpin was recovered by Ted Mangum. At the 20-yard line, he lateralled to Wayne Garner, but he fumbled back to Tylertown. Still, before halftime, Hughes tallied four times while McMillan added another on a keeper. Carmichael was credited with 3 points on the night.

GAME 9: MAGEE (8-0) vs MORTON (8-0)
MAGEE 7 MORTON 0
November 8, 1963

The Panthers had a solid 7-3 season under Dale Brasher but finished 2nd in the LDC North thanks to a 6-0 loss to Forest Hill. This season, the blue and gold were the pick as winners of the division and had their entire backfield returning. They were true to expectations at kickoff and all eyes were focused on this particular Friday night tilt. Writers accurately noted that it may very well be a preview of the soon-to-be-played Little Dixie Championship. The Magee Courier called the Panthers *"unquestionably the strongest opponent of the season"*.

"Two big lines with a lot of determination, leather-popping and sometimes a little holding and jumping the gun pretty well sums up the hard-nosed activity which almost completely stymied the offensive play of both teams". The game was essentially won just four plays into the contest. A Magee kick was touched by Morton and Thomas McAlpin alertly fell on the pigskin at the 12-yard line. Hughes' 4-yard plunge and Carmichael's PAT would be all that was needed.

The Panthers *"fought desperately until the final whistle to equal the score. But from end-to-end, Jack McAlpin, Ted Mangum, Wayne Garner, Larry Tolbert, Terreal Garner, Pat Smith and Kelly Roberts said 'no' as they held the ground game to only four first downs. In the air, the defensive backfield would not allow but two completions out of nineteen tries"*. Magee led 174-44 in total yardage (124 from rushing) and in first downs (6-4).

GAME 10: MAGEE (9-0) @ MENDENHALL (7-0-2)
MAGEE 26 MENDENHALL 0
November 15, 1963

Little Dixie voters had Coach Troy Greer's Tigers only 7 votes behind Magee in South predictions. Mendenhall hadn't lost a game yet, but they had been tied by Crystal Springs (13-13) and Brandon (7-7). Strangely, it was stated that the winner would represent the division in the title contest against Morton. Despite the 9-0 start, the UPI poll could put Magee only as high as 6th. Again, that was without merit as three teams (Meridian, Greenville and Hattiesburg) each had a loss and had played fewer games.

Mendy was more than prepared, out-dueling Magee in the first half with most of the game played on the Trojan side of the field. But it was Hughes with the first touchdown before intermission on a 12-yard dash. Carmichael's PAT was blocked by Phillips to keep it 6-0. In the 3rd, McMillan hit Jack McAlpin on fourth down for the second TD and 12-0 lead. In the final frame, McMillan pitched to Roberts who then found Wells for the TD. Carmichael converted.

Garner put the exclamation point on things before the final whistle by picking off an H.N. Shows throw and returning it to the 5-yard line. Hughes did the rest from there and Magee now held claim to the LDC South title.

GAME 11: MAGEE (10-0) vs MORTON (8-2)
MAGEE 14 MORTON 0
November 21, 1963: PEARL HIGH SCHOOL; PEARL, MS

For the second time in three weeks, Magee would be on the field with powerful Morton. The last game had come down to an early Magee touchdown that resulted from an error on the opening kick. Said Williams, *"They know they have a real tough ball game on their hands and we are going into the game with that in mind"*. Morton had last won the bragging rights in 1958, though playing for it multiple times. All players were reported healthy for the game at Pearl High School. As a side note, the Trojans still sat 6th in the UPI poll. Every team in front of them had losses or ties with the exception of first-place Gulfport (10-0).

The first quarter in front of 4,000 fans was deadlocked, but Magee changed that in the ensuing quarter. Eerily, it was set up by a touched-punt that was recovered at the 45-yard line by Donald Cowart. Successful runs got the ball to the 10 from where McMillan hit Thomas McAlpin *"in the right hand coffin corner"*. Carmichael booted the PAT for a 7-0 halftime advantage. Magee got to the Panther 1-yard line in the 3rd, but Morton *"slammed an iron-clad defense"* to stop any further advance.

Now in the final quarter, Roberts *"found a gaping hole over Ted Mangum and Wayne Garner on the left side of the line and struck a trot to the right sideline for a 68-yard scamper to the Panther 2"*. He capitalized later from there and Carmichael *"put the icing on the cake"*. The Magee Courier said that *"With the sound of the final whistle, up in the air went Coach John Williams and Assistant Coaches Malcolm Nesmith and Orland Everett atop the big broad shoulders which had paved the way for another championship, and with a great deal of enthusiasm, Williams placed a kiss on the Championship Trophy…"*

Magee led in first downs (13-7), rushing (286-144) and passing (72-38). Magee picked off 3 passes while Morton had one theft. The Panthers, however, lost two fumbles. The following day turned joy into sadness with the assassination of President John F. Kennedy.

The All-State list included Jack McAlpin on the Third Team. All Little Dixie First Team members counted McAlpin, Ted Mangum, Terreal Garner, Larry Tolbert and Mickey Hughes. Pat Smith and Kelly Roberts were Honorable Mentions. Coach John Williams earned the prestigious Coach of the Year award.

1964 (7-2) LITTLE DIXIE CHAMPIONS

After just two seasons, John Williams had departed Magee for the mentorship of the Biloxi football team. In his place was former assistant Malcolm Nesmith. Nesmith would be joined in coaching by Orland Everett and C.B. Hawkins. Thirty-one varsity players were ready for practices. Nesmith thought *"his squad to be a much-lighter squad than last season"* but they *"have the desire and speed … to win games"*.

The team made their way to Copiah-Lincoln Junior College in late August for practices and team-building. *"The boys stayed together as a unit, got to know each other better, and it is a tremendous asset to team morale"*. Unlike past years, the Trojans were picked an amazing 5th in the Little Dixie South. Rival Mendenhall was the clear favorite to take bragging rights this season.

Magee had lost 16 senior players to graduation and now had only 7 lettermen on hand. *"An overall lack of experience will hurt us, but I believe this is the best-conditioned boys I have seen at Magee and they will give 100% on the field"*. The line averaged 170 pounds while the backfield was at 140 pounds.

GAME 1: MAGEE (0-0) @ MORTON (1-0)
MAGEE 7 MORTON 13
September 11, 1964

Another surprise for this season was that the Panthers were picked 4th in the LDC North. They hadn't shown signs of that placement as they whipped Newton the first week of the season 32-14. The Clarion-Ledger said that they were *"light this season but should have good speed"*. Nesmith called it an *"acid test"* and said *"The Panthers have some real fine backs and are strong up front, but our boys have the best desire, spirit and work harder than any group I have ever coached at Magee"*. It would mark the third meeting with Morton in Magee's last four games.

The Magee Courier said that Morton *"found the Trojans, even though inexperienced and untested, to be a determined and stubborn opponent who put up a 'bulldog' battle right to the final whistle"*. A first-play fumble by Magee did no damage but Morton did score first in the 2nd quarter on Melvin Westerfield's 3-yard plunge to make halftime 6-0. In the 3rd, Magee tied things on a solid drive capped by Earnest McAlpin's 1-yard pass to Tom McAlpin. Then, Royce Foster split the uprights for the 7-6 lead.

Unfortunately, the Panthers came right back with a 30-yard Larry McCrory strike to Jerry McCrory and, with the point-after, took the lead they would not relinquish. Near the game's end, Magee drove for a game-winning score but barely missed. It served as only the second loss for the Trojans since November of 1959.

GAME 2: MAGEE (0-1) @ CRYSTAL SPRINGS (2-1)
MAGEE 13 CRYSTAL SPRINGS 7
September 25, 1964

A week's rest due to a bye week allowed Magee to prepare for their pre-season 4th place LDCS opponent. The Trojans had put up a respectable 9-2-1 record against them since 1946, but The Magee Courier called them *"the heaviest team in the South Little Dixie and a battle-tested eleven..."* The Tigers had beaten Forest Hill and Pearl, but dropped a 14-7 decision to Mendenhall.

Another 13-7 final was at hand, but this time it favored Magee. In the opening frame, they drove 60 yards with Earnest McAlpin capping it with a 2-yard sweep around the left. Foster's PAT made it 7-0. McAlpin then picked off George Thornton football and raced 98 yards for the fan-pleasing score. Wyck Neely assisted by *"throwing a key block on the Tiger 40 to shake the fleet-footed quarterback into the open"*. Crystal Springs took advantage of a Magee fumble before intermission when Tommy Traxler escaped from the 10. Buddy Donahoe's point-after would finish scoring for each team.

In the second half, *"The Trojan line displayed tremendous aggressiveness on both offense and defense and did a beautiful job all night in holding Crystal Springs' crack 190lb fullback scoreless and to minimum gains. From end-to-end, every lineman turned in a brilliant performance in containing the 200lb-plus line and in the backfield the backs were clicking with precision to give the Trojans an outstanding performance for the evening..."*

First downs were even (8-8), Magee lost one more fumble (2-1) and overall yardage barely went to Crystal Springs (162-153). Magee also did themselves no favors, putting up 65 penalty yards against none for the Tigers.

GAME 3: MAGEE (1-1) vs PRENTISS (UNREPORTED)
MAGEE 14 PRENTISS 7
October 2, 1964: HOMECOMING

Coach Ken Bramlett's Bulldogs were picked 3rd in the LDC South and called *"a definite dark horse ... with a lot of talent on hand"*. It was a rebuilding year in Prentiss after a 3-7 campaign in 1963. In Magee, it was Homecoming for the rainy alumni and the Trojans gave them reason to be glad they came.

Robert Landrum hit the board first on a 10-yard rush and Foster toed the PAT. Prentiss drove in response in the 2nd quarter, but Jim McAlpin killed the threat by recovering a fumble at the 36-yard line. It took two plays before Earnest McAlpin *"uncorked his tossing arm"* to find Neely from the 45-yard line for the touchdown. Foster made halftime a 14-0 affair. The Dogs answered in the 3rd on a short Demery Grubbs run and a Rory Lee point-after to make the 4th quarter a nervous one. But Magee's defense *"settled down to hard-nosed football and prevented the necessary penetration to change the score"*.

GAME 4: MAGEE (2-1) @ HAZLEHURST (2-2)
MAGEE 14 HAZLEHURST 6
October 8, 1964

Ex-Trojan Coach Charlie Callaway's Indians were *"expected to be greatly-improved"* and his *"rebuilding program show signs of bearing fruit"*. As such, voters had the team 2nd in the South. The game was played on Thursday due to the State Fair, and stayed that way even though the event in Jackson was altered.

A scoreless opening frame led to Magee crossing the goal on a 50-yard Earnest McAlpin strike to Tom McAlpin and a 7-0 lead. Hazlehurst responded last in the quarter on a 1-yard Pat Amos plunge and halftime sat 7-6. The Indians went to the air in the 3rd with numerous completions but could not get to paydirt. Carter, however, added some insurance on his 40-yard escape. The Lawrence County Press said that *"There were several plays when the Indians had the Magee QB caught for a loss, only to have him step by for a nice gain"*.

It was evident that the Trojan offense needed to get more productive. In four contests, they had put up no more than 14 points while the defense did their job by holding teams to no more than 13 points. That would change in the following week.

GAME 5: MAGEE (3-1) vs MONTICELLO (1-5)
MAGEE 42 MONTICELLO 0
October 15, 1964

It was a good time to play the pre-season last-placed Red Devils. A win could catapult a team picked 5th in the LDCS to solidify a first-place division spot. It took only a few minutes before Landrum began the assault with a 3-yard run and Foster added the PAT. They tacked on a pair of touchdowns in the following frame; both by Landrum with Foster topping each. The last came after Kelly Herrington recovered a loose Red Devil ball on the Monticello 43. Another reference says that it could have been Neely with the second TD on a pass from Earnest McAlpin.

Landrum opened the 3rd with another score and Foster made it 28-0. Before the end of the 3rd, Bubba Carter *"danced and twisted his way for 62 yards for another"*. McAlpin and Neely definitely hooked up later on a 34-yard connection and Foster maintained his perfect mark. The Magee Courier said *"it was a big (win) for the Trojans and a thriller all the way through"*.

GAME 6: MAGEE (4-1) @ PETAL (4-3)
MAGEE 28 PETAL 0
October 23, 1964

The Trojans now faced a team outside of The Little Dixie; thus ensuring that regardless of the outcome, they would maintain top spot in the South division of the conference. They had played 4 times since 1935 with the overall record being in favor of Petal 2-1-1.

Neely proved early that this one belonged to Magee when he took the opening kick 90 yards to paydirt. He *"jogged at three-quarter speed to the midfield stripe where he cut back to the left sideline and then shifted into high gear to literally outrun two downfield defenders"*. Foster made his first of four extra points. Petal then fumbled to Tom McAlpin to set up a 1-yard Earnest McAlpin plunge. In the 2nd, Carter did the honors from the 5-yard line and halftime was 21-0.

In the 3rd quarter, Neely picked off an errant Dickie Carpenter throw. With second-team members in, Jock Allen *"rammed it over"* from the 5-yard line for the final tally. Another solid drive later was hampered by penalties and the Foster FG attempt was unsuccessful. One more failed FG attempt followed before the final whistle. First downs (18-5) and rushing (264-41) were solidly in Magee's favor while passing went to Petal 48-29. Both lost a fumble on the night and Magee never punted.

GAME 7: MAGEE (5-1) vs SAINT ALOYSIUS (2-5)
MAGEE 0 SAINT ALOYSIUS 10
November 6, 1964

The Flashes, under former LSU Chinese Bandit and now Coach Andy Bourgeois, had been struggling this season. Currently members of the Mississippi Catholic Conference, he had petitioned unsuccessfully to be in The Little Dixie. He was cautious but optimistic about his chances on the field. They had 13 seniors, but Bourgeois said *"We could have the finest team since I've been at St Aloysius and still have my worst record yet. You win with seniors and we have 13 this year. So, we expect to win our share"*. Until the week before, all of their losses had been by a combined 14 points.

Saint Al took their first possession to the Magee 35 before Eddie Ray fumbled to Neely. Magee drove to the Flash 40 but lost the chance on an incomplete 4th down pass. In the 2nd, Neely fumbled a Flash punt that was recovered by Joe Maggio. Ray then hit George Zorn for the touchdown on the next play, but a flag brought it back. Ray then rushed to the 1-yard line and then into the end zone for the score. The PAT was good. In the 3rd, Carter fumbled to Tom Balzli, but Neely subsequently picked off a Ray pass at the 15 shortly after.

In the final frame, Saint Al marched 89 yards to the 3-yard line. Charles Antoine was called upon to add the 19-yard FG and he delivered. Magee nearly scored on their next possession on a drive to the Flash 1-yard line behind plays by McAlpin, Neely and David Tedford. However, the 4th downs pass was overthrown and *"the Saint Aloysius stands rocked"*. Saint Al led in first downs (11-10) and passing (123-68) while Magee held the ground (149-117). Magee had one more lost fumble (2-1) but had a pair of interceptions. Eddie Ray went on to LSU and eventually the NFL.

GAME 8: MAGEE (5-2) vs MENDENHALL (7-0-1)
MAGEE 14 MENDENHALL 5
November 13, 1964

The edition of the rivalry game, like so many others recently, had the two teams fighting for their place in the Little Dixie championship game. Both teams were 4-0 in conference and the winner would likewise advance. In fact, the title of the conference was held in Simpson County a reported twelve-straight years. Mendy held the trophy in 1953, 1956-1959 and 1961.

Coach Troy Greer was an obvious favorite; having been ranked tops to start the season and now holding a better record overall. Despite having only 3 seniors, they had given up only 21 points on the year. Both teams had made the Others Receiving Votes category in the UPI poll. What others may not have known in that a *"virus bug"* had *"weakened five of Coach Greer's starting eleven"*.

The 5,000 fans saw what was called *"one of the most spectacular gridiron performances to ever be witnessed in Little Dixie circles"*. Magee opened scoring when Earnest McAlpin hit Neely from the 38-yard line. Neely *"grabbed at the Mendenhall 25 and dashed all the way to put the Trojans out front"*. Foster made it 7-0. Mendenhall came close to tying the game before halftime, but Tom McAlpin *"leaped high into the air to deflect Allen Gary's would-be touchdown pass"*. Jaris Patrick was called upon for the 27-yard FG and intermission sat 7-3.

Magee nearly cost themselves the game in the 3rd quarter when they fumbled to James Phillips at their 8-yard line. *"At this point, one of the most outstanding goal line defenses was displayed by the Trojan defensive line when, after three thrusts, big Jim McAlpin halted Donnie Caughman on the 1-yard line to stop an apparent 7 points for a 2-point safety on the next play when Frankie Barrett (or Jackie Mullins) downed Earnest McAlpin in the end zone"*. Mendenhall, down only 7-5, began their final-frame march for the win. As time wound down to roughly 7:00, they had moved deep into Trojan territory. But Neely pulled in an errant Gary throw at the 10-yard line and raced 90 yards to paydirt.

Mendenhall led all around: first downs (16-6), passing (96-56) and rushing (125-72). Landrum paced Trojan runners with 37 yards. But Magee picked off a pair of throws with one score as a direct result. Mendy recovered the only fumble of the night.

GAME 9: MAGEE (6-2) vs MORTON (9-1)
MAGEE 7 MORTON 6
November 20, 1964: PEARL HIGH SCHOOL

This game was not only a rematch of the first meeting of 1964, but also of the Little Dixie Championship in 1963. Morton made the dance with a 28-6 defeat of rival Forest. The Clarion-Ledger said that *"Both ball clubs pack strong, explosive running attacks coupled with air arms that are capable of breaking a game wide open anything the opportunity arises"*.

The game was essentially over late in the 2nd quarter when Earnest McAlpin's 50-yard run put the ball on the 10-yard line. Neely *"raked in a toss from McAlpin in the end zone"* and Foster converted. That 7-0 score held until the final frame. A McAlpin fumble at the Magee 18 was recovered by Tommy Harrell. Jerry McCrory's 4-yard dive made it 7-6. *"At this point, the Trojan defense moved in, putting the rush on Vernon Crotwell, causing his attempt to go wide of the uprights and keeping the Trojans alive by a shoestring for the championship"*. Magee would end up holding for a long drive and punting as the whistle indicated yet another Magee Little Dixie Championship.

McAlpin led rushers with 62 yards while all papers praised the play of a host of Trojans. Morton led in first downs (7-5) but it was Magee holding the ground (121-109) and the air (35-0). The only turnover of the night was the lost Magee fumble to set up Morton's lone tally. It was a clean game as neither team went over 20 yards in penalties.

End-of-year First Team All Little Dixie honors went to Thomas McAlpin, Donnie McNair, Earnest McAlpin and Lamar Carter.

1965 (11-0) LITTLE DIXIE CHAMPIONS

After an inaugural year as head coach with a Little Dixie Championship, Malcolm Nesmith returned to the Trojans as mentor alongside C.B. Hawkins and Orland Everett. The 45-man team again journeyed to Copiah-Lincoln Junior College for pre-season workouts in late August, with Nesmith saying that *"he was encouraged over his prospects for this year, but realized that there was a lot of hard work ahead of them before getting into the season's opener"*. It's not sure when he understood what could be accomplished by this band of scarlet and silver in their 40th year of organized football, but it must have been a pleasant realization.

Voters must have seen the writing on the wall as they picked them tops in the Little Dixie Conference South division by 6 votes over Hazlehurst. They expected them to end up playing Forest Hill for the title but Nesmith still had to replace Earnest and Tom McAlpin in key roles. While he had 15 lettermen back and 13 seniors, he stated that *"they just don't seem to have the desire that we had this time last year and that concerns me a great deal"*.

GAME 1: MAGEE (0-0) vs MORTON (1-0)
MAGEE 13 MORTON 0
September 11, 1965

Back-to-back games with Morton was again on the menu for Magee. Coach Dale Brashier's team was picked 2nd in the Little Dixie North this year, but the coach was concerned. He stated that they were *"weak at tackle, end and guard but should have a better passing game"*. Nesmith told the Magee Touchdown Club that *"This is going to be a tough one. With 21 seniors on their 31-man squad and only having lost 5 boys last year, the Panthers are strong in all positions and are capable of an aggressive passing and running game with plenty of depth in every position"*.

Magee would ensure that there was no repeat of the 1964 opener against Morton that gave them one of their two losses before marching to the LDC title against the same team. The Magee Courier said *"Only once in the night did the Panthers invade Trojan territory and that was a penetration to the 49-yard line…"* Meanwhile, Magee drove 38 yards on their opening possession with Lamar Carter dozing in from the 3 and Royce Foster providing the point-after. Before halftime, Foster found Jim McAlpin for a second touchdown. The point-after *"was thwarted by Stovall"*.

Magee rushed for 129 yards, led in passing (129-0) and first downs (13-9) and intercepted 2 errant Panther throws. The game was originally scheduled for a Friday affair, but Hurricane Betsy changed plans and they held the tilt on Saturday.

GAME 2: MAGEE (1-0) @ SOUTH JONES (UNREPORTED)
MAGEE 40 SOUTH JONES 0
September 17, 1965

The Ellisville, MS Braves were somewhat new. This was their *"first football team"*; though an Ellisville-based high school had played Magee as early as 1947. South Jones was formed as a high school after the merging Ellisville High and Moselle. Their team, like Magee, had 45 players and 11 of them had experience. Norman Roberts said that his Rebel Conference team *"lacks experience, size and speed, but hoped that spirit and hustle can make up for lack of physical attributes"*.

This one got out of hand early, with Magee holding a 20-0 lead after a quarter of play before substitutes came on the field. Thomas McAlpin's 58-yard scamper was followed by Mike Benefield recovering the onside kick. Foster hit Jim McAlpin for another quick TD from the 6-yard line while Wyck Neely *"dashed one over from 13 yards* out" for the third score. Carter then escaped South Jones defenders for a 55-yard tally while Foster hit Neely for a 69-yard strike thereafter. Foster's PAT made it 33-0. In the last frame, Foster hit Thomas McAlpin for 60 yards and a final score.

South Jones had driven to the Magee 1 in the final quarter before a fumble erased the threat. Magee, with no punts, put up 280 rushing yards and 161 passing yards while holding their opponent to 177 rushing.

GAME 3: MAGEE (2-0) vs CRYSTAL SPRINGS (0-3)
MAGEE 28 CRYSTAL SPRINGS 0
September 24, 1965

Coach Wade Alexander's blue and gold were 6-4 the previous season. They had 7 lettermen back but had lost 14 others. Thus, the Tigers were picked 5th in the Little Dixie South pre-season. So far, they had been outscored 45-14 on the season. Nesmith said that the Tigers *"have a fine ball club and a group of big boys who have been faced with some mighty tough competition this season and they can't be judged on the base of their win and loss ratio"*.

The Magee Courier said that the defense *"was as stubborn as a mule"* on the evening. A first-drive march to the 6-yard line produced no points, but on their next possession, Neely rushed 40 yards to paydirt. He added a 62-yard dash in the 2nd quarter *"behind a key block by Tom McAlpin"* while Carter provided a 3rd quarter score from 1 yard away. In the 4th quarter, Foster hit Thomas McAlpin from the 25-yard line for the finale. Foster and Mike Taylor added the points after touchdowns.

The defense held Crystal Springs to 80 rushing and 38 passing yards while rushing for 343 and passed for an amazing 236 yards. Crystal Springs got into Magee territory three times; once on a fumble recovery. Magee led in first downs 11-3. The Trojans did suffer 100 yards of penalties, and due to that, Nesmith and Hawkins *"designed a Bone Head hat which the players who are guilty of the most-costly infractions will have to wear around the clock following the game"*. Four players were the first to sport the new headwear.

GAME 4: MAGEE (3-0) @ PRENTISS (2-2)
MAGEE 14 PRENTISS 6
October 1, 1965

Coach Ken Bramlett's red and white Bulldogs finished 6-3-1 the previous year. Now, with 9 returning lettermen, the were picked 4th in the LDCS. The Clarion-Ledger said that they had an *"explosive backfield this season (and) will have good team speed (and) spirit is high. The only weak spot appears to be lack of experience in the line and possibly lack of depth at tackle"*. They added later that the Dogs had *"good backs and good speed but an inexperienced line may bug the Bulldogs"*.

Nesmith told fans beforehand that *"the Bulldogs will definitely be one of the toughest teams we will face this season. They are aggressive offensively and very strong defensively. Penalties can be a very costly things and we have just got to keep from drawing that much yardage by unnecessary errors"*.

The coach was not kidding as this one was, by far, the toughest battle of the season. The Magee Courier said that Prentiss *"displayed a fast and forceful offense and an alert and stubborn defense from end-to-end"*. Despite 20 yards in penalties, Magee still drove 76 yards for a first-possession TD with Neely doing the honors on a screen pass from Foster. Though driving to the Prentiss 8-yard line before halftime, the march failed and kept intermission 7-0. In the 3rd, Carter and Foster carried the pigskin to the 8-yard line from where Carter went in *"standing up"*. Foster's second PAT was true.

Prentiss punched right back with a drive culminating early in the final quarter. Jim Polk's (or Vic Carter's) 27-yard connection with Louis Grubbs *"deep in the end zone"* would be the first TD allowed this season. Their last drive was moving steadily downfield but gave with the whistle. Magee had 153 rushing yards and 62 passing (2-6) while Prentiss had 114 on the ground and 107 in the air. First downs went to Magee 10-7.

GAME 5: MAGEE (4-0) vs HAZLEHURST (3-1)
MAGEE 46 HAZLEHURST 0
October 8, 1965

Another tough conference game waited against former Coach Charlie Callaway's maroon and white Indians. Though 3-6-1 the previous season, they were marked 2nd in the LDC South this season and called *"the division dark horse"*. *"Hazlehurst presents an unpredictable offense by using a great variety of formations. They have suffered very few losses in the season and will present a threat to the Trojan record"*. Magee had moved to 8th from 9th in the UPI poll.

In the end, it was called *"their best effort of the season"* by The Clarion-Ledger. It took 7 plays before Foster hit Neely for a long scoring scamper. Foster then found Thomas McAlpin for the next from the 3-yard line (Foster PAT) in the same quarter. Magee then put up 21 more points before halftime, including a 1-yarder by Carter and an 80-yard pick-six by Benefield. Neely later picked off a pass to set up a 1-yard Danny Ashley plunge, Steve Creel also had a theft of an Indian pass and the final score came from a 49-yard Neely dash.

First downs were 11-8 in favor of Magee. They had 312 rushing, added 42 passing, and 180 yards in interception returns while holding Hazlehurst to a total of 110 yards. Said Callaway, *"The boys were too tense, too eager to win, that they could make no plays or even move"*.

GAME 6: MAGEE (5-0) @ MONTICELLO (3-3)
MAGEE 36 MONTICELLO 0
October 15, 1965

Though Coach Dawsey's maroon and white lost only a lone letterman, they still went 2-7 the previous season. Voters in the LDC didn't expect it to improve despite the experience returning, and picked them last in the LDC South. Ironically, they did better against Magee than the team picked 2nd in the division. This marked the last LDC South competition before meeting Mendenhall in the crucial season-closer.

Magee held a 13-0 lead after a quarter and 20-0 advantage at halftime. Three minutes in, Carter was into the end zone from the 2-yard line while Foster hit Neely from the 26-yard line later. Foster and Jock Allen connected in the next frame from the 15 while Taylor notched the PAT. Other details are hard to comprehend, but Foster did add a 20-yard FG to finalize scoring. Carter was later credited with 109 rushing yards.

Dawsey said afterwards *"It's tough to play a team their caliber. I'm glad that no one was hurt"*. The Lawrence County Press said that *"Well, as far as I'm concerned, Magee is the most powerful football team that I have ever seen. I was impressed by their quietness when they arrived and after the game. Old Chinese proverb say, 'he who walks softly carries a big stick'. I wonder what they carried? In fact, I was happy to see them miss a few extra point conversions. It proved they were human"*.

GAME 7: MAGEE (6-0) vs PETAL (?-1)
MAGEE 28 PETAL 0
October 22, 1965: HOMECOMING

Magee had moved to 7th in the UPI poll, but like other years, they appeared better than most above them. Four of the teams had tie games while three of them (Columbus, Greenville and Hattiesburg) had losses. As for Petal, Nesmith said that *"Petal is a passing team, has a QB with two years of successful experience and heavy linemen"*. Steve Mangum suffered a *"badly sprained ankle"* in the Prentiss game and was likely out.

Coach Ed Walker remembered the 28-0 defeat from 1964. He called Foster *"a capable passer as he mixes the plays"*. Ironically, this game would match the last tilt. But, Foster would be responsible for throwing all four touchdowns. Jim McAlpin's second-quarter fumble recovery at the 28-yard line led two plays later to Foster finding Allen from the 18. Foster then hit Neely from 26 yards that, with Foster PATs, finished the first half 14-0. His 3rd quarter throw was from 23 yards to Jim McAlpin while his last came in the final quarter on a 29-yard toss to Thomas McAlpin.

Petal's only threats came via two missed FG attempts. Magee led in rushing (177 yards) and passing (166 yards) versus 103 rushing and 33 passing. First downs were also in favor of the Trojans 10-4. Mendenhall's surprising loss to Hazlehurst that night was welcome news to Magee to increase the odds of heading back for another LDC title. Still, they would have to beat the Tigers to claim bragging rights.

GAME 8: MAGEE (7-0) @ WARREN CENTRAL (UNREPORTED)
MAGEE 28 WARREN CENTRAL 0
October 28, 1965

Warren Central was a newly-formed school after consolidation in Vicksburg. Originally scheduled for Friday, it was moved to Thursday on the Saint Aloysius field as they could not play on the local turf. The trip to Warren County would bring up memories of the 1964 trip to Warren County where Magee notched their second defeat of the year against Saint Al. The Magee Courier stated that *"spectators literally got the living daylights scared out of them"* as it *"looked like it had come pay day for the Trojans…"*

Warren Central took the opening kick on a drive to the Trojan 2 before the defense put up a solid goal-line stand. In fact, the Vikings stayed in Magee territory the entire first half, but each time the defense would repeal the threat. The Trojans, meanwhile, had only a lone entry across the midfield stripe. A different Trojan team came out of the lockers for the 3rd quarter.

Thomas McAlpin made a statement by taking the opening kick 85 yards *"up the middle"* to paydirt. Neely then picked off a Viking pass and returned it 57 (or 43) yards for another tally.

Like the 3rd quarter, Magee scored on the opening play of the final frame on a Carter plunge from 6-yard line *"without being touched"*. With 1:00 left in the game, Foster *"went up the middle, cut to the left sideline and split two defenders on the goal line"* for the last touchdown. He also added all four extra points. Benefield had joined Mangum on the sidelines due to a knee injury.

Magee put up 288 yards of offense (32 passing) while Warren Central had 117 markers (80 in the air). They also led in first downs 13-6. The Vicksburg Evening Post said that *"The Little Dixie powerhouse was fought to a draw in the first two quarters, but the second half followed the form charts all the way with Magee finally living up to its press clippings"*.

GAME 9: MAGEE (8-0) vs SAINT ALOYSIUS (7-0)
MAGEE 13 SAINT ALOYSIUS 0
November 5, 1965

Saint Al was introducing a new head coach (Elmo Broussard) and had lost 13 of 19 lettermen. Still, they sat undefeated by game day and had already upset the Magee cart in 1964. The Vicksburg Evening Post said that *"The defending Little Dixie champs will be ready. We believe the Flashes will go all-out, too. They realize what's riding on the outcome and it's not altogether just an undefeated, untied season"*. Said Broussard, *"We're just going to do the best we can and if the boys will give ... 100% effort like they have done all season, that's all we can ask"*.

Flash fumbles in what Phil Maclin called *"a backyard mud puddle"* started immediately. Eddie Ray lost the handle on the first drive for a loss, suffered a penalty, and lost the ball a couple of other times before Magee recovered at the Flash 4. It took 4 plays before Carter dove in from the 2 and Foster made it 7-0. Foster then capped a second half 62-yard drive with a 2-yard plunge. Ray was picked off later, received more penalties to move them back, Saint Al recovered a Foster fumble, but dropped it right back to Magee. The Trojans then fumbled again, but Saint Al could get only to the 3-yard line before the whistle.

The Vicksburg Evening Post said that the game was *"played on a field standing several inches deep in water in many places"*. Said Broussard, *"I am truly proud of the entire squad for their fine spirit, hustle and determination this season. It has been one of my finest hours"*. Saint Al went on to accept the bid to the Mississippi Bowl; a game they lost to Forest Hill 7-6.

GAME 10: MAGEE (9-0) @ MENDENHALL (8-1)
MAGEE 20 MENDENHALL 0
November 12, 1965

Although Troy Greer's Tigers were picked 3rd in the LDC South after losing 11 lettermen, they still had 7 returning from a 7-2-1 campaign. The Clarion-Ledger said that the black and gold *"lost so heavily to graduation that the Tigs will be rebuilding this year"*. But as had been the case almost without exception, the two teams would wrap up the season with a trip to the Little Dixie championship on the line. Canton had already solidified their spot in the contest.

The Simpson County News called Magee *"heavy favorites"* but said that in this game, *"the dope bucket can be kicked over"*. A prime example came the previous year when Mendenhall entered the fray as the favorite only to lose to the Trojans. Mendy opened with a bang, taking the first possession as far as the Trojan 15-yard line before giving way. After holding, they inadvertently touched the ensuing punt to give Magee the ball inside the 50. It took 9 plays before Carter banged in from the 2-yard line and Foster converted.

Carter then picked off a Mendenhall pass and Magee used 5 plays to score again. A long Foster pass to Neely put the ball at the 3-yard line and Carter capitalized on a 1-yard plunge. Foster's toe made it 14-0. After recovering another Tiger fumble, Magee moved quickly to the Tiger 1-yard line but failed to cross before the halftime whistle. The 3rd quarter was a defensive battle, but early in the last quarter, Tom McAlpin *"went over right tackle and cut back to the sidelines and raced 48 yards for the final score of the game"*. Mendenhall made their second entry into Magee territory on their last drive, but time was not on their side.

Carter rushed for 97 yards while Tom McAlpin added 63 yards. Magee led in first downs (11-7), rushing (191-82) and passing (66-47). The Trojans picked off one ball (Neely) and recovered two fumbles. They had no turnovers themselves.

GAME 11: MAGEE (10-0) vs CANTON (8-2)
MAGEE 27 CANTON 0
November 19, 1965: CRYSTAL SPRINGS, MS

Magee, though undefeated with just 6 points allowed against them, was still just 8th in the UPI poll. Murrah was 9-0 and held the top spot, but each team after had a blemished record. Four teams (Biloxi, Jackson Central, McComb and Pascagoula) even had 2 losses on the season. It was apparent that the UPI poll continued their yearly streak of having more unknowledgeable voters than otherwise.

That was of no concern. What was of utmost importance was Billy Cooper's black and gold Tigers. They had gone a woeful 3-7 the previous year but did return 17 letter-winners. Voters expected them to be better and placed them 3rd in the Little Dixie South. Now, the Madison County team could make a statement against powerful Magee. The Clarion-Ledger called it a *"dream game"* that matched *"two of the strongest prep squads in Mississippi grid circles"*.

The Trojans' first score came late in the opening frame on a 5-yard Foster throw to Jim McAlpin. Neely uncharacteristically fumbled a punt to Mickey George, but the defense held and got the ball back at the 22-yard line. Twelve plays later, Carter plunged in from the 3-yard line and Foster's kick put halftime 13-0. Canton drove to the Magee 4 in the 3rd quarter but could not advance. Magee then drove 95 yards to paydirt with Foster's 37-yard connection with Tom McAlpin *"all alone in the right flat"*. Foster converted the point-after.

The final touchdown on the season came in the 4th quarter when a host of Trojans caused Lane Cook to fumble the ball at the 16-yard line. Steve Kennedy recovered for the Magee touchdown and Foster brought an end to the season. It may have been different as Magee was preparing to cross again from the 17-yard line as time expired. Magee dominated in first downs (12-6), rushing (112-28) and passing (106-57).

All-State awards were led by First Team nominee Lamar "Bubba" Carter and Honorable Mention Jim McAlpin. In the LDC, Carter was named Most Outstanding Back while McAlpin was Most Outstanding Lineman. Other First Team All-Little Dixie members were Steve Mangum, Wyck Neely, Mike Benefield, Kelly Herrington, Larry Creel and Thomas McAlpin. Honorable Mentions included Jock Allen, Paul Hughes and Royce Foster. Malcolm Nesmith was voted as Coach of the Year by the Mississippi Sportscasters Organization.

1966 (9-1) LITTLE DIXIE RUNNER-UP

Third-year Coach Malcolm Nesmith came into the 1966 season picked by his peers as front-runner for the Little Dixie Conference title. Still, he thought there was work to be done before that could happen. *"We have a lack of experience due to the loss of 14 lettermen. This will be a problem at several positions, especially in the interior line"*. The Trojans had amassed a 60-3-1 record in the 1960s and were looking to continue their domination in the LDC. Paul Davis, MSU head coach, addressed the Magee Touchdown Club on August 16th to kick off the season.

GAME 1: MAGEE (0-0) @ MORTON (0-1)
MAGEE 26 MORTON 6
September 9, 1966

New head man Reggie Robertson's Panthers were decimated by graduation. As such, voters had Morton picked 5th in the Little Dixie South. They had not fared well in their opener, dropping a 39-13 decision to Newton. The Magee Courier said that *"the Panthers will be fighting back viciously to get into the win column"*.

Four fumbles in the opening frame kept the game scoreless, but Chuck Akers broke the drought in the 2nd quarter to make it 6-0. One more touchdown before the half, followed by Royce Foster's PAT sent the teams to the locker 13-0. Magee continued to press in the 3rd when Wyck Neely broke away around his right end for a 65-yard scoring scamper. With reserves in play, Lannie Stewart notched the next score on a 1-yard run and Mike Taylor booted the PAT. Morton avoided the shutout with just :35 remaining when Tommie Harrell *"plunged across"*.

GAME 2: MAGEE (1-0) vs SOUTH JONES (UNREPORTED)
MAGEE 33 SOUTH JONES 13
September 16, 1966

In Ellisville, Coach Norman Roberts had the services of 9 senior lettermen back from a 5-5 campaign. Magee was now ranked 10th in the UPI poll and they made an early statement in their first home tilt. They started the game with a 53-yard march powered largely by Neely and Akers runs. "*With South Jones zeroed in on the two running backs, Foster finessed them off their feet as he rolled out to the right to go across standing up*" and then added the point-after.

Neely added another in the frame on a 26-yard end-run and Foster converted. In the 2nd, Foster hit Neely from the 43-yard line to make it 20-0. With :05 left before intermission, South Jones found paydirt on a 16-yard Sanford toss to Kyzar and Powell's conversion. The visitors appeared game to start the 3rd by blocking a Trojan punt and returning for a score. But Neely was again to cross the goal before the quarter ended on a 42-yard escape. Foster added the last in the final frame when he hit Ronnie Garner from the 5-yard line. Taylor's point-after was true.

The Clarion-Ledger noted that "*Jim McAlpin was outstanding on defense for the Trojans*".

GAME 3: MAGEE (2-0) @ CRYSTAL SPRINGS (0-3)
MAGEE 32 CRYSTAL SPRINGS 13
September 23, 1966

This game would be important as it was a divisional contest. Wade Alexander and his Tigers were picked 5th in the South and had yet to break into the win column according to one report. Nesmith gave a different indication on game week when he said "*Big Crystal is a tough one. Forest Hill will attest to that after bowing to them in their first game*".

Neely brought Trojan fans to their feet when he took the opening kickoff 90 yards to paydirt and Foster converted. To close the quarter, Garner forced a punt fumble that was recovered by McAlpin and Steve Kennedy. Foster then found Don Beatty from 15 yards away to make it 13-0. "*The Tigers then suffered an acute attack of 'fumbleitis' as a result of an overdose of Trojan tonic*". Beatty recovered a pair of those fumbles; one to set up a 4-yard Akers plunge.

Back came Crystal Springs with a 95-yard kick return by Tim Knight and Nelson PAT that put the game 19-7 at the half. Magee drove 76 yards in the 3rd quarter with Foster hitting Garner for the touchdown and nailing the point-after. While Knight later picked off a Foster throw, Neely returned the favor by intercepting Bob Knight. Akers capitalized with an 11-yard scoring run. Unbelievably, Crystal Springs bested their previous effort when Bob Knight took the ensuing kickoff 98 yards to the end zone.

First downs (14-7 or 15-9) went to Magee. Foster threw for 98 yards and the ground game churned out 260 (or 273) markers. In all, Crystal Springs suffered 5 turnovers.

GAME 4: MAGEE (3-0) vs PRENTISS (3-0)
MAGEE 20 PRENTISS 6
September 30, 1966

Tommy Alexander's 15 Bulldog letter-winners included "*some big, tough linemen and prospects are bright for a successful season*". Though 5-5 the previous year and picked only 4th in the LDCS, the big squad reportedly sat undefeated as they rolled into Simpson County.

The visitors were first into the end zone in a game called "*rain-soaked*" when Lewis Grubbs dashed 36 yards for the score. That 6-0 score surprisingly held until the 3rd quarter when Neely raced in from the 25-yard line to cap a march of 60 yards. Now in the final moments and with the score 6-6, Akers gave Magee all they would need on a 35-yard run. The icing on the cake came shortly after as Magee picked off a desperation pass and took it to the 1-yard line. Foster got in from there.

GAME 5: MAGEE (4-0) @ HAZLEHURST (4-1)
MAGEE 13 HAZLEHURST 7
October 7, 1966

Charlie Callaway, picked 3rd in the LDCS, would love nothing more than to beat his old team. The Magee Courier said that "*Callaway's bag of tricks has been stacked for this game and he will dig just as deep as necessary…*" The Trojans once again found themselves in a weight disadvantage, but it had thus far not seemed to be an issue.

After a lost fumble followed by a deep drive into Indian territory, the home team made it interesting when Billy Wyatt raced 98 yards to paydirt and Ray Bridges converted. Later, a Magee pass was picked off by Charlie Callaway to set up a drive to the Trojan 6-yard line. But, an Indian fumble killed the effort. Despite a Neely interception, halftime still sat in favor of Hazlehurst

7-0. Now in the 4th, Neely found the end zone via a pass from Foster. The crucial PAT was blocked by Skip Petrich.

Magee put the game away with just 2:00 remaining when Foster found Jim McAlpin from the 35 and then notched the point-after. Akers iced things away afterwards by picking off a Callaway throw. First downs (11-8) went to the Indians as did rushing (209-89). Passing was in favor of the visitors 117-16.

GAME 6: MAGEE (5-0) vs MONTICELLO (0-6)
MAGEE 28 MONTICELLO 0
October 13, 1966: HOMECOMING

The Red Devils had a new coach leading them into 1966. Harold Morris was in no enviable position, having lost 19 lettermen and returning only seven. Voters understandably had them picked last in the LDCS and they sat winless by kickoff. The Enterprise Journal said that *"Monticello will step from the frying pan into the fire by going to Magee"* and picked the Trojans 40-13.

Akers broke the game open early when he escaped for a 58-yard touchdown on the first play. Ronnie Duhon got his first TD of the season afterwards on a 1-yard plunge. The last two scores were provided by Akers (6 yards) and Foster (45 yards). Taylor booted 3 extra points while Foster provided the last.

GAME 7: MAGEE (6-0) vs WARREN CENTRAL (0-?)
MAGEE 35 WARREN CENTRAL 0
October 28, 1966

Magee used their open date to prepare for the red and white Vikings. The Vicksburg team, led by Coach Donald Oakes, was less than impressive the previous year, going 3-8. On top of that, they had lost 23 lettermen and returned only 3 experienced players. The Vicksburg Evening Post noted that Magee led 21-0 after the initial quarter and added touchdowns in the 2nd and 4th periods. Akers had scoring runs of 40 and 10 yards while Foster hit Neely (18 yards) and Terrell Stubbs (23 yards) for the others.

Warren Central's only glimmer came in the 2nd quarter after Robin Stroud's interception put them in FG range. But, Ernest Myer's 29-yard attempt was no good. Magee led 16-7 in first downs.

GAME 8: MAGEE (7-0) @ SAINT ALOYSIUS (2-4-1)
MAGEE 19 SAINT ALOYSIUS 0
November 4, 1966

Anyone expecting a 7-2 repeat season for Saint Al would be in for disappointment by season's end. Gone were Eddie Ray, Tom Balzli, and others to graduation. Additionally, the Flashes lost three more players as a result of moves. That left 13 lettermen on the squad. Said Coach Elmo Broussard, *"We just haven't got that 'zip' we had last year, but I'm hoping it will come around ... we'll just have to take things as they come and hope for the best."*

Because of 13 Flash injuries, The Vicksburg Evening Post predicted a 20-13 loss. Magee opened the game with the kickoff, but fumbled it to Saint Al. Three plays later, however, a Mike Booth pass was picked off by Don Beatty and taken to midfield. Saint Al later moved to the Trojan 34, but again Booth was intercepted; this time by Neely. Magee dented the scoreboard for the first time in the 2nd quarter when Akers converted a 3rd down at the 5-yard line. He was hit hard as he crossed the goal and fumbled, but officials ruled that he had gotten over the line. Foster made it 7-0. The Flashes desperately tried to score before halftime but could get only to the Magee 19.

Akers hit the board again in the 3rd quarter on a 31-yard run to finish a 78-yard march. Then, a Booth fumble was picked up by Bob Everett and taken 25 yards to paydirt. Not giving up, Saint Al used a fumble recovery and a pass interference call to get to within inches of the goal. But Booth's fumble was recovered by Magee to end the game.

GAME 9: MAGEE (8-0) vs MENDENHALL (8-1)
MAGEE 14 MENDENHALL 0
November 12, 1966

As always, this end-of-the-regular-season rivalry was for more than just bragging rights. Mendenhall, under Coach Troy Greer, could throw the entire Little Dixie South into turmoil with a win. That would produce a three-way tie and the conference executive committee would be forced to pick the winner. Magee had beaten Prentiss, but the Bulldogs had bested the Tigers 7-6. To add to the drama, the game would be pushed back to Saturday due to rain.

On a field still wet from days of downfall, Mendy garnered the first golden opportunity when Randy Reed picked off an errant Trojan throw. However, they fumbled it back to Magee deep in their territory to set up a 2-yard Foster dive and his PAT. The home team picked off another Tiger throw in the 2nd quarter to thwart a drive while McAlpin also fell on a dropped punt. Neither would produce points. Mendy opened the 3rd with a drive to the Trojan 31 but fumbled the ball away. Magee generously did the same with Thomas Jones falling on the loose pigskin.

Magee later picked off a throw but promptly gave it back in the same manner to Charlie Powell. They marched all the way to the Magee 11-yard line but could not get into the end zone. Akers, however, would cross the goal afterwards when he *"went between his left tackle and end, pulled away from three Tigers and went down the west sidelines for the final Magee touchdown"*. Akers rushed for 146 yards on the evening while Neely pitched in 61.

First downs (11-10) and passing (98-29) went to Mendenhall while Magee led the ground game 231-58.

GAME 10: MAGEE (9-0) vs BRANDON (8-2)
MAGEE 7 BRANDON 12
November 18, 1966: LITTLE DIXIE CHAMPIONSHSIP

Louis Strickland returned for his 8th overall season as mentor of the Bulldogs. The Clarion-Ledger noted before the season that his squad *"could be rugged this season; even after losing heavily at graduation. The Bulldogs have a nucleus of 16 seniors who want to play football"*. The Bulldogs were rated 3rd-best in the Little Dixie North division and The Vicksburg Evening Post called the team *"reported with a solid foundation with 10 lettermen returning and 9 of the veterans are seniors"*.

The contest, one that could give Magee yet another LDC crown, would be played at Magee due to their win of a coin-flip. The Magee Courier noted that *"those of us who used to oppose the boys from Rankin County will agree that they demand respect on the gridiron"*. Both coaches were also respectful. Said Nesmith, *"Brandon has a real fine ball club ... They are a real tough foe for our kids and I look for a hard-fought, crowd-pleasing game"*. Added Strickland, *"Magee has a big, strong team. Our boys welcome the challenge and they know they are going to have to put out in order to win. We will try to match our power with theirs and it should really be a fine ball game"*.

The opening period ended scoreless, but Brandon put a scare into the Trojans when a Jim McBrayer punt *"glanced off a Magee player and was promptly recovered by Richard Newman"*. Magee's defense held. In the 2nd, the home team spurred the crowd when Neely *"broke through his own right tackle and headed for the left sideline ... for the score"*. That 87-yarder, plus the PAT by Foster, made it 7-0 with 3:30 left. As the halftime horn wailed, David Tigrett spotted Newman from the 16. Fortunately, he got only as far as the 1-yard line.

Brandon took control of the second half starting with their first drive. The 67-yard march was capped by a 12-yard Tigrett run. Carl Swilley's kick *"was just wide to the right"*. The Dogs then took advantage of a Buster McVey fumble after being *"hit hard by a host of Brandon linemen"*, that was recovered by Swilley. Seven plays later, Robbie McLeod *"burst off tackle"* for the 4-yard TD and final points of the game. Brandon led all in stats: rushing (157-126), passing (64-3), first downs (12-3), penalties (0-50) and fumbles (0-2). It was a disappointing end to such a wonderful season.

All Little Dixie honors included a host of Trojans. First Team members included Jim McAlpin, Chuck Akers, Steve Kennedy, and Steve Creel. Second Team members included Greg Hall, Gary Parker, Billy Everett and Wyck Neely. Don Beatty and Royce Foster were selected as Honorable Mentions. McAlpin was again Most Outstanding Lineman.

1967 (8-3) LITTLE DIXIE CHAMPIONS

Voters had once again picked Coach Malcolm Nesmith's Trojans as tops in the Little Dixie South division. But, Nesmith had concerns. *"Injuries are killing us. We had had a rash of injuries that has hampered our practice sessions and we still have two boys sidelined"*. He was also worried about his depth. *"We lost some good boys from last year's squad and our major trouble spots are finding capable replacements at halfback, QB and end"*. Captains for the season were Ronnie Garner and Steve Kennedy.

GAME 1: MAGEE (0-0) @ COLUMBIA (0-0)
MAGEE 19 COLUMBIA 0
September 8, 1967

The Big Eight Wildcats under second-year Coach Jerry Wilkinson were 3-6 the previous season. They did, however, return 9 regulars and prospects were bright. Said Wilkinson, *"We're better now than last year at this time and are shooting for a better mark…"* He expanded his thoughts on the team's weaknesses. One report said that *"lack of depth, inexperience on the squad and the lack to speed are his biggest handicaps"*. The Clarion-Ledger said that this contest *"could go a long way toward determining just how rugged the always-rugged Trojans are going to be this autumn"*.

After losing an opening-possession fumble, the defense stood tall and a failed Cat FG kept the game scoreless. It took only four plays to move 80 yards on their next possession. Chuck Akers raced 60 yards to set up a Tommy Meador 4-yard scoring run and Mike Taylor PAT. Though Columbia once again drove deep into Magee territory, the defense again stood tall. The next Trojan touchdown looked similar to the first. Solid Akers runs set up Meador's 4-yard dash. A Columbia fumble, their third of the night, led to the last score. Like the others, Akers runs allowed Meador a 3-yard tally.

"The entire Magee defensive line looked good and Mike Taylor and Ronnie Garner, in the defensive secondary, were in on many tackles. Offensively it was a case of too much Akers".

GAME 2: MAGEE (1-0) vs MORTON (1-0)
MAGEE 0 MORTON 7
September 15, 1967

Once perineal power Morton had posted a miserable 2-7-1 record in 1966. Coach Reggie Robertson lost 8 lettermen but did return 12 others. The Clarion-Ledger called the blue and gold a possible *"dark horse"*. It was evident from the start that this contest would be a slugfest.

"The entire first half was spent deep in Magee's territory, with the Magee defensive until throwing Morton back three times within the 10-yard line". A Trojan fumble inside the 10-yard line early was given back the same way. Again Magee fumbled, but the defense held. Morton then picked off a pass in the 2nd quarter and drove to the 3-yard line before Kennedy caused a fumble that was recovered by Taylor. It appeared destined for a tie, but with :04 left, David Roberts picked off a Magee pass and raced 45 yards to paydirt. Ricky Rector's PAT iced the cake.

GAME 3: MAGEE (1-1) @ SOUTH JONES (1-0-1)
MAGEE 0 SOUTH JONES 7
September 22, 1967

Coach Tuffy Roberts' Braves from Ellisville had gone down in defeat to Magee two years in a row. It had been since 1956 that Magee had opened a football season with a 1-2 record, so expectations were high for a Trojan win. However, Magee would find themselves on the short end of back-to-back 7-0 losses.

That score came in the opening frame when David Cooley found Emmitt Lewis from the 16-yard line for a touchdown. *"From that point on, the game turned into a defensive battle with neither team able to score"*. Magee led on the ground (204-68) while South Jones held the air (35-11). The only turnover came from an intercepted Magee throw.

GAME 4: MAGEE (1-2) vs CRYSTAL SPRINGS (2-1)
MAGEE 14 CRYSTAL SPRINGS 6
September 29, 1967

The gold and blue under Leon Canoy went 7-3 on the previous campaign. They lost 10 lettermen and returned 6 for this year's edition of Tiger football. Said Nesmith, *"Speed is the key to the Crystal Springs team. They have two of the fastest boys in the conference in Bob and Tim Knight, and their line is big and fast"*. Meanwhile in Simpson County, the Trojans were still enduring a rash of injuries. Nesmith mentioned at least four players who would not be available for the contest. *"We have had so much trouble with injuries that our state of training is not as good now as it was at the time of our pre-season scrimmage"*.

True to form, Bob Knight opened scoring in the first quarter when he picked up a Trojan fumble and darted 75 yards to the end zone for a 6-0 lead. But the home team *"electrified the highly-partisan Magee crowd with a touchdown drive the first time they handled the ball following the second half kickoff"*. The only notation of the pair of Magee scores said that it was Akers who crossed for the first touchdown (2 yards) while Donald Barrett recovered a fumble for the last. Taylor provided both extra points.

The Copiah County paper reported Magee with 11 fumbles on the evening. Magee led in first downs (12-4).

GAME 5: MAGEE (2-2) @ PRENTISS (3-0)
MAGEE 0 PRENTISS 20
October 6, 1967

An admirable 9-2 record with 9 lettermen returning put Tommy Alexander's team one that would not be as easy as the previous seven-straight victories. He had lost 14 letter-winners due to graduation, but they were undefeated while Magee was in an unusual break-even period after four contests. The loss would mark the first time the Trojans suffered 3 losses in a year since Charlie Callaway's team went 5-5 in 1958.

The Magee Courier said *"Mix a rock-ribbed defense with a fast, hard-charging running offense, stir in a generous helping of Lewis Grubbs add a pinch of piping-hot on the Prentiss gridiron and you have the recipe for defeating the Magee Trojans"*. Grubbs opened scoring in the 2nd quarter with a 25-yard race to paydirt that, along with Johnny Stamps' conversion, made it 7-0. John Carter stopped the next drive with an interception at the Magee 15 to keep intermission the same score.

In the 3rd quarter, they drove 77 yards in 12 plays with Johnny Green (or Talsie Dearman) *"rolling over"* from the 4-yard line and Stamps converting. Their final march went 51 yards with Grubbs *"doing most of the damage, then hit paydirt in 5 plays"* from the 3-yard line. The same paper said *"Ronnie Garner did yeoman-like work in the defensive secondary and John Carter helped the cause with two key interceptions. Steve Kennedy, Lannie Stewart and Donald Barrett looked best in the line"*.

Prentiss controlled first downs (13-8) and rushing (257-78) while Magee was best in the air (34-9). Both teams suffered a pair of interceptions.

GAME 6: MAGEE (2-3) vs HAZLEHURST (2-3)
MAGEE 18 HAZLEHURST 6
October 13, 1967: HOMECOMING

Familiar Charlie Callaway was now replaced by Emmett Smith as Indian mentor. They went 6-4 in Callaway's last season and had lost 11 lettermen with only 4 back. At kickoff, the team that had lost ten-straight since 1956 against Magee was under the .500 mark thus far.

In front of alums for Homecoming, Akers *"ran wild"*. In the 2nd quarter, Magee went 48 yards with Akers bulldozing in from the 3-yard line. Magee then recovered a fumble at the Trojan 38 and Akers eventually made it count from the 5-yard line. Now in the final frame, Akers added the last touchdown to cap scoring. Hazlehurst's only points came in the second half from Frank Ford.

GAME 7: MAGEE (3-3) @ MONTICELLO (2-4)
MAGEE 26 MONTICELLO 14
October 20, 1967

The Red Devils under Coach Harold Morris were already better than their 1-9 record from the previous year, but they had 11 letter-winners back. Still, and despite a 2-4 record, The Magee Courier said it was a game where the Trojans *"shocked"* the home team. The win would be significant in that Prentiss went down to Crystal Springs to vault Magee into the driver's seat (3-1) in the LDC South.

Magee drove 80 yards in the opening frame. Akers ran for 65 yards to the Monticello 15-yard line. Garner thought he had finished the effort from there but a penalty called it back. Akers still managed to steadily drive into paydirt from the 4-yard line. Monticello responded and took the lead when Randy Foster hit Mike Hearn from midfield. Before the half, Akers got in again from the 8-yard line. In the second half, both teams hit paydirt. Akers did the trick again from the 3 while Monticello's last came from a Foster pick-six of 50 yards. One Trojan tally is unreported.

GAME 8: MAGEE (4-3) vs CANTON (4-3)
MAGEE 21 CANTON 6
November 3, 1967

The Trojans enjoyed an off-week to recuperate an ailing and injured team. Their opponent would be at home against Wesley Reed's Canton squad coming off a 6-4 season. They lost a whopping 14 players while bringing back 8. The voters had the Tigers 3rd in the LDC South. The Magee Courier noted that Canton was "*dangerous*" but that the Trojans were now at "*full strength for the first time since the beginning of the season*" and "*in the best physical condition*" since pre-season. Said Nesmith, "*They throw the ball about 40% of the time and run it the other 60%. Their backs are all capable boys and they do not have to depend on any one man*".

The head Trojan went on to say that "*They run the same plays from many different formations and it gives each play a different look. They keep you continually off-balance. We have Carter back at QB and we are going to throw the ball more to keep the defense from messing up on us*". Magee was still in the hunt for the LDC South chase with Prentiss, Crystal Springs and Mendenhall.

Though it was near-freezing, The Magee Courier said that the Trojans "*were as hot as a firecracker*". Though details are sketchy, it was again Akers with the three Magee touchdowns. His first came on a 5-yarder along with Taylor's kick. The Panthers scored in the next frame when Charles Weems hit Hank Joyner from 25 yards to make it 7-6. In the 3rd quarter, Akers moved in from the 3-yard line and added his last on a 36-yard scamper in the final period. Taylor was true on both PATs.

GAME 9: MAGEE (5-3) vs SAINT ALOYSIUS (4-1-2)
MAGEE 14 SAINT ALOYSIUS 6
November 10, 1967

Coach Elmo Broussard's Flashes now visited Magee to continue a series that had been hard-fought and close going back to 1929. The Vicksburg Evening Post picked Magee in another tight game 7-6. An early Flash march moved to the Trojan 20 before being stopped. A fumble later to Magee allowed them to move to the 5-yard line, but the Saint Al defense stopped the approach. In the 3rd and after a series of punts, Tommy Ray put the Flashes up on a 75-yard dash.

But Magee responded on the ensuing drive as Magee crossed the stripe thanks to a 2-yard pass and Taylor PAT. In the 4th, Magee moved to just inches from the goal, but fumbled to Jimmy Salmon in the end zone. Eventually, Akers put up an insurance touchdown from the 3-yard line with just minutes left to play. Ray said of Akers, "*He's not that fast or hard to bring down, but he's got some moves. He's hard to catch*".

GAME 10: MAGEE (6-3) @ MENDENHALL (3-3-2)
MAGEE 33 MENDENHALL 0
November 17, 1967

Coach Ralph Sanders' 8-2 Tigers had 11 returners, but this one would be like every game played for a decade in that there was much more on the line than just bragging rights. Magee and Crystal Springs were tied at 3-1 in the division. So, a Magee loss could mean a multitude of outcomes; none of which were advantageous to the 6-3 Trojans. Mendy and Prentiss were both 2-1-1. However, Magee had beaten Crystal Springs earlier in the year, so all they needed was a win to go once again to the championship. Both teams were hampered by starters out for the game.

In the end, in front of a capacity crowd and "*amid all the excitement and anticipation which always accompanies this high-spirited meeting*", it wouldn't be close. And, it would give Magee their sixth-straight Little Dixie championship tilt. Akers opened scoring from the 10-yard line "*around right end with big Steve Kennedy clearing the way with a key block to send him across standing up*". Garner got in from the 4-yard line in the 2nd quarter and Taylor made it 13-0. Later, Butch McKenzie's sack set up Garner's next TD from inside the 6-yard line and Taylor made intermission 20-0.

Akers drove in from the 7 after halftime following a Jerry Sturm interception. Finally, Ricky Lane and Ronnie Cockrell took turns plowing through the Mendy line to set up a Cockrell 4-yarder. The paper noted too many "*standouts*" for Magee to mention. "*Akers gained (182 yards), more than four-times as much yardage as all the Tigers on rushing plays"*. First downs (15-7) and rushing (302-41) went to Magee while the Tigers held serve in the air (91-14).

GAME 11: MAGEE (7-3) vs FOREST HILL (9-0-1)
MAGEE 21 FOREST HILL 14
November 23, 1967

These same two teams met for the 1962 Little Dixie championship, with Magee coming out on top 26-6. Coach Billy Templeton had done well in the Jackson area; going 8-2 the previous season and starting the year with 12 returning letter-winners. They clearly had to be the favorites this time with only a tie to blemish their record (Morton 20-20). But Magee could brag of the same thing or better in 1966 when they were undefeated to a Brandon team that beat them for the title. Forest Hill had last won a conference championship in 1954 while Magee was after their sixth LDC ring.

Akers, with 84 points and 14 touchdowns, worried Templeton. *"(He) is a really tough, hard-nosed running back. He doesn't have great speed, but he does have great moves. I respect their team and I look for a real good game on the part of both clubs"*. Nesmith was respectful and *"impressed with their balance, both offensively and defensively"*.

As was Templeton's expectation, Akers was the workhorse on the evening; scoring all three Magee touchdowns. His runs of 77, 69 and 4 yards all ended in the end zone and Taylor was true on all conversions. Akers first scored early in the 2nd to make halftime 7-0. Forest Hill answered on a 52-yard Rodney Lingle strike to George Morris. Akers then rattled off his 69-yarder while Forest Hill responded in the final frame on a 58-yard Lingle connection with James Simms. Garner then picked off a later Forest Hill throw to set up Akers' last touchdown. Ray Wright notched both PATs for the eventual runner-up.

Magee was behind in first downs (8-6) and passing (209-3) but rushing went their way (282-30). Magee had a pair of interceptions to seal the title. The Magee Courier said that *"Teams of the past have been fortified with more weight, more depth and a larger number of veteran returnees than was the team of 1967. But no team of any year has ever been known to offset their inadequacies with greater desire than the ... squad that has just emerged Little Dixie champions"*.

All LDC players from Magee include Steve Kennedy and Chuck Akers. Honorable Mentions went to Ronnie Garner and Mike Taylor. Internal awards included to Akers (Best Blocker) and Ronnie Cockrell (Best Sportsmanship).

1968 (7-3)

Malcolm Nesmith, now in his fifth season at Magee, opened practices on August 12th with *"the toughest schedule since (he's) been head coach"*. Former Clinton assistant Jerry Sullivan was now on the staff alongside Orland Everett. There were a few less players for 1968 but 8 starters were back along with 13 lettermen. It would be the first year in quite a while that the Trojans were not expected to repeat as Little Dixie South champions; instead picked second to Prentiss.

The Clarion-Ledger though Magee would be *"counting heavily on its experienced line to offset the lack of experience in the backfield"*. Individual positions were under evaluation by the coaches leading up to kickoff. Jerry Sullivan though that the line had *"the size and strength and could become a good line if they are willing to develop quickness and learn fundamentals as well as learning their assignments"*.

The same paper said later that *"There aren't any established stars in the lineup, but Coach Malcolm Nesmith has been known to produce a top-notch lineup over the years. The Trojans could very well claim it all again this time"*.

GAME 1: MAGEE (0-0) @ MORTON (1-0)
MAGEE 6 MORTON 7
September 13, 1968

Morton, under Coach Reggie Robertson, gave the Trojans a setback in 1967 by a last-play 7-0 score en-route to an 8-1-1 campaign. This year, with four starters and twelve lettermen back, the Panthers were picked in a tie with Canton for LDC North bragging rights. They opened well the week before with a 33-7 whipping of Newton. Said Nesmith, *"We are experienced in our offensive line but inexperienced in our offense backfield. Friday night's game will be a test to see if our offensive backs can move the ball. Our offensive success will hinge a great deal on making use of our experience in the line. We feel that we have got to stop Morton's outside game with the QB and the inside game with the fullback*".

The Trojans' only score came in the 2nd quarter after a strange kick actually put them at the Panther 5-yard line. On the second play, Ricky Lane hit the hole "*in good fullback fashion*" for the touchdown and 6-0 halftime lead. However, the game was decided in the 3rd quarter when Tommy Strahan "*plunged across from the one and Rick Phillips added the point*".

Morton led in first downs (9-2) and rushing (147-39) while Magee held the air 37-0. Donald Barrett won Magee Touchdown Club Player of the Week.

GAME 2: MAGEE (0-1) vs SOUTH JONES (2-0)
MAGEE 6 SOUTH JONES 7
September 20, 1968

Coach Herschel Hathorne thought he had "*a very inexperienced interior line and a veteran backfield*". He had lost 8 linemen and 4 backfield players from a 4-3-1 season, but the DeSoto Conference Braves were "*reported to be extremely tough*" with 16 letter-winners on the team. They opened the season with wins against Northeast Jones (25-6) and Forrest AHS (20-0).

Magee was unexpectedly in for another 7-6 loss, though The Magee Courier said that the Trojans "*took full control of the running, passing and kicking game and gave them a rather comfortable feeling that victory was around the corner*". Early in the 3rd quarter, Magee recovered a Brave fumble to set up a pair of Tommy Meador throws. The first was for 24 yards to James Windham and the last a 7-yard TD strike to Butch McKenzie. But shortly afterwards, Jackie Simpson blocked a Barrett punt. Wayne Easterling picked up the loose ball and raced the necessary 10 yards (or 35 yards) for the touchdown. Jerry Powell's conversion made the difference.

The home team got inside the South Jones 20-yard line two times before the game was over, but they could not get across the goal line. Magee gave up no first downs (or one according to The Progress Item) and allowed only 23 rushing yards. Meanwhile, the Trojans had 10 first downs and 165 yards on the ground. Player of the Week went to Joe Fortenberry.

GAME 3: MAGEE (0-2) @ CRYSTAL SPRINGS (1-2)
MAGEE 33 CRYSTAL SPRINGS 0
September 27, 1968

Leon Canoy's Tigers had put up a respectable 7-2-2 record the previous year, but were picked 4th in the LDC South to start this season. They opened with a win over Forest Hill but then dropped close games to Mendenhall (6-3) and Pearl (14-13). Said Nesmith, "*The Tigers are a real good defensive club and a hard team to run against*". The paper added that they were "*also an average or better passing team*".

An opening fumble by Magee gave Crystal Springs a golden opportunity to get on the board first, but their FG hit the crossbar. The Trojans then began to take out frustrations on the home team. Lannie Stewart capped a 6-play drive with a run from inside the 24-yard line and Jonathan Styron notched the PAT. They scored on their next possession via Meador's connection with Eddie Dickey and Styron again converted. Now 14-0 in the 3rd quarter, Meador picked up a punt at the Tiger 30 and took it to the house with Styron making it 21-0.

The next came after a drive of 60 yards where McKenzie "*hit left tackle and went in standing up*" from the 21-yard line. Their last came before the quarter ended when Stewart picked off a pass to set up a 16-yard Windham dash. They moved to the 3-yard line unsuccessfully later and Meador finished things with an interception of Sumrall. Magee led in first downs (8-4), rushing (153-60) and passing (111-0). Stewart was awarded Player of the Week by the touchdown club.

GAME 4: MAGEE (1-2) vs PRENTISS (2-1)
MAGEE 7 PRENTISS 13
October 4, 1968

As mentioned previously, there was a new prediction for top spot in the 1968 LDC North. Coach Tommy Alexander's team had 7 returning starters and 15 lettermen, including the LDC's second-leading scorer (93 points) in Lewis Grubbs. They had posted an 8-1-1 record last year and opened with a shocking loss to Pearl before winning against Columbia and Warren Central. "*I was pleased with the effort and desire displayed by the entire Trojan squad in last Friday's game and can only hope they will not become complacent and will show the same characteristics in Friday's night game with Prentiss".*

The first half was scoreless but not without opportunities. Magee blocked a Bulldog punt at the 33-yard line, but gave it back via an interception by Charles Hutchins. Prentiss managed a march to the Magee 6 just before halftime, but Stewart's interception killed the threat. Prentiss moved 63 yards to start the 3rd quarter with Grubbs hitting paydirt from the 2-yard line. Magee responded with a 58-yard Meador scoring pass to McKenzie. Styron's toe put them up 7-6. Now with 2:46 left in the game, Donald Wayne Bridges picked off a Meador pass. With :51 left, Grubbs found the end zone from the 2-yard line and David Maynard converted.

GAME 5: MAGEE (1-3) @ HAZLEHURST (4-1)
MAGEE 19 HAZLEHURST 16
October 11, 1968

This was unusual territory for Magee. Their three losses had been by 8 total points and put them 1-3 for the first time since 1956. It seemed that Hazlehurst would be just the medicine needed as Emmett Smith's Indians went 2-6-2 the previous year and were slotted 5th in the LDC South. But with a surprising 4-1 record despite losing 15 lettermen, it would not be as easy as earlier thought.

The 7-0 Magee lead at halftime came courtesy of Windham's 22-yard sweep and Styron's PAT. *"But the ulcer action started in the third quarter"*. Goodman's run from the 5-yard line cut into the lead, but Barrett's block of the extra point kept it 7-6. The Indians took the lead, however, when Simmons pulled in a 67-yard bomb and the point-after put things 13-7. Before the quarter was over, a McEleavey FG was tacked on to their advantage.

McKenzie followed that with a 30-yarder off-tackle but the PAT failed. Now it was down to 1:00 remaining after holding Hazlehurst threats. That's when Lane *"swept right end from 4 yards out to pull the Trojans out front 19-16"*. Magee dominated first downs (14-5) and rushing (311-1) but the passing contest was held by Hazlehurst (164-57). Lane, Player of the Week, led rushers with 100 yards while McKenzie chipped in 85 yards.

GAME 6: MAGEE (2-3) @ MONTICELLO (2-3)
MAGEE 20 MONTICELLO 0
October 18, 1968

The last game had taken a toll relative to injuries. Fortenberry was now out for the season with two broken bones in his foot while Bob Everett was hampered by an ankle sprain. The opponent this week was Coach Harold Morris' Red Devils. They had 7 starters and 10 lettermen back from a 3-7 team, but were picked 7th in the division. After dropping their first three tilts, they bounced back with wins over Mendenhall and North Pike. The Magee Courier thought them *"stronger this year than they have been in past seasons"*.

Though Monticello stopped Magee at the 6-yard line early in the game, the Trojans still garnered the lead with :23 left before halftime when Meador found McKenzie from the 49-yard line and Styron converted. Lane added another in the 3rd quarter on a 31-yard sweep before dodging in from the 6-yard line in the last frame. With one Styron PAT good, the scoring was done. Magee led in first downs (9-5) and overall yardage (230-94).

GAME 7: MAGEE (3-3) vs COLUMBIA (2-4)
MAGEE 13 COLUMBIA 6
October 25, 1968

There was new life for Magee as Prentiss had dropped a South division contest to Crystal Springs. That gave hope for a surprising division title in Simpson County. Still, they needed to win the rest of their contests, and that included Coach Jerry Wilkinson's Cats. Columbia had recently re-joined the Little Dixie after a short stint in the Big Eight conference. With 5 starters and 13 letter-winners, they were slotted 6th in the division.

An early fumble by Magee did no damage, nor did a sustained drive by Columbia as the first quarter ended. However, they did reach the scoreboard in the next quarter via a 31-yard Randy Branch throw to Forbes (or Roberts). The PAT snap was botched to keep it 6-0. The defense bailed out the team in the 3rd quarter after Magee lost another ball via fumble. Before the end of the quarter, Lane brought fans to their feet when he broke through the line for a 55-yard scoring dash. Styron's conversion was true.

Late in the contest, Dwayne Yates picked off an errant throw and took it to the Cat 12. Meador tallied from there to finalize scoring. Desperately trying to come back, they went to the air only to have a throw intercepted to seal the evening. Windham received Player of the Week.

GAME 8: MAGEE (4-3) @ CANTON (7-1)
MAGEE 14 CANTON 13
November 1, 1968

A pre-season ranking at Number 1 in the LDC North appeared to be accurate as the Tigers entered the game with only a lone loss. Coach Wesley Reed had 6 starters and 13 lettermen back from a 5-4-1 team. Magee desperately needed to pull out the win to keep any hopes alive of a title.

The game would be somewhat of a "payback" for the first two losses where Magee went down due to missed extra points. They held a 14-0 advantage at halftime thanks to a 38-yard drive capped by a Meador pass to Barrett from the 8-yard line, a 27-yard pick-six by Stewart off of a Charlie Weems throw, and a pair of Styron extra points. Canton, meanwhile, added a 9-yard David Wesley (or Roger Whitehead) run and Roger Willis PAT in the 3rd. Then, with 2:19 remaining, Weems "*rolled around his own right end from eight yards out*" for the touchdown. Willis booted the extra point, but a penalty backed them up. His next effort went left and Magee had taken the surprise road victory. Another report notes that the Canton extra points were from Mosby. Yates received The Touchdown Club Player of the Week.

GAME 9: MAGEE (5-3) @ SAINT ALOYSIUS (3-4-1)
MAGEE 39 SAINT ALOYSIUS 0
November 8, 1968

Coach Elmo Broussard had only 5 seniors in his starting lineup and already had a number of players out with injuries; some season-ending. The Magee Courier said that "*Saint Aloysius is always considered a tough foe, especially when they play at home. The quick, aggressive and hard-hitting defense seems to be their main asset this season. Offensively, St Aloysius often uses its passing attack*".

The Vicksburg Evening Post added that "*This one could be close. Magee hasn't been as powerful this season as in the past. St. Aloysius has had its ups and downs and they're still not in the best shape of the season. Make it Magee 14-3 and hope it's the other way around*". It would definitely not be that close in a heavy downpour that created a "*rain-drenched field*".

Magee opened with a safety when a punt snap went over Joe Gerache's head. Later in the frame, Meador got in from the 5-yard line to make it 8-0 before the point-after. In the 3rd quarter, Magee recovered a Flash fumble to set up a Lane Stewart run from the 3. Barrett's toe made it 15-0. Stewart scored twice more in the 4th quarter. One was set up by an interception that allowed him a 35-yard dash and he added another run from the same distance later.

The Magee Touchdown Club named Jerry Craft as Player of the Week.

GAME 10: MAGEE (6-3) vs MENDENHALL (3-6)
MAGEE 34 MENDENHALL 0
November 15, 1968

This season, Magee's fate was now out of their hands. A Prentiss win over Hazlehurst would put the Bulldogs in the LDC finale. It seemed unlikely, but stranger things had happened in the past. In Mendenhall, Coach Ralph Sanders' Tigers were feeling the bite of injuries. That was bad news as they started the season with only 4 regulars back and 8 lettermen. That season, they went a dismal 3-4-2. A loss here would make this season worse.

Playing conditions were just as miserable, with the teams enduring a "*steady downpour*" of rain. A Trojan fumble in the opening frame was remedied when Meador picked off a Thompson throw. Magee put up 14 points in the 2nd quarter; the first after recovering a Tiger fumble. Meador hit Barrett on a pass to the 2-yard line and then Stewart went in from there. Later, they drove 55 yards with Stewart finishing what Lane had started from the 1-yard line. Styron was true on both points-after.

Bruce Smith's fumble recovery in the 3rd quarter gave Lane an eventual 8-yard score. Late in the same quarter, Meador and Barrett hooked up from the 40 for the touchdown and Styron made it 27-0. Early in the last frame, Lynn Steele's stop of Glyn Boggan on fourth down set up Meador's throw to McKenzie from 37 yards out. Styron's PAT marked the end of Trojan scoring for 1968. Magee led in first downs (10-9), rushing (167-43) and passing (164-54). Mendy suffered

2 interceptions and 3 lost fumbles. Jerry Sturm was the final Player of the Week. Unfortunately, Prentiss' defeat of Hazlehurst meant that the season was over for the Trojans.

Barrett was named to the All-Little Dixie team. Canton whipped Prentiss 28-6 for the Little Dixie Championship.

1969 (8-3)

Filling in for the departed Malcolm Nesmith was a familiar name; albeit for very a unique reason. Troy Carroll Greer, former head man for rival Mendenhall, now became the 18th Head Coach for Magee High School. Jerry Sullivan and Orland Everett were still alongside as assistants. First practices began on August 11th before heading to Co-Lin Junior College for a week of fundamentals. Greer noted later that *"We're pleased with the attitude and desire shown so far by the Trojans. However, we still have a lot of work before our first game"*.

The team had 6 returning letter-winners but had lost 12 others to graduation. With more sophomores than juniors and seniors combined, it was expected to be a rebuilding year in Simpson County. But, voters amazingly picked them to actually take the Little Dixie South crown at season's end.

GAME 1: MAGEE (0-0) vs SAINT ALOYSIUS (0-0)
MAGEE 22 SAINT ALOYSIUS 14
September 4, 1969

With the departure of Elmo Broussard, the Flashes were now led by 16-year veteran coach Don Alonzo. He started practices late with 13 lettermen, but had quickly lost at least 6 players before the first kickoff. Said Alonzo, *"Nevertheless, we'll show up and hope for the best. This is the worst shape I've ever been in for an opener"*. He would not know that QB Eddie Dickey and Jory Thompson would miss for Magee; also with injuries.

Though fumbling and recovering 3 times on their opening drive, Magee still got points when Jonathan Styron hit a 24-yard FG. They added a next-drive TD on a 97-yard (of 51-yard) Butch McKenzie escape. A solid march got Saint Al to the 1-yard line from where Jerry Hosemann dove in. Magee promptly fumbled to Ronnie Muffaletto and they made it count on a 3-yard Jimmy Salmon plunge with :53 left in the half. Donnie Price found Muffaletto for the two pointer and intermission sat in favor of Saint Al 14-10.

On the third play of the 3rd quarter, Ronnie Herrington blasted *"up center"* for a 48-yard score. Then, with just :15 remaining, Butch McKenzie iced the contest on a 1-yard dive. McKenzie amassed 98 yards in rushing. First downs (14-5) and rushing (336-62) went to Magee while Saint Al dominated (67-0) the air.

GAME 2: MAGEE (1-0) vs MORTON (1-0)
MAGEE 13 MORTON 0
September 12, 1969

The only thing that kept Reggie Robertson's 9-1 Panthers from playing for the Little Dixie title had been their loss to Canton. Though they lost 10 lettermen, they brought 12 back into camp. Voters had them 3rd in the Little Dixie North pre-season. Magee had suffered losses of 7-0 and 7-6 to the Scott County eleven the last two years and were hoping to get going on the right foot in the LDC.

Early in the opening quarter, Dickey found Jimmy Harris from the 47-yard line for a quick 6-0 lead. It could have been worse as Gary Nichols fell on a Panther fumble before halftime, but the Styron FG attempt was unsuccessful. Morton had their chances on a fumbled Trojan punt and missed FG from close-in. Another Magee FG effort in the 3rd quarter produced the same result to keep the score 6-0. More frustration came later when Dickey and Harris hooked up one more time, this from 30 yards, for a touchdown. But, a motion penalty brought the score back.

As the clock was running down, Morton's Larry Waggoner picked off a Dickey pass to set up a possible scoring march. But on the next play, McKenzie fell on a fumble at their 6-yard line. With 1:02 on the clock, McKenzie crossed for the touchdown and Styron converted. Magee led in first downs (17-8), rushing (206-92) and passing (72-0).

GAME 3: MAGEE (2-0) @ CLINTON (1-0)
MAGEE 7 CLINTON 12
September 19, 1969

Now in his 14th year as Arrow mentor, Roy Burkett would be trying to bring the title of Little Dixie Champions to Clinton. He had 8 returning lettermen on campus but had lost 12 to graduation. His peers had slotted the Arrows as fifth-best in the North. Like Magee, they had started off the year with a game against Saint Aloysius and came away with a victory.

Magee jumped out early on the Arrows on a rain-soaked field with just 3:10 off of the clock when Harris ripped off a 97-yard touchdown up the left sideline past Clinton defenders. The successful extra point by Styron gave them a 7-0 lead. But it would last just :50. Boyd Sullivan responded with his own breakaway; a dash of 67 yards *"after breaking five tackles"*. The missed extra point meant Magee was still up 7-6. Sullivan added another in the 3rd from the 3-yard line for the game's final points. Clinton failed to connect on either of their two extra point attempts.

First downs were even (6-6), rushing went to Magee (216-138) and passing to the Arrows (84-66).

GAME 4: MAGEE (2-1) vs CRYSTAL SPRINGS (1-2)
MAGEE 20 CRYSTAL SPRINGS 8
September 26, 1969: HOMECOMING

Leon Canoy's blue and gold was unpredictable on offense *"as varied types of formations are utilized"*. They lost heavily to graduation with 16 lettermen gone from Crystal Springs, claiming only 7 returners. With their 4-6 effort the previous year, voters put them 7th in the South. The Clarion-Ledger said that they would *"be an underdog to Magee, especially since the Trojans will be on home ground and also since they will likely be on the rebound after losing to Clinton"*.

It was tenuous early as a Sam Sumrall block of a Lynn Steele punt put the Dogs at the Magee 8. Four plays later, Mike Barlow dove in on a QB sneak from the 1-yard line. They then went for two points and made it on a Mike Barlow connection with Eddie Thames. Back came Magee with a touchdown via Dickey's pass to Charles Adcox, but the two-pointer failed and kept halftime 8-6. In the 3rd, two TD passes from Barlow to Albert Harris were called back on penalties. The Trojans took advantage when McKenzie *"hit the right side of the Trojan line, cut to his left and in a beautiful piece of broken-field running, scampered 82 yards for a Trojan TD with DeWayne Harris springing him free with a key block…"*. Styron connected on the PAT.

Later, a bad snap went over the head of Tiger punter William Teasley and was recovered in a pile by a number of Magee players at the 5-yard line. McKenzie made it count on a plunge and Styron notched the final point. Late in the contest, strong play by Ronnie Herrington, Tim Everett, Styron and Steele kept Crystal Springs out of the end zone to seal the win. Magee led in first downs (10-7), rushing (183-55) and passing (405-96). McKenzie rushed for 138 markers on the night.

The Crystal Springs newspaper called it *"one of the poorest excuses for officiating that Tiger fans have seen in years. Statistics will not show the determination of the Tigers. Tiger fans for the first time in a long time saw the Trojans beaten before the red flags gave them hope"*.

GAME 5: MAGEE (3-1) @ PRENTISS (3-0)
MAGEE 15 PRENTISS 14
October 3, 1969

New head man Richard Dossett had *"plenty (of talent) and also fares well in the experience category with 13 returning lettermen"*. The red and white Bulldog team, picked second behind Magee in the South, went 6-5 the previous season but were looking to beat Magee three times in a row. As for the contest, The Magee Courier said *"regardless of where the game may be played or who the teams are that are playing, spectators just won't get an opportunity to see a better and more exciting football game than they saw … when the Magee Trojans squeezed by the south division Prentiss Bulldogs"*.

Excitement for Magee fans suddenly changed early in the opening quarter when Magee fumbled at the Dog 15 and Charles Hutchins *"picked it up and raced 85 yards for a TD and then followed with a pass (to Joe Lee) into the end zone to make it 8 points"*. Then, David Weaver fell on a loose Trojan ball to set up Larry Fike's 46-yard bomb to John Polk. That 14-0 score ended the opening frame. McKenzie punched back by taking the kickoff 90 yards to paydirt with Harris skirting left for the conversion. That wasn't all. After forcing a punt, Harris took the ball on the first play the same distance to the end zone and Styron made it 15-14.

Prentiss had one chance to snatch the win, but Mike Harrison's long run was stopped by *"the last man who had a chance to get him... A few more inches and defeat would have been turned into victory"*. First downs (14-8) and rushing (316-118) went to Magee while the Dogs got the best in the air (117-20).

GAME 6: MAGEE (4-1) vs HAZLEHURST (2-2-1)
MAGEE 27 HAZLEHURST 6
October 10, 1969

The sixth-place team in the South under Coach Emmett Smith had two wins to their credit thus far. The first had been 16-6 over Florence and the last against Warren Central 9-7. They had 13 letter-winners back from a 6-4 team. The Magee Courier said that *"As the scores indicate thus far, Hazlehurst's defense is certainly a prominent feature in their game strategy"*.

Early in the opening quarter, Harris *"cracked it over from 1 yard out and Steve Gaskin polished up his kicking toe to split the uprights to make it 7 points for the Trojans at halftime"*. After intermission, Harris got in again (this time from the 2-yard line) and Gaskin converted. Their next came when Dickey found McKenzie *"on the run with David Ware paving the way to the end zone with a key block"*. Gaskin made it 21-0. Hazlehurst did not lay down; instead Jimmy Green picked off a Dickey throw to set up Graham Jasper's 35-yard scamper. Another report said that it came from Mike Rainer. Bruce Smith foiled an onside kick attempt and Harris made it count on a later run from inside the 15-yard line.

"The Indian running backs found the going tough with Mike Varner, Mike Sullivan and Tim Everett camping in their backyard along with Gary Nichols and Bruce Steele..." Dickey ended any hopes of more points with :22 left by picking off a Myers throw. Magee dominated first downs (12-2) and rushing (192-62) while Hazlehurst led in the air (74-61).

GAME 7: MAGEE (5-1) @ MONTICELLO (5-0)
MAGEE 14 MONTICELLO 10
October 17, 1969

Coach Harold Morris may have been picked 4th in the South after a 2-8 season, but he had *"an experienced ball team with 14 returning lettermen, including 13 seniors"*. The Magee Courier said before the game that *"the toughest of toughies ... is supposed to be the Monticello Red Devils..."*. The Devils had given up only 12 reported points thus far on an undefeated campaign. Added Greer, *"Monticello has a fine, well-balanced football team with plenty of size and experience"*.

Magee fans barely had a chance to get their seats before McKenzie took the opening kick 90 yards to the end zone *"with Joe Smith catching him from behind as he crossed pay dirt"*. Gaskin's PAT was true. But Magee's penchant for fumbling came back again with Dennis Rushing the recipient of the gift. Cletus Hux snuck in from the 1 a few plays later and James Wilson's toe tied the contest. In the 3rd quarter, Don Boyles picked off a Dickey throw to give James Wilson an eventual 31-yard FG.

McKenzie saved the day for Trojan fans, however, as he capitalized on a solid Magee drive with a 5-yard TD around left end. Gaskin's point-after ended the affair. Magee led in first downs (10-7) and rushing (178-102) while the Devils barely squeaked by in the air (20-8).

GAME 8: MAGEE (6-1) @ COLUMBIA (3-3)
MAGEE 13 COLUMBIA 14
October 24, 1969

The win against Monticello put Magee in first place in the LDC South. It appeared they would have somewhat of a breather this week as Jerry Wilkinson's club started the season 5th in the South. They had lost 12 players from a 4-5 team but did return 13 lettermen. Magee had won six-straight since their last loss in 1952 against the Cats, but it was on the road with Columbia having an off-week to prepare and get healthy. Meanwhile, Harris appeared out with an injured foot from the Monticello contest.

On this night, it was David surprising Goliath and statistics bore that out. In the 2nd quarter, a McKenzie fumble was recovered by Rusty Knight. Rick Taylor (or Haddox) then found Al Watts for a 6-0 advantage. Magee rebounded a few plays later when Dickey hit McKenzie from 53 yards away to tie it at halftime. Columbia actually scored once more, but it was called back. In the 3rd quarter, a Cat fumble was recovered by Gary Nichols. Dickey and McKenzie hooked up again and Styron put the contest 13-6.

In the final frame, Watts connected with Paul Berry for a touchdown. Electing for two points, they got it on a Taylor throw to Watts. That would be the margin of error on the night. Jesse Ford's interception as time neared ending sealed the upset. Columbia dominated first downs (16-0) and rushing (179-31). Magee barely held the air 110-100. Magee lost one fumble and had two passes picked off to aid the cause.

GAME 9: MAGEE (6-2) vs WARREN CENTRAL (3-3-1)
MAGEE 24 WARREN CENTRAL 13
October 31, 1969

The Vikings under Coach Dewey Partridge were slotted 3rd in the division after a 4-6 campaign. They returned only 8 letter-winners and sat with a mediocre year thus far. For Magee, they would still be without Harris, now joined by David Ware. Each win now for Magee was crucial in order to earn their way back to a Little Dixie championship. It didn't hurt that Warren Central had lost both games played all-time (1965-1966).

Gaskin opened scoring in the 1st with a 25-yard FG after Bruce Steele fell on a loose Viking football. McKenzie later returned a Bill Mendrop punt 56 yards to the 4-yard line and then took it the rest of the way on the next play. Gaskin made it 10-0. But it was Mendrop taking the ensuing kick 90 yards to the end zone with Frank Ford notching the 10-7 PAT. In the 2nd, Ford's 58-yard QB keeper put the game 13-10. With :28 left, Dickey spotted Gaskin from the 14-yard line and then he finished the half with the point-after.

Now in the final quarter, Styron recovered a WC fumble at their 23-yard line. Ronnie Herrington's 3-yard plunge and Gaskin's PAT marked the end of scoring. Warren Central had a chance for more points but a Jerry Childers fumble inside the 5-yard line gave Magee the ball. *"Gary Nichols and Mike Sullivan (were) tough company as they held the Vikings to only 4 first downs"*. Magee notched 10. They also led on the ground (173-85) and the air (61-33). The Vicksburg Evening Post put first downs 7-5.

GAME 10: MAGEE (7-2) @ MENDENHALL (1-7-1)
MAGEE 21 MENDENHALL 0
November 14, 1969

Paul Pounds' Tigers went 3-7 the year before but were not improving. With 14 lettermen gone and 11 back, they were slotted early in 5th place in the LDC South but had only a lone win on the year. *"Injuries of key players have plagued the Mendenhall team throughout the season"*. Only Crystal Springs (1-8) was worse. Magee knew that the game was critical as Monticello was also 5-1 in division play, but the Trojans did have a week of rest to prepare.

It wasn't until the 2nd quarter that Magee broke the scoreless tilt when they drove 71 yards and capped it on a 1-yard Harris dive and the first of 3 Styron PATs. McKenzie opened the 3rd quarter with an 80-yard kickoff return for a touchdown. Mendy threatened in the 4th when Ricky Warren picked off a Dickey throw, but they could march only to the Trojan 4-yard line. Magee, meanwhile, went the other way and, with :23 left, got into the end zone on a 2-yard McKenzie blast around the right.

Magee led in first downs (18-3) and rushing (245-21) while the Tigers held serve in passing (75-27). McKenzie rushed for 111 yards and Harris added another 97. Monticello also won, but Magee took the tiebreaker thanks to their head-to-head victory.

GAME 11: MAGEE (8-2) vs FOREST (9-0-1)
MAGEE 13 FOREST 46
November 21, 1969: LITTLE DIXIE CHAMPIONSHIP

The Bearcats under Coach Ken Bramlett started with 17 returning lettermen from an 8-3 squad and were rightfully picked first in the Little Dixie North to begin the season. After an opening-day 6-6 tie with Warren Central, they had marched on to dominant victories. *"With a team big in size and big in numbers, Forest is loaded with plenty of talent in both offense and defense. The big Bearcat line has held four of their opponents scoreless this season while not allowing more than 14 points against them in one game"*.

Forest was once a regular opponent, suiting up against a Magee team at least 22 times. That series, led by Forest 11-9-2, ended in 1958. *"We are tickled to be in the game. We think Forest is a fine football team and we'll have to be at our very best to stay in the game. But our kids have done a good job of motivating themselves and we hope to be ready"*. Added Bramlett, *"I have a lot of respect for Magee and I look for a tough game"*.

Despite the outcome, The Clarion-Ledger said "*Magee, though out-manned this night, played a whale of a game and showed a well-coached team with plenty of fight*". In fact, it was Magee on the board first when McKenzie rushed in from the 9-yard line and converted the PAT. Early in the 2nd quarter, Freddie Bagley found Jimmy Wright and then converted the two-pointer. Back came Magee with a 65-yard McKenzie dash and it was now 13-8. But from there, the Cats began to pull away. That started with an 11-yard Bagley toss to Richard Austin and Wright's two-point conversion reception with 1:49 left in the half.

In the 3rd, David Calhoun dodged in from the 8 and Wright converted the two-points. Steve Clark then plunged in from the 3-yard line and Thompson ran in the conversion. The final two tallies came from Ralph Brown runs of 1-yard each. First downs (15-6), rushing (198—149) and passing (168-41) all favored Forest. After the contest, Greer went to the Forest locker room and told the Cats, "*We lost to the best team tonight. I am sure your coaches and your boosters are proud of you*".

When All Little Dixie honors were announced, Butch McKenzie was named First Teamer. Jonathan Styron, Tim Everett, Dewayne Harris, Charles Hutchins and Jimmy Harris made the Second Team. For Honorable Mentions, the list included David Ware, Gary Nichols, Lynn Steele, Bruce Smith, and Eddie Dickey. Forest was dominant in the North, claiming 7 of the 12 First Team slots.

1970-1979

1971 (10-1): Little Dixie Champions

1970 (7-1-2)

Troy Greer, back for his second stint, said of pre-season practices "*The boys have a good attitude and are working hard*". His squad had 12 out of 24 lettermen returning and were picked a solid first in the Little Dixie South division. The team continued their week-long off-campus training routine and headed to Co-Lin Junior College before the season to work on fundamentals and team-building exercises. Afterwards, Greer said "*Our players have worked real hard in practice*". By game week, he noted his team had 37 players consisting of 7 seniors and 20 juniors.

GAME 1: MAGEE (0-0) @ WEST JONES (0-0)
MAGEE 12 WEST JONES 0
September 4, 1970

Coach Rex Todd's Mustangs were considered a "*good passing team (with) several linemen weighing in over 200 pounds*". Senior Bruce Smith had sustained an injury at Co-Lin and would miss the inaugural contest between the two clubs. Still, Magee would open the campaign with a road victory.

In the 2nd quarter, Jerry McNair pulled in a Jake Russell toss from the 15-yard line for the opening volley while Russell would add the last touchdown in the last frame from the 2-yard line. The first had been set up by a blocked West Jones kick by Joey Hughes while the last was the result of a Mustang fumble. Russell had thrown another touchdown to McNair along the way but it had been called back due to penalty.

First downs were reported by Magee as favoring the Trojans 6-5. The (Laurel) Leader-Call called them for West Jones 8-5. Magee led in total yards 119-98 and the Mustangs ventured past midfield only twice. Jimmy Adcox was credited with a pick-six that came back due to a penalty. One negative would be that Mike Sullivan suffered "*fractured ribs*". Greer "*appeared pleased with the defensive game*" and singled out a number of players for their efforts.

GAME 2: MAGEE (1-0) @ MORTON (1-0)
MAGEE 7 MORTON 0
September 11, 1970

Traditional opponent Morton was picked second in the North under Coach Reggie Robertson. The Clarion-Ledger said that the Panthers had "*size but lacks speed among 15 of 28 lettermen back from an 8-2 team*". They opened the 1970 season with a slight 14-13 win over Newton. Both Smith and Mike Sullivan would miss the contest.

Despite a solid running game and a Bernie Herrington interception in the 2nd quarter, the first half closed 0-0. However, Magee was more successful in the 3rd quarter thanks to continuous ground and air movement that resulted in a Russell 5-yard keeper for the touchdown. David Hopkins' PAT would finish scoring. But it wasn't without action. Morton moved inside the 1-yard line in the frame but could not cross the goal after three attempts. Magee, on the other hand, also put a goal-line drive together late but couldn't score.

"*I thought the whole team played a good ball game Friday night*". Greer elaborated by noting that "*the team had improved greatly since last week ... especially ... the defensive secondary not allowing a single pass completion and the defense as a whole allowing only four first downs; two of which were by penalties*". Magee had 11 first downs and had 194 total yards (104 rushing). Morton gained 93 on the night; all coming on the ground. Mike Stewart now joined the ailing Trojan list with an inflamed knee and would miss the next game.

GAME 3: MAGEE (2-0) vs CLINTON (1-1)
MAGEE 6 CLINTON 0
September 18, 1970

Practices under Roy Burkett began on August 10th and the team worked twice-a-day thru August 21st. He had seven lettermen back but had lost upwards of 17 to graduation. As such, the LDC coaches voted his team 4th in the North Division. On August 25th, the Arrows unveiled their team to the fans in the form of a two-hour scrimmage. Admission was "*bath towels or bars of soap*". By game day, the Arrows had beaten Jackson Saint Joe while falling the next week to Saint Aloysius.

The game would come down to one series late in the opening quarter. Magee used nine runs and two passes to move to the Arrow 3 and Bill Carter managed to avoid Clinton defenders for the touchdown from there. The PAT missed. The Arrows had chances to win. They marched to the 8 in the 3rd and to the 5 in the 4th, but both drives fizzled. Added to the problems was the fact that three Clinton passes were picked off by the Trojans; all factors which sealed the loss. The Magee Courier said that *"The second half was plagued with fumbles and incomplete passes which held the Trojans to their initial score, but the Trojan line made two exciting stands with their backs to the goalposts and stopped two desperate attempts by the Arrows…"*

Magee led in first downs (16-5), rushing (152-134) and passing (38-13).

GAME 4: MAGEE (3-0) @ CRYSTAL SPRINGS (3-0)
MAGEE 14 CRYSTAL SPRINGS 14
September 25, 1970

Surprisingly after a 3-8 season, Coach Leon Canoy's team was picked 3rd in the South and stood undefeated by kickoff. They had given up only 13 points; that in the opener to Forest Hill. Said Greer, *"Friday's opponent is an explosive team capable of breaking from anywhere, anytime, but (we seem) to be up for the game and should do well…."*

The Tigers came ready to play and opened with an 81-yard Mike Barlow dash and his PAT to make it 7-0. Magee responded in the 2nd quarter with a 5-yard Bob Roberts run up the middle to cut it to 7-6 at halftime. That had been set up by a fumble by Tiger William Teasley. Crystal Springs threatened before intermission with a march to the Magee 8-yard line before fumbling yet again. Rain began to change conditions in the second half; hampering play for both quarters. The visitors had the first opportunity but a short FG failed. Barlow then notched his second score in the 3rd quarter on a 28-yard keeper and PAT, but *"Coach Troy C. Greer's determined Trojans fought back in the final period…"* Their touchdown came on a 46-yard toss from Russell to Roberts. Russell then plunged over for the crucial two-pointer and game-tying conversion.

The Tigers had the last two chances to beat Magee on drives to the one-inch line and the 4-yard line. But, again, the defense held. *"Both the offensive and defensive lines blocked well. We feel that our boys are improving each week and hope they continue to improve as the season progresses"*. Crystal Springs held first downs (13-10) and rushing (274-113) while Magee gained the advantage in the air (112-48). Magee picked off one Tiger throw and they lost 3 more balls on fumbles. Additionally, they suffered 105 penalty yards against Magee's 35 yards.

GAME 5: MAGEE (3-0-1) vs PRENTISS (2-2)
MAGEE 9 PRENTISS 7
October 2, 1970: HOMECOMING

It was thought that the 5-5 team with 10 returning lettermen for Coach Richard Dossett *"could be the surprise team … with three all-conference returnees"*. Yet, they were picked 5th in the South division and sat in last place by Friday night. The Magee Courier said that Prentiss *"is certainly not going to be easy"*. And, they weren't.

Much of the problem lay with fumbles as Magee dropped the football three times in their first four drives. Two times, it was in their own territory but the defense stood tall. Russell picked off a pass on their second march while Larry Maddox recovered a Dog fumble in the end zone on the surprise touchdown. Now 6-0, Prentiss bounced back with a George Jones 40-yard scoring reception. Their PAT by T.J. Ross put them ahead 7-6 at the half. In the second half, a Hopkins 30-yard FG gave the Trojans the lead back and it held thanks to solid defense and a Hughes interception.

Prentiss held first downs (10-8) and dominated passing (115-0) while Magee's success came on the ground (237-43). The home team lost four fumbles on the night.

GAME 6: MAGEE (4-0-1) @ HAZLEHURST (2-3)
MAGEE 0 HAZLEHURST 0
October 9, 1970

Not much was expected of Coach Emmett Smith's Indians. They were picked 6th in the LDC South after a 5-4-1 season and had just one LDC win; that coming the week before against Warren Central. Greer noted that *"the Indian squad is a strong one and the Trojans will have to play good football to beat them"*. Though on the road, not many Magee fans expected the outcome.

It appeared that Magee was on the right track on their first drive as Russell peeled off a punt return touchdown. However, it was called back due to clipping. Later, they moved as far as the 10-yard line but the FG opportunity was unsuccessful. *"For the rest of the game, the Trojans and Indians did a lot of hitting ... but the scoreboard came through the evening untouched except to record downs, yardage and quarters"*. Expectedly, the stat line was unimpressive. First downs (5-4) and rushing (73-24) went to Magee while passing fell to the Indians (61-20)

GAME 7: MAGEE (4-0-2) vs MONTICELLO (4-1)
MAGEE 6 MONTICELLO 17
October 16, 1970

Though 10-1 in 1969, the Red Devils had only 3 returning lettermen and were picked last in the South division. First-year Coach Parker Dykes had surprised everyone, though, with a loss only to Mendenhall. Monticello was called *"a strong threat to Magee's undefeated string. The team is known to have several explosive offensive players who have the capability to put it together for points on the scoreboard"*.

The home team had a bad break on the opening play as McNair's fumble to Monticello at the 32-yard line led four plays later to a James Wilson field goal. A 2nd quarter drive looked promising, but another fumble killed the opportunity. There was confusion on the play on an inadvertent whistle but it probably saved a Devil touchdown as Emmitt Madison had picked up the ball and raced to the end zone. Halftime stood 3-0. An early 3rd quarter Monticello fumble led to a 50-yard scoring drive with Smith dodging in. The PAT failed but Magee was up 6-3.

The Red Devils responded quickly, with Madison taking a punt back 70 yards for the touchdown. Now 10-6, Monticello put up insurance points on a Joe Smith dash to the 2-yard line from where Willie Harris scored. For good measure, they picked off a Trojan throw on the next march to essentially ice the contest. Greer still felt that the game *"was one of the best the Trojans have played all season discounting fumbles and penalties which seemed to come at inopportune times. The team was well-prepared and stopped the Monticello running and passing games"*.

In fact, Magee led in first downs (14-4), rushing (214-180) and passing (30-7). But five fumbles (3 lost), a pair of interceptions and six penalties derailed hopes. Monticello scoring came from James Wilson, Emmett Madison and Willie Harold Harris.

GAME 8: MAGEE (4-1-2) vs COLUMBIA (7-0)
MAGEE 17 COLUMBIA 8
October 23, 1970

Picked 4th in the South and with 11 lettermen back from a 7-4 team, first-year Coach Tommy Davis' Wildcats were said to open the season *"with a monkey on its back"*. They had gotten a late start due to the coaching change and Davis said that *"They'll just have to prove themselves. If we can do OK in our first few games, then we'll be alright during this season. The line from last year was lost to graduation and we must rebuild it completely. We have 36 boys on our roster now and that's small for a Little Dixie Conference team"*.

By game night, the Cats looked very strong. Their backfield was said to be the best faced thus far. Said The Magee Courier, *"The Trojans will have to be up to win this one, but the team seems to have good morale at this point and will definitely be out to win it Friday night"*. Columbia featured a running back named Walter Payton.

Columbia opened play with a long kickoff return to the Magee 30 but could not move further. In return, Magee drove steadily to the Cat 13-yard line but could do no better. In the 2nd quarter, Carter dented the scoreboard on a TD run to cap a 56-yard march and Hopkins made it 7-0. Hopkins added three more points via a 12-yard FG in the 3rd after Carter snagged an errant throw. Columbia came right back in the frame after a Trojan fumble with Payton's 9-yard scamper and his two-point conversion. That made it 10-8. In the final period, Hughes added an interception for Magee that led to a Russell scoring run. Hopkins' kick marked the end of scoring.

Magee dominated first downs (13-1) and rushing (198-27) while also holding the passing attack (32-12). Columbia's three intercepted passes did not help their cause.

GAME 9: MAGEE (5-1-2) @ WARREN CENTRAL (2-4)
MAGEE 20 WARREN CENTRAL 7
October 30, 1970

Coach Dewey Partridge's Vikings were having a strange season. They had been picked 2nd in the LDC South, but with only 4 lettermen back, they struggled early before winning their last two games against Prentiss and Crystal Springs. The Magee Courier said that *"The Vicksburg team has a good defensive squad and is a big team, and the Trojans are not taking the coming game lightly*".

Magee wasted little time in finding paydirt, driving on their first march to set up Roberts' 18-yard escape and Hopkins PAT. Roberts found daylight again later in the frame from six yards to pad the lead with Hopkins again converting. Warren Central pulled in a midfield fumble before halftime and used it to allow Butch Newman a 50-yard pass to Dean Hearn. With Bo Oakes adding the PAT, it sat 14-7. The last score came in the 3rd quarter when a McNair 4-yard run was fumbled into the end zone where Bernie Herrington recovered for the score.

Statistics were closer than the previous week, but Magee held first downs (11-9 or 13-11), rushing (171-136 or 173-119) and passing (175-70). The Trojans suffered four lost fumbles on the evening. The Vicksburg Evening Post credited Roberts with 117 rushing yards and Adcox with 131 receiving.

GAME 10: MAGEE (6-1-2) vs MENDENHALL (5-4)
MAGEE 3 MENDENHALL 0
November 13, 1970

Mendenhall was picked next-to-last in the South to start the season. Coach Paul Pounds' Tigers had gone 1-8-1 last year, but they had the services of 12 returning letter-winners. Said Greer, "*We'll have to play top-notch ball to beat them. (Our players) know they are going to play a good team and they'll have*

to hustle to win". The playoff picture was murky. Columbia had lost another game (Monticello) to move them to 5-2 in the division. So, wins by Magee and Monticello would force a three-way deadlock. It would take a Monticello loss for Magee to face North champion Forest in post-season play.

Rain that dampened play from start to finish was symbolic of the mixed feelings after the final whistle. Fumbles, slips and penalties forced a punting duel that raged the entire opening half of the game. Mendenhall had actually kicked away the ball before fourth down on a few drives. Magee did the same in the 3rd quarter after finding themselves at the 3-yard line. The Trojans did have their second FG attempt in the frame, but like the first, it was unsuccessful.

As the game neared close, Mendy ended a pair of promising drives by fumbling the football. With only seconds left, and after a Russell completion to Charles Adcox, the Trojans lined up for the game-winning FG. Hopkins' 20-yard kick was true. The last play resulted in a Russell interception to seal the win. Magee led in first downs (9-4), rushing (125-46) and passing (58-11). Monticello's 7-0 win over Prentiss gave them the playoff spot with wins over both Columbia and Magee.

First Team All-Little Dixie honors went to Joey Hughes, J. Mike Smith, Bruce Steele, Bruce Smith, and Bob Roberts. Honorable Mentions included Charles Adcox, Mike Sullivan, Bernie Herrington, Jerry McNair, Jake Russell and Bill Carter. Undefeated Forest beat Monticello 22-10 to capture the Little Dixie Championship for 1970.

1971 (10-1) LITTLE DIXIE CHAMPIONS

Sixteen lettermen were on hand to start Troy Greer's third year in Magee. He had lost 10 key players but had 18 seniors on the team that had grown to 50 participants. "*We're glad that we have (that many). That's the most we've had in a long time*". The Trojans were picked tops in the Little Dixie South but had a tough schedule. "*Especially our first three games which will be outside the South Little Dixie. These three football teams are real fine ones. Of course, the whole schedule is comprised of real tough teams, so we're looking for a real good fight this* year".

The guys made their annual trek to Co-Lin Junior College to work on a multitude of things. As the first game approached, Greer said "*They've worked hard and have a real good attitude. The seniors have shown a lot of leadership, which is essential to have a good football team. The competition for starting positions is real keen*".

GAME 1: MAGEE (0-0) vs WEST JONES (0-0)
MAGEE 40 WEST JONES 6
September 3, 1971

Coach Rex Todd's Mustangs were picked preseason in the top three DeSoto Conference rankings. In their first-ever meeting the previous year, Magee had escaped by a 12-0 score. *"We expect (them) to have a good football team. And we know that we will have to play well to win"*. This one would not be nearly as close.

It took only two plays before a Mustang fumble recovered by Mike Stewart put Magee on the 2-yard line. Bob Roberts went into the end zone on the next play and David Hopkins converted. On the next drive, Jake Russell dashed 48 yards to paydirt and Hopkins again converted. It didn't take much longer for Russell to find Billy Bishop for the next TD and Hopkins made it 21-0. A second quarter push by West Jones was thwarted by Charles Thames' interception. Before the end of the half, Russell added his own interception to set up Jerry McNair's toss to Danny Welch. The Hopkins PAT put intermission 28-0.

Magee opened the 3rd quarter with another solid effort but fumbled out of the end zone from the 9-yard line. But Jerry Winn *"who with good blocking from the right side of the line"*, eventually galloped 6 yards for another score. After a McNair interception, the 3rd quarter ended 34-0. In the final frame, a Mustang fumble to Thames resulted in a 45-yard Winn run and 1-yard Roberts plunge. In the closing seconds, a deflected punt resulted in a 1-yard Archie Harper sneak for the finale.

"The coaching staff was pleased with the overall performance of the team, both offensively and defensively. We know that we made a few mistakes, but we're going to try to eliminate those mistakes before we play Morton". Magee dominated on the stat line in first downs (12-3), rushing (221-38) and passing (69-15). There were 95 yards of penalties, however.

GAME 2: MAGEE (1-0) vs MORTON (1-0)
MAGEE 3 MORTON 0
September 10, 1971

The Panthers under Coach Reggie Robertson went 8-2 the previous season. With 15 of 25 lettermen back, they were chosen the LDC North favorites. In their opener, they had beaten Newton 33-21. As expected, a tussle between the top teams from each division would be a close battle. The Magee Courier said afterwards, *"An inch is as good as a mile and three points are as good as 30 as Magee proved Friday night in edging Morton"*.

An opening quarter march moved into Panther territory, but a Ray Harvey interception at the 1-yard line proved costly. However, Magee moved to the 10-yard line in the next frame and Hopkins nailed an eventual 25-yard FG for what would be the game-winning tally. The Trojans stopped second half drives with fumbles recovered by Tony Heriard and Ralph Brown. *"We will have to improve in certain areas. We hope that our offense will improve with each game. We're always happy to win, naturally, by a small or large score"*.

First downs (8-2), rushing (125-51) and passing (77-0) all went to the Trojans. Morton lost a pair of fumbles while Magee had the lone pass intercepted. Morton never moved past midfield and attempted only two passes.

GAME 3: MAGEE (2-0) @ CLINTON (0-1)
MAGEE 22 CLINTON 0
September 17, 1971

Unbeknownst to everyone in the program, this would be the final year for Coach Roy Burkett as health problems had begun to take their toll on the Arrow mentor. The team had 10 returning lettermen and received a commendable 24 votes in the Little Dixie North voting from other coaches. That put them in fourth place; just 4 votes shy of Forest Hill. The good news for Clinton was that leading scorers in Bill Sellari, Phil Frazier, T.Y. Gunter and Terry Harrison were among the returnees.

Magee took the lead they wouldn't give up in the 1st when Russell hit Welch from the 9 and Hopkins converted the PAT. Clinton had their best attempt at points afterwards when Warren Green fell on a dropped punt by Russell at the Magee 5. The FG attempt by Jim Blackwell, however, was missed to keep halftime 7-0. The next Trojan score came in the 3rd on a 12-yard Russell pass to Thames, while the final came in the 4th quarter via a 7-yard Russell pass to Bishop and his two-pointer to McNair.

"We were pleased with our defensive effort and with our passing game. We hope to improve on our running game as time goes on". First downs were even (10-10) but Magee controlled the offensive numbers in rushing (134-70) and passing (136-114). Clinton had the one fumble recovery on the turnover ledger.

GAME 4: MAGEE (3-0) vs CRYSTAL SPRINGS (0-4)
MAGEE 48 CRYSTAL SPRINGS 0
September 24, 1971

Big Crystal went 7-3-1 the previous year and claimed a Crystal Bowl championship. Leon Canoy's blue and gold were slotted 5th in the South due to just 7 of 18 lettermen back on the team. Magee would make it tougher, scoring on an opening 65-yard drive and 12-yard run by Roberts. McNair then picked off a Crystal Springs pass to set up Russell's 18-yard dash and the second Hopkins PAT.

Just 6:00 into the game, Roberts then took a Tiger punt 42 yards to paydirt and McNair did the same from 32 yards out soon after. Crystal then fumbled to Roberts and it took two plays before McNair turned it into a 62-yard dash. With Hopkins' conversions, it was now 35-0 still in the opening quarter. Russell actually did the same as Roberts and McNair to open the 2nd quarter, but it was called back. Now, Greer substituted freely. Magee opened the 3rd with an 8-yard Hopkins run and, two minutes later, Larry Maddox picked off a Tiger pass. Winn got in from the 6-yard line and Hopkins converted.

"Against Crystal Springs, we were pleased with the overall play of the offense and defense. We were glad to be able to play a lot of our younger players. We thought that our offensive backs and linemen blocked better and we hope they continue to improve". Even with reserves, first downs (11-4 or 11-0) and rushing (305-47) went to Magee. The Tigers took the air (23-0).

GAME 5: MAGEE (4-0) @ PRENTISS (1-2-1)
MAGEE 34 PRENTISS 0
October 1, 1971

Coach Richard Hall would have a tough road for 1971. His team, which had *"lost most of its offense"* was slotted last in the South due to just 5 lettermen returning of 27 that earned letters that year. For clarity, Magee had bested Prentiss only 9-7 that season.

This time it took a second drive before scoring; that an 18-yard McNair run *"with fine blocking from the left side of the Trojan line, consisting of Mike Martin, Danny Welch, Mike Shelton Smith and Jory Thompson".* After Hopkins converted, Prentiss thwarted the next offensive drive with an interception. But, Russell later hit McNair from 63 yards away and Hopkins converted. Magee drove 50 yards in the next frame with Russell doing the honors on a sneak. A 70-yard Mike Varner punt ensure that halftime stayed 20-0.

They increased it to 27-0 in the 3rd on a 3-yard Roberts plunge and Hopkins kick. Prentiss picked off a 4th quarter pass and recovered a Russell fumble to stall more scoring. Finally, with :21 remaining, Russell snuck in from the 1 and Hopkins nailed the PAT. McNair finished the night with a pickoff. *"We were pleased with our overall play both offensively and defensively. Our backs and linemen blocked better and we hope they will continue to work hard and have a positive attitude. Our defensive linemen and backs did a real fine job holding Prentiss to one first down and no completions".*

Indeed, Magee had 13 first downs to only 1 for Prentiss. Rushing (271-31) and passing (106-0) were gaudy in favor of the Trojans. Magee did lose the two fumbles and had the same number via interceptions.

GAME 6: MAGEE (5-0) vs HAZLEHURST (0-4)
MAGEE 42 HAZLEHURST 6
October 8, 1971: HOMECOMING

In Hazlehurst, Coach Mason Denham had only 6 lettermen back to improve on a 3-6-1 campaign. But voters thought them to be only sixth-best in the South pre-season. Their 0-4 start did not give prospects much hope, and only a tie the previous year had stopped 13-straight Magee wins over the program.

A 63-yard drive and 1-yard Russell dive opened play while Thames then recovered a next-drive Indian fumble. Roberts made it count from the 1-yard line and Hopkins drilled his second PAT. Roberts added another in the 2nd quarter from the 8-yard line and Hopkins made halftime 21-0 despite a deep Indian drive later to the goal line. In the 3rd quarter, Russell moved in from the 1 over the center of the line and Hopkins put up the point-after. Thames finished the frame with an interception.

Jimmy Stuard got into the scoring books with a 1-yarder while Russell added an 84-yard dash afterwards. Hopkins' toe made it 42-0. Hazlehurst avoided the shutout on the ensuing kickoff when Jerry Killingsworth took the pigskin 79 yards to the end zone. *"We were glad to win against Hazlehurst... Each boy that participated gave a good account of himself. We hope that we can improve this week in all phases... Monticello will have the best team, by far, that we have faced in Little Dixie play"*.

First downs (14-5), rushing 239-130) and passing (26-2) favored Magee. Both teams lost a fumble and the Trojans had only 3 penalties.

GAME 7: MAGEE (6-0) @ MONTICELLO (2-3)
MAGEE 6 MONTICELLO 17
October 15, 1971

The Red Devils, under Coach Parker Dykes, had spoiled another Magee run to the LDC title the previous year with a win over the Trojans before losing in the finale against Forest. *"The potential is there for another crack at the LDC trophy, but we have a lot of work to do. We won't have the speed we had last year, but we do have some experienced players with some size on them"*. Voters had them 2nd in the South with 12 of 25 returning lettermen. Monticello had beaten Magee in a critical game last year 17-6. Unfortunately, it would be same score in an upset this season.

Against *"the toughest team in the Little Dixie we've faced"*, the Trojans found themselves behind Warren Central in the division lead when the game was over. An early Russell fumble was returned the same way to Thames. Monticello's James Wilson tried a 2nd quarter FG unsuccessfully, but they got the ball back on a Russell interception by Warren Cross that was taken back to paydirt only to have it called back. Still, they found the end zone on a 10-yard Cecil Lewis pass to Retius Standfield. Wilson notched the PAT and it was 7-0.

Only seconds before halftime, Wilson redeemed himself with a 30-yard FG to make intermission 10-0. A 3rd quarter Hopkins FG attempt was not good, but Monticello fumbled the ball back to the Trojans. Roberts made the most of the gift from the 1-yard line and it was 10-6. In the final frame, McNair picked off a Red Devil throw but Magee could not get into the end zone. The Devils put the icing on the cake afterwards on a 3-yard Lewis pass to Cross and Wilson kicked the PAT. Magee picked up one last fumble, but it was not to result in points.

"It's always discouraging to lose, but we did not perform well. We hope we can do better this week against Columbia". Magee was bested in all phases: first downs (12-9), rushing (155-115) and passing (46-7). Monticello lost 3 fumbles and had 14 penalties for 117 yards on the evening.

GAME 8: MAGEE (6-1) @ COLUMBIA (1-5-1)
MAGEE 14 COLUMBIA 0
October 22, 1971

This week against the 4th-ranked LDCS team of Coach Charles Beall was critical. They had 12 of 26 lettermen back but had lost the services of Walter Payton in the backfield. They could not take this one for granted as their only loss had come the week before to a 2-3 squad. It would be closer than expected at Gardner Stadium.

Varner got the Trojans out of an opening-quarter jam with a 69-yard punt. After holding, a bad snap on the John Wilson punt caused by Billy Bishop and Jory Thompson forced a safety. In the 2nd quarter, McNair picked off a Cat pass and raced 70 yards (or 86 yards) for the TD and 8-0 lead. Before halftime, the defense *"got to the Columbia punter for the second time"*. From the 15-yard line, Roberts cashed in on a 4-yard run *"with excellent blocking from the Trojan line"* for the last score.

Despite a number of fumbles that opened doors for both teams in the second half, scoring was over. *"Our defense played well. Our offense was not effective"*. In fact, Columbia led in first downs (7-6) and passing (39-19). Rushing favored Magee (107-81). Columbia fumbled 7 times but lost only a lone football.

GAME 9: MAGEE (7-1) vs WARREN CENTRAL (6-1)
MAGEE 17 WARREN CENTRAL 8
October 29, 1971

Of the surprise teams in 1971, the boys in red from Vicksburg had to be among the biggest. Picked 7th in the LDC South, they were now 6-1 under Coach Lum Wright with just 14 of 31 lettermen back in camp. Said Greer, "*They're good. We're just going to have to play really fine football to beat them*". If Magee wanted any shot at returning to the title game, they would have to get past the Vikings.

Hopkins started things off in the opening quarter with a 43-yard FG. Dwight McWilliams then recovered a fumble to stop a WC drive but, though they couldn't score, Varner pinned the Vikings at their own 1-yard line. A Hopkins FG attempt failed before the end of the quarter and kept the game 3-0. In the 2nd quarter, Magee drove 42 yards with Russell providing the last 11 yards and Hopkins the conversion. In the 3rd quarter, Russell picked off a pass, but it would lead only to another missed FG attempt. The frame ended with a Thames pickoff of the Vikes. In the final segment, Roberts "*with excellent downfield blocking from the Magee line*" raced 24 yards for a touchdown and Hopkins notched the 17-0 PAT.

Later, a Roberts fumble gave Warren Central the ball at the 14-yard line and they managed to eventually avoid the goose egg when (future Magee head coach) Lummy Wright darted in from the 8-yard line and then found Eliot Tillison for the two-point conversion. That had come as a result of a deep Magee fumble. The game ended when Russell picked off a Viking football.

"*We were extremely proud of the way our boys played football and conducted themselves against Warren Central. Our defense was real sharp and the blocking and running was a pleasure to watch. It was a real fine team effort*". First downs (13-7) and rushing (234-119 or 243-199) went to Magee while the Warren County squad held the air 46-0.

GAME 10: MAGEE (8-1) @ MENDENHALL (8-1)
MAGEE 21 MENDENHALL 7
November 12, 1971

Coach Paul Pounds had troubles in the past with his results, moving them up to a break-even 5-5 the season before. Now with 11 lettermen back, and picked 3rd in the LDCS, they were one game out of first place with only a lone loss. However, it would be Magee with the crown via a win and Warren Central moving forward should they lose. That was due to the Vikings 10-7 win over the Tigers. Roberts sat 6th in LDC scoring with 60 points, but Mendy's Arthur Phillips was by far the best in the category. Clinton was already in place for the opponent.

Said Pounds, "*We respect Coach Greer and the Trojan team. We're expecting a good game*". His team would hit the board first in the opening quarter on a 70-yard drive capped by Phillip's 22-yard strike to Charles Jerry Williams. Don Coleman's PAT put them up 7-0. Magee stormed back with an 82-yard march in 8 plays and Russell's 20-yard run "*around left end*", combined with Hopkins' PAT, tied the game. Magee's next score started with a Russell pass to McNair that put them eventually within the 5-yard line. Russell and Bishop connected with 1:01 left but Jack May's blocked PAT kept intermission 13-7.

In the second half, a Russell toss to Bishop put the Trojans at the 6-yard line. They got to the 1-yard line before being stopped on a fourth down play. Later, Larry Maddox recovered a Tiger fumble at the Mendy 33. Though producing no points, Roberts would end things in the 4th quarter on a 64-yard escape and then added the two-pointer. That made up for his earlier fumble to George Washington. The visitors' final gasp throw was picked off by McNair. Magee led in first downs (11-8), rushing (237-96) and passing (240-98). "*We felt like it was a good team effort; both offensively and defensively*".

GAME 11: MAGEE (9-1) vs CLINTON (7-2)
MAGEE 10 CLINTON 6
November 19, 1971

Magee had already shut out the Arrows earlier in the season. To Clinton's credit, they had given up only 12 points in their last 6 games. Said Greer, "*We're proud of our football team because of the way they work and perform. Clinton has a real fine football team. We'll have to have a determined effort to beat them. Even though we beat them one time this year, they have improved and have gotten better.*" By now, the Arrows were led by interim coach Bob Neblett; substituting for an ailing Burkett. The Clarion-Ledger thought Magee best 14-13, saying "*Magee's Trojans shouldn't let the fact that they blanked the Arrows 22-0 in an earlier meeting make them overconfident*".

A Russell interception and a Joey Hughes fumble recovery did nothing for the Trojans as Clinton also got a turnover via fumble. In the 2nd quarter, Dwight McWilliams found a loose football at the 16-yard line that led to a Hopkins 27-yard FG. Clinton came right back to take a 6-3 halftime lead when Mickey McMurtry hit Bill Sellari from the 33. With the exception of the fumble,

Clinton had the advantage in the first half. They held Magee without a single first down and outgained them 181-29. The two teams then traded interceptions with Russell accounting for Magee's theft. Clinton would attempt one more Jim Blackwell 31-yard FG before intermission, but it failed.

Magee came to life in the 3rd quarter, but started with a trade of interceptions. Again, Russell had the pickoff for the Trojans. Roberts then did the same to set up the final Trojan scoring drive. In the final frame, Roberts put them at the 3-yard line from where he later went in from the 1-yard line for the touchdown. Hopkins' boot marked the eventual winning point. Mike Stewart added a late pickoff, as did Thames. Clinton won in first downs (10-6) and passing (162-7) while Magee out-rushed the Arrows 154-63.

"We were glad of the way our boys came back in the second half. They showed a lot of poise and self-determination. And a real team effort. We were extremely proud of them all season for the way they conducted themselves; both on and off the football field. We were proud of the way the student body and townspeople got behind our football players. And we were surely glad to win the Little Dixie Conference championship".

First Team All-LDC nods went to Mike Smith, Joey Hughes, Jake Russell, Bob Roberts, Dwight McWilliams and Jerry McNair. Smith also received the Most Valuable Lineman award. Russell had previously been selected Most Outstanding Player in the LDC playoff and had received the first annual Fred L. Gaddis Memorial Trophy. Honorable Mentions included Charles Thames, Mike Varner, Jory Thompson, Mike Stewart, and David Hopkins.

1972 (8-2)

Troy Greer had 7 lettermen and 11 seniors for his fourth season as Trojan mentor. His squad was picked an unusual 3rd in the Little Dixie Conference South for the coming season; a departure from their usual first or second spot. By the later part of practice weeks, he said *"Our boys have shown a lot of enthusiasm and hustle and we have been getting fine leadership from the seniors that we have. We have made a lot of progress so far, but we still have a lot of work to do before our opening game. We are having some keen competition for different starting positions and we hope this competition will make us a better football team. We will have some boys that will have to play both offense and defense. This will be especially tough on them in the early games because of heat".*

The Magee Touchdown Club hosted the team and parents at a supper the night before kickoff. There were at least 13 less Trojans on the roster than the year before.

GAME 1: MAGEE (0-0) @ WEST JONES (0-0)
MAGEE 21 WEST JONES 0
September 8, 1972

The Mustangs from the DeSoto Conference had new leadership in Coach Fred Kirkland and were picked 7th in that division after returning 17 lettermen from a 2-8 season. Though Magee had beaten them a combined 52-6 in the past two seasons, Greer noted that *"You always go into the first game kind of blind and hope you're better prepared than the other team. But we've tried to prepare for them".*

Magee had an opportunity to take a first quarter lead, but a 27-yard David Hopkins FG was just left of its mark. But with good line blocking, Keith Grubbs put the Trojans on the board in the next frame via his 43-yard dash. Hopkins' PAT made it 7-0 at halftime. They opened the 3rd quarter with a solid 78-yard drive capped by a 1-yard Bob Roberts dive. A few plays later, Fredrick Lee picked off a Mustang throw. That would lead to Grubbs' 30-yard strike to Billy Bishop. Hopkins converted on both point-after attempts. An interception killed a last-frame drive and the Trojans made it only to the 1-yard line as time expired.

"We made a lot of mistakes against West Jones but was still able to move the football real well. We will have to eliminate some of our mistakes and move the ball better against Morton. We had a good number of young linemen and we believe that they are the kind of people that want to get better each week. We were proud of our defensive play as a unit".

GAME 2: MAGEE (1-0) @ MORTON (0-1)
MAGEE 14 MORTON 0
September 15, 1972

Coach Cotton Robertson, in his first year as Panther head man, was picked to take his 6-4 team to a second-place LDC North spot. Some reports put him with 8 returning lettermen while others boast of 12 players. Magee was 11-3 against Morton since 1960 and was looking to prove voters wrong about a third-place prediction to start the season.

It seemed that Morton would be first to the scoreboard, but a Bishop interception of Jeffery Halley led to his 86-yard pick-six and, along with Hopkins, a 7-0 lead. Early in the 2nd quarter, Roberts found paydirt on a run that capped a 71-yard march. Hopkins' kick would prove to be the last points. Magee would add three more interceptions before the final whistle; those coming from Ted Hart, Donald Magee, and Roberts. The Trojans could have scored again, but a missed FG and suffered a TD called back from Glenn Smith to Grubbs. Magee led in first downs (15-6), rushing (208-70) and passing (36-19).

"We were happy to have a good team effort against Morton. We improved our blocking from the first to the second game. Our linemen moved off the football much better and showed a lot of determination. Our defensive team showed a good effort in holding Morton to 89 yards running and passing. We still made some mistakes, though, and hope to do better. We will have to continue to improve this week... We have a couple of boys who have been sick. We hope all will be in good shape and ready to give 100% against a good Clinton football team this Friday".

GAME 3: MAGEE (2-0) vs CLINTON (1-1)
MAGEE 20 CLINTON 22
September 22, 1972

With the retirement of Roy Burkett, the defending North Little Dixie champion Arrows had a new head man for the first time since 1955. James Sloan called for players on August 3rd and hoped they would come in good condition due to the limited amount of practices available. *"There is a lot of unfinished work, unfilled positions and much-needed leadership. Certainly I am looking for a good team at Clinton. I'm optimistic, that is the only way I know how to approach the coming season; that's the only way I know how to coach it. Therefore, I will draw these conclusions from the above statement. If we get the unfinished work finished, the unfilled positions filled, and the fellows come up with the needed leadership, we could be tough. If not, well I don't even want to think about it."*

Sloan would start his first year with the loss of four quality players from the 7-3 season but ranked number one by his peers in LDC predictions. *"That poll is just for sportswriters. The pressure is not only on me now, but the kids and my assistants. I hope we can fulfill the confidence the coaches have placed in us."* It would start with highly-favored Arrow player Fred Rainer suffering a knee injury in practice during the week and requiring surgery. *"The loss of Rainer was a severe blow."*

The Trojans were finally playing at home after two conference road wins. Called *"one of the more interesting scraps of the evening"*, it put the North and South winners from 1971 against one-another. The Clarion-Ledger called it 7-6 for the Arrows. Magee, unscored-upon thus far, had beaten Clinton twice that year to take home the title. The game would come down to the last play.

Magee's defense provided the first score of the night when Hart snagged an errant Mickey McMurtry pass and took it 33 yards for a touchdown. Clinton came right back with two 2nd quarter scores to make halftime 10-6. The first was a McMurtry one-yard sneak set up by a Barry McKay run 21 yards to the 1-yard line. Another McKay run of 21 allowed a Richard Keyes 27-yard FG. The second half *"was played under an on-off downpour."* Magee had the only points of the 3rd when Jerry Winn dashed for 50 yards to the Arrow 20 and later took it in from the 5. Hopkins' extra point made it 13-10. They added the first score of the 4th to give them a *"commanding"* 20-10 lead on a Roberts fumble return of 63 yards.

As the game neared completion, McMurtry hit Bill Sellari from the 9 to tighten the contest 20-16. Now with :06 on the clock and time for one more play, the two hooked up again. From the 20, McMurtry hit Sellari in the corner of the end zone to give the Arrows *"a heart-pounding 22-20 win."* Said Greer, *"It was real tough on our football team to lose in the manner in which we lost to Clinton."* McKay had 95 yards of Clinton's 134 in rushing (Magee had 198 yards). Passing definitely favored Clinton 186-12.

GAME 4: MAGEE (2-1) @ CRYSTAL SPRINGS (2-1)
MAGEE 30 CRYSTAL SPRINGS 0
September 29, 1972

In a series stretching back to 1928, Magee had gone 14-0-1 against Crystal Springs since 1957. Odds were good that the streak would continue as Coach Terry Randolph's team went 1-9 last season and were picked last in the South. They had 12 lettermen back and their 2-1 record could be a problem, but that wasn't the only issue. *"We had some boys who were banged up in the Clinton game. But I hope they will be ready to play against Crystal Springs"*.

Roberts started the scoring midway through the 1st quarter on a 4-yard plunge. Hopkins added the PAT and a 33-yard FG later (after a Magee fumble recovery) to make it 10-0. In the 2nd, Roberts *"with excellent blocking from the right side of the Trojan line"* dove in from the 1 and Hopkins converted for a 17-0 halftime lead. Now in the final quarter, Grubbs hit Smith on a *"miraculous catch"* from the 30. With under 4:00 to play, Roberts again found daylight from the 2-yard line. That had come after an interception of Steve Lingle. Hopkins nailed the final point.

"We were glad to win our first South Division game against Crystal Springs. We were especially glad to see improvement in our kicking game. Our kickoffs and place-kicking were extremely good. Our linemen moved off the football real well on offense and blocked people. Our running backs ran better and their blocking was improved. We hope our blocking and picking up on our assignments on different defenses will continue to improve as we get ready for the Prentiss game".

Stats from The (Crystal Springs) Meteor show Magee losing the air 120-60 but holding the ground 148-81.

GAME 5: MAGEE (3-1) vs PRENTISS (3-1)
MAGEE 36 PRENTISS 8
October 6 ,1972

The cardinal and white under Coach Richard Hall were an unimpressive 4-5-1 the previous year but did have 17 returning lettermen to push them to a 3-1 record thus far. They had been picked 4th in the South by voters pre-season.

Roberts found the end zone in the opening quarter from the 2-yard line to open scoring. On the PAT, the snap was low, but Hopkins managed to find Fredrick Lee for the surprise two-point conversion. Roberts made it 14-0 on a 7-yarder in the same period and Hopkins converted. Grubb's 68-yard bomb to Smith in the 2nd quarter was topped by the pair's connection from 75 yards out later. Hopkins made the first PAT but the second was blocked to make it 28-0 at intermission.

In the 3rd quarter, it was Hopkins with the 2-yard rush and Roberts with the two-point conversion. Prentiss avoided the shutout later when Larry Pace dodged in from the 1-yard line. Steve Terrell's two-pointer to Terry Stein finished Bulldog scoring. Magee led in first downs (14-12), rushing (174-81) and passing (184-95). *"We were proud to see our offensive football team perform in the manner that they did against Prentiss. They had a lot of poise and the execution and blocking was much better. Our offensive line has improved each week and we hope they will continue to improve each week. The defense played well, also. They hit real good and our tackling was much better"*.

GAME 6: MAGEE (4-1) @ HAZLEHURST (1-3)
MAGEE 42 HAZLEHURST 13
October 13, 1972

Picked 6th in the South, Coach Mason Denham had little reason to expect to better that position. He returned only 6 letter-winners from a 3-7 team and, predictably, was 1-3 by kickoff. Said Greer, *"We will have to be ready for Hazlehurst this week. They have played some good football and we know they will be up for us"*.

The initial score early in the game came via Dwight McWilliams' tackle of Alex Stovall for a safety. An ensuing kickoff fumble by Bishop was recovered by Herbert McMillian and, one play later, Sidney Wiley found Sam Easterling from 58 yards out for the score. Ricky Tanner's PAT put the Indians up 7-2. Roberts quickly erased the deficit with a 20-yard touchdown run and his two-pointer. In the 2nd quarter, Lee broke away for 63 yards to the Indian 4-yard line before Roberts drove in from there. Hopkins added the PAT. Then, Grubbs hit Smith from the 7 and it was now 23-7 at halftime.

Winn got into the books in the 3rd quarter on a *"dazzling"* 37-yard dash and Hopkins converted for the 30-7 advantage. Hazlehurst's Stovall then scored from the 8-yard line to cut into the lead. In the same period, Hopkins dove in from the 2-yard line to gain the points back. Finally, and in the last frame, Roberts put icing on the cake with a 3-yarder. *"In general, we are pleased with the offensive performance of our team. Both linemen and backs blocked well on offense, but we made some mistakes on defense against the running and passing game that we hope we can correct this week"*. Magee dominated in first downs (23-7) and rushing (343-69) while the Indians gained the air 166-20.

GAME 7: MAGEE (5-1) vs MONTICELLO (3-2-1)
MAGEE 14 MONTICELLO 8
October 20, 1972

The Red Devils had become a recent menace to Magee; keeping them out of the LDC playoffs in 1970 and ruining a perfect record in 1971. Coach Malcolm Courtney finished 7-4 that 1971 season and was now picked 5th in the South. *"The Monticello game will be a tough football game. We will have to be well-prepared for them. Monticello had defeated us two consecutive years. They are the only team to have done this. Our kids should be up for this one"*.

Magee marched straight down to the 1-yard line before fumbling to Brooks Martin in the end zone, but came back in the 2nd quarter via a 10-yard Grubbs toss to Smith. Later, a Lee run of 23 yards made it possible for Grubbs and Roberts to hook up from the 11. Hopkins converted both PATs and halftime sat 14-0. Monticello cut into the lead early in the last quarter on Ernest Thomas' 7-yard escape and added two more points on a Cecil Lewis toss to Ulysses Bridges. In the end, the Red Devils forced 5 Trojan turnovers while Magee forced 4. McWilliams and Bishop recovered fumbles while Roberts and Hopkins picked off passes.

"We were happy that we were able to beat a real sound Monticello football team. We made some mistakes at times that hurt us, but our boys had enough poise to hang in and preserve the victory". The Lawrence County Press noted that Magee could have scored more in the first half but had a Frankie Baylis inception on the 3-yard line and missed a FG. First downs (12-7) and rushing (144-78) went to the Trojans; passing (102-73) to the Red Devils.

GAME 8: MAGEE (6-1) vs COLUMBIA (2-5)
MAGEE 21 COLUMBIA 6
October 27, 1972: HOMECOMING

First-year Coach Charles Coggins inherited a 2-8 team with 13 returning lettermen. Voters expected little; slotting them 7th in the South. Said Greer, *"Columbia has some good football players. They have quickness and some of their backs are relatively big folks. It should be a good game"*. Roberts sat just four points behind Arthur Phillips (Mendenhall) for the LDC scoring lead with 76 points. Bishop would have to miss the contest with a knee injury.

An early McWilliams fumble recovery at the Cat 19 set up a Roberts touchdown run from there and Hopkins converted. In the same frame, Grubbs and Smith teamed up for good yardage to allow Hopkins a 7-yard scoring run a few plays later. Hopkins was again true. Columbia responded in the 2nd quarter on a Bruce Threadgill pass to Jerry Holloway to put halftime 14-6. The final points came in the 3rd quarter when Winn *"made a 60-yard gallop through a tremendous hole made by the Trojan line"*. Hopkins' PAT finished scoring. Magee (interception) and Virgil Overby (fumble recovery) ended any Columbia threats.

Magee led in first downs (18-13) and rushing (280-113) while Columbia and Threadgill held passing 143-48. *"We were glad to win our game against Columbia, but we were not satisfied with our inconsistency on offense and defense. We will have to be more consistent and have more enthusiasm in order to beat Warren Central, which is in our opinion, one of the most improved football teams we have seen"*.

GAME 9: MAGEE (7-1) @ WARREN CENTRAL (2-4-2)
MAGEE 8 WARREN CENTRAL 7
November 3, 1972

This game, perhaps even more than the Clinton contest which gave Magee their only loss, would be the toughest of the year to date. The Vikings under Coach Lum Wright had started disappointingly. Picked 2nd pre-season in the LDC South with 13 lettermen, they now stood with only a pair of victories. But Greer knew what was in store. *"We hope that our players will accept the challenge Warren Central presents us by preparing for them during this week"*. Roberts had suffered a separated elbow in the Columbia tussle and would be unavailable.

The slugfest between the two teams in Vicksburg in intermittent rain was a stalemate until the 3rd quarter. That's when Don Kitchens picked off an errant Grubbs toss and took it to the Trojan 12. From there, Keith Wright *"scampered and slid in"* and Kitchens notched the point-after. In the same quarter, Grubbs *"behind the beautiful blocking of the Trojan line"* went 5 yards to paydirt. Deciding to go for the lead, Winn (or Glenn Smith) drove into the end zone for the two-point conversion that would eventually give them the honors.

The visitors had opened with a push to the Viking 3-yard line but a fumble to Gary Grant killed the threat. In the next frame they moved to the 1-yard line but the Warren Central defense held strong. *"The last couple of plays in the first half saw the valiant Vikings putting the stops to the Trojan offense again"*. The last came as Magee was at the 3-yard line before the clock expired. The Vikes fumbled to Magee in the 4th quarter, but Wright got the ball back via interception. The Trojans finished the contest with a pickoff.

Magee led in first downs (11-4), rushing (159-50 or 200-119) and passing (54-49). The defense forced 4 turnovers. Smith, Grubbs, Bishop and McWilliams were noted for their defensive play. *"We were happy to win against Warren Central. The game was played under conditions, too. Our defensive unit played extremely well, holding Warren Central to four first downs, 50 yards rushing and 49 yards passing. Our offense had other opportunities to score, but when we needed to come from behind, they had the determination to do it. We need the week off for two or three of our boys who have slight injuries to get better"*.

GAME 10: MAGEE (8-1) vs MENDENHALL (9-0)
MAGEE 0 MENDENHALL 21
November 17, 1972

Paul Pounds' team lost 10 lettermen from an 8-3 team, but they were now picked as front-runners in the LDC South. And with good reason. By game night, they were tied with Magee for that spot and a win would send them to the championship. The same held true for the Trojans. As was becoming customary, this contest always had implications. Magee had won 10 straight, starting after their 1961 shocking 13-6 defeat. *"We are working real hard in preparation for the game. We expect it to be real tough"*.

It didn't take long for Mendenhall to strike; that on a 24-yard Joe Boyles strike to Charles Jerry Williams to cap a 73-yard drive. Stennis Bridges' PAT put it 7-0. On the last play before halftime, Bridges found Williams again from 59 yards away and Stennis sent the teams to the lockers 14-0. The combination hooked up again late in the 3rd quarter from 27 yards out and Stennis finished the scoring. Hart and McWilliams did recover Tiger fumbles, but Magee could not make them pay.

Mendy led across the board: first downs (12-10), rushing (170-110) and passing (121-40). Said Pounds, *"We were very happy to have won the football game. But we were also very humble at the same time ... We had all the luck and a lot of breaks; all that goes into winning the championship. I think Coach Greer is one of the finest coaches in the conference. It was a pleasure to beat him and to beat Magee"*.

The Trojans were once thought to be playing in The Mississippi Bowl at season's end. But, both Magee and Forest Hill had *"decided against post-season action"*. All-Little Dixie First Team awards went to Glenn Smith, Dwight McWilliams, Donald Magee, Virgil Overby Bob Roberts, Keith Grubbs and David Hopkins. Honorable Mentions included Billy Bishop, Ted Hart and James Parish. Hopkins won All-Conference Place Kicker. Clinton beat Mendenhall 7-0 to claim bragging rights in the Little Dixie Conference.

1973 (1-9)

Troy Greer entered his fifth, and final, season as head coach with a bleak situation. Gone were many starters (many All Little Dixie players) and key pieces at QB, kicking, etc. But, they did have 15 seniors suited up. The head man had taken his Trojans to an overall 33-7-2 record in his tenure and nobody could take a Greer-led football team like Magee for granted. Amazingly, the LDC picked Magee second to Warren Central in the South for the coming season.

GAME 1: MAGEE (0-0) vs WEST JONES (0-0)
MAGEE 26 WEST JONES 8
September 7, 1973

The DeSoto Conference Mustangs, now under the leadership of ex-Laurel Coach Jim Gatwood, went 3-7 the previous season and had lost 17 lettermen for the upcoming campaign. Said Greer, *"This first game is always a little hard to anticipate because of the unknown factors. We don't know anything about the team. They have a new coach ... however, their roster shows some pretty large linemen, larger than ours, and we know they have a good running back in Rickey McKenzie"*. The Hattiesburg American picked Magee 24-7 and said that West Jones *"should provide limited opposition for Magee"*. Their prediction was eerily accurate.

Halftime ended 6-0 in favor of Magee after Ted Hart plowed in from the 5-yard line for the opening tally in the first frame. They moved to the Mustang 2-yard line later on a fumble but fumbled it back. Before halftime, West Jones picked off another pass to kill a threat. Hart then took a 3rd quarter punt back 72 yards to paydirt while Fredrick Lee converted the two-pointer. The ensuing West Jones drive was killed by a Virgil Overby interception. A few minutes later, Melvin Smith found James Parish from 21 yards out to make it 20-0. After another Mustang fumble at their 35-yard line, Lee added the last Trojan points in the same quarter on a 1-yard plunge. West Jones avoided the shutout with 1:57 remaining when Bernard Knight got in from the 2-yard line and George Smith notched the two-point conversion.

First downs (11-9), rushing (110-101) and passing (55-36) went to the home team. *"It's always encouraging to win the first game of the season. As expected, we had a lot of mistakes on offense and defense and hope that the boys will be determined to correct their mistakes. We hope to improve on our blocking (and) both backs and linemen need to be consistent with our passing game. We believe we can have a winning football team if the players are willing to work hard and keep a winning attitude"*.

GAME 2: MAGEE (1-0) vs MORTON (0-1)
MAGEE 0 MORTON 6
September 14, 1973

Like West Jones, Morton was also under new leadership after a 2-7-1 record. Fred Foster now held the whistle and was upset 26-6 in his opener the previous week against Newton. The Panthers had been picked second-to-last in the LDC North. It didn't help things that they had lost two players via knee injury and appendectomy. Meanwhile, Magee was riding a four-game winning streak against the Scott County eleven.

The only score of the contest came in the 3rd quarter after Richard Latham recovered a loose Trojan football. After three tries inside the 10-yard line, Ricky Hatch plunged in from the 2. The two-point conversion by Howard Smith *"was stopped ...by a stingy interior Trojan defensive line"*. Morton came close to scoring more, but a Ricky Walker punt-block that was recovered by Charles Keeton for the touchdown was called back. In all, Magee fumbled three times.

Magee led in all categories: first downs (12-6), rushing (142-86) and passing (30-0). *"It's disappointing to lose in the manner that we did. We beat ourselves by committing too many mistakes. We hope that we can get a lot more aggressiveness and a more positive attitude by the Clinton game"*.

GAME 3: MAGEE (1-1) @ CLINTON (2-0)
MAGEE 6 CLINTON 21
September 21, 1973

James Sloan was coming off of a Little Dixie Championship, had 5 returning All Little Dixie performers, had won 12 straight games by kickoff, featured 22 of 39 lettermen in camp, and was picked 1st in the LDC North *"with strong competition from Forest Hill and Pearl."*

The first possession for the Arrows resulted in a drive of 63 yards with Johnny Everett going in from the 1. Magee fumbled to Perry Tanksley at their 32 to set up an Everett run to the 14. Barry McKay dashed in from the 4 for the next score afterwards. The Clinton News said that Tim Harper and Larry McMurty both recorded interceptions in the 2nd to kill Magee drives. In the 3rd, McKay did it again with a 65-yard run to daylight to make it 21-0. Warren Green had hit all 3 PATs. Two Clinton punt fumbles finally resulted with Magee at the Arrow 32. But McMurtry picked off one of two passes on the night to kill the drive.

Magee managed to get on the board before the whistle when Smith hit Lee from the 36 with just :45 remaining in the game. Clinton had 180 yards rushing and 107 passing versus Magee's 72 and 73 yards. Said Greer, *"We are working hard to get over what happened at Clinton and to get ready for Crystal Springs."*

GAME 4: MAGEE (1-2) vs CRYSTAL SPRINGS (3-0)
MAGEE 0 CRYSTAL SPRINGS 22
September 28, 1973

Magee had gone 15-0-1 against Big Crystal since 1957. But this season, the team with 22 returning lettermen from a 6-3-1 season were undefeated. Pre-season voters had the Tigers 3rd in the South division. *"Crystal Springs has a fine football team with plenty of speed, quickness and size. Because they have 17 returning lettermen this year, and because (they) are undefeated with wins over Mendenhall, Canton and Pearl, we will need a good effort in order to win"*. It would be tougher than normal as Magee would now be without Terry Tutor, Ted Hart, and QB Melvin Smith due to season-ending injuries. Smith suffered a broken leg during practice week.

The Magee Courier said that Magee *"couldn't find the right formula"* during the rainy affair. The visitors' first score came in the opening quarter after Clarence Pendleton's fumble recovery on a 35-yard Steve Lingle toss to Larry Singletary. Jimmy Mangum blocked the PAT. Before halftime, Jimmy Kennedy fell on a blocked Joe Stephens punt by Lee Roy Yarn at the 5-yard line to set up a Michael Wilson dive from the 2. Marcunes Newell raced in for the two-pointer and 14-0 lead. In the final frame, and after another Pendleton fumble recovery at midfield, Wilson broke away from the 20-yard line and then notched the two-point conversion.

Crystal Springs led in first downs (12-10), rushing (172-76) and passing (61-12). It was becoming clear that injuries to starters would spell troubles for the remainder of the season.

GAME 5: MAGEE (1-3) @ PRENTISS (3-2)
MAGEE 7 PRENTISS 18
October 5, 1973

Prentiss went a break-even 5-5 the previous year and, with 14 returning letter-winners, was picked 6th in the South. But nothing would make them happier than to beat Magee for only the 4th time since 1958. Midway through the 2nd quarter, they hit the board on a 6-yard run by Charles Loftin. Mangum blocked another PAT; this by Terry Stein. Heartbreak followed as, with just :01 on the clock before halftime, Larry Thompson picked off Al Styron and sped 71 yards to paydirt for a 12-0 lead.

Magee responded with their only score in the 3rd on a 65-yard drive capped by David Williamson's 1-yard plunge. Preston Maddox converted for the Trojans. With just :01 left in the 3rd quarter, the Dogs' Baldwin Butler drove in from the 2-yard line to end scoring. Prentiss led in first downs (14-9), rushing (204-108) and passing (31-22).

GAME 6: MAGEE (1-4) vs HAZLEHURST (1-3)
MAGEE 0 HAZLEHURST 7
October 12, 1973: HOMECOMING

Hazlehurst had beaten Magee only 4 times since 1948, though they recorded a tie in 1970. As it was Homecoming, it was hoped that the injured Trojans would find enough to continue the streak. But *"bad luck on fumbles, errors, penalties and interceptions"* thwarted the plans in front of alums.

The lone tally of the night was set up on the game's very first play when Herbert McMillan hit Sam Easterling for a 51-yard gain to the Trojan 21-yard line. Melvin Jordan ended the drive with his 1-yard run and Fredrick Tanner booted what would be a 37-yard point-after. *"The Trojans made several thrusts at the Indian goal, but were stymied by two interceptions, two lost fumbles and penalties which came in crucial situations"*. Magee did lead in first downs (9-8) and rushing (102-84) but were dominated in the air (-5 to 60). They lost 2 fumbles and suffered a pair of interceptions.

GAME 7: MAGEE (1-5) @ MONTICELLO (4-2)
MAGEE 0 MONTICELLO 13
October 19, 1973

Monticello was proving voters wrong as they had gone from 1-9 the previous year and voted last in the South to a 4-2 spot and 3rd-place tie. If Magee wanted a break-even season, this game was critical.

They had a chance in the first half to break a scoreless affair, but their drive to the Devil 19-yard line was spoiled by a fumble to Ricky Barnes. Then, they drove to the Monticello 23-yard line but lost a fourth-down play. In the 2nd quarter and after a fumble recovery, Magee was held to a 28-yard Maddox FG attempt, but it was wide right. The Red Devils got it going in the 3rd quarter after a Jeff Ball fumble recovery ended in their 52-yard march and his 22-yard escape. In the final frame, they went 69 yards with Tommy Siler doing the honors from the 1-yard line. Kevin Stamps provided the point-after.

Monticello led in first downs (15-9), rushing (207-136) and passing (19-0). Magee had one pass picked off and lost two fumbles.

GAME 8: MAGEE (1-6) @ COLUMBIA (3-4)
MAGEE 19 COLUMBIA 22
October 26, 1973

The outlook for second-year Coach Charles Coggins' Wildcats depended upon what you read. The Columbian Progress said that they were *"expected to have good depth"* with *"experienced linebackers and returnees at every position"*. The Clarion-Ledger said that Columbia, 3-7 the previous year with 17 lettermen returning, should still *"be strong"* but noted that they were chosen 5th in the LDCS. In fairness, they also said that Columbia could be *"a surprise contender"*. The Hattiesburg American picked Columbia 24-14.

It was an exciting tilt at Gardner Stadium with Dwight McWilliams falling on a loose Cat fumble at the 2-yard line early in the opening frame. Lee ran in from there and Maddox converted. In the 2nd quarter, Columbia came back with a Lonnie Allen 1-yarder and the Bruce Livingston two-point conversion. Back came the Trojans with Williamson's strike to Gary Herrington. With the two-pointer, it was 13-8. But a later Trojan fumble was picked up by Bobby Hartwell and taken 15 yards to the end zone. With Livingston's two-pointer, halftime ended 16-13.

Williamson opened the 3rd quarter, after a Jimmy Mangum fumble recovery, with a 4-yard scoring pass to him to make it 19-16. With 6:07 remaining, Allen escaped from 47 yards out for what would be the final score. Magee didn't quit, moving to the Cat 19. But a Maddox FG attempt was off-target. Still, Magee was better on the evening in first downs (11-10) and rushing (127-114). Passing went to Columbia (189-171). The Trojans did recover 4 fumbles and added a pass interception. As a side note, two sources (The Hattiesburg American and The Clarion-Ledger) gave touchdown pass credit to Frank Wade.

GAME 9: MAGEE (1-7) vs WARREN CENTRAL (8-1)
MAGEE 7 WARREN CENTRAL 36
November 2, 1973

The Viking started the season as overwhelming favorites for the LDC South and would secure that honor when the game was over. It was impressive as they had gone only 3-5-2 the previous year. They were able to count 17 lettermen back, however. Said Greer, *"We are well-pleased with the enthusiasm, desire and hard hitting in the Columbia game. We hope to get an equally good effort against Warren Central. Of course, they have a real fine team and we hope that we can get ready to play them"*.

The season-spiral would continue with their worst loss of the year. But, it was Magee first on the scoreboard with :27 left in the opening quarter with Williamson's 11-yard pass to David Dunn and Maddox's PAT. The team from Vicksburg controlled the remainder of the contest. Keith Wright's 1-yarder and James Mills' PAT put things even at halftime. Wright ran in again from the 1-yard line in the 3rd quarter and Mills again found the uprights.

Late in the frame, Wright broke away from 53 yards for a touchdown. One minute later, Bobby Smithhart picked up a dropped Lee football and returned it 6 yards to paydirt. Jim Grisham's two-pointer to Wright ended the frame 28-7. In the final stanza, Wright picked off a Williamson throw and took it 57 yards. Martin Chaney notched the two-point conversion to ice the LDC South title for the red and white. First downs (14-10) and passing (31-0) went to Magee. WC took the ground 198-161. Magee had a pair of interceptions and a pair of fumbles lost.

GAME 10: MAGEE (1-8) @ MENDENHALL (6-3)
MAGEE 0 MENDENHALL 13
November 15, 1973

For the first time in recent memory, the game meant nothing other than bragging rights to either team as Warren Central had already locked up the division. Mendy was slotted 4th pre-season in the group with *"severe gradation losses wiping out eight starters, including the entire backfield"*. That was quite a change from a team that went 10-1 the previous season; losing only in the championship game. The Simpson County News said that *"Sixteen out of the last 21 years found either Mendenhall or Magee in the championship game and hardly a year went by without the champ in the South Division being decided in the Mendenhall-Magee tussle"*.

The Tigers struck just two plays into the game when Larry Harper dashed 77 yards to the end zone and Bob Bridges converted. The Simpson County News noted that *"If this run by Harper got the fans' spirits running high, all soon settled down to a tune of defense, fumbles, punts and mistakes"*. Now late in the 3rd quarter, Harper dove in from the 2-yard line to finish a game called *"filled with mistakes and miscues on both sides"*. Magee led in first downs (10-8) and passing (62-22) while losing the ground 191-6.

All-Little Dixie First Teamers included Fredrick Lee and Jimmy Mangum. Honorable Mentions included Dwight McWilliams and Virgil Overby. Warren Central would go on to beat Forest 15-8 for the Little Dixie title.

1974 (5-5)

It was a new day for the Trojans as Jerry Sullivan was now the 19th head man for Magee football. He was no stranger to the team as he had served as an assistant for years and principal of the school the year before. *"We are strictly rebuilding, there's no doubt about it. But we've got some good prospects and these young men are working hard to come up with a better record than we had last year. Their attitude is great"*. He based that on the fact that only three of his 13 lettermen *"held down starting assignments in last year's squad"* and the team had only 8 seniors. Strangely enough, voters had the 1-9 team picked 3rd in the Little Dixie South for the coming year.

GAME 1: MAGEE (0-0) @ GEORGE COUNTY (0-0)
MAGEE 14 GEORGE COUNTY 20
September 6, 1974

George County, under tenth-year Coach Bill Martin, went 4-5-1 in the DeSoto Conference the previous year but was picked a contender for the title according to sources. Martin told the paper that the Rebels *"must find replacements for several outstanding gridders lost through graduation"*. For this inaugural scrap, The Hattiesburg American picked the home team 20-17; once again eerily accurate.

Said Sullivan before the game *"We've had our share of bruises and two of our top players (Jimmy Mangum and Joe Stephens) have missed several practice sessions due to injury or sickness. But, they're fine now and our entire squad is in good condition. And, we're overdue for a win. So, we'll be fielding a hungry squad down in George County"*.

The Magee Courier said afterwards that *"Five turnovers helped to account for two of George County's touchdowns…"* Midway through the opening frame, GCHS went 70 yards and capped the drive with a Vince Reed (or Jason Fallon) 1-yard run and Rusty Martin PAT. Back came Magee with a 40-yard Roger Maddox pass to Hal Berry at the 4-yard line. Melvin Smith got in from the 1-yard line and Preston Maddox tied things early in the 2nd quarter. With :37 left in the half, a fumble recovered by Bruce Ward put the Rebs at the 11-yard line. Reed dove in from the 1-yard line to make it 13-7. To make matters worse, Davy Sellers pulled a pick-six with just :09 remaining for 44 yards and a 20-7 score at intermission.

Overcoming numerous turnovers in the 3rd quarter, Magee was able to hold GCHS scoreless. Late in the final frame, David Williamson hit Berry for an 8-yard touchdown. Maddox's PAT put it 20-14. But time was not on the Trojans' side. Magee lost the race for first downs (10-9) and rushing (113-28) but led in the air (125-40). *"With all the turnovers, they didn't get discouraged and kept their composure. We definitely need to work this week polishing up on offense and working out some of our problems"*. Jimmy Mangum won Player of the Week in a game captained by him and Berry.

GAME 2: MAGEE (0-1) @ MORTON (1-0)
MAGEE 28 MORTON 8
September 13, 1974

Like Magee, Morton had a new mentor for 1974. Glenn Rhodes, former head coach at Saint Aloysius in Vicksburg, now led a team picked pre-season 6th in the South. They had finished just 4-6 the year before but had 12 lettermen back. Their opener was good as they beat Newton 15-0. Said Sullivan, *"They may not have many, but you can count on them being top-quality ball players. Morton is always tough and this year will be no exception"*.

In this game, it was Magee with an aerial theft; this time by Williamson. That led to a 6-yard Smith score and Preston Maddox PAT. In the 2nd quarter, Mangum found a loose football at their 14-yard line. Williamson then hit Berry from the 14 and Stephens *"scrambled for the two-point conversion"*. The defense then took two more takeovers via J.L. Robinson (fumble) and

Stephens (interception) but couldn't turn them into points. But with :17 left before halftime, Dale Berry picked off another pass and turned it into a 14-yard pick-six. With Maddox's kick, it was 22-0.

Williamson and Ronnie Yates continued the parade of interceptions in the 3rd quarter, but it was Morton putting up points on Jack Ficklin's 49-yard pick-six. Bobby Roberts' pass to Benny Tillis for the two-pointer put things 22-8 as the 3rd quarter ended. Finally, Smith burst away for 54 yards to set up a FG attempt, but it was unsuccessful. Seconds later, Kenny Gray picked off a Panther pass and took it the necessary 20 yards for the last score.

"I thought they played super defensively. We need to play offensively as well. Our offense was too erratic ... and that is due to inexperience of our players. But they're getting better with each game and we'll work this week brushing up on our offensive plays". Dale Berry was named Player of the Week by the coaches.

GAME 3: MAGEE (1-1) vs CLINTON (1-1)
MAGEE 7 CLINTON 3
September 20, 1974

With 30 lettermen returning from an 8-2 team, the Arrows were unanimous vote-getters for first place in the LDC North with veteran returnees. Everyone was optimistic except Coach James Sloan. *"We have a long way to go. We're small on defense and we'll have to depend on desire from the players to carry us through a rugged slate"*. A week or so later, he said that *"We have a long way to go. We lost some fine kids"*.

Perhaps due to their South Pike win the week before, The Clarion-Ledger predicted a 20-14 Clinton victory. *"Clinton tunes up for its North Little Dixie encounter with Forest next week by getting past South Little Dixie foe Magee."* Said Sloan, *"We think Magee is the best team we've faced yet."* He would now be without key RB Johnny Everett for the season as he underwent knee surgery during the week. *"You don't replace a guy like that. But our kids won't quit and they keep coming back."*

All of the scoring was done by halftime. The Arrows got to the 20 and the 11 in the opening frame, but the last march would be lost via a fumble. Clinton captured the lead later in the 1st quarter when Greg Powell, after a Magee fumble, hit a 32-yard FG. That would be short-lived as an Arrow fumble was recovered by Mangum. Williamson found him for the go-ahead touchdown from the 6-yard line in the 2nd. Maddox nailed the PAT. A 3rd quarter FG attempt by the Trojans was missed. The Arrows attempted a comeback in the 4th frame. With :23 remaining, Gary McMurtry hit Bill Maxey and the running back went 60 yards to the Magee 20 before being tackled by Robinson as time expired.

The Clinton News reported that Magee picked off three McMurtry passes and recovered 4 Arrow fumbles. Clinton could muster only two fumble recoveries and a Fasano interception. *"What can you say about your defense when they hold a team to just three points? They played almost flawlessly and our entire defensive unit deserves plenty of praise. We made a lot of mistakes offensively, but so did Clinton. But our offensive unit improves weekly"*. Williamson was picked as Player of the Week for his efforts.

GAME 4: MAGEE (2-1) @ CRYSTAL SPRINGS (3-0)
MAGEE 0 CRYSTAL SPRINGS 3
September 27, 1974

The blue and gold under Coach Terry Randolph were going to provide tough competition for the Trojans. They went 9-2 the year before, returned 12 letter-winners and were picked 2nd in the South pre-season. Fans making the trip would stay on the edge of their seats the entire game as the visitors put up a valiant fight. They also left *"disgusted with what some called poor officiating while others used much stronger language"*. In fact, an official protest to the MHSAA (Mississippi High School Activities Association) would be filed later.

The only score of the game came with 2:18 in the 2nd quarter after a Tiger interception of an errant Trojan throw. With a solid defense hampering progress, they opted for a Scott Jones 19-yard FG; a kick that would make the difference on the night. Joseph West stopped another CS drive with a 3rd quarter interception. In the final frame, trouble began. As the game neared ending, the football had been blown dead; thus stopping the clock. But it continued to count down despite pleas from Magee coaches that it should be stopped. It ticked away and Magee had lost. The Crystal Springs Meteor noted that Magee had moved to the 6-yard line; thus making the game-tying FG a "chip shot".

Magee led in passing (76-26) while rushing (195-16) and first downs (10-3) were dominated by the Tigers. *"We definitely had some calls during the game but we did have several opportunities that we failed to take advantage of ... I don't want our fellows thinking that poor officiating lost us the game. Had we executed our plays more effectively earlier in the game, the time would not have played such a factor. We can beat any team in the LDC if the boys just make up their minds to win. They're a hard-hitting bunch of fellows and are coming along very well. I think we're in for some more fine football during the rest of the season"*. Berry was voted Player of the Week.

GAME 5: MAGEE (2-2) vs PRENTISS (3-1)
MAGEE 6 PRENTISS 12
October 4, 1974

Coach Richard Hall's Bulldogs were predicted to finish 5th in the South after a 6-4 season as there was only 8 lettermen back in red and white. Thus far they had lost only to Warren Central. It would once again be a fight to the finish for the Trojans.

Like the week before, the opening score came in the 2nd quarter. Williamson, back to pass at his own 18-yard line, was hit from the blind side by Allan Craft and Jessie Newsome and fumbled. Larry Thompson grabbed the pigskin and raced the 18 yards to paydirt. Jeffery Butler's block of the PAT kept it 6-0 at halftime. Berry's fumble recovery in the 3rd quarter allowed an eventual *"hotly-disputed"* Stephens 1-yard dive. Maddox's PAT was blocked by Malcolm Armstrong; thus keeping the game 6-6. Prentiss got all they needed with 3:40 left when Anthony Iovino hit Larry Donaldson from the 14-yard line. The PAT was blocked by Mangum. With 1:45 remaining, a Williamson pass was intercepted by Jerry Bryant to ice the game.

Magee led in first downs (6-5) and rushing (75-42 or 82-71) but lost the air (46-39 or 62-40). Prentiss lost 3 fumbles while Magee lost a pair. Kenny Gray, six solo tackles and four assists, was voted Player of the Week.

GAME 6: MAGEE (2-3) @ HAZLEHURST (2-2)
MAGEE 14 HAZLEHURST 6
October 11, 1974

It should have been looked upon as a breather for Magee as Coach Mason Denham's Indians were not expected to improve on their 4-6 campaign. They had only 8 lettermen back and voters slotted them last in the South. But with Homecoming in Hazlehurst, anything could happen.

Things didn't start of well for the home team as Stephens picked off a Kenneth Roberts pass at the 38-yard line on the first play. He eventually ran it in from the 9-yard line and Magee led 6-0. Ronnie Yates then recovered a fumble at the 30-yard line and Stephens again hit the end zone from the 6-yard line. Late in the 2nd quarter, a bad punt snap sailed out of the end zone and the Trojans had a safety to make halftime 14-0. Hazlehurst avoided the goose-egg with 2:15 remaining on Roberts (or Herbert McMillan's) 6-yard TD toss to Michael Welch. Stephens rushed for 100 yards in the affair. Smith would have accomplished the same feat had not rushes of 48 and 53 yards not been called back.

GAME 7: MAGEE (3-3) vs MONTICELLO (0-5-1)
MAGEE 30 MONTICELLO 6
October 18, 1974: HOMECOMING

The Monticello coach was Doug Merchant. He later became a force at Pearl High; leading that team to success for numerous years with his fiery approach and attention to detail. The Red Devils had gone 5-5 the previous year and were ranked just 6th pre-season in the division. But, this year would be substantially different as they sat winless with just a lone tie game.

Maddox ended a drive from the 22-yard line with an opening-quarter FG. Williamson *"unloaded a bomb"* to Hal Berry from 55 yards out in the same frame and Maddox made it 10-0. Williamson added a 1-yard sneak in the next stanza and Maddox put things 17-0 at halftime. In between, Monticello got their lone score on a 4-yard run by Tommy Siler. In the 3rd, Williamson capped a 59-yard drive with his 1-yard plunge while he also hit Mangum in the final quarter from the 30. That had come as the result of a fumble recovery. Maddox hit the initial PAT but the last was blocked.

First downs (10-4), rushing (133-30) and passing (103-69) favored the Trojans. Monticello lost 2 of their 4 fumbles while Magee lost one of their two. Terry Green, causing two fumbles in the game, was named Player of the Week.

GAME 8: MAGEE (4-3) vs COLUMBIA (4-2-1)
MAGEE 23 COLUMBIA 8
October 25, 1974

First-year Larry Hancock had only 5 lettermen and 6 seniors to help him match the 7-3 campaign from the year before. Voters thought he would not and picked them 7th in the LDCS. *"I expect this to be a rebuilding year since we are so young and lost 12 players to graduation"*, he said preseason. They weren't as bad as expected with a 4-2-1 tally, but it was still going to be a tough road. They had won three-straight and were hoping to keep moving upward in LDC games. Meanwhile, Magee was fighting for second place in the division.

Smith put the Trojans up in the opening quarter by capping a 71-yard drive with his 5-yard run. Maddox was true on the conversion. In the next quarter, and despite a Magee fumble at the 5-yard line, he hit a 31-yard FG before Steve Ashley hit Quinn Belk on an 11-yard toss with just :01 left before halftime. Ashley converted for the 10-8 score. Stephens' 1-yard dive in the 3rd quarter was paired with his 2-yarder in the 4th quarter that, along with both Maddox PATs, ended scoring. Stephens garnered 118 markers on the night before a home crowd.

Magee led in first downs (14-8) and rushing (214-81) while the Cats held passing 38-0. Columbia had one pass picked off in the game.

GAME 9: MAGEE (5-3) @ WARREN CENTRAL (8-0)
MAGEE 0 WARREN CENTRAL 16
November 1, 1974

Much like 1973, Warren Central was dominant. Coach Lum Wright, picked 1st in the LDCS with only 5 lettermen, went 10-1 that season. By game day, they had already wrapped up the South and Magee was playing for second place. That was a big improvement over the previous 1-9 campaign that was so hampered by key injuries. *"We have a chance to beat Warren Central. We've improved with every game and our defense is the best in the conference. We just need to make up our minds and we can win"*.

All of the scoring had been done before halftime. A bad break in opening frame punting put the Vikings at the 39-yard line. Josh Rogers capitalized from the 2-yard line and Jim Grisham *"caught the Trojans napping on the fake kick"* for the two-point conversion. In the next quarter, Rogers found Sam Price from the 13-yard line and Leo Cage did the two-point honors to end scoring. Williamson's 53-yard pass to Smith in the 3rd quarter gave a ray of hope but it did not end with points.

Warren Central led in first downs (14-8) and rushing (175-51 or 219-8) while Magee was leader in the air (148-51). Two Magee passes were picked off in the game. Jerry Barnard, called by his coaches *"outstanding all year"*, was chosen as Player of the Week.

GAME 10: MAGEE (5-4) vs MENDENHALL (4-4-1)
MAGEE 7 MENDENHALL 10
November 8, 1974

Coach Hamp Gaston's Tigers were slotted 4th pre-season in the division. They had gone 8-3 the year before, but returned only 4 lettermen according to sources. Their 4-4-1 record reflected what voters expected. But, this game would not depend on records, returning lettermen, or what was a stake for either school. Bragging rights for the Simpson County teams were at hand for a series that stretched back to at least 1929. The Simpson County News put it best when they said *"Who's going to win? That's a good question as it is impossible to tell what will happen when these two schools meet. Past records, wins and defeats don't mean a thing in this annual classic"*.

This one, like others, would come down to the last seconds of the game. But, it would end in heartbreak in more than one way. Williamson put the Trojans into the end zone on a 3-yard dive topping an 80-yard march in the opening frame. Maddox gave Magee the 7-0 lead with just :36 left. In the 2nd, Stephens picked off a ball to kill a drive that had actually resulted in a score before a penalty erased a Keith Coleman run. But, the Tigers fell on a loose Trojan football. Reports differ afterwards. The Magee Courier says that Coleman took it 31 yards for a touchdown while The Simpson County News says it was a 60-yarder. Either way, Gary Hilton's PAT provided the game-tying point.

Before halftime, disaster struck for Magee as Williamson suffered a broken leg and Stephens was also lost to injury. Both teams were scoreless for the 3rd quarter *"and the game was all defense"*. Gregory Walker had recovered a fumble for the Tigers to kill a drive and Mendy had actually gone as far as the Magee 6-yard line in the 4th quarter. But, a FG attempt *"was wide to the left*". With 1:41 remaining, the Tigers started moving from their own 26-yard line. With :03 remaining, and at their own 21-yard line, Mike Smith was called upon. He drilled the kick and the game was over.

Said Gaston, "*Coaches for both teams knew it would be a close ball game. We told our players all week that the kicking game would win it*". Stats differ depending on the source. The Magee Courier said that first downs (12-7), rushing (128-120) and passing (85-0) all favored the visitor. The Simpson County News had it pretty close to the same except rushing (172-123). Williamson and Dale Berry won co-Player of the Week honors for the last game of the 1974 season.

All-Little Dixie honors on First Team went to Jimmy Mangum, Dale Berry and Preston Maddox. Honorable Mentions included David Williamson, Freddie Hansbrough, Terry Green and Hal Berry. Warren Central beat Clinton 33-14 for the Little Dixie Championship.

1975 (8-2-2)

In his first year, Coach Jerry Sullivan did what others were skeptical of being accomplished. He took a 1-9 team that had been struck hard by injuries and turned them into a break-even (5-5) squad. This season, peers had placed a second-place mantle upon the Trojans in the Little Dixie South division though they lost 9 lettermen. The Hattiesburg American said that Magee had "*Strength and quickness but lack of speed…*"

Sullivan told the paper "*We plan to throw the ball more this year because we have some good receivers. If we can avoid crippling injuries and get off to a good start, I think we will be a factor in the race for the Little Dixie champions. We will be big and strong. We'll have a lot of quickness but not a lot of breakaway speed*". Reports put his line at an average 209 pounds.

Another report said before the first game of the year, "*Sullivan will take advantage of the non-conference opener against Florence to see where each player fits best into the Trojan picture for 1975. Many positions are still undecided and up-for-grabs as they go into the season opener. The Trojans have good passing ability and with that big line should see plenty of hard running right up the middle*".

GAME 1: MAGEE (0-0) vs FLORENCE (0-0)
MAGEE 32 FLORENCE 0
September 5, 1975

Florence was not a first-time opponent, but those who remember previous games were few. In 1932 and 1935, the Burrheads had faced Florence and came away with wins. Coach Terry Brister's red and black Eagles went 1-9 the previous season but did have 11 letter-winners back in camp. The Clarion-Ledger predicted a Magee win, saying "*Coach Terry Brister has the Florence Eagles flying high in practice this fall, but the Birds' opening opponent will be too much. Tab the Trojans 28-7*".

In a game plagued by "*bad weather and a strong team*", Magee opened the 1975 season with a bang. Despite a trade of punts and a Magee drive that failed at the 2-yard line, the Trojans came up with a fumble a few plays later and Hal Berry made it count from the 6-yard line. Berry then found Melvin Smith from 60 yards away for another score and Joe Stephens converted the two-pointer for the 14-0 advantage at halftime. In the 3rd, Berry took the kickoff 78 yards for a tally and later Smith "*scored on a sneak set up by a pass from Smith to Roger Maddox*". Stephens had the last tally in the frame to ice scoring.

"*I was pleased with the performance of our team and we will be looking forward to another good game when we face Morton*". Magee led in first downs (10-4), rushing (103-66) and passing (74-0). The Trojans picked off a pair of Eagle throws and recovered the same number of fumbles. Berry was the obvious choice for the very first Player of the Week award.

GAME 2: MAGEE (1-0) vs MORTON (1-0)
MAGEE 14 MORTON 14
September 12, 175

After just one season, Coach Glenn Rhodes was gone from the Morton team and replaced by ex-coach Reggie Robertson. Like Sullivan, Robertson had also served as principal of the school before coming out of "retirement". He would hope to build on the 5-4-1 record with 9 blue and gold lettermen. His first outing had been a success, beating Newton 29-6.

A 2nd quarter fumble by Stephens set up Morton's first score when Ray Massey picked up the loose ball and raced the necessary yardage for the touchdown. In the 3rd, Magee went 62 yards with Smith dodging in from the 1-yard line. Preston Maddox's PAT put them ahead 7-6. Morton fumbled the ensuing kick and Magee not only recovered, but used it to move to the 16-yard line from where Roger Maddox escaped for the touchdown. Back came Morton with a Dwight Hughes 22-yard toss to Willie Ray McDonald. The crucial two-pointer was converted by Hughes.

Fumbles killed opportunities on both sides in the last frame. The Panthers actually got to the Magee 1-yard line before a penalty and fumble killed their chance for the victory. Magee led in first downs (11-9) and rushing (203-92) while Morton dominated passing 118-7. Two players, Kenny Gray and Danny Thompson, shared Player of the Week.

GAME 3: MAGEE (1-0-1) @ CLINTON (1-1)
MAGEE 0 CLINTON 30
September 19, 1975

While winning the entire LDC outright only once (1972), the Arrows had won or shared the NLDC title in 1971, 1972, 1973, and 1974. This year was no surprise that their peers selected them first in conference play. They had 18 returning lettermen, including LDC honorees Gary Ferreri, Steve Miller and Steve Fasano. Gary McMurtry was back at QB along with David Lee and Jimmy Givens. Those three had been at or near the lead in their categories in 1974.

Coach James Sloan, as always, wasn't so sure. *"This is really going to be a tough year; an interesting season. We have four rugged games outside the conference and you know our conference schedule. It's going to be a Battle of the Bulge every week. Most of these teams are going to just pin back their ears and say come and get us."* As for depth, Sloan said, "We *have good competition for most of our positions with a super group of sophomores and backup players."*

The Arrows bounced back from their previous week 27-0 loss to Kosciusko in fantastic fashion. They shut out the Trojans while putting up 17 points in the first half and 13 in the 3rd. David Lee provided the first points with a 28-yard FG and, two plays later, Bruce Hulitt recovered a Smith fumble and returned it 31 yards for the score. Lee made it 10-0. The FG was set up by an Arrow interception. The two teams traded turnovers afterwards; Clinton's Donnie Hill picked off a pass but Clinton gave it back via fumble at the Arrow 9.

In the 2nd, Hulitt capped a 42-yard drive with a run from the 1 and Lee made halftime 17-0. The last two Arrow scores came from a 38-yard Gary McMurtry pass to Greg Frazier and a Mitch Elliot 2-yard plunge. Clinton had 175 rushing yards to Magee's 28, though The Magee Courier thought it 159-41. In passing, Clinton outpaced the Trojans 102-78. Elliot had 114 yards on the ground while McMurtry went 6-15. The Clinton defense came through with 5 interceptions on the night. Manuel Beasley had 2 while Donnie Hill, Steve Marshalek and Mark Green each had another. Stephens was named Player of the Week for Magee.

GAME 4: MAGEE (1-1-1) vs CRYSTAL SPRINGS (2-0)
MAGEE 24 CRYSTAL SPRINGS 13
September 26, 1975

Things would seemingly get no easier for the Trojans as Coach Terry Randolph's blue and gold had gone 9-2 the season before, were undefeated and picked 3rd in the South. The game proved as tough as anticipated, but Magee was up to the task and never gave up in their first LDC South matchup.

The Magee Courier said that *"time after time during the entire first half, the Trojans had the opportunity but couldn't put the formula together for the score"*. It was Preston Maddox with a pair of FGs that kept Magee in the ballgame; down 7-6 at intermission. The Crystal Springs TD came from Ricky Pickett's pass to Robert Bennett and Randy Moulder's PAT. In the 3rd quarter, Smith hit Randy Garner from 16 yards away to change that, but the Tigers wasted no time in response. Keith Ainsworth bulled in from 5-yards out on their next drive and made it 13-12.

Robert Maddox then recovered a Marcus Harper fumble that he returned a few yards to the 19-yard line and then drove in from the 3-yard line. Five minutes later, he dove in from the 4-yard line for his second touchdown and gave Magee the insurance they needed for the upset. His team led in first downs (14-7) and rushing (213-108) while Big Crystal held a 48-23 passing margin. But it was Smith who garnered Player of the Week.

GAME 5: MAGEE (2-1-1) @ PRENTISS (1-1-1)
MAGEE 13 PRENTISS 6
October 3, 1975

This game was important as it would give the Trojans a lead over yet another LDC South opponent. Coach Richard Hall's Bulldogs were 6-3 the previous season and picked to end 5th in the division. He had an uphill battle for the coming season in his mind, saying "*We lack a proven QB and we're hurting in the defensive line*".

Magee wasted no time with their opening 63-yard drive capped by Smith's 1-yard plunge and Preston Maddox's PAT. Back came the Dogs with a 67-yard march and Vicky Sexton touchdown. In the 2nd quarter, Smith gained his second tally of the evening on a 58-yard drive. "*The second half of the game was back and forth with no score change. Magee carried to the 10-yard line once and attempted a FG but it was declared no good*". Roger Maddox was awarded Player of the Week.

GAME 6: MAGEE (3-1-1) vs HAZLEHURST (1-3)
MAGEE 41 HAZLEHURST 0
October 10, 1975: HOMECOMING

The Trojans had now moved up to 2nd place in the LDC South. Now up on the schedule was Coach Mason Denham's Indians. They were only 3-7 the year before and had a limited five lettermen. As such, they were picked last in the division pre-season. If you removed the 1970 tie game and the 1973 loss, Magee had not lost to Hazlehurst since 1956. This game continued the bragging rights in a big way.

Scoring came early and often, starting with a 39-yard Smith pass to Bill Griffith starting the parade. In the 2nd quarter, Roger Maddox rushed in for a TD, added another, Stephens recovered a fumble on a punt, Williamson hit David Heriard with :10 left, and halftime sat 28-0. Another Indian fumble set up Smith's late 3rd quarter TD run. In the last frame, Bobby Hamilton got into the end zone from the 3-yard line for the finale. Magee led in first downs (11-8), rushing (158-118) and passing (132-6). Griffith was named Player of the Week.

GAME 7: MAGEE (4-1-1) @ MONTICELLO (2-4)
MAGEE 28 MONTICELLO 0
October 17, 1975

After playing the last-place LDCS team, Magee now had the 7th place team on the docket. Coach Doug Merchant's team went 0-9-1 in the previous campaign but he did have 12 lettermen back in Monticello. They had already outpaced the win column from that season, but would not improve on it this night in front of home fans.

On their first drive, Roger Maddox found paydirt from 40 yards while Preston Maddox notched the PAT. The next Magee score came from the 5-yard line after "*a combination of Bill Griffith and Preston Maddox*" runs to make halftime 14-0 in part due to a missed FG by the Trojans. Garner picked up the next TD in the 3rd quarter via a pass from Smith from 34 yards, while Smith provided the last tally on a 1-yard dive after his significant run set up the opportunity.

Magee out-rushed Monticello 201-77 and held first downs 10-7. They also held the air 56-15 (or 56-0). Freddy Hansbrough and Joseph West were awarded co-Players of the Week for their efforts.

GAME 8: MAGEE (5-1-1) @ COLUMBIA (2-5)
MAGEE 14 COLUMBIA 7
October 24, 1975

Coach Larry Hancock's Wildcats had nearly beaten Long Beach the week before. But the 4th-place pre-season LDC South team could still brag of only a pair of victories on the year. They did have 13 letter-winners back from a 6-3-1 squad and were hosting Magee at Gardner Stadium. But The Columbian Progress said that "*The Trojans will bring to town enough opposition to keep Columbia's hands full. Pick Magee by 8*".

The initial volley from Magee came after a Cat fumble on the 17-yard line was returned to the 1-yard line. Smith "*saw daylight and ran it over*" to make intermission 6-0. Smith later hit Griffith from the 21-yard line and then the Trojans iced it with a Roger Maddox two-point play. Late in the game, David Riley (or Ellis Griffin) hit Richie Bullock from 65 yards out and Randall Lewis provided the PAT. Williamson was credited with two fumble recoveries out of Columbia's three.

First downs (10-4) and rushing (158-65) favored Magee. The Cats gained the edge in passing 98-21. Williamson and Mike Keith shared Player of the Week awards for Magee.

GAME 9: MAGEE (6-1-1) vs WARREN CENTRAL (7-1)
MAGEE 7 WARREN CENTRAL 7
October 31, 1975

While Magee had won the first 6 matchups against the Vikings, the Vicksburg eleven had taken the last two games. That was not much of a surprise. The Vikings under Coach Lum Wright finished the previous season 11-0 and were understandably (again) picked tops in the South. That marked two-straight Little Dixie titles. The difference in this game would be that the LDC South (and therefore the LDC) hung in the balance this time. Like Magee, they had lost to Clinton (7-0). Of the top 4 scoring leaders in the Little Dixie, Warren Central counted two of them. But this night in Simpson County would prove only that each team was hungry. Nothing more.

Magee was first to the scoreboard when Roger Maddox dove in from the 2-yard line in the 2nd quarter to cap a 72-yard march. Preston Maddox nailed the PAT and it appeared that the score would remain as in lights until the closing seconds. To be accurate, Warren Central actually scored in the opening frame on a Mike Dawson 54-yard dash but it was called back on a penalty. In the final frame, with a minute to go, Magee was penalized a total of 45 yards to put the Vikings within sight of the end zone. That came via 3 personal fouls and an interference call. Finally, Jim Grisham hit Dawson for the touchdown and the game-tying PAT from Eugene Wiley was true.

First downs favored Warren Central 12-11 (or 15-8). Magee won both the ground (156-116) and the air (57-39). The Vicksburg Evening Post noted that the Vikes held the ground 182-180. The Magee Courier noted that Warren Central had "*decided in a pre-game vote to refuse a playoff in the event of a tie*"; thus resulting in fans "*gathered on the field to say 'We're number one*!" But, that would not matter until the last game was played and a decision by the Executive Committee of the Little Dixie Conference met. David Heriard and Keith Jackson won Players of the Week.

GAME 10: MAGEE (6-1-2) @ MENDENHALL (4-5)
MAGEE 37 MENDENHALL 0
November 7, 1975

If the Warren Central contest proved anything, it was that Magee could not lose this contest. Mendenhall went 5-4-1 the previous year and could only hope to somewhat match that result under Coach Hamp Gaston this season. With only 8 lettermen, he had thought it a rebuilding year for 1975 and was validated by his peers in their 6th place LDC South spot pre-season. Said The Simpson County News, "*The Trojans are loaded in size and depth and have played outstanding football this season. They are well-coached and appear to have regained the pride that has characterized so many of their fine teams in years past. Our team will have to give its best effort to date if we are to stay in the ball game*".

The Vikings were playing outside of the South against Forest Hill, and with a one-game LDCS advantage, Magee could not falter if they wanted to see another Little Dixie game. It was rumored in a November 9th Clarion-Ledger article that should Magee lose, they could be pitted against Saint Aloysius in the Mississippi Bowl. But that was of no interest versus beating a rival for bigger spoils.

Griffith started things early with a 3-yard dive. Preston Maddox converted and then notched a late 2nd quarter 39-yard FG to make it 10-0. A Mendy fumble in the 3rd put Magee at their 15-yard line from where Roger Maddox crashed over. Preston's kick put it 17-0. Stephens ended the frame with a scoring run, Williamson notched the next from 43 yards and Joe Harold Smith hooked up with Larry McDonald from 39 yards out for the last. Maddox converted on two of the points-after.

First downs (14-5), rushing (285-52) and passing (52-0) all went to Magee. Now, there was no decision. Warren Central and Magee would again face off to see who would play again.

GAME 11: MAGEE (7-1-2) vs WARREN CENTRAL (8-1-1)
MAGEE 20 WARREN CENTRAL 14
November 13, 1975: CLINTON, MS

Despite the claims of fans back on the last day of October, Warren Central would again face the Trojans to see who actually was "*number 1*". This time the game would be in Clinton; a neutral field for a shot at another Little Dixie title for both. Each had reasons to claim importance.

Magee had won the ring 7 times but Warren Central had bragging rights two years in a row after being in existence in a much shorter time period.

The Magee Courier said that, in front of 6,000 spectators, *"It was obvious that Magee had come to play football and that the Magee fans had come to cheer their fans"*. The Trojans wasted no time in marching 73 yards and topping the drive on a 1-yard Smith dive and Preston Maddox PAT. In the 2nd, Roger Maddox dove in from the 3-yard line to finish a 53-yard march and Preston converted for a 14-0 advantage. They struck again in the 3rd quarter on Roger's 27-yard dash that highlighted a 75-yard move but the PAT failed and kept things 20-0.

Warren Central came back with a 75-yard Jim Grisham escape that, along with the PAT, made it 20-7. With 2:58 remaining, Grisham hit Russell Richards from the 5-yard line and it was suddenly 20-14. Magee fumbled to Tom Gay with 1:40 left to go to give the Vikings new life. But Garner sacked the QB for a 15-yard loss and time ran out on the red and white after a last-gasp pass was overthrown.

Rushing went to Magee (284-136) while passing (121-8) went to the Vikings. Both suffered an interception and a lost fumble. Said Sullivan afterwards, *"That was a tough, hard-fought ball game and we're hurting. Anytime you play a game like that, you'll come out with plenty of bruises that take some time to heal"*.

GAME 12: MAGEE (8-1-2) vs CLINTON (9-1)
MAGEE 7 CLINTON 8
November 21, 1975

On November 19th, Clinton entertained Magee and beat them 30-0. But this was a different Magee football team. Coach Jerry Sullivan called Clinton *"a great football team whose strong suit is defense. They have the finest pair of defensive tackles in the conference and they have simply taken away everyone's inside running game. It will take a super effort for us to move the ball offensively and to win."* Coach Sloan returned the favor. *"They are not the same ball club. I saw them in the playoffs against Warren Central and they are much more impressive then there were earlier in the season. They are much stronger offensively"*.

Nash Nunnery wrote that *"The Cardiac Kids were at it again Friday night."* That reference was to Clinton's miraculous ability to come back in contests. Magee had the first half's only score after Mike Marshall fumbled a punt to Keith Jackson at the Arrow 48. Smith eventually hit Garner from the 8 and Preston Maddox's PAT made it a 7-0 Trojan lead with 4:37 left in the 1st. That score would hold until the last seconds of the game, though Magee had missed two FGs in the first half. Clinton threatened to even up the contest with 4:25 left, but Hulitt was short on a 4th and 5 play. The defense held Magee and forced a punt.

With 1:17 remaining, Mike Bishop broke through the line and blocked a Stephens punt. Wayne Hudson chased down the loose ball and fell on it in the end zone for the touchdown. Now down 7-6, Sloan would have to choose between the tie and the potential win. Nunnery reported that Coach Sloan commented *"Coach Monroe and Coach Farrar changed my mind about going for one, thank goodness', said the jovial leader, murmuring through tears."* Hulitt would take a Steve Jordan pitch and walk into the end zone for the Little Dixie Championship. Said Hulitt, *"A truck could have gone through there."*

Clinton won in first downs (9-6) and rushing (113-67). Magee barely held the passing game (55-51). Keith Jackson won the Fred Gaddis, Jr. Award for MVP.

At season's end, Sullivan garnered the Little Dixie Coach of the Year honor, to which he replied that he was *"very much surprised and very pleased, of course"*. All-Little Dixie awards went to Mike Keith, Kenny Gray, Danny Thompson, Melvin Smith, Robert Maddox, Keith Jackson and Joe Stephens. The team was given a trip to The Liberty Bowl in Memphis as a reward from the Magee Touchdown Club to see USC play Texas A&M.

1976 (7-4)

Jerry Sullivan returned for his third year confident of what his Trojans could accomplish. *"We've got a good football team and we know it. We have good experience, good speed and good size returning for this fall. But we do have a problem of depth and that is what we will be trying to develop before our first ball game. Our ends are 160 and 198, our tackles are 190 and 238, our guards are 241 and 173, our center weighed in at 164, our guard 160 and our backs average all in at 157. We are looking for a good season. We are working to have one and are expecting it"*.

His team, *"sprinkled with college prospects...",* consisted of 12 seniors and 12 letter-winners. Eighteen key lettermen were now lost to graduation. The Hattiesburg American noted that *"some replacements must be found soon if the Trojans are to make another bid for the (Little Dixie) title"*. Voters still though the Trojans the pick for South honors.

GAME 1: MAGEE (0-0) @ FLORENCE (0-0)
MAGEE 36 FLORENCE 0
September 3, 1976

If you listened to Sullivan, this game would be closer than the 32-0 shutout from 1975. *"They are better this year than when we beat them and they have a good passing attack which they will launch against us"*. In the end, and on the road, it would not be.

Magee opened the contest with a steady drive to the 2-yard line from which Roger Maddox dove in. He added another from the 3-yard line and then put up the two-point conversion for good measure in the same quarter. That 14-0 score held through halftime as the 2nd quarter was *"marred by penalties and sloppy offensive play"*. Joe Harold Smith dove in from the 1-yard line in the 3rd quarter thanks to his 30-yard escape earlier. Now 20-0, they went to the air with Smith finding Randy Garner for a pair of touchdowns from 29 and 47 yards. Bill Griffith added two-point conversions after each.

After watching the game film, Sullivan said *"We played better than I thought we did. However, we must play better this week to win at Morton"*. First downs (12-7), rushing (229 to -1), and passing (76-42) favored the Trojans. Both teams lost a fumble and Florence had a pass picked off.

GAME 2: MAGEE (1-0) @ MORTON (1-0)
MAGEE 13 MORTON 0
September 10, 1976

Magee was 13-4-1 against Morton since 1960. The lone tie ball game came the year before. The Panthers opened the regular season with a 38-6 win over Newton and Sullivan knew he was against tough competition. In fact, the Panthers under Coach Reggie Robertson were predicted to win the Little Dixie North this season. *"Morton has collegiate prospects at quarterback and tailback, so we must play super defense"*.

The visitors' first score came in the 2nd quarter when Pat Herrington took a Panther punt 41 yards to paydirt and Maddox converted. Their last came in the final frame when Maddox used *"beautiful blocking"* to get the necessary 16 yards. With 1:00 remaining, Magee fumbled to Morton at their own 15-yard line. However, the defense held for their second-straight shutout to start the season.

Said Sullivan, *"We played a super ball game. I am very pleased and I thought we played as well as we possibly could have"*. Added Robertson, *"They just came out after us. That's all there was to it. Magee had a tough, tough football team"*. First downs were even 9-9; rushing (143-54) went to Magee and passing (44-12) to Morton. Maddox recorded 103 of those rushing markers. Magee had the lone lost fumble in the game. Maddox won Player of the Week for his efforts.

GAME 3: MAGEE (2-0) vs CLINTON (2-0)
MAGEE 11 CLINTON 27
September 17, 1976

James Sloan's *"Cardiac Kids"* were preparing with two-a-days, but Sloan would rather have the name obsolete with huge early victories instead of last-second comebacks. The squad had lost a number of graduates but the head coach was still optimistic. *"Have our kids gone stale? No, they haven't. The seniors have worked just as hard this season and that kind of spirit and dedication rubs off on the younger players. Our goal is to produce and improve every day. It's one thing to win a title, but to defend it is something quite different."* Sullivan told The Magee Courier that *"it would take an equal or better effort (than in the past) to defeat Clinton..."* The two teams met for the Little Dixie championship in 1975 with Clinton winning 8-7 with under 2:00 left in that contest.

Clinton's first possession, aided by Magee penalties, resulted in a Steve Jordan touchdown from the 3. Magee drove as far as the Arrow 2 in the 2nd, but had to settle for a 32-yard Maddox FG. They also blocked a Clinton punt with just 1:30 left, but could do no damage. Said Sullivan, *"If we could have scored from there, the game might have been different."* An Arrow interception in the 3rd led to a Jordan pass to Edgar Jackson from the 36. They struck next in the 4th when Jordan found Scott Dickerson from the 42 and followed it with a 6-yard run by Mike Paul Marshall. With the game ending, Smith scored from the 1-yard line and Maddox provided the two-point conversion.

Sullivan said afterwards, "*We played with no intensity and certainly no concentration. Mental mistakes will kill you as quickly as physical mistakes, and we made more than our share*." Clinton picked off 3 Magee passes, and out-rushed (117-56) and out-passed (98-42) the Trojans. Griffith won Player of the Week in the loss.

GAME 4: MAGEE (2-1) @ CRYSTAL SPRINGS (1-1)
MAGEE 42 CRYSTAL SPRINGS 6
September 24, 1976

Long-time opponent Crystal Springs had beaten South Pike this season while also suffering a loss to Mendenhall. The Simpson County News said that the Tigers had "*tremendous speed and a QB who likes to throw the ball to some very good receivers*". It was finally time to start play in the Little Dixie South.

After a 60-yard punt return by Herrington, Smith made it count with a 2-yard rushing TD and Maddox converted. Griffith then took an option pitch 21 yards to the end zone, Maddox dove in from the 1-yard line, Griffith added a two-point conversion, and it was 21-0 to end the opening quarter. They added an 85-yard march and 5-yard Maddox plunge for their lone TD before halftime and Herrington kicked the PAT. It could have been worse as Magee sat on the 4-yard line when the whistle blew.

A 3rd quarter Trojan fumble set up Big Crystal for their only score, but Magee responded quickly. Maddox escaped from 17 yards out and Griffith converted the two points. Larry McDonald got into the scoring column to wrap things up with his 5-yarder. Magee led in first downs (11-7) and rushing (242-4). What Crystal Springs lacked on the ground, they got in the air (142-65). With all of the enthusiasm and concentration, Sullivan noted that "*It looked like they enjoyed playing again*". Randy Garner (65 receiving yards) was voted Player of the Week.

GAME 5: MAGEE (3-1) vs PRENTISS (UNREPORTED)
MAGEE 30 PRENTISS 0
October 1, 1976

The Simpson County News said that "*The Bulldogs are reported to have excellent speed and a hard-nosed defense*" and were "*expected to give the Trojans plenty of trouble…*" The two teams had played annually since 1952 with Magee holding a 13-4 edge since 1959. For a game that was expected by some to be close, Magee proved them wrong with their third shutout of the season.

Magee opened the contest with a 77-yard drive with Griffith going the final 24 yards and Maddox converting. A later fumble in the frame and a missed FG with just seconds left in the half kept it 7-0. A Dog fumble in the 3rd quarter led to a 25-yard drive with Griffith getting in from the 6-yard line and Maddox notching the kick. After an ugly skirmish early in the final quarter, Magee managed a pair of scores. Maddox had the first from the 6-yard line with Griffith adding two points. Maddox also had the last as the game was nearing completion when he ran in from the 14-yard line. Smith found Garner for the "*one-handed*" two-pointer.

Magee led in first downs (16-9), rushing (234-125) and passing (78-8). Prentiss lost 3 fumbles while Magee dropped just one. "*We were happy to win because through the years, Prentiss has been one of our toughest opponents. We also have to keep winning because Warren Central already has a 4-0 conference record*". Added Prentiss Coach Richard Hall, "*We were beaten by an excellent team*". Joe Harold Smith was awarded Player of the Week.

GAME 6: MAGEE (4-1) @ HAZLEHURST (UNREPORTED)
MAGEE 17 HAZLEHURST 0
October 8, 1976

Hazlehurst was an abysmal 1-17-1 against the Trojans going back to 1957. Magee would not only add to that misery, but keep their LDC South record unblemished when it was all over. An opening fumble recovered by Allen Maddox at midfield led to a 29-yard Roger Maddox FG. Before halftime, Roger would dash 17 yards to paydirt to make halftime 9-0. It didn't come without a scare as the Indians made it to the Trojan 3-yard line as the whistle sounded.

Magee opened the 3rd quarter with a 74-yard drive capped by a 3-yard Griffith TD and Smith two-pointer "*off right tackle*". Hazlehurst had two solid marches before the final horn, but both ended deep in Magee territory due to interceptions. Smith picked off the first while David Heriard snagged the last. "*Our running game went real well for us. Hazlehurst played well and I'm just proud of the effort of our kids. We gave up too many yards on defense against the Indians and we'll have to work on that this week*".

Magee led in first downs (18-15) and rushing (255-134) but lost the air 106-50. Maddox claimed 110 rushing yards and Griffith garnered 107 yards but it was Heriard as Player of the Week.

GAME 7: MAGEE (5-1) vs MONTICELLO (UNREPORTED)
MAGEE 21 MONTICELLO 8
October 15, 1976: HOMECOMING

Magee had a record somewhat similar in recent history to that against Hazlehurst. Since 1959, the Trojans had dropped only 3 contests. It took only one play before they jumped in front in front of home fans in this one. That came on a 59-yard Smith connection with Heriard and Roger Maddox's PAT. Before long, Charles Cooper stepped in front of an errant Rocky Arnau throw and raced 29 yards to the end zone. Maddox's conversion made it 14-0.

Before the halftime whistle, Magee recovered a Mike Nelson fumble that would lead to a 6-yard Griffith run. The successful PAT finalized Magee scoring. With 6:48 remaining, A.D. Madison took a reverse 75 yards to paydirt for Monticello and they converted the two-pointer on Arnau's pass to Ford Wall. Sullivan "*was proud of the win but disappointed in the performance in some of the Trojan players. However, give credit to Monticello for taking the game to us. What really matters now is the physical condition of our squad*".

Magee led in first downs (8-7) and passing (91-58) but lost the ground (133-130). The Monticello report puts passing 118-114. Magee lost a pair of fumbles while Monticello lost 3.

GAME 8: MAGEE (6-1) vs COLUMBIA (3-?)
MAGEE 19 COLUMBIA 14
October 22, 1976

Sullivan was right to be over-confident about the upcoming contest against the Wildcats. "*We're concerned about them. They have had some great games this year, especially against Warren Central. We hope to have our people back (from injury and sickness). We need a good game for our confidence*".

Things seemed to be going well when Roger Maddox finished a drive from the 6-yard line and added the PAT. Then, he drove in from the 13-yard line to make it 13-0. Just 1:36 before halftime, Columbia scored on a 39-yard Greg Pittman pass to Bobby Wilks and Randall Lewis added the PAT to make it 13-7. In the 3rd, they marched 67 yards and got in from the 12-yard line via a Pittman toss to Billy Holmes. With the Lewis PAT, it was 14-13. Now with 3:05 left in the game, Magee went 74 yards and finished the march on a 2-yard Maddox dive on fourth down.

First downs (24-9) and rushing (257-80) favored the Trojans while Columbia led in passing 70-29. Pat Herrington was named Player of the Week for his efforts.

GAME 9: MAGEE (7-1) @ WARREN CENTRAL (8-0)
MAGEE 6 WARREN CENTRAL 7
October 30, 1976

The previous year, these two teams played twice in three weeks to see who would claim the LDC South title. After an initial 7-7 tie, Magee pulled out a 20-14 win to send them to their eventual LDC title. This season would look much like that one. The winner of this contest would claim the title regardless of what happened later. "*We are pleased to be in position to settle the championship without having to depend on someone else to beat Warren Central. We know it will take a super effort but believe we have one to give. We are about the same physically. We just hope we're larger mentally. We do know we'll have to play better defensively than we did (against Columbia)*".

The game, without Roger Maddox, was exactly as everyone from fans to sportswriters thought it would be. A 2nd quarter Viking punt hit a Trojan at midfield and was recovered by the home team. They marched the 50 yards in 9 plays with Dale Erves capping it from the 1-yard line and Russ Richards converting. Warren Central had a chance to increase the lead before halftime, but Wylie's 42-yard FG failed. With 4:30 left in the game, Magee began an 80-yard drive. Two Smith passes to Herrington moved the ball to the 6-yard line and Smith went in from there for the touchdown. Electing to go for the game-winning two-point conversion, a quick pitch to Herrington fell just a few feet short.

"The Warren Central defeat was a bitter one. We gambled and lost in the last minute, falling short by two feet on an attempted two-point conversion. (Erves' 55 rushing yards) was a great tribute to Magee; holding the highly-coveted collegiate prospect to more than 100 yards below his per-game average". Warren Central did lead in first downs (10-6) and passing (55-50) while Magee held the ground 94-70. Allen Maddox was voted Player of the Week.

GAME 10: MAGEE (7-2) vs MENDENHALL (6-3)
MAGEE 12 MENDENHALL 15
November 5, 1976

Without a Little Dixie title to play for, Magee accepted a bid to play Laurel in the Mississippi Bowl. Still, this rivalry game against Coach David Abercrombie's Tigers was for much more than just another number in the win column. Magee had finally ended a three-game losing streak the previous year but had run off ten in a row before that.

Much like other games this season, Magee started strong. Benny Anderson's 1st quarter interception set up a 29-yard drive with Smith plunging in from the 1-yard line. Solid defense kept halftime 6-0. In the 3rd quarter, Magee fumbled the ball away to Mendy at the 14-yard line. Six plays later, David Walker drove in from 3 yards for the touchdown. The Norman Standfield PAT was successful. Magee responded with a 44-yard march ended on Smith's 1-yarder and, again with a missed PAT, it was 12-7.

Late in the game, and pinned deep in their territory, the Trojans gave up an intentional safety. With 1:03 remaining, Jon Munn found Joe Saxon from the 11-yard line for what would be enough to claim the rivalry win. A last-gasp throw by Magee was picked off by Cleveland Holmes to ice things. First downs (14-9), rushing (138-66) and passing (104-19) went to the Tigers. Both teams lost two fumbles. Magee had two passes intercepted; Mendy just the lone Anderson pick.

"We played a poor game. We didn't deserve to win. We didn't execute offensively or defensively, but I suppose you can credit Mendenhall for that. They played with more enthusiasm, more concentration and much more desire. We hope we can get ourselves back up for the Mississippi Bowl game. If we have the character I think we have, we'll bounce back and make ourselves and our fans proud of us again".

GAME 11: MAGEE (7-3) vs LAUREL (6-4)
MAGEE 12 LAUREL 14
November 20, 1976: MISSISSIPPI BOWL; CLINTON, MS

Coach George Blair's Tornadoes were members of the Big Eight conference. No Laurel team had ever faced a Magee squad. Said Blair, *"This is our third bowl appearance in the last three years. Two years ago we participated in the Shrimp Bowl and, last year, we were fortunate enough to defeat Jackson Murrah in the Capital Bowl. Magee had a tradition of being tough and aggressive and they are members of a tough conference. We are really going to have to work hard if we're going to win"*.

Added Sullivan, *"Although it has been a long time since we participated in a bowl, we're looking forward to meeting Laurel. They are a very formidable foe and I hope that Magee can win this year as it won in 1961. The two losses that we suffered at the end of the season have given us additional incentive to win this game. We'll have to play our best game of the season to win"*. They would have to do it without Roger Maddox and David Heriard; both out with injuries.

In the rainy opening minutes, Johnny Gregory (or McCollum) blocked a Tornado punt. The loose ball was picked up by Griffith who ran it 35 yards to paydirt to make it 6-0. Laurel answered in the half on a 58-yard drive capped by Alvin Gore from the 12-yard line and Tony Taylor converted the two-points after the PAT snap was off its mark. Magee drove steadily in the 3rd both on the ground and in the air. From the 15-yard line, Griffith *"blasted into the end zone"*. The two-point attempt by Smith *"was inches short"*.

Late in the final frame, Laurel began what would be the winning drive. It was finished by a tight-end screen from Taylor to Bo Myrick from 42 yards out. Laurel's Gore was named MVP of the contest. Laurel led in rushing (112-67), passing (52-37) and first downs (11-4). *"We played well. We played well enough to win. If a team always gave the effort our kids gave, they would seldom lose a game. We feel like Laurel was the best team we played all year and we are proud to have played them to the last minute"*.

All Little Dixie honors included Mike Keith, Keith Jackson, Roger Maddox, Bill Griffith, Joe Harold Smith and (Honorable Mention) Pat Herrington. Jackson was named Most Valuable Lineman. Morton would lose to Warren Central 15-0 for the Little Dixie Championship.

1977 (7-4) SOUTHERN ATHLETIC CONFERENCE CHAMPS

Huge changes were in store for fourth-year Coach Jerry Sullivan and his team of 40 players. After what seemed a lifetime in the prestigious Little Dixie Conference, the Trojans entered the inaugural season of the Southern Athletic Conference. A small report noted that there was disagreement on the conference alignment as it pitted much smaller schools against far-larger ones. Sullivan also noted that *"We feel like we would be better off financially in the conference"*.

"We realize our road to success is rocky, but we have a lot of desire and we are not afraid of hard work. We are enthusiastic about our chances. Our size will be the smallest in years and our experience is very limited. We do have a super attitude, however, and we expect this to propel us toward another fine season. We are excited about our new conference".

Gone were a number of key players that shot the Trojans to within one point of another Little Dixie South title. But, at least 9 lettermen that played significant time were back in Simpson County. Sullivan actually started spring training with 63 players but that number had dwindled. *"We are disappointed in our numbers. We have 15 seniors, 13 juniors and 12 sophomores"*. The Hattiesburg American said that the 2nd place pre-season Trojans, would have a hard time matching their past record.

GAME 1: MAGEE (0-0) vs GEORGE COUNTY (0-0)
MAGEE 12 GEORGE COUNTY 18
September 2, 1977

Magee had actually played George County in a losing (20-14) cause in 1974. Coach Bill Martin, now in his 13th season, had been Gulf Coast champions with a 10-1 season and among Mississippi's Top 10 teams, but lost 18 lettermen and 17 starters for the coming season. *"I think our strong point will be our offensive line. We are having to replace all our linebackers, two defensive ends, one down lineman and two people in the secondary. We open with Magee and we don't know too much about them"*.

Said Sullivan, *"This will be the toughest opener since I've been here. We are looking forward to the game and the season. We lost our size and we have very little experience. If we are to win, it will be because of our togetherness and our team quickness. We think we have a lot of heart. We'll see in the next few Friday nights. Our kids have worked hard"*. The Hattiesburg American predicted a 21-20 Magee upset.

The Trojans were first to the scoreboard on their third possession when Joe Harold Smith hit Bernard Lofton from 79 yards away. Then, they ran the clock and ended another march with a 3-yard Pat Herrington run and 12-0 lead. Costly mistakes then changed the ball game via penalties and dropped opportunities. With 1:00 left in the half, George County cut into the lead with Gordon Fryfogle's 8-yard toss to John Goff. In the 3rd quarter, a fumbled snap to Winfred Riley put the visitors at the 25. Fryfogle then found Steve Martin from the 5-yard line to tie the game. Another fumble later at the 35-yard line led to a 9-yard Curtis Bivens dash for what would be the winning score.

Magee led only in passing (108-48) while George County held first downs (8-6) and rushing (94-58). Willie McCollum led tacklers with 5 solo and 10 assists. *"It was a bitter defeat for us because we needed this win for our lack of confidence due to our youth and inexperience. We should have won. We had control of the ball game for the first half, but we let it slip away. I think it was obvious we were a tired ball club; especially in the fourth quarter. I realize they were playing two platoon ball while all of our players were going both ways. However, if that is the situation, you must play harder and be in better shape. We offer no excuses, but we dedicate ourselves to playing better"*.

GAME 2: MAGEE (0-1) vs MORTON (0-0)
MAGEE 6 MORTON 0
September 9, 1977

Morton, old nemesis still in the Little Dixie, played for the title last season before finishing 8-2 with a loss to Warren Central. They had 43 players featuring 17 letter-winners from 1976. Said Sullivan, *"They are extremely big. For example, their tackles weigh 250 and 260 pounds. We expect a tough game but look forward to playing"*. The two prognosticators for The Simpson County News called it for Morton; one 14-6.

Though Morton picked off a Magee pass on their first drive, the defense held. Back came Magee with a scoring drive (after a short Greg Hawkins punt) ending with Smith's 20-yard toss to Benny Anderson and Herrington's 11-yard plunge into the end zone. Morton had actually picked off a Magee pass the drive before, but garnered a penalty after spiking the ball in celebration. Their two-point conversion attempt failed and kept things 6-0. Magee recovered a fumble before halftime at the 20-yard line but the FG attempt was wide.

In the 3rd, Morton staged their best effort with a drive to the Trojan 4-yard line. But, the defense rose up and held. *"The remainder of the game was played around midfield with neither team seriously threatening"*. Morton led in first downs (12-7) and rushing (108-60) while Magee held the air (80-46). Said Coach Reggie Robertson, *"We just got our tails whipped. The Panthers played good defense but did a sorry job on offense. It just killed us"*. The Simpson County News said that Morton lost 3 of 4 fumbles and had 2 passes intercepted

Sullivan called it a *"bitter defensive struggle"* with his team *"breaking out early, muffing several opportunities to put the game away and then fighting for their life. Twice we were denied because of our own mistakes. The first, a long run to the 15 was nullified because of a motion penalty. The second, a first and goal opportunity from the 3 (was) negated by a clipping penalty. We played a good opponent. We made some mistakes that hurt but we played with great intensity and motivation."*

GAME 3: MAGEE (1-1) vs HARRISON CENTRAL (UNREPORTED)
MAGEE 25 HARRISON CENTRAL 6
September 16, 1977

This would be the first-ever meeting between Harrison Central and Magee. But expectations were not very high. Sullivan noted on game week that *"They have one of the largest schools in the state with 80 players on their squad. Their personnel is super, they have good size and some good speed (and) we are expecting another bitter struggle"*. When it was over, The Magee Courier said *"The bigger they are, the harder they fall"*.

The home team opened play with a 62-yard march capped by Herrington's 6-yard escape. On their next drive, Charles Cooper did the honors from the 4-yard line and it was 12-0. After falling on a 2nd quarter fumble, Magee gained their third TD when Cooper dove in once again from the 4-yard line. Before halftime, Harrison Central moved steadily before throwing an interception to Randy Smith near the goal line to make intermission 18-0.

Magee added their last points in the 3rd quarter when Smith snuck in from the 1-yard line. David Weathersby notched the PAT. In the last frame, Harrison Central moved across the goal on a 32-yard Kent Jones pass to Ronald Buckley. First downs (12-7) and rushing (189-61) favored Magee while their visitors led in the air (83-59). *"We are exceptionally proud of our defense. We have a lot of pride in our defense and as long as we play like this, we feel we will be in every game. We are very excited now about our chances. We have progressed much faster and further than we anticipated. We now begin our conference schedule as we play Petal here this week"*.

GAME 4: MAGEE (2-1) vs PETAL (0-3)
MAGEE 47 PETAL 7
September 23, 1977

Petal, under new head man Ronnie McNair, was slotted 4th in the SAC. That was strange as they had finished 4-5-1 the previous season and lost 22 seniors for the upcoming season. He called his team *"young and inexperienced. Most of the boys have never had any playing time and that's going to hurt us. We don't have a lot of size and our offensive and defensive line has needed the most work in preseason workouts. Defensively, we do not have any starters coming back. Therefore, we will have a lot of people going both ways"*. Added Sullivan, *"Petal hasn't won a game yet, but with their coach being a native of Magee, I'm sure they will come prepared to play"*.

Petal had at least one good thing after the dismantling loss at Trojan Field: they now were outscored only 152-7 but had finally crossed the goal in the season. The scoring was called *"rampant"*, with touchdowns in each frame. Late in the 1st quarter, Cooper dodged in from 8 yards and Weathersby converted his first of 5 PATs. In the next frame, Harvey Magee's punt block was picked up by Scottye Holloway and taken the 10 yards to paydirt. A later errant punt snap gave Magee the ball, and one play later, Herrington ran in from the 3-yard line. Petal's only score of the night came after Tommy Minter picked off a Trojan throw to set up Jody Simon's run from inside the 3-yard line with :15 left. Carey Barlow added the point-after.

In the 3rd quarter, Smith got in from the 9-yard line and added another from the 1-yard line before the frame ended. Finally, McCollum grabbed a ball for a 33-yard pick-six. Garfield Turner took advantage of a Trojan fumble recovery afterwards on his later 50-yard dash. Stats were closer than expected. First downs were even (8-8), while Magee held the ground (217-155) and the air (20-14). *"All of our kids executed real well. It was just a great team effort. It was a big win for us as we prepare for the critical part of our schedule..."*.

GAME 5: MAGEE (3-1) @ SOUTH JONES (3-1)
MAGEE 6 SOUTH JONES 13
September 30, 1977

Pre-season SAC favorites were the Ellisville, MS Braves under Coach Sonny Farrar. He was 7-2 the previous season and his team was called *"rulers in the DeSoto Conference for many years and will have a team loaded with experience, especially on defense"*. The Hattiesburg American said that it should be *"a good one"* with South Jones pulling out a 21-20 victory.

Said Sullivan, *"They have super personnel ... We know we must play our best and certainly our kids are prepared to do this. We have been practicing very carefully. We are working hard, too. Defensively, we are playing fine. But most of our kids have to go both ways instead of two-platooning. I think the main thing we have to do to improve is quit making mistakes and having so many penalties"*. The winner of this game was expected to have the edge in overall SAC title hopes.

After holding the Braves on their first drive, Turner took the ensuing punt 91 yards to paydirt but the missed PAT kept it 6-0. South Jones punched right back with an 8:00 drive and a Donald Ray King touchdown. With the Marty James PAT, it was 7-6. A costly fumble in the 2nd quarter in Brave territory led to a South Jones drive to the Trojan 3-yard line. But the Magee defense held. After a trade of fumbles in the 3rd quarter, Magee had a chance to take the lead, but the *"short field goal"* from 26 yards was unsuccessful. In the final portion of the contest, Magee fumbled yet again. Once more, the defense held. South Jones added one more touchdown in the contest again after a fumble recovery; that from Ronnie Harper's 1-yard dive.

South Jones led in first downs (16-7) and rushing (220-20) but Magee held led in passing (145-30 or 59-17). *"We played pretty well but we can play better. Our defense played extremely well in spots. I don't believe anyone can keep them from scoring less than 13 points. Our offense was our disappointment. We just couldn't hold on to the ball to maintain any ball control. They were two-platooning. Maybe that had something to do with our ragged look offensively. We aren't discouraged. We know we can be in the playoffs if we win the rest of our conference games"*.

GAME 6: MAGEE (3-2) vs NORTHEAST JONES (3-2)
MAGEE 12 NORTHEAST JONES 3
October 7, 1977

Coach Tom Boszor was *"facing a rebuilding year"* from their 5-5 campaign. With 18 lettermen lost, voters had them slotted 7th in the SAC in pre-season. In the end, they put up a valiant fight against a Magee team with the same record.

Herrington dotted the scoreboard first after a Smith interception when he nailed a 28-yard FG. The (Laurel) Leader-Call thought it from 17 yards. That kept intermission at just 3-0. He then picked off a Northeast Jones throw and set up a 7-yard Smith TD toss to Lofton. Jones put up their only points afterwards when Bruce Strickland hit a 23-yard FG. Magee came right back with a drive to the 20-yard line but fumbled it away. But the next possession ended in another Herrington FG (25 yards) for what would be the last points.

Magee led in first downs (12-5) and rushing (188-35) while passing was even at 40 yards for both teams. Magee had only one pass picked off while Jones had five. *"Friday's game was a hard-fought defensive struggle with Magee showing good offense in the second half. Our defense controlled the game. We took away the two things they did best: the veer option and their passing game. We intercepted 5 passes; three by Joe Harold Smith. We were also very happy about our kicking game and, by this I mean, all facets of it: kickoffs, punts and field goals"*.

Added Boszor, *"We felt like we got a good defensive effort against a powerful team. But our offense just got a good old-fashioned whipping. We couldn't generate any kind of offense consistently. Their kicking game was excellent all night and kept us bottled up and we had too many turnovers against a team as good as Magee. You can't give that kind of team the ball and still expect to beat them"*.

GAME 7: MAGEE (4-2) @ MONTICELLO (5-1)
MAGEE 42 MONTICELLO 8
October 14, 1977

Before the season, Coach Doug Merchant's team was picked to finish 6th in the conference after a 6-5 season. However, it was also said that they *"could be a surprise to many teams"*. Merchant proved them right as they sat undefeated in conference play and with an overall 5-1 mark. *"Right now, Monticello is the most important game of the year for us. They have a super defense and no one has really penetrated this fine unit all fall. Offensively, they have good speed, an outstanding QB, and good receivers. It should be a great game. We just can't afford another loss and we'll just have to play them one game at a time"*.

Magee took advantage of a 1st quarter fumble with Smith's 1-yard dive and his two-point pass to Turner. They moved 89 yards in the next quarter with *"beautiful pass receptions by Bernard Lofton and Benny Anderson"*. Smith once again got in (from the 17-yard line) and Herrington hit the PAT. The last play of the half was a missed FG to keep intermission 15-0.

They put up a pair of 3rd quarter scores on a 5-yard Herrington run and an 8-yard Cooper escape. The first came after a failed fake punt by the Red Devils while the last was set up by a fumble recovery. Weathersby's PAT put it 28-0. Cooper dashed in from 51 yards in the final frame and Weathersby converted. Monticello's only tally came after as Donnie Peyton ran 75 yards on a Keith Blackwell pass and Blackwell dove in for two points. Finally, Turner eluded Monticello defenders for an 80-yard blast and Weathersby finished things.

"We completely dominated a very good ball club. Our defense played well, but it was our offense that pleased us so much. In our past few games, our offense had sputtered. But Friday night it really came alive. It was a big victory for us and kept us in the conference race. I'm just real pleased with our effort".

GAME 8: MAGEE (5-2) @ COLUMBIA (3-3)
MAGEE 0 COLUMBIA 6
October 21, 1977

It was expected by many to be somewhat of a "breather" this week. Fourth-year Coach Larry Hancock had lost 15 letter-winners from his 3-7 Wildcats and was slotted 5th in the SAC. Hancock did say that *"enthusiasm and hustle is greater than it has been the previous three years"*. But The Hattiesburg American was also expecting Magee would do what they had done the previous week to Monticello. Calling it 28-16, they said *"Jerry Sullivan's Trojans are destined to make a valiant shot at the SAC playoffs and Columbia doesn't have enough to stand in the way. Somebody's in trouble ... this week, Columbia"*. Said Sullivan, *"We must keep winning to make the playoffs and this week's game will certainly be a challenge. We play Columbia, a team that always plays us off our feet. In addition, we must go (there) so we expect the fight of our lives"*.

The game's lone score came in the opening frame after losing a previous trip at the Trojan 5 due to a fumble. Mike Landrum's 13-yard keeper set up his 33-yard strike to Eric McLendon for the tally. *"Little did they realize six would be the winning margin"*. After that, it was simply frustration for the Trojans. They would suffer 3 turnovers and end 4 trips to the Columbia goal without points. They once got to the Columbia 8 but lost it via fumble. Hancock said afterwards, *"We've been pushed around all year on defense and giving up a lot of points. But tonight they really rose to the occasion. We were somewhat fortunate in the fact that we made them turn the ball over"*. First downs (14-10) and rushing (189-147) favored Magee. Passing (60-45) went to Columbia.

"We have a shot at the playoffs but we have to get some help from someone else. If we beat West Jones and Columbia beats Monticello, we would be in the playoff. Also, if we beat West Jones and West Jones beats South Jones, we would be in. I don't know why we played below par. I suppose the credit for our performance would have to go to Columbia for they wanted to play a little bit more than we did. Give me some credit for our performance, too. I should have gotten us higher for the game. In a sense it's frustrating. I've been here 10 years and it seems we've never played well at Columbia. We're still proud of our players".

GAME 9: MAGEE (5-3) vs WEST JONES (7-1)
MAGEE 20 WEST JONES 3
October 28, 1977

The road would get no easier in their last gasps to stay relevant in the playoff chase. Coach Mike Taylor was *"expected to field a reasonable team"* at West Jones. Picked 3rd in the conference due to 14 lost lettermen from a 7-4 team, they had done much better than *"reasonable"*. Now, they were in a three-way tie for top spot with their only loss coming the week before in a 24-15 loss to Monticello. Said Sullivan, *"We've got to pull ourselves up off the ground and get going again. We think we know these young men well enough to know they will give a good effort".*

The early back-and-forth resulted only in a short Stan Lyon FG to give West Jones their last lead of the game. Herrington broke it open with a 65-yard punt return for a touchdown and added the PAT to make it 7-3 at halftime. The visitors marched to the Magee 4-yard line in the 3rd quarter but the "*Trojans refused to yield anymore and for three straight downs they held off the Mustang charge*". In response, they moved 99 yards with Herrington providing the last 62 yards on a "*beautiful move on the WJ safety*".

Cooper had the last points of the night when he "*roared 45 yards*" to put them in scoring position and then dove in for the last 2 yards for the touchdown. Herrington's conversion was true. "*We were fortunate because they outplayed us the first half. We couldn't get anything going offensively. We survived because we played defense when we had to. We played well. Our defense held them on a goal line stand on three downs from the 1-yard line. Charles Cooper and Joe Harold Smith played outstanding on defense*".

GAME 10: MAGEE (6-3) @ MENDENHALL (8-1)
MAGEE 3 MENDENHALL 21
November 7, 1977

There was a bright glimmer of hope for Magee as a fumbled snap on a two-point conversion gave West Jones a 13-12 win over South Jones the week before. That meant that there was now a four-way tie for top spot in the SAC. Though this rivalry contest didn't mean much relative to Trojan chances for the SAC playoffs, it did mean something for citizens and players in Simpson County.

"*This game means a lot to us. To win this game, we'll have to play our best game of the year. I think their line will probably outweigh us 35 or 40 pounds to the man, so we will have to win with desire and quickness. It will be a great game, of that I'm sure. We are looking forward to playing and I'm sure Mendenhall is, too*". Originally scheduled for the normal Friday spot, the game was moved to Monday; presumably due to weather.

Recaps of the contest are more scarce than normal. All Magee could muster was a 25-yard Herrington FG. Billy Welch did the same for the Tigers while Tommy Hamilton returned a punt 64 yards for another Mendenhall tally in the 3rd quarter. They also notched a pass interception that paid dividends and turned a Magee fumble into a fake FG attempt for points. "*We were playing over our heads, in my opinion. I was so proud of our kids for the fight they were putting out and the punt return took away our enthusiasm. Mendenhall has a great team. They were so big (that) we just couldn't move them out. We knew we would have to play with more enthusiasm and intensity than they did in order to win. We also thought we would have to prevent the big play on their part*".

Magee was now waiting to see their fate. If Monticello beat Petal, it could be a rematch. If they lost, it may be the Trojans against one of the Jones County teams. "*We will sure need all this time to get well. In all my years here, I've never seen so many injuries. What scares me even more is that I'm afraid some of them won't be well for the playoff game. Nevertheless, we are real excited about (it) and look forward to playing*".

GAME 11: MAGEE (6-4) vs MONTICELLO (7-3)
MAGEE 16 MONTICELLO 9
November 18, 1977

Trojans wishes came true after the Mendy game when Columbia beat Monticello 20-12. Though scenarios changed, that would mean that the Friday following the Mendenhall scrap, Columbia would play George County while Monticello would play Petal. When it was over, it would be Monticello (20-7 over Petal) and Magee as both had 4-2 divisional records, Magee losing to South Jones while Monticello lost to Magee. The math also depended on the point system of one point for a home win and two for a road victory.

"*We are elated that we are in the playoff. We haven't had our best record this year but we have gotten a great effort from kids that have had to play over their heads many times. We probably played our best game of the year when we played Monticello the first time. We know they want revenge (and) that they will come to kill or be killed. We think we will be mentally prepared for the game but the physical part is something else again. Monday afternoon, our tailback, fullback, center, one guard and split end couldn't dress out for practice. We hope most of them will be well by game time*".

An opening onside kick, recovered by the Red Devils, proved to be fruitless. The defense held again after a punt fumble deep in their territory. But Monticello eventually turned in a 58-yard march resulting in Rocky Arnau's 13-yard strike to A.D. Madison for a 6-0 lead. Yet another fumble in the 2nd quarter eventually gave way to a Red Devil 26-yard FG by Arnau and 9-0 lead. On the next possession, Magee responded with a 68-yard Turner dash to paydirt. That cut into the lead with the scoreboard showing 9-6. Then, they fell on a loose Monticello football but could turn it only into a 31-yard Herrington game-tying FG.

The 3rd quarter opened with a pair of Trojan fumbles but neither gave the Red Devils points. Now in the final frame, Monticello fumbled again to Anderson (or Stanley Jordan). Herrington, Turner and Smith moved the ball to the 1-yard line from where Smith *"sneaked over for the winning TD"* with 1:00 remaining. Herrington converted. With time running out, Monticello went to the air. But McCollum, *"who had been outstanding all night defensively"*, picked off the last-gasp throw to seal the win.

"It was an especially satisfying win because it was a total team effort. We don't have as much talent as many Magee teams of the past, but we've never had a group to give a better effort. We are so proud of our players and think they deserved to win. We were worried about this game. Monticello had so much initiative because we beat them badly the first time we played this season. We also felt they might have had an advantage because of our injuries, but all our people pulled together and won our biggest game of the year".

When it was all over, it would quickly mark Magee's only diversion from the Little Dixie Conference as they were already planning on being back the next year. Magee had been a charter member of the conference. *"This is a public school and we believe our public wanted to be a part of the Little Dixie Conference"*, said Principal Ray Blackledge. *"Had the Little Dixie realigned last year when we asked them to, we never would have left the conference".*

Pat Herrington, Charles Cooper, Ricky Maddox and Joe Harold Smith were all named to the Southern Athletic Conference All-Star list. Willie McCollum was named an Honorable Mention.

1978 (9-3) NORTH LITTLE DIXIE CHAMPIONS

After just one year in the Southern Athletic Conference, fifth-year Coach Jerry Sullivan took the practice field with 12 lettermen back in red and gray. They had won that championship the year before and were now picked 2nd in the newly-reorganized Little Dixie Conference North. Many schools that were perineal opponents were shuffled to the LDC South. Said Sullivan about the move back, *"Our people are happier with the Little Dixie Conference. Most of the teams in the SAC are from around Hattiesburg and Laurel. The Jackson papers cover the Little Dixie and most our local Magee people subscribe to the Jackson papers. Next to the Big Eight, I think the LDC is recognized as the best conference in the state".*

Relative to his team and prospects, he noted that *"We're small, but we've got good overall quickness. We hope to use this quickness in stunting defenses and running wide offensively. The interior line is small (and) inexperienced, but has good quickness. We have a long way to go, but we're slowly getting there. The offense is ahead of the defense but that's to be expected. Our schedule will be tougher".*

GAME 1: MAGEE (0-0) vs PEARL (0-0)
MAGEE 12 PEARL 3
August 25, 1978

With the departure of two-year Coach Joe Edwards, another familiar face held the whistle. Coach Doug Merchant had faced off against Magee numerous time in other stints; namely Monticello. Voters had the Pirates 4th in the Little Dixie South. They also featured a squad of 66 players with 7 returning starters. Two of them had achieved All-Conference status the previous year. Pearl had broken the four-win mark only three times since 1957 and Merchant was determined to reverse the trend. He was forthright about what needed to be done.

"Since this school hasn't had a winning football team in a decade, we felt like we had to instill confidence into the players and we feel we have. They honestly think they can be winners this season. It's probably the toughest schedule Pearl's had in a few years. I feel like we'll be better, though, than last year. Our kids are workers and have done everything we've asked of them. A lot of them have improved, too. Our strong point right now would have to be team enthusiasm. Our kids are really looking forward to the season".

"The Magee game will mean a lot to us. If we can play with them and whip them, we'll be off to a great season. Magee is expecting about the same ball club as ... a year ago. We'd really not rather open with them, but financially it'll help us in the long run. (The game) will tell us quick what kind of ball club we've got." Said Sullivan, *"Yes, they are bigger than we are, but that doesn't necessarily mean they are tougher. We have been practicing for a long time and we need to play"*.

A *"standing room only crowd"* was in for a treat on opening night. Magee churned toward the end zone only to lose the ball at the 10 on a Charles Cooper fumble. Pearl added an interception of Brooks Sullivan in the 2nd to kill another drive and took a 3-0 lead into the lockers thanks to a 25-yard Larry Echols FG. That lead would hold until the 4th quarter thanks to a missed Garfield Turner 30-yard FG as the half expired. The 3rd was a scoreless affair. Pearl fumbled at the 35-yard line but another FG (25 yards) effort failed.

In the 4th, Magee took the lead they would not relinquish. An 88-yard drive was capped by a Turner dash of 51 yards to the end zone. Now with :30 left in the contest, and after a Turner interception proved not to produce points, Patrick Brown picked up a Pirate fumble and took it 38 yards for a TD and opening-day win. *"We moved the ball real well, but crucial errors killed us. I'm not taking anything away from Magee, but our mistakes were the difference in the ball game"*. First downs were even (12-12). Pearl led in the air 138-25 while Magee held the ground 221-81. The Pirates lost 2 fumbles while the Trojans lost only 1.

Said Sullivan, *"We played a good team and were fortunate to win. It was a big win for us. We were worried about our inexperience, especially on the offensive line, but they performed well although our offense did sputter at time. We were also concerned about the depth because Pearl only played two men both ways while we had to play eight"*. Turner rushed for 185 yards while Jack Everett (13) and Cooper (12) led tacklers.

GAME 2: MAGEE (1-0) @ GEORGE COUNTY (0-0)
MAGEE 26 GEORGE COUNTY 6
September 1, 1978

George County had beaten Magee 18-12 in the season-opener last year and ended 7th in state polling. Said Sullivan, *"We think we will improve and we will have to be to win at their place"*. The Clarion-Ledger said that *"Observers are split on which one of these teams has the better squad, so the game should be a good one"*. When over, The Magee Courier would call the win *"a combination of Magee defense, George County fumbles and a game-breaking kickoff return"*.

A 2nd quarter fumble set up Everett's 9-yard TD run and Turner PAT. The Rebels responded on a 70-yard march with Craig Havard finding the end zone from 8 yards, but the Trojans blocked the PAT. *"On the ensuing kickoff, Turner fielded the ball on his own 18 and, after breaking a tackle and making beautiful open-field cuts, bolted 82 yards for a TD"*. Halftime now sat 13-6. The Rebs fumbled again to Paul Arnold in the 3rd quarter at the GC 11-yard line. Cooper made it count from the 1-yard line. Late in the 4th, Magee grabbed another loose pigskin. Two plays later, Sullivan found Arnold from 30 yards out and Turner converted.

First downs were even 11-11 but Magee held the ground (128-74) and the air (71-63). George County suffered 7 lost fumbles while Magee had only a lone drop. *"It was an impressive win for us. In fact, we played a little better than I thought we would. We are extremely proud of our kids. Their efforts in both games thus far have been outstanding"*.

GAME 3: MAGEE (2-0) @ WEST JONES (0-1)
MAGEE 0 WEST JONES 7
September 8, 1978

Sullivan smartly knew that the next two games would mark the start of better competition. He said that the Mustangs would be *"Our toughest opponent yet. We'll have to play our best game to win. Other than Clinton, I think West Jones will probably be about as good as anyone we play. It will take a total team effort"*. Magee had beaten them 20-3 the previous year and were hoping to stay undefeated.

The head man thought that *"right away the pattern was established"* after the kickoff. Both teams threatened in the first half; Magee even getting to the Mustang 10-yard line but lost the opportunity on a fake FG attempt. Defenses again dominated the contest until late. A solid drive was killed by penalties and sacks. With 2:00 left, and having to punt to West Jones, a host of Mustangs blocked the kick. Jeff Soley picked up the loose pigskin and took it to the end zone for the game's only touchdown. Eric Johnston provided the PAT. First downs favored WJ (13-6) as did rushing (193-72). Passing went to Magee 107-10. The Mustangs lost 3 fumbles and Magee a pair.

"With the people we have to play each week, we must be mentally prepared and that's awful hard to do every Friday. I'm not trying to take anything away from West Jones, though. They certainly deserved to win. We never seemed to have the football. In fact, we only touched the ball three times in the first half. When we did get the ball, it was never with any field position. To be frank, they just shut us down. I don't know why we couldn't move the ball better.".

GAME 4: MAGEE (2-1) @ CLINTON (2-0)
MAGEE 6 CLINTON 7
September 15, 1978

Coming off an undefeated season brought high expectations for James Sloan's Arrows. But he was not setting the team's goal as one of replicating the previous season. *"Sure, we'd like to be undefeated, it's just that when you set a goal like that and you get your tail beat, your whole bubble is shot. Now, the Little Dixie championship is a more realistic goal and that will be our goal for this year."* The team had 19 returning lettermen, 7 of which started the previous year.

The Clarion-Ledger and Jackson Daily News pre-season poll had the Arrows 1st in their division of the LDC. This was despite Sloan's thoughts that he had no superstars on the team. *"We don't have any players that major colleges can't wait to get their hands on, but we have something to make up for that: Team unity. We have a saying that nobody is going to out-work or out-prepare us and the team is living up to that."*

It would be the first conference game for the 6th ranked Arrows. The Clarion-Ledger thought the game may be a *"preview of the Little Dixie Conference championship playoff."* Said Sloan, *"Magee is bad tough. We have had several dog fights with Magee. Come Friday night, we will see what we are made of. This will be the biggest challenge of the year."*

Clinton fans at a rainy Roy Burkett Field held their breath for 4 quarters in this one. Danny Rasberry said, *"When Clinton hit the field last Friday night against the Magee Trojans, they had their gun loaded and fired it on the first play. However, that was the only bullet in the gun."* That first play was a Mickey Marshall strike to Terry Sorey from 56 yards away and a Charles Farmer PAT. That 7-0 lead would give Clinton all they eventually needed to escape with a win. *"After we got that easy one, I guess we figured they were all going to be that easy."* The usually-reliable offense turned the ball over three consecutive times in the 2nd frame deep in Arrow territory. The defense won the game for Clinton by standing firm. The Arrow defense stopped Magee on the evening *"twice inside the 10 and five times inside their own 30."* Said Sloan, *"We can't keep laying down the ball."*

But with less than 1:00 before halftime, Cooper blocked a Clinton punt and pulled it in at the Arrow 4. After losing 4 yards, Sullivan hit Cooper for the touchdown. Turner's missed extra point would make the difference in the contest. The remainder of the game was sloppy on both sides. Clinton fumbled a total of 11 times, losing 3. Magee only lost 1 of 3 fumbles but was picked off 3 times. Rushing went to Clinton (80-71) as did passing (86-49).

Said Sloan afterwards, *"They whipped us in every department. They brought it to us. We knew it when they hit us. About the only thing I can say good about us is that our defense played well. I have nothing but praise for them. But (the defense) stayed out on the field three quarters and you can't win doing that. The party is over. There's not gonna be any more games like the first two."* Added Sullivan, *"We had nine boys playing both ways and they were completely two-platooning. We did the best we could but I guess winning just wasn't in the cards. But I'm still real happy with them"*.

GAME 5: MAGEE (2-2) @ MORTON (1-2)
MAGEE 9 MORTON 0
September 22, 1978

Coach Reggie Robertson's Panthers were 6-3 the previous year but picked tops in the Little Dixie North for the coming season. *"Our major weakness will be inexperience at QB and the offensive ends and running back* positions". Said Sullivan, *"Morton has a great team but we desperately need a win to begin our conference play and we're going to try to be ready for them"*. One Scott County Times prognosticator felt a 23-22 Morton win was to come.

Magee took their second possession 60 yards to the end zone with Cooper racing away for a 37-yard tally to make it 6-0. *"Magee kept field position and actually came close to scoring three more times but costly interceptions and penalties blunted each attempt"*. Eddie Evans nabbed a pair of pickoffs for Morton while Randy Ficklin added another. In the 3rd, the same thing happed as penalties and a blocked FG by Arthur Ragsdale kept more points off the board. Late,

Magee moved to the 12-yard line from where Turner nailed a 29-yard FG with 3:00 left. The Trojans got as far as the 4-yard line before the final whistle sounded.

"It was certainly a big win for us. We needed a win for our morale because we had lost those two close ones and we especially needed to win because it was a conference game. If our offense ever jells, I think we will be a great ball club and hopefully that has begun to materialize". Morton crossed midfield only one time during the game. All stats went to Magee: first downs (11-5), rushing (180-69) and passing (22-0).

GAME 6: MAGEE (3-2) vs SOUTH JONES (4-1)
MAGEE 18 SOUTH JONES 13
September 29, 1978

At South Jones, they had a new mentor. Stanley Matthews, minus 14 seniors from an 8-2 team, had lost some *"outstanding players"*. The SAC coach said, *"We are looking for depth both offensive and defensively. We don't have any experience in the offensive or defensive backfields. We have got to have some help in both lines. If everyone works hard, we could be competitive in a few of our games"*. Still, he had 65 men on his roster. Sullivan noted that, *"They have their entire line back from last year and their tight end is considered one of the top athletes in the state. We must be mentally prepared to play these folks and hopefully we will be"*.

Magee struck quickly to give them the lead they would hold throughout. Cooper had the first tally from the 6-yard line, South Jones fumbled the ensuing kick at their 11-yard line, and Everett spotted Turner later from the 20 to make it 12-0 in the opening frame. They notched their third TD before halftime on a 93-yard march and Cooper 1-yarder to make things 18-0.

The Trojans opened the 3rd with a fumbled kickoff to kill an opportunity. Late in the game, a blocked punt gave Simmie Cooley a 2-yard QB sneak (Sherman Wells PAT) and South's last came with :20 left after a Cooley "bomb" to Robbie Lawson. From the 5-yard line, Cooley hit Marty James for the finale. Magee led in first downs (11-8) while rushing (150-141) and passing (93-73) went to South Jones.

GAME 7: MAGEE (4-2) @ MADISON RIDGELAND (1-5)
MAGEE 36 MADISON RIDGELAND 0
October 6, 1978

One-win Madison Ridgeland was a newcomer to Magee football. They were picked 5th in the LDC North with 17 of 26 lettermen back from a 5-4 squad. They would prove no match to the LDC stalwart of Simpson County. In fact, Magee moved to paydirt on their first drive of 6 plays with Cooper dashing the last 35 yards for the score. Shortly after, Turner was *"slamming over left guard"* from the 18-yard line to make it 12-0.

MR moved to the Trojan 7-yard line before the defense held. In response, Turner capped a drive from the 21-yard line for a touchdown. Kirby Turner then stole a football from a returner and dashed 30 yards to the end zone and suddenly it was 24-0. They kept pace in the 3rd quarter with a 68-yard Everett screen pass to Turner. Finally, Steve McCollum found the goal from the 3-yard line to end scoring. Magee led in first downs (16-9), rushing (330-59) and passing (9-40). *"We were pleased with our play. We must now play a much tougher opponent in Forest"*.

GAME 8: MAGEE (5-2) vs FOREST (5-2)
MAGEE 19 FOREST 6
October 13, 1978

Coach Gary Risher was pleased with his Bearcat football team going into the season. Though they had been slotted 4th in the North with 23 lettermen back from a 6-4 team, he said that *"They've got a good attitude and there are some mighty fine ball players out there"*. Risher added that the 43-man roster was of *"adequate size and strength'*. The Scott County Times, picking Magee 21-7, said that *"We hate to pick the Bearcats to lose this week, but all signs point to a setback unless the Cats can really be fired up"*. The Hattiesburg American shared the opinion and picked Magee 27-12.

Sullivan was quoted on game week as saying *"They had some key injuries earlier in the year but I understand they are almost at full strength now. They've now won three in a row since they lost to Mendenhall so I'm sure they have a lot of confidence going for them. They are experienced... The conference race is still up for grabs and we certainly need to beat Forest to stay tied with Mendenhall. On the other hand, Forest knows that they must win or they will have two (conference) losses and be eliminated from the title chase. We know they will come to kill or be killed and I think we will respond to the challenge".*

Turner controlled the first drive with a 39-yard touchdown run and his PAT. His subsequent fumble set up Forest's opening 3-yard touchdown from Ben Lassetter but it was still 7-6. Solid running by Everett and Cooper allowed Everett a toss to Pat Brown to the Wildcat 5. Cooper notched the last couple of yards to make it 13-6. Forest had a chance to add points before halftime but Kenny Brumfield missed a FG from their own 10-yard line. Now in the final frame, Magee drove to the half-yard line with no points. But, a Bruce Langston 20-yard Allen Smith fumble recovery taken into the end zone made up for it.

It was not without controversy. Forest coaches and players thought Smith down before the fumble, but officials thought otherwise and gave the points to Magee. First downs were even (7-7), Magee held the ground (232-95) and Forest the air (55-11). *"I'm sure Turner will be out for the rest of the season with a broken arm. I am especially complimentary of our offensive line. I thought we played well. As we expected, Forest came to play ball. They had a good game plan and a burning desire to win. We're glad to have this one behind us".*

GAME 9: MAGEE (6-2) vs PRENTISS (1-7)
MAGEE 27 PRENTISS 7
October 20, 1978: HOMECOMING

Magee had begun playing Prentiss in 1928; a game that ended in a tie. Aside from a lull in 1977 due to the SAC, these two teams faced each other annually since 1952. The Trojans had won 14 of 18 matchups since 1959. Prentiss was picked low (6th) in the North with 13 of 24 lettermen back from a 2-8 campaign. Said Sullivan, *"This week is Homecoming for us and surely this will be a big boost to win this one. They always play Magee tough and we don't expect this year to be any different. I would certainly think that we'll try to look good for our alumni"*.

A first-drive fumble by the Dogs was recovered at the 15-yard line and Cooper made good on the gift via his 3-yard plunge. Everett's PAT put it 7-0. Prentiss dropped the ball again late in the 2nd quarter and Magee drove 92 yards in response. The last 70 yards came on Everett's throw to Langston and Everett's toe made intermission 14-0. Harvey Magee then got involved in the 3rd quarter by blocking a Bulldog punt. Steve McCallum recovered in the end zone and Everett converted.

Before the frame was over, Langston capped a 47-yard march with a 30-yard dash. Prentiss avoided the shutout later after recovering a Trojan fumble. Ira Johnson's 20-yard run was followed by a successful PAT. Magee led in first downs (11-7), rushing (143-58) and passing (84-61). Langston rushed for 104 yards. *"Although we looked ragged at times, I thought we played well. Our main concern now is for our injured players. We lost another defensive back Friday night which leaves us extremely thin in the secondary. We also have a couple of linemen hurt..."*

GAME 10: MAGEE (7-2) @ JACKSON SAINT JOSEPH (2-6)
MAGEE 13 JACKSON SAINT JOSEPH 0
October 27, 1978

The Jackson team under Coach Bill Raphael was a newcomer to the Magee history. It was noted that *"A small squad with few returning starters wasn't enough of a challenge for the Saint Joseph HS football team. Coach Bill Raphael had to get them a tough schedule to boot"*. Added Raphael about a team with 11 lettermen from a 3-7 team, 39 players including 12 freshmen, and a small line, *"I honestly don't know if we will have a winning season. We certain want to, but have lost some people who would have helped us. We have no size, experience and depth. All of that hurts us"*.

Said Sullivan before the game, *"We must now go to Saint Joseph and everyone knows how close they came to beating Mendenhall Friday night (14-9). Hopefully we can get ourselves up one more time for there surely won't be any problems getting up for that last game against Mendenhall. We've had a super year up until now and if we are winners like I think we are, the last games won't be any exception"*.

Langston got things going in the 2nd quarter by picking off a Joe Rooks throw. His 45-yard escape and Everett PAT made halftime 7-0. Cooper put the finishing touches on the game in the 3rd quarter when he got in from the 7-yard line. Despite a Trojan fumble later, the defense held and *"hopes of at least getting on the scoreboard flared once again when Luna intercepted an Everett throw"*. However, the Magee defense again proved up to the task.

Sullivan was less upbeat after penalties stopped key drives. *"We will have to discipline ourselves mentally if we hope to have any chance against Mendenhall this week. We will have to do a much better job on our blocking. We were just going through the motions last week"*.

GAME 11: MAGEE (8-2) vs MENDENHALL (8-1)
MAGEE 20 MENDENHALL 0
November 3, 1978

With 8 lettermen back, including 3 starters, Coach David Abercrombie's Tigers were picked 3rd to start the LDCN season. *"We're young this year and the most important factor will be the kind of leadership we get from our (18) seniors. We're going to be small overall; not nearly as large as we have been in other years. I'm talking about 170 pounds up front compared to, say, 220 last year. We're optimistic about the season but we know we've got our job cut out for us"*. By game day, he had far-exceeded expectations and sat 10th in the state.

As in years past, this game was for a lot more than just another win as the victor claimed the division title and played for the championship. Said Sullivan, *"This is the game of the year for both teams. The NLDC championship is at stake... In addition, the county championship is at stake and even more important: bragging rights for a full year. We are aware that Mendenhall has a great team. With an even split in the breaks, they would have beaten Warren Central. We know we'll have to play super defense and improve our offensive execution. Considering how explosive their offense is, we'll be in bad trouble if the defense breaks down. But we've relied on them all year and they've come through every time"*.

A Tiger fumble to Magee on their second drive did no damage, but another gave Magee a glimmer of hope. The Trojans attempted a fake FG but were caught short and left halftime scoreless. Mendenhall opened the 3rd with a drive to the 15-yard line, but their FG attempt was blocked by Mark Marbury (or J.C. Smith) and recovered by Brooks Sullivan. Cooper *"broke off right tackle for 55 yards"* and Langston finalized the drive with an 18-yard run. Everett's PAT put Magee up 7-0.

Midway through the final frame, another Mendy fumble went to Magee. Langston turned that into an 8-yard TD. Then, Patrick Brown found yet another loose ball (this by Jon Munn), picked it up and raced 3 yards for the touchdown. Everett's conversion marked the last points. First downs (10-7) and rushing (206-36) went to Magee. The visitors held passing 105-4. Mendy had 4 lost fumbles while Magee had one pass intercepted.

"Our defense just played super. We've been counting on them all year and they really came through tonight. Of course I'm pleased with the offense, too. After being kind of sluggish in the first half, it really got going. It was the most important game of the year. It's a bitter rivalry. It determined the conference championship, the Simpson County championship and who has the bragging rights for the year. But I think the pride element was more important than even the championship". The paper estimated the crowd, five-deep round the fences, to be near 7,000.

GAME 12: MAGEE (9-2) vs WARREN CENTRAL (10-0)
MAGEE 13 WARREN CENTRAL 24
November 10, 1978

To begin the week, the team and cheerleaders were treated with a trip to Hattiesburg to see USM take on Bowling Green as a reward for their season thus far. As for this tilt, the two teams had met for the big prize before reconfiguration of the Little Dixie. In 1975, it was Magee finally beating the Vikings in their second meeting to go to the LDC championship game. Warren Central, under Coach Lum Wright, got their revenge in 1976 by a lone point in a game that had serious implications. Now? They were meeting for all of the marbles in the finale.

Warren Central took their first possession and mixed a *"devastating running game with a precision option attack"* to move to the 10-yard line before fumbling to Magee. After a short punt, the Vikings moved close enough to nail a 37-yard Art Mordecai FG. Langston took the ensuing kick deep, but it was called back due to clipping. Carl Blue returned a punt later to the Trojan 15 and then Kenny Bolden scored from the 1-yard line.

Magee stormed back with Everett notching the last yard. Back came WC with a touchdown drive, Bolden 4-yard run, and two-pointer from Scott Allen, but again Magee found paydirt. Everett's 59-yard strike to Paul Arnold did the damage and Everett's kick made it 18-13 at halftime. Magee could get only to the WC 10-yard line in the 3rd while Warren Central got a late touchdown after Clyde Shelley's interception with the last Bolden 1-yard run to ice the title.

First downs (18-11) and rushing (260-139) favored Magee but Warren Central had passing (70-0) and the score on their side. Said Wright, *"That interception was the big play of the game for us"*. Added Sullivan, *"Naturally we are disappointed but we had a good year and we are proud of our kids. I thought 13 points would have won it"*.

1979 (9-2)

After five years at the helm of Magee football, Jerry Sullivan was now gone and replaced by former player John Mangum. The 20th head coach of team had played at USM and the NFL (Boston Patriots) after graduation and had roughly 12 out of 22 lettermen back in camp. That number differed according to reports. But, he did have *"all but seven starters from last year coming back"*. As such, his Trojans were picked tops in the Little Dixie North.

Said Mangum, *"This is an adequate size (42 players) to work with. We had had a lot of good practices and luckily we haven't had any injuries. We are working very hard and we hope to have a good team this year. We have good team speed and team spirit. That's an advantage on our part. We have been practicing very hard so we shouldn't have any excuses. We are looking forward to the upcoming season and are anxious to get started. We have a great bunch of boys to work with and have utmost respect for our opponents"*.

GAME 1: MAGEE (0-0) @ PEARL (0-0)
MAGEE 13 PEARL 20
August 31, 1979

First-year coach Doug Merchant had produced the first winning Pirate season (6-5) since 1968. Now, he was back for his second year and ready to make a giant leap forward with 22 lettermen on board. And, according to The Clarion-Ledger, he was ready to *"rid (the) squad of "whipping boy" status"*. Merchant, as would be his style for years to follow, was confident about the process and his team. *"This year, we're capable of lining up with people and just whipping them. We've got more talent than we know what to do with. But, we've got to be more consistent this year. I think Pearl is approaching the point where it's playing winning, exciting football that will traditionally be in demand for bowl games if we can't win the conference. When I first came here, the kids didn't have self-confidence, and there were several cliques. They weren't playing as a team. We still have to combat that. We still need to always put the team first"*.

Said Merchant of Magee, *"Their speed scares me. I don't think they'll be able to punch it down the field on us, but we've got to prevent the big play. That's important because I look for a low-scoring defensive struggle. Magee is heads-and-shoulders above the teams in their division. I think they'll win the North going away with little trouble"*.

The huge season-opener sat tied 6-6 going to the lockers with both teams putting up points in the 2nd. Magee was first after Patrick Brown recovered an Ive Burnett fumble. That led to a 2-yard Garfield Turner run. Turner actually put up another afterwards (53 yards) but it was called back for holding. Pearl knotted the contest after Wayne Mitchell recovered a loose football. Ricky Sutton escaped from the 27 for the tally. Turner accounted for Magee's next TD, *"bursting through the middle and then outracing several defenders down the left sideline (from 90 yards)"*. David Ham's PAT made it 13-6.

Now in the 4th, a tipped Magee punt put the Pirates in position to drive 50 yards, with Doug Washington accounting for the 4-yard score. Mike Carr's toe tied the contest. Late in the game, a personal foul gave Pearl new life at midfield. It took 5 plays before Mike Sills darted in from the 7 with 1:55 left. Carr's PAT finished scoring. Turner put up 208 yards on the ground of their total 250. Pearl had 183. The Pirates also led in first downs (15-12) and passing (70-38). Said Merchant, *"Our offense was ragged. I was impatient with our offense, but it takes these guys time to warm up. I was trying to create a big play for us. Fortunately, we finally got clicking. This is truly a great victory. I am some kind of proud of this game"*.

Added Mangum, *"Penalties and mistakes hurt us. I felt we played well enough to win. That third touchdown by Garfield Turner was the make-or-break point in the game. Unfortunately, a holding penalty called the TD back and the tide seemed to turn in their favor. But all of that aside, the Trojans led most of the way and the game could have gone either way. The kids gave us their total effort and played very well, but penalties cost us the ball game"*.

GAME 2: MAGEE (0-1) vs GEORGE COUNTY (0-0)
MAGEE 35 GEORGE COUNTY 14
September 7, 1979

Magee had lost two-straight to George County before rebounding the year before with a decisive victory. After an opening loss to Pearl, The Magee Courier said that Magnum planned *"to work the Trojans harder this week in preparation..."* Like Pearl, their opponent would have many more players. One report had George County with 90 players on the team.

Turner put in the only score of the opening frame on a 25-yard run followed by the first of 5 Ham point-after efforts. In the next quarter, Jerome Williamson hit Paul Arnold from 71 yards out to make it 14-0 at intermission. Turner's 3rd quarter dash of 54 yards was followed by the first George County score; that a Ricky Havard run topped with the Vaughn Fryfogle PAT. In the final session, Turner tallied from the 15-yard line and Ed Nelson topped it later from 41 yards out. As time was expiring and after a Trojan fumble, Havard dashed in from the 21-yard line that, along with the point-after, ended scoring.

While George County led in first downs (13-10), Magee held rushing (194-65) and passing (157-89). Turner had 157 of the ground markers. *"Coach Mangum commended the entire Trojan defense for never letting up against a fine football team"*. He said *"The line ... blocked and ran real well. The QB is improving each week and we are pleased with his progress. It was a big night for us because we felt like George County had a good team"*. He also noted a number of player individually as *"bright spots in the game"*.

GAME 3: MAGEE (1-1) vs WEST JONES (1-0)
MAGEE 21 WEST JONES 7
September 14, 1979

Fourth-year coach Mike Taylor led not only the defending Southern Athletic Conference champions, but returned 10 lettermen and 18 seniors for the 1979 season. He did, however, only have 5 starters back. It would not be a problem as voters had them in first place in the SAC. *"It's a challenge being the champions. We've got to work hard to fill in the losses through graduation"*. Turner was tied with Carl Blue (Warren Central) for Little Dixie scoring leader honors with 30 points.

West Jones hit the board first on a 41-yard Adolph Ducksworth scamper and Chip Geiger's (or Pat Odom's) PAT. Magee responded with a 60-yard Turner touchdown run, but it was called back and kept halftime 7-0. He did, however, get in from the 17-yard line in the 3rd quarter and Ham converted. Later, he burst away for 75 yards with Ham again true on the kick. Brown's final-quarter dive from the 1-yard line and Ham PAT would finish things on the evening. That had been set up by a West Jones fumble to Magee.

Marbury led tacklers with 15 and Turner ran for 174 yards. First downs were even (10-10), rushing went to Magee by 3 yards (194-191) and passing favored the Trojans (46-4). *"We felt that the team has character to win in the last half"*. Added Coach Taylor, *"We did our scoring in the first half. Then, it was the Garfield Turner show. We played pretty good football the first half, but they came out there in the second half and just whipped us good."*.

GAME 4: MAGEE (2-1) vs CLINTON (2-1)
MAGEE 16 CLINTON 6
September 21, 1979

Clinton had the services of only two head coaches since 1956. With the departure of James Sloan to Co-Lin Junior College, they would now have their third in Jerry Lyons. Lyons had been a standout player at Clinton through 1960. *"I feel real excited about our prospects. Our number one strength this year will be the senior leadership. Our defensive front is strong. I feel that they will do a good job for us this year. Our defensive secondary has come on. They have really improved. We are going to make mistakes, but win, lose or draw, we are going to give it our best. We are representing the community. The red and white is going to mean something but it will take dedication, sacrifice and determination."*

His team started the season picked second in the South Little Dixie behind the obvious-choice Vikings. He had 16 lettermen back including a number of starters. One, Ike Tyre, was selected as one of the best prospects in the state. *"I have to keep a separate mailbox for him just to keep all the mail he gets from recruiters."* As for Magee, Lyons noted, *"Magee is the same class of Mendenhall. There's no difference between the teams. It's going to be a tough game; no doubt about it."* In the end, the contest would look similar to the one against the Arrows played against Mendenhall on opening day. Magee would put up all of their points before Clinton could reach the scoreboard.

The paper said that *"...they grow boys mean and tough in Simpson County."* The Trojans nearly crossed in the 1st after having the ball at the Arrow 1. But a stout Clinton defense held to keep them out. Magee took a 6-0 lead into the locker room courtesy of a 2nd quarter 34-yard Williamson pass to Brooks Sullivan. The 3rd quarter was a defensive struggle with neither team gaining either momentum or an advantage. In the 4th, however, the Trojans scored twice before the Arrows hit once. Ham pointed a 27-yard FG for the first and Turner took an Arrow punt 68 yards for their last. In the waning minutes of the game, Danny Tanksley plunged in from the 1.

John Mangum said afterwards, *"At times against Clinton we showed signs of being a really good ball club. We are very proud of this win. It's been a long time since we've beaten Clinton."* Said Lyons, *"We were ... disappointed that we lost, but I saw a lot of good things out there. After the Mendenhall game, we set a timetable of where we wanted to be. Our defense is past that goal and our offense has yet to reach it. We plan to make several personnel changes on offense this week. We have to get (the) offense going"*.

GAME 5: MAGEE (3-1) vs MORTON (1-2)
MAGEE 29 MORTON 27
September 28, 1979

Though they had played in 1927, this meeting had been continuous since 1945. For Morton, they were picked 3rd in the division with 14 of 32 lettermen back from a 6-4 team. Magee was 8-1-1 against them since 1969 and 16-4-1 since 1960. Still, The Scott County Times thought it a Panther win 28-7.

It was Morton setting the pace in the first quarter with a 60-yard escape by Tim Aycock and a Terry Miles PAT. Turner brought Magee right back on the ensuing kick with a return of 85 yards and Ham tied the tilt. Greg Gray put Morton back up with a 15-yard reception from Jon Burham and Miles PAT. But again Turner would punch back with a 91-yard TD turn and Ham's kick put halftime even at 14-14. In the 3rd, Burnham and Randy Ficklin hooked up from 60 yards out for the next Morton score. It was Turner who had the ensuing score from the 15-yard line and the missed PAT kept it tied 20-20.

Magee gained their first lead of the game (26-20) in the final quarter on a 3-yard Brown plunge. With 5:00 left, Burnham hit Gray from the 18-yard line and, with the Miles kick, it was 27-26. Now with :55 left and on fourth down, Ham came in to attempt to win the game from the 24-yard line. *"The players lined up and the ball was put in place. As the ball was snapped, thousands of spectators stood in hushed silence awaiting the outcome of the game. The ball drifted lazily though the air and floated gracefully through the goal posts"*. Magee picked off a desperation pass in the end and had come back to win.

The Trojans led in first down (15-10) and rushing (206-172) while Morton led in passing (155-71). *"The coaches were far from satisfied with the overall performance of the Trojans. We are not taking anything away from Morton and their ball club. They were well-prepared and they came to Magee to win. We intend to shape our defense and go back to basics. Our offense needs to be more consistent. We played well offensively the last half. Our ground game was very effective"*.

GAME 6: MAGEE (4-1) @ SOUTH JONES (3-1)
MAGEE 30 SOUTH JONES 22
October 5, 1979

Coach Stanley Matthews' South Jones team was expected by voters to be a good squad this season. In the SAC, they were picked 2nd, and Mangum noted that *"They are a fine football team. They are one of the top four teams that we will play this year"*. The boys had been playing an Ellisville, MS team since as early as 1947 and had been 3-3 since 1965 against them.

The Magee Courier called it *"a scary win"*. The Braves struck on their first drive via a 1-yard run by Leo Shelby to make it 6-0. Donnie Bender then picked off a 2nd quarter pass to set up Simmy Cooley's 6-yard pass to Dan Ashley and a Cooley two-point conversion. Magee cut into the lead with Kelvin Langston's 16-yard keeper and Ham conversion. Before halftime, with just :43 remaining, Williamson found Arnold (or Brooks Sullivan) from the 9-yard line and intermission sat 14-13.

South threatened in the 3rd quarter with a Shelby dash to the Magee 14-yard line but they fumbled it away on the next play. Turner got things going with a 51-yard dash and his two-point tally. He added another from the 5-yard line in the final frame and Ham later hit a 17-yard FG to end Trojan scoring. The Braves had one final score with :37 left when Cooley hit Rocky Purvis (or Sherman Wells) from 23 yards away. Magee led in first downs (15-12) and rushing (303-156) but lost the air (55-78). The Braves may have lost 4 fumbles in the game. The Laurel Leader-Call gave Turner credit for 237 rushing yards.

"(We) moved the ball real well but penalties (12 for 138 yards) kept the game from being broken open earlier. Defensively after the half, the Trojans lightened their pads and held South Jones from crossing their goal line until the last few minutes of the game. It was a big victory for us because we were on their home field and we beat a fine ball club. Both offensively and defensively we showed good character by coming from behind 14-0 to a 30-22 victory".

GAME 7: MAGEE (5-1) vs MADISON RIDGELAND (0-6)
MAGEE 41 MADISON RIDGELAND 6
October 12, 1979: HOMECOMING

Even with 16 lettermen back in Madison County, the upcoming opponent was picked last in the North. The previous year, Magee had shut them out 36-0. Magee's last win now put them number 10 in A-AA state rankings just behind Mendenhall. *"We have received votes in the past but I don't think that we have ever been listed in the top 10. This is a real honor for us. We always play to win ball games and something like this is just a sidebar but we are honored. I think it says something for the conference we play in to have three teams listed in the top 10 in the state"*.

It was Ricky Barnes putting up the first points for Madison Ridgeland in the 2nd quarter on a 1-yard run. But Magee would awaken and control the rest of the contest. Turner's 1-yard dive and Ham's PAT put Magee up 7-6 at halftime. Williamson opened the 3rd with a 1-yard dive and Turner added a 7-yarder later. Both PATs by Ham made it 21-6. Finally, Turner dodged in from the 18-yard line, Patrick Brown did the same from the 4-yard line and Turner put the icing on the cake with a 1-yard plunge. Ham notched a pair of PATs.

Turner rushed for 153 markers while Brooks Sullivan pulled in 52 yards on 4 receptions. Randy Cook, Mark Marbury, Greg Green, Harvey Magee, Jeff Craft and Steve McCollum led tacklers. *"Defensively we played well all night. Late in the second quarter the offense came alive and moved, scoring on nearly every possession in the last half. We have to become a four-quarter team to be considered a top-notch ball club. We've got to play 48 minutes. I would like to commend coaches Ernest Jaynes, Mike Smith and Charles Keeton on a job well-done in preparation... Our next four games are conference games and should be crucial in every aspect"*.

GAME 8: MAGEE (6-1) @ FOREST (1-6)
MAGEE 46 FOREST 13
October 19, 1979

Gary Risher's Bearcats were having a horrendous year. They were 7-4 the season before and had 18 lettermen back. Picked 4th in the LDC North, they had beaten only Brandon (27-17). In their last game against Monticello, they put up only 47 passing yards and 25 rushing. The Scott County Times *"sadly predicts a Forest defeat, probably at the tune of 28-6"*. Meanwhile, Magee moved to 8th in the A-AA state poll. Turner was 16 points behind LDC leader Carl Blue in total points scored (120-104). Said Risher, *"Magee has as good a team (as) I have ever seen"*.

This week the Trojans would not be a come-from-behind team. Turner opened scoring with a 74-yard dash and, in the 2nd quarter, he added a 5-yarder. His next was from 6 yards and, before halftime, Brown dove in from the 5-yard line. With Ham PATs, it was 27-0. Turner opened the 3rd with a 97-yard kickoff return of Perry Qualls' boot to make it a quick 33-0. In the final frame, Randy Cook notched a 31-yard tally and Ed Nelson escaped from 91 yards. Forest added points when Brian Kaskie hit Danny Battle from 80 yards and 6 yards. Paul Bridges had the PAT for the Cats.

Rushing (330-163) favored Magee while passing (125-88) was in favor of Forest. Marbury led tacklers, Nelson (132) led rushers and Sullivan (50) paced receivers. Cliff McGinty recovered a Magee fumble in the contest. Though they had 160 penalty yards, Mangum said *"This was a complete ball game for us. We are happy that many of our younger players got to play but we need to look ahead to Prentiss. They are an up-and-down team with great potential"*.

GAME 9: MAGEE (7-1) @ PRENTISS (3-5)
MAGEE 14 PRENTISS 7
October 26, 1979

Though they were just 2-9 the last year, Coach Richard Hall's 16 returning players had them 5th in the LDC North. He said, *"We should be experienced. But we will have a lack of depth in the line. And the schedule is very tough"*. Added Mangum, *"We feel like they will be up for us but we have the utmost respect for them"*. Turner had closed the gap in second place LDC scoring to Blue 134-128.

After tough goal-line stands on both sides, Magee took the 7-0 halftime lead in the 2nd quarter on Turner's 63-yard reception from Williamson and Ham's PAT. Turner added the last Trojan points in the 3rd quarter when he rushed 83 yards to paydirt and Ham converted. Prentiss notched a final-frame touchdown on Joe Dampier's 1-yard dive and Chester Longino's extra point.

Turner rushed for 122 (or 115) yards on the night and Sullivan pulled in 52 reception yards. Sullivan and Harvey Magee led tacklers with 8 each. Green and Brown were close behind with 7. *"It was a very physical football game. We are very happy with our win at Prentiss. We met an inspired football team and we are happy to win the game. The season is winding down and every game becomes important"*.

GAME 10: MAGEE (8-1) vs JACKSON SAINT JOSEPH (5-4)
MAGEE 8 JACKSON SAINT JOSEPH 7
November 2, 1979

Coach Bill Raphael thought his pre-season 6th place LDC North team better than the 3-7 year before. *"I feel like we're stronger and improved over last year. Our chances of having a better record is very good this season because the boys are a lot stronger. When a player gets more experience under his belt, he gets stronger"*. His team returned 8 starters and *"several defensive regulars"*. Magee had actually dropped a spot to 9th in the A-AA poll behind a pair of teams (Murrah and Picayune) with two losses. Meanwhile, the race between Blue and Turner had widened 152-140.

It was a lackluster Friday night in anybody's opinion that was not sitting in the visitors' stands. In fact, it was Saint Joe with a 7-0 lead via their 2nd quarter touchdown by Joe Rook from one yard out and his extra point kick. Magee got all they needed in the 3rd quarter when Turner dodged in from the 10-yard line and then converted the two-pointer. *"The fourth quarter was the make-or break point of the game. The Trojan defense held as the Bruins made several unsuccessful attempts to reach the end zone"*.

Turner led rushers with 181 yards, Sullivan caught 36 markers, and tacklers were paced by Cook, Brown and Magee. Said Sullivan afterwards, *"After reviewing last week's game film, we found very little to be happy about. Saint Joseph came to play. We didn't. We were unemotional"*. Jeff Craft sustained a broken arm in the tilt to mark his last game as a Trojan.

GAME 11: MAGEE (9-1) @ MENDENHALL (9-1)
MAGEE 7 MENDENHALL 20
November 9, 1979

With few exceptions in over 50 years of meetings, there was always something of importance even more than the bragging rights that naturally existed in the communities for a yearly post-game. Coach David Abercrombie's Tigers were picked 2nd in the North and with good right. They held the same record as Magee, even though the head man thought his prospects low as the season began. *"We lost many people (14 lettermen) at key positions and we have inexperienced replacements"*.

The winner faced Warren Central in the South; the only team that had beaten Mendy. The paper said *"Both teams have been labeled as opportunistic because of the wide-open brand of football they have played this season. The Trojans are a little larger this year than in the past and the Tigers a little smaller. Both teams' play is characterized with long runs, kickoff and punt returns for touchdowns"*. Said Abercrombie, *"We are not going to do anything new. Our game plan this year has worked successfully and we'll continue with what we've been doing. If we can (execute) then we'll be okay"*.

Added Mangum, *"We believe that each team member has the character to dedicate himself to put forth their best effort against Mendenhall. This final game of the year is very important to both schools. I'm sure that both teams are looking forward to setting the big question. We are looking forward to playing Mendenhall and have the utmost respect for them"*.

The Magee Courier said that *"tempers flared at times because of the title and team pride at stake on the outcome of the game"*. Willie Holmes' 1-yard dive and Mark Herrington's PAT put Mendy up 7-0 in the opening quarter after an interception. They put up one more in the frame when Holmes bulled in from the 3-yard line after a blocked Magee kick. The Trojans responded in the 2nd quarter when Williamson and Arnold connected from 12 yards away. Ham's PAT made it 14-7. Before the halftime whistle, Holmes pulled in a 13-yard toss from Greg Paes that would mark the eventual end of scoring.

Mendenhall controlled first downs (10-9) and rushing (147-47) while Magee held only the air (88-69). *"I don't know of anything that we did exceptionally well. We did not play our best game of the season by any means. We have a lot of ability but it just didn't show through. The game was definitely won on the field ... I thought that we were ready to play before the game started. I think the boys were really high but the turning point was definitely the blocked punt and the pass interception. A good team, it is said, makes its breaks and I guess Mendenhall took advantage of the ones (we) made*".

Abercrombie noted that "*We were very happy with the win. We felt we had a good chance of winning going into the contest. To be honest, I didn't think the score would be that far apart but otherwise it was a very even contest. I thought both teams played well and it was by, no means, a one-sided game as many people might say. I believe we got a super effort out of our football players*".

The North Little Dixie All-Conference team was led by Garfield Turner (Most Outstanding Back), Mark Marbury, Harvey Magee and Kelvin Williams. Honorable Mentions went to Brooks Sullivan, Jeff Craft and Patrick Brown. WC grabbed the overall title with a 34-0 win over Clinton.

1980-1989

1989 Team (15-0): 3A State Champions

1980 (6-3-1)

Coach John Mangum noted before his second season at the helm of Magee football that *"We're going to have a good football team but it's just going to take some time. The talent is there, it's just young talent. They're going to have to play a few games to become a seasoned ball club, but by the time the conference schedule comes around, they should have become a seasoned team"*. One report noted that 8 of 11 starters had never stated a game.

His outlook improved somewhat by game week, saying that *"our chances of winning the conference are as good as anybody's. We play most of our big games at home. Right now our strong suit is defense. We're not sure how far we've come"*. Mangum and his team with 15 lettermen attended a Magee Touchdown Club dinner the Thursday before kickoff of the season.

GAME 1: MAGEE (0-0) @ CLINTON (0-0)
MAGEE 6 CLINTON 31
September 5, 1980

Coach Jerry Lyons entered his second year hoping and expecting to improve on his first-year 7-4 record. He had 17 seniors, including many who played pivotal roles in 1979, but wasn't about to take the opening game lightly. But, he was high on his kids. *"This group of seniors has never played on the real championship Clinton teams. They were 7-4 as sophomores and 7-4 last year. I think this group is ready to play up to their credibility. They're better than they think they are, but it may be good that they think like that. They don't sit back and wait for things to happen."*

As for Magee, Lyons said *"I'd compare them to Mendenhall. They've got speed and size and can score points in a hurry."* Clinton would start the successful year with a bang and play as aggressive against Magee as anyone the remainder of the year.

The game was under-reported by all three newspapers. Dwayne Malloy got things going for Magee in the 1st with a 1-yard plunge while Clinton tied the game 6-6 on Scott Failor's 8-yarder. After a Magee fumble at their 18, Failor had yet another touchdown on opening day to make halftime 12-6. Wayne Gasson crossed the goal in the 3rd from the 5 and the Arrows added a couple of others in the last quarter. Gary Gleason ran in from the 5 and a Barry Bedells interception set up Failor from the 1 for another. Andy Palmer added a PAT in the win.

Clinton's rushing (305-220) made part of the difference as Magee had 175 yards to the Arrows' 70 in the air. Magee shot themselves in the foot with penalty yardage (140 yards) and made 7 turnovers to Clinton's 4. Said Coach Mangum, *"We made mistakes, both coaching mistakes and playing mistakes, and we paid for it. And their two-platoon system just wore us down. They played a good football game and we had seven turnovers to their three. Our objective now is to play Clinton again or to play the team that beats them."*

GAME 2: MAGEE (0-1) @ WEST JONES (1-0)
MAGEE 14 WEST JONES 14
September 12, 1980

The last time a team had put up 31 points or more on Magee had been in 1973 against Warren Central. Mangum was still optimistic about his team and the season. *"We've had a good practice this week and we're going to get better. Let's face it. We play a rough opening schedule but the coaches and players have regrouped and decided to become a good football team. And we intend to be shortly. We intend to be a factor in our conference. We will be back. We got embarrassed but we don't think it will happen again"*.

James Williams suffered a broken left arm in the opener and would be lost for the foreseeable future. Still, the Trojans hit the road in an attempt to get on the right track. Both teams traded touchdowns in the opening frame. Magee hit paydirt on a Malloy 11-yard pass to Robert Dixon while the Mustangs hit on Mitch Reynolds' 55-yard pass from Julius DeLoach. Pat Odom's PAT put them up 7-6. Kevin Williams turned a fumble into a 65-yard TD return and Ed Nelson converted the two pointer to make halftime 14-7. Magee could have increased the advantage but a FG effort by Patrick Brown failed.

Now in the final quarter, West Jones hit the end zone on DeLoach's 29-yard scamper and Odom's PAT. They could have won the game late but missed a final FG attempt as time waned. *"We knew all along we were going to have to suffer through the first two or three games but, as we expected, we're seeing super improvement each week. I think in ten games we'll see ten different teams. We're improving that much each week"*.

GAME 3: MAGEE (0-1-1) vs PEARL (2-0)
MAGEE 7 PEARL 10
September 19, 1980

Doug Merchant, back for his third year at the helm of Pirate football, was confident about his chances to match or improve upon his 10-1 season. He and his assistants would have the services of up to 81 players. *"We're young and inexperienced. At least 7 or 8 sophomores will play and perhaps 20 juniors. We'll probably start slow but should come on strong by the end of the season. I think we can be as good as last year. We've got super talent from one end of the squad to the other. Speed will be our long suit. If we can get by the first couple of games, we should be all right because we should get stronger as the season goes on".*

The only issue of concern for Merchant was the youth. *"Our inexperience worries me. I'm worried how we'll react under pressure situations and if we can win the close games early in the year. If those games go against us, it will be disastrous".* Voters had Pearl 2nd in the LDC South behind Warren Central and ranked 8th in Class A-AA overall. By kickoff, the Pirates' 2-0 start had Pearl 4th in The Super 10 and in the ORV of the AP Poll.

Said Mangum, *"We're going to go after them with both feet and both hands. I know they will be hard to go against".* Merchant added *"Magee has a good football team. They don't have the experience they've had in the past, but I would really disregard their showing to this point. Magee has revenge in their eyes. It will be a tough ball game. If our kids don't get ready to play, we'll get our britches wore off".*

Pearl's big-play defense came through again; this time a 1st quarter Willie Griffith fumble recovery taken 67 yards to the end zone. Mike Carr notched the extra point. In the same frame, Magee tied it on a 52-yard Nelson run and Dan Quick PAT. The only points added to the scoreboard afterwards came in the 3rd when Carr drilled a 37-yard FG for the eventual win. Pearl won the rushing game 188-152 while the Trojans had one more first down (12-11). Magee passed for 12 yards but had 2 picked off. Daron Trigg was credited with an interception.

"We're not pleased with the loss, of course, but we feel we're becoming a good football team. Our execution is a lot better. We getting into shape". Magee rushed for 152 yards (Nelson 106) and passed for 27 more. Brown led the team with 13 tackles.

GAME 4: MAGEE (0-2-1) @ MORTON (1-2)
MAGEE 20 MORTON 0
September 26, 1980

Mangum noted during game week that *"They are a real good team with one of the best backs (Leo Shelby) around. We're interested now in making a run for the division title and we think we can do it. We're not down by any means".* The Scott County Times thought Magee a winner either 28-21 or 17-16.

Brown was the leader in scoring, first with a 15-yard TD in the opening frame. He added another from the 10-yard line in the 3rd and Williams added the two-pointer. Nelson's last-quarter dodge from the 8-yard line finished things. Magee led in first downs (17-7), rushing (264-43), and passing (64-54). Brown had 104 yards on the night. *"Once again the whole squad pulled together to win this one. We'll have to work on those mistakes. We just had too many turnovers. Right now our defensive unit is as good as it has been in the past several years. They just shut Morton down".*

GAME 5: MAGEE (1-2-1) vs SOUTH JONES (2-2)
MAGEE 17 SOUTH JONES 14
October 3, 1980: HOMECOMING

The Southern Athletic Conference opponent finished 6-6 the previous year with their last being a defeat in the Jaycee Bowl. They lost 12 lettermen, so expectations may have been a bit low. But Mangum was wary. *"Last year we went down there and won 30-22. They'll be looking for us this year so we should have a real fine football game. We're trying to get the team to understand that the Jones County schools are really tough. We want to instill in them that it is going to be a barn-burner Friday night or a knock-down-drag-em-out".*

In a game marred by yellow flags, Magee hit paydirt first on a 1-yarder by Brown. South Jones punched back with a 42-yard Earl Bridges escape and Gary Vanderslice PAT to make it 7-6. Nelson then opened the 2nd quarter with a 12-yard run (12-7) but South Jones answered with a 3-yard Shelby dive and point-after. In the 3rd quarter, Brown nailed a 33-yard FG that would be the difference in the game. Donald Smith finished things with a safety.

Magee led in first downs (13-5) and rushing (220-52) while the visitors held the air 40-11. Magee had 90 yards in penalties; South Jones had 67 yards. Nelson led Magee rushers with 98 yards while Brown led tacklers. *"We just did not play with enthusiasm. We won but we didn't do a super job. South Jones has a good team and we almost weren't ready for them. The defense played well, though; limiting South Jones to less than 100 total yards, and the line blocked well".*

GAME 6: MAGEE (2-2-1) @ MADISON RIDGELAND (2-3)
MAGEE 41 MADISON RIDGELAND 0
October 10, 1980

The Trojans had won their only two meetings; both in the last two years. *"Everything from now on out is conference competition and we must be ready. We're looking forward to the Madison Ridgeland game this week. Although the record doesn't indicate it, this team can be up and give you a lot of trouble. We can't afford to take them lightly. We're not the big play team we were last year and can't afford to make mistakes".*

Magee made quick work of the Braves with a pair of opening quarter touchdowns. Nelson's came from 55 yards while Williams got in from the 1-yard line. Malloy followed with a 20-yarder, Williams converted the two points and then moved in later from the 11, and Brown added the 27-0 halftime PAT. Malloy hit Williams from the 35-yard line in the 3rd quarter and Brown added a 50-yard fumble return in the final frame. He also booted both extra points.

Nelson led on the ground with 109 yards. *"Our defense was able to hold. This is the third-straight game that our defense has allowed the opponent less than 100 yards. All 46 players had a chance to play in this game and we feel like this is good for the whole team. We got a lot of experience".*

GAME 7: MAGEE (3-2-1) vs FOREST (1-4)
MAGEE 27 FOREST 21
October 17, 1980

Everyone thought that this week would be much easier than it turned out. Even The Scott County Times predicted a Magee win of 22-3. But it took four quarters before the Trojans could finally relax. Brown got 8 yards of his 122 rushing for the first touchdown (Quick PAT) and Williams added a 15-yarder to make it 13-0. The Bearcats, meanwhile, added a pair of touchdowns in the next frame. Eric Chancellor hit Danny Battle from 27 yards and Perry Qualls booted the PAT. Then, Chancellor found Bill Sadler from 26 yards and, with Qualls' PAT, it was 14-13 at halftime.

Heavy rain returned for the second half. Qualls found paydirt from 8 yards and added the PAT. Brown responded for Magee in the 4th quarter with a 4-yard run and two-pointer to tie the game 21-21. Brown iced the nail-biter afterwards when he edged in from the 1-yard line with 4:00 remaining. Forest led in first downs (9-7) while Magee led on the ground (205-136). *"The first quarter was a good game and the last quarter was a good game. But, the middle two were extremely weak. We are pleased with the comeback that our kids made. They really showed some good character to come from behind and win it".*

GAME 8: MAGEE (4-2-1) vs PRENTISS (3-3)
MAGEE 42 PRENTISS 12
October 24, 1980

Coach Richard Hall lost 18 of 22 starters from a 4-7 ball club. But, they had won 3 games thus far to be somewhat of a surprise. Said Mangum, *"They always have a good team and always put up a good fight".* While possibly true, Magee had lost to Prentiss only 4 times since 1959.

Nelson got the machine going in the 2nd quarter with a 66-yard dash and Brown hit Scott Rankin for the two-point play. Later, Malloy hooked up with Robert Dixon from the 30 and Quick added the 15-0 PAT. In the 3rd, Brown rushed in from the 2-yard line and grabbed a 49-yard Malloy throw for another touchdown. Quick's toe put it 28-0. Brown then ran in from the 9-yard line and Magee was cruising into the final quarter up 34-0.

The last Magee tally came on Wallace Langston's 14-yard run and Quick's kick. Prentiss avoided the shutout with a pair of scores. James Smith hit Marvin Gray from the 11-yard line and Theodore Lampton connected with Anthony Wiggins from the 13-yard line for their last. Magee led in first downs (12-7) and completely dominated rushing (356-18) and passing (127-45). Steve McCollum grabbed two fumbles, Brown had another, and Donald Smith led in tackles.

"We're pleased but we're not complacent. When you limit the opposition to 63 total yards, you just have to be pleased. Once the game got started, our QB Dwayne Malloy turned in a good performance".

GAME 9: MAGEE (5-2-1) @ JACKSON SAINT JOSEPH (5-3)
MAGEE 37 JACKSON SAINT JOSEPH 8
October 31, 1980

Jackson Saint Joe was still under the leadership of legendary coach Bill Raphael. Ever the optimist, he had 13 lettermen from a 6-5 team and said that his team had *"a good attitude and will have a good backfield"*.

Understandably, there was little reported as to details of the game. One box score had Magee with 15 opening frame points from Brown runs of 5 and 3 yards, a Brown two-pointer and a Quick kick. Robert Dixon added an 85-yard dash in the 2nd quarter and Quick converted. Saint Joe had their only response on Mark Trebotich's 5-yarder and Paul Harkins' conversion, but Magee added two more before the final quarter. Those came from Williams (1 yard and a two-pointer) and Brown (60 yards and a Quick kick).

"We're pleased with the overall performance of the team. We're happy to win this one. Though we did make a lot of mistakes, it was a great effort on the part of each player. All facets of our team looked good. The kids showed good tackling, blocking and running; just good all-around football".

GAME 10: MAGEE (6-2-1) vs MENDENHALL (8-1)
MAGEE 3 MENDENHALL 14
November 7, 1980

Mendenhall had been oh-so-close to a title in 1979, losing in the championship game to Warren Central 16-12 to finish 10-1. Coach David Abercrombie expected them to be pretty good again with 18 lettermen and numerous returners on both sides of the ball. The winner of this game would end up facing the Clinton/Warren Central winner for the LDC Championship. It was only fitting as the Simpson County Super Bowl almost always had serious implications on the line aside from bragging rights.

"We'll be running our first unit against them and working on what they do well. They do a good job with quick pitches and dives. They just have an outstanding football team and we know that". Mendy was ranked 6th in the Super 10 list of teams and the A-AA poll.

The first points in the game came on a 35-yard Brown FG to give Magee a 3-0 lead. But Mendenhall had enough left to gain the upper hand. In the 2nd quarter, Willie Holmes dove in from the 1-yard line and Gerald Hilton knocked home the extra point. That 7-3 score stood until the final quarter. Curtis May inserted the dagger on a 1-yarder and Hilton again drilled the PAT. Said Abercrombie afterwards, *"We are just elated to win that game. The Magee game is one we work for all year. I just hope we play with the same intensity this week"*.

Mangum noted that *"We are proud of our young kids through the year. Especially in putting themselves in a game like that. That shows a lot of character on their part. (Mendy) just came out on top. We couldn't capitalize on their errors. We didn't turn our breaks into points. That was the difference in the ball game. We see the Mendenhall squad as a quick and well-balanced team. They really have a bunch of outstanding athletes and we wish them well in next week's championship match. Looking at the year in perspective, we think (we) did a fine job"*.

All North Little Dixie honors included Steve McCollum, Steve Smith, Donald Smith and Patrick Brown. Honorable Mentions went to Greg Green, Danny Quick and Robert Dixon. Clinton beat Mendenhall 20-13 to claim the Little Dixie championship.

1981 (5-5)

The Trojans started 1981 with not only a new coach, but also a new playoff system. Johnny Woitt had come from Pascagoula after seven years to be head man for Magee football after the departure of John Magnum to private business. *"I felt like I needed to make a change. Moving to Magee was a spiritual decision. I simply felt like this is where I needed to be after considering a lot of other possibilities"*.

The Simpson County News said that *"Overall the Trojans are a small but fairly quick team"*. After going through their first practice on August 10th, he said near game week that *"We'll be small this year but, as always, Magee will field a strong defensive team. That's always been true of Magee and this year will be no different. Defense is definitely our strong point"*. The good news was that the Trojans were picked 2nd in a four-team 6A South division. *"We'll use a lot of options of every kind... We're going to throw the ball a lot, too"*.

GAME 1: MAGEE (0-0) vs ROSEDALE (0-0)
MAGEE 12 ROSEDALE 8
September 4, 1981

First-time opponent Rosedale under Coach Leland Young was no team to be overly-confident of playing. Having won their conference two years in a row, they were called by the paper *"a perineal power in the Mississippi delta"*. Said Woitt, *"Rosedale is a two-year conference winner and a good team. Traditionally they're tough and are the same size as Magee. They are small physically which will be a disadvantage to us because we don't know what they'll do offensively or defensively. They'll be well-disciplined ... but quick and aggressive"*.

After a late rain, the game began *"with a new set of offensive plays installed on Monday"*. A promising first drive fizzled but Jeff McDonald picked off an ensuing pass to get the ball back. Unable to move, they gave it to Rosedale on the 2-yard line. Their ensuing fumble was recovered by Efron Benson and Terrell Luckey capitalized on a run from there for the 6-0 lead at halftime. Rosedale responded in the 3rd with a 42-yard touchdown and two-point conversion *"on a sweep"* to take the lead.

Magee was able to answer afterward with Keith Green's 20-yard (or 42-yard) connection with Donald Smith. Their two-pointer failed but all of the necessary scoring was done. First downs (16-11) favored Magee. Erndaryl Jaynes led rushers with 61 yards and Smith led tacklers with 19. The Trojans had a total of 123 rushing yards; 41 passing, and four lost fumbles. They picked off one pass. *"We made a lot of mental and physical mistakes but I was very pleased with the courage the kids showing in coming back. That showed a lot of character. I was well-pleased with the conditioning and thought our boys showed a fine effort"*.

He added later, *"Rosedale kept pulling (us) off with what I thought was a technically illegal type snap. But our defense finally adjusted to their style and the officials called them on it a couple of times. We let them have the ball too long that first quarter. Most of the first quarter was theirs. My coaches did a great job... I was also pleased with the effort in the hearts of our young team. They could have given up, folded in the third quarter, but they didn't"*.

GAME 2: MAGEE (1-0) vs WEST JONES (0-1)
MAGEE 0 WEST JONES 20
September 11, 1981

West Jones, who lost their opener to Columbia 13-12, was 1-6-1 against Magee since they started playing in 1970. But Woitt knew that they had athletes. *"West Jones is bigger than (us) with a fine back whose specialty is power running and sweep running. We'll have to play super against them"*. Their coach, Mike Taylor, was a native of Magee and a person Woitt called *"a nice guy"*.

The visitors held a 6-0 lead in the opening frame behind Ronnie Duckworth's 23-yarder and added to it before halftime with a 25-yard Duckworth touchdown and two-point conversion from Frankie McBride to Bubba Hathorn. Now in the final frame and completely out-played despite the score, West Jones added their last on a *"surprising pass play"* from McBride to Hathorn. Magee blocked the extra point. In all, West Jones controlled first downs (17-8) and dominated the ground game 287-10. The Trojans held the air 75-35.

"We were out-classed; totally out-manned. And Ronnie Duckworth was awesome. He gained 200 of their yards. I thought our passing game went fairly well. They should have scored more but we had 155 yards in penalties between us. We'll use (upcoming) Pearl and West Jones as learning experiences. We're in pretty good shape after (the game). And I can assure you one thing: you can look for a good effort from our boys against Pearl Friday night".

GAME 3: MAGEE (1-1) @ PEARL (2-0)
MAGEE 6 PEARL 26
September 18, 1981

Fourth-year Coach Doug Merchant had the benefit of 25 returning lettermen including starters on defense (8) and offense (6). *"With so many kids back, we will have lettermen at all the starting positions which means that our sophomores will have difficulty breaking in as regulars"*.

The previous season had ended with disappointment as his Pirates had risen to the top spot in state polling before losing their last four contests. But, with the landscape in Rankin County, he was "*expecting to have one of our best teams ever. We've got a lot of experience*". Voters felt the same and slid Pearl into 4th in Class A-AA voting.

Their previous win gave Pearl an ORV spot in the AP Poll and kept them 3rd in The Super 10. Johnny Carr was tied for 2nd in 6-AA scoring. The two teams started play in 1958 and Magee had a commanding lead overall in the series. But Pearl had won their only two games against the Trojans in back-to-back seasons. "*Magee is a good, strong team, running out of a Power-I set. Nothing too fancy. Just power right at you*".

A scoreless opening quarter led to a pair of Pearl touchdowns in the next. Danny Brunson found Mike Stewart from the 10-yard line and Mike Stutzman converted his first of 3 PATs. That had been set up by a Fredrick Rogers fumble and Mike Miller recovery at the Magee 20. After stopping a promising Trojan drive with just :55 left, Ive Burnett broke away for 16 yards and then pitched to Milton Bryant. Bryant "*raced down the sideline to complete an 81-yard scoring play with :02 left*". The Magee Courier said of the play, "*The game film Saturday shows Burnett guilty of a forward lateral. Unfortunately, the officials missed that and Pearl got the break*".

In the 3rd, Magee put up their points on a 30-yard Dewayne Malloy run. But Pearl immediately answered with a 66-yard Burnett pass to Willie Griffith. "*The Magee defensive back went for the interception and Griffith … raced untouched to the end zone*". The last Pirate score came in the frame on a 15-yard run by Bryant. Magee led in first downs (14-10) but lost rushing (224-185) and passing (82-67). The unfortunate side of the victory for Pearl was that Scott Pierce broke his leg and would miss the remainder of the season.

Said Merchant, "*We played spotty. There were some good points and some bad points, but I've never seen a perfect team or a perfect game. We will try to improve ourselves. Magee was sky-high; very emotionally charged*". Added Woitt, "*They played well and I saw maturity we haven't seen. Other than a couple of really bad mistakes, I was well-pleased with their play*".

GAME 4: MAGEE (1-2) vs MORTON (2-1)
MAGEE 12 MORTON 9
September 25, 1981: HOMECOMING

It was Homecoming down in Simpson County. Their opponent had been picked to win 6A North and was no unfamiliar foe. In fact, this was their 42nd meeting since 1927. The Scott County Times picked the Panthers by either 14-13 or 18-6, saying "*Morton is having its problems. Now it appears that the team is once again unified under Coach Ed Amis*".

"*They are a tough team and it's time for us to cut down on our mental mistakes and get in on the winning side. We played a real spirited, emotional game (last week), but made several mental mistakes. Those were defensively costly and wound up in long touchdown runs. On the offensive, we dropped crucial passes and made two critical fumbles that set up scores and kept us from scoring. Other than that, we played a hard-nosed football game*".

While the Trojans put up a 25-yard Freddie Rogers touchdown in the 1st quarter and a 2-yard Jaynes run in the next, both points-after failed. The Panthers cut into the lead before halftime on Jeff Robertson's 1-yard run, but like Magee, they missed their PAT. The final tally of the game came in the second half as Jeff Busby hit a 28-yard FG. The Clarion-Ledger said it was in the 3rd quarter; The Magee Courier thought it the final frame.

Magee held first downs (11-7) and rushing (168-131) while Morton led in passing (153-83). Rogers paced rushers with 78 yards and Donald Smith led tacklers with 17. "*(I'm) well-pleased with the overall effort. Defensively there were some breakdowns along the way as we allowed them to run the ball but we held our composure late in the game and kept them from scoring. Offensively we didn't move the ball in the second half the way I know we can but I don't know why. Overall, we're pleased with the win*".

GAME 5: MAGEE (2-2) @ FLORENCE (0-3)
MAGEE 34 FLORENCE 0
October 2, 1981

Coach Doug Bramlett had improved his record in each of his three years (0-10 to 4-6 to 7-4) and taken his team to their first bowl since 1961. Still, he was picked last in 6A South due to circumstances outside of his control. The school district had undergone reorganization and taken many players away. Though he had 15 lettermen back, he said "*This is a tough situation we face but it's one we have to live with so there is no need to take a negative attitude*". For their first home game of the year, he said "*Magee has a younger team than it usually does but still was good enough to beat Morton last week so I'm not looking for anything too much easier than we've been facing"*.

In the end, he was right. Magee finally hit the board in the 2nd quarter on a 10-yard Malloy toss to Robert Dixon and Green PAT. They soon turned up the heat. Malloy then added a 35-yard dash and found Chris Roberts from 15 yards for another. Jeff McDonald's two-pointer made halftime 21-0. Like the opening quarter, the 3rd was scoreless. But Magee again began churning with McDonald's 2-yarder and Rogers' 78-yard escape and Green PAT.

Tyrone Stapleton led tacklers with 17 and Rogers had 137 rushing yards. Magee put up 22 first downs, 328 rushing yards and Malloy was 10-11 for 151 yards. *"We didn't score the first quarter because of fumbles and penalties, which hurt us offensively. In the second quarter we finally started a drive that ended in the end zone"*.

GAME 6: MAGEE (3-2) vs PORT GIBSON (UNREPORTED)
MAGEE 42 PORT GIBSON 24
October 9, 1981

Next up in Simpson County was the third-ranked 6A South Port Gibson squad. Said Woitt, *"I know that Port Gibson is a very big football team. They have a lot of speed and have traditionally been a real fine football team. We'll throw the ball against them and hope that our defense can shut down their power running attack. This is a must game. We must win this one to even stay in the running. It's a good game and we're looking for a large crowd"*.

The home team opened with a 78-yard march capped by Jaynes' 29-yard run and Green's PAT. Port Gibson fumbled the kickoff to Tracy Robinson to set up a 9-yard Rogers dart. On the next PG drive, Stapleton forced a fumble to McDonald and Jaynes made it pay from the 2-yard line. Rogers added to the board in the 2nd quarter on a 14-yarder while Jaynes notched the two points. Even though Port Gibson added a 72-yard Charlie Barr dash to make it 27-6, it appeared to be a run-away.

Port Gibson had other ideas, opening the 3rd with a 53-yard Ronnie Polk run. While reports differ, it appears that the score soon became 27-24 on a 12-yard Barr fumble return and a Willie Edwards 1-yarder. Magee was still up to the task with Jaynes plunging in from the 3-yard line and Malloy finding Rogers for the two points. A Green interception set up the final tally; that a 1-yard Rogers run and Green PAT.

Rogers led rushers with 87 yards and Donald Smith was best with 56 receiving yards and 11 tackles and assists. Magee led in first downs (19-15) and passing (130-18). *"They did good and they did bad. I was pleased with our offensive efforts and disappointed in our defense. We're going to have to get better for the rest of the schedule…"*

GAME 7: MAGEE (4-2) @ FOREST (3-3)
MAGEE 0 FOREST 28
October 16, 1981

The three losses suffered by Coach Lawrence Wesson's Bearcats had been against three solid teams. The Simpson County News picked Forest 8-7, saying *"Now 3-0 in sub-district, the Bearcats will be playing their hearts out to show Magee that football is still played tough on Atkins Field"*. Added Woitt, *"(We will) have to play heads-up football for all four quarters Friday night if (we) plan to stay in the game"*.

The game was all Cats, with their first score coming in the opening frame on Woodrow Longmire's 11-yard run and Perry Qualls' PAT. They tacked on two more before halftime when Eric Chancellor hit Leroy Robinson from midfield and Qualls ran in the PAT. Then, with seconds to go, Chancellor found Chris Watts and Qualls made it 22-0. Finally, a Longmire interception late in the game set the stage for Qualls' 5-yard plunge. The Cats led in first downs 14-12 and rushing (250-144).

"Totally one of the most embarrassing moments in coaching football. We experienced a total mental breakdown. I don't know what was on their minds but they were definitely not thinking about football. I don't want to take anything away from Forest by making excuses for our play. Forest really got after us and gave a fine effort. They were very enthusiastic and just whipped the dog out of us".

GAME 8: MAGEE (4-3) @ COLUMBIA (4-3)
MAGEE 0 COLUMBIA 21
October 23, 1981

These two teams had played often since their first encounter in 1929. Though not in the district, it was still a big game for Magee as they needed to recover from the shutout at Forest. *"Columbia is a big, big football team … They throw the ball a lot and have a run-and-shoot offense using two wide receivers, two slot backs and one set-back"*. The Hattiesburg American picked Magee 13-12, saying *"I'm going out on a limb on this one. The main reason for the selection being the fact that Columbia was practically run out of the stadium last week and I don't think it has recuperated yet"*.

Things took a decidedly bad turn early as Magee lost both Robinson and Donald Ray Smith to injuries before the third plays of the game. Columbia had the only tally of the opening half on an 85-yard Rosco Medious run and David Newsome PAT to make it 7-0. After sitting in the end zone during the cold intermission, the tilt picked up where it left off. The 3rd quarter was scoreless as Magee couldn't find paydirt. In the final frame, the hosts put up a pair of scores. Ronald Harvey (or Randy Franklin) had the first on a 55-yard dash while Franklin put up a 60-yarder afterwards. A two-pointer from Chip Loftin to Ricky Flowers was true.

Magee led in first downs (12-8) and passing (126-59); Columbia in rushing (228-109). *"We had a good effort and we played much-improved football. What can I say? We came back after a disappointing performance a week ago and played good football only to find ourselves losing 21-0. Next week we have another tough one against Saint Joseph. What we've got to do is regain our confidence"*.

GAME 9: MAGEE (4-4) vs JACKSON SAINT JOSEPH (4-3)
MAGEE 24 JACKSON SAINT JOSEPH 0
October 30, 1981

Saint Joe might have been expected to give a better account of themselves against Magee in their fourth all-time meeting. The Trojans had buried Saint Joe in the last three. Said Woitt, *"They're big, physical, and tough defensively. It's going to take a super effort. This game Friday is our last home game and I'm trying to keep everybody thinking about Saint Joe (and not looking ahead to Mendenhall)"*.

That held true as the first half was scoreless thanks to a missed Saint Joe FG attempt. McDonald broke scoring open in the 3rd on a 4-yard plunge and the Trojans added three more in the last quarter. Malloy and Dixon hooked up from 10 yards, Jaynes ran in from 5 yards and finally a 37-yard Rogers scamper. Rogers led rushers with 89 yards and Stapleton and McDonald each had 13 tackles. Magee led in first downs (16-9) and rushing (210-113).

"We found a defensive alignment that was giving them a big hole and finally got it across to the boys during halftime. When we came back, we shut them down; allowing only 30 yards rushing in the second half and only two first downs. I'm so glad we came alive offensively. They were supposed to be good defensively and we moved the ball on them. This has to mean something to our team".

GAME 10: MAGEE (5-4) @ MENDENHALL (9-0)
MAGEE 14 MENDENHALL 41
November 6, 1981

With 19 letter-winners in camp from a 9-2 team, Mendy under first-year Coach Tommy Lucas was picked first in the 6A South voting. But, as usual, their 9-0 record would mean very little should Magee upset them. The winner would make their way to play the Forest-Morton winner before taking a swing at a State Championship.

The paper said that Woitt *"discovered two black and gold bows on the door knob of his office Tuesday morning with an accompanying note claiming 'With Deepest Sympathy from The Mendenhall Tigers"*. Said he, *"I've been told so much about this rivalry and I'm really looking forward to my first Magee-Mendenhall encounter. Mendenhall is a fine football team. They're rated Number 5 in the AP Poll and Number 4 in The Clarion-Ledger Super 10 poll. They'll get nothing but respect from me. We're going to have to play four quarters of football against them; none of this wait-til-the-second-half business. We're going to have to avoid turnovers and mistakes against this strong team"*.

Mendenhall scored early and often. Tim Smith garnered 3 touchdowns; one in the 2nd quarter from 71 yards away. The others were from 2 and 3 yards out. Greg Dampeer added a rushing touchdown from 17 yards and a score via the air from the same distance. Kelly Greer notched 5 PATs on the night. One Malloy fumble ended up in the hands of Anthony Buckhalter who raced 41 yards for a tally to make it 41-0. Magee scored twice in the last minute of play.

Green hit Dixon from the 10-yard line for the first, the Trojans recovered an onside kick, and Green spotted Dixon from 47 yards for the last.

Mendenhall dominated rushing (295-73) with Tim Smith gaining 207 of those markers. Overall yardage went to the Tigers 324-199 as did first downs (14-8). Donald Smith (15) and Stapleton (14) led tacklers. Said Lucas, "*The players worked real hard and were ready. The defense really controlled the Magee passing game and the team took charge on a couple of turnovers and cashed in on them early in the game. Offensively we had some of the hardest running and most aggressive blocking all year*".

Added Woitt, "(*They) were very aggressive. Mendenhall just beat us physically and the scoreboard whipped us. They just got after us. I don't want to take anything away from Mendenhall; they are a super team. But I thought we have played better in many games throughout the year. We certainly didn't have our best performance Friday night*".

West Bolivar topped Forest 48-33 for the State A championship.

1982 (7-6)

For the third time in four years, Magee football now had a new mentor. Coach Woitt had actually conducted spring drills before leaving for Choctawhatchee High in Fort Walton, FL. Former Hattiesburg coach David Bradley called for first practices on August 10th and said immediately afterwards that "*Our first practice went well. The kids had a lot of enthusiasm and exhibited a willingness to work hard. We have a very fine group of kids with a number of fine athletes who are better than your average group of high school athletes. It's too early to make a prediction about the season. But the team we field for the first game will be a competitive team. We will take the season one game at a time…*"

His roster included 21 seniors, 12 juniors and 19 sophomores. Pressure was high as the Trojans were picked South 6A favorites. "*I was surprised to hear that. But I think we will be good because we'll challenge our kids with four games before we play any district games. Of those four, Starkville, Brandon and West Jones are ranked in the top ten in state polls and Brookhaven is a AA school. If we're going to do well, we will find out fast playing against those teams*".

GAME 1: MAGEE (0-0) @ BROOKHAVEN (0-0)
MAGEE 12 BROOKHAVEN 28
September 3, 1982

The trip to Lincoln County marked the first meeting between Ole Brook and Magee; two traditionally-tough football schools. Said Bradley, "*Brookhaven has always played real tough schedules and I'm sure they are used to tough competition*".

Brookhaven jumped out early with a pair of first quarter touchdowns after a fumble recovery and 17-yard march. One score came via a Roger Connley 4-yard run and the next a 20-yard Todd Self pass to Billy Smith. They added another touchdown in the 2nd quarter on Mike Ellis' 1-yard plunge after

Magee fumbled on the 22-yard line to Mike Ingle. The Trojans responded with two scores thanks to Michael Green's 4-yard run in the 3rd quarter and Frederick Rogers' 1-yarder in the next. Late in the game, Brookhaven put up an insurance score via Self's 1-yard dive to finish things. Brookhaven led in first downs (16-14) and rushing (150-132). Rogers led rushers with 72 yards.

"*We started off okay. I guess we had a case of the first-game jitters. We didn't know what to expect and we made several costly errors before we decided to settle down in the second half and play ball. After we got over the jitters, we settled down and proved we could play ball. We made some costly errors in the ball game but they were aggressive mistakes; not passive ones*".

The bad news for the Trojans was that Dwayne Malloy sustained a broken jaw "*due to an illegal blow to the head*" and would be gone for the majority, if not all, of the season. Larry Stubbs was the Player of the Week for Magee.

GAME 2: MAGEE (0-1) @ WEST JONES (1-0)
MAGEE 0 WEST JONES 20
September 10, 1982

West Jones was no stranger to the schedule. Since 1970, Magee had posted a 6-2-1 record against them. The home team opened with a 28-22 win over a strong Columbia squad and posed no small task for the Trojans. *"They have the best running back in the state (Ronnie Ducksworth). I'm not saying that West Jones is a one-man team, but he is good and in order for us to do well Friday night, we will have to contain him"*.

Ducksworth opened play in the 1st quarter with a 20-yard touchdown run and John Easterling converted. That had been set up by Greg Amerson's interception. In the next frame, he ran in from 14 yards and Easterling made it 14-0. That, too, had been the result of an interception by Jeff Clark. The final tally came in the 3rd quarter via John Clark's 9-yard escape. West Jones held first downs (12-10) and rushing (150-84) while Magee won the air (62-30). Rogers was Magee's leading rusher with 44 markers. Frank Smith was voted Player of the Week.

"We were completely disappointed with the outcome of Friday night's game. We felt we had a chance if we could stop Ducksworth and we did stop him with less than 100 yards. I don't think that's been done very often. But consistency offensively was not there. We had three interceptions that really hurt us. We were very pleased with defensive play. Our defense was very aggressive".

GAME 3: MAGEE (0-2) vs STARKVILLE (2-0)
MAGEE 0 STARKVILLE 19
September 17, 1982

The Oktibbeha County group won the AA North State Championship the previous year *"and forecasts are predicting a repeat"*. By game day, Starkville sat 8th in the Super 10. *"Starkville is very quick, larger than we are, and run their offense with a lot of faking (and) cross-action in the backfield. They have 20 seniors on their team and are a veteran, experienced football team. We feel if we can adjust to their offense and play defense as well as we did against West Jones, we'll have a chance of defeating them"*.

The Magee Courier said that the Trojans played an *"impressive first half against a squad that outweighed, outmanned and outgained them"*. Halftime sat only 7-0; that touchdown coming midway through the opening quarter on Ken Rogers' 3-yard run. Magee drove to the Starkville 26-yard line in the 3rd, but the fourth-down play was picked off by Willie Kelly. The Jackets added their next tally in the 3rd on Scott Chesser's 10-yard escape and finished things in the final quarter on a 7-yard Chesser run. Both points-after were unsuccessful. The first of those scores came via Jerome Walker's pickoff.

Starkville led in first downs (12-9) and total yardage (237-157). Erndaryl Jaynes led rushers with 61 yards. *"I'm pleased with their efforts in the first half. They played well. But in the second half, some breakdowns cost us a chance of winning the (half)". Those mistakes included falling for a long count and jumping offside twice on critical downs, and pass interceptions..."*

GAME 4: MAGEE (0-3) @ NORTHEAST JONES (2-1)
MAGEE 12 NORTHEAST JONES 14
September 24, 1982

It had been since 1954 that Magee started out 0-3. Bradley was optimistic that things were going to change. *"We're looking to have a good game. The team really has good spirit and are looking for a win. We feel like with the right preparation this week, we can do it. I think we have a good shot at them. They don't have the tradition that West Jones and Starkville have and that might offset their home-stand advantage"*.

The game was a tale of two quarters, though it would not be enough in the end. Northeast held a 14-0 lead at halftime thanks to a 3-yard Bradley Blakeney run, a 77-yard dash by Robert Franklin and a pair of Stan Livingston PATs. But Magee did not quit. In the final quarter, they moved to the 6-yard line but couldn't punch it in. However, Northeast fumbled and tenth-grader Tony Forrest picked up the loose ball and raced 43 yards to paydirt. They then drove 94 yards with the big play a Green pass to Jimbo Nowell, who then found Forrest for a 91-yard dash to daylight. The on-side kick was successful but time was not on their side.

Magee led in first downs (10-7) and total yardage 240-143). *"We started off playing very uninspired football and we let them score twice, leaving us two touchdowns behind at halftime. We fought back and came very close to winning"*. Terrell Luckey was named Player of the Week for his defensive efforts. Northeast Coach Danny Adams said after, *"Give Magee credit. They never quit. They are the best 0-4 team in the state"*.

GAME 5: MAGEE (0-4) vs FLORENCE (1-3)
MAGEE 46 FLORENCE 14
October 1, 1982: HOMECOMING

It was Homecoming in Simpson County and time to finally get the important part of the season underway. Said Bradley, "*Florence is a good, big team and they've played competitively against other teams. We're looking forward to starting our district play on a winning note*". The nearby team had never beaten Magee on the football field.

Scoring was rampant. Rogers was first on a 3-yard run and James Brinson notched the PAT. Louis McCollum had the next on a fumble return, Forrest broke away for 65 yards (Brinson) and then Jaynes plunged in from the 1-yard line to make it 27-0 after one quarter of play. With reserves now in play, Rogers dashed 81 yards for a score and Brinson converted. Florence cut into the lead with a 65-yard Jerome Young pass to Jerry Lewis and Harris' PAT, but Wallace Langston returned the kick 88 yards in response. Before halftime, Florence found points on an 18-yard Young pass to Lewis and point-after.

Neither team found the end zone in the 3rd quarter, but Magee tallied once more in the final frame when Terry Holloway galloped 63 yards to finish things. Magee dominated statistically with 454 rushing yards. Forrest counted 137 and Rogers another 105 yards. "*I think they were hungry for success and played really good football. We were even able to play substitutes during the first quarter and more in the second quarter and that made us all feel good*". Forrest, also with an interception, was named Player of the Week.

GAME 6: MAGEE (1-4) @ PORT GIBSON (3-1)
MAGEE 27 PORT GIBSON 18
October 8, 1982

In their inaugural meeting the year before, Magee had taken Port Gibson 42-24. "*They have a fine team and we've seen them in action on film and have had them scouted. They'll be hard to handle down there. And they're probably the largest and fastest group we've played*".

With under 5:00 to go in the opening quarter, Brinson started the scoring with a 27-yard FG. Port Gibson rallied on a 25-yard Charlie Banks run to take a 6-3 lead. In the 2nd quarter, they scored on a 21-yard pass but again missed the PAT. Before halftime, Rogers found the end zone and Brinson put the game 12-10. Now in the 3rd, Rogers moved in from the 3-yard line and Brinson converted. The home team was awarded a touchdown on a 1-yard QB sneak though the Trojans contested that it was short. Still, it counted and the game was 18-17.

Back came Brinson with a 4th quarter FG from 23 yards. Rogers broke loose from the 47 with just over 2:00 remaining and Brinson put the cap on the night. Magee edged Port Gibson in first downs (15-10) and total yards (279-265). "*I think, overall, we probably played our most aggressive game this year. We have to overcome a lot of adversities and a lot of penalties that tend to get us down. It seemed like we stayed behind all game and got started a little poorly in the first quarter, but after that we came through with a good effort. They opened up with a passing attack which left our defensive backs extremely busy most of the night*". McCollum and Forrest each had interceptions.

Both Rogers and Brinson garnered Player of the Week honors.

GAME 7: MAGEE (2-4) vs FOREST (3-3)
MAGEE 34 FOREST 0
October 15, 1982

After two-straight district wins, Magee was looking to keep the momentum going against long-time nemesis Forest. Assistant Coach Gary Risher once held the whistle for the Cats. The Simpson County News was split on the outcome. One prognosticator favored Forest 14-13 while another picked Magee 21-3. Said Bradley, "*They started off kind of slow but they've come on strong during their recent games. They'll definitely be up and play some kind of tough game. We'll do our best to make sure they don't keep up their streak*".

The Trojans hit the scoreboard in every quarter; their first a 26-yard Keith Green throw to Donald Green. Brinson nailed his first of four PATs. Magee put up a pair of scores in the 2nd quarter on a 10-yard Jaynes run and Green's 30-yard toss to Tracy Robinson. In the 3rd, Jaynes broke away from 67 yards and, finally, Luckey dodged in from the 11-yard line to wrap things up. First downs favored Magee 10-4 and Magee out-gained the Cats 194-112 in total yardage. Jaynes racked up 124 rushing yards. Keith Green was tabbed as Player of the Week for Magee.

"*We played an outstanding defensive football game. It was the fourth quarter before Forest ever had a first down. Probably the best defensive effort all year. Offensively, we did well. Forest never gave up and played tough, though the team is down a little this year. Forest was harder to move the ball on that we anticipated but our kids did real well. We've improved quite a bit. We're playing as a team and if we continue to do so, we should have an outstanding chance of knocking off Brandon".*

GAME 8: MAGEE (3-4) vs BRANDON (5-2)
MAGEE 6 BRANDON 0
October 22, 1982

Wally Bumpas, back for his 3rd year, was chosen 1st in the 6-AA North with 19 seniors, 16 lettermen and 12 starters. Things had changed as there were now two divisions (North and South) and Brandon had erased Florence, Hinds AHS, Morton, Forest and Vicksburg. *"The obvious difference between this season and last is the schedule. At least four of the five new opponents will be stronger than any of four that have gone off the schedule. Another thing quite as uncertain would be the matter of intangibles. Things like senior leadership, which we had so abundantly in 1981. Another would be injuries; something that can turn a season around in an instant".*

In 1981, the paper had continuous notations about the best future team for Brandon being that of the coming season. That year was at hand. Additionally, The Clarion-Ledger put two of the Bulldogs as members of The Top 25 Seniors to Watch: Kelvin McLaurin and Steve Joyner. They also put Brandon 4th in The Super 10 to start the campaign. *"I don't take too much stock in those polls. We're not that good right now, but I would hope we will get that good. But we're not right now. Our schedule is extremely tough ... There aren't any easy ones on the schedule".* Bradley noted that *"It should be a good ball game and I think we've got a good chance of beating them even though they're picked to win. I believe they will be the best and strongest team all year".*

Despite a Dog fumble on their first drive, the defense held. The only tally of the contest came at 11:09 of the 2nd when Rogers capped a 65-yard march from the 3. The two-pointer failed but the scoring would be over. Late in the final frame, Brandon had a chance deep in their own territory. A 4th down pass from Brian Hutson to Steve Joyner moved the ball to the Trojan 25. But, a last-ditch attempt by Hutson was picked off by Michael Green on the 1-yard line.

Magee led in first downs (10-7) and rushing (126-11) while passing (82-68) favored the Dogs. Both teams suffered interceptions. Said Bumpas, *"The team played very good defense. We were up against a mighty fine team that had been scoring a lot of points. But, we held them to under 100 yards of offense. The kids played as best as they could. It just came down to they were ready to play and we weren't. Defensively we played well enough to win, but Magee got stronger as the game went on and we went flat".*

Added Magee's mentor, *"This was the best defensive effort of any team I've ever coached. It was our best overall effort this season. They all had a super night. We were up against a mighty fine team that had been scoring a lot of points. But we held them to under 100 yards of offense".* John Hosey and Lewis McCollum gathered Player of the Week nods for defensive efforts.

GAME 9: MAGEE (4-4) @ MORTON (6-2)
MAGEE 0 MORTON 13
October 29, 1982

The North 6A favorite Panthers were living up to expectations with a 6-2 record. The Scott County Times was again split on the outcome, picking Morton 21-19 and Magee 6-0. Said Bradley, *"Morton has a lot of size and quickness. We know we will have to be well-prepared to play in the same ball park with them".* Little did they know that it would be the first of two games between the clubs in a two-week span.

It didn't take long for Morton to take a lead when Ken Warnsley took a 1st quarter punt 55 yards to paydirt and Randy Crapps converted the point-after. In the next frame, Harold Chambers upped the score to 13-0 on an 8-yard scamper. The Magee Courier said that *"then Magee got the idea that if Morton scored first, it was all over. And that's the way they played the rest of the night".*

Despite the shutout, Magee still led in total yards 131-48. Rogers was Magee's leading rusher with only 30 yards. Michael Green, with 9 tackles and an interception, was named Player of the Week. *"Our concentration was poor, as was our kicking game. I think we were emotionally low after the emotional high we had experienced last week against Brandon. Plus, our kids were already thinking about Mendenhall. We played real good defensive football but just didn't have any drive about us to go out and do what it took to win the game".*

With Madison Ridgeland's upset of Forest, Morton now was assured of the district title.

GAME 10: MAGEE (4-5) vs MENDENHALL (8-1)
MAGEE 13 MENDENHALL 0
November 5, 1982

Coach Tommy Lucas' Tigers were picked 2nd in South 6A, but he underplayed his season expectations. He said that they had *"young players lacking in a lot of experience but with competitiveness and attitude of winning which carries the potential of victory every week. We will be playing a lot of young boys which doesn't mean we're weak, but if we had all of them a year from now, it would be a lot different. Our season will depend on how fast our 10th and 11th graders can move in and learn what to do and gain confidence while perfecting their skills"*.

Now, it was winner-take-all for the South sub-district with Mendy second-ranked in Class A. *"This is one of the toughest games of the year and a lot is at stake here. Magee has an outstanding team. They have played some of the most outstanding teams in the state and have played them well. When it comes to this game, you have to throw out all of the records. We are hoping this will be an exciting game as it is every year"*.

Added Magee's mentor, *"Mendenhall is, without a doubt, the toughest team we will play this season. They have quickness and are very impressive. (They are) aggressive; probably more aggressive than any team we've played. They've had more successes this year than any other team we've played and success builds confidence. We're trying to get our offensive execution down. We're working on our blocking and tackling and working on being in the right place at the right time. This late in the season, you don't try anything new. You go with what's already done the job for you. We've done alright offensively and defensively, but what we're looking for is consistency"*.

This rivalry would mark the inaugural Wally Beach Challenge Trophy, named for a respected former coach. Suffering from ALS, he would still be on hand to make the initial presentation to the winner. With Magee now retaining the services of Dwayne Malloy from his opening-game injury, and despite his earlier fumble to the Tigers, Havard McDonald came up with a return gift via a fumble near midfield. That resulted in a Brinson 35-yard FG and 3-0 lead. Another promising Mendenhall drive was also killed via a fumble.

Magee tacked on their next score in the 2nd quarter after yet another dropped ball. Rogers did the damage on a 25-yard dash and Brinson put halftime 10-0. A 3rd quarter Trojan fumble gave the Tigers a chance but uncharacteristically Mendy fumbled it back. With 5:25 left on the clock, Brinson nailed another FG from 36 yards and the game was effectively over. The Trojans had led in first downs (11-5) rushing (227-19) and passing (85-51). Rogers rushed for 82 yards and caught 51 yards more. Both Rogers and Frank Smith were tabbed Players of the Week while the Magee Touchdown Club gave honors to Luckey (defense) and Keith Green (offense).

"We had a very aggressive defense and probably the best defensive effort all year. We are just real pleased with the overall effort. We know we beat a good football team in Mendenhall and that makes us feel much better. No doubt Mendenhall is one of the best teams we've played all year; if not the best". Said Lucas, *"A lot of credit should go to their players and coaching staff for a tough ball game. We felt like their desire to win was the best we've seen all year. They were real keyed up. They outplayed us and won the game"*.

GAME 11: MAGEE (5-5) @ MORTON (8-2)
MAGEE 13 MORTON 7
November 12, 1982

The rematch was now on tap; once again on Morton's home turf. The Simpson County Times, as usual this season, was split on who the winner would be. One picked Coach Mickey Burton's Morton squad 21-20, saying *"Although Magee players said they were not ready for Morton and were looking ahead to Mendenhall, we still think the Panther team is better and by playing at home will have a definite advantage"*. The other prognosticator picked Magee 14-12. Said Bradley, *"We were not mentally prepared to play Morton, but are working on being ready this time"*.

This one was worth the price of admission at R.H. Watkins Stadium, with the score 7-7 until the final minutes. Despite an opening drive fumble and the ball on the 6-yard line after a bad punt snap, their FG attempt failed and kept the game scoreless. In the 2nd quarter, Morton found paydirt on a 26-yard pass and the PAT to give them the halftime edge. Midway through the 3rd quarter, a fake punt set up Rogers' 28-yard scamper and Brinson's PAT. Each team threw interceptions as the game neared expiration. But with :51 on the clock, Rogers found daylight from 25 yards for the game-winner.

"We had a really good second half offensively and defensively. I was extremely happy with the good blocking from Tommy Manning, Clifton Walker, Havard McDonald and Erndaryl James. Their blocking set up many of Green's exciting runs". Lewis McCollum was named defensive player of the game with an interception and was accompanied by Michael Green with his 116 rushing yards.

GAME 12: MAGEE (6-5) vs STONE COUNTY (9-2)
MAGEE 20 STONE COUNTY 9
November 19, 1982

Magee had never met up with Stone County High, but had faced Wiggins in 1939 (loss 12-6). The Magee Courier said that *"The group from Wiggins will bring probably the biggest, strongest team the Trojans have faced all year. Some have compared them to Brandon"*. Bradley noted that *"We're trying to prepare ourselves mentally to play and are working on total concentration. They are a very fast team according to what all the coaches I've talked to and, probably with the most speed of any of them. They have a lot of size and use a misdirection offense... it will be kind of different than what we have seen. They must be good or they wouldn't be here"*.

Now ranked 5th in Class A, Magee made a quick statement when Rogers took the opening kick 89 yards to the end zone and Brinson converted. Fumbles began to take their toll as the Trojans gave the Tomcats the ball back later on the 29-yard line to lead to a Harold Tillman 27-yard run to daylight. Another fumble gave Randy Geiger a 30-yard FG to put the Tomcats up 9-7. In the 3rd quarter, it was the Tomcats' turn to fumble to Magee. Jaynes would make it count with a 2-yard run but the two-pointer failed. Finally, in the last frame, Rogers ended things with a 42-yard (or 25-yard) dash and Brinson converted.

Statistics vary depending on the report. The Magee Courier said that Rogers put up 245 yards of rushing on the night. That counted the kick return. The box score showed the Trojans leading in rushing (195-163) while Stone County held the air 67-35. First downs were even 11-11. *"The entire front wall ... has improved week-after-week and our offense looked exceptional this week. We took control in the 3rd quarter and simply wrapped up the game. You would have thought that kickoff return would get us pumped up but we never got any momentum in the first half. We hurt ourselves on every drive with turnovers and we just told the kids at halftime to be more aggressive on defense and quit making silly mistakes. Thankfully they did just that in the second half"*.

Coach Buddy Emmanuel said *"They (Magee) just wanted to win this one more than our folks did. It was just a simple lack of character on our part"*.

GAME 13: MAGEE (7-5) vs COLUMBIA (11-1)
MAGEE 8 COLUMBIA 26
November 26, 1982

The Class A State Championship was up for grabs at D.I. Patrick Stadium in Hattiesburg. Magee had taken an unusual route to the title game with a 7-5 record. Meanwhile, Columbia was steamrolling at Number 1 in The Clarion-Ledger and Jackson Daily News Class A poll. *"They lost their first ball game 27-22 to West Jones and won the next 11. They have three top college prospects ... and they'll probably throw more than any team we've seen this year. They'll run a lot of options and misdirection sweeps to the outside. Our defense is quick, and if they will play with quickness and determination, we can win the south title"*.

After a scoreless opening quarter, Columbia took advantage of an interception to march 45 yards with Randy Franklin doing the damage on a 10-yard run and Chip Loftin hitting Ricky Flowers for the two-points. With about 2:00 left, Rogers *"burst through the line breaking loose for 74 yards to paydirt"*. His two-pointer made it an 8-8 game. An ensuing squib kick gave Columbia a chance to hit a 41-yard Flowers FG and give them an 11-8 halftime advantage.

Columbia controlled the second half, with The Magee Courier noting that the Trojans had only *"eight plays during the entire second half, two of those punts"*. The Cats were able to score in the 3rd quarter on Roscoe Medious' 52-yard breakaway, a Loftin two pointer to Flowers, and Loftin's 1-yard run (with :04 remaining) and Edward Daniel's PAT. Said Bradley, *"I thought it was kind of tacky. It wasn't their coach. The QB called the timeout. He made an error in judgement but he'll learn as he gets older. We didn't play real well on defense. Any time a team stays on the field that long, they are going to get tired. They just kept the ball away from us in the second half"*.

According to The Columbian Progress, Coach Jerry Drane disagreed. *"Chip did not call the timeout. We had not planned a timeout but with one play left, you do the best you can. We had whipped them all over the field and 19-8 would not have been indicative"*. Columbia dominated in first downs (16-5), rushing (224-124) and passing (86-11).

The South sub-district team include Terrell Luckey, James Brinson, Frank Smith, Clifton Walker, Larry Stubbs, Havard McDonald, Darren Easterling, and John Hosey. Honorable Mentions went to Michael Green, Fred Rogers, Dwayne Malloy, Keith Green and Erndaryl Jaynes. Columbia beat New Albany 20-0 for the Class A championship.

1983 (6-4)

Second-year Coach David Bradley lost between 15-17 lettermen from the 1982 team including 12 starters. The Trojans now found themselves back in the Southern Athletic Conference but were picked 5th out of the six teams. *"We will have a team which has a lot of experience in some areas, but is inexperienced in the line. We have good linemen who, given experience and time, could turn the team into a competitive one"*. They held a Meet the Trojans event on August 25th complete with a scrimmage.

He said afterwards, *"Since we've been hitting, we've found out that we are definitely going to be inexperienced and young in the line. Once they get experience, I think we'll be pretty good. We have good football players and good kids that work hard. That's usually all it takes. We should be a very competitive team as the season progresses. We should be pretty competitive with a chance at vying for the district championship"*.

GAME 1: MAGEE (0-0) vs BROOKHAVEN (0-0)
MAGEE 0 BROOKHAVEN 15
September 2, 1983

The inaugural game between the teams had been the previous year where Brookhaven took the victory 28-12. Ole Brook had finished 7-3 that season. The Hattiesburg American predicted a Brookhaven win 14-6, saying that the home team *"expected to be a tough opponent with three players being watched closely by major colleges"*. For this encounter, the same paper would say afterwards, *"The Trojans were victims of their own mistakes, fumbling the ball nine times and throwing 3 interceptions."*

The Daily Leader said that the … *"Trojans committed gridiron suicide with eight turnovers (3 interceptions and 5 lost fumbles)"*. Brookhaven's first score came in the 2nd quarter after Cammie Collins recovered a fumble. Bill Smith did the honors with a 1-yard plunge to make it 6-0 at halftime. Another fumble, this time in the 3rd quarter, set up another Smith one-yarder. He also notched a 47-yard FG to close out scoring. That came after a Bobby Hathorne interception. Magee led in first downs (11-9) and passing (62-13) while losing the ground 169-121. Willie Williams led tacklers with 10 solo.

"We started off in pretty good shape until we started making mistakes. We had a good offensive and defensive effort but those turnovers were our downfall. We had bad quarterback pitches and our receivers dropped passes which were in their hands. I guess you could call it first-game jitters. We'll work on this aspect of the game this week".

GAME 2: MAGEE (0-1) @ FOREST HILL (0-1)
MAGEE 40 FOREST HILL 6
September 9, 1983

Coach Billy Templeton was now in his 17th year as Forest Hill mentor. After a 3-7 season, he was not overly optimistic about the chances for the coming campaign. *"I'm not going to say that we are going to win any more games than last year, but I am pleased with our attitude so far. If things keep improving, we will be respectable. We've got a long way to go, but we are definitely on the right road. The kids are hungry. They really want to win"*. The two teams met often between 1944 and 1956, but only twice since. Both (1962 and 1967) were victories for Magee.

Forest Hill's opener had been a tight 6-0 loss to Clinton in a storm-delayed contest. Said Bradley, *"We'll be the first Class A school to play them in a number of years. Their defensive and offensive lines have been pointed out to us as being very comparable to Brookhaven"*. The Hattiesburg American predicted a Forest Hill victory 14-8.

This game was a tale of two halves. Forest Hill held a 6-0 lead after one half of play thanks to two interceptions and two fumbles by Magee. Scott Mayes' 1-yard run in the opening quarter would be the last they would get. The Trojans notched three touchdowns in response after halftime. Erndaryl Jaynes had the first on a 35-yard run and Lazar Stubbs converted. Dwayne King then found a loose football and raced 17 yards to paydirt. Stubbs was again true. Finally, a John Hosey fumble recovery set up Jaynes' second TD; that from 40 yards out.

But the scoring assault was not over. In the final frame, King and Donny Malloy found another loose ball to set up Fred Rogers' 20-yard effort. After yet another King fumble recovery, Terry Holloway connected with Fred Newsome from 5 yards. An ensuing fumble to James May allowed one final Magee score when King raced in from 22 yards out. Magee led in first downs (14-8) and rushing (317-49) while Forest Hill held passing 78-59. The home team fumbled 5 times to Magee's 3.

GAME 3: MAGEE (1-1) @ COLUMBIA (1-1)
MAGEE 20 COLUMBIA 13
September 16, 1983

Columbia had been not only the team to end Magee's improbable 1982 run, but also did it with just seconds left. This year, Coach Jerry Drane *"lost so many fine athletes off last season's Class A state championship team he has trouble remembering all of their names"*. Said he, *"Last year we were worried about our second and third strings and didn't have to worry about the first string. This year we're worried about the first string. We must find replacements for the graduated starters in a hurry"*.

Though they lost 22 lost lettermen, they were still picked second in the SAC. Said Bradley, *"Columbia has a very raw, talented football team ... They have quickness and as much talent as any team we'll play this year. They're also fielding a team with 14 who started at various times during the season"*.

Columbia threated first on a short FG effort but it failed. Magee shortly thereafter fumbled right back to the Wildcats and Otis Franklin made it count on a 6-yard run. Edward Daniels notched the 7-0 point-after. Magee went to the bag of tricks before halftime, faking a punt and handing off to Jaynes. His first down run led a few plays later to his 2-yard dive into the end zone. Ronald Harvey broke through the Magee line to block what would have been the game-tying PAT at halftime.

The home team opened scoring in the 3rd quarter on a 40-yard Eddie Brakefield toss to Franklin. Now in the final period, the special teams gave the Trojans the spark. John Mangum's block of a Cat punt fell into the arms of Tony Forest and he raced 41 yards for the score. Keith Green's kick evened the scoreboard. With just 2:55 remaining, Green hit Forest in stride from 42 yards for the last touchdown. Green converted to finish scoring. Magee led in first downs (11-10) and passing (156-41). Columbia held the ground 100-56.

GAME 4: MAGEE (2-1) vs NORTHEAST JONES (2-1)
MAGEE 20 NORTHEAST JONES 7
September 23, 1983: HOMECOMING

Fifth-year Coach Danny Adams had surprised many with a good season in 1982 but *"ended on a sour note"*. Still, they were 8-3 and had lots of reasons to be optimistic for 1983. Adams was picked 4th in the SAC after losing 15 starters, but did have five seniors back. *"They're a tough, physical team and they'll come out passing. Their QB has completed 68% of his passes this year. He's very accurate"*.

Magee got off to a great start with a game-opening drive to paydirt with Jaynes capping it from the 6-yard line. An ensuing Mangum interception set up shop at the 32-yard line. Green did the damage from the 1-yard line four plays later and then kicked his second extra point to make halftime 14-0. Northwest managed their only response in the 3rd on a 15-yard Chris Thornton strike to Bobby Martin and Stan Livingston's PAT.

The visitors actually picked up a Trojan fumble in the last frame for a touchdown, but it was called back for clipping. Now on 4th down and going to the air again, their throw found Forest instead of a Jones receiver. He raced 101 yards to paydirt in what may have been the longest pick-six in Magee football history. Jaynes, tied for 1st in 6A scoring, finished with 90 rushing yards while King (defense), Keith Hall (offense) and Willie Kemp (special teams) were named Players of the Week.

"We got a little complacent after the first half. But they came back late in the game and played heads-up football. I'm especially proud of our defensive unit. They've scored a touchdown

in each of the last three games. That'll make a difference in a ball game". First downs (12-2) and rushing (187-3) favored Magee. Jones dominated the air 155-0. Said assistant NEJ assistant Cliff Herrington, *"We feel like Magee is the best team we have played"*.

GAME 5: MAGEE (3-1) vs WEST JONES (3-1)
MAGEE 7 WEST JONES 14
September 30, 1983

Former Magee native Mike Taylor was in his 9th year as Mustang mentor. Though he graduated 12 seniors from their 8-2 team, he was still the pre-season favorite in the SAC. By kickoff, Magee and West Jones were tied for top spot. *"They have a fine football team and are well-coached. They have a tremendous winning tradition. We are expecting a battle"*. The Hattiesburg American called it 20-13 in favor of the 5th ranked Class A Trojans.

A very early Trojan fumble to West Jones was all they needed. Five plays later, John Easterling dove in from the 1-yard line and then provided the PAT. They added to that advantage before the end of the quarter after a Trojan fumble via Gary Amerson's 3-yard run and Easterling's kick. Unbelievably, scoring for the night ended in the 2nd quarter when Rogers escaped defenders for a 54-yard tally. Green's kick was good. The second half was a defensive battle for both clubs.

Rogers (offense), Michael Green (defense) and Holloway (special teams) received praise from the coaches. *"We did not play a good game against an excellent ball club. Our execution was not good. And you certainly don't give a team like West Jones a break. They'll take advantage every time. Their kicking game kept us bottled up. We didn't have real good field position... They just managed to put together that one drive and took advantage of one fumble. It was a hard-fought game on both sides"*. West Jones led in first downs (8-5) and rushing (156-120). Passing went to Magee 34-24.

GAME 6: MAGEE (3-2) @ SOUTH JONES (2-3)
MAGEE 12 SOUTH JONES 10
October 7, 1983

Magee had reeled off three-straight wins against the Ellisville, MS squad before taking a two-year hiatus. South Jones was picked 6th in the SAC for the coming season and were battling to stay .500. Said Bradley, *"This is the first time in my coaching career that I've had a chance to play in my home territory. I'd like very much to win over there Friday night. But we're going to have to balance out, play better overall and execute offensively to win"*.

The visitors hit the board late in the opening quarter on a Rogers run from inside the 2-yard line. In the 2nd quarter, Green found Jimbo Nowell from 64 yards away and Magee now held a 12-0 lead. But before halftime, South Jones managed a Fred Cooley 24-yard FG to cut into the lead. They cut deeper in the 3rd quarter via a 3-yard Bobbie Rae Rodgers blast for what would be their final tally. South Jones actually drove to the Trojan 10-yard line in the last frame after Wayne Tanner's fumble recovery and attempted a 27-yard FG for the lead. To Trojan fans' delight, the attempt failed.

The Laurel Leader-Call provides insight into a controversial ending to the game. *"After being held by the tough Magee defense, the Braves lined up in punt formation at their own 43-yard line. Fred Cooley punted to Magee ... (the receiver) rushed forward to receive the punt, but suddenly changed his mind. The ball landed just in from of (him) and appeared to touch the confused senior as it headed toward the end zone. The pigskin rolled across the goal line and was recovered by Mike Newell"*. The play was eventually called a touchback.

Edward Lockhart (defense) Keith Hall (offense) and Kemp (special teams) were players of the week. Jaynes rushed for 149 and Rogers added 107 more. First downs (10-8) and rushing (262-30) went to Magee. South Jones held the air 97-64. *"South Jones played a good game and were really fired up. They really got after us as far as aggressiveness. We got more bruised up, bumped up and beat up in this game than in any we've played so far this year"*.

GAME 7: MAGEE (4-2) @ FOREST (4-2)
MAGEE 38 FOREST 6
October 14, 1983

These two teams had played only once (1969) between 1959-1977. Since they resumed play, Magee was 4-1 against the Bearcats. Said Bradley about Forest, *"They make mistakes, but they play with reckless abandon and make up for those mistakes. We're simply going to have to play football all four quarters; something we have not done all year long. It will be a tough game with some kind of tough football".*

Magee's furious-paced scoring in the opening frame at L.O. Atkins Field closed the door on any Forest hopes. King blocked a Cat punt and Mangum picked it and raced 25 yards for a touchdown. Ed Lockhart then picked off a Forest throw to set up a 17-yard Rogers dash. Michael Green then joined in the interception parade and Rogers made the most of it from 15 yards. Stubbs notched PATs after the first and last touchdown. Finally, Green hit Darren Easterling from the 23-yard line and it was 26-0.

The Trojans added their next score in the 3rd on a fake punt run by Mangum 54 yards. Their last came in the final frame after a series of passes set the ball at the 1-yard line from where Jaynes burst through. Forest avoided the shutout late on Fonzie Odom's 1-yard plunge. First downs (14-12), rushing (226-95) and passing (120-48) all went to Magee. Rogers (138 rushing yards), Hosey (14 solo tackles) and Holloway were Players of the Week.

"Forest ... made some mistakes. We intercepted some passes and scored right after the turnovers. Our defense played real well, giving us the ball with good field position. You've got to be pleased with that sort of thing. Forest was a tough opponent, though".

GAME 8: MAGEE (5-2) @ BRANDON (6-1)
MAGEE 23 BRANDON 37
October 21, 1983

Wally Bumpas, now in his 4th season as head coach, thought his team to be in a rebuilding year. *"We have so many new and young players that we need to see in a game situation so that we can evaluate them".* The Dogs lost 16 starters from the 1982 squad but were, according to The Copiah County Courier, ranked as high as 4th. The team featured a pre-season All-State player in Don Palmer. The Clarion-Ledger said that he was *"one of the best players to ever suit up for the Bulldogs. A defensive end, he also will probably move from fullback to tailback".* Said Bumpas *"We've had some good players here and he's probably as good or better than anybody we've had".*

Now, Brandon had moved to 5th (Super 10) and 4th (AP) in preparation. The Magee Courier noted that the Trojans would face tougher competition. *"Brandon is tough with a capital T. It could be a long night for the Trojans. I pick Brandon by 14".* That forecast would be deadly accurate. Bradley called Brandon *"probably the most aggressive team we'll meet. We're going to have to play aggressively with a lot of emotion to stay with them".*

The Dogs put up two 1st quarter TDs from Albert McCray (45) and Palmer (16) to go along with the first of 4 Phillip Patureau extra points. Magee responded with a 3-yard Jaynes run and Green PAT to make it 14-7. In the 2nd, Magee tied the game on a 2-yard Rogers run (Green PAT) before Palmer put up his second TD with 1:10 left on a 16-yarder. That had been set up by a Henry McKay interception.

The only score of the 3rd came via a 28-yard Patureau FG that made it 24-14. Now in the final frame, Gerald McAllister hit Carl Volz from 29 to make it 31-14. It was here that Magee attempted their comeback. Green found Easterling for a 67-yard connection and then nailed a 25-yard FG with 2:51 remaining. But, after a key fumble recovery by David Ford, Palmer iced things with a 37-yard run. Wayne Spann picked off a last-gasp throw by Magee.

Brandon led in first downs (16-14) and rushing (313-113) while the Trojans held the air (179-29). Palmer put up 124 yards on the night. Strangely, The Magee Courier put rushing at 127-30 (Brandon); probably intending to reflect passing. Said Bumpas, *"I think we relaxed a little bit. Even I relaxed when it was 31-14. We don't have a very physical football team and we don't have a killer instinct. We haven't been able to knock anybody out early".* Added Bradley, *"Brandon exhibited more speed than anyone we've played. If we had played more consistently on defense, we had a chance to win".*

GAME 9: MAGEE (5-3) vs MORTON (3-5)
MAGEE 40 MORTON 0
October 28, 1983

Though the two teams split games the previous year, Magee had a 20-5-1 record against Morton since 1960. *"They've got a good, scrappy team and do a lot of stunting. We're going to have to find a way to move the ball. Morton has been trying to throw the ball deep a lot, so we're going to have to play good pass defense. If we can do those two things, we feel like we can win".*

The game would never be in doubt. King opened play with a strip and return 65 yards for a touchdown. Green converted on his first of 4 PATs. Green and Easterling added to the board on a 9-yard pass and it was 14-0. In the 2nd, Jaynes burst through from 8 yards and then Green added another from 3 yards. Halftime sat 27-0. Jaynes notched a 65-yard dash in the 3rd quarter while Forest claimed a 40-yard pick-six to ice things in the final frame. Jaynes (104 yards), Vince Burgess and Hosey were all players of the week. First downs (14-8), rushing (262-102) and passing (55-7) understandably went to the Trojans.

GAME 10: MAGEE (6-3) @ MENDENHALL (8-1)
MAGEE 17 MENDENHALL 20 (3OT)
November 4, 1983

Tommy Lucas thought that his 35-man roster was still enough to win. The paper said that *"The Tigers have good overall size (and) morale is high…"*. By kickoff, they sat 8-1. But, as was customary, nothing mattered except for this rivalry tilt. The winner would go on to play Forest the following week for championship dreams. Said Bradley, *"We have a lot of respect for their team and players"*. The Hattiesburg American called this game, the 58th all-time, for Mendenhall 34-13. *"Mendenhall has had the better season and I can't see them losing this key contest at home"*.

Regulation play for the Wally Beach Challenge Trophy ended in a scoreless tie though each team had opportunities. Mendenhall missed a pair of FGs while Magee made threats that continuously ended in fumbles. Mendy's last-gasp was picked off by Forest to send the contest into the first OT. Magee, with the ball first, scored on a 10-yard pass from Green to Easterling and Green's PAT. Louis Womack responded on the Tigers' first play and the Ronnie Magee PAT evened things. Roches Johnson put Mendy on top in the 2nd OT on a 1-yard plunge and Magee made it 14-7. Rogers answered on his own 1-yarder and Green sent the contest to the third OT.

The Trojans were forced to take a 25-yard Green FG for the short-lived lead. Mendenhall claimed the South sub-district afterward when Ray Hobbs got in from the 2-yard line. The try for the PAT was unnecessary. Green (67) and Rogers (62) led in rushing for Magee. First downs were even (10-10) while Magee led in overall yardage (193-152). Rushing favored Magee 156-132.

Said Lucas, *"It was probably one of the closest games that I've ever coached. It was a very exciting game for all the people involved. We feel like they were one of the best teams we've played all year and we played one of our best games of the year. We knew it was going to be one of our toughest games. I think everybody realized that. We were just pleased that our youngsters never gave up; especially in the OT when we were down 7-0"*.

Magee had originally signed up for the East Central Bowl to be played in Decatur against Waynesboro. But soon after, the game was cancelled as Waynesboro and Newton decided to forego any further play. All Conference nods went to First Team members Jerry Keys, Dwayne King, Tony Forest, Keith Hall, Dwayne Luke and Fred Rogers. Second Teamers included John Mangum, Michael Green, John Hosey, and Erndaryl Jaynes. Green also had a Second-Team nod for kicking. Honorable Mentions included Darron Easterling, Vince Burgess, James May, Willie Williams and Ed Lockhart. Mendenhall beat Eupora 17-7 for the Class A championship.

1984 (12-2) 3A STATE CHAMPIONS

Coach David Bradley returned for his third year as mentor of the Trojans highly optimistic about the upcoming campaign. He had the services of 11 starters and 16 overall letter-winners on the team and had been picked 3rd in the SAC behind defending state champion Mendenhall. They were also picked 3rd in the 6-3A South Sub-District. *"If the kicking games become sound, we should field a very strong AAA team. We lost the entire kicking game from last year. The punter, place kicker, snapper, holder and returner all graduated. I expect this team to be my strongest at Magee. One of the team's strengths is we have excellent returning starters that are equally balanced between offense and defense"*.

To prepare for the season, the team held a "Meet the Trojans" event on August 30th accompanied with a scrimmage.

GAME 1: MAGEE (0-0) vs FOREST HILL (0-0)
MAGEE 38 FOREST HILL 0
September 7, 1984

Since their first match in 1944, this series had been pretty close with Magee holding an all-time 8-5 advantage. The previous season, Magee had embarrassed the Rebels 40-6. Unfortunately for the visitors, this one would be worse as the Trojans steadily counted points in each of the four quarters while holding Forest Hill to just 52 total yards.

First it was a 48-yard Terry Holloway strike to John Mangum followed in the next frame by their connection from 3 yards. Chip Holbrook added the PAT and, later, Michael Hayes hit a 38-yard FG to make halftime 16-0. Michael Green added more in the 3rd quarter on a 1-yard run while Donnie Malloy did the same from 2 yards. Billy Hubbard then recorded a QB safety and it was now 31-0. The final points came in the 4th quarter when Estus Barron hit Richard Forest from 58 yards and Hayes converted.

Michael Pittman's 6 solo and 6 assists led tacklers. Malloy rushed for 115 yards of Magee's 229 and Mangum paced receivers with 51 yards of the 146 total. *"I was very pleased with the defensive performance. Forest Hill changed their offense in the offseason and we really didn't know what to expect. All we could do was guess, but the defense held... We made a lot of first-game mistakes. Fortunately, the score wasn't close. This time we came back in the second half and played just as hard and put the game out of reach. We're really proud of that and the fact we didn't let down after our lead"*.

GAME 2: MAGEE (1-0) vs FLORENCE (0-1)
MAGEE 29 FLORENCE 6
September 14, 1984

Florence and Magee had faced each other only 5 times since 1933 and the Trojans (and Burrheads) had won each one of them. This edition of Florence football would be a bit stronger as Coach Lee Bramlett had taken his Eagles to a 9-2 record the previous season. With 12 lettermen back and 6 starters, they were picked 3rd in the South sub-district but had had dropped their opener to Byram. In Magee, the Trojans had now moved to 18th in the AP poll.

The home team put up a pair of 1st quarter scores on Michael Green's 3-yard drive and Malloy's 28-yard scamper. Hayes converted on both attempts. They added a few more before halftime on Holloway's 37-yard pass to Malloy and Pittman's 37-yard dash. One Hayes conversion made it 27-0. Now in the final frame, an Eagle snap went out of the end zone for a safety. They avoided the shutout with just 1:28 left on a 4-yard Robby Grantham pass to Marvin Cousin.

"We were well-pleased with our play in the first half. In the second half, we were a little sluggish, but we did have a big lead and had begun to substitute a great deal. Florence is real young with only 6 seniors playing but they never gave up and deserve a lot of credit for staying in there and pitching". Magee out-rushed Florence 167-29 and led in first downs 10-6.

GAME 3: MAGEE (2-0) vs COLUMBIA (0-2)
MAGEE 10 COLUMBIA 7 (OT)
September 21, 1984

Voted 5th in the SAC after a 5-5 season, Columbia now had a new leader. James McCollum had posted a 30-5 record at Taylorsville and was expected to provide the offensive spark for the team. *"The offensive line should be a strong point. Another should be our depth in the backfield. We need to start off strong because our tough schedule. The key to success is getting off to a good start"*. Said Bradley about their opponent, *"They are a very big team up front, fast and with more speed than anybody else we've played. They are hungry for a win... We know we will have our work cut out and will have to be prepared"*.

The Wildcats were at a disadvantage with key players sidelined due to injuries. Said McCollum, *"They're (Magee) probably better than either of the two we've played so far. West Jones relied on the passing game, but Magee just has an overall good team, good size, good speed and good strength. They're a good, balanced team that doesn't rely on any one aspect"*.

Despite the praise and injuries, Columbia wasn't prepared to quit. After a scoreless first half, Malloy broke things open with an *"electrifying"* 85-yard gallop and Hayes notched the PAT. Back punched Columbia with a 60-yard march capped by a 12-yard Ivan Daniel pass to Daniel Flowers and Gregg Gonzales' PAT. That's the way it stood through regulation. In the OT, Magee settled for a 33-yard Hayes FG. With a chance to upset the Trojans, Dwayne King picked off a second-down throw to seal the victory.

Malloy led rushers with 136 yards. Magee led in first downs (11-7) and rushing (185-55). Columbia held passing 36-25. *"We were proud of the way we played under pressure and were tired late in the game. However, the team made too many mistakes and had too many penalties. We must eliminate those mistakes before the next game..."*

GAME 4: MAGEE (3-0) @ NORTHEAST JONES (3-0)
MAGEE 7 NORTHEAST JONES 16
September 28, 1984

Picked 2nd in the SAC with 25-30 lettermen back and 14 starters, Coach Danny Adams noted before the season, *"The key to our success will be the overall play and leadership of our seniors. We're going to have some senior leadership and experience this year that we didn't have last year. We don't have any breakaway speed on offense and we're going to be smaller on defense than we have been in the past"*.

By game day, they were undefeated and ranked 14th in the state. Said Bradley, *"They are very strong on defense, having allowed only 10 points in three games. They are very explosive on offense with a fine QB and a good group of receivers..."*

Magee started the night with a pair of fumbles; the last allowing the Tiger QB Chris Thornton a 6-yard sweep for the TD and, with Stan Livingston's PAT, a 7-0 lead at halftime. In the 3rd quarter, Magee drove 48 yards behind gutsy fourth-down calls and solid running with Malloy plunging in from a yard out and Hayes converting. Northeast inserted the dagger with 1:04 remaining on Thornton's 25-yard strike off the fingertips of Darron Easterling to Rodney Kirby. Livingston added the PAT. On Magee's last gasp, Holloway ran into a referee in the end zone to set up a safety sack.

"We put out an excellent team effort; one of the best ever in a losing game. The entire team is to be commended for never giving up until the final horn". Added Adams, *"Both teams made mistakes. But I'm proud of the kids hanging in there against a tough team like Magee. This was one of the most physical ball games I've seen. Offensively, we were whipped up front"*. Jerry Keys suffered a broken arm in the game and was probably lost for the season. Magee led in first downs (8-7) and rushing (99-51) but lost the air 144-44.

GAME 5: MAGEE (3-1) @ WEST JONES (3-1)
MAGEE 7 WEST JONES 17
October 5, 1984

Coach Mike Taylor had taken his team to a 9-2 record the previous year, had 11 starters and 12 lettermen back, and were overwhelming favorites for SAC honors. For Magee, it was their second-straight road trip against a quality opponent. Thoughts of the 14-7 loss in 1983 were still on the minds of many of the Trojans. *"They are perennially a fine football team and Coach Taylor does a fine job"*.

It appeared that Magee would drive for a first-possession touchdown but a fumble deep in West Jones territory ended the threat. Meanwhile, the home team notched two touchdowns in the 2nd quarter on Howard McDonald's 8-yard run, Aubrey Cooper's 39-yard reception from John Easterling and two Jim Taylor PATs. After a scoreless third period, West Jones added a 30-yard Taylor FG to make it 17-0. Magee's only tally came with just 2:55 left when Holloway hit Mangum for an 80-yard touchdown and Hayes converted.

Magee led in first downs (14-8) and passing (179-52) while losing the ground 147-127. King led rushers with 72 yards while Mangum caught 97 yards. *"The game wasn't the best of efforts for the defensive squad and, on offense, though we moved the ball, we still didn't make the plays to score. We must play the way a Magee Trojan team is supposed to play. This week will be dedicated to making sure we play like Magee this Friday night"*.

GAME 6: MAGEE (3-2) vs SOUTH JONES (1-4)
MAGEE 47 SOUTH JONES 0
October 12, 1984

The Braves under new head man Tom Moore were picked 6th in the SAC after a forgettable 2-8 campaign. They did have 21 lettermen back, causing Moore to say *"We've got a good group of seniors. Several of them played a lot last year. I'm looking for our seniors to provide us with some leadership. Our offensive line should be tough if we can keep them healthy"*. They had just gotten their first win of the season against Bay Springs. Added Bradley, *"We feel like they are improving week-by-week and we're expecting a tough game"*.

Magee methodically tallied in each quarter to provide the runaway victory over South Jones. Malloy made it 6-0 in the opening frame on his 1-yard run, King added a 3-yarder in the 2nd quarter followed by a 5-yard Malloy dash. That made halftime 18-0. In the 3rd quarter, Holloway and Hayes hooked up from 11 yards and Holloway hit Easterling for the two-pointer. Pittman had the next late in the quarter on a 9-yard jaunt and Hayes converted his first of two extra points. Finally, Pittman (42 yards) and Calvin Womack (31 yards) put the nails in the coffin.

Magee led on the ground (226-62), the air (96-27) and first downs (17-4). South Jones lost two fumbles on the night. Malloy led rushers (91 yards), Holbrook receivers (59 yards) and Willie Williams tacklers (7). "*We needed a big win and we were lucky enough to get it. A lot of the win had to do with the way we started out. Our play was consistent and we had no letdown. We just stayed on top of our game*".

GAME 7: MAGEE (4-2) vs FOREST (4-2)
MAGEE 34 FOREST 7
October 19, 1984: HOMECOMING

Coach L.M. Wesson had the services of only 5 starters and 8 lettermen back for the Bearcats. Still, they were 4-2 and picked 2nd in the North sub-district pre-season. "*They are real aggressive, play good defense and don't allow many points to be scored against them. Forest is a team that plays power football and they don't make many mistakes*". This would be the 31st meeting in series that stretched back to 1926.

Though Magee struck first on a 55-yard Malloy dash and Hayes kick, Forest responded with Jamie Derrick's 60-yard fumble return and Mike Courtney's PAT to tie things 7-7. Back came Malloy with a 47-yard romp and Hayes made it 14-7. The Trojans gave themselves a bit of breathing room in the 2nd quarter on a 67-yard drive with King going in from the 1-yard line to cap it. Hayes' toe was true and halftime stood 21-7. In the final frame, Magee paired the board on runs by Green (1) and Mangum (4).

Forest was held to only 37 yards of total offense while Magee put up 367 yards. First downs were an amazing 15-1 for Magee and rushing 308-12. Malloy rushed for either 164 or 157 yards. "*We seemed really ready from the start as the offense took control and the defense followed and played another outstanding game. It was a good team effort*".

GAME 8: MAGEE (5-2) @ PROVINE (5-2)
MAGEE 15 PROVINE 0
October 25, 1984

This marked the inaugural meeting between the Jackson-area Provine team and Magee. Provine, under Coach Stanley Blackmon, had gone only 4-6 the year before, but did return 10 starters. Said Bradley, "*They'll have more depth and will keep fresh players on the field all night. We must be able to play a full 48 minutes of hard, aggressive football*".

The scoreless first half was a true defensive slugfest, with Magee having only 1 first down and 2 yards of offense. Provine was worse with -7 yards thus far. In the 3rd quarter, Malloy got in from 5 yards out to end a 77-yard drive. King surprised the opponent by taking the PAT snap into the end zone for the two points. Early in the final frame, Magee marched a short 28 yards following a Provine fumble recovered by King. Pittman capped it from 5 yards and Hayes added the final point.

First downs were a jaw-dropping 11-0. The Hattiesburg American and Clarksdale Press Register, among others, made it their headlines on the game article. But Magee also led in rushing (158-13) and passing (9 to -2). Said Blackmon, "*We have no alibis. Magee just destroyed everything that we tried offensively. Nothing else can be said. Sure, I feel bad about not getting a first down, but I would have felt bad if we had gotten 20 first downs. If we lost, we still didn't accomplish anything*".

Added Bradley, "*We usually don't give up too many first downs or yards. These guys are hungry and they were determined tonight. If we had played like this all season, we would be undefeated. (We played) a pretty much perfect game. The second half especially showed the best ball-control the team has shown, with players responding to a challenge and playing one heck of a ball game*".

GAME 9: MAGEE (6-2) @ MORTON (1-7)
MAGEE 43 MORTON 0
November 2, 1984

Magee had embarrassed the Panthers the year before by a 40-0 tally. Coach Gary Risher, finishing 3-7 that year, would be in a worse situation now. Though they had won only over Decatur, they had lost 3 games in OT. He returned 8 starters and 22 lettermen in the North sub-district and voters initially had chosen Morton 3rd in that grouping.

The Magee Courier called the conditions *"a mud bath"*, but the Trojans made a statement in Scott County. They put up their first TD in the opening quarter on Green's 4-yard run and Holbrook's kick. They then added a 24-yard Malloy dash, a 33-yard Holloway toss to Mangum, and another 24-yard Malloy run. Holbrook converted on two more extra points and halftime sat 27-0. The last scores came in the 3rd. Mangum and King blocked a punt that rolled out of the end zone for a safety. Russ May drove in from 2 yards away and Easterling darted in from 7 yards.

The defense put up interceptions from Barron, Womack, Malloy and King. Malloy rushed for 135 yards to put him at 896 on the season.

GAME 10: MAGEE (7-2) vs MENDENHALL (7-2)
MAGEE 40 MENDENHALL 0
November 9, 1984

Coach Tommy Lucas had taken his Tigers to a 13-1 record and state championship the year before. Now he had 15 lettermen back, but was initially hesitant about the chances for 1984. *"We'll have a tough season this year with only 6 veterans returning. The others are younger, inexperienced players. The outcome of the season will depend on how our young players progress"*. But when kickoff rolled around, it proved to be the same story as almost every other year. The winner moved on; the loser lost bragging rights and would hang up their gear for another year.

Said Lucas, *"They have one of the most physical teams we'll see and that applies position-wide: offensively and defensively. Also, playing Provine and not giving up a first down, beyond a shadow of doubt, they play top defense. Only one or two teams have gained over 100 yards against them. They have threats at every position and have a fine line with blocking up front, a QB that throws well, controls and handles the ball, and runs the option well. I know both teams will be up and excited. It should be one of the best games of this area so far this year"*.

Mendenhall got in their own way on their first two drives; both ending with fumbles. After the second, Holloway dashed in from 10 yards to cap the initial scoring drive. Hayes nailed his first of 4 extra points. Barron stopped the next drive with a phenomenal interception but the gift ended in a failed FG attempt. But Tim Wright did his part afterwards with a 15-yard fumble return for the 13-0 lead. With :27 left before intermission, Green picked off a Tiger throw and took it 45 yards to paydirt. Halftime now stood 20-0 for Magee.

Magee opened the 3rd with a drive to the 1-yard line, most from a 50-yard Holloway run to that point, from where he dove in for points. Now in the 4th quarter, Holloway got his third touchdown on a 1-yard keeper and it was already 33-0. Later, Mangum picked off a Mendy throw to set up Holloways 13-yard throw to Easterling. Magee led in first downs (14-9) and rushing (284-104 or 299-101) but the Tigers held the air 49-13. Mendy lost 3 fumbles on the night. Holloway, with 106 rushing yards, was Player of the Week by The Jackson Daily News.

"When it's Magee and Mendenhall, you never know what to expect. We really thought we could stop their running game. But they threw in a blocking scheme they hadn't used all year. When we adjusted, that took care of that. This was one of the finest efforts we've had. What's so significant about this team is the way we've become more consistent this late in the season. That's the way a team should be".

GAME 11: MAGEE (8-2) @ FOREST (7-3)
MAGEE 28 FOREST 0
November 16, 1984

Magee had already faced the Bearcats less than a month before and had controlled the contest. Said Bradley, *"That early season 34-7 victory over Forest worries me. This is the biggest problem: looking past a team we've already defeated. We've got to respect them now and we've got to make sure we're ready for them Friday night"*. The winner not only claimed the 6-3A title, but also had the chance to go further. Magee was now 5th in The Clarion-Ledger/Jackson Daily News Class 3A poll.

Halftime stood 6-0; a score that was surprising to most that felt Magee may have held a bit bigger margin. The score came late in the opening frame when Holloway hit Mangum from the 15 to cap an 80-yard march. But in the 3rd, they pushed the lead out when Holloway found King from 12 yards, Mangum ran in for the two-pointer, and Barron picked off a Cat throw and took it 32 yards to the end zone. Hayes' kick made it 21-0. Finally, in the last frame, Holloway went in from a yard out and Hayes converted.

Malloy garnered 119 rushing yards while Mangum had 40 yards of receiving. Mangum also had an interception. Magee led in first downs (17-4) and rushing (224-17) while Forest led in the air 75-56. The Cats lost two fumbles on the night with recoveries by Mangum and Vince Burgess. Interceptions were also recorded by Michael Green and Malloy.

GAME 12: MAGEE (9-2) @ WEST LAUDERDALE (10-1)
MAGEE 33 WEST LAUDERDALE 0
November 23, 1984

Coach Joe Williford's West Lauderdale squad had gone far the previous year and were on track to match or better that performance. He said before the season, "*We lost in the south state finals last year and these kids have dedicated themselves to getting at least that far again this year. We're almost there now*". The two teams had not met in previous years. Bradley called them "*large, strong and a perpetual contender*". Before kickoff, it was determined that West Lauderdale would be without four starters for disciplinary reasons.

The Trojans had allowed only 7 points since the first week of October, and that streak of stifling defense continued when it counted. In temperatures around the freezing mark, they used only three plays to strike first. That came on a 15-yard Malloy dash and the first of three Hayes PATs. They made it 14-0 before halftime when Malloy notched a 76-yarder. Green opened the 3rd quarter with a 1-yard dive to send the teams to the final quarter 20-0. There, Holloway and Mangum connected from 9 yards while Holloway darted in from 11 yards to finish things.

Malloy led rushers with 154 markers and Holbrook led receivers with 51 yards. Barron notched an interception in the contest. First downs (17-5), rushing (277-48) and passing (111-8) favored Magee. Said Williford, "*Magee is just a tough team. They had us outmanned and we couldn't do anything with them*".

GAME 13: MAGEE (10-2) vs COLUMBIA (8-4)
MAGEE 12 COLUMBIA 7
November 30, 1984: D.I. PATRICK FIELD; HATTIESBURG, MS

In the third game of the season, these two teams battled mightily before Magee pulled out a 10-7 overtime win thanks to Hayes' 33-yard FG. Now, the two teams faced one another again, this time for the South 3A Championship. Said Coach James McCollum of the previous encounter, "*Nobody did much of anything on offense; we just beat the fool out of each other*". Columbia had punched their ticket by beating Poplarville 12-7.

Magee would be wounded for the tilt as many players were injured. Said Bradley, "*The only real difference in the two teams could be the depth of Columbia. They run several backs and can alternate their receivers. It should be a very competitive ball game and I look for it to be a real defensive battle*". Both The Hattiesburg American (21-6) and The Newton Record called it for Magee.

In the end, the game was much like the first with defense leading the way. Columbia scared Magee in the opening frame before Mangum chased down Otis Franklin after a 64-yard gain. The defense dug in at the 7-yard line and Columbia's 22-yard FG effort was unsuccessful. The remainder of the half found neither team dent the scoreboard and intermission sat 0-0. Magee, however, drove 80 yards on their first play of the next quarter when King dodged in from 13 yards to make it 6-0. Columbia responded in the frame with a 70-yard Edward Daniels escape and the PAT by Greg Gonzales put the Cats up 7-6.

In the 4th quarter, Magee produced the final tally on "*a score that really looked a little bit like a miracle*". Malloy, hemmed up by five defenders, found his way out of the scrum and dashed 33 yards to paydirt. After a late Trojan fumble, Columbia had one more shot. But, their deep pass into a mass of players was tipped and May came away with the game-saving interception. "*This win says a lot about the character of our kids. We were uptight the first half but came back and won. We were here two years ago and it was like a wall in front of us. We have broken through the wall now and I really feel we have a good chance of winning the state championship*".

Added McCollum afterwards, "*You have got to hand it to Magee. They came back after we scored, got the ball back and rammed it down our throats*". Magee led in first downs (13-7) and rushing (223-172) while Columbia held the passing lanes (39-5). King led rushers with 114 yards while May and Green led tacklers with 12 solo and 6 assists each.

GAME 14: MAGEE (11-2) vs KOSCIUSKO (9-3)
MAGEE 49 KOSCIUSKO 0
December 7, 1984: HINDS JUNIOR COLLEGE; RAYMOND, MS

The two teams had actually met once before. In 1940, Kosciusko had given Magee their second-worst beating of their 5-5-1 season by a 47-12 final. A familiar face awaited the Trojans as former Mendenhall mentor David Abercrombie held the whistle for the Whippets. *"Magee has an awesome defense. They are the best defensive team we've seen this year and that includes Louisville. They have more quickness and they're pretty big. They're not fat folks. They're lean and mean people. We've been looking for a player or a scheme to hurt them and we haven't seen anything"*.

Said Bradley, *"Kosciusko will show us the most versatile offense we've seen all year. They'll run from the shotgun or the I-formation. They'll be throwing different stuff at us all night. I know Kosciusko has a football tradition. We expect it to be a defensive game"*. Though both had come close in the past, this would be the first time one of these two teams could claim a state championship.

What was expected by most to be perhaps the toughest battle of the season ended with Magee's biggest blowout since 1961. The Clarion-Ledger called the game *"a lot worse"* than what the scoreboard reflected. In front of 3,500 freezing fans, Malloy got it going with a 55-yard dash and Hayes connected on the PAT. After Mangum picked off an ensuing Whippet pass, Green got in from the 14-yard line and Holbrook did the honors. It was his first of 6 extra points.

In the 2nd quarter, Barron joined in the interception parade to set up a 13-yard King blast. Holloway then hit Holbrook from the 10-yard line and, with :06 left before halftime, Holloway found King from the 35-yard line for yet another score. To make it worse for Kosciusko, Michael Pittman opened the 3rd quarter with a 56-yard scoring dash. The dagger came in the final frame when Malloy grabbed an errant throw at the 1-yard line and stepped into paydirt.

Said Abercrombie afterwards, *"It was a nightmare of the worst kind. We didn't play good at all and they really took it to us. We just couldn't do anything with them all night. They came out and intimidated us early and that was about it"*. Stats differ depending on the source. First downs were roughly 14-3 for Magee. But, the rushing numbers were nothing short of jaw-dropping. Magee rushed for 338 yards and held Kosciusko to -65. Even with their 50 yards of passing, they still ended with (roughly) -15 total offensive yards.

"Fantastic. It's hard to explain just how good we played tonight. I knew that the kids were keyed up all week. I just hoped that they wouldn't make mistakes. They didn't. Everything we did worked. It was great. The defense played super. We wanted to put a lot of pressure on their quarterback. We did that. The defensive line and the linebackers are real quick and get by the line in a hurry. Everything took care of itself. (It) was probably the most gratifying victory that I've ever been involved in. It was a thrill to see our kids in the biggest game of their life playing up to their full potential".

The 3A South Sub-District First Team included Willie Williams, Vince Burgess, James May, Michael Green, John Mangum, Terry Holloway, Dwayne King, Donnie Malloy, Darron Easterling, Keith Hall, Jerry Keys, Willie Kemp, and Michael Hayes. Most Valuable Back was Malloy while Williams was Most Valuable Lineman. Honorable Mentions went to Tim Wright, Billy Hubbard and Chip Holbrook.

In the SAC, Williams was named "Most Valuable Defensive Player" and Malloy "Most Valuable Offensive Player". Other First Team members were Burgess, May, Mangum, and Hall. Second Team honorees included King, Kemp and Holloway.

1985 (12-2)

It would take a lot to improve on the 3A title-winning Trojan club of 1984, but fourth-year Coach David Bradley had reason to be confident. They were selected tops in their South Sub-District, first in Class 3A (Jackson Daily News/Clarion-Ledger poll) and 6th on The Clarion-Ledger Super 10 poll. The team consisted of 14 returning lettermen, 2 returners on the offensive line and 7 on the defensive side of the football.

Bradley said before the season, *"It's going to take a while to get the kids playing together. We do a lot of team defense, whereas it's a whole team situation as well as the player having his own individual responsibility. They all have to do their part so that the whole team works together"*. Before kickoff, he was pleased with how they had progressed. *"I believe we have a fine football team this year. With nine starters back and with our juniors and other younger players playing backup roles, we are coming along real well and have great prospects for another winning season. Our team will have a lot of aggression and quickness, but we still have a tough schedule ahead of us".*

GAME 1: MAGEE (0-0) vs PORT GIBSON (0-0)
MAGEE 48 PORT GIBSON 0
September 6, 1985

The two teams had faced one-another in 1981 and 1982 with Magee winning both, but not by such an overwhelming margin. The Blue Wave was now led for the first time by legendary ex-Warren Central mentor Lum Wright. Bradley noted that *"I believe they will be a tremendously improved team (over previous years)".* The Hattiesburg American still predicted a 33-6 shellacking by the Trojans.

Magee held a 15-0 lead after one quarter thanks to a John Mangum 29-yard dash, a Donnie Malloy two-point conversion, Malloy's 18-yard escape and Chip Holbrook's PAT. The next frame was no better for Port Gibson as Malloy got in from the 8-yard line, King from the 6-yard line, and Calvin Womack from a yard away. Holbrook converted on all PATs to make it 36-0. They added another tally in the 3rd from Michael Pittman (12 yards) and finally in the 4th quarter on Dexter Berry's 2-yard dive.

Magee led in rushing (247-60) and first downs (16-6). Port Gibson held the air 108-7. *"We were real pleased with the team and they played good football. There were limited mistakes on the offense and defense. I was really surprised at the extent of the score, so it's difficult to tell exactly what our overall team picture looks like. I wasn't expecting that big a margin".*

GAME 2: MAGEE (1-0) @ FLORENCE (0-1)
MAGEE 34 FLORENCE 0
September 13, 1985

In six games going back to 1935, Florence had walked off the field against Magee on the losing side of the ledger. This year, Coach David Bramlett's team was predicted 3rd in the South Sub-District with Bradley saying *"They are an experienced team, only losing five seniors (from) last year. We were surprised they lost 3-0 to Byram last week".* Meanwhile, Magee now sat 7th in the AP Poll but down two spots to 8th in the Super 10.

Mangum began the scoring the initial quarter on a 61-yard dash and Holbrook put through his first of 4 extra points. Malloy then ran 37 yards to paydirt and it was 14-0. With 2:02 before intermission, Malloy got in from the 5–yard line after a Womack interception of QB Robbie Grantham. Malloy crossed from 6 yards out and 1 yard out to finish scoring in the 3rd quarter. Said Bramlett, *"Magee is out of our league right now. Their defense was just awesome tonight. They beat us off the ball and turned us inside-out. They were too much".*

Statistics were surprisingly gaudy. Magee not only dominated first downs (18-2) but decimated the Eagles in rushing (358 to -13) and passing (26-0). Florence fumbled 5 times (losing two). Mangum chalked up 125 rushing yards and Malloy had 121 all-purpose yards.

GAME 3: MAGEE (2-0) @ ESCAMBIA HIGH (PENSACOLA), FL (1-0)
MAGEE 6 ESCAMBIA HIGH 7
September 20, 1985

About three weeks before schedules were released, Columbia dropped the Magee contest from their schedule. So, Bradley went all around the state to find a replacement. He was unsuccessful. So, who did he find to take their spot? The Hattiesburg American summed it up best during game week. *"Assume you are a coach and your school's in 3A Mississippi, which is only medium-size. And there are 350 total students in the school. And your football team is playing a team whose student population was 1,450. And there might be more than 10,000 fans at the game; most pulling against you. And that team you were playing was ranked third in the nation. What would you do?".*

Said Bradley, *"I'm tickled to death and scared all at the same time. Yeah, I believe we can win. I have a great deal of confidence in our players and coaches. I don't think their first 11 will be better than our first 11 all the time. But we play all eleven at the same time. They (have a different eleven for each phase)".* Though Magee had moved to 7th in the AP and 5th in the Super 10, The Hattiesburg American still thought it an Escambia win 17-7. *"Nothing would be finer than to see the little ole Mississippi team beat up on the great big Florida team".*

Indeed, it was Magee with the first opportunity on a drive to the Gator 18-yard line before fumbling away. Likewise, Escambia blew two chances in the 2nd quarter with they missed field goal attempts by Alan Ward. But in the 3rd quarter, a John Brady throw was picked off by Malloy and he ran *"untouched"* to paydirt from 38 yards away. The PAT was unsuccessful but the Trojans were up 6-0. Escambia tied things as the last frame started when a running back named Emmitt Smith plunged in from 3 yards out. The crucial point-after by Ward was true.

Magee did not quit. They moved deep into Gator territory but again missed a FG. After stopping their hosts, Magee had another chance. With :11, the Trojans lined up for one more FG attempt. That, too, went awry and the game was over. Said Coach Dwight Thomas afterwards, *"We dodged a bullet. That's what we did tonight. They hung tough on every down, every kick, every play. They are tough. I am totally impressed with Magee"*.

Magee led in rushing (226-112) but lost the passing game (66-10). Escambia also held first downs (13-12). King rushed for 102 yards while the defense held Emmitt Smith to only 86 yards. *"We played hard and didn't give up. The loss really hurt us because we were so close. Our kids fought hard and had a chance to win. We felt like we should have won, but it will give our kids confidence to play anyone. The defense did a fine job. We played our regular defensive game, which is pressure defense. We had several tackles behind the line that put them in the situation that they weren't used to being in"*.

GAME 4: MAGEE (2-1) vs NORTHEAST JONES (3-0)
MAGEE 17 NORTHEAST JONES 7
September 27, 1985

Northeast Jones, now ranked 5th in 3A and undefeated, would be no easy Friday night opponent. *"They are one of the best teams left on our schedule. They beat Columbia pretty bad. They have enough players for eleven on offense and eleven more on defense"*. The series sat 2-2 since their first meeting in 1977. The loss against Escambia had not taken Magee completely out of rating respect. In fact, they had actually risen to 4th in the Super 10 while dropping only to 8th in the AP. The Hattiesburg American called it 13-12 in favor of the Trojans.

The nail-biter began in the opening frame on Mangum's 39-yard pass to Malloy and Holbrook's kick. In the next frame, Bobby Martin pulled in a 40-yard Stacy Carson throw and the PAT made it 7-7 at halftime. Magee notched a 23-yard Holbrook FG for the only score of the 3rd quarter, and Magee added to it before the final whistle after a fumble recovery when Malloy dodged in from the 3-yard line. Holbrook's kick iced the contest.

Magee led in first downs (10-7) and rushing (170-85) while Jones held passing (81-51). *"They just about beat us. We just didn't do well during the first half. I think all of them were living on the memories of the week before and it's hard to get that 'up' two weeks in a row. We kind of settled down and played with more sense during the second half. We didn't give them nearly as much scoring effort"*.

GAME 5: MAGEE (3-1) vs WEST JONES (3-1)
MAGEE 27 WEST JONES 19
October 4, 1985

Magee had won the first 5 encounters with West Jones before going 1-5-1 since. Now, WJ was ranked 5th in 4A. Said Bradley, *"They are just tough. They know what they are doing"*. The Hattiesburg American picked Magee in a close one 19-17. As for rankings, the Trojans were now 6th in the AP and 4th in the Super 10.

The home team struck first in the initial quarter when Mangum got in from 5 yards away and Holbrook converted. West Jones cut into the lead as the quarter ended via Jim Taylor's 28-yard FG. It could actually have been tied save for Calvin Womack's touchdown-saving tackle and the Trojan defensive stand. Malloy's 5-yard run and Holbrook's kick put halftime 14-3. It wasn't as pretty to start the 3rd quarter. A fumbled kickoff put the Mustangs at the 19-yard line. Mark Chapman's (or Harold McDonald's) run capped the opportunity and Taylor made it 14-10.

Magee punched back soon after on Mangum's 67-yard dash and Holbrook's kick, but WJ answered with a 4-yard McDonald dive. That had also been set up by a Magee fumble. Now in the final frame, the Trojans dodged a serious bullet when a bad snap to Malloy was finally picked up on the 5-yard line and he hit Richard Forrest for an 80-yard touchdown. But, Magee yet again fumbled the pigskin to their visitors. West Jones was able to add a 19-yard Taylor FG, but it would be all they could muster throughout the rest of the game.

Rushing (241-138), first downs (10-7) and passing (80-23) favored Magee. Mangum had the two touchdowns, an interception, 56 rushing yards and 11 individual (10 assist) tackle evening.

For that, he was Player of the Week by The Clarion-Ledger and the Jackson Touchdown Club. *"Then (up 14-3) is when the trouble began. We just got excited and began fumbling and it scared me pretty bad. We lucked out. We had three costly fumbles against a real fine football team and for a while it looked like we were absolutely going to fumble the game away. Our kids just played on out with determination and some measure of poise to win this one"*.

GAME 6: MAGEE (4-1) @ SOUTH JONES (0-5)
MAGEE 34 SOUTH JONES 0
October 11, 1985

Though on the road, this week seemed to bring some measure of relief. The Braves were winless and had been outscored 129-7 thus far. The result was predictable. Mangum had touchdown runs of 5 yards and 38 yards, Malloy added a two-pointer and Holbrook a PAT to make it 15-0. In the 2nd quarter, King burst in from 7 yards, Malloy from 6 yards, Holbrook added a PAT, and halftime was 28-0. The last touchdown had been set up by Richard Forrest's blocked punt and Jerry King's recovery. Malloy add another from 27 yards in the 3rd to end scoring.

"It wasn't as easy as it looks like the score says it is. They are a very well-coached team, even though they are young and fairly inexperienced, and we got a few lucky breaks. But we played them hard. The game was a very good win for us and all of our players were able to play. We were glad our younger players got some experience. We played a little sloppy and made several mistakes but we will try to improve this week". Magee led in rushing (320-51) and first downs (13-4). Passing went to South Jones 70-48. Said Coach Gregg Jefcoat, *"Their big backs just ran through us ... Magee has an outstanding team and they just physically whipped us"*.

GAME 7: MAGEE (5-1) vs PETAL (2-4)
MAGEE 41 PETAL 0
October 18, 1985: HOMECOMING

Magee had played Petal in 1935 and came back with a loss. Since then, and counting that contest, the series sat 4-2-1 in favor of the Trojans. The Panthers were having troubles this season. They had endured a 3-game losing streak before beating Perry Central 9-6 the previous week. Now they were probably playing without the services of starting QB Tony Russell with a hand injury. *"They are a young team and they have a new coach, but they are improving every week. They will have a lot of incentive to beat us"*. Magee was now 5th (AP) and 4th (Super 10).

Estus Barron's interception in the initial frame provided the impetus for King to run in later from the 9-yard line and Holbrook to convert. King did it again from 3 yards in the 2nd quarter to make halftime 14-0. In the 3rd, Pittman escaped from 44 yards and, later, Malloy *"broke loose and jumped over the white mark for the TD"*. Holbrook converted on both. With substitutes taking the field in the 4th quarter, Womack jumped a route and sailed 80 yards to daylight. Finally, Monique Craft got in from 3 yards and Holbrook iced scoring.

Rushing (329-45), passing (12-0) and first downs (16-2) went to the winners. *"We just didn't play well during the first half. I guess it was the excitement of the parade and Homecoming in general, but the boys went into the game without real concentration, with not much enthusiasm or emotion as far as football. It was just an all-around good team effort once we got started. I would just say the first half was flat, but during the second half the kids got crisp and played better ball"*.

GAME 8: MAGEE (6-1) @ HINDS COUNTY AHS (2-4-1)
MAGEE 41 HINDS COUNTY AHS 0
October 25, 1985

First-time opponent Hinds AHS was now on the schedule. It was a bad match-up on paper as Magee was 3rd in the Super 10 and AP while HCAHS was picked last in the South Sub-District. Bradley knew that the Trojans could be looking ahead. *"We've got to beat Hinds AHS and then Rolling Fork before we even begin to think about Mendenhall. We still have to gear up and stay tough"*.

Very much like the week before, the game was out of control early. Malloy started it with a 3-yard run in the opening frame (after a Barron interception) alongside the first Holbrook PAT, while King added a 5-yarder in the next quarter. King then pulled off a 75-yard pick-six and it was 20-0 at halftime. Mangum then went 76 yards in the 3rd and Malloy from 3 yards to make it 34-0 with Holbrook boots. In the last frame, Barron hit Holbrook from 8 yards and Holbrook put the final point on the scoreboard.

Malloy led rushers with 89 yards and Mangum was just behind with 87 yards. Magee led in rushing (372-102) and passing (50-12). *"Our team played real well and we are very proud of the offense because we didn't have to punt all night. The offense moved the ball quite well and did a very good job on blocking and faking. The defense played very good, also"*.

GAME 9: MAGEE (7-1) vs ROLLING FORK (4-4)
MAGEE 55 ROLLING FORK 6
November 1, 1985

While Magee was number one in 3A football, Rolling Fork had been picked a lowly 4th in the South Sub-District. It would mark their first-ever meeting on the football field. *"Rolling Fork has a good team with experience. Offensively they run misdirection plays and we will have to contend with that this week and defensively they are pretty big. We will have to be sharp this week in order to beat them"*. Bradley could not have been wrong.

The Trojans were up 20-0 in the opening frame alone thanks to a Malloy 6-yard run and Mangum runs of 59 and 4 yards. Holbrook converted on two of his 7 extra points. The delta team did avoid the shutout on a 1-yard William Bell sneak but Womack picked off their two-point attempt. Before intermission, Malloy scored from the 4-yard line and King from 31 yards. Pittman (3 yards and 2 yards) and Barron (6 yards) provided three more touchdowns in the 3rd quarter to mercifully end scoring.

Said Bradley after, *"(We) were not really trying to run up the score. Offensively we were real pleased at how we moved the ball and the defense played very well, especially in the second half"*. Magee led in rushing (301-68) and first downs (14-6). Rolling Fork led in passing 17-7.

GAME 10: MAGEE (8-1) @ MENDENHALL (8-1)
MAGEE 27 MENDENHALL 6
November 8, 1985

After a 7-5 season, Coach Tommy Lucas' Tigers entered 1985 second in the South Sub-District. They had 40 players with 22 lettermen back, but only 6 seniors. *"We have 15 eleventh graders that got considerable playing time as 10th graders last year. Most of these will be playing this year. It's like I've told them: You have to grow up"*. He and his staff had done a remarkable job thus far as they now held the same record as Magee. Thus, the winner would advance toward a state championship and maintain bragging rights.

The Trojans were still solidly in 3rd in both the AP and Super 10 polls. The Hattiesburg American thought it would be a close contest and picked Magee 13-12. Said Bradley, *"This is always a tough game and Coach Lucas and his staff have done an outstanding job this year. It doesn't really matter about the scores or records or anything else for the rest of the year. This is the game for all the marbles (and) all of the bragging rights. This will necessarily be a hard, rough, tough, rock-em, sock-em football game. We would surely like to keep (the Beach Trophy). The trophy and the championship. Both would be nice"*.

For the first time this year, Magee's opponent was first to the scoreboard. That came in the 2nd quarter when Danny Ray Hobbs bulldozed in from the 1-yard line to make it 6-0. With a minute left before halftime and after a fumble recovery, Malloy crashed in from the 2-yard line. The blocked PAT kept it a 6-6 contest. Magee began to roll in the second half with Malloy starting things with his 29-yard dash along with a Holbrook PAT. In the last frame, they notched a pair of scores. Mangum found Malloy from the 14-yard line and Willie Kemp picked off a pass to set up King's 15-yard escape. Holbrook booted both points-after.

King led Magee tacklers with 9 solo and 4 assists. Rushing (185-87), passing (87-15) and first downs (10-7) went to the Trojans. *"It was just a good, well-played ball game. I am absolutely satisfied with our team's performance. I just couldn't be more pleased that we beat such a fine, 8-1 team with all the tension and pressure on both teams and coaching staffs. I want to commend Coach Lucas, his coaching staff and the players. They were an outstandingly prepared team, well-coached and disciplined"*.

GAME 11: MAGEE (9-1) vs FOREST (9-1)
MAGEE 27 FOREST 0
November 15, 1985

The Bearcats under Coach L.M. "Bozie" Wesson had been chosen first pre-season in the North Sub-District. *"We will take the ranking as an honor and try to do the best we can. We are small and don't have any depth. Magee has it all. Talent, depth, coaching and tradition. They will win it all this year*". One report noted that Forest had lost 20 players and had only 20 on the team. Both The Union Appeal and The Hattiesburg American (30-13) called it for the Trojans. Said Bradley, "*They are probably the most aggressive and fastest team we will meet*".

The 34th meeting between the teams had obvious implications for the season as it was now "win or go home". Unfortunately, Wesson would miss the contest as he was having surgery for a ruptured disc. Mangum got things started by blocking a Cat punt to set up Malloy's 8-yard run and 6-0 lead. Just before halftime, Pittman recovered a Forest fumble and allowed Holbrook a 33-yard FG. In the 3rd, Magee drove 67 yards and topped it with Mangum's 10-yard dart. He also contributed to the next touchdown in the 4th quarter when he returned a punt 81 yards. Malloy finished it off from the 6-yard line. Finally, King dove in from 2 yards as the game neared expiration.

The Trojans led in rushing (177-27), passing (60-27) and first downs (13-4). "*Right up to (Mangum's 3rd quarter TD), nobody was sure about the game. That drive seemed to restore us, give us confidence and shake them up at the same time. I think the warmer weather had some effect on our players. We didn't have as much snap as we should have and maybe looking over on the Forest bench and seeing 19 players on the entire team may have been a factor. It may have caused us to not key up tight enough. They don't have many players, but they are tough.*".

GAME 12: MAGEE (10-1) vs BAY SAINT LOUIS (9-1)
MAGEE 41 BAY SAINT LOUIS 0
November 22, 1985: HATTIESBURG, MS

Next on the schedule was the Bay Saint Louis squad coached by Cleveland Williams. They had taken the 8-3A title and now traveled to Hattiesburg to face the Trojans. Old-timers would have remembered a string of games between 1938-1940 where Magee had actually beaten BSL two of three meetings. The Hattiesburg American called it for Magee 27-17, saying "*If Magee doesn't repeat as AAA state champ, it will be an upset*". Added Bradley, "*We are taking it one game at a time. Bay High has a lot of team speed and will probably be the fastest the Trojans have faced all year. We will have to have our defensive game plan down in order to stop them*".

King had the first of many opening half points when he topped a 71-yard march with his 8-yard run in the 1st quarter. Mangum then added a 7-yarder, Pittman took advantage of a Quintin Bell fumble to Willie Kemp with his 1-yarder, and Willie Lewis' fumble to Charlie Magee led to a 4-yard King run. Now 27-0 after Holbrook kicks, the Trojans went to work after halftime with Malloy galloping 58 yards to daylight. Mangum wrapped things up with a touchdown pass to Holbrook. First downs (10-5), passing (45-12) and rushing (267-78) went to Magee. Malloy had 133 rushing yards on the night.

Said Williams, "*Those two fumbles took a lot out of our offense. But give Magee credit; they have nothing but a solid ball club*". Added Bradley, "*Playing real physical football is one of the characteristics of our team. We teach our kids to play tough and aggressive and they do it. I think teams make more mistakes if you put pressure on them. As aggressive as our kids are, we tend to make the other team kind of nervous. It was just one of the best games we have played all year. Almost all of the boys played up to their potential. We had outstanding blocking on offense and a fine defensive effort by the whole team*".

GAME 13: MAGEE (11-1) vs BAY SPRINGS (11-1)
MAGEE 45 BAY SPRINGS 8
November 29, 1985: MM ROBERTS STADIUM; HATTIESBURG

Much like the previous week, it had been some time since the two teams had met previously. But, the squads did compete three times between 1943-1946. Coach Joe Williford said of his upcoming opponent, "*For a 3A school, they certainly have some outstanding talent. If they have a weakness, I haven't found it. But I don't feel like the Lone Ranger. They have pretty much dominated the people they have played*".

Bradley was complimentary of his opponent. "*Bay Springs is fast, quick and defensive. We will have to play on our toes because they have two running backs that are highly probably recruits, along with a very impressive offense. They run the option more than any football team we have played. Once you make the championship game, you can kind of turn it loose because either way there is no tomorrow. The pressure to make the championship game is right here on this game*".

An early Bay Springs fumble by Jerry Crawford led later to Malloy's 1-yard dive and his two-point conversion. The Bulldogs fumbled again, this time to Pittman, and he took it the 15 yards to paydirt. Holbrook converted his first of 3 point-after kicks. In the 2nd quarter, they drove

74 yards with King doing the honors from the 4-yard line and Malloy added two more points. The opponent avoided the shutout when Ricky Bradley hit J.B. McCurtis from 66 yards out and Jerry Crawford converted the two-point play.

Magee stormed right back with a 59-yard march and Malloy 5-yard run. The two-pointer by Pittman put it 31-8. Another Dog fumble was picked up by Womack and taken the necessary 20 yards. Halftime stood 38-8. The final tally came in the last quarter as rain began to fall. The 75-yard drive, set up by a King interception, was ended when Mangum found Creston Berch from 23 yards away. The game was essentially over.

Bay Springs held only passing (123-54) while Magee led in first downs (17-8) and rushing (187-30). Said Williford, "*We got our butts whipped. We spotted them too much early. I would have liked to have seen if we could play with them*". Said Bradley, "*I think it's a mark of a good bunch when you can take advantage of the other team's mistakes. This has been a great year*".

GAME 14: MAGEE (12-1) vs ROSEDALE (13-0)
MAGEE 14 ROSEDALE 28
December 7, 1985: JACKSON, MS

Rosedale, a town of roughly 4,000 residents at the time, is in the Mississippi Delta. Of late, their program had begun to produce significantly impressive football seasons. This would not be the first meeting between the Eagles and Trojans. In 1981, Magee opened with them and took home a hard-fought 12-8 victory. Said Coach Leland Young about Magee, "*I don't know if we can play with them this year. Magee may have the best team in the state. One sports writer told me they can play with Meridian, but that depth might be the thing that would get them. Magee is in a situation where you have an awful lot of talent on one football team*".

Bradley was well-aware of his opponent. "*I don't think the kids will be afraid. Anxious, enthusiastic, excited, but not afraid of Rosedale or the fact that this is the state 3A championship game. (Rosedale's) strong suit is speed on offense. We will have to hold them. We thought we'd be playing Rosedale last year and we also felt they would be the team to beat this year. I said long ago that if we made it back, we'd be playing Rosedale. That just shows that they have a fine a fine program. I expect a real fight and it should be a battle all the way*".

The truth is that most fans in Simpson County, sports writers from around the state, and others following high school football thought Magee a favorite to repeat as state champions. The Hattiesburg American picked the Trojans 27-17, saying "*Magee may have a worse record than Rosedale, but that doesn't mean the Trojans are the worse team. Magee will successfully defend its 3A championship*". The Newton Record among others also picked Magee.

It took only one play for the Eagles to grab the lead when Michael Honorable's 75-yard bomb to Tim Barnett put them up a quick 6-0. They added another touchdown before the quarter was done on Aundra Lambert's 3-yard plunge. Back punched Magee in the 2nd quarter with a 1-yard King dive and Holbrook's kick. But up 12-7, Rosedale padded the halftime lead after recovering a fumble. Lambert went in from the 1-yard line and Honorable hit Greg Robb for the two-pointer. Intermission sat a surprising 20-7.

In the 3rd, Rosedale added their last score on a 2-yard Lambert run and Honorable two-pointer. Magee's last points of an astounding season came afterwards when Malloy broke through from 6 yards out and Holbrook converted. That had been set up by King's recovery of a Rosedale fumble. For the first time this season, the opponent led in all categories: first downs (13-9), rushing (176-117) and passing (94-62). The Trojans finished 9th in the Super 10.

"*Rosedale was emotionally peaked up and ready to play. I simply failed to get the kids motivated. I just didn't have them believing it was going to be so tough. Rosedale did a super job. They deserved to win that game. Some people thought we had the better team, but they proved they were the best in the state tonight. We fully expected to win and that's what makes it so disappointing. But I'm still proud of our boys*".

All SAC honors at the end of the season included Bradley as Coach of the Year. John Mangum was the league MVP. Others making the list were Billy Hubbard, Willie Kemp, Michael Pittman, Donny Malloy, Calvin Womack, DeWayne King and Jerry King. Second team members were Gail Wyatt, Danny Smith, Dwayne King, Chip Holbrook, Eric Jaynes, Richard Forrest, Lazar Stubbs and Estus Barron. Honorable Mentions went to James David, Dexter Berry and Doug Cox.

1986 (9-1)

Fifth-year Coach David Bradley's Trojans had moved from 6-3A to 5-3A along with Mendenhall. Still a member of the SAC, he said early, *"We had 65 guys out the first day; now we have 58 and I hope we keep that many. We lost 12 seniors, lost a starter due to eligibility, one senior decided not to play and Dexter Berry is out with a knee injury, making us lose about 15 in all. We had 23 players come up from 9th grade and we have some fine young athletes. The only problem I can see is that they have not had much field time, but I think they will gain the experience along the way. We will have more or less an inexperienced line"*.

Magee was picked 2nd pre-season to Mendenhall, but he still liked what he saw as game week neared. *"I think I have seen the best results in early practice in the four years I have been here. We timed them in the mile run and other stamina and endurance tests and they could really tell the difference. People are going to be surprised when I say this, considering the players we lost. But we're going to be competitive this year. I believe we can be a very good team"*.

GAME 1: MAGEE (0-0) vs PORT GIBSON (0-0)
MAGEE 35 PORT GIBSON 6
September 5, 1986

Port Gibson, under Coach Lum Wright, was picked second behind Florence in their division. Said Bradley about the upcoming tilt, *"We're running about even with Port Gibson in that they lost 12 seniors also and they won five out of their last six games. They have a reputation of starting off slow and finishing fast and they did real well in the spring games... We'll just have to wait and see"*.

Magee started 1986 scoring with Monique Craft's 6-yard run and David Garner made it 9-0 in the next frame with his 27-yard FG. After halftime, they drove 68 yards with Estus Barron dodging in from 8 yards and Garner providing the PAT. The game was back-and-forth afterwards due to fumbles and interceptions on a wet field. Russ May provided the final Magee touchdown on a 10-yard run (Garner kick) while the Blue Wave avoided the shutout on a 6-yard Kenneth Tarleton scamper. The Clarion-Ledger called it a pass from Arthur Randall while The (Port Gibson) Reveille said it was Arthur Brandon to Lemon Johnson.

May rushed for 72 yards to lead the Trojans. Magee led in first downs (16-8), rushing (171-87) and passing (153-21). Richard Forrest was credited with a pair of interceptions. *"I thought the team effort was excellent. The desire was strong; the enthusiasm was outstanding. I was just very pleased. We just played to win. The field was wet, of course, and the footing was pretty unsteady, but we held our own"*.

GAME 2: MAGEE (1-0) @ HEIDELBERG (1-0)
MAGEE 21 HEIDELBERG 6
September 12, 1986

First-time opponent Heidelberg was voted a lowly fifth pre-season in the district but started the season with a 21-14 win over Bay Springs. Still, Bradley was confident. *"We will do our best. I think we can contain them without too much trouble"*.

Barron wasted no time getting Magee started with a scoring run and Garner notched the PAT. Their next threat was lost via fumble at the Oiler 1-yard line. In the ensuing frame, Forrest took a *"bouncing (punt) at midfield and sped down the sidelines for another Trojan touchdown"*. Garner provided the 14-0 PAT that extended to halftime. Another fumble deep by Magee took away another opportunity in the 3rd quarter and Heidelberg took advantage. Reginald Martin's 52-yard bomb to either Anthony Milsaps or Ron Cooley cut into the lead 14-6.

In the final quarter, the Oilers threatened deep in Trojan territory twice but lost both on fumbles. Magee inserted the dagger on Barron's throw to May and Garner iced things.

GAME 3: MAGEE (2-0) vs COLLINS (0-2)
MAGEE 27 COLLINS 3
September 19, 1986

From 1926-1938, the two teams had faced one-another six times. Surprisingly in the early years of Magee football, the record sat 2-3-1. Collins had started 3rd in the division pre-season but opened with a pair of losses. The last had come against Bay Springs 28-20. The Hattiesburg American called their schedule *"Murderers' row"*.

Magee opened with a 62-yard drive that finished on May's 2-yard run and the first of 3 Garner kicks. Collins moved right back to the Trojan 10-yard line in the 2nd quarter and counted a FG by Billy Shoemake. However, back punched the Trojans with Sammy Phillips providing the last 23 yards of the drive to make halftime 13-3. Collins may have had another shot at the scoreboard had Marcus Bowen not picked off an errant Shoemake throw. In the 3rd quarter, and after suffering a goal-line fumble earlier, Darrell Russell moved in from a yard out to make it 20-3. Finally, with reserves in play, Monique Craft rushed in from 2 yards to finish any threats.

Russell had 91 rushing yards to lead Magee. *"We are showing signs of improvement offensively with a lot more consistency than we have had before, although we have to eliminate some of our mistakes. Our defense played pretty good in most spots with three interceptions and we had some big plays behind the line of scrimmage when they were needed. But we need to get more consistent. (Collins is) just a good, young team and they are scrappers. Coach Thames had them very-well prepared"*.

GAME 4: MAGEE (3-0) @ NORTHEAST JONES (3-0)
MAGEE 14 NORTHEAST JONES 12
September 26, 1986

The 4A team picked pre-season 1st in their division and sitting 8th in the AP statewide poll now hosted the Trojans for their Homecoming. Said Bradley, *"They are ranked in the top 10 of the state and have one of the five best teams statewide. They have power and speed with a good QB and running backs"*.

The Tigers made a statement early by running *"through the Trojan defense like they owned it"*. Raymond Williams' 2-yard dive capped a 65-yard march to make it 6-0. They increased the lead with a 62-yard drive when Steve Peavey got in from a yard out to put it 12-0. In the 2nd quarter, a fumbled punt was recovered by Dalton Bradley to give Magee a chance. Craft ran for 25 yards to the 5-yard line and Phillips went in from there. Garner's PAT put intermission 12-7.

Northeast Jones' next drive ended with a fumble deep in Trojan territory. Now in the final frame, another Tiger fumble gave a glimmer of hope to players and fans. Barron *"unloaded a pass under a heavy rush and Richard Forrest was leaping, almost parallel to the ground, and the football reached his fingertips. He pulled the ball in to his chest as he hit the ground, sliding to a halt at the back of the end zone"*. Garner's PAT would prove to be the final point. Northeast could not muster a response. Lost in the victory was a knee injury to May; now out for perhaps a month.

Magee led only in passing (59-32) while losing first downs (8-12) and rushing (44-210). *"There were some miracles out on that field tonight. Through our first four games, we've gone out and done what we had to do to win. With our inexperience and lack of any great players, I believe we have a bunch of overachievers. They came out in the first quarter and scored touchdowns on us and made us look like we weren't even there. But we came back and scored ... and held them scoreless the last three quarters. We seemed to get stronger as the game wore on and were fortunate to come away with a very emotional win"*.

GAME 5: MAGEE (4-0) @ WEST JONES (3-1)
MAGEE 21 WEST JONES 6
October 3, 1986

West Jones finished 5-5 the previous year under long-time Coach Mike Taylor. With 12 lettermen back, the Mustangs were ranked 2nd in their division pre-season. Said Taylor then, *"Our strengths will be in our returning offensive linemen and defensive backs. Inexperience at linebacker and running back would be our weak points"*. Despite a 31-8 win over Petal the previous week, The Hattiesburg American predicted a 19-14 Magee win, saying *"Oughta be a good 'un. Does Magee have enough left after last week's intense encounter to do away with West?"*. Added Bradley, *"They seem to have gotten it back together after losing to Starkville. They are big and strong and come straight at you. We'll have to play our best game of the year to stay with them"*.

Barron kicked off scoring with a 24-yard scamper and Garner knocked through his first of 3 PATs. In the next quarter, he found Forrest from 35 yards and halftime sat 14-0. After a scoreless 3rd quarter, Richard Johnson got in from the 9-yard line to make it interesting, but Magee responded with a Craft 3-yard run and the game was effectively over. Magee led in first downs (13-8), rushing (211-140) and passing (61-0). Barron rushed for 121 yards. *"I thought we played our best ball game since the season began. We had a good team effort. They executed well on every play. What more can we ask of them"?*

GAME 6: MAGEE (5-0) vs SOUTH JONES (1-4)
MAGEE 35 SOUTH JONES 14
October 10, 1986: HOMECOMING

South Jones had gone a lowly 0-10 the previous year and were predictably picked last in the division. New coach Jack Thompson said, *"You've only got one way to go, and that's up. We feel we'll be fairly competitive. I don't know if that will be reflected in our record, but that doesn't mean we're looking to lose. We feel like we can put a pretty good defense on the field. Our offense is not going to be real explosive, so our defense needs to play well. Our young people have got to come through for us and we've got to play good defense. Those are musts"*.

Bradley summed up his Homecoming opponent by saying *"(They are) a good team that has lost some close games. They have a young team and have shown excellent ability"*. In fact, they had only been outscored this year 100-70. The Hattiesburg American noted that South would *"have its hands full again this week…"* after losing to Laurel 24-0.

South Jones did themselves no favors by fumbling the kickoff to the Trojans and Barron took advantage on a 1-yard keeper. Garner made it 7-0 quickly. They fumbled on their next two drives and Russell made short work of one from the 4-yard line. South did put up points in the 2nd quarter on Randy Duhon's 5-yard plunge and Glynn Branch's two-point conversion, but Magee came back with a 67-yard drive and Barron 7-yard pass to Quincy Talley for the score. Barron's run put halftime 21-8.

The opponent opened the 3rd quarter with an interception leading to Chris Wade's 1-yard dive, but back came the Trojans with a march ending in Craft's 17-yard escape and Garner kick. Following another Brave fumble, James Davis continued to lug the ball until he broke in from a yard out. Garner finished the scoring.

GAME 7: MAGEE (6-0) @ PETAL (3-3)
MAGEE 16 PETAL 14
October 17, 1986

The Panthers were picked 4th in their division pre-season while undefeated Magee was now tied for 20th in the AP poll. Said Coach Rush McKay, *"This is a new ball game (comparing the 41-0 loss of the previous year). This is a different team. You can't dwell on the past. We're going out there and play hard. We're looking for a real good ball game"*. Added Bradley, *"They are sound fundamentally. I haven't seen them do anything that wasn't sound. If we have a let-up, anybody can beat us. I feel like the rest of the way, and Petal especially, teams will be ready for us. Petal would like to be a prime example"*.

Petal proved to be just as strong as Bradley predicted, scoring on their first drive of 55 yards when Bill Lott hit Billy Reynolds from 28 yards away. Michael Hogan's PAT put it 7-0. It took only as long as the kickoff before Davis dodged Panther defenders for a 98-yard touchdown return and Garner tied the ball game. The only score of the first half came later when a snap over the Petal punter went out of the end zone for a safety and 9-7 Trojan lead.

Magee put together a 65-yard drive in the 3rd quarter when Barron hit Doug Cox from 10 yards and Garner converted. Petal found the end zone in the last frame with 6:25 remaining on a 1-yard Bill Lott dive and Hogan extra point. *"Magee reached down and found something extra and held the Panthers at bay for the remainder of the game"*. Mike Kelly was credited with one potential score-saving fumble recovery.

Magee led in first downs (11-7) and passing (106-67) while Petal held the ground (93-91). Said Bradley after his Trojans had clinched the SAC championship, *"Petal is better than a 3-4 team. I told our players Petal was good. It would have taken a nut to believe they weren't a good team. Petal's defense was real aggressive. We couldn't protect our quarterback"*.

GAME 8: MAGEE (7-0) vs BAY SPRINGS (4-3)
MAGEE 12 BAY SPRINGS 0
October 24, 1986

Bay Springs had made the playoffs last year but was now picked 6th pre-season. They were a touch better than that now. Meanwhile, despite a perfect 7-0, Magee had climbed only to 18th in the AP. As for this contest, Magee hoped to make it a two-game streak against their opponent after having broken a winless stretch the previous season.

On a rain-soaked field, it was Magee with the first error; that a fumble on their second drive. However, the Bulldogs could only muster a 44-yard Ingo Ihlbrock FG attempt. That sailed *"far right of the goal post"*. The Trojans then marched 80 yards for the first touchdown, with

Barron doing the honors from a yard away. That PAT, like so many other opportunities, was lost due to a fumbled wet football. The last score came in the final quarter, but could have been different after a Magee fumble. But Marcus Bowen stepped in front of a *"desperate pass"* by Anthony Myers to get the ball back.

Again, Magee fumbled away the opportunity. Forrest, however, picked off the Dog throw and put the home team in scoring position after his 65-yard return. Craft turned it into a 5-yard touchdown for what would be the final points. Another interception sealed the final score. First downs (11-9) and rushing (161-69) went to Magee. Bay Springs held the air 68-16. In all, there were four lost Trojan fumbles.

GAME 9: MAGEE (8-0) @ WAYNESBORO (5-3)
MAGEE 35 WAYNESBORO 7
October 31, 1986

Picked 4th pre-season in the district, Waynesboro was tied with Magee as they were undefeated in district play. Another report had their overall record at 6-2. While the winner would not claim the district title, the loser was almost assuredly out of contention. Magee had faced Waynesboro in their very first year of organized football (1926) and only in 1948-1949 after.

Magee was the recipient of great field position after a bad snap on fourth down. They turned that into a 1st quarter score when Barron outran the defense 37 yards to daylight. Garner converted his first of 5 points-after. They added more in the next quarter on a 60-yard march capped by Barron's 13-yard run. They moved the same distance before halftime to set up Craft's 6-yarder to make it 21-0. A Trojan fumble in the 3rd gave way to a 2-yard Sammy Chambers run and Daryl Stevens conversion.

The Trojans put the game away in the final period with a 25-yard Barron pass to Forrest and Amie Green's 12-yard effort. The last had been set up by a Waynesboro fumble. Magee led all the way around: first downs (9-3), rushing (152-52) and passing (102-0). *"The Trojans never cease to amaze me. They never gave up. Who would have thought we would be 9-0 at this point?"*

GAME 10: MAGEE (9-0) vs MENDENHALL (7-2)
MAGEE 0 MENDENHALL 22
November 7, 1986

Mendenhall had lost Coach Tommy Lucas to Starkville just a couple of weeks before the season. In stepped Neil Hitchcock to take control of the team picked first in pre-season with 21 returning lettermen. This 61st edition of the Simpson County Super Bowl would be much like most of the past contests. Regardless of the records, bragging rights, the Wally Beach Memorial Trophy and the district championship hung in the balance.

Said Hitchcock, *"Magee is the best team we will play this year and they have the best record. So far, we haven't played an undefeated team. I knew that the game was a real big one before I came here. I have seen the spirit at school. It's the biggest game of the year. We just want to play Magee and win the district championship"*. As a side note, Magee had finally entered the Top 10 of the AP Poll.

The rivalry battle was a defensive one. The only score of the first half came 6:35 before halftime when Mark Johnson burst in from a yard out to make it 6-0. Like the opening frame, the third was scoreless. But the Tigers put the contest away in the 4th quarter with touchdowns. Their first came on a 35-yard drive capped by Johnson from the 11-yard line. Tracy Easterling's 3-yard leap into the end zone made it 14-0. Then, Easterling picked off an errant Barron throw and took it 25 yards to paydirt. Another two-point conversion would be the dagger. Gayle Williams' last-gasp interception ended things.

Mendenhall led in first downs (15-5) and rushing (217-69). Magee held on the passing stats (58-14). While Mendy fumbled three times without losing any, Magee lost a pair to the Tigers and suffered 3 interceptions. *"We didn't go very well. We made too many mistakes. Maybe they were keyed up too much. Mendenhall has a fine football team. They executed real well. It was not so much the lack of defensive play as our not making the big plays when we had to have them and the offense not doing anything. That put too much pressure on the defense. I still am very proud of our team, the players, coaching staff, fans and everyone who has supported us this whole season"*.

Added Hitchcock, *"Magee surprised me throwing the ball so much. We expected them to run, but before the first half they were back in the shotgun and that sort of surprised us. But we adjusted"*.

District 5-3A South honors went to Estus Barron (Most Outstanding Back), Doug Cox, Richard Forrest, Eric Jaynes, Alan Mangum and Sammy Phillips. West Bolivar beat Mendenhall 26-15 for the 3A championship.

1987 (6-4)

David Bradley returned for his sixth, and final, year as head man in Magee. The previous season had been disappointing in that despite a 9-1 record, their last-game shutout loss to rival Mendenhall had ended their season. Still, a 33-5 record over the past three years had served to re-establish Magee as a perennial football power. Uncharacteristically, very little was reported on the team or its activities as the season kicked off.

GAME 1: MAGEE (0-0) @ COLLINS (0-0)
MAGEE 21 COLLINS 0
September 4, 1987

The Tigers had started 0-7 in 1986 including a 27-3 loss to Magee. Though not a division contest, both teams wanted to get the season started off on the right foot.

Collins was nearly the first team to get it going when Charles Posey took the kickoff 90 yards to the end zone. But, a clipping penalty brought the ball back and they never seemed to recover. A fumble by Billy Shoemake at the 13-yard line set up Tony Tatum's 2-yard run and the first of 3 David Garner extra points. In the 2nd, Tatum blasted in from 2 yards and halftime was 14-0. The final points came in the 3rd quarter on a 68-yard march topped by Tatum's 39-yard dash.

First downs (10-5), rushing (240-80) and passing (50-12) went to Magee. Stats vary by the publication. Tatum rushed for 113 (Hattiesburg American) yards while Amie Green and Marty McWilliams added interceptions. *"We didn't plan it that way, but Tony has a lot of quickness. Collins had some real fine plays on their kicking game but penalties brought them back each time and that kind of broke their back"*. Added Collins' Coach Thames, *"Anytime you get an opening break on a kick and they bring it back on a penalty, it's going to deflate you a little. For everything we tried, nothing would go. But it boils down to (the fact) that we didn't block at all. None"*.

GAME 2: MAGEE (1-0) vs HEIDELBERG (1-0)
MAGEE 20 HEIDELBERG 12
September 10, 1987

In their first-ever game in 1986, Magee had taken the measure of the Oilers 21-6. Unlike the previous season, it was Heidelberg first to the scoreboard when Reginald Martin's delay handoff to Dupree McGee ended 89 yards later in the end zone to make it a quick 6-0. Midway through the 2nd quarter, and after an Oiler penalty, Magee responded with Monique Craft's 1-yard dive and Garner's PAT. That 7-6 lead would hold until the final frame.

Jerry King's fumble recovery soon led to Napoleon Sharble's 16-yard connection with Quincy Talley. The Trojans found another loose football late in the game at the Oiler 20-yard line. Green did the honors *"up the middle"* for the 9-yard score and Garner converted. Heidelberg mustered an answer with a little over 1:00 remaining on Martin's 55-yard strike to Ron Cooley but their ensuing on-side kick was recovered by Magee. First downs (13-3) and rushing (177-87) went to Magee while the Oilers led in passing (110-26). Tatum galloped for 109 yards.

GAME 3: MAGEE (2-0) @ RALEIGH (1-0)
MAGEE 47 RALEIGH 0
September 18, 1987

Magee had played Raleigh only one time in their history. In 1938, the team from Simpson County hosted Raleigh and defeated them 32-0 en-route to a 5-4-1 season. As a side note, Bradley had actually coached at Raleigh in 1978 and 1979. Now sharing the division with the Trojans, they would meet again. Using *"a bone-cracking defense and some great play by the punt return team"*, they bettered that result of nearly 50 years past.

Despite the score, it would be a tale of two halves. The only tally of the opening half of play came in the 2nd quarter when Sharble found Chaucer Funchess from 18 yards out and Garner nailed his first of 5 extra points. They exploded in the 3rd quarter, starting with Green's 17-yard dart. Tony Smith then added a 58-yard punt return to the board and Sharble hit Craft from 42-

yards. Douglas King's fumble recovery shortly afterwards led to a 1-yard Craft plunge. It was now 33-0.

In the final frame, Smith burst 58 yards for another punt-return touchdown. Finally, Kevin Malloy found the end zone from a yard away and Magee's third-straight win and second shutout was in the books. Green led Magee rushers with 74 markers.

GAME 4: MAGEE (3-0) vs NORTHEAST JONES (3-0)
MAGEE 16 NORTHEAST JONES 13
September 25, 1987

Fourth-ranked Class 4A Northeast Jones had outscored opponents 71-35 thus far on the season, including a previous-week win over Number 10 Laurel 16-14. It would undoubtedly be the toughest game thus far for the Trojans, and The Hattiesburg American predicted a Northeast win 21-20. It marked the fourth-straight undefeated opponent for Magee.

Things looked gloomy after just 2:00 of play when Kenny Jordon burst through Trojan defenders for a 76-yard scoring scamper and the PAT by Raymond Williams was true. After a trade of interceptions, Williams booted a 38-yard FG and the quarter ended 10-0. Magee's Michael Warren then found a loose ball at the Tiger 25-yard line and Sharble hit Talley from 7 yards for the response. Garner's kick cut the lead to 10-7. Just :12 before halftime, Williams kicked a partially-blocked 35-yard FG to make intermission 13-7.

In the final quarter, Magee started punching back. Green drove in from 15 yards and, with Garner's kick, it was 14-13. Now late in the game, Rob Holbrook's punt was downed at the 1-yard line with :02 left. The Trojan defense *"swarmed all over the Tiger QB (Stacy Carson) in his own end zone. Darryl Collins led the charge that ended the game with a safety"*. The Hattiesburg American also gave credit to Kevin Jackson and Dale Collins.

Magee led in all categories: first downs (15-4), rushing (189-142) and passing (45-16). Each team had an interception. *"This team showed some kind of courage out there tonight. It was unbelievable. The players' intensity was all we could ask for... When we held them to a field goal on their second drive, the team knew we could stop them and got really fired up"*.

GAME 5: MAGEE (4-0) vs WEST JONES (2-2)
MAGEE 0 WEST JONES 16
October 2, 1987

Though their next opponent was 2-2, the Mustangs under long-time Coach Mike Taylor had dropped those games to Mendenhall and Starkville. *"They are such a large, physical team and it is their style to run the ball right at you. But our strength on defense is against the run. But we can adjust to a passing attack, also. We will have to rely on our passing game and finesse, because I don't think we are going to get much between the tackles. We have to force them to do something different, something they are not used to doing, to beat us"*.

The tough defensive struggle took a turn in the 2nd quarter when a bad snap sailed over the Holbrook's head for a West Jones safety. West Jones followed that with a 41-yard drive capped by Kenny Craven's 1-yard dive and Brad Holifield's PAT. The 9-0 score held until the 4th quarter when a bad exchange bounced into the waiting hands of Craven and he raced the necessary 12 yards. Holifield's kick would mark the final point. Holifield and Terry Ulmer picked off last-gasp Magee attempts. West Jones led in first downs (8-5), rushing (143-24) and passing (10-8).

GAME 6: MAGEE (4-1) @ SOUTH JONES (3-2)
MAGEE 0 SOUTH JONES 14
October 9, 1987

It would get no easier this week as 6-4A South Jones had won three-straight and outscored opponents 122-14. Yet again, Magee would be facing higher-classification teams and The Hattiesburg American predicted a close game but 12-10 loss for the Trojans.

Magee drove deep into Brave territory twice but could put no points on the board. South Jones fared no better and halftime stood scoreless. But, they opened the 3rd quarter with an 80-yard march with Jason Simpson diving in from a yard away and converting for the 7-0 lead. Late in the game, and after a Doug Coleman fumble recovery, Michael Ross bounced off would-be Trojan defenders and raced 29 yards to paydirt and Simpson again provided the point-after. Magee moved to inside the Brave 10-yard line but could not penetrate the white stripe.

Magee led in first downs (13-10) and passing (40-18) while South Jones barely held the ground (187-172). Said Coach Jack Thompson, *"Any time you can shut out a team like Magee, you have had a total team effort"*.

GAME 7: MAGEE (4-2) vs PETAL (4-2)
MAGEE 21 PETAL 7
October 16, 1987: HOMECOMING

Coach Pat Davis' Petal squad was looking good after a previous-week 44-14 drubbing of Oak Grove. After dropping two-straight, The Hattiesburg American picked the Panthers 17-14. *"Petal is on a hot streak and Magee is on a cold one, so look for the Panthers to come out on top. Barely"*. Since the first game in 1935, Magee held a 6-2-1 advantage in meetings. They would move that in the right direction on this evening.

On Petal's second possession of the night, they moved 77 yards with Timbo Oglesby (or Melvin Cooper) dodging in from a yard out and Tracy Montague notching the PAT. But the tide of scoreless football for Magee changed after that. In the 2nd quarter, they moved 65 yards with Tatum diving in from a yard and Garner converting his first of three PATs. Magee notched a touchdown on a 61-yard drive in the 3rd quarter via Green's 9-yard escape and, after turnovers by both teams, put up their last on Tatum's 1-yarder. One other report gave credit to Funchess.

First downs (11-10) and rushing (194-108) belonged to Magee. Petal had the passing game an amazing 5-0. Said Davis, *"Our defense had to stay on the field too long tonight. Both times the defense has had to stay on the field too long, we've lost the game"*.

GAME 8: MAGEE (5-2) @ BAY SPRINGS (3-4)
MAGEE 21 BAY SPRINGS 0
October 23, 1987

After going 0-2-1 against Bay Springs between 1943 and 1946, Magee had come on to win the last two years. This time, they opened with a drive to the 11-yard line but fumbled the ball away. Bay Springs returned the gift the same way at their 14-yard line and Garner used the opportunity to dodge in from 4 yards out. His PAT was his first of four. The only threat by the home team came and went on an unsuccessful Bubba Brown FG effort.

Penalties overtook the Trojans as they marked 61 yards in flags before halftime. Late in the 3rd quarter, Funchess found a loose football at the Dog 15-yard line. Green capitalized with a 1-yard scoring run. Now in the final quarter and after a Daniel Rice interception of a Billy Caston pass, Magee went 73 yards with Garner pitching in the last 38 yards for the touchdown. Magee led in first downs (10-4), rushing (151-49) and passing (32-23). *"This was not a crisp ball game. There were a lot of mental mistakes on both sides of the ball. Neither team really had their mind on the ball game"*.

GAME 9: MAGEE (6-2) vs WAYNESBORO (3-5)
MAGEE 0 WAYNESBORO 6
October 30, 1987

Notwithstanding the two losses, the good news for Magee was that they were 3-0 in district play. That put them in the same position Mendenhall was in the year before when, despite a worse record, they were able to claim the district title. There were only four games in history with Waynesboro; the first coming in Magee's initial season of football. The series sat 2-2 but none of that mattered on this evening. A playoff spot was at stake.

Despite three interceptions in the first half of play, the Trojans could not capitalize. In fact, they had only 2 first downs and 11 rushing yards by intermission. The Panthers' passing game was not getting better, but their one completion came in the 3rd quarter when Jerrell Rankin found Steve Powe for a 24-yard touchdown. Their two-point attempt failed. Afterwards, it was a *"battle of fumbles and interceptions"*. Magee led in first downs (6-4), passing (48-24) and rushing (53-52). There were 10 turnovers in the contest.

GAME 10: MAGEE (6-3) @ MENDENHALL (8-1)
MAGEE 0 MENDENHALL 14
November 6, 1987

The defending 5-3A champions, and now 3rd-ranked 3A Tigers, under second-year Coach Neil Hitchcock lost 14 lettermen to start the year but returned 14 others. Said he, *"We don't seem to have quite as much speed this year as we did last year so we are going to have to play smarter. This will be a young team. We figure we will probably start four seniors, three juniors and three or four sophomores with one freshman to begin with. We have been working mighty hard"*. By game day, they were one game better than the last time they faced the Trojans. Said Hitchcock, "*Not only is it a good rivalry, but it's real good high school football*".

It was called a "*titanic defensive battle before an estimated 5,500 wild and enthusiastic fans*". The first score came in the 2nd quarter when Maurice Norwood "*scrambled to his right and hit senior tight end Donald Mays at the Magee 15-yard line*". In stride, he hit the end zone and Chris Berry provided the point-after. Magee's best opportunity came in the 3rd quarter when Sharble hooked up with Green for 44 yards, but would go for naught at the 25-yard line. Now in the final 5:00, the Tigers moved 48 yards and sealed things with Mark Johnson's 2-yard plunge with :22 on the clock. Berry's PAT was academic.

Mendy won the battle of first downs (8-4) and rushing while Magee held passing 51-42. Said Hitchcock, "*You have got to give Magee credit. They played us tough. It was just our year. Magee gave us one of the hardest games we had this season. They were every bit as good as we thought they were*". Bradley told his players afterwards, "*We played as hard as we could play. That's all you can ask. Every one of you did us proud. You did yourselves proud and you did Magee proud. You have nothing to be ashamed of tonight*".

All SAC honorees at the end of the year included James Davis, Michael Warren, Quincy Talley and Rob Holbrook. Second Team members were Scott Edwards, Jerry King and John Lee. The Honorable Mention list noted Michael Brown, Harold Russell, Amie Green, Tony Tatum, David Garner, Chaucer Funchess and Darryl Collins. Mendenhall's 34-14 win over Amory gave them the 3A championship.

1988 (10-3)

With the resignation of David Bradley for a position at Woodham High in Pensacola, Magee how had their 23rd head coach in place. Lum Wright, Jr., formerly head man in Yazoo City and Biloxi, now made the move to Simpson County. "*Magee's been strong for quite some time. We hope to continue that tradition and build on that. If we play sound football and not make mistakes, we should have a pretty good season. I know that they boys have been working hard with the weights and conditioning program that has been initiated here in Magee and they have shown good effort. The boys believe in themselves and the coaching staff as well*".

The red and gray had high expectations for a good year as even though they had lost 16 lettermen, they returned 15.

GAME 1: MAGEE (0-0) vs COLLINS (0-0)
MAGEE 24 COLLINS 6
September 2, 1988

The green and white Tigers under Coach Richard Thames finished 4-6 the previous season. Graduation had taken 15 letter-winners, but they did have the services of 20 returning. Said Thames, "*The kids all came back from the winter in great shape and the right frame of mind about working hard. That's all I can ask of them. This season we fully expect to get over the hump, but we're not going to be satisfied with that*".

After stopping their head-to-head contests in 1938, the two teams re-established meetings in 1986. Magee had won both tilts. Said Wright, "*We had better be ready when Collins comes to town*".

On a wet field, Magee struck on their opening drive by marching 48 yards with David Garner crashing in from 3 yards out to make it 6-0. They increased the lead shortly afterwards when Delvin Rankin recovered a fumble to set up Garner's 28-yard FG. In the 2nd quarter, Chuckie Allen struck with an 85-yard punt return. Amie Green's two-point conversion made halftime 17-0. Collins notched their only score in the 3rd on a 62-yard march and Charles Posey's 1-yard dive. Now in the 4th quarter, Green "*raced untouched*" the 55 yards to daylight and Garner converted.

Magee led in first downs (10-8) and rushing (128-76) while Collins held the air (32-13). "*We had a couple of drives stopped by penalties and fumbles, but considering the wet field, these fellows played a good game. This was our first game and win. We have to play them one game at a time*".

GAME 2: MAGEE (1-0) @ HEIDELBERG (1-0)
MAGEE 28 HEIDELBERG 10
September 9, 1988

Much like Collins, Magee had played Heidelberg the past two years and came out with wins in each. Magee opened well with an 80-yard drive and 5-yard Garner touchdown. He added the first of 3 extra points afterward. The Oilers answered quickly via a 9-yard Reginald Martin strike to Anthony MIlsap and their two-point conversion via a Martin pass to Milsay. That put Heidelberg ahead 8-7 after a quarter.

A bad snap/fumble in the next quarter was picked up by Daniel Rice to set up Garner's 5-yard TD. Before intermission, another fumble at the Oiler 19-yard line made it possible for Tony Smith to get in from 6 yards out. The Trojans added another score in the rainy 3rd quarter on Smith's 51-yard dash to make it 28-8. Heidelberg's only other points came late via a safety when Magee intentionally downed to run the clock.

The visitors held first downs (14-11) and rushing (301-12) while Martin's 198 yards of passing bested the 5 yards from Magee. Smith racked up 156 yards of rushing while Chaun Barron recorded a pair of interceptions.

GAME 3: MAGEE (2-0) vs RALEIGH (0-2)
MAGEE 29 RALEIGH 6
September 16, 1988

Coach Durwood Anderson was in his 3rd year at Raleigh. After putting up a 21-3 record at Lake High, he had finished the last season with the Lions at 1-9. *"We have 12 seniors and 10 juniors returning, which includes 15 lettermen, so we have a lot of experienced players. Right now we're just looking for improvements and to get our minds right"*. In the end, this one would go the same way as the only other two meetings (1938 and 1987).

Magee tallied first on a 50-yard march and Smith 1-yarder. Garner converted his first of 3 PATs. Before the end of the frame, Smith raced 47 yards to paydirt. Two Raleigh drives before halftime ended on interceptions by John Lee and Rice. A snap over the Lion punter's head in the 3rd quarter resulted in a safety. Raleigh posted their only points in the quarter on either Chris Thurman's or Ernest Barber's 1-yard plunge, but Magee responded with Chuckie Allen's 50-yard race. Finally, in the final quarter and after a Lion fumble, Kyle Gordy snuck though for the touchdown.

For the third time, Magee led in first downs (9-4) and rushing (192-9) but lost the passing attack (68-7). Marty McWilliams recorded an interception in the tilt. Smith rushed for 133 to pace Trojan runners.

GAME 4: MAGEE (3-0) @ NORTHEAST JONES (1-2)
MAGEE 7 NORTHEAST JONES 14
September 23, 1988

The black and gold under Coach Danny Adams finished 6-3 the year before. With 17 lost lettermen and 12 returning, he said *"How quickly we can get the QB situation settled and how well our defense performs early in the season are the keys to success this year"*. The Tigers were described as *"strong"* despite their 1-2 record this year.

It was the home team striking first on David Waters' 63-yard misdirection run minus his shoe and Scott Landry's PAT. The 7-0 score held until the 3rd quarter when Ken Jordan raced 40 yards to the end zone and Landry converted. Magee began to put things together in the final period when Tony Tatum crashed in from a yard out and Garner converted. Their last chance with 1:24 remaining failed to produce points.

Magee suffered 9 sacks in the contest and rushed for only 16 yards. Gordy, however, did pass for over 100 yards. Chaucer Funchess (6 solo and 3 assists) led tacklers while Napoleon Sharble added an interception.

GAME 5: MAGEE (3-1) @ WEST JONES (1-3)
MAGEE 35 WEST JONES 7
September 30, 1988

West Jones had 12 lettermen back from a 6-5 campaign for long-time Coach Mike Taylor. Said Taylor in pre-season about his green and gold Mustangs, *"The offensive line is our strong point, which is important because we rely so heavily on our running attack. But if we have a lot of injuries early in the season, it could ruin our division performance; especially because most of our guys play both ways".* The Hattiesburg American predicted a Trojan win 21-20.

Magee was quick to the scoreboard on Smith's 2-yard leap and the first of 5 Garner PATs. But West Jones punched back immediately when Terry Duckworth took the kickoff 95 yards to the end zone and Michael Sims converted. It would be all they would get. The Trojans, meanwhile, matched the WJ feat when Tatum took their kickoff 95 yards up the middle. They added another score in the 2nd quarter on Gordy's 35-yard pass to Green to make halftime 21-7.

The final points came in the 3rd quarter on Green's 17-yard dash and Garner's 1-yard plunge. The last had been set up by a Funchess punt block off kicker Sammy Ray. Magee led in all categories: first downs (9-7), rushing (97-79) and passing (89-0). Rice had an interception while Rankin led tacklers (8 solo and 3 assists).

GAME 6: MAGEE (4-1) vs SOUTH JONES (5-0)
MAGEE 7 SOUTH JONES 0
October 7, 1988

Next up would be the defending 4A South champions. Jack Thompson's Braves had gone 11-3 that season and returned 12 lettermen in red and blue. *"Of course we were pleased with last season's performance, but it doesn't make a bit of difference this year. All of that is history and we can't live on last year".* Magee had won 7 straight against South Jones before dropping their matchup the previous season. Now, South Jones had already clinched 6-4A and sat 2nd in the 4A poll and 6th in the AP.

The game was solely a defensive struggle. In fact, the only score of the game came in the 2nd quarter when their fumble was picked up by Darryl Collins and returned 35 yards to the end zone. Garner's conversion was true. Collins also prevented a possible score before halftime by picking off a pass. Before it was over, Funchess found another loose ball to stop a drive and Collins added a big sack. Magee led in first downs (6-3) and rushing (87-0) while South Jones held the air (24-13).

Said Thompson, *"Magee played a good game. They shut us down and played well. Magee was ready to play. They got the one big break in the game and used it to score".*

GAME 7: MAGEE (5-1) @ PETAL (3-2)
MAGEE 23 PETAL 14
October 14, 1988

The Panthers had not put two-straight wins together this year, but had just beaten 6-4A Oak Grove 29-6 the week before. It had been the most points they had scored thus far this season. Historically, Magee had taken the last six contests and were trying to get refocused after such a big win.

A determined Petal team hit the board in the opening quarter on Bill Lott's 8-yard run. Magee answered late in the 2nd quarter after a Petal fumble via either a Garner 1-yard play or *"a touchdown pass to Amie Green".* Garner's PAT made halftime 7-6. Back came Petal afterwards with a 3-yard Melvin Cooper dive and it was 12-7. Magee responded with a 33-yard Gordy pass to Funchess and Garner PAT. Before the frame ended, Magee added a safety courtesy of a blocked punt.

Midway through the final quarter, the Trojans tallied their last on a Green's 5-yard score and Garner's kick. After a Lee interception, Magee gave a deliberate safety to Petal to run out the clock. First downs went to Magee (16-9) while Petal led in rushing (85-68) and passing (134-128).

GAME 8: MAGEE (6-1) vs BAY SPRINGS (5-2)
MAGEE 35 BAY SPRINGS 0
October 21, 1988

The Trojans had finally moved into the Others Receiving Votes category in the AP poll. Their opponent, a familiar face from the 1940s, had re-entered the Magee schedule in 1985. The Trojans had won each of those tilts. The Hattiesburg American predicted a Trojan win 14-7.

Without some players due to injury, the opening quarter was a back-and-forth affair. But Funchess' 10-yard reception from Gordy to open the 2nd quarter was followed by the first of 5 Garner kicks. That scant 7-0 lead held until the 3rd quarter when Green took a punt 55 yards to paydirt. Now in the final quarter, the Trojans put it away. Tony Bullock's pickoff set up Darryl Lomax's 2-yard drive. A few minutes later, Gordy hit Green from the 12-yard line. Before it was over, Randy Meadows picked up a Bay Springs fumble by Kevin Winfrey and raced 80 yards for the last. The Jasper County News questioned whether that particular score should have been called an incomplete pass.

Bay Springs apparently led in first downs (12-9 or 9-5) and rushing (168-82) while Magee led uncharacteristically in passing (115-31). Rice put 2 interceptions in the books for Magee. *"We were flat tonight. We have some people hurt and we were not up for this game"*.

GAME 9: MAGEE (7-1) @ WAYNESBORO (2-6)
MAGEE 27 WAYNESBORO 6
October 28, 1988

The green and white lost 11 lettermen but returned a whopping 19 from a 5-5 season. Said Coach Jim McCain before the season, *"Experience in key positions should make the defense strong..."* The Hattiesburg American picked Magee 21-7 over their 2-6 opponent. Still, they had moved no further in the polls than the Others Receiving Votes.

Magee started strong with an 80-yard drive capped by Gordy's 15-yard TD pass to Allen. Garner's kick was good. Lee then picked off a Waynesboro pass, but the Trojans fumbled it back later at the 15-yard line. In the next frame, Ronald Cunningham dove in from 2 yards in the 2nd quarter for the Panthers for what would be their only points. Magee came back with a 77-yard march with Tatum going in from 2 yards and Garner making halftime 14-6.

Waynesboro stopped an early 3rd quarter threat with an interception, but the Trojans still managed a tally on their next possession via a Garner run. Now in the final period, Green pulled in a 12-yarder from Gordy and Garner tacked on the PAT. Magee led in first downs (15-10), rushing (160-117) and passing (156-29). More importantly, Magee had a playoff berth regardless of the outcome the following week.

GAME 10: MAGEE (8-1) vs MENDENHALL (9-0)
MAGEE 3 MENDENHALL 14
November 4, 1988

Up in Mendenhall, things sat similar to the previous season. Coach Neil Hitchcock came into that rivalry game 8-1 before going on to win the 3A championship. Now, he had 14 lettermen back from that Tiger team. *"I think my biggest concern this season is whether or not we can accept the challenge of being defending state champs. It's going to be a battle every week because all of our opponents will be shooting for us"*. For this game, he said *"Magee is a very well-coached, very disciplined team. They don't beat themselves. We've got our work cut out for us"*. The Trojans now sat 17th in the AP poll while Mendenhall was 9th in The Super 10.

In a rainy battle for the Wally Beach Trophy, it was Magee first on the board with Garner's 28-yard FG. His next attempt in the 2nd quarter from the Mendy 22 was unsuccessful and halftime sat 3-0. A Trojan miscue in the 3rd via a fumble at their 1-yard line was erased when Mendy fumbled it right back. But Magee put it on the ground again three plays later to set up Mark Johnson's 3-yard blast to put it 6-3. The Trojans moved the football in response to the Mendy 4-yard line, but it ended in another missed FG attempt.

In the final quarter, the Tigers put the game away with a 45-yard march ending in Cory Lott's 8-yarder. Their 2-point play on a pass from Maurice Norwood to Chris Funchess put the nail in the grudge-match coffin. Mendenhall led in first downs (12-8) and rushing (186-47) while Magee held the air attack (82-2). In all, there were four lost fumbles and an interception.

Said Wright, *"We had our chances to win the game and didn't. Mendenhall did"*. Added Hitchcock, *"Both teams played hard. Magee was extremely well-coached and all of the boys, both teams, played just as hard as they could. I am very proud of our boys"*.

GAME 11: MAGEE (8-2) @ POPLARVILLE (8-2)
MAGEE 21 POPLARVILLE 7
November 11, 1988: PEARL RIVER JUNIOR COLLEGE

The Hornets were 15-3A champions with losses only to Hancock North Central and Forrest County AHS. Coach Pat Morris' team had outscored opponents 260-63 thus far and had just defeated Perry Central 42-9. Picking Magee 17-14, The Hattiesburg American said that *"Poplarville might be able to pull this one out with its ability to run and throw, but it won't be easy"*.

A Poplarville fumble in the opening quarter set up Magee's first score; that an 8-yard Green run and Garner kick. Defenses held to make intermission just 7-0. However, Magee put up more points quickly when Green *"took a pitch from the center and raced 82 yards before anyone knew he had the ball"*. Both teams hit the board in the 4th quarter. Magee got in on an 8-yard

Smith dart while the Hornets crossed on a 32-yard Melvin Henry throw to Don Butler. Arthur Poole provided the last point.

Green rushed for 106 yards of Magee's 175 yards, Allen pulled in 60 yards via the pass, and Gordy (playing with a broken hand) threw for 88 yards. *"Poplarville played a good ball game. We changed our offensive strategy for the second half and that helped us"*.

GAME 12: MAGEE (9-2) vs PHILADELPHIA (UNREPORTED)
MAGEE 21 PHILADELPHIA 7
November 18, 1988

Despite numerous erroneous reports, Magee's next opponent was Philadelphia instead of Kosciusko. Said Wright about the Tornadoes, *"On film, they are very fast and run the veer option offense"*. As for injuries, he said *"We are healthy"*. This marked the first meeting between the two teams; both ending regular season as runner-up in their divisions.

The first score came in the 2nd quarter after a Philadelphia interception. They moved 59 yards with Wayne Kelly finding Terry Houston from 25 yards and Bruce Thames converting for a 7-0 lead. Back came Magee with an 87-yard drive ending in Garner's 2-yarder and his PAT. Halftime stood even 7-7. In the 3rd quarter, Magee moved all the way to the Tornado 1-yard line but couldn't get across. But on their next possession, Smith ran 43 yards to the 2-yard line and Green finished things with a 5-yarder (after a penalty). Garner's kick put it 14-7.

Philadelphia moved as far as the Trojan 15-yard line in the 4th, but could not go any further. Marty McWilliams' interception later put Magee in good position and Gordy used the gift to find Funchess from 17 yards. Again, Garner was true with the extra point. Magee led in first downs (15-11), rushing (227-162) and passing (93-39). Smith ran for 197 of those yards. *"Some mistakes hurt us, but we will work on that this week. (Our position in the playoff race) is the result of the efforts our kids and coaches. They were all very attentive and were ready to play. Winning football games is a lot of fun"*!

GAME 13: MAGEE (10-2) @ COLUMBIA (10-1)
MAGEE 16 COLUMBIA 22
November 25, 1988

The Wildcats may have had a new coach in Joey Porter, but they weren't an unknown opponent. In fact, the two had faced one-another 32 times since 1928. *"The key to Columbia right now are those three athletes they have running the football. There are no great athletes on this football team. Every one of them contributes something every week on this team. It seems like we'll have one standout who will make the big plays as far as leadership goes. Every week it's somebody else. Defense had been our strong suit. The defense has played exceptional. I'm one of those that just doesn't change things. We're going to just line up and do what we've been doing. At this time of year, that's just about all you'll see from teams"*.

The Hattiesburg American picked Columbia 24-21, saying *"These two teams have played great football all season long. Columbia's only loss was to Northeast Jones 10-6. Magee's only loss also was to Northeast Jones 14-7. In my book, that means Columbia is favored by three"*. Said Porter, *"We are excited about being here. At the beginning of the year, we set our goals to make the playoffs. I don't think we ever thought we would go this far"*.

It took only as long as the football could be kicked before Columbia had their first points. Steve Simon pulled in the boot and raced 87 yards to the end zone before fans could get their seats. The two-point conversion by Anthony Preston put it 8-0. The Trojans punched back in the frame with a 73-yard march capped by a 2-yard Smith run. Magee grabbed the halftime lead in the 2nd quarter when a stalled drive at the Columbia 9-yard line resulted in Garners 26-yard FG and 9-8 lead.

Columbia had the only tally of the 3rd quarter courtesy of Phillip Holloway's 14-yard burst up the middle, and both found paydirt in the final frame. The heart-breaker for Magee came when Calvin Newsome grabbed a 77-yard pick-six untouched. The two-pointer by Holloway made it 22-9. The Trojans came back with 3:56 left on a 71-yard drive in only 5 plays. Gordy's 40-yard strike to Funchess crossed the goal and Garner booted what would be the final point of the 1988 season. A last-gasp glimmer was snuffed on a touched-punt turnover.

Stats differ depending on the source. But Magee led in first downs (15-9) and passing (155-21) while barely losing the ground (123-120). The Magee Courier had rushing (114-91) and passing (176-20). Smith was the leading ball-carrier for Magee with 91 yards. Said Porter of Magee, *"I'll tell you, they're the best football team we've played all year. No doubt about it"*. Added Wright, *"They scored seven points and we gave them 14. We lost the ball game because we gave away points on errors, not because Columbia whipped our tails. But take nothing away from Columbia. They controlled the ball and contained us well".*

All Division 5-3A honors went to Kyle Gordy, Amie Green, Chaucer Funchess, Daniel Rice and Napoleon Sharble. Mendenhall beat Amory 14-7 in a rematch for the 3A title.

1989 (15-0) 3A STATE CHAMPIONS

Second-year Coach Lum Wright, Jr. would have to work hard to better his inaugural season. Despite the loss of 20 seniors, he said *"I feel like if you play or coach football in Magee, you have to shoot to be one of the best teams in the state of Mississippi. If our young people come along like I expect they will, then we should be just as good as we were last year. Overall, we have more athletic talent, but it's inexperienced"*.

As for the season outlook, he said *"For us to go 10-0 would mean the ball would have to take a lot of positive bounces in our favor. I don't think that any team in our district can go undefeated without a certain degree of luck because the competition is so intense. However, my kids will be prepared in every possible way so that when the ball bounces our way, we will be able to take advantage of it. This team will be fundamentally sound and that's what it takes to win games. If we can work together as a team, there's no telling where we could end up at the end of the season"*.

In their 11-3A division, the red and gray were picked 2nd behind Mendenhall; a rival team who had become perineal championship attendees of late.

GAME 1: MAGEE (0-0) @ COLLINS (0-0)
MAGEE 28 COLLINS 14
September 1, 1989

The green and white had a new mentor in ex-Vicksburg legend Jim Sizemore. But he knew that his inaugural season would be tough with 22 letter-winners lost from a 2-8 season. He was definitely expecting a rebuilding season. *"I'm not even sure we know how to practice. This first year, we're going to lay a foundation and get the work habits correct and get them pointed in the right direction. Any victories this year is kind of like the old saying: icing on the cake"*.

Despite an opening-drive interception deep in Tiger territory and a failed 30-yard FG, Magee came back in the 2nd quarter with a 1-yard Tony Bullock dive and his first-of-four extra points. That slight lead held through intermission. Bullock increased the lead afterwards on a 2-yarder and then, after a Sedrick Durr interception, Tony Smith shook off tacklers for a 23-yard tally. They could have made it more, but a fumble at the Collins 7 ended the opportunity.

Still in the period, Smith notched the last Trojan score with a 1-yarder. Collins came back in the final frame with a pair of scores against Magee reserves. The first was a 12-yard Larry Manning or Nario Owens reception from Kevin Conner while the last was a 42-yard Darryl Simmons escape. Hathorne converted on both PATs. Smith rushed for 142 yards, while Marty McWilliams led in tackles. *"We moved the ball pretty good, but did not execute well while in scoring position. We had too many turnovers. The score could have been 21-0 at halftime. We have a long way to go"*.

GAME 2: MAGEE (1-0) vs HEIDELBERG (1-0)
MAGEE 28 HEIDELBERG 0
September 8, 1989

The Oilers opened the year with a win, but were still expected to bring up the rear in 11-3A. The Hattiesburg American thought the Trojans slightly better for this tilt 22-6 and the prediction wasn't far off. Magee started as if they would run away with the game; scoring twice in the opening quarter. First was a 67-yard drive capped by Bullock's 3-yard plunge. They then went 56 yards with Bullock escaping from 32 yards. With his extra points, it was 14-0.

Two fumbles thereafter kept the game unchanged until the final quarter. Smith added a 17-yard scamper and Marcus Hayes provided the PAT. Durr then picked off an errant Oiler throw and took it to the Heidelberg 13-yard line. Randy Pace then hit Shelby from 11 yards and Hayes converted to seal things. Smith put up 109 yards on the ground while the defense limited the Oilers to just one first down and 37 total yards.

GAME 3: MAGEE (2-0) @ RALEIGH (1-1)
MAGEE 36 RALEIGH 9
September 15, 1989

Like Heidelberg the previous week, Raleigh had never beaten a Magee football team. This year, they were picked 3rd in the division behind Magee and Mendenhall. Unlike the past week, this one would never be in doubt. Durr started things with a long interception return off of Johnny Evans to set up Shelby's 2-yard plunge and the first of 4 Bullock kicks. An errant snap on the next Lion possession went out of the end zone for a safety.

In the 2nd quarter, and after a 25-yard Chris Dukes FG, Smith took handoff 61 yards to paydirt to make it 15-3. Next, Pace outran defenders for a 35-yard score to put halftime 22-3. Smith opened the 3rd quarter with a 43-yard scoring scamper. The game wrapped up with an 80-yard Trojan drive topped by Pace's 20-yard strike to Shelby. Raleigh added their lone touchdown afterwards on a 24-yard Earnest Barber run.

Raleigh led in first downs (6-5) while Magee led on the ground (173-89) and the air (74-66). Those stats came from The Smith County Reformer. Smith had 136 rushing yards, while Kevin Jackson, Hayes, Kris Mangum, James Cockrell, Chuckie Allen and Durr led tacklers.

GAME 4: MAGEE (3-0) vs NORTHEAST JONES (0-3)
MAGEE 49 NORTHEAST JONES 14
September 22, 1989

The black and gold under Coach Carlton Dillard had a dilemma. He lost 19 lettermen from a 6-4 team and brought back only 6 letter-winners. Said he, *"Everybody, including the assistant coaches, has been working really hard. Everyone has a real positive attitude"*. Magee was now up to 20th in the AP. And much like previous week, it would be over early.

Magee scored twice in the opening frame; the first on a 34-yard Shelby dash and the next on a 13-yard Smith run *"up the middle"*. Bullock added his first of 7 extra points. They matched that in the next quarter on Smith runs of 7 and 55 yards to put halftime 28-0. Jones started the 3rd quarter with a bad punt snap that caused the punter to be downed by a host of Trojans. Pace then hit Shelby from 22 yards for a touchdown. NEJ avoided the shutout in the final frame first on an 18-yard double-reverse David Holifield run and Rex Cooley PAT.

With Trojan reserves in play, Magee still answered with Mickey Berry's 15-yard dash. Back came NEJ with a 60-yard march and Holifield 16-yard TD, but Magee had the last points when Karrell Dampeer escaped defenders from 34 yards away. Smith, a Clarion-Ledger Star of the Week, put up 128 rushing yards while Pace threw for 91 more. Hayes led tacklers with 5 solo and 5 assists. *"(We are) improving each week. We are gaining experience every week and we are looking forward to the game next week..."*

GAME 5: MAGEE (4-0) vs WEST JONES (3-1)
MAGEE 35 WEST JONES 9
September 29, 1989

Coach Mike Taylor, now in his 14th season at West Jones, had reason to be wary early of his green and white team. They had gone only 2-8 the previous year and had only 10 lettermen and 28 players nearing the start of the season. Still he said, *"We're going to be young and exciting. We'll work hard and play hard. The kids have a good attitude. If we can stay healthy, then we can be successful. We'll be in the hunt if we hustle and do things right"*.

But by game day, the Mustangs (10th) were ranked ahead of Magee (14th) in the AP Poll. Said Taylor, *"Magee's got a good football team. They always have a good football team"*. Added Wright, *"They are winning and they will give us some problems. (It's not the formation, but) the athletes that bother me. This will be our first true test. We'll find out what kind of team we have this Friday. We really haven't had to play anyone yet"*. The Hattiesburg American thought it 28-21 for the Trojans.

A steady rain kept the first quarter scoreless. Early in the next, the Mustangs grabbed the lead on a 23-yard Stan Holifield FG. Not long after, Darrin Ulmer was sacked by a host of Trojans in the end zone for a safety. Magee then marched 45 yards with Smith notching the last 5 yards for the score and 8-3 halftime advantage. Magee turned up the heat in the 3rd quarter after falling on another Ulmer fumble. Shelby found the end zone from 20 yards and Bullock converted.

Then, Bullock picked off an ensuing Ulmer pass and took it the necessary 40 yards to daylight. With the PAT, it was now 22-3. In the final quarter, Pace hit Allen from 7 yards for the touchdown. Recovering another Mustang fumble, Pace found Hayes from 10 yards and, with

Hayes' PAT, made it 35-3. As the game neared the whistle, West Jones drove to their touchdown with Ulmer hitting Renard Harper from 22 yards out. First downs (11-5), rushing (119-80) and passing (82-28) went to Magee.

GAME 6: MAGEE (5-0) @ SOUTH JONES (4-1)
MAGEE 7 SOUTH JONES 0
October 6, 1989

Coach Jack Thompson's red and blue were picked tops in their division, thanks in part to their 10-2 record from the previous season. This year, the Braves had 10 returning lettermen after losing 19 to graduation. Said he, "*I haven't got a clue about this team. They don't show much emotion at practice. We've lost a lot of players, but we've got some that will hit you. We'll just have to see what happens*". What had happened was that they had lost only to Laurel 14-0 while outscoring opponents 96-28. While The Hattiesburg American picked the Trojans (8th AP) 13-12 over the Braves (14th), The Clarion-Ledger picked South Jones.

South Jones put a scare into Magee with an opening drive that moved to the 1-yard line. But the defense stood strong and held them out of the end zone. A 2nd quarter bad snap was recovered by Magee deep in Brave territory, but the 32-yard FG failed. However, on their next possession, Dampeer and Allen hooked up from 20 yards out for the score. Bullock's PAT would unknowingly add the final point of the night. A late drive by Jones before halftime ended when Dampeer picked off a throw at the 2-yard line.

The Braves moved again into Trojan territory, reaching the 11-yard line. But Allen's interception thwarted that threat. Again they began a drive before yet another interception by Dampeer. Magee could have scored once again from 7 yards out as the game ended, but decided to take a knee instead. First downs (13-6) and passing (128-45) favored South while Magee held the ground (106-63).

GAME 7: MAGEE (6-0) vs KOSCIUSKO (5-1)
MAGEE 35 KOSCIUSKO 7
October 13, 1989: HOMECOMING

There had been only two games between the teams in the history of the programs. The first was a Magee loss in 1940. The last was a win in 1984 to give Magee the 3A title. This edition of Whippet football was a team coming off of a 9-3 season with 18 lettermen and 13 starters back. Said Coach Jeff Terrill, "*We want our kids to play hard and for us to turn into a good football team by the end*". Magee, now 7th in the AP, was picked by The Hattiesburg American winners 28-6. Counting this contest, the last three Trojan opponents entered the games a combined 12-3.

Magee jumped out of Kosciusko early and continued the pressure through three quarters of play. An early Allen interception set up an 8-yard Shelby touchdown while Bullock picked off another shortly after. Smith turned that into a 34-yard scoring run. Kosy fumbled in the 2nd quarter and Magee used it to go 65 yards with Smith going in from 18 yards. The two-pointer by Dampeer made it 21-0. Before intermission, Magee moved 47 yards with Dampeer and Bullock hooking up for a 35-yard tally. Bullock's kick was true.

A Whippet interception by Steve Brantley killed a 3rd quarter threat, but Magee added a score in the final frame on Dampeer's 19-yard throw to Allen and Bullock's PAT. Kosciusko avoided the whitewash afterwards on a 69-yard drive with Shane Pullen getting in from the 1-yard line. Eugene Harmon notched the PAT. Dampeer threw for 107 yards and Smith rushed for 161 markers. The defense held Kosy to just 21 rushing yards.

GAME 8: MAGEE (7-0) @ MORTON (5-2)
MAGEE 20 MORTON 3
October 20, 1989

After playing each other every year since 1945, the rivalry had taken a break between 1985-1988. Now, the Panthers were back on the slate. Morton was predicted to win their division this season. The Clarion-Ledger picked Magee 32-17, saying "*Magee has a great team and Morton has a great back. The match between Morton's Michael Davis against a rugged Trojan defense should be interesting*".

Morton used a tremendous amount of clock in the opening quarter and actually found the end zone. But a holding penalty brought it back and they settled for a 35-yard Pete Porter FG. They made another move to the Trojan 13-yard line but failed on a fourth-down run. Magee used the stand to their advantage, with Dampeer hitting "*a streaking*" Shelby for a 55-yard touchdown in the 2nd quarter. McWilliams' PAT kick made it 7-3. Now in the 4th quarter, Magee drove 86 yards with Shelby scoring *"standing up"* from 10 yards out. After stopping Morton at the Trojan 17-yard line, Magee moved the other way and capped the march with Smith's 14-yard escape and McWilliams' PAT.

The defense held Davis to just 65 yards on the ground. Dampeer threw for 185 yards while Smith ran for 86 more. *"When you are number 5 in the state, you have to battle, battle, battle because everyone wants to beat you. Morton has a good football team and we had to play 48 minutes of football to beat them"*.

GAME 9: MAGEE (8-0) vs WAYNE COUNTY (5-3)
MAGEE 37 WAYNE COUNTY 7
October 27, 1989

Though not frequent, a Waynesboro team had been on the schedule since the first year Magee fielded a team. The Trojans were 2-1 over the last three years against them. The War Eagles had just pulled a 15-6 upset over Hancock North Central the week before and now made the trip to Simpson County. Magee sat 6th in the AP with three larger 6A schools above them (Warren Central, Pearl and Meridian) each having one loss.

The home team was now hitting its stride and was quick to establish the lead. They moved 74 yards on their second possession with Dampeer finding Shelby from the 9-yard line. Allen then picked off an Eagle pass and Dampeer turned it into a 19-yard strike to Allen. Berry's two-point conversion put it 14-0. After a penalty nullified a Wayne County touchdown, Magee drove 83 yards with Dampeer and Kris Mangum connecting from 21 yards. McWilliams' PAT made it 21-0. A Pace interception before intermission kept it the same.

In the 3rd, a bad punt snap went out of the end zone to give Magee a safety. Dampeer and Mangum turned the next possession into a 10-yard touchdown and McWilliams put it a commanding 30-0. Wayne County then got their only score on a 75-yard drive and Thomas Smith 34-yard touchdown run. Chris Pitts' kick was good. Magee's finale came on a 64-yard drive capped by Roy Rigsby's 8-yarder and McWilliams' kick. Dampeer threw for 194 yards on the evening. Magee led offensively 480-343 in yardage.

GAME 10: MAGEE (9-0) @ MENDENHALL (8-1)
MAGEE 13 MENDENHALL 10 (OT)
November 3, 1989

Regardless of the records, which were almost always phenomenal, this one usually carried more importance. The bragging rights were high, but so was the race for home-field playoff position. Mendenhall, two-time defending 3A champions, was pre-season number 1 in 3A and picked 1st in the division. By kickoff, Magee sat one position (6th) ahead of Mendy in the AP poll. Picking Magee 21-20, The Clarion-Ledger said that *"This might be the best rivalry in the state. Both teams are usually good. Real good. These teams have dominated the 3A championship game with one getting there six of the eight years since the playoffs were resumed"*.

The game went just as everyone on both sides of the stadium thought it would. Except for one play; that being the first from scrimmage for the home-standing Tigers. Cory Lott took the pigskin from Darrell Benson, *"broke free into the Magee secondary and was off to the races on a 63-yard touchdown run"*. Brandon Barlow's PAT put them up with just :39 off of the clock. The remainder of the quarter gave both teams opportunities. A Tiger fumble was recovered by Magee, but a bad snap by the Trojans gave Mendy life. Additionally, a 29-yard McWilliams FG attempt was wide-right.

Before halftime, Mendy had picked off a Trojan pass to dodge yet another bullet. Now in the 3rd quarter, Bullock recovered a Tiger fumble. It took four plays before Dampeer hit Allen from 5 yards out and McWilliams' toe provided the tying point. Lott found a loose Magee football in the final frame but the visitor's defense held at the Magee 24-yard line. The end of regulation showed both teams knotted at seven. Mendy had the first crack in overtime, settling for a 26-yard Barlow FG. Magee's response was one of the lucky bounces Wright had foreseen before the season. Pace, now in for Dampeer, tossed a pass to Mangum but it bounced into the waiting hands of Allen in the end zone for the game-winner.

Both teams had turned the ball over four times. First downs (6-4) and passing (113-0) went to Magee while Mendy led in rushing (168-60). Said Neil Hitchcock, *"We made too many mistakes. You can't make those kinds of mistakes. I lost this one"*.

GAME 11: MAGEE (10-0) vs FRANKLIN COUNTY (6-3)
MAGEE 35 FRANKLIN COUNTY 14
November 10, 1989

Magee had never faced a Franklin County program in their history, and their opponent would come to Simpson County to face a red-hot, undefeated team. The Trojans had also moved to number 10 in The Clarion-Ledger Super 10 and sat 2nd in 3A polling. The Hattiesburg American thought Magee best 27-10.

Bulldog hopes of moving further were put to rest fairly early. An Allen interception set up a 91-yard drive with Dampeer notching the last 13 yards and McWilliams kicking his first of five extra points. Their next move came in the 2nd quarter with Smith finishing a 47-yard drive from 5 yards out. In the 3rd quarter, they padded the lead with two scores. Smith got in from the 15-yard line and the 12-yard line to set up reserves for entry into the contest.

Mark Patterson's interception of a FCHS pass allowed Curtis Hayes a 7-yard reception from Dampeer for their final points. The Dogs put up two touchdowns in the frame afterwards. Arthur Jackson's fumble recovery of teammate Shane Mann's (or Arthur Sykes') drop was taken the necessary 22 yards while Robbie Pernell rushed in from 10 yards later. Smith led rushers with 160 yards. Magee led in first downs (17-12), rushing (237-197) and passing (78-25).

GAME 12: MAGEE (11-0) @ PEARL RIVER CENTRAL (7-3)
MAGEE 32 PEARL RIVER CENTRAL 0
November 17, 1989

The first-time team from Carriere had earned their playoff entry as runner-up in 16-3A. In their last contest, they bested Newton 45-14. In the end, it would be no contest.

A deep 1st quarter drive ended with a Trojan fumble, but Allen got it back in the form of an interception to race 15 yards to paydirt. Another fumble deep on their next possession did no damage as the defense held at midfield. One play later, Smith "*hit the Pearl River defense like a lightning rod on a 48-yard touchdown run*" to make it 13-0. Then, Bullock grabbed an errant Blue Devil pass and Dampeer counted it on a 21-yard strike to Berry. The 19-0 advantage held through halftime.

Pearl River's 3rd quarter drive got only to the 8-yard line before being stopped. Magee would go on later to march 70 yards with Dampeer finding Smith for a 41-yard tally. Finally, in the last period, Dampeer found Smith again from 11 yards and the PAT ended scoring. Jason Rankin picked off the final effort to run out the clock for Magee. Smith had 77 yards on the ground. First downs (12-10) and rushing (114-37) went to Magee while passing was even (171-171).

GAME 13: MAGEE (12-0) vs WEST MARION (11-1)
MAGEE 41 WEST MARION 8
November 24, 1989

Another brand of Trojans now filled Magee's schedule for the first time. Their opener had been a loss to East Marion, but they had gone on to win each of the other games thus far. They were not in the best shape after their 18-10 win over Kosciusko, with three starters out with injuries. Said Coach Perry Coggin, "*Kosciusko was so big, they just physically annihilated us. When you've got only 29 kids on the team and you lose three starters, it hurts you really bad*". The Hattiesburg American picked Magee 21-13.

The result, therefore, was probably predictable. Shelby's 8-yard run and McWilliams' PAT put Magee up 7-0, but shockingly not for long. West Marion's Derek Daniels picked off a Dampeer pass at the 18-yard line and took it the distance. Walter Husband's two-point pass to Tracey Blansett put them up 8-7. A center-snap to Smith caught West Marion off-guard and Smith "*rambled 36 yards before the surprised defense caught him*". Smith finished the effort a few plays later from 37 yards and McWilliams made it 14-8.

Magee added another 6 points before halftime on a 52-yard march topped by Dampeer's 15-yard toss to Allen. In the 3rd quarter, they drove 77 yards with Dampeer doing the honors from a yard out. Then, a Durr pickoff set up Smith's 25-yard effort and McWilliams converted. Finally, in the last quarter, they moved 79 yards with Berry darting in from the 33-yard line and McWilliams booting the PAT. Magee rushed for 347 yards with Smith grabbing 199 of them.

"Our defense has played well all year. Tonight our kids came back and held them. I made a bad call (on the West Marion pick-six) and put the offense in a deep hole. Our guy threw the interception. That was my call. That was a bad error on my part".

GAME 14: MAGEE (13-0) vs MENDENHALL (11-2)
MAGEE 16 MENDENHALL 14
December 1, 1989

Nothing much needs to be said about this matchup. Magee had squeezed by Mendenhall 13-10 less than a month before in overtime. But Mendenhall had still made the playoffs and had bested Forrest County AHS 41-8 the previous week to set up the re-match. If it were even possible, this game was bigger than the last. The Hattiesburg American thought it tough to beat the Tigers twice in a season and picked them 13-10.

With 7,000 fans crowding Trojan Field, the game proved to be just as exciting as the first meeting. Smith brought home fans to their feet on the first drive with a 52-yard escape to the end zone and McWilliams knocked home the PAT. Kenny Miller gave Mendy hopes in the 2nd quarter with an interception of Dampeer. But, their drive to the Trojan 20-yard line ended on fourth down by the solid Magee defense to keep halftime 7-0. Magee padded the lead in the 3rd quarter by driving 83 yards with Dampeer arching a 16-yard aerial to Allen for the touchdown. The PAT was blocked.

Now in the frenzied final quarter, the Tigers began their comeback. They drove 55 yards with Cory Lott crashing in from a yard out and Brandon Barlow converting. Magee promptly fumbled the ensuing kickoff and Mendy was there to grab it. Lott *"went over the top for the one-yard touchdown"* and Barlow's toe put it 14-13. With the season in the balance, and with 2:33 remaining, Magee wound up a 74-yard drive with a 32-yard McWilliams FG to grab the 16-14 lead. Allen sealed the night with an interception of a desperation pass.

First downs were even at 11 each. Mendy led in rushing (159-153) while Magee held the air (99-62). Each team picked off a pass while Magee had the lone fumble. Smith rushed for 132 markers. Said Hitchcock afterwards, *"They're a good team and good teams make the plays when they have to. We didn't play football for four quarters"*.

GAME 15: MAGEE (14-0) vs ROSEDALE (12-2)
MAGEE 7 ROSEDALE 6
December 8, 1989: CLINTON, MS

In 1985, the Rosedale Eagles had beaten Magee 28-14 to rob them of what would have been their 12th championship title. Magee was 12-1 while Rosedale was a perfect 13-0. The only other meeting had been in 1981 where Magee won 12-8. Now the two teams met again at Robinson-Hale Stadium (Mississippi College) in Clinton. Coach Leland Young's team had lost only to Leland (7-6) and Pascagoula (12-7) this season. For the seventh-straight year, a Simpson County team would be competing for the state championship.

Young, a 22-year mentor in Rosedale, noted that a victory *"would take a miracle. It'd be great to start and end the '80s with a championship. We want to. I just don't know if we can or not. I don't want to scare them. We can't find any weaknesses. Their coaches have done an excellent job that that bunch"*. The Eagles had won the title three times in the 1980s. Added Wright, *"I think we have to play good defense. You can tell they are well-coached. They haven't made too many mistakes at all"*. The Clarion-Ledger picked Magee 28-24.

It was 30 degrees and muddy in Clinton on championship night. Magee looked to strike early on a Bullock interception and return to the 19-yard line, but it went for naught. But on their next drive, they moved 56 yards in 7 plays with Smith diving in from a yard away. McWilliams' PAT proved to be their final point of the season. An early 3rd quarter fumble to Melvin Jackson got the Eagles later to the Magee 7-yard line. Two plays later, Ward Gilbert evaded Trojans for their only score. The crucial PAT by Calvin Brooks was unsuccessful. Magee could have scored twice more, but fumbled at the Rosedale 15-yard and 2-yard lines. Bullock put the dagger in any come-from-behind threats with a pair of sacks.

Smith rushed for 101 yards on the evening. Magee led in first downs (13-6) and rushing (225-48) while Rosedale held the air (40-13). While the perfect 15-0 wasn't the first for a Simpson County team (see Mendenhall in 1988), it did mark a milestone for Magee football. Four teams (1960, 1962, 1963 and 1965) had gone undefeated. But all ended just 11-0. Said Coach Young, *"They controlled the ball all night. It was just hard to tackle them. They were wet and muddy and strong. They just broke away from us"*.

Wright told reporters afterwards, *"It might be more than we can stand. That (undefeated record) might be more pressure (than) if we had had a pretty good season. It's going to be hard to run out there in September. I don't know if we did anything special on offense. We lost our throwing game early. That's been a big part of our offense. They lined up in that eight-man line and got after us. We ran the same running game we've had all year. We didn't add anything for this game. The kids started winning and kept improving and never gave up; never quit*".

At season's end, Wright was named Coach of the Year by The Mississippi Association of Coaches. The banquet for the team was held in the Magee Middle School cafeteria with Joe Lee as emcee and Terry McMillan as speaker. Tony Smith, Marty McWilliams, Kevin Jackson and David McLean were named permanent team captains.

The first-team SAC members included Smith, McWilliams, Jackson, McLean, Travis May, Chuckie Allen and James Cockrell. Second teamers were Sedrick Durr, Roy Rigsby, Tony Bullock, Randy Pace and Bob Curtis. Division All-Stars included Jackson, McWilliams, Bullock, Cockrelll, McLean, May, Smith and Allen.

Other award winners were Pace (Scholastic), Cockrell and Pace (Achievement), May (Most Consistent), Jackson (Game Performance), McWilliams (Headhunter), Jackson (Defensive Lineman and Mr. Trojan), McLean (Offensive Lineman), Allen (Most Valuable Defensive Back), and Smith (Most Valuable Offensive Back). Trainer Lynn Boardman and team doctor Frank Wade were also recognized.

1990-1999

1997 Team (14-1): 3A State Champions

1990 (5-6)

Lum Wright, Jr. came into his third season at Magee picked tops in 11-3A and 9th (AP) with 20 letter-winners. And even though he had 5 offensive and 6 defensive starters back, he wasn't as optimistic after a 15-0 season. *"You try to tell them that even though last year's team had a lot of success, this year will be different. I've told them that before every practice. I feel like we don't have the depth on offense and we're going to have to use some sophomores before the season is over to come in and help us"*.

After some of those practices, his view hadn't changed. *"During the spring, our kids didn't look as good as we should have. I don't know if it was because of the (streak), but we weren't solid and we are not now. But when we open up, we have the chance to be a very good football team. I used to wish the expectations weren't as high. But maybe when they are, we will work a little harder to reach those goals. If we drag our tails, we won't win against a lot of the teams on our schedule"*.

GAME 1: MAGEE (0-0) vs COLLINS (0-0)
MAGEE 13 COLLINS 26
August 31, 1990

Picked fourth in 4-3A after a 4-6 season, Jim Sizemore's green Tigers were hoping to improve with 7 offensive starters back. *"We're going to be better, but so is everybody else"*. The Hattiesburg American called it 20-14 for Magee, noting *"People are saying that the Collins Tigers are a 3A dark horse this season. If the Tigers knock off Magee, the 3A defending state champions, they'll be more than a dark horse. They'll be a legitimate contender"*. Added Wright, *"If we lose, it makes for a long season trying to-regroup and gather ourselves. We have to be ready and hyped to play Collins"*.

It would be an unfortunate opener to the 1990 season after winning four-straight in the series. The last lid-lifter lost by the Trojans was 1983 against Brookhaven 15-0. The Tigers held a 26-0 lead at halftime in what appeared to be a runaway contest. They had a 12-yard Darrell Simmons pass to Larry Manning or Byron Watson and Simmons 66-yard bomb to Manning (or Simmons) in the opening frame to make it 12-0. In the next, they put up a 19-yard Curtis Magee dash and Simmons' 60-yard punt return and two-point conversion pass to Jason Graves.

Magee's only response came with a pair of 3rd quarter scores on Mickey Berry's 6-yard run and Kris Mangum's 9-yard reception from Karrell Dampeer. Tony Bullock converted the first of the point-after attempts. Magee actually led in first downs (10-4) and passing (109-88) while losing rushing (113-95). Said Sizemore, *"This was a super win for our program. But it's like I told the kids after the game. If Magee is 9-1, then we have reason to be excited. If they are 5-5, then we don't. We're not trying to get too excited about it"*.

GAME 2: MAGEE (0-1) @ HEIDELBERG (1-0)
MAGEE 34 HEIDELBERG 0
September 7, 1990

In the all-time four meetings since 1986, Magee hadn't lost to the Oilers. This year, they were picked 3rd in their division, and Magee was trying to recover from a devastating opener. Though the opening quarter was scoreless, the Trojans began to turn it on before intermission.

With 4:29 left, Bullock romped in from 22 yards out and converted on his PAT. Dampeer then hit Mangum from 9 yards with :15 left to make it 13-0. Dampeer added another in the 3rd quarter on a 4-yard run and two-pointer, while in the final quarter, Bullock raced in from the 3. The two-pointer to Mangum was good. With just 7:00 left, Roy Rigsby dove in from a yard away for the final tally.

Magee rushed for 226 yards and passed for 75 more. Bullock ran for 159 yards and pulled 35 yards. *"We aren't executing. We missed several third down plays and some fourth-and-one situations. I feel like the personnel we changed around made a big difference. I feel the seniors came forth Friday night. They made the big plays. But more than anything, we got back to being that 'common' football team concerned with winning; not trying to stay on top"*.

GAME 3: MAGEE (1-1) vs RALEIGH (2-0)
MAGEE 27 RALEIGH 6
September 14, 1990

Picked last in the division, and never having defeated Magee all the way back to 1938, Wright was still wary of his opponent. *"They are a misdirection team, very similar to Collins. I imagine when they see what Collins did to us, they'll do the same and we'll have to stop that"*.

Magee jumped out with scores in each of the two opening quarters. First was a 49-yard Dampeer toss to Mangum and the next a 7-yard Bullock escape. Bullock also converted both PATs for a 14-0 advantage. The last Trojan points came in the 3rd quarter on Bob Curtis' 4-yard plunge and later from 7 yards. The last was set up by a Dampeer interception. Raleigh avoided the shutout in the final frame when Rick Barrer found Jimbo Evans from 20 yards out. Their local paper called it a Johnny Evans pass to Donnell Barnes. Magee had 13 first downs, 215 rushing yards and 163 passing.

"We played a lot better. The kids seem to have adjusted to us moving them back to other positions. (They) played extremely well against Raleigh and the guys played with a lot of intensity. There are still a few areas we will have to work on this week to improve. Physically we have good athletes. Right now the youth of our team has a lot to do with our mental attitude. We gear ourselves to be mentally ready to play Friday nights".

GAME 4: MAGEE (2-1) @ NORTHEAST JONES (0-3)
MAGEE 19 NORTHEAST JONES 0
September 21, 1990

Despite losing only 6 lettermen and having the services of 22 others back in black and gold, Coach Carlton Dillard's Tigers were picked 3rd in Division 5-4A. Perhaps that was due to the 2-7 campaign from the previous season. *"Last season we really didn't have a strength. It was just one of those years. Hopefully the players gained a lot of experience from that"*. Said Wright, *"Over the next three weeks, we have three games which will go a long way in determining what kind of season we will have"*.

Magee got most of their points in the opening frame on Dampeer's 10-yard dash, a Bullock PAT, and Rigsby's *"nifty 15-yard run"* with :45 left. Now in the final frame, Curtis went in from 15 yards and scoring was done. *"We did not play well as a football team. I was upset Friday night, not so much at the guys' execution, but there were times they decided they were going to play the game the way they wanted to. We have to play a team-concept in the type offense and defense we have. Everybody had to do what is called for on a given situation. I saw people doing what they weren't supposed to do and I got onto them"*.

"They have a lot of guts. They are fighters. If we can play that bad and still win, then they're fighting. We have a lot of heart. We're struggling, but we're on a three-game win streak. We have come a long way". Dane Hosey was named Player of the Week.

GAME 5: MAGEE (3-1) @ WEST JONES (3-1)
MAGEE 0 WEST JONES 7
September 28, 1990

Voted 2nd in 5-4A, Coach Mike Taylors Mustangs had 12 lettermen back while graduating 12 others. The Mustang coach said, *"We've got inexperience in some spots and we've got to find some offensive linemen. The offensive line is the main thing. We've graduated a lot of players there. We'll be adequate if we can block and improve running the football"*. Said Wright, *"I see West Jones being very physical. They bring a tremendous amount of punch on defense. We are going to have to control the line of scrimmage. They will be geared to stop us and we'll have to do some things to offset their defense."*

It was a devastating gut-punch to Magee as the green and gold took the opening kickoff and J.P. Varnell (or Marsea Jones) raced 84 yards to the end zone. Stan Holifield's PAT would be the last point scored on the night. The Hattiesburg American reported that Magee had a chance with 3:00 remaining, but Wayne Musgrove's interception killed the threat. Magee was inside the West Jones 10-yard line 3 times but could not produce points. Unbelievably, first downs (15-3), rushing (138-81) and passing (8-0) favored Magee. Terry Ducksworth had 56 of the Mustang yards.

"A break-down in the kicking game is like a break-down on defense. It's like a play from scrimmage. We didn't execute and they did. I thought we would beat West Jones. I didn't think that would be all the scoring. We dropped seven footballs. It's cut and dried. We dropped three

passes in the end zone and four in the open field on crucial third and fourth down plays. That's where you lose".

GAME 6: MAGEE (3-2) vs SOUTH JONES (4-1)
MAGEE 17 SOUTH JONES 21
October 5, 1990

Things would get no easier as the 4-1 Braves, next on the schedule, were picked first in 6-4A. Jack Thompson's red and blue finished 10-3 the previous year, one game short of the South 4A championship, with 12 lettermen back from 33 winners. *"We're just real inexperienced. We've got a lot of juniors and seniors playing and lost some real fine players from last season. These guys just didn't get much playing time... We're just going to have to work hard this season and the key is we have to maintain ball control of offense. We just need to play consistent".*

It took only twelve minutes for Magee to hold a 14-0 thanks to a 63-yard Rigsby run, a 13-yard Bullock run and Bullock's two PATs. Bullock then notched a 42-yard FG early in the 2nd quarter. After halftime, Jones' Scott Phillips rushed in from 3 yards and converted the point-after. Then, he took a punt back 60 yards to paydirt and converted to make it 17-14. The last score came on Chris Pitts' 20-yard reception from Ira Berry late in the final frame to put the game away. That culminated a 96-yard drive from the Braves. Jason Maskew converted on the point-after. Magee lost the race for first downs (12-10) and passing (72-61) but won the ground (156-77). Byron Gibson led tacklers with 12 unassisted. Bullock (81) and Rigsby (71) led rushers.

"(South Jones) did not quit. They wore us out and our kids were tired. This was another game where, when you add up statistics, we should have won. We went in ahead 17-0 at halftime and once we got on top, we just seemed to go flat. We didn't put any pressure on them and allowed them to gain momentum. We have lost the last two games with the kicking game. I have reworked and shuffled the kicking game trying to put people on the kicking team who want to play. We have not gotten a commitment from any one player who wants to come forward and be a leader of the team. We have to find someone to pay the price and make the decision to be a leader and be dedicated".

GAME 7: MAGEE (3-3) @ KOSCIUSKO (5-0)
MAGEE 7 KOSCIUSKO 41
October 12, 1990

Magee was 2-1 since 1940 against Kosy and had won the last two contests. The Whippets were picked 2nd in their district, but only by two votes to New Hope. *"(Their) offense is not complicated. We have to be able to defend but they have to be able execute. My kids still have a chance. They haven't quit on me and they've played hard. I look forward to the rest of the season. There's a lot of pressure on the coaches and the kids. There's a lot that is demanded. There are four games left. I'm not going to quit and the kids aren't either. We are going to win these last four games".*

Kosciusko apparently picked correctly for their Homecoming affair as the game was not in question before their alums. Midway through the 2nd quarter, Kelvin Gladney plunged in from 2 yards" *up the middle"* and added the PAT. After a turnover, he did it again from 4 yards out and his PAT put it 14-0. Before halftime, Dampeer hit Mark Walker from 18 yards away to cut into the lead. Bullock's PAT made it 14-7. But Kosy would go on to put up 21-unanswered points in the 3rd quarter.

Troy Nickerson ran in from 9 yards on a keeper, Gladney from 3 yards, and Chad Jackson pulled in a 30-yard toss from Nickerson. Gladney had the first and last PAT while Rodney Fuller added the one in between. Fred Adams' final touchdown in the final frame from 3 yards finished the scoring. First downs (18-9) and rushing (253-83) went to the Whippets while passing fell on the side of Magee (143-45). Said Coach Jeff Terrill, *"I consider Magee a tremendous program and I had no stretch of the imagination that we would win the way we did..."*

Said Wright, *"We have to eliminate the kind of mistakes we made. I think the three fumbles we had made the game look worse that it was. You just can't fumble the ball three times, once inside the 15 and twice inside the 5 (with) the strength and size that they have. They were the dominate team as far as size, then we let the game get blown out of proportion by making those thee big mistakes which let them score. That made it look like it was ragged game on our part. But their dominance on the offensive line was big factor in the game, too".*

GAME 8: MAGEE (3-4) vs MORTON (4-3)
MAGEE 21 MORTON 14
October 19, 1990: HOMECOMING

Long-time opponent Morton was next on the schedule for Homecoming. The Panthers had been chosen 2nd in their division pre-season to Forest by a lone vote. Thus far, the Scott County team had dropped all three of their road tilts. *"They have a good football team. I think we will match up well size-wise with them. Right now, we are a little banged up. But I think our kids will bounce back for Homecoming. By Friday night, we should be healthy and ready to go. We can't look past anyone but we have a chance to win"*. The Hattiesburg American came very close to perfection, calling it 21-17 for the Trojans.

Magee opened the game with a 3-yard Dampeer touchdown run, but Morton came right back via Stan Crotwell's (or Leonard Sanders') 25-yard strike to Andre Hollis. Both teams failed on the extra points. In the 2nd quarter, Berry gave Magee the lead again on his 2-yard run and his two-point conversion. After halftime, he pulled in a Morton punt *"en route to a nifty 65-yard return"*. Bullock's PAT marked the last Trojan point. Morton closed the gap in the final frame on Crotwell's 15-yard pass to Hollis and his two-pointer to Simpson.

The Trojans held the ground (121-44) while Morton had the air (138-88). Berry led rushers with 64 yards while Hosey led tacklers with 5. *"The kids have been down and getting back (into the win column) was a real boost. The kids came out with a lot of enthusiasm and played hard and we were successful. We were able to block them well and threw the ball a good bit. They didn't do anything we weren't ready for. Morton has a good team and they played us a good game"*.

GAME 9: MAGEE (4-4) @ WAYNE COUNTY (5-2)
MAGEE 13 WAYNE COUNTY 6
October 26, 1990

Amazingly, Magee had already clinched a playoff berth since they were 2-0 in division play. Mendenhall had solidified the other spot.
"I'm sure they (Wayne County) have seen the film of the Kosciusko game and they'll set their offensive scheme as such. Their defense does a lot of slanting in the holes and there are no patterns. We have to be able to block zones and areas. We'll throw the football Friday night. We always have". The Hattiesburg American called it a squeaker for Wayne County 14-12.

The halftime score was 7-0 thanks to a 2nd quarter 58-yard Dampeer pass to Walker and the Bullock PAT. Magee had missed an early FG courtesy of a Bobby Hogan block but had fumbled back to the Trojans later at the Magee 24. Wayne County got on the board in the 3rd quarter on a 4-yard Kevin Lofton (or

Ricky Ballard) plunge but the PAT failed. Finally, in the last quarter, Dampeer spotted Mangum from 23 yards out for the last tally. Wayne County's last chance to score ended on a fumble at the Magee 20-yard line.

Magee led 278-239 in total yardage; 145 of which came via passing. Said Coach Jim McCain, *"(Wright) just out-coached us. He really did a good job preparing for us. You have to give Magee credit. They have a good football team"*. Added Wright, *"It was really an up-and-down game. But overall I was pleased with our effort. (The game) was very tough. We matched up well size-wise with (them). But they had tremendous team speed and had skilled athletes. It was a very hard-fought game by our kids. We insured ourselves of a .500 season"*.

GAME 10: MAGEE (5-4) vs MENDENHALL (7-2)
MAGEE 7 MENDENHALL 27
November 2, 1990

The Tigers had not let up in their results despite a having new head man. With Neil Hitchcock's departure for Grenada, Mendenhall hired former Magee coach Eddie Pierce. Winning the state championship in 1987 and 1988, they had posted an 11-3 record the following season. With 10 returning starters and 22 seniors, they were tabbed tops in 11-3A pre-season. Said Pierce, *"Both of these teams will play hard. I feel we're gonna be ready and I know Lum will have his guys ready, too"*.

Wright stated that *"This is an intense series. It has a way of juggling itself out. It's been an even series through the years. The odds are against us. We're really banged up right now. We haven't looked real good, but we've won. We'll be ready to battle Friday night".* The Hattiesburg American though Mendenhall best 14-13.

A Tiger fumble midway through the 1st quarter led to Rigsby's 3-yard dive and Bullock's PAT. But it would be all Mendenhall afterwards. They came right back with Darrell Benson's 19-yard scamper and Darren Overby conversion. In the next quarter, they notched a pair of scores. First was a 29-yard Brandon Barlow pass to Benson followed by Wayne Gholar's 30-yard dash and Barlow PAT. The last score came in the final frame when Kenny Miller got into the end zone from 10 yards and Barlow converted.

"They just whipped us. They played a great game on both sides of the football. There were three plays in the ball game I felt like we gave to them. The second touchdown they scored and the fake reverse they ran, each time we had people in position but failed to make the play. And on their fake punt, we just missed the tackle. We didn't do anything offensively. (We) couldn't get the pass off. They were a better football team than we were. We are not a great football team and we just cannot give those plays away".

GAME 11: MAGEE (5-5) @ STONE COUNTY (8-2)
MAGEE 9 STONE COUNTY 42
November 9, 1990: GULF COAST CC; PERKINSTON, MS

The Trojans had faced Stone County only once before. In 1983, Magee met the Tomcats in post-season play and won 20-9. Coach Larry Easterling's team would be much tougher this time around. *"I told the kids that everything we do from here on out can only make us better and improve our record. We're really pumped up for the game and, as far as I'm concerned, if we have a chance to play, we'll play to win. They've got an extremely well-balanced game. To stop Stone, we've got to have containment on the line and we've got to gang tackle on every play".* The Hattiesburg American picked Stone County 14-7, saying *"Magee does not have the team it had last season. Stone is better".*

The opening quarter at A.L. May Stadium saw Artie Moore get away from 42 yards for Stone and Bullock nail a 33-yard FG in response to keep it 6-3. The next quarter was disastrous for the Trojans. Moore crossed from 5 yards, added a two-point conversion and then broke away from 25 yards for another touchdown. Brent Huff provided the PAT. While Curtis Hayes found paydirt for Magee from 25 yards out on a fumble return, Stone still managed another tally on Jerry Fletcher's 33-yard strike to Marcus Hinton. Huff's kick was good.

They put up touchdowns in each of the last two quarters against many younger Trojan players who were gaining valuable experience. First was a 44-yard Moore run and then Fletcher and Hinton hooked up from 40 yards. Huff provided both conversions. Moore, with 218 rushing yards, was named Hattiesburg American Prep Player of the Week. *"I thought we would probably play better than we did. We were coming off the Mendenhall loss and were not carrying any momentum into the game. We were just an average football team. They've got a good football team and just took it to us".*

The 1990 campaign finished with the Trojans notching the first losing season since 1973 and only the second since 1953. Water Valley beat Stone County 20-14 for the state championship.

1991 (10-1)

With the departure of Lum Wright Jr. for Mount Pleasant (TX) HS, former Morton mentor Johnny Mills now held the head spot in Magee. Said he, *"There is no doubt in my mind that that we're going to have a good football team. But what people need to understand is we have moved up in classification and we're going to be playing other good football teams. It's going to be a challenge. But let me tell you something about these Trojans. They are not real big but they get after you. This has been a trademark of Magee football for as long as I can remember and these guys are no different".*

While he had some key returners, he noted generally about his team *"We are still little (on the offensive line). We don't even compare with Mendenhall, Laurel and those folks. We'll run a lot of misdirection. We will do a lot of trapping and run some play action passes to keep the defenses off balance. As for the defense, I think the people around here will be real pleased with what we do in our defensive package. Our defense is going to be exciting".*

The Trojans would now be up in classification from 3A to 4A football while keeping some of the same faces on the schedule. Kris Mangum was voted as a Clarion-Ledger Dandy Dozen player.

GAME 1: MAGEE (0-0) @ COLLINS (0-0)
MAGEE 7 COLLINS 6
September 6, 1991

First-year Coach Raymond Buffington's Tigers had also made the jump from 3A to 4A, but did not share the same division as the Trojans. They had shocked Magee the previous year 26-13; one of only three wins against them since 1938. Said Mills, *"I can tell you right now it's be a battle again. I know they got the Trojans last year. We are not going to take them lightly, but this is a new year"*.

Though Magee opened the tilt with a 1-yard dive and Steven Willis conversion, it took almost no time before Rodney Hawthorne escaped Trojan defenders from 80 yards away for a touchdown. As it turned out, the critical point-after *"sailed wide"*; eventually giving Magee their season-opening win. The News-Commercial of Collins put the scoring in the opposite order. The remainder of the game was a solid defensive struggle. Mangum was voted Bank of Simpson County Player of the Week.

GAME 2: MAGEE (1-0) vs NORTHEAST JONES (0-1)
MAGEE 56 NORTHEAST JONES 20
September 13, 1991

Northeast Jones had been stymied by South Jones 32-7 in their led-lifter. They now traveled to Simpson County to see if they could put up only their fourth all-time win over Magee. Previously described as a *"powder keg"*, the Trojans finally lived up to expectations in front of home fans.

Harold Shaw's big night began immediately a with a 42-yard dash to paydirt. The Tigers responded well with a 7-yard Chris Thompson (or Michael Merrill) run and Chisholm PAT for the 7-6 lead. The rest of the frame was Magee via Karrell Dampeer's 35-yard strike to Curtis Hayes, his two-pointer to Chris Coward, and Shaw's 24-yard blast. Willis converted on the last and numerous others. Back came NEJ with a 73-yard Narrell McCann dash and Chisholm kick.

Dampeer then ran in from the 3-yard line and Shaw pulled in a 67-yard pass from Mark Walker. Now 34-14 in the 3rd, Mark Patterson blocked a Tiger punt and Dana Turner recovered for a 15-yard tally. Shaw then escaped from 34 yards out for Magee. While Northeast put up their last points in the final frame on Merrill's 2-yard run, Josh Sanders did the same from that yardage later. Willis was 7-7 on PATs and Dampeer was McDonalds Player of the Week.

"Northeast Jones is not as bad as they showed. We just did some things differently offensively and they did not adjust. Down in Collins, we weren't quite ready to do our offense from lack of time in practice because we didn't get a chance to do any two-a-day practices. Since then, we have our complete offense in and we have 15 different sets we can run our offense out of. Our guys have adjusted to our system".

GAME 3: MAGEE (2-0) @ QUITMAN (1-1)
MAGEE 35 QUITMAN 13
September 20, 1991

These two teams had played four times between 1939-1944 with Magee holding a 2-1-1 record. Mills said of his Trojans' opponent *"They have an up-and-coming program. They run the two veer option and have two extremely fast backs. I don't think they're that strong defensively (but) they are capable of beating us"*. The Hattiesburg American thought it a Magee squeaker 22-20. The Trojans were now 19th in the AP poll.

Midway through the opening period, Walker *"cut through the Panther line en-route to a 19-yard touchdown"*. Willis' conversion was the first of many. In the next quarter, Mickey Berry punched in from a yard to make it 14-0. A determined Quitman team answered with David Nelson's 60-yard dash and James Nelson's PAT. Then, Jeffrey Nelson (or Greg Smith) topped the effort with a 76-yard gallop. But the blocked PAT kept it in Magee's favor 14-13. Shortly before halftime, Berry got in from 19 yards and Willis put it 21-13.

Dampeer started the next half with a 7-yard run. Then, his pitch to Eldwyn Harvey was *"lofted downfield where Mangum out-jumped three Panther defenders, cut right, immediately cut back left and raced to the end zone for the score"*. Willis' fifth extra point was good.

GAME 4: MAGEE (3-0) vs LAUREL (1-2)
MAGEE 21 LAUREL 0
September 27, 1991

Next up for a Trojan team now ranked 8th in the Super 10 was the defending class state champion Tornadoes. But, they were now *"in jeopardy of sinking even lower unless it knocks off undefeated Magee"*. They had just notched their first win of the year the previous week with a 17-14 nail-biter against McComb. The Hattiesburg American picked the Trojans 23-20, saying *"Magee looks good; at this point better than Laurel"*.

Laurel was determined to change the course of their season; holding the Magee offense in a defensive battle for the entire first half. However, Magee broke things open in the 3rd quarter with a pair of touchdowns. First was Dampeer's 30-yard pass to Mangum while Chris Easterling claimed the next on a 1-yard Russell Ross-fumbled kick return. Willis was true on both extra point efforts. Finally, in the 4th quarter, Dampeer dove in from a yard away and Willis again converted. Laurel's best last-chance came on a drive to the Trojan 28-yard line before faltering.

"Magee's defense, which was a bend-but-don't-break style, thwarted two Golden Tornado drives; the first coming after Laurel had driven down the field only to fumble the ball out of the end zone". Magee led in first downs (7-6) and rushing (87-55) while losing the air (89-51). Laurel lost 2 fumbles while Magee gave up just one. *"We have improved game-by-game. We knew this would be a low-scoring game. Laurel has a good football team"*. Mangum was elected the McDonalds Player of the Week.

GAME 5: MAGEE (4-0) @ LONG BEACH (0-4)
MAGEE 53 LONG BEACH 0
October 4, 1991

The Trojans now moved up to 16th in the AP poll and 7th in the Super Ten and would take on first-time Mississippi Gulf Coast opponent Long Beach. The game would be a scoring fest for the road Trojans.

Touchdowns came quickly and often. First was a 65-yard Berry punt return, Shaw's 21-yarder and then Berry's 2-yard effort. Two Willis PATs made it 20-0. In the next frame, a 2-yard Johnson run, Willis PAT and his FG made halftime 32-0. One score was not reported. They continued the pressure in the 3rd quarter with a 21-yard Walker run. Finally, Allen rushed in while Tony Clements hit Easterling for the last. Mangum pulled in 82 yards of Dampeer's 87 passing markers. Berry was named Player of the Week.

GAME 6: MAGEE (5-0) @ NORTHEAST LAUDERDALE (2-3)
MAGEE 56 NORTHEAST LAUDERDALE 7
October 11, 1991

Northeast Lauderdale was also a newcomer to Magee football scheduling. Much like the previous week, it would not be close. Their 21 first quarter points came from Berry runs of 5 and 2 yards and a 1-yard Johnson dive. Willis was true on those extra points, and five more later. The first was set up by a fumble recovery. In the next frame, and after a blocked punt, Dampeer hit Mangum from 15 yards before Northeast Lauderdale garnered their only score on a 36-yard David Bararseh toss to Travis Porter and their PAT.

Magee put up another score in the 3rd quarter on Shaw's 24-yard dash, but finished the evening with three more tallies. Berry plunged in from a yard, Harvey from 2 yards and Josh Sanders from 3 yards. Like many scores before, these had been set up by fumbles. Magee led in rushing (251-94) and passing (50-35). Berry led rushers with 123 yards. Jason Yates was voted Player of the Week. It was the second time this year that Magee had put up 56 points on a team with Long Beach being only 3 points behind that feat.

GAME 7: MAGEE (6-0) vs WAYNE COUNTY (4-2)
MAGEE 40 WAYNE COUNTY 14
October 18, 1991: HOMECOMING

The Trojans now found themselves undefeated, ranked 8th in the AP poll and 6th in the Super 10. Since 1986, Magee was 4-1 against a Waynesboro squad; losing only 6-0 in 1987. The Hattiesburg American picked Magee 28-21 for the Homecoming affair.

Mangum had the only score of the opening quarter on Dampeer's 24-yard pass and the PAT. Then, a touched punt by WC put Magee at the 1-yard line and Berry dove in from there. The

War Eagles answered with a 3-yard Bobby Glover plunge and Richie Nicholson PAT to make it 14-7. Before halftime, Berry escaped defenders from 70 yards and intermission sat 21-7. Shaw then took the opening kick of the second half 96 yards to daylight. Berry would add a 9-yarder and Shaw a 55-yarder for more scores while Wayne County could only counter with a Ricky Ballard 55-yard dash and Gil Queen PAT.

Said Coach Jim McCain, "*There is no doubt in my mind at all: Magee is the best football team we have played this year. They just have it all. They did not seem to have any weakness*". WCHS led in first downs (9-8) but stats differ tremendously after. The best guess is that Dampeer threw for 96 yards and Magee rushed for 213 more. The Trojan defense held Wayne County to 156 rushing and 30 passing yards. David Warren and Harold Shaw were elected Players of the Week.

GAME 8: MAGEE (7-0) vs WEST JONES (4-3)
MAGEE 38 WEST JONES 6
October 25, 1991

The climb continued up the polls with Magee now 5th in the AP and Super 10. Unlike many opponents, West Jones had held their own historically against the Trojans. But they would find themselves out-gunned in this affair.

Magee went up 13-0 in the opening quarter on Shaw's 52-yard punt return and Dampeer's 25-yard strike to Mangum. Willis converted on the last touchdown. They did the same in before halftime on Dampeer's 14-yard throw to Mangum and Shaw's 3-yarder. West Jones had the only tally of the 3rd quarter on a 53-yard connection between Chris Wright and Monoleto Keys, but Magee answered with a pair of scores before the final whistle. Walker dodged in from a yard away while Shaw returned a punt 76 yards for his second special teams score.

"*The defense played excellent. The only time that West Jones scored was when we missed the tackle and coverage all in the same play*". West Jones had 80 passing yards and put up only 13 yards of rushing on 31 carries. Magee led in first downs (11-2) and rushed for 245 yards. Yates and Mangum led tacklers with 8 each while Harvey, Mark Patterson and Neal Warren grabbed interceptions. Mangum was named Player of the Week.

GAME 9: MAGEE (8-0) vs MENDENHALL (7-1)
MAGEE 14 MENDENHALL 0
November 9, 1991: JACKSON, MS

Like Magee, rival Mendenhall had a first-year coach on the sidelines. Former Tiger assistant Royce Foster had stepped in after Eddie Pierce went to join Jackie Sherrill at Mississippi State. They had lost 19 lettermen from an 11-3 squad but were solid at just one defeat. Said Foster, "*I have a lot of respect for those guys (Magee) and the school and the athletic program. They really have some super athletes*". As for Magee, they were now 2nd in the Super 10 and 3rd in the AP.

This marked the first game between the two teams outside of Simpson County. Mills knew it was potentially unpopular, but said "*When the stadium offered us the chance to play up there and showcase our kids, there was no doubt in my mind that was the best thing for us. These kids won't get another chance to play in that stadium...*" The Clarion-Ledger projected the potential attendance at roughly 20,000 attendees. Said Foster, "*It definitely takes away the home-field advantage. But at the same time, you can't take away the opportunity of playing in Memorial Stadium. Not many of these kids will ever have the opportunity to play (there)*".

Both teams had open dates to prepare. "*I'm optimistic, but we're being cautious. Mendenhall always has a good football team*". The Hattiesburg American called the 5-4A championship scrap for Magee 22-21 while The Clarion-Ledger predicted 26-20.

The Magee Courier said that "*Neither team played well during the first half with the score tied at zero going into the locker rooms*". But the Trojans finally started their march to dent the scoreboard with about 5:00 left in the 3rd quarter on an 11-play possession. After an 11-yard touchdown run by Shaw was called back for illegal motion, Dampeer hit Mangum for 12 yards to the Tiger 6. Berry got 3 yards and Dampeer punched it in on fourth down from there with :34 left. Mendy threatened but couldn't convert a fake punt. Now with 5:00 left in the game, Magee drove 65 yards and sealed the rivalry when Shaw "*danced into the end zone on a 17-yard carry*".

Dampeer, Player of the Week, picked off a pair of Brandon Barlow passes to claim the 5-4A title. "*We were just sitting back and waiting for something to happen. It was a big to-do playing over here. We finally got that out of us and started playing ball*".

GAME 10: MAGEE (9-0) vs PORT GIBSON (9-1)
MAGEE 21 PORT GIBSON 14
November 15, 1991

Port Gibson was led by former Magee Coach Lum Wright, Jr's father. The long-time Mississippi coaching legend was going for his 307th career win. Mills anticipated another "*tough ball game*" against Port Gibson. "*The key to (the game) is the Trojan offensive line. The defensive line will have to stop Port Gibson's running attack*". For Magee, they now had scaled the mountain and were 1st in the AP poll. "*I don't know if we're the best team in the state, but we have worked hard and improved every week. After the way things wound up last year, people were waiting to see what would happen*".

Lum Wright, Sr. had a runner (Tyrone Shorter) with 1,751 yards thus far and 22 touchdowns. But he respected the Magee program. "*Magee is a good football team. It's going to be a challenge. The offensive and defensive lines will be where the game is won or lost. We're healthy and ready to roll*". Added Mills, "*We're certainly counting on the playoff experience helping us. We had excellent senior leadership. Port Gibson is no slouch*". The Clarion-Ledger picked Magee 21-20 while The Hattiesburg American thought it larger by a 26-13 final.

Things did not look good for home-standing Magee initially as Port Gibson tallied on their first two possessions. Shorter's 11-yard pass to Keith Beasley ended an 87-yard drive with Enos Tisdale converting for the 7-0 lead. They then marched 62 yards in 13 plays. Enrico Banks' 10-yard run to the 3-yard line was fumbled, but Maurice Jackson picked it up and made the end zone. Tisdale's PAT marked what would be their final point. Later, Dampeer cut into the lead with his 33-yard dash, but Wright wasn't happy. "*I know damn well they clipped on that play. I saw two of them*".

In the 3rd quarter, the Trojans tied things 14-14 with a 65-yard drive capped by Dampeer's 38-yard toss to Shaw. The dagger for the Port Gibson squad came later when Shaw took a punt 45 yards. "*He caught the ball and backpedaled, hit the right sideline, cut back inside and headed for the flag at the left corner of the end zone*". Officials ruled him out of bounds at the 1-yard line, but Berry got in on the next play and Willis again converted. Said Wright, "*Magee has a good football team and a lot of tradition. This one is a hard one to lose. I guarantee you it hurts. Shaw is an excellent broken-field runner. He was the difference in the game*".

GAME 11: MAGEE (10-0) vs STONE COUNTY (10-1)
MAGEE 7 STONE COUNTY 14
November 22, 1991

Magee fans well-remembered the previous year when Stone County destroyed the Trojans 42-9 in the opening round of the playoffs. The Clarion-Ledger picked Magee 21-14 in the rematch but said that the Trojans "*almost didn't make it to this game. If Magee really wants to add a 4A state title to the two 3A crowns it won in 1984 and 1989, (they) can't afford to keep playing catch-up football*". The Hattiesburg American was close to The Clarion-Ledger, picking Magee 16-13.

What was perhaps unknown at the time was that Magee was unable to practice either Thursday or Friday due to a flu bug. Additionally, Dampeer had separated his shoulder. Mills noted afterwards that it "*negatively affected the Trojans' performance*".

Coach Larry Easterling's Tomcats found the end zone first in the opening frame on Pierre Monroe's 30-yard bullet to Sheldon Nelson. Brent Huff's PAT was true. Magee came back to knot the game before halftime on a 68-yard drive capped by Berry's 2-yard run and Willis' PAT. Magee's only other opportunity came after a Clements recovery of their kickoff. But Willis' 32-yard FG effort was unsuccessful. Stone County would get all they needed in the 3rd quarter, however, when Monroe found Chris Stokes from 26 yards away and Huff converted.

Magee led in first downs (10-7 or 11-9). Rushing (82-77) and passing (70-34) went to Stone County. Berry led Trojan rushers with either 97 or 75 rushing yards. Said Easterling, "*We had to tackle well and pursue well. We knew coming into the ball game we couldn't give them the big plays*". Mills added, "*It wasn't their fault. They were giving everything they had. It goes back to being sick all week. The timing wasn't there on our offense*".

Kris Mangum, pulling 640 receiving yards on the season, was named First Team All-State. Louisville beat Stone County 6-3 for the 4A title.

1992 (9-2)

Magee was in store for yet another head coach as Johnny Mills had left the Trojans early in the year to take a defensive back coaching role at Mississippi College. In his place was former Forrest County AHS mentor Perry Wheat. His 5-4A Trojans had 11 lettermen back and 13 seniors. Peers had picked Magee to finish first in the division. *"We're excited about the season and will be observing each player to determine where they can best be used. Our strong point will be our good speed in the offensive backfield, but we're inexperienced in both the offensive and defensive lines".*

GAME 1: MAGEE (0-0) vs TAYLORSVILLE (0-0)
MAGEE 26 TAYLORSVILLE 40
August 28, 1992

In 1938, Magee opened with Taylorsville and came away a 12-0 winner. The two teams had avoided each other on the gridiron for the next 53 years but now met again in Simpson County. For Wheat, it would not be the season-opener he or the overflow of fans had been anxiously awaiting.

Things did start well, however, as Harold Shaw rushed in for a 33-yard score and Steven Willis converted the PAT. Shaw then picked off a Tartar throw and raced the 18 yards to paydirt and Willis made it 14-0. The strong Taylorsville squad did not roll over; instead driving 75 yards with Gary McGill catching an Andrew Autry throw. Their fumbled PAT snap was picked up by Ted Duckworth and tossed to Autry for the two-pointer. Magee answered in the 2nd quarter with Eldwyn Harvey's 11-yard strike to Shaw to put them up 20-8. But things went horribly wrong afterwards.

Taylorsville drove 69 yards and capped it with a 4-yard McGill run. They then picked off a Harvey pass leading to another 4-yard McGill escape. A later Shaw fumble set up a 4-yard Duckworth pass to John Jennings and Autry found the end zone on the two-point play. Halftime now sat 28-20. Magee's last tally came in the 3rd quarter on Chad Grayson's 23-yard toss to Jarius Milton, but the Tartars had two more in them. First was Duckworth's 38-yard pass to Larry Campbell following later by Autry's 6-yard plunge. The last came after yet another Trojan fumble.

Shaw, a Clarion-Ledger Top Performer, rushed for 101 yards with Josh Sanders pitching in another 86 yards. Taylorsville led in first downs (19-14), rushing (199-193) and passing (145-37). Magee had 6 lost fumbles and an interception. Said Coach Bruce Merchant, *"The gambling just was doing what I felt we had to do. I've got a lot of confidence in the offense, but the defense is real young. When it showed the second half it could do the job, our confidence steadily rose".*

GAME 2: MAGEE (0-1) vs COLLINS (0-0)
MAGEE 21 COLLINS 0
September 4, 1992

First-year Coach David Abercrombie inherited a Tiger team coming off of a 4-5 season. He had lost 8 lettermen but did have the same number back. *"We need to re-establish the work ethic that was here a couple of years ago. That's what has been the problem. Pride in a team comes from winning. We hope to be competitive early, win some ball games and have some early success".* The Hattiesburg American picked Magee 21-14.

Collins' first drive pushed them to the Trojan 10-yard line but Deshaun Sim's interception thwarted the effort. Shaw made the best of it on the return drive by getting into paydirt from 15 yards out. Harvey picked off a 2nd quarter throw and Sims did the honors later from the 16-yard line. Shaw converted the two-point play and halftime sat 14-0. Though Magee moved to the 1-yard line before a 3rd quarter fumble to Shaft Booth, Shaw picked off yet another Tiger throw and ran in from 22 yards. Willis' kick ended scoring. Magee led in first downs (14-10), rushing (188-88) and passing (43-27). Sanders rushed for 100 yards on the evening.

GAME 3: MAGEE (1-1) @ NORTHEAST JONES (0-2)
MAGEE 42 NORTHEAST JONES 14
September 11, 1992

Northeast had gone a lowly 2-8 the previous campaign. Now picked 6th in 5-4A, they had a new head coach in Larry Ishee. To make matters worse, he had lost 19 letter-winners while returning only 3 starters and 7 lettermen. *"The key for us will be our younger players to come around and our being able to stay healthy"*. This game, with the Trojans up 8-3 all-time, marked the division opener for Magee.

Harvey started the onslaught by intercepting a ball at midfield to allow Grayson a 10-yard throw to Shaw and Willis' PAT. Northeast responded with Chad Chisholm's 78-yard shocker to Patera Jones but Magee blocked the point-after. As the opening frame ended, Sanders dodged in from 20 yards and Willis converted. Magee then dropped the NEJ punter at the 27 and, one play later, Sims ran in to make it 21-6. Halftime ended after Shaw's 5-yard plunge and Willis' kick.

Though Willis missed a 32-yard FG in the 3rd quarter, Shaw took their ensuing punt 61 yards to paydirt. Clements then picked off a Jones throw to set up Tremayne Williams' 3-yarder. Willis was true on both PATs. With reserves in play in the final period, Northeast drove 78 yards for a final score via Shannon Ishee's 27-yard pass to Brad Hancock. Ishee ran in for their two points. Sanders led rushers with 71 yards. Magee lost the first down race (9-8) and passing (120-83) but led in rushing (174-77).

GAME 4: MAGEE (2-1) vs QUITMAN (1-1)
MAGEE 28 QUITMAN 8
September 18, 1992

Next on the schedule was a Quitman team picked 5th in the division to start the year. For Magee, Shaw had racked up 62 points thus far on the campaign to set himself in the race for scoring leader. In this contest, it would start much slower than fans may have anticipated.

Solid defense stood out in the opening quarter as Harvey's fumble recovery at the 21-yard line killed a Quitman drive, but Magee gave it back at their 11-yard line shortly afterwards. In the 2nd quarter, Grayson found Shaw for their first tally and Willis converted his first of 4 extra points. Shaw got his next in the 3rd quarter on a 25-yard dash. *"He was pinned in against the sidelines, ... showed some Timex moves as he took a licking but kept on ticking, reversing his field, circled back to the 40 and then outran everyone untouched to the end zone"*.

Only four plays later, Corey Swain fell on a loose Quitman ball. That allowed Williams a 1-yard plunge. The visitors tallied their only points in the final frame on a 58-yard march with Shannon Wallace doing the honors from 2 yards and Maurice Evans diving in for the conversion. Late in the contest, Sanders dashed in from 24 yards to finish scoring. Swain grabbed an errant throw to seal the win. Sanders rushed for 92 yards and Sanders for 73 more. Grayson threw for 73 yards.

GAME 5: MAGEE (3-1) @ LAUREL (0-3)
MAGEE 14 LAUREL 7
September 25, 1992

Coach George Blair's Golden Tornadoes were expected to give Magee the biggest threat in 5-4A as they were picked second in the division pre-season. He had lost 12 lettermen but had 12 back for the year. *"We've always had a tough schedule in years past. The kids realize it when they come out. We'll just have to work hard and get them ready. We'll have seven or eight players going both ways. This is as thin as we've been in a long time"*. Their second all-time meeting the season before ended with a Trojan win 21-0. Despite their winless record, this one would be tighter in Jones County.

After an Anthony Fagan fumble was recovered near the Tornado 33-yard line in the opening quarter, Grayson found Shaw from 15 yards and Willis added the PAT. In the next frame, they moved 76 yards with Sanders bursting in from a yard. Again Willis was true to make halftime 14-0. A solid drive after by Laurel got to the Trojan 9 but Chad Dozier's errant throw was nabbed by Marcus Allen to kill the opportunity. Finally, in the last period, Laurel found paydirt on Dozier's 16-yard connection with Ralph Stinson. John Satcher's PAT made it 14-7, but that would be all they would get as Magee recovered the on-side kick.

Laurel led in first downs (13-11) and passing (167-142) while Magee was best on the ground (74-51). Another report had Grayson throwing for 125 markers on the night.

GAME 6: MAGEE (4-1) vs NORTHEAST LAUDERDALE (0-6)
MAGEE 57 NORTHEAST LAUDERDALE 0
October 9, 1992: HOMECOMING

The result was somewhat predictable as Magee was playing a winless team projected to finish 7th in the division; and at home. Scoring came early and often. In fact, though numerous editions of Magee football had put up over 50 points in a contest, this one sat second at the time on the all-time list. The only team with more was the 1961 squad that beat Monticello 59-0.

Shaw had the first pair of running touchdowns, Allen recovered a fumble, Clements got in from a yard and Williams grabbed a 40-yarder to make halftime 28-0. Shaw then added a 20-yard dash, Clements notched the two-pointer, Allen put in a 26-yard effort and Harvey bested it from 57 yards. In the final quarter of play, Harvey picked off a pass but Magee fumbled it right back. But, Lonnie Leggett grabbed a bad NEL throw and raced 85 yards to the end zone. Willis added the PATs except for one made by Ray Brinson.

Of note would be a 3rd quarter injury to Sanders, who *"lay motionless on the ground following a bruising tackle of a NE ball carrier"*.

GAME 7: MAGEE (5-1) @ WAYNE COUNTY (4-2)
MAGEE 35 WAYNE COUNTY 0
October 16, 1992

The War Eagles were expecting a brighter year than their 4-6 record from 1991. Coach Jim McCain lost and kept 11 letter-winners but had the services of 55 players. *"This year we have more guys who played the year before. We only lost two starters on offense"*. At 4-2, it was critical that they pull out a win over Magee to keep playoff hopes alive. Magee now sat 5th in the AP poll.

Magee quickly put this one away in just the opening quarter with 21 points. A first-play Eagle fumble led 5 plays later to Grayson's 1-yard sneak. Just four plays later, they fumbled again and Grayson hit Charles Johnson from 46 yards to make it 13-0. An ensuing kick fumble to Magee allowed Sanders a 44-yard streak to paydirt and Willis made it 21-0. That score held through halftime. Yet another War Eagle fumble to Magee in the 3rd quarter resulted in Shaw's 76-yard dash. Unbelievably, Wayne County fumbled again to Magee and Shaw made them pay to open the 4th quarter with a 2-yard plunge.

Shaw rushed for 114 yards to lead the Trojans; Grayson threw for 127; while the defense held Wayne County to just 149 yards of offensive output. They also picked off a pass while pulling in 7 of 11 War Eagle fumbles. *"Turnovers got them into trouble real quick. The turnovers went to our favor. It's part of the game"*.

GAME 8: MAGEE (6-1) @ WEST JONES (4-4)
MAGEE 21 WEST JONES 0
October 23, 1992

West Jones under seventeenth-year Coach Mike Taylor lost as many lettermen (11) as he had back. The Mustangs had put up a break-even 5-5 record the previous year and were projected as a third-place tie in the division. *"We're kind of spotty right now in certain areas. Maybe our early games will help us develop our skills. If the seniors do the things they're capable of, we can have a pretty good year"*. The Hattiesburg American picked Magee 29-22. A win would give them a guaranteed playoff spot and the odds-on favorite for 5-4A honors.

On their second possession, Grayson hit Shaw on a pass to set up Shaw's 1-yard dive and Willis' PAT. Magee tried to put it away before intermission on a march to the 11-yard line but gave the ball away via interception to Anthony McDonald. The Trojans held the 7-0 lead into halftime thanks to a defensive stand at their 9-yard line. Magee put up a touchdown in each of the following quarters to put the game away. The first was on a 53-yard drive with Sanders out-pacing defenders from 43 yards. Then, Grayson hit Shaw from the 25-yard line on fourth down and Willis added his third PAT.

Interceptions by Allen and Sims of last-gasp throws put things on ice. Magee held West Jones to just 156 total yards while putting up 321 of their own. *"(We) did a good job blocking. We had some opportunities that we missed. We dropped some passes we should have caught"*. The game was the 700th reported contest for a Magee football team.

GAME 9: MAGEE (7-1) vs MENDENHALL (5-4)
MAGEE 28 MENDENHALL 0
November 7, 1992: JACKSON, MS

Coach Royce Foster's Tigers were picked 3rd in the division with 5 starters back from a 7-3 season. *"The keys to success for us will be to stay injury-free and to beat Magee"*. Mendy was 4-1 in the division, thus making this one for the district title. Should Mendenhall lose, there would be no guarantee since Laurel would take the runner-up spot. But as history had shown almost yearly, this game could go either way. And, it was almost always for division bragging rights regardless of either record. The Clarion-Ledger picked Magee 20-6.

At Mississippi Memorial Veterans Stadium, the Trojan fans were rewarded for their patience as Magee scored in the 2nd quarter on a 77-yard drive capped by a 1-yard Grayson sneak and the first of 4 Willis extra points. Williams added a 5-yarder before intermission to pad the lead. In the 3rd, Williams *"ran for 22 yards and scored standing up on his following 12-yard run"*. Now in the final frame, the Tigers put the ball on the ground to Magee but it did no damage. However, midway through the final frame, Harvey picked off a David Posey throw to set up a 4-yard Williams plunge.

Magee dominated in first downs (20-6), rushing (277-79) and passing (36-13). Said Foster, *"You can't turn the ball over that much against a team like Magee. Our kids played hard, but it was the turnovers that killed us. Their defense did a super job"*. Added Wheat, *"I thought it would be tougher than it was. We got some breaks early and were able to score 14 in the first half. I thought that we played pretty well defensively"*. Williams rushed for 146 yards and was Trojan MVP.

GAME 10: MAGEE (8-1) vs PEARL RIVER CENTRAL (8-2)
MAGEE 45 PEARL RIVER CENTRAL 6
November 14, 1992

Pearl River Central had been on the Magee schedule before. In 1989, Magee had shut them out 32-0 in the second round of the playoffs on their march to the state championship. This contest would not even be that close.

Magee, behind a *"tenacious defense and explosive offense"*, put up a pair of opening quarter scores. Their first was a 74-yard march and Sanders 25-yard run while the next was a 61-yard drive with Sanders getting in from 15 yards. Willis was true on both extra points. In the next frame, Magee scored on a 7-yard Grayson toss to Easterling and Grayson's 23-yarder to Milton. Now 28-0 in the 3rd quarter, Willis nailed a 35-yard FG. Harvey then picked off a pass and Shaw used it to romp 75 yards to the end zone. After Willis extra points, reserves came on the field.

Pearl River avoided the shutout in the final quarter on Jonathan Mitchell's 1-yard effort but Magee then drove 54 yards in response with Allen dodging in from 8 yards away. Shaw had either 186 or 160 rushing yards and was awarded a Clarion-Ledger Top Performer. Grayson threw for 64 yards of Magee's total 394 output. Pearl River mustered 149 offensive markers.

GAME 11: MAGEE (9-1) @ SOUTH PIKE (10-1)
MAGEE 14 SOUTH PIKE 21
November 22, 1992

The two tradition-rich teams had never faced one-another on the field. South Pike, playing at home on Colee Field, was ranked 7th in the Super 10 with a single loss. Unfortunately for the players and those Simpson County fans making the trip, it would be a heartbreaking end to their first encounter with such huge stakes at hand.

Magee appeared ready to go as they held a 7-0 lead after a quarter thanks to Sanders' 27-yard run to the Eagle 3 followed by Grayson's 1-yard sneak and Willis' PAT. Before the quarter ended, Donnie Ashley (or Kendrick Matthews) picked off an errant throw to set up Derrick Pounds' 3-yard plunge and Ernest Jackson's extra point. With :47 showing before intermission, South Pike capped a 97-yard drive with a Tyson Taplin 4-yard pass to Ashley. The Jackson point-after put them up 14-7.

A time-consuming drive to open the 3rd quarter went 72 yards with Grayson hooking up with Charles Johnson from 35 yards and Willis tying the ball game. Defense took over *"with each team desperately looking for the knockout punch to win the game"*. Shaw picked off an Eagle throw in his end zone to stop one threat, and Maurice Johnson did likewise with time running out. However, it was *"erased on a questionable late defensive holding penalty"*. Taplin found Ashley from 5 yards with just :27 remaining and the season was over.

Said Coach Greg Wall, *"We did a good job. Our defense played tough and we had to hang in there to win. Our defense did a good job and we kept Shaw under control. Our defense gave up one big play. They found a soft spot on our corners and scored a touchdown"*. South Pike led in first downs (14-11) and rushing (141-97) while Magee held the air (108-90). Sanders led Trojan rushers with 48 yards on the ground.

The Simpson All-County football team included Eldwyn Harvey, Harold Shaw, Justin Cockrell, Maurice Johnson, Tommy Smith, Neal Warren, Tremayne Williams, Chris Easterling,

Donny Welch, Jerry McGuire and Steven Willis. South Pike beat Neshoba Central 14-13 for the 4A championship.

1993 (13-1)

After putting up a 9-2 record in his first season, Perry Wheat returned to lead the Trojans. He had high hopes as Magee was picked first pre-season in 5-4A, fifth in overall 4A polling, and 14th in the AP. He had the services of 20 lettermen and 12 starters, including Harold Shaw. Shaw had been named not only to the Top 100 Seniors and Dandy Dozen lists, but also made the Reebok and Pigskin Picks Preseason All-American lists.

"(Our strong points are that we have) good size and speed in our running backs and an experienced quarterback and receivers. An inexperienced defense (is of concern) but the defense will be better than last year. This is the second year with the staff together, so things should be more settled. We should understand everything a little better. Now we can concentrate on playing football". By the week of their first game, Wheat added, *"If we stay healthy we can score some points. Right now, we're better offensively than defensively"*.

GAME 1: MAGEE (0-0) @ BASSFIELD (0-0)
MAGEE 39 BASSFIELD 0
August 27, 1993

This wasn't only their first meeting, but also the first game for Coach Barry Sharpe. His Yellow Jackets were well-regarded in football circles; having put up 19 consecutive winning seasons and finishing the previous campaign 12-1. But this edition would be different. Bassfield had lost 18 lettermen from that team and returned only three. *"We are not reloading. We're rebuilding. Most of the starters have no experience. We have no depth to go to..."*

Wheat was still wary. *"Bassfield is traditionally a power in their class. They've lost two regular season games in the past two years. I don't know what to expect because of the coaching change. I do know they have a good football tradition"*. The Hattiesburg American picked Magee 27-13.

It was a strong opener for the Trojans against the out-matched Jackets with scores in each quarter. Tremayne Williams opened things with a 39-yard gallop. Magee then recovered a Bassfield fumble to set up Shaw's 5-yard blast. Now 12-0, Chad Grayson found Chris Easterling *"all alone on a 24-yard TD pass"* and Cory Swain notched the two-point play. Grayson's 70-yard hook up with Eddie Shaw and Steven Willis' PAT were the only points of the 3rd quarter, but the Trojans added a pair in the last stanza. Grayson and Shaw hooked up from 61 yards while Grayson hit Charles Johnson from 57 yards for the last.

Williams led rushers with 84 yards while Grayson, Clarion-Ledger Star of the Week, threw for 255 more. The Trojan defense limited Bassfield to just 153 total yards.

GAME 2: MAGEE (1-0) vs GREENWOOD (0-0)
MAGEE 29 GREENWOOD 12
September 3, 1993

Coach Bill Ingersoll's Bulldogs were picked 5th in their division this year after going 2-8 the previous year. Said Wheat, *"We're hoping the fact that we've played a game will give us a little edge. Normally you make a lot of mistakes your first game and this will give us an opportunity to correct them. We know very little about them except that they know what big-time football is all amount and that they have a lot of big kids"*.

Magee partially blocked a Greenwood punt after their first drive and Tony Clements recovered. Shaw made the most of it from 9 yards and Willis converted his first of 3 extra points. In the same frame, Grayson and Johnson connected from 31 yards for the next tally. The Trojans added one more before halftime via Shaw's 4-yard run. Swain added two points and it was now 22-0. The Bulldogs didn't quit fighting; scoring in the 3rd quarter on a 5-yard David Watkins keeper. Their last came in the 4th quarter when Watkins hit Sherrod Gideon from the 21-yard line. Jarius Milton finished things with a 40-yard pick-six.

Magee led in first downs (15-7), rushing (151-62) and passing (93-59). Shaw rushed for 107 yards and was Athlete of the Week. Said Ingersoll, *"We made too many mistakes. You can't do that against a team like Magee"*.

GAME 3: MAGEE (2-0) @ QUITMAN (1-1)
MAGEE 34 QUITMAN 6
September 17, 1993

The Trojans, now 11th in the AP, had Quitman next on the schedule. Ranked 6th in the division preseason, they had opened with a loss before destroying West Lauderdale 42-8. That luck wouldn't continue as Magee scored on their opening possession, marching 75 yards with Grayson hitting Shaw from 24 yards. Wills added the PAT. In the 2nd, Shaw rushed in from 21 yards (Willis extra point) before Quitman responded with a 40-yard Corey Wallace toss to Maurice Evans.

Halftime stood 14-6 thanks in part to a pair of Trojan turnovers in Panther territory. But in the 3rd quarter, Shaw capped a 60-yard drive with his 3-yard run and Willis converted. Shaw did it again in the frame *"untouched from midfield"* to make it 27-6. In the final quarter, he added his last on a 22-yard reception from Grayson. Willis' point-after finished things. Magee led in first downs (18-9), rushing (376-124) and passing (125-81). Shaw, Athlete of the Week, had 223 rushing and 46 receiving yards while Josh Sanders added another 97 on the ground. Eddie Shaw and James Mangum were credited with interceptions.

"We needed this type of performance from our guys going into the heart of our tough division schedule. Offensively and defensively, we did a lot of fundamentally-sound things that our coaching staff has worked so hard to get the kids to execute during the last month or so".

GAME 4: MAGEE (3-0) vs NORTHEAST JONES (3-1)
MAGEE 22 NORTHEAST JONES 15
September 24, 1993

The Tigers, picked 5th in division play and had lost 14 lettermen from their 2-9 team. But, they did return 16 letter-winners to give them hope. *"We're improved. We're still awfully small. All we can do is ask them to give us all they've got"*. They had done just that by game time with a 3-1 record. Said Wheat, *"I have constantly reminded our players that Northeast is well-prepared and fired up to come here and win this game. This game will definitely be the toughest one for us so far…"*.

Wheat had not underplayed the toughness of their opponent. They turned an early Trojan fumble into a 12-yard Darryl Carter touchdown throw to Brent Westin. Penalized on a 2nd quarter FG attempt, the Tigers used the gift to score again; this time Carter's 12-yarder to Brad Hancock (or Ishee). Northeast then picked off a Magee pass before halftime to stall a drive and keep the score 12-0.

Momentum changed in the 3rd quarter, first with a 76-yard Magee drive capped by Sanders from the 7. Willis' PAT was good. Now in the final stanza with under 8:00 left, Northeast's Jamie Jones booted a 25-yard FG. Back came Magee with an 80-yard march topped by Grayson's 50-yard strike to Eddie Shaw and Harold's two-point conversion tied the contest. With less than 3:00 remaining, Shaw finished a solid march with his 1-yard burst and Willis converted.

Magee actually led in first downs (19-11), rushing (242-94) and passing (129-77). Shaw rushed for 154 markers.

GAME 5: MAGEE (4-0) vs LAUREL (2-2)
MAGEE 18 LAUREL 13
October 1, 1993

Second-ranked pre-season Laurel had just ended a two-game win streak with a 15-7 loss to Wayne County. In this, the fourth all-time meeting between the teams, it would be as hard-fought as anticipated.

Though Magee had the first score on Shaw's 1-yarder, it would be the Tornadoes taking over before intermission. In the 2nd quarter, Yahmani Adams took a Trojan punt 55 yards to paydirt. Six plays later, Corey Brown picked off a pass and raced 42 yards for the pick-six. Will Renovich's PAT put them up 13-6. Magee had a chance to tie before the whistle but could get only to the Laurel 5-yard line. The home team responded with two 3rd quarter scores; the first via Grayson's 9-yard pass to Easterling. An ensuing Tornado fumble recovered by Maurice Tatum set up Grayson's 29-yard pass to Johnson. That would finish scoring.

First downs (17-7), rushing (178-62) and passing (101-29) went to the Trojans. Said Coach Joel Speed, *"We knew they were a good team coming in and we had to play faultless ball. We gave two excellent opportunities off our kicking game and we can't do that to a fine football team"*.

GAME 6: MAGEE (5-0) @ NORTHEAST LAUDERDALE (3-3)
MAGEE 33 NORTHEAST LAUDERDALE 8
October 8, 1993

Northeast Lauderdale had been unsuccessful in beating Magee the last two seasons. Ranked 7th pre-season in the division and sitting at .500, the woes would continue against the now-ranked 7th AP team. The Hattiesburg American had predicted a 27-12 final.

The Trojans raced out to a 14-0 lead after a quarter via Shaw's 1-yard and David Williams' 10-yard efforts. Willis was good on those kicks and another later. A bad punt snap in the 2nd quarter resulted in a 15-yard pick-six by Williams. Shaw's 1-yard tally in the 3rd quarter signaled the start of reserve players on the field. Clements blocked a punt on the home team's next possession to allow Fred Patrick a 9-yard touchdown. With :58 remaining, and after Brian Bell fell on a fumbled Magee punt, Fred Peters escaped from 24 yards for Northeast's only touchdown and Jacques Gordon notched the two-pointer.

Magee led in first downs (181-4), rushing (190-70) and passing (111-5). Williams was Athlete of the Week.

GAME 7: MAGEE (6-0) vs LEFLORE COUNTY (2-4)
MAGEE 41 LEFLORE COUNTY 24
October 15, 1993

After winning their first two games, the Tigers had dropped the next four. That trend did not appear to be changing as they traveled to 8th (AP) Magee for a rainy affair. The marked the first meeting between the two teams.

Grayson and Harold Shaw hooked up from inside the 14-yard line, Maurice Johnson recovered a fumble, Shaw burst in from 4 yards and notched another soon after from 25 yards, and Willis converted on all the PATs. In the 2nd quarter, Leflore got on the board with Rodney Singleton's 60-yard bomb to Reginald Brownlee. Surprisingly, Brownlee then picked off a Trojan throw and raced 53 yards for the pick-six. Now 21-12, Magee drove 68 yards with Shaw running the last 12 and Willis converting.

They opened the 3rd quarter with a 69-yard march and 8-yard James Mangum touchdown. But the Tigers weren't going away. They moved 94 yards with Christopher Fisher capping it with a 5-yard reception. Again the Trojans turned the ball over and Leflore made it count with a 14-yard Singleton throw to Starks. With :44 left, Shaw iced the contest with a 15-yard dash and Willis booted home the extra point. Magee led in first downs (17-8) and rushing (337-59) while Leflore dominated in passing (172-19). Shaw rushed for 179 yards on 11 carries to put him at 827 for the season.

GAME 8: MAGEE (7-0) vs WEST JONES (3-5)
MAGEE 51 WEST JONES 10
October 22, 1993: HOMECOMING

Coach Mike Taylor's Mustangs were picked 3rd in the division after going 6-5 in 1992. They had 11 returning lettermen, causing Taylor to say "*We return an experienced ball club. We have several starters that return with valuable playing time. Granted we did have some key losses from last year's team. But for the most part, we are able to fill the holes and should display a veteran ball club that should be able to win some games*". This game, the Trojans' last regular-season home game was important for a couple of reasons. First, it was Homecoming. And, a win would give Magee the outright 5-4A title.

It wasn't the best opening for Magee as an early fumble set up a 37-yard Joe Teagle FG. Back came Magee with Grayson's 59-yard strike to Milton and Willis PAT, but West Jones hung in and drove 69 yards for a response; that a 3-yard Melvin Thomas dive and Teagle PAT. After that, it was all Trojans. Grayson found Sanders from 66 yards, Clements ran in the two-pointer, Grayson hit Milton from the 37-yard line and Willis converted to make halftime 22-10.

In the 3rd frame, Eddie Shaw's interception set up Sanders' 12-yard effort and Harold Shaw added a 56-yard dash. Willis converted on both. Finally, Williams blocked a Magee punt to allow Marcus Allen a later 1-yard dive and Swain notched the two-point conversion. Harold Shaw put things away late with an 81-yard punt return and Willis added the PAT. First downs (10-8) and passing (247-43) favored Magee while the Mustangs held the ground (144-132).

GAME 9: MAGEE (8-0) @ COLLINS (3-4-1)
MAGEE 7 COLLINS 0
October 29, 1993

The Tigers under Coach David Abercrombie, 4th preseason in district polling, were 6-4 the previous campaign and with 14 lettermen returning. However, they had only a reported 32 players. "*They're good enough to play the positions, but we had a little more depth last season. Our concern is how effective they'll be playing on both sides of the ball; especially in the second half of our early games*". By game day, Collins had been impressive at times but lost three games by a touchdown.

Magee now found themselves 10th in The Clarion-Ledger Super 10. Said Wheat, "*I really don't feel like we've played up to our potential. Our schedule is reasonably tough, but more of the teams we've played are not playoff caliber. You've got to play 48 minutes against teams you'll play in the playoffs. We've played pretty well in spurts, but we've got to play 48 minutes*". The Hattiesburg American picked Magee 20-13.

Unbeknownst to everyone watching in Collins, Magee garnered the only score of the game on their first drive. In rainy and muddy conditions, they moved 68 yards in 11 plays with Grayson's 5-yard pass to Allen and Willis' conversion giving the Trojans all they would need. As the rain came heavier, the contest became one of turnovers. In all, there were 9 fumbles and a pair of interceptions. The Magee Courier said that in the second half, "*it was almost impossible to identify either team by uniform numbers*". First downs (13-5), rushing (126-49) and passing (40-0) favored Magee.

GAME 10: MAGEE (9-0) vs MENDENHALL (6-4)
MAGEE 24 MENDENHALL 7
November 5, 1993: VETERANS MEMORIAL STADIUM, JACKSON

Things hadn't gone as anticipated in Mendenhall thus far. Coach Royce Foster's Tigers were picked initially tops in 4-4A after a 5-5 year. They had 22 lettermen back in his 3rd season and said before the year, "*We've very young as we lost all four (DBs) from last year. How quick our secondary matures will be a key for us*". Unlike most years, this one would not be for much more than bragging rights as the Trojans had already sewn up division honors. The Hattiesburg American called it for the Trojans 21-15 while The Clarion-Ledger thought it more like 24-10.

In Memorial Stadium, it was Mendenhall with the first mistake when they fumbled at midfield to Magee. Seven plays later, Grayson hit Sanders for the touchdown. Then, Grayson and Allen hooked up from 47 yards and, with a pair of Willis kicks, it was 14-0. They added another score in the 2nd quarter via Grayson's 24-yarder to Eddie Shaw and Willis kick. A 3rd quarter Trojan drive was stymied by a fumble to set up a 47-yard Tiger march capped by Darnell Norwood's 4-yard scamper and Brian Barlow's PAT. Early in the 4th quarter, Magee tacked on what would be the final point when Willis nailed a 31-yard FG.

Magee led in first downs (17-11) and passing (187-20). Mendy led in rushing 148-141. Shaw paced Trojan rushers with 80 yards, but it was Grayson winning the game MVP with his 187 passing. Said Foster, "*The two fumbles in the first half hurt us. Our defense did a hell of a job in the second half, but you go down 21 against a team like Magee and it's hard to come back*". With Canton's defeat of Northwest Rankin, Mendy's playoff hopes were over.

GAME 11: MAGEE (10-0) vs McCOMB (9-1)
MAGEE 21 McCOMB 7
November 12, 1993

This would be a powerhouse high school football game; especially for the first round of the playoffs. Magee was 9th in the Super 10 while McComb sat 8th. As for the AP, Magee was higher at 4th versus their 11th spot. Said Coach Lee Bramlett, "*It's the start of a new season. We had a great year. Now we start a new season and start climbing a new ladder. It's week-to-week now. Lose and you're out. When you get in the playoffs, you play good football teams, so we might as well play one of the best right off*".

Added Wheat, "*You're probably going to meet them (McComb) some time. At least we get them at home. They're better than any team we've played this season. They are definitely a playoff-caliber team. I think we're a pretty good football team. Whether we're better than McComb and South Pike and those other folks, we'll find out*". The Clarion-Ledger thought it a close one favoring the Trojans 21-20.

McComb seemed to have the momentum as they scored on the first play of the 2nd quarter. That came on a 10-yard Kirk Allen run and Ben Jeffcoat PAT. "*This seemed to wake the slumbering giant*" and Magee went on to put up three touchdowns of their own. The first was set up by a 59-yard Grayson toss to Eddie Shaw to allow Harold a 1-yard dive. Their next was a 66-yard march with Harold going in from 5 yards. Finally, and after Maurice Johnson picked off an Alden Kirk pass, Grayson hit Harold from 19 yards for another. Willis was true on all of the kicks and scoring was done. Though they fumbled in the 3rd quarter, the defense held and even threw in an Eddie Shaw interception.

Magee led in first downs (14-13), rushing (187-114) and passing (102-101). "*Early we didn't seem ready to play, but our team adjusted well. The entire team picked it up to another level. The offensive line did a good job. The defense played well the whole game. Hopefully people will believe in us now. This shows everybody that we can play with the best*". Shaw rushed for 151 markers. Said Bramlett, "*In close ball games, usually it's two or three plays or different things that you can look back and say that was the turning point. Unfortunately, tonight, most of those went the other way*".

GAME 12: MAGEE (11-0) @ COLUMBIA (7-4)
MAGEE 19 COLUMBIA 8
November 19, 1993

Though they hadn't played since 1988, the Wildcats were not unfamiliar. In fact, they had first started meeting in 1928 and had played 32 times after that initial encounter. Columbia earned the right to host the second round game with a come-from-behind win over previously undefeated East Central 36-28. The Clarion-Ledger called this edition for Magee 27-6.

On their first possession, Magee traveled 74 yards with Harold Shaw doing the honors from the 2-yard line. Down 6-0, Columbia roared back with Michael Oatis finding Tim Pittman from 18 yards out to tie things. Then, Derrick Burton rushed in for the two-pointer. With just 1:41 before halftime, Grayson spotted Eddie Shaw from the 16-yard line to make it 12-8 at intermission. Defenses stood tall in the 3rd quarter, but Magee managed one more tally with 6:00 remaining on Harold's 4-yard effort. Willis' kick was good.

Statistics vary by source. Magee led in first downs (18-11), rushing (230-112) and passing (88-64). Columbia had the only turnover of the night on a fumble. Shaw rushed for 104 yards.

GAME 13: MAGEE (12-0) vs SOUTH PIKE (11-1)
MAGEE 21 SOUTH PIKE 18
November 26, 1993

The Eagles had ended Trojan dreams the previous year on their way to the state championship title. Said Coach Greg Wall about this one, "*It will be a pretty tough one. We can't let Shaw get turned loose. I thought we did a good job of gang-tackling on him last year. If we can get pressure on (Grayson) and still contain the sweep and the trap, we'll still be in there with them. I think*".

This game was everything that sports writers had predicted that it would be. South Pike took their first possession 61 yards with Donnie Ashley dashing in from the 5-yard line. Clements' block of Isaac Green's PAT kept it 6-0. Magee punched back with a 69-yard drive with Harold Shaw adding the last 11 yards and Willis giving the Trojans the lead. In the 2nd quarter, Narleski Lewis found Ashley from 7 yards out to re-take the lead, but again Magee responded. After an Eagle punt fumble to Clements, Grayson hit Eddie Shaw from 27 yards and Willis converted. Thanks in part to another South Pike fumble, halftime stood 14-12.

South Pike gained the upper hand in the 3rd quarter on Lewis' 2-yard keeper. They could have inserted the dagger in the final frame, but sacks by Tommy Ashley and Sanders were accompanied by a Harold Shaw pass breakup. With about 5:00 remaining, Grayson caught the Eagles napping on a throw-back to Harold and he darted 83 yards to paydirt. Willis provided the PAT. South Pike had one last chance on a drive to the Trojan 8, but Lewis' fumble ended hopes.

South Pike had dominated stats; first downs (19-8), rushing (177-86) and passing (203-138). Said Wall, "*Turnovers were the thing that stopped us. Magee really didn't stop us. But give them credit. They are ae good football team. They have speed at every position. Their defense bent but it didn't break*". Added Wheat, "*We're lucky to win*".

GAME 14: MAGEE (13-0) vs LOUISVILLE (13-1)
MAGEE 6 LOUISVILLE 25
December 4, 1993: JACKSON, MS

Unbelievably, this was the inaugural matchup for these two teams on the football field. Louisville was a traditional power with three state championships in hand. In their last contest, Louisville beat Neshoba Central 27-0. That was remarkable as NCHS had gone to the state championship three times in four years. Said Wheat, *"They're the best team, by far, we will have played. We have a lot of respect for them. We know what we're up against"*. The Winston County (Louisville) Journal picked Louisville 20-13 as did The Clarion-Ledger 19-16.

Magee ran into a first-half buzz saw on this Saturday morning. Louisville took their opening drive to paydirt on Darrell Robbins' 30-yard keeper. The Trojans moved as far as the Louisville 13 before faltering. In the 2nd quarter, they went 73 yards in 6 plays with Travis Coats bursting in from a yard out. Later, they moved 72 yards in only 3 plays with Coby Miller escaping from 57 yards for the touchdown to make halftime 18-0. In the 3rd quarter, Grayson hit Johnson from 46 yards away to cut into the lead. But Louisville had another left in them when Dandy Dozen Monte Nicholson darted 62 yards on a QB keeper. Peyton Weems's extra point was true.

Magee led in first downs (16-8) and passing (180-72) but were dominated on the ground 250-94. *"We knew Louisville would move the ball on us. We gave up three long runs and a long pass. You just can't do that against Louisville. They physically took the ball game. We had hoped to throw the ball a good bit, but our pass protection broke down. Defensively, we just didn't get the job done early"*.

1994 (6-3)

Perry Wheat was back for his third and final season in Magee. During his tenure thus far, his Trojans had put up a remarkable 22-3 record. This edition had his squad picked first preseason in 5-4A. But he had lost 13 lettermen that included numerous star players. *"It's going to be difficult to repeat (13-1). We lost a lot of good seniors. I think that we are going to have a good football team, but it's not every year that you can win 13 games. Our kids that are returning, I think that the loss really stuck in this minds. I think it made them determined to work hard and to prepare. It was a tough loss for us. This is a hard-working group. They are improving each day and I think that they are going to become a good team of their own"*.

One player returning was Dandy Dozen QB Chad Grayson. The senior had posted 1,789 passing yards and 23 touchdowns on the previous campaign. Magee entered their first game at 14th in the AP.

GAME 1: MAGEE (0-0) @ GREENWOOD (1-0)
MAGEE 6 GREENWOOD 27
September 2, 1994

Initially, Magee was to play a home game against Bassfield. But somewhere before the end of August, that game was scrapped. It would cause the Trojans to find a later replacement opponent to avoid an eight-game season. With an extra week to prepare, Magee made the trip to Leflore County to take on Greenwood. The Bulldogs would be much stronger this year than when Magee beat them 29-12 in 1993 as Coach Terry Moore's squad opened the season with a 19-15 win over Number 3 Moss Point.

Now, Greenwood had jumped to 7th in the AP. The Clarion-Ledger thought them slight 20-14 favorites to continue their solid ball play. Said Moore, *"I'm excited about playing at home against a quality program like Magee. They have a lot of speed at the skill positions. It should be a good football game"*. Like every-other season since 1989, Magee dropped their kickoff contest. This one would have a lot to do with the Trojans' four fumbles and one interception off of a reverse.

The Dogs had the only score of the initial half as Anthony Erving dove in from a yard out with 1:48 left. Marcus Singleton's kick made halftime 7-0. On their second possession of the 3rd quarter, they went 44 yards with Antowoine Williams bursting in from the 1-yard line. They followed that with an interception to kill a Trojan march and a fumble recovery to stop another. Now in the last stanza, Sherrod Gideon found Terrell Adams from 26 yards and they converted the two-pointer on Zucchineus Carruth's pass to Von McClee.

On the next Trojan drive, Tron Reed picked up a dropped ball and raced 24 yards to paydirt. Magee avoided the shutout with a 1-yard James Mangum run but the kick failed.

Greenwood led in first downs (11-10) and rushing (104-34) while passing was equal at 82 yards. *"We just got whipped up front. They were real physical. Their defense was the ball game. We'll have to put some emphasis on pass protection. That's something we can correct".*

GAME 2: MAGEE (0-1) vs QUITMAN (1-2)
MAGEE 27 QUITMAN 7
September 16, 1994

Coach Mike Weather's Panthers were picked 6th in 5-4A to start the season and had just gotten their first win the previous week. Still it would not be an impressive home opening for the Trojans.

An opening turnover for Quitman led to a 45-yard Grayson strike to Jeremy Clark. Then, Anthony Floyd to set up James Mangum's 12-yarder to make it 12-0. Magee dropped the football in the 2nd quarter at the Trojan 13 to allow a 1-yard Antonio Smith dive and Albert Green (or Leggett) PAT. That made halftime 12-7. The home team put up scores in each of the next two frames to seal the win. The first with a 3-yard Mangum run and Fred Patrick two-point conversion, while Clark dodged in from 3 yards and Corey Easterling booted the PAT.

Magee led in first downs (15-9) and passing (136-21). The Panthers held the ground 161-141. Magee suffered 3 fumbles but Quitman threw 3 interceptions and lost a fumble. Mangum was named Athlete of the Week.

GAME 3: MAGEE (1-1) @ NORTHEAST JONES (3-0)
MAGEE 20 NORTHEAST JONES 21
September 23, 1994

After putting together their first winning season (8-3) since 1988 and returning 15 lettermen, Coach Larry Ishee's Tigers were picked just behind Magee in the division. *"Hopefully last year was something to build on. One season does not turn a program around. It does heal some wounds but we still have a long way to go. We haven't accomplished anything yet. My biggest concern would be size and strength and depth at certain positions".* The implications were obvious as Northeast was 3-0 already and 12th in the AP. The Hattiesburg American picked it deadly accurate 21-20.

A surprise on-side kick by NEJ was recovered by Magee. They used the short field to find the end zone via Clark's (or Patrick's) 21-yard dash. Magee then moved 72 yards in 6 plays with Mangum finding paydirt from 2 yards to make it 12-0. The home team cut into the lead in the 2nd quarter with Shannon Ishee's 2-yard plunge and his PAT, but the Trojans answered with an 86-yard drive capped by a 2-yard Magnum dive and Grayson's two-point pass to Etoya Traxler. That made halftime 20-7.

Magee seemed to be poised to finish things in the 3rd quarter but could get no further than the 7-yard line. NEJ then went 88 yards and scored on a 7-yard Darryl Carter throw to Brent Rustin. In the final quarter, a questionable pass interception by Jamie Jones ended another threat. The home team pulled out the critical win with less than 1:30 left when Carter hit Jones from 42 yards away. Going for the win, Ishee kept on a two-point play and crossed the stripe. First downs were even at 17 each. Rushing (257-245) and passing (97-67) went to Northeast.

GAME 4: MAGEE (1-2) @ LAUREL (1-2)
MAGEE 7 LAUREL 3
September 30, 1994

Though there were 11 lettermen back from a 5-6 team, Coach George Blair had lost 16 to graduation. Still, they were picked 3rd in the division. *"This year we're going to be young. We have some talented people but they just haven't played much together. We're experimenting every day".* On the positive side, they had an open date to prepare after beating Wayne County 14-12. Magee had posted a 3-0 record in the series in the last 3 games. A loss here would kill any hopes for the Trojans.

The first half was highlighted only by a long FG missed by Tornado kicker Will Renovich. Magee recovered a fumble later but could do nothing with the opportunity. Fred Thomas put up the only touchdown of the evening on a 4-yard run and Marcus Myers knocked home the PAT. Laurel got into Magee territory on the ensuing possession, but had to settle for a 32-yard Renovich FG.

GAME 5: MAGEE (2-2) vs NORTHEAST LAUDERDALE (3-3)
MAGEE 45 NORTHEAST LAUDERDALE 30
October 7, 1994: HOMECOMING

Northeast Lauderdale had never bested a Trojan team, and now picked last in 5-4A. It seemed probable that the streak would continue for Magee's Homecoming affair. The Hattiesburg American picked Magee 26-6, but was well-off-of-the-mark on the total points scored.

Magee went up 21-0 in the opening quarter with scores coming from Grayson passes to Jarius Milton (33 yards), Traxler (29 yards) and Milton's indescribable 30-yard pick-six on the kickoff. Fred Peters had attempted a surprise pass back after receiving only to have Milton grab the errant throw instead. Myers was true on all extra points. Tim Sertin's 55-yard escape and 9-yard touchdown after was accompanied by Brian Bell's two-pointer. That made it 21-8 going into the next frame.

Grayson and Mangum hooked up from 4 yards and Floyd converted via the run. Four minutes later, Grayson found Clark from 39 yards and Myers made it 36-8. Before halftime, NEL managed a 6-yard Ricky Nicks run and PAT to make it 36-15. In the 3rd quarter, Grayson and Johnson connected from 20 yards, Myers converted and substitutions began. Northeast managed two more scores later when Sertin dodged in from 40 yards, Bell converted, Bell then got in from a yard for Lauderdale and Peters converted. Grayson went 14-17 for 244 yards and won The Jackson TD Club Player of the Week.

GAME 6: MAGEE (3-2) vs WOODLAWN HIGH, LA (1-4)
MAGEE 47 WOODLAWN HIGH 7
October 14, 1994

With the vacancy from the season-opener against Bassfield, Magee was forced to find a replacement. The only thing known about Woodlawn was they had won the 7-4A Louisiana title the year before. Their trip from Baton Rouge would not be a pleasant one.

Clark's 9-yarder was the only score of the opening frame, but Magee had more in them. Grayson added to that on a 40-yard pass to Easterling to make it 12-0, but Woodlawn efforted a touchdown after on Lance Mayeux's 5-yarder to Derrick Anderson and Matt Cody's PAT. Before intermission, Grayson found Traxler from 7 yards to make it 18-7.

The 3rd quarter was a disaster for the visitors. Magee opened with Clark's 90-yard kick return, Patrick's 24-yard run, a Myers PAT and his ensuing 23-yard FG. Then, Mangum dove in from 2 yards and the score was 40-7 going into the final frame. Floyd managed a 6-yard pass to Gerald Payne in that quarter and Myers converted for the final point. Patrick led rushers with 132 yards. Magee dominated in first downs (22-10) and especially rushing (403-24). Woodlawn did hold serve in the air (198-86).

GAME 7: MAGEE (4-2) @ WEST JONES (5-3)
MAGEE 6 WEST JONES 7
October 21, 1994

The importance of this game could not be overstated. The winner would take the second spot in the playoffs while the loser knew their fate. West Jones, picked 4th in the division, had 14 lettermen back from a 4-7 season. Said their coach, "*We are going to be counting on an awful lot of 10th and 11th graders this year. The key for us will be to develop our young players early in the season. Hopefully many of them will be ready to help us by midseason*".

Magee held a 6-0 lead at halftime thanks to Grayson's 16-yard pass to Traxler. But the eventual dagger came in the 3rd quarter when a Trojan fumble was picked up by Larenzo Page and taken 39 yards to the end zone. Wesley Keyes' PAT put them ahead. First downs (14-6), rushing (145-116) and passing (124-23) favored Magee in a losing effort. Magee had 3 fumbles lost while West Jones suffered a pair.

GAME 8: MAGEE (4-3) vs COLLINS (2-6)
MAGEE 46 COLLINS 14
October 28, 1994

The Tigers had been picked 5th pre-season and had now lost five-straight games. The remainder of the season was for pride as they would not have a post-season game for the first time since 1987.

Frustrations were released on Collins in the form of 19 points in the 1st quarter alone. Grayson found Easterling from 10 yards, Mangum ran in from 19 yards, and Grayson's long pass to Milton set up a 1-yard Mangum dive. The last two touchdowns were result of Tiger fumbles. They added another before halftime when Mangum turned in a pick-six. With two Myers PATs, it was 26-0. Collins reached the end zone in the 3rd on Marlon Firle's 1-yarder and Anthony Owens' two-point play, but Magee did the same on Clark's 4-yard effort and Johnson's conversion.

Clark opened the last quarter with a 44-yard dash, Collins answered with Anthony Magee's 80-yard escape, and Magee finished things on Floyd's 38-yard run. Clark led rushers with 124 yards while Mangum added another 103 yards. Magee led in first downs (22-10), rushing (414-260) and passing (156-23).

GAME 9: MAGEE (5-3) vs MENDENHALL (8-2)
MAGEE 21 MENDENHALL 0
November 4, 1994

After a number of years of contests in Jackson, the game was back in Simpson County. But this one would also be different in that Mendenhall had the much-better record and was guaranteed a spot in the playoffs. Still, this one was for much more than post-season play.

Roughly 5,000 fans were on hand to see the rivalry. Magee hit paydirt first early in the 2nd quarter on a 64-yard march capped by Thomas' 15-yard dash and a Myers PAT. Traxler then picked up a loose football and raced 30 yards for the next touchdown. That made halftime 13-0 despite turnovers on both sides. Mendenhall threatened in the 3rd quarter before Traxler picked off a Perry Miley pass in the end zone to thwart the threat. Magee then drove the other direction and capped the drive in the final frame on Patrick's 3-yard effort and Johnson's pass to Floyd for the two-pointer. Floyd and Mangum ended any Tiger hopes with interceptions.

Magee led in first downs (17-14) and rushing (225-139) while Mendy led in passing (84-26). Clark (65), Thomas (63) and Mangum (57) led rushers. *"We got the breaks and took advantage of them to win. The defense took over and played tough football in the second half. I want to congratulate Coach Steve Pruitt and his staff on the game. Mendenhall has a good team and good kids. They are to be commended"*.

Starkville defeated South Pike 16-13 to claim the 4A title.

1995 (9-4)

Perry Wheat's departure to Forrest County AHS meant a change in Magee. Now holding the whistle was Danny Cowart. He had been coaching for 18 years with stops in Tishomingo, Perry and George Counties. At Biloxi, Cowart headed up the number 2 team in the state of Mississippi. The move to 4-4A brought new opponents for the red and gray. Picked 2nd to Pearl, Cowart said, *"Our offense will be a take-what-they-give-us type of offense. We're going to have a balanced attack. Our defensive strength will be speed. We could get in trouble by thinking only of (a few opponents). We've got to get to those games in position for those games to mean something"*.

GAME 1: MAGEE (0-0) @ COLLINS (0-0)
MAGEE 6 COLLINS 14
August 25, 1995

The Tigers' coach was Royce Foster; formerly at rival Mendenhall. Their 2-7 record the previous season was bolstered by 24 returning lettermen to put them pre-season tops in 7-3A. *"The size of our offensive and defensive lines should be a strong point for us"*. Said Cowart, *"It's very important to get momentum. Remind the public that in 1993, the score of the Collins game was 7-0"*. The Hattiesburg American still picked the Trojans 27-0.

Turnovers spelled defeat in the road lid-lifter. Their second drive ended in a fumble while another ended with a Cory Haynes interception. That led four plays later to Marcus Thompson's 1-yard burst and Pat Pipkins' PAT. Magee couldn't take advantage of a Tiger fumble in the 3rd and then fumbled to Collins in the last stanza. They turned that gift into a 7-yard Andre Pickering dart and Pipkins extra point. Magee avoided the goose egg with 1:40 left when James Mangum dodged in from 11 yards.

Said Foster, *"We were very pleased to beat Magee. They have a good football team and they are going to win a lot of games"*.

GAME 2: MAGEE (0-1) vs BROOKHAVEN (1-0)
MAGEE 25 BROOKHAVEN 12
September 1, 1995

Magee had been bested by Brookhaven in their only two meetings (1982-1983). It was imperative that the Trojans avoid coming out of the gates 0-2 for the first time since 1982. In front of home fans, they did so. Their initial score came via a Brookhaven fumble by Kelby Bowman picked up by Fred Patrick and taken 34 yards to paydirt. Mangum added another in the 2nd quarter on a 15-yard run to cap a 76-yard drive to make it 12-0. Brookhaven got on the board before halftime when Chuck Brown scampered in from 5 yards out. That score had been set up by a Terrance Bates interception.

Brookhaven had one more chance for points before halftime but John Grissom's 32-yard FG was blocked by Etoya Traxler. Now in the final frame, and with rain falling, Patrick broke away for a 67-yard scoring dash and Marcus Myers converted. An ensuing Panther fumble to Magee at the 1-yard line gave way to Traxler's touchdown dive. Brookhaven managed a final tally by going 79 yards with Bowman providing the last 4 yards. First downs (17-4) and passing (149-20) went to Brookhaven while rushing was even at 150 yards each.

"I'm proud for our seniors. We made the most of our opportunities with those turnovers. Defensively, we played real well and ran to the football. Offensively we made some mistakes, but it's early in the season. Our offense will catch up".

GAME 3: MAGEE (1-1) @ FOREST (0-1)
MAGEE 15 FOREST 20
September 8, 1995

Forest and Magee had played 32 times from 1926-1985. Now, the Bearcats were back on the schedule. They had been picked 2nd in their division, but, like Magee, had dropped their opener. Magee had won 8 of the last 9 contests, but this one would change that trend at L.O. Atkins Field.

Things started well with Magee stopping the Cats at the Trojan 10 and heading the other way to paydirt. The TD came via Taraki Collins' 13-yard toss to Gerald Payne and Myers knocked home the PAT. Forest again drove deep but Magee held at the 9-yard line and Traxler blocked a 33-yard Rhett Simmons FG attempt. But the Cats' Foreman would pick off an ensuing pass to set up a Billy Lyles 9-yard run. Traxler again blocked a kick to keep it 7-6 at halftime.

With 1:04 left in the 3rd quarter, Regi Moore found the end zone from 2 yards and Clint Wilkerson added the two-point play. Now with 1:43 left to play, Lyles got in from a yard away. Never quitting, the Trojans punched back with a 43-yard Collins strike to Traxler. Tyler McAlpin dove in for the two-pointer with :27 remaining. Julius Barnes then recovered the onside kick but Magee could get only to the Forest 39 before Joey Pinkston picked off a desperation pass.

GAME 4: MAGEE (1-2) @ WEST JONES (1-2)
MAGEE 35 WEST JONES 14
September 15, 1995

The Mustangs finished 1994 at 9-4 but lost 13 starters to graduation. Said Coach Mike Taylor, *"We return 14 lettermen... The key for us is to build a strong defensive team and stay healthy. Depth is not great. We have a lot of talented returnees on offense. The key is to play defense to the level we did last season"*. The Hattiesburg American picked Magee by a slight 7-0, saying *"The handshakes may last longer than the game"*.

The opening quarter was an exchange of touchdowns. Collins and Traxler hooked up from 18 yards but Melvin Thomas evened things from a yard away. Both Myers and Armando Avila provided PATs. Magee exploded before halftime with three touchdowns. Julius Griffith pulled a 34-yard pick-six off of Darren Welch, Mangum escaped from 57 yards, and Griffith grabbed his phenomenal second pick-six (55 yards) of the quarter. With Myers PATs, it was 28-7.

An opening-kick fumble by West Jones led to a 1-yard Mangum plunge and Myers kick. With reserves in play, West Jones added their last late on Alrekus Graves' 1-yarder and Avila kick. West led in first downs (13-7) while Magee held rushing (174-173) and passing (54-7). *"We were able to create some breaks that gave us a lot of confidence. We've had a lot of injuries early and we're just beginning to get everyone back healthy. This has helped us a lot"*.

GAME 5: MAGEE (2-2) vs NORTHWEST RANKIN (2-1)
MAGEE 28 NORTHWEST RANKIN 13
September 22, 1995

This marked the first meeting between the Trojans and Coach David Coates' Cougars, a team picked 4th in the division. Said Coates, *"This is the first time we face the Wing T this season. Magee looks awful good on film. They run like a deer"*.

The Trojans put up two touchdowns in the opening stanza on a Mangum 4-yarder and 71-yard Patrick dash. Myers was good on those extra points and two more later. Their third score came on Patrick's 1-yard plunge before Northwest found the scoreboard. They did so on a 62-yard drive and Davie Lewis run of 7 yards and a Scott Westerfield PAT. Following a Trojan fumble at the Magee 16, Westerfield booted 30-yard FG to make halftime 21-10.

Westerfield opened 3rd quarter scoring via his 40-yard FG, but the Trojans effectively put things away afterwards on Jeremy Clark's 55-yard run and Mangum's 25-yard finish. Magee managed a later drive to the NWR 6 but lost the effort via fumble. Clark ran for 168 yards while Patrick added another 135.

GAME 6: MAGEE (3-2) @ WINGFIELD (1-4)
MAGEE 54 WINGFIELD 7
September 29, 1995

This marked the Trojans' second-straight road trip to take on a first-time opponent. The Jackson-area school was picked just below Northwest Rankin (5th) in pre-season rankings. The game would nearly break the 1992 mark (57 points) against Northeast Lauderdale for most points scored in a game.

Scoring came early and often. Opening quarter touchdowns came from Mangum (58) and Anthony Floyd's 47-yard strike to Traxler. Myers would knock through 6 PATs on the night. Clark then got in from 16 yards, Floyd picked off an errant Falcon throw, and Patrick *"barreled 11 yards up the middle"* for the touchdown. After halftime, Traxler escaped from 61 yards and Clark from 16 yards. With reserves in play, Magee still added two more touchdowns.

The first was from James King (18 yards). Wingfield avoided the zero on a 57-yard Johnnie Lindsay run and Wes Thomas PAT. But Magee came back with a 61-yard move with Dante Durr dodging into the end zone from 16 yards away. Mangum (167), Clark (118) and Patrick (108) led Trojan rushers.

GAME 7: MAGEE (4-2) vs BYRAM (4-1)
MAGEE 46 BYRAM 14
October 6, 1995

Believe it or not, this was not the first meeting between Magee and the Bulldogs. Back in 1941, the Burrheads entertained the Byram eleven and drummed them 47-0 on their way to a 5-5-1 record. Byram had been picked last in division play but had surprised folks by sitting 4-1 by kickoff. Coach David Virgil said, *"We can't make any mistakes. Magee is so quick"*. The Clarion-Ledger called it for Magee 24-14.

This tilt was a tale of two halves. Traxler fell on a loose Dog ball in the opening frame to set up Patrick's 11-yard touchdown. Byram stormed back in the 2nd quarter via Leon Willis' 52-yard scamper and, later, Cedric Harris' 4-yarder. Two Jason VanLandingham PATs made halftime 14-6. But in the 3rd quarter, things changed dramatically. Justin Griffith's 27-yard run made it 14-12. Then, after David Hubbard recovered a Byram fumble, Traxler got in from 28 yards and it was now 18-14.

Following a Mangum interception, Magee moved 80 yards with Patrick providing the last 50 yards. An unintentional onside kick was recovered by Barnes. Patrick rushed in from 17 yards for another touchdown. Tomone Johnson then *"broke through to sack the Byram QB, jarring the football loose"*. He picked up the pigskin and raced 38 yards to the end zone. Myers converted on the last four touchdowns. Finally, a Traxler pickoff set up Mangum's 23-yard effort and the game was over.

First downs were even (10-10), Magee led in rushing (391-155) and Byram in passing (24-10). Clark rushed for 145 yards and Traxler eclipsed the 100-yard mark with 101 yards. *"The (penalty) calls hurt both teams. But I think over 48 minutes they evened out. The offensive line play and the running of the backs got us the second-half domination. We had a few lucky breaks, like that muffed kick that hit their man and we recovered. But mostly we did well"*.

GAME 8: MAGEE (5-2) vs PORT GIBSON (1-6)
MAGEE 49 PORT GIBSON 0
October 13, 1995

Port Gibson, picked 6th in the division, had tried five times since 1981 to defeat Magee but had yet to do so. They wouldn't come close to pulling it off this season. Magee started quickly with Traxler's punt return touchdown from roughly midfield. Clark then moved in from 14 yards and Myers made it 13-0. Chris Langston forced a QB safety to end the first quarter.

A lateral pass from Payne to Patrick meant 88 yards of green grass, Clark intercepted a Blue Wave throw to set up Floyd's 25-yard strike to Payne, Hubbard recovered a fumble to allow Mangum a 1-yard effort, Myers converted on the touchdowns, and halftime sat 36-0. The only score of the 3rd quarter came on Clark's 22-yard dash while Fred Thomas finished things with a 1-yard plunge. Mangum (72), Patrick (70) and Clark (68) led rushers.

GAME 9: MAGEE (6-2) @ PEARL (6-2)
MAGEE 24 PEARL 22
October 20, 1995

After making a run to the South State 5A Championship the year before, 12th-year head man Bruce Merchant now found his Pirates back in 4A competition. Expectations were high for Pearl, ranked first in the division after such a powerful 5A showing, but Merchant was cautious. *"One of the things we're having to deal with is that expectations are high. But if the kids don't continue to work, we'll get our tails kicked. If we're not careful, we'll play down to the level of the people we're playing"*.

Merchant added, *"Based on the strength of our schedule, this year is different from last year because we have a little breathing room. Last year we didn't have any breathing room at all. Our kids have worked hard. They have a good attitude and are excited about the season. This year we have more depth at the skill positions. We have a lot of experienced kids back on defense. We feel good about our offense, as well. We may be a little more inexperienced on offense to start, but we have the potential to do some good things"*.

This game was of great importance. A win by the Pirates gave them the 4-4A title. For Magee, a win meant that they would make the playoffs. The Clarion-Ledger picked Pearl a winner 17-14. Said Merchant, *"Magee is extremely tough with a lot of speed"*. The Rankin County News noted that *"Early in the game, Pearl seemed to be in a mental fog"*. An opening kick fumble to Johnson set up a 5-yard Justin Griffith scoring run. An ensuing fumble to Marcus Floyd at the 34 led four plays later to Patrick's 22-yard run. Heath Morgigno picked off the conversion but the score sat a quick 12-0.

Magee opened the 2nd with a 72-yard drive completed by Clark's 15-yard touchdown run. Pearl's response came when Dandy Dozen Robbie Staten *"took a handoff at the Pearl 41, spun out of a tackle at midfield, then ran into the end zone on a 59-yard touchdown play"*. Chris Davidson cut into the lead with the PAT. The teams traded turnovers after. Pearl fumbled at the Magee 37, Morgigno picked off a pass, but Pearl fumbled back. A Magee punt snap to Tim Brown then *"sailed over the punter's head"* and into the end zone for a safety. Now 18-9, they had another chance but fumbled at the Trojan 3 to end the half.

Magee opened the 3rd with a 1-yard Mangum plunge for the frame's only points. Pearl mounted a comeback in the 4th, starting with another bad punt snap. Tory Alexander's 2-yard dive was followed by Rodrecus Rand's 7-yard toss to Brad Raphelt. Davidson made it 24-22, but the onside kick was covered by the Trojans' Anthony Floyd and the game was over.

Magee led in first downs (13-9) and rushing (208-148) while Pearl held passing (98-16). Said Merchant, *"I think turnovers led to both teams getting in trouble. Magee was up for us and we were flat from the start. The turnovers we had in the first half were mental. Magee did a good job. They have a good football team. They took advantage of our mistakes and it was 18-0 before we showed up. We didn't quit and we came back to make a ball game out of it. There was some hitting going on out there"*.

GAME 10: MAGEE (7-2) vs CRYSTAL SPRINGS (0-9)
MAGEE 34 CRYSTAL SPRINGS 7
October 27, 1995

Crystal Springs had been on the schedule 31 times between 1928-1976. The last twenty games found Magee holding a 17-2-1 record against the Tigers. This year, they had been picked 7th in the division and sat winless on the campaign.

Magee put up a touchdown in each of the first two rainy quarters. The first was a 49-yard Mangum run up the middle while Clark had the next from 5 yards. Myers was true on both conversions. Magee had another opportunity foiled by a fumble at the Tiger 14. Clark notched the lone score of the 3rd quarter on a 4-yard effort while Anthony Floyd found Johnson from 41 yards for their next. Up 27-0, reserves took the field. Byron Magee recorded his first touchdown from the 3-yard line and Myers finished Trojans scoring. Michael Catching's 1-yard dive and Jeffery Smith's PAT kept the Tigers from being shut out.

Mangum led rushers with 142 markers. The defense gave up just one first down, 11 rushing yards and 6 passing yards. Johnson, Langston, Brown, Marcus Floyd, Andre Hayes and Mangum *"played well on defense"*. Said Coach Carl Cole, *"We knew they had a powerful offense. So we tried to keep the ball away from them and slow them down"*.

GAME 11: MAGEE (8-2) @ MENDENHALL (5-5)
MAGEE 9 MENDENHALL 14
November 3, 1995

The previous year, Magee had been 5-3 as they faced the 8-2 Mendenhall squad. But to illustrate the relative unimportance of records in the rivalry, Magee shut out the Tigers 21-0. Now, the roles were reversed on the Tigers' home field. In fact, it was probably more common than not that the underdog stood a good chance of winning. This year was no exception. The season would end for the Tigers either way, but bragging rights stayed in Mendenhall.

Magee jumped on the scoreboard in the opening frame when Anthony Floyd eluded Tiger defenders for a 57-yard touchdown and 6-0 lead; an advantage that held through halftime. Mendenhall grabbed the lead in the 3rd quarter on Larry Magee's 1-yard plunge and Barlow's extra point. Now in the final quarter with time ticking, Patrick broke away for 65 yards to the 12-yard line before Bershard Tillman caught him. But the Trojans could only muster a 27-yard Myers FG. Disaster struck later when Mendy fell on a fumbled punt snap. Larry Magee's 7-yard dash and Barlow kick sealed the upset.

Said Coach Steve Pruett, *"That play (Tillman tackle) saved the game. Our kids, they never quit. They need to be commended"*. Larry Magee, playing with a chipped thumb bone from the opening series, rushed for 115 yards against the Trojans.

GAME 12: MAGEE (8-3) vs LAFAYETTE (8-3)
MAGEE 14 LAFAYETTE 6
November 10, 1995

Back in the playoffs, the Trojans would face yet another first-time opponent. Conditions for the game against the Commodores would not be ideal, as rain fell continuously. That would keep scoring down, and contribute to an opening fumble by the Trojans at their 29. But the defense stood tall and held.

They provided the lone score of the first half on a 74-yard drive with Anthony Floyd keeping for a 36-yard score and Patrick two-point conversion. Lafayette muscled their way to the Trojan 5 in response, but again the defense held. In all, there were 7 fumbles and an interception in the half. A 3rd quarter fumble by Lafayette led early in the next stanza to Floyd's toss to Payne from 10 yards away. The Commodores managed a touchdown before the end on Kinte Brannon's 1-yard plunge. Traxler ended any Lafayette hopes under 2:00 with an interception.

GAME 13: MAGEE (9-3) @ LOUISVILLE (8-3)
MAGEE 13 LOUISVILLE 17
November 17, 1995

There were still some Trojans from the 1993 squad that remembered the first meeting against Louisville. In that game, the Wildcats beat the undefeated Trojans for the state championship. For a long while, it looked as if Magee would get their revenge.

Midway through the 1st quarter, Steve Henly got through numerous defenders for a 33-yard Cat touchdown and Martin Rajevski converted for the 7-0 lead. Three minutes later, Patrick bested the effort with a 69-yard dash and Myers tied the contest. Louisville's return drive stopped inside the 20-yard line and Rajevski nailed a 35-yard FG. But, Magee punched back with a 70-yard march capped by Mangum's 1-yard plunge. That kept made halftime 13-10 in favor of Magee.

The best chance for a score in the 3rd quarter came from Magee but they could move only to the 16-yard line. Early in the final quarter, Tyler Peterson found Mark Clemens for 39 yards to put the ball at the 10. From there, Henly ran in from 7 yards and Rajevski provided the PAT.

After recovering a fumble with 2:35 remaining, Magee was unable to move and ran out of downs to end their season. First downs (7-6) and rushing went to Louisville while Magee led on the ground (182-171). Patrick led Trojan rushers with 78 yards.

All-District awards included Fred Patrick (Best Offensive Back) and David Hubbard (Best Defensive Lineman). Other first team members were Jeremy Clark, Tyler McAlpin, James Mangum, Andre Hayes and Etoya Traxler. Second Team honorees included Aundrial Turner, Fred Thomas, Tomone Johnson, Chris Langston, Anthony Floyd, Taraki Colins and Tim Brown. Magee also garnered Coaching Staff of the Year. Louisville beat McComb 14-7 for the state title.

1996 (11-2)

Danny Cowart's second edition of red and gray wasn't expected to be extremely strong. Though they had 18 lettermen (8 offensive and 4 defensive starters) back, voters had the Trojans third in 4-4A pre-season. Pearl had garnered the top spot while rival Mendenhall held second place. Cowart was quoted only as saying *"We are expecting good team leadership... Injuries will be a key factor this season. If we can stay healthy and the kids play like they are capable of playing, we'll be OK. Right now we are picked third in the division behind Mendenhall and Pearl"*.

GAME 1: MAGEE (0-0) vs COLLINS (0-0)
MAGEE 28 COLLINS 6
August 30, 1996

In Collins, Coach Royce Foster had a substantial 25 lettermen back from an 8-3 team. That included thousand-yard rusher Correll Buckhalter. Their opening-season game the previous year had been a victory for Collins, but it had been only the second against Magee since 1986.

A solid drive to the Collins 2 to start the game ended there, but they reached paydirt on the next. Justin Griffith's 12-yard dive made it 6-0 to start the 2nd quarter. An ensuing Buckhalter fumble was picked up by Julius Barnes at the 25-yard line. That lead to Griffith's touchdown dash on the next play. Taraki Collins hit Dante Durr for the two-points. After holding, Collins punted to Gerald Payne. He *"picked up the punt at his own 30, was hit several times, (and) broke out of the pack to outrace everyone 70 yards for the touchdown"*. Marcus Myer's PAT made it 21-0.

Before halftime, the Tigers notched their only points on a 73-yard drive capped by Jay Johnson's 24-yard pass to Meaco Duckworth. Midway through the final frame, a hit on the QB by Tim Brown allowed Magee their final score. Griffith did the honors from seven yards and Myers converted. Magee led in first downs (16-11) and rushing (214-93) but lost the air (48-15). Griffith tallied 156 rushing yards on the night.

GAME 2: MAGEE (1-0) @ BROOKHAVEN (0-1)
MAGEE 27 BROOKHAVEN 0
September 6, 1996

The Panthers were picked 2nd pre-season in their division. Magee, on the other hand, was now 5th in 4A schools but noted only in the Others Receiving Votes category of the AP. The Trojans had broken a two-game losing streak to Brookhaven the year before. In Brookhaven, they had dropped their opener to Laurel 14-7.

Griffith got things going early with an 8-yard escape and Myers converted. In the next frame, and after a pair of touchdowns were called back, he tallied another and Myers made halftime 14-0. Magee also had another touchdown called back before the whistle. Fumbles at the 14-yard line and 15-yard line killed two more opportunities. But Griffith still managed a 76-yard touchdown dash with Myers notching the PAT. With reserves now in play, they scored once more. Bruisha Hubbard evaded Panthers from 22 yards and the game was effectively over.

The Trojans dropped a total of four footballs on the night and committed 110 yards of penalties. Griffith put up 256 yards on the ground while Collins threw for 112 more.

GAME 3: MAGEE (2-0) vs FOREST (1-0)
MAGEE 50 FOREST 29
September 13, 1996

Though the Trojans had won eight of the last ten contests, it was Forest with the win the previous season. The Bearcats were picked 3rd in 3A and had just defeated Neshoba Central

28-8 but The Clarion-Ledger still thought Magee best 16-14. The amount of scoring put up in this game would come as a surprise to all.

On the first play of the game, Collins hit James King for a 65-yard touchdown. Forest punched back with a 53-yard Clint Wilkerson strike to Jeff Brown to set up Regi Moores' 6-yard plunge. Wilkerson's keeper for two points was good. Back came Magee with two more tallies. King rushed in from 8 yards, Griffith provided the two-pointer, Julius Griffith picked off a Cat pass, and King dashed in from 20 yards with Myers converting. In the next quarter, Wilkerson snuck in from a yard and Rhett Simmons kicked the PAT. Seconds before halftime, Payne grabbed a punt and raced 82 yards to the end zone and Myers made it 28-15.

Forest cut into the lead in the 3rd quarter when Wilkerson found Jeff Brown from 29 yards and Simmons made it 28-22. Magee answered on a 25-yard Collins throw to Justin Griffith and Justin added the two points. Wilkerson and Brown again hooked up from 15 yards (Simmons) but Julius Griffith picked off another throw to allow Justin a 55-yard reception from Collins (Myers). Julius Barnes then added another theft and, seven plays later, Justin rushed in from 3 yards. Myers closed things out with his kick.

Griffith rushed for 101 yards to put him at 503 on the season. King ran for 75 more yards while Collins threw for 152 yards. *"I figured it would be one of those 21-14 games. I wouldn't have thought it would have been a high-scoring game"*.

GAME 4: MAGEE (3-0) vs WEST JONES (2-1)
MAGEE 26 WEST JONES 27 (OT)
September 20, 1996

Coach Mike Taylor had lost 11 lettermen but returned the same number for the Mustangs' 5-7 campaign. That season had ended in a first-round playoff loss to D'Iberville. *"Every week it's going to be a battle. We've got a good group of players back from that team. We have experience on both sides of the ball. Hopefully we will develop some more depth on the line. If we stay injury-free, we'll be OK"*.

An opening fumble by West Jones recovered by Fernando Patrick gave Magee an opportunity, but the 31-yard FG was unsuccessful. Still, they drove 65 yards on their next touch with Durr bulling in from 5 yards and Myers converting. In the 2nd quarter, Lafayette Keyes picked off an errant Trojan throw to set up Alrekus Graves' 13-yard effort and James Wildman PAT. That score held through halftime. Both teams hit the board in the 3rd quarter. A Magee fumble at the WJ 11 killed one opportunity but Justin Griffith still got through later from 25 yards.

The Mustangs were quick with an answer when Graves escaped from 66 yards and Wildman connected. Magee started the final stanza with an 83-yard drive capped by Justin's 24-yarder. West Jones moved 63 yards in response with Darren Welch finding Mark Barron from 10 yards to tie things 20-20 at the whistle. In overtime, WJ scored first on Cedric McDonald's 5-yard run and Wildman's kick. The Trojans then matched it with Collins' 7-yard pass to Payne, but the critical PAT exchange was low and the attempt to convert failed.

Justin rushed for 169 yards while Durr also passed the 100-yard mark (101). *"You have to give all the credit to Coach Taylor and his staff. They came in here and never gave up. Whatever he told them at halftime worked"*.

GAME 5: MAGEE (3-1) @ NORTHWEST RANKIN (0-3)
MAGEE 13 NORTHWEST RANKIN 12
September 27, 1996

Magee had won the only other meeting between the two teams the previous year 28-13. This year's match against the fourth-place pre-season divisional opponent would be much closer. In fact, all twelve NWR points came in the opening frame. Terry Wray had the first on a 22-yard escape while David Lewis counted the next from 10-yards to make it 12-0.

Magee's first answer came before halftime on a 57-yard drive and Justin Griffith 10-yard dash. Myers' kick cut the lead to 12-7. The Trojans had two more opportunities before the break, but both ended on fumbles. In the 3rd, Magee got inside the NWR 1-yard line, but could not cross the stripe. Now in the final frame, Durr got away from 9 yards for the touchdown and final score. The last Cougar effort to get into field position ended on a Chris Langston interception. Magee fumbled 9 times on the night, losing 5 of them. Northwest lost 2 of the 6 they dropped. Griffith rushed for 163 yards on the night.

GAME 6: MAGEE (4-1) vs WINGFIELD (2-3)
MAGEE 18 WINGFIELD 0
October 4, 1996: HOMECOMING

Like Northwest Rankin, the only other meeting between these two teams occurred the previous year where Magee walked away victorious. The Falcons were picked near the bottom of the division pre-season (6th) and now sat below .500 on the year. But, the game would not be a run-away.

All of the scoring was done before intermission. Magee carried a 6-0 lead into the 2nd quarter via Justin Griffith's 22-yard run and added more afterwards. Though Wingfield's Gary Derrick returned the ensuing kick 86 yards to paydirt, it was called back for clipping. Magee had also experienced futility; getting to the Falcon 1-yard line before fumbling. Byron Magee later sacked the Falcon QB for a safety, Griffith dove in from 3 yards, Myers converted the PAT and then added a 22-yard FG. Griffith led Trojan rushers with 123 yards.

GAME 7: MAGEE (5-1) @ TERRY (4-1)
MAGEE 43 TERRY 12
October 11, 1996

The game against division opponent Terry, ranked 5th preseason, would take place at Hinds Community College in Raymond. For the first time since the Forest contest, the Trojan offense came to life.

An opening Barnes interception of Les Myrick led four plays later to Justin's 3-yard dive. Terry moved into Magee territory in response, but their 25-yard FG was blocked by Langston. In the 2nd, Griffith got in from 3 yards again, Payne picked off a pass, and Durr found paydirt from the 14-yard line. Terry managed their first tally thereafter with :45 left when Dennis Steed dove in from the 1-yard line to make intermission 18-6. Though Payne returned the opening kick of the 3rd quarter 91 yards to the end zone, it was brought back. Still, Durr found purchase with his 24-yard effort.

Terry then moved 67 yards with Steed hitting Jarod Green from 4 yards. Magee struck back with a 58-yard march with Griffith getting in from 10 yards to make it 30-12. In the final frame, the Trojans put up two more scores. Collins hit Raynold Kinslow from 11 yards, Myers converted, Hubbard picked off another Terry throw, and Thomas Brown snuck in from a yard away. Magee rushed for 368 yards with Griffith (132) and Durr (114) leading the way. Magee held Terry to 56 rushing yards.

GAME 8: MAGEE (6-1) @ PORT GIBSON (2-5)
MAGEE 70 PORT GIBSON 6
October 18, 1996

In 1992, Magee broke their all-time scoring record by whipping North Lauderdale 57-0. On this night against the team picked last in the division, they obliterated that mark. Scoring came at a rapid pace with no less than two touchdowns by the Trojans in each frame. Justin had the first score from 9 yards, Durr added the two points, Durr got in from 8 yards, a fumble to Magee led to Justin's 6-yarder and Myers ended the opening stanza up 21-0.

Justin rushed from the 6-yard line, Durr from the 20-yard line Brown hit James Grubbs from 25 yards and Myers converted after each touchdown. In the 3rd, Justin got in from a yard and Kedric McDonald did the same from 24 yards and 8 yards. Myers was again true on each. Port Gibson got on the board in the final quarter on Bobby Jones' 1-yard dive, but Magee had a few more left. Langston pulled a 45-yard pick-six and Edison Lee hit Byron Magee for the two points.

Justin rushed for 229 yards to put his mark at 1,329 on the season. Durr added 109 on his own. Magee rushed for a total of 430 yards while holding Port Gibson to an amazing -51 yards.

GAME 9: MAGEE (7-1) vs PEARL (6-2)
MAGEE 33 PEARL 16
October 25, 1996

Bruce Merchant was back for his 13th season in Pearl. The previous year had them 9-5 but with a deep run to the state championship. Said Merchant, *"There is more speed on this team than we have had in several years. Overall, our defense will be better. We have a lot of kids back who started last year. All of our secondary started at some point last year. We have an experienced offensive line. We're young, but also have a lot of experienced people returning"*.

He added, "*We'll be tested early. If we survive the early games, we have the potential to be a better-than-average ball team. No doubt, we're a green team, but this is a team that will get better as the season progresses. If we can avoid injuries, we have the makings of a pretty good football team. This group is young and energetic. They have worked hard for us and kept a good attitude through some tough pre-season practices. They have a lot of cohesion and they really like playing football together*".

The Pirates were hoping to redeem their 24-22 loss from the previous season. "*Magee is tough with a good defense and real good offense that likes to go after people*". Things started well for Pearl as they took the opening drive 79 yards to the end zone. Justin Jenkins' 38-yard pass to Rodrecus Rand provided the points but Chris Davidson's PAT was blocked. A snap went over the head of Magee's punter later to put the Pirates in position for Davidson to hit a 28-yard FG for the 9-0 lead. The Trojans responded in the 2nd with an 82-yard drive capped by King's 7-yard run and Myers' kick. The final points of the half, and of the remainder of the game for Pearl, came on a 2-yard Jenkins run and Davidson PAT. That made halftime 16-7.

The Rankin County News said that afterwards, "*the Pearl offense should have gone to the bus*". Magee cut into the lead in the 3rd when Justin got in from the 4 and Myers converted. The wheels came off in the 4th as the Trojans put up 19 unanswered points. A touched punt by Pearl and recovered by Langston set up another Griffith TD; this from 7 yards. Durr added a score from the 22 while Griffith plunged in from the 1 for their last. The win gave the Trojans the 4-4A title.

Pearl managed just 88 rushing and 83 yards passing in the contest. Griffith rushed for 216 markers for Magee. Said Merchant, "*Up to (a certain point), we did what we had to do. We had them on the ropes and let them off. Our defense spent so much time on the field the second half that finally they just gave out. We played a good first half, but we made a couple of mistakes in the second half to give Magee good field position. You can't do that against a team like Magee and win*".

Added Cowart, "*This bunch of kids proved tonight that they have character. When the chips were down, they did not quit. We used more personnel at different positions tonight. I am so proud of these kids*".

GAME 10: MAGEE (8-1) @ CRYSTAL SPRINGS (2-7)
MAGEE 53 CRYSTAL SPRINGS 14
November 1, 1996

With a two-win team ranked 7th in the division preseason next on the schedule, the offensive output would continue. And it would continue in a hurry with Justin's 66-yard first-play run up the middle and the first of many Myers PATs. He did it again from 1-yard away in the frame before Crystal Springs hit the board on an 8-yard James Robinson dash. Tomone Johnson blocked their point-after attempt.

Before halftime, Justin again found the end zone; this time from the 9-yard line. Two minutes later, he raced 86 yards and halftime was 26-6. His next was from 62-yards out and Myers made it 33-6. Barnes then picked off pass and turned it into a 57-yard pick-six. McDonald found daylight from 18 yards in the final frame for Magee's final reported score. Crystal Springs wrapped things up in the final seconds on a 62-yard touchdown pass between Robert Young and Michael Catchings and two-point conversion by Jasma Wheeler.

Griffith blew away any previous rushing best with 347 yards. That put him at an amazing 1,902 yards with 29 touchdowns. Said Coach Carl Cole, "*If there's a better 4A team out there, I don't want to play them: ever. They are by far the best team we've played all year. We were simply outmatched. We were as prepared as we could be. But they were so big and strong ... and fast*".

GAME 11: MAGEE (9-1) vs MENDENHALL (3-7)
MAGEE 35 MENDENHALL 6
November 8, 1996

Up in Mendenhall, third-year Coach Steve Pruett's Tigers looked to be poised for a breakout season. They had been picked 2nd in the division and had 30 lettermen back on the team. However, by kickoff, the long-time rival sat an amazing 3-7. Still, that would not guarantee a Trojan win, as history had shown so many times. This game marked the 750th all-time contest for a Magee football team.

Scoring by the home team was spaced fairly evenly, with 15 points coming in the initial frame. A Tiger fumble recovered by Byron Magee led to a 28-yard Collins toss to King. Justin ran in for the two points. Then, they drove 84 yards with King breaking in from 27 yards and Myers converting. In the next frame, Lee picked off a Mendy pass. Fourteen plays later, Justin dodged in from 7 yards and Myers made halftime 22-0. It could have been different after the Tigers recovered a Trojan fumble, but they failed on their FG attempt.

Justin passed the 2,000-yard mark on a 32-yard run before adding 1 more for a touchdown. Myers finished with the kick. Later, he burst in from 7 yards for his last. Finally, in the last stanza, Kenneth Bates' 14-yard run gave Mendy their six points, but Magee's second team hit the field and prevented any further scores.

GAME 12: MAGEE (10-1) vs CLEVELAND (8-3)
MAGEE 12 CLEVELAND 8
November 15, 1996

These two teams had never faced one-another on the gridiron. They would now do so in the opening round of the playoffs. The Delta team made a solid impression despite their second drive to the Magee 10 failing due to a fumble. Magee returned the favor but Cleveland could get only to the 15-yard line. However, a punt snap over the head of the punter put Cleveland at the 1-yard line. From there, Cedric Arrington dove into the end zone and John Jones ran in for the two points and 8-0 lead.

Magee's responses came in each of the next two quarters. First was an 89-yard drive capped by Justin from 2 yards. Magee later forced a Wildcat fumble that was recovered by the Trojans. Justin took the ball to the 1 and then into the end zone. *"The Magee defense began to smell the roses and dug in with all the determination they could muster"*. In the second half, the Cats gained only 9 offensive yards and a lone first down. Justin ran for 126 yards but Marcus Floyd won Player of the Week.

GAME 13: MAGEE (11-1) vs KOSCIUSKO (11-1)
MAGEE 14 KOSCIUSKO 17
November 22, 1996

The last four contests, starting in 1940, sat deadlocked 2-2. This one would be for much more than just the advantage in all-time victories. The Whippets earned their trip to the game by beating Oxford 19-17. They were now ranked 3rd in 4A polling. *"Magee has a lot of speed. We can't run with them so we're going to have to work hard and make our tackles. It's going to be a good, physical game"*. The Clarion-Ledger called it in favor of Magee 21-17.

This nail-biter saw the Whippets first to the scoreboard via Sam Potts' 21-yard throw to Billy Roundtree. Potts' PAT made it 7-0. Halftime remained the same despite two Kosciusko drives deep into Trojan territory that failed on downs. A Tim Brown fumble recovery in the 3rd quarter led one play later to Durr's reverse to King and handoff back to Collins. Collins then found Grubbs for 32 yards to the 9-yard line from where Justin dodged in to make it 7-6.

Another deep drive by Kosy failed deep and Magee used the gift to drive the other way with Justin escaping from 6 yards in the 4th quarter. He then ran in the two-point conversion to make it a 14-7 affair. Kosciusko moved 54 yards and capped the game-tying effort with Armon Quarles' 12-yard scamper and Pott's PAT. Now with :23 remaining, and after numerous Trojan penalties, Kosy was in FG range. Potts' 22-yard FG split the uprights and the season was over. Griffith added 117 in his final contest of the season.

The Touchdown Club honored the team with a banquet at the high school with Melvin Smith serving as guest speaker. Griffith was named to the All-State Team, MVP of the All-District Team, and First Team Division 4-4A. He also became the first 4A player in Mississippi to break the 2,000-yard mark. His final number was 2,261 per The Clarion-Ledger. Terrance Logan (Best Offensive Lineman), Tomone Johnson (Best Defensive Lineman) and Gerald Payne (Best Defensive Bank) received Special Awards in All-District Voting. The coaching staff were also named Coaching Staff of the Year.

All 4-4A honorees included First Teamers Chris Langston, Aundrial Turner, Logan, Terrance King, Payne, Johnson and Tim Brown. Second Team members were Taraki Collins, Marcus Floyd, Byron Magee, Dante Durr, Fernando Patrick, Logan and Eric Smith. Honorable Mentions went to Willie Franks, Raynold Kinslow, Edison Lee, James King and Marcus Myers. Northeast Jones beat Kosciusko 13-9 for the 4A title.

1997 (14-1) 3A STATE CHAMPIONS

With a move back to 3A due to realignment, the red and gray under third-year Coach Danny Cowart were expected to be dominant. Peers had them 1st in 7-3A, the AP put them 8th to start, The Clarion-Ledger had them 10th in The Super 10, and also picked them the number one team in 3A overall. In addition, they featured phenomenal runner Justin Griffith on the Dandy Dozen list. *"We'll be alright if we don't have too many injuries. We will have a very good defensive front and will be two-deep at QB. Our team speed will be good and the weak side of the offensive line returns with quality and experience. We will have the best running back in the state returning. Our defensive backfield should be alright".*

The Clarion-Ledger called them the *"favorite to win a state championship"* since they moved down from 4A. Magee had 14 seniors that included 8 sophomores who had started. Some new opponents were now found on the Magee schedule. *"We are new in the division and don't know too much about the other teams".*

GAME 1: MAGEE (0-0) @ PEARL (0-0)
MAGEE 22 PEARL 7
August 29, 1997

Bruce Merchant returned for his 14th, and what would be his last, season as mentor of Pirate football. The team was coming off the heels of a 7-5 season that ended unfortunately to Cleveland East Side in the opening round of the playoffs. Voters had Pearl slotted 3rd in the division pre-season. *"The kids have given us three weeks of good practice. It's been hot but they have done exactly what we asked them to do, which is all they can do. They have had good preparation time, but practice gets old. They're ready to play some games. We've talked to our kids about our overall schedule. At 5A, we have got to play well every week. We have to be ready to play every Friday night. There are no weak teams. We've got some pretty good seniors. I think our defensive line and our secondary are the strengths of the defense".*

The Trojans had won two-straight since they resumed playing in 1981. Said Merchant, *"Magee is the only non-5A team on our schedule, but they may be as good as any team that we play".* His words wouldn't be exaggerated, while The Rankin County News said that *"The Pirates proved their own worst enemies at time as they dropped passes and committed penalties at the most inopportune times".*

A fine opening drive to the Trojan 7 failed on downs, but Steven Alexander gave Pearl hope when he recovered a loose Magee fumble. The Pirates promptly fumbled it back to Eric Smith near the Magee 45, leading later to Kedric McDonald's dash from the 20 for the score. They moved to the Pearl 17 in the 2nd but lost the ball again; this time to Aaron Lewis. But their third drive resulted in points when Griffith broke loose from the 26. Bruisha Hubbard's two-point conversion made it 14-0. Pearl's response came when Justin Jenkins *"caught the Magee secondary napping"* and hit Rodrecus Rand from 52 yards out. Michael Beam sent the teams to halftime 14-7.

Magee put up the last points of the game in the 3rd quarter. A Pirate drive got to the 23 but failed and the Trojans marched the other way and capitalized on a Taraki Collins 26-yard scamper. Hubbard was again successful on the two-point play. Chris Knight was credited with an interception in the 4th at the Pearl 9 to kill another Magee threat.

Merchant noted afterwards, *"They executed well. They didn't make any mistakes. They have one of the top running backs in the state and he proved it tonight. They're a senior-dominated team while we're still young. We dropped a couple of passes and had some penalties that really hurt us. We played hard and did a good job for the most part. We're the type of team that is going to get better week after week".*

GAME 2: MAGEE (1-0) vs McCOMB (1-0)
MAGEE 21 McCOMB 7
September 5, 1997

In their last meeting in 1993, Magee had evened the all-time series to 1-1. Their first tilt came in 1940 when McComb blew out Magee 55-0. It would be a dandy as the Tigers were ranked 2nd in 4A while the Trojans were still the top-rated 3A team and now 6th in the AP. Though McComb opened with a 28-18 win over Wayne County, The Clarion-Ledger picked Magee 22-21.

Said Coach Lee Bramlett, *"They're good; real good. They're definitely a Top 10 team as far as the state rankings are concerned. They've got great skill people and an outstanding running back*". Added Cowart, "*The key will be stopping their run. If we do, we'll have a pretty good night. If we don't, it'll be a slugfest*".

The billing was everything it was supposed to be, with both teams fighting a defensive war until just :26 remained before halftime. That's when Magee finished an 86-yard drive with Griffith's 2-yard dive to make it 6-0. The McComb Enterprise gave credit to Hubbard. After the kickoff in the 3rd quarter, he "*smashed over his left tackle, ran over several defenders, and outran everyone else to the end zone*". Jason Robertson's PAT put the Trojans up 13-0. Then, he did it again with a 49-yard dash to paydirt and it was suddenly 20-0. A Trojan fumble deep in McComb territory did no damage, but a block of Tim Brown's punt attempt by Quentin Mullins and recovered in the end zone by Kevin Gray gave them their only score and Carmus Haynes (or Mac Hart) added the PAT.

McComb had other chances after Paul Taylor recovered a muffed Trojan punt and Derrick Wansley recovered a Trojan fumble. Anthony Bonds also gave them a chance with a fumble recovery, but the final frame was a defensive struggle with neither team scoring. Magee led in first downs (11-10) and rushing (334-120) while McComb held passing 53-0. Griffith, Clarion-Ledger Top Performer, ran for 236 yards while Hubbard added another 109 yards. "*This story of the ball game tonight was our defense. Except for some mistakes, they didn't come close to scoring. We played a good part of the ball game between the 30 yard lines*".

GAME 3: MAGEE (2-0) vs BILOXI (2-0)
MAGEE 21 BILOXI 11
September 12, 1997

Next up was the Biloxi Indian team under Coach John Williams fresh from an 8-3 campaign. Though they were undefeated thus far and currently 3rd after being projected 4th in the division preseason, The Clarion-Ledger predicted a Magee win 21-19. "*We've got to be ready. Our schedule is nothing to play with and we've got to come to play every night*". If John Williams sounded familiar to Magee fans, it was because he was the head coach of the 1962 and 1963 squads that went a combined 22-0.

On the initial Indian possession, they fumbled to Magee's Chris Langston at the Indian 28. Griffith took advantage of the gift with a 4-yard rush six plays later and Robertson made it 7-0. Scott Virgil cut into the lead before the end of the quarter on his 34-yard FG. In the 2nd quarter, Griffith capped a 72-yard march with his 1-yard plunge and Robertson converted. Magee hit the end zone again in the 3rd quarter on McDonald's 27-yard escape and Robertson's kick. Now in the final frame, Louis Hengen dove in from a yard out and Lorenzo Diamond's two-pointer to Kendrell Smyers was successful.

Stats vary wildly. The Clarion-Ledger had Magee leading in first downs (13-12) while The Magee Courier had them 17-9. Magee led in rushing roughly 250-104 while Biloxi led in passing 77-12. Griffith was credited with 113 rushing yards. Said Williams, "*I give Magee all the credit in the word. They played hard and took advantage of our mistakes. That's the mark of a good team*". Cowart was voted as Clarion-Ledger Coach of the Week. "*We must be pretty good. I think we'll be recognized for this*".

GAME 4: MAGEE (3-0) @ WEST JONES (0-2)
MAGEE 27 WEST JONES 6
September 19, 1997

The green and gold under Coach Mike Taylor had gone 9-3 the previous year and were now picked 2nd their division preseason. They had 6 offensive and 6 defensive starters back; thus giving them a change for a great season. "*We feel good about our team's chances this year. We should be able to compete*". However, at kickoff they sat winless. Meanwhile, Magee was now up to 4th in the AP poll and 7th in The Super 10.

In the 25th meeting, it would be a tale of two quarters. West Jones struck first late in the opening quarter when Clifton Pittman dove in from a yard. Their local paper gave credit to Vincent Brown for setting it up on a "*36-yard rampage up the middle*". Six plays later, Hubbard broke away from 28 yards to tie the game 6-6 at halftime. Midway through the 3rd quarter, Raynold Kinslow was taken to a Laurel hospital with a neck injury. Afterwards, Griffith dodged in from 20 yards for the touchdown.

In the last frame, Magee added a few more scores for insurance. Griffith got in from 12 yards and Thomas Brown "*went airborne at the two and landed just inside the end zone*" for two more points. Finally, Hubbard "*did his thing*" from 15 yards and Robertson converted. That touchdown had been set up by a Ricky Funchess interception. First downs (14-10), rushing (25-

138) and passing (30-11) went to Magee with Griffith rushing for 159 markers. Hubbard added another 80 on the ground.

GAME 5: MAGEE (4-0) vs COLLINS (2-2)
MAGEE 33 COLLINS 13
September 26, 1997

Collins was picked 6th in the division after a 6-4 season. Coach Todd Mangum's Tigers now sat break-even by kickoff on their trip to Simpson County. But they showed that they came to play when Daryl Carney took the opening kick 88 yards to paydirt and Courtney Clark converted.

An unintentional onside kick recovered by Eddie Bell gave them possession again and Jerome Hales shocked Trojan fans with an eventual 10-yard scoring run and 13-0 lead. In the next frame, a Tiger fumble was picked up by Julius Barnes and taken 65 yards to paydirt. Griffith's two-pointer put it 13-8. Before halftime, Eric Smith's safety-tackle cut into the lead 13-10. A deep drive to the Tiger 8 was fruitless, but Byron Magee ended up tackling Jerry Easterling in the end zone for yet another safety.

It took six plays before Magee hit the board again on Griffith's 11-yarder and Hubbard's two-point conversion. With 4:48 left in the contest, Funchess *"picked up a loose football and outran everyone 48 yards for another Trojan touchdown"*. Smith ended things with a 70-yayrd pick-six and Bill Shivers knocked home his first PAT. Magee led in first down (14-9) and had more in offensive production (259-156). Griffith rushed for 127 yards. *"We've got a lot of speed on defense"*.

GAME 6: MAGEE (5-0) @ HEIDELBERG (0-5)
MAGEE 59 HEIDELBERG 0
October 3, 1997

Heidelberg had faced Magee 5 times between 1986-1990 and never been victorious. This season, they had a new coach in Christopher Gale. Picked 4th in the division, they had only 4 starters back from a 4-6 team. *"We're thin in numbers but the guys have been putting up a good effort in practice. Pure talent-wise, we're not as strong as in the past, but we're strong mentally. This is a hard-working group of young kids"*. The result was predictable. In fact, it made one of the all-time highest scoring output contests (tied for 4th) of Magee's history.

Scoring came in bunches. Brent Walkers' opening-kick fumble recovery allowed Griffith an 11-yarder. Smith picked up a next-possession fumble and took it 41 yards to paydirt. With a Robertson PAT on the first TD, it was 13-0. Magee then tackled the Oiler punter to set up McDonald's 10-yard run and Robertson's PAT. The first play of the next quarter had Griffith finding success from a yard and later he got in from 3 yards to cap a 21-yard march. Robertson made things 33-0 at halftime.

The 3rd quarter was no kinder to the Oilers. A four-play opening drive ended with McDonald's 38-yard score and Josh Chatman *"set sail down the sideline"* for 76 yards for the next. Robertson and Shivers added the PATs. Griffith came in for one play and ran in from 27 yards, Shivers converted, and Julius Griffith pulled in an 80-yard pick-six on the final play of the game. Smith led with 12 tackles while Julius Griffith added 7 more. Justin Griffith rushed for 121 yards, followed by McDonald (80) and Chatman (78).

GAME 7: MAGEE (6-0) vs PRENTISS (1-5)
MAGEE 34 PRENTISS 0
October 10, 1997: HOMECOMING

Prentiss had high expectations before the season began. Picked 2nd in the division under Coach Alvin Gray, they had just played for the state championship the year before. The red and white had 9 offensive and 10 defensive starters back, causing Gray to say *"The way everyone around here is talking, why don't we just go on and give the title to Magee? We're going to have a lot of young ones, especially on the interior line that are going to have to grow up real quick. If we can get them to hang in long enough after some of the early whippins' we're going to take, then we're going to be alright once the division schedule starts"*. Magee was now ranked 3rd in the AP.

It would be the second-straight shutout for the Trojans, with Magee putting up a pair of scores in the initial stanza. Griffith capped the last 16 yards of the 87-yard march to open things. Later, McDonald got in from 21 yards and Robertson nailed both points-after to make halftime 14-0. In the 3rd quarter, Magee drove 55 yards with McDonald going in from 4 yards. Zanyon Dampier's ensuing fumble recovery set up Brown's 10-yard throw to McDonald and Robertson converted on both. Finally, Chatman rushed in for the final touchdown from 30 yards and Robertson made the PAT count. McDonald rushed for 95 yards while Griffith ran for 112 yards. It was his 20th consecutive 100-yard rushing game. Julius Griffith led tacklers with 9 solo and 6 assists.

GAME 8: MAGEE (7-0) @ WEST MARION (7-0)
MAGEE 6 WEST MARION 14
October 17, 1997

The big shocker of the season came from Coach Perry Coggins' West Marion team. At the start of the season, they were picked dead last in the division. Now, they were undefeated and coming off of a 40-6 whipping of nearby East Marion. The battle of the unbeatens would come down to the last quarter in front of *"the largest crowd to ever witness a football game at West Marion"*.

A defensive battle took place over a full half of football. The decisiveness of the defenses showed in that each team had 5 first downs while Magee barely held the advantage on the ground 79-75. West was first to the board in the 3rd quarter on Shaun Magee's 80-yard escape through Trojan defenders. Mark Broom added the two-point play to make it 8-0. Justin returned the favor with his own 80-yarder but it was called back for holding. However, early in the final frame, Julius Griffith found a loose West Marion ball. Three plays elapsed before Brown drove over from 2 yards. With the failed two-pointer, things stood 8-6.

A faulty punt exchange by the visitors that was recovered by Jamie Baughman put West in good position. They turned that into a halfback pass from Broom to Magee from 15 yards out for what would be the final points. Magee responded spectacularly with Barnes' 81-yard kick return for a touchdown. But, like Justin's run from earlier, it was called back for clipping. The drive fizzled and West simply ran out the clock.

First downs (13-7), rushing (217-133) and passing (67-21) went to the home team. Griffith ran for 106 yards while Smith led tacklers with 13. *"We'll have to watch the films and see if we committed the fouls. I don't think this team is as good as we are. (But) you've got to give West Marion credit. They controlled the clock by moving the football"*.

GAME 9: MAGEE (7-1) vs RALEIGH (0-8)
MAGEE 68 RALEIGH 0
October 24, 1997

Former Trojan assistant coach Terrell Luckey headed up the Raleigh team picked 5th pre-season in the division. They had finished 4-6 the previous year but now sat a dismal 0-8. Magee would have no sympathy for one of their own and go on to getting within two points of their all-time high in points. The game against Port Gibson (70-0) still held that high-water mark.

First quarter scoring came in bunches. Griffith ran in from 6 yards, Julius Griffith returned a punt 52 yards to paydirt, Justin drove in from 16 yards and Taraki Collins swept in from 18 yards for the last. Robertson booted three PATs for a 27-0 lead. Both Hubbard (8) and McDonald (40) also crossed before halftime and Robertson was true on the kicks.

After blocking a 3rd quarter Lion punt, Justin got in from 9 yards. Then, Julius picked up a blocked FG attempt by Charlie Goodwin and took it 80 yards. Robertson converted after the first TD while Shivers did the same on the last. Jason Rankin got into the books on a 10-yard punt return and Brown added the finale from 37 yards. Shivers was true on both kicks for the whitewash.

GAME 10: MAGEE (8-1) @ EAST MARION (4-4)
MAGEE 28 EAST MARION 0
October 31, 1997

A win here against Coach Les Peters' East Marion team would guarantee the Trojans a playoff berth. His team was picked 3rd in the division preseason and now sat 4th by kickoff. They had finished 3-7 the previous year but had not played against Magee.

The only score of the opening frame was set up by Collins' 14-yard pass to James Grubbs to set up Justin's 1-yard drive. Langston then recovered an Eagle fumble and Justin broke up the middle from 37 yards for the score. Late in the half, Collins found Grubbs from 24 yards and, with Robertson kicks, it was 21-0. A 3rd quarter Langston fumble recovery allowed McDonald to find the end zone from 25 yards and Robertson ended scoring.

Griffith rushed for 108 yards, Julius Griffith added an interception and Terrie Logan also recovered a fumble. Smith led tacklers with 6 solo while Brown had 5 solo and 3 assists. Said Peters afterwards, *"The turnovers killed us against Magee. You have to go be consistent when you play a team like Magee".*

GAME 11: MAGEE (9-1) @ MENDENHALL (4-5)
MAGEE 34 MENDENHALL 28 (OT)
November 7, 1997

Though Steve Pruett's Tigers went 3-8 the previous year, he did return 15 lettermen. Those included 4 offensive and 5 defensive starters.
"We'll be better this season if our younger players contribute. We have some experienced players returning at some positions but will need some help from the younger players to be successful". It was the 73rd meeting between the two teams and, while playoff positions were already established, bragging rights were not.

The Magee Courier said that Tiger Field *"was not the place for the weak at heart".* Midway through the opening quarter, Justin burst through the line for a 60-yard touchdown. He added to it before the end of the frame on a 1-yard plunge and Robertson nailed both PATs. The Tigers responded with a 70-yard drive capped by Alex McCullum's 20-yard strike to Marcus Winn and James' extra point. Before intermission, they tied the contest when McCullum *"faked everyone on a keeper"* for a 73-yard tally. James' toe squared things.

After recovering a Mendy fumble in the 3rd quarter, Hubbard found paydirt from 26 yards and Robertson made it 21-14. Mendenhall's only answer was a 25-yard FG. But an ensuing Magee fumble put the Tigers at the 29. That resulted in a 26-yard James FG and the score was 21-20. Julius Barnes quickly punched back with a 90-yard kickoff return and Robertson was true. Back came the Tigers with a 60-yard drive and Reggie McLaurin's 3-yard score. The critical two-pointer was converted when McCullum hit Jamie Sullivan. Magee could have won in regulation, but Robertson's 42-yard FG effort was just short.

Justin's 3-yard plunge in OT put Magee up 34-28. The PAT was unsuccessful. Now with a chance, Mendy marched as far as the 13-yard line but their *"fourth down pass fell incomplete".* Justin rushed for 201 yards on 25 carries. Magee also claimed the 7-3A championship thanks to finals in other contests.

GAME 12: MAGEE (10-1) vs VELMA JACKSON (10-1)
MAGEE 34 VELMA JACKSON 8
November 14, 1997

Like Magee, Velma Jackson also featured a Dandy Dozen running back in Albert Jones. The first-time opponent had a very strong record to date and made the trip to Simpson County for their inaugural meeting with such big stakes on the line. Coach Willie Young said, *"I think it's going to be a great matchup. We're going to go after them like we've gone after everybody. What it's going to boil down to is the team that makes the fewest mistakes. They've had a good program for years while a lot of this is new to us".* The Clarion-Ledger though Magee better 17-14.

The first half was every bit as tough as the records would indicate. Magee had the only tally, that coming early in the 2nd quarter on Collins' 24-yard pass to Kinslow to make it 6-0. It may have been better except for a drive-killing interception and a missed FG. In the 3rd quarter, Magee blocked a VJ punt but couldn't make it count. But on their next possession, Justin found paydirt from a yard away and then added the two pointer to make it 14-0.

Julius Griffith then forced a QB fumble that allowed Justin a 9-yard tally and 20-0 advantage. Velma Jackson responded with a 74-yard drive and Marvin Vaughn ended the march with a 22-yard run and two-point conversion. But Julius Barnes took the ensuing kickoff 91 yards to paydirt and Robertson made it a 27-8 affair. The game ended on a QB fumble in the end zone that was recovered by Langston for the score. Magee held VJ to just 3 first downs and 64 offensive yards. Justin's rushing numbers vary. The Clarion-Ledger called it 202 yards while The Magee Courier said it was 133.

GAME 13: MAGEE (11-1) @ FRANKLIN COUNTY (10-1)
MAGEE 42 FRANKLIN COUNTY 12
November 21, 1997

Magee had squared up against the team from Meadville only once previously. In 1989, they were the first-round opponent in the playoffs and the Trojans left with a 35-14 victory. Coach

Mike Goff's team had since gone on to be runner-up in the state in 1994. Now sitting 5th in 3A, their only loss had come 23-19 to undefeated Brookhaven. Said Cowart, *"Our defense has played well this season. Most of the time when it gets down to championship games and both teams have good defenses like this game, the defenses usually rule the roost"*.

In the mud and fog, Magee would improve on their previous encounter with the Falcons. A FCHS fumble to Smith at the 18 set up Justin's 8-yard run and Robertson PAT. They fumbled again, this time to Langston, and Robertson added a 28-yard FG. In the next quarter, Justin drove in from 4 yards to make it 17-0. Franklin County again fumbled and Brown picked it up *"and lumbered in for his first varsity touchdown"*. The Falcons added one of their two touchdowns before halftime when Bobby Hunt broke away from 41 yards and intermission sat 23-6.

The Trojans put the game away in the 3rd quarter. Justin dashed 67 yards to the end zone, *"literally ran over four Falcon players and one of his teammates"* for a 20-yarder, and Brown darted in from 6 yards. One Robertson PAT made it 42-6. In the final stanza, Marcus Briggs plunged in from a yard out. First downs (20-11) and rushing (312-187) went to Magee while FCHS led in passing (30-4). In all, the Falcons lost 5 fumbles. Griffith ran for either 206, 216, or 233 yards depending on the source.

"The muddy field let us take advantage of our size more. We are a power team and we just were able to out-power them. They have some small linemen but they gave a gutsy performance this year and this game".

GAME 14: MAGEE (12-1) vs PURVIS (12-0)
MAGEE 14 PURVIS 7
November 28, 1997

Things would not get easier for Magee as they now took on the undefeated and 2nd ranked 3A team. The previous week, Coach Jim Sizemore's team had pulled out a 17-14 OT win over Forest. The Hattiesburg American picked Magee 21-14, saying, *"Purvis has played well in earning its first south state title shot. The Tornadoes have depth, skill and a lot of heart. It will take all that and more for Purvis to pull off one more victory..."*

An early Magee drive to the Tornado 5 fizzled, and Purvis responded with a 2nd quarter march to the end zone. Derrell Burkett dashed in from 7 yards and Derek Swan gave Purvis the 7-0 lead. A later short punt by the visitors set the table for Justin's 28th touchdown; that coming on a 1-yard dive. Robertson tied the game before halftime. A 3rd quarter move deep in Purvis territory ended when Jeremy Chance picked off an errant throw at the 15. Magee also fumbled to them later at the Magee 33. But a bad pitch between Burkett and Lorenzo Young was fumbled to Tim Brown. That led directly to Thomas Brown's 1-yard sneak and Robertson kick.

The defense went to work to ensure that their scant lead held. Julius Griffith picked off a pass, Langston recorded a sack and Barnes pitched in with another pickoff. First downs (12-8) and rushing (208-77) went to Magee. Passing favored Purvis 72-26. Griffith had either 125, 135 or 145 yards on the ground. *"We had only given up two long scoring drives in our 13 games and when they put that long drive on us, we knew we were in for a game"*.

GAME 15: MAGEE (13-1) vs SENTABOBIA (12-1)
MAGEE 20 SENATOBIA 6
December 6, 1997: JACKSON, MS

Magee had never faced the Tate County team, but they knew it would not be easy. The Warriors under eighth-year Coach Jerry Barrett were solid defensively, giving up on 69 points all year. Said Cowart, *"That (West Marion loss) served as a pretty good wake-up call. We put it in cruise after those first four games and that loss might have served us good"*. The Clarion-Ledger called it 17-14 for Magee.

Senatobia proved they were ready to play on their second possession when Brooks Oakley found Josh Brunt from 17 yards to make it a quick 6-0. The PAT by Shae Orrell was blocked by Julius Griffith. It would be all they would get as the Trojan defense took control. In the 2nd quarter, Smith blocked a Warrior punt, Barnes picked it up and then raced 8 yards to the end zone. Robertson's kick gave Magee the lead they wouldn't lose. After halftime, Justin ran in from 8 yards after having a 24-yarder called back. Finally, with 1:15 remaining, he *"broke through a tired Senatobia defense, broke five tackles in the secondary"* and raced 42 yards for his last TD of the season. Robertson's kick finished the season.

First downs (10-8) and rushing (252-72) went to Magee. Senatobia held the air 112-0. Griffith ran for between 172-185 yards. *"I've said all season that the strength of our ball club is our defense. This is most special for the seniors. It won't be said that they came close three years and didn't get one (championship)".* Added Coach Barrett, *"Magee was just too big and too physical. They are the best team we have played all year. They wore us down ..."*

Justin Griffith ended the year as a Clarion-Ledger Athlete of the Year for his 2,533 rushing yards and 30 touchdowns. All 7-3A Special Awards included him as MVP, Danny Cowart (Coach of the Year), Eric Smith (Defensive MVP), Chris Langston (Defensive Lineman MVP), and Julius Barnes (MVP Defensive Back). All-Division players included Griffith, Langston, Terrie Logan, Smith, Tim Brown, Barnes, Willie Franks and Byron Magee.

1998 (13-2)

There was turmoil surrounding the program as the season began. Danny Cowart, popular coach who had put up a 34-7 record in his three years at Magee, was now in a legal dispute with the school. Details surrounding the circumstances are unimportant for this purpose, but both sides had valid points both legally and otherwise. The Trojans were now led by ex-assistant coach Larry Kinslow. He had been former head man at Parklane Academy and Southwest Mississippi Community College, among others, before joining the Trojans.

"I hate this for the kids to have to be in the middle of all this. Right now we're in the business of playing football. We can't worry about all this other stuff going on. We're going forward". Going forward meant having to better their 3A State Championship from the previous season. To do that, they had only 4 offensive and 3 defensive starters back. *"At Magee, you always think you can do it. We're not nearly as physical as we were last year, so we'll have to try and get outside and play more of a finesse game. But I think we'll still be able to play with a lot of people".*

While Kinslow's 7-3A squad had been decimated by key players, he still felt good as pre-season practices continued. *"If we don't get someone hurt, we'll be alright".*

GAME 1: MAGEE (0-0) vs PEARL (0-0)
MAGEE 14 PEARL 22
August 28, 1998

For the first time since 1978, Pearl did not have a head coach with the last name of Merchant. Doug had rebuilt the Pirate program from 1978-1983 while his brother Bruce put his stamp on the team starting in 1984. The latter had decided to take a new job in Collins to be closer to family. The new mentor was Marcus Boyles, former head man in Taylorsville. There, he had not only won 2 state championships in 5 years, but he amassed an amazing 67-4 record in the process. His take on the new opportunity was one of lofty expectations.

"I knew when I took this job that the expectations were high, as they are here every year. I attribute that to what Bruce has done here. All coaches put more expectations on themselves than the fans do. It's important for the coaches to keep the players from getting caught up in that so they don't start thinking that they have got to win this game. At times, the players feel the expectations more than the coaches do. We need to keep the game fun for them so that they can stay focused on the task at hand".

Voters expected Pearl to be strong, picking them 2nd in 3-5A, 13th in the AP, and 9th in The Clarion-Ledger Super 10. *"After the first five games, we'll know what kind of team we'll have this year. Those are some good football teams. 5A teams always have good players. On our front seven, we lost some players. But we've got some kids who will step up and meet that challenge. Some kids are great in practice but freeze up under the lights. Others don't show much in practice, but when the lights come on, they become great football players".*

The Magee Courier said of the game against the 15th (AP) Trojans, *"(Pearl has) not beaten Magee in several years and I don't think they can do it this year..."* The new coach said the week of the game, *"I think the biggest thing at Taylorsville is the kids expected to win every game. I'm anxious to see if it's going to be that way here. I don't know if we're a Top 10 team or not, but we're not going to back down. We're going to try to go down to Magee and whip 'em".*

Magee raced out to a 14-0 lead on a first-possession drive capped by a 3-yard Kedrick McDonald run and followed it with a 1-yard Thomas Brown dive. After a missed PAT on the initial score, they went for two points and got it via a Brown toss to Josh Chatman. Pearl cut into the lead in the 2nd on a 28-yard Justin Jenkins pass to Dray Bridges. An ensuing bad punt snap by Magee put Pearl at the 36. Two plays later, Michael Johnson rushed in from the 20. A missed PAT and a two-point conversion failure kept it 14-12 at halftime.

Magee opened the 3rd with a fumbled kickoff reception to Lawrence Jackson, putting Pearl at their 15. But the Trojan defense held and Aaron Tew nailed a 32-yarder for their first lead. Before the end of the frame, Steven Alexander crossed from the 9. Tew's PAT finished scoring on the night. Both teams fumbled in the final frame. Magee's was at the Pirate 24 while Pearl's was at the Magee 3. Michael Larry fell on the Magee fumble. The Trojans led in first downs (16-12) and total yardage (358-246).

Said Boyles, *"After the first two series, I was real concerned. We don't need to spot anybody two touchdowns. We made some adjustments on defense and they shut them down. Our defense played a good game. I was anxious to see how the kids would respond after we got down two touchdowns. They didn't quit and I'm proud of that. That showed a lot of heart"*. Added Kinslow, *"You can't make the kind of mistakes we made against a team like Pearl and win. But I expect us to get better each week. I just don't want the people to give up on us"*.

GAME 2: MAGEE (0-1) @ McCOMB (0-0)
MAGEE 21 McCOMB 17
September 4, 1998

The Tigers were in unfamiliar territory in 1997; finishing 7-4 and sitting home for the playoffs. Now, Lee Bramlett had 14 returning lettermen for this lid-lifter. *"I hope we're ready. With a young team like we have, you never know for sure. My biggest fear is to go out and make a lot of mistakes"*. The two teams had actually faced one-another in a spring scrimmage with Magee winning 14-0.

Magee would jump out to a 21-7 halftime lead at C.C. Moore Stadium and then *"held on with all they had"* to avoid an 0-2 start. Nine plays into the game, Thomas Brown dove in from close range to cap a 94-yard march and Bill Shivers converted. Back punched McComb via Patrick Miller's 52-yard touchdown scamper and Brad Boyd PAT. Magee responded with a 77-yard movement and McDonald 24-yard dash to make it 13-7. The only other score before halftime came from Brown's 55-yard dash to set up his 1-yard sneak. Bruisha Hubbard pulled the *"old swinging gate"* to add the two points.

Now in the final frame, Magee fumbled a Tiger punt to Paul Taylor. Miller passed to Chavel Williams from 6 yards and Boyd made it a 21-14 contest. The Trojans fumbled yet again on the kickoff to Tory Lewis, but the defense held Boyd to a 35-yard FG with 7:00 remaining. Again, Magee fumbled back to McComb, but the resilient defense held together. Leon Nelson's interception ended any McComb chance of a comeback. First downs (21-4), rushing (232-110) and passing (136-34) went to Magee. Tate McAlpin and Ricky Funchess led tacklers with 6 solo each.

"We hung in there and McComb played well. We had a couple of turnovers and couldn't get our offense back on the field and McComb took advantage of it. McComb is going to get better as the year goes along. We knew it was going to be tough coming in here".

GAME 3: MAGEE (1-1) @ BILOXI (0-2)
MAGEE 28 BILOXI 8
September 11, 1998

After losing back-to-back games in 1948-1949, Magee had come back with a win in 1997. Though they would be going on the road, Biloxi under Coach Mike Battles had yet to win a game thus far. In a *"mud battle"*, it was Magee recovering an early Biloxi punt fumble at the 20 to set up Hubbard's run from there and his two-point conversion.

In the next quarter, Thomas Brown *"struck paydirt again"* when he dashed 55 yards untouched. That 15-0 score held through halftime. Then, with the rain slackening, the Indians drove 55 yards with Bernard Vinson diving in from 2 yards and Ricardo Smith finding Kendrick Richards for the two-point conversion. Magee still had more in the tank, however, as Hubbard dashed in from 3 yards and Shivers converted. With 3:03 remaining, the lights went out. After a delay, Jeremy Williamson bulled up the middle, *"broke two tackles, veered off to his left and into the open field"* for the 38-yard touchdown.

First downs (11-8), rushing (324-171) and passing (27-14) went to Magee. Brown was credited with 141 rushing yards while Hubbard ran for 96 yards. Biloxi lost 3 of their 6 fumbles on the night. Said Battles, *"They have a good football team and you can't help a good football team like we did. We fumbled the football right off the bat and set them up"*.

GAME 4: MAGEE (2-1) vs WEST JONES (0-2)
MAGEE 29 WEST JONES 13
September 18, 1998

The 25 games played previously against West Jones showed a pretty competitive matching (15-9-1). Jones had just lost to perennial power Hattiesburg the week before 26-13. Though the Trojans were now 3rd in 3A voting, nothing could be taken for granted.

Chatman's 47-yard dash and Mitch Mangum's two-point pass to Hubbard put Magee up 8-0 in the opening quarter. In the 2nd, Zanyon Dampier fell on a dropped Mustang football. That led to Brown hitting Hubbard only to have him flip the ball to McDonald. Kedric ran untouched for the 35-yard score and Shivers made it 15-0. Before halftime, Clifton Pittman hit Mark Barron at the 1-yard line and then Jerome Crosby dove it for the touchdown. Luke Johnson's PAT put intermission 15-7.

The Trojans had the only score of the 3rd quarter on Brown's 15-yard run and Shivers' PAT. West Jones recovered a later fumble and Crosby made it count with a 6-yard tally. A bobbled PAT snap meant disaster for the point-after. West did not give up, driving late before Jason Rankin picked off a Mustang throw. Brown attempted to simply run the clock, but moved around the end where he found 95 yards of open field in front of him.

Though Magee led in rushing (324-140) and passing (63-33), they lost first downs (11-10). Brown rushed for 135 yards and Chatman 116 yards. Funchess led tacklers with 5 solo and 5 assists. Nelson, Lacarlos Winn and Slovokia Griffith were close behind. Dampier recorded 3 QB sacks. *"It's a real special win for me, personally. You always want to win for the home crowd. I'm glad we got this win. With the exception of a couple of series, we moved the ball pretty well"*.

GAME 5: MAGEE (3-1) @ COLLINS (3-1)
MAGEE 23 COLLINS 7
September 25, 1998

Bruce Merchant had left Pearl and now headed up long-time opponent Collins. They finished 7-4 the previous year but returned only 2 offensive and 2 defensive starters from that club. Merchant was the third coach in Collins in the past three seasons. *"We don't have a lot of people back, but those who do return should benefit greatly from last season's experience"*. The previous week, the Tigers had beaten Wilkinson County 27-6 to put their mark equal to that of Magee.

It wasn't the best showing for the Trojans, but they were able to do enough to win. Their only score of the first half came when Nick Williams grabbed a fumble at the 32-yard line and *"lumbered 68 yards for the first touchdown of his varsity career"*. Shivers' kick was true. In the 3rd quarter, Brown ran in from 37 yards and Shivers converted. Antonio Spencer's 45-yard surprise to Kentrael Goudy cut into the lead and Lester Magee knocked home the PAT to make things 14-7.

They then picked off a Brown throw in the end zone to kill a Magee response. But, they would end up fumbling a punt snap out of the end zone for a safety. With 2:48 left and in an attempt to come back, Spencer was intercepted by Rankin for a 42-yard pick-six. Shivers' kick spelled the end of the night. First downs (11-5) and rushing (225-72) went to Magee. Collins out-passed them 54-33. Brown rushed for 84 yards while numerous Trojans players were credited with tackles.

Said Merchant, *"We made three turnovers. On those, they scored 16 points. You can take those mistakes away and it's an even game. I guess that's why you play the games on the field. They made big plays and forced our hand at time. Other times our inept offense killed us. Magee dominated the line of scrimmage. Offensively we have a long way to go"*.

GAME 6: MAGEE (4-1) vs HEIDELBERG (1-4)
MAGEE 28 HEIDELBERG 0
October 2, 1998: HOMECOMING

Though Chris Gale's Oilers had gone 2-9 in his first year as head man, he said that *"I think that we played great defense last year. I also think that great defense helped us stay in ball games, but we just didn't score enough"*. In six meetings, they had never beaten a Magee team. And with the Trojans now 20th in the AP poll, that would not change.

An opening kick fumble to Tony Floyd set up Brown's 1-yard sneak and Shivers' PAT. Dampier then found another fumble and Williamson used it to bust through from the 1 for the next TD. Again Shivers was true. Before the end of the quarter, Magee drove 62 yards with Brown hitting Novak Traxler for the touchdown. Shivers' PAT marked the end of scoring until the 3rd quarter. With substitutions in play, McDonald got in from 2 yards and Shivers ended scoring. One more opportunity was lost due to a fumble at the Oiler 10.

Magee dominated statistics. First downs (23-3), passing (39-38) and rushing (304 to -6) showed what the final could have been. Brown ran for 82 yards while McDonald added 63 more. Funchess had 3 QB sacks, Nick Williams had 6 solo tackles, while many others also had good numbers.

GAME 7: MAGEE (5-1) @ PRENTISS (1-5)
MAGEE 41 PRENTISS 6
October 9, 1998

Prentiss had a miserable season the year before as Coach Alvin Gray's Bulldogs finished just 1-9 on their campaign. *"(Last season) is motivating me. I hope it's motivating the kids. I know they don't want to go through another season like that and neither do I. We just didn't have the skill people we had the year before. I feel like we are bigger on the lines and have more team speed this year"*. Meanwhile, Magee had moved to 18th in the AP.

Scoring was early and often for the Trojans. They put up two opening-quarter touchdowns on Brown's 47-yard pass to Traxler and Brown's 1-yard dive. The last touchdown was set up by a Williams fumble recovery. Shivers was true on the kicks and another later. Brown added another in the next frame from 8 yards and they pulled a *"swinging gate"* pitch from Traxler to McDonald *"who ran untouched the final 32 yards on the 53-yard play"*. Halftime sat 28-0.

Reserves now took the field for the Trojans. Slovakia Griffith added a 2-yard keeper and Tomario Weathersby dove in from 4 yards for the last. Midway through the final quarter, Omar Robinson found Eddie Ratliff from 7 yards to avoid the shutout. Magee led in first downs (18-8), rushing (262-26) and passing (91-43). Funchess recorded 10 solo tackles, 3 assists and 2 sacks.

GAME 8: MAGEE (6-1) vs WEST MARION (5-2)
MAGEE 25 WEST MARION 14
October 16, 1998

The previous season was still in the minds of the Trojans when they welcomed West Marion to Simpson County as their only loss of that year had come at the hands of the visitors. The Hattiesburg American picked Magee 21-6, saying *"Remember last year? West Marion won 14-6. Even if you don't, rest assured Magee does"*.

It looked as if Magee would strike early after a WM fumble, but their drive ended in futile at the 10-yard line. Hubbard, however, found the end zone from 5 yards on the next possession and Shivers converted. Then, James May blocked a later West Marion punt and Mario Weathersby recovered for Magee in the end zone. Halftime now sat 13-0. The Trojans opened the 3rd with a 75-yard march with McDonald covering the last 20 yards *"up the middle"*. Now in the 4th quarter, West Marion found paydirt on a 14-yard Mark Broom run and Terrance Brister two-pointer. That had been set up by a fumble recovered by Jason Graham.

An ensuing Magee fumble recovered by Thomas Johnson allowed the visitors to strike again when Broom hit Chester Toney from 35 yards. On the kickoff, McDonald *"took the kick on his own three and set sail straight up the middle 97 yards for the back-breaking touchdown"*. First downs (16-9), rushing (209-63) and passing (135-43) went to Magee. Michael Magee led tacklers with 9 solo and 2 assists. Funchess, Dampier, Jamie Ingram and James Pittman added sacks.

GAME 9: MAGEE (7-1) @ RALEIGH (2-6)
MAGEE 21 RALEIGH 13
October 23, 1998

The previous year had been a brutal one for Raleigh. Magee put up their second-most points in a contest in their 68-0 beating and the Lions surely had that encounter in their minds.

Magee opened scoring midway through the 1st quarter on Brown's 6-yard run and Shivers' PAT. Raleigh then punched back with Jerry Nixon's 11-yard escape and Charlie Goodman's PAT. Magee added one more before halftime when Brown got in from 5 yards away. Now in the final frame, both teams found paydirt. Griffith dodged in from 11 yards with 1:48 left but Jafus McCullum took the ensuing kick 85 yards to the end zone. Now 21-13, they attempted the onside kick, but it hit Matthew Keller and Magee ran out the clock.

Despite the score, stats were gaudy. Magee led in first downs (19-5), rushing (302-106) and passing (36-9). Chatman (95) and Brown (91) led rushers. Leon Nelson had 7 solo and 2 assists to lead tacklers. Williams recorded a pair of sacks. Raleigh had an interception by Jason Hughes, but their 47-yard FG attempt failed.

GAME 10: MAGEE (8-1) vs EAST MARION (4-5)
MAGEE 34 EAST MARION 18
October 30, 1998

In a game that would give Magee yet another division title, they did not fail to grab it. They scored twice in the opening frame on Brown's 58-yard dash and McDonald's 1-yard dive. Shivers provided both points-after. In the 2nd, Brown and Traxler connected from 30 yards before East Marion responded with Jamie Powell's 32-yard pass to Sh'ron Chisolm. That play had been a multi-reverse and halfback pass. Before halftime, Magee drove 85 yards with Brown and Traxler hooking up from 8 yards and Shivers connecting.

East added the only score of the 3rd quarter when Powell hit Brian Ducre from 33 yards. Midway through the final stanza, Powell dove in from a yard for their last score. Magee answered with a 67-yard march capped by Hubbard's 9-yarder and Shivers' kick. Magee led in first downs (22-9) and rushing (305-81) while East led in passing (131-65). Brown rushed for 101 yards while Griffith led tacklers with 6 solo, 4 assists and a sack.

Coach Les Peters' assistant Greg Ellzey said afterward, *"When Magee came out on the field to warm up, it looked like an ant bed with a bunch of players going everywhere"*.

GAME 11: MAGEE (9-1) vs MENDENHALL (4-6)
MAGEE 35 MENDENHALL 16
November 6, 1998

Unexpectedly, this would be another year where Magee held a decisive record over rival Mendenhall. The Tigers' last 5-4A game ended the previous week with a 34-17 win over Quitman. While records mattered as much as a newspaper picks, The Clarion-Ledger chose the Trojans 28-14. Still, there were bragging rights on the line at Trojan Field in front of an estimated 5,500 fans.

Midway through the 1st quarter, McDonald got through Tiger defenders for a 24-yard touchdown and Shivers connected. Mendy came right back with James Hobbs' 13-yarder to Jeffery Hobbs. Matt Powers booted the extra point to tie the game. Quickly, McDonald took a handoff 70 yards for another TD and Shivers was again true. In the 2nd, Powers nailed a 42-yard FG to cut into the lead, but Magee then went 57 yards with Hubbard doing the damage from 20 yards. Shivers put halftime 21-10.

Alex McCullum's 5-yard dash in the 3rd quarter made it an interesting 21-16 going into the final stanza. But Magee would let them go no further. Hugh Pace's hit on McCullum at the goal line forced a fumble recovered by Michael Magee for a score. Griffith then picked off a Tiger pass and Chatman made it worthwhile with his 67-yard dash to paydirt. Shivers provided both extra points for the rivalry win.

Mendy led in first downs (15-12) and passing (58-0). But Magee held firmly on the ground 333-128. McDonald ran for 174 markers while Chatman added 82 more. Nelson had 7 solo tackles and 5 assists while Dampier and Griffith pitched in with 6 each. *"A lot of people didn't think we would be where we are right now. We lost a lot of talent last year but these kids can play. They made their minds up to move on and have played well and done a creditable job under the circumstances"*. Added the Tigers' Coach Steve Pruett, *"We wanted to come down here and do two things. That was stop the big plays and not turn the ball over. We didn't do either"*.

GAME 12: MAGEE (10-1) vs HAZLEHURST (9-2)
MAGEE 30 HAZLEHURST 24
November 13, 1998

With one lone exception (1946), Magee and Hazlehurst had squared off against one-another from 1943-1976. They had played earlier (1931 and 1940) but had not met since that last game some 22 years earlier. Hazlehurst had put up a fantastic 9-2 record thus far and had a chance to win just their second game in 21 attempts against Magee. The Hattiesburg American picked the Trojans 28-14.

This would not be the same Indian team that Magee had bested for so long. They drove 57 yards to start and capped it with Corey Stewart's 2-yard run and Andrew Burks' two-point conversion. After holding the Trojans, they fumbled the punt to Hubbard. McDonald managed a 5-yard touchdown and then added the two-pointer to tie the game. In the 2nd quarter, Hazlehurst scored again when Michael Jenkins dove in from 3 yards. Again they converted the two points on Stewart's pass to Cory Murray. But Dampier's later fumble recovery at the Indian 33 led to Brown's 25-yard toss to Traxler. Still, they were behind 16-14.

Before halftime, Hubbard *"broke free up the middle"* for a 35-yard touchdown and McDonald notched the two points. In the 3rd quarter, Michael Jenkins found paydirt from 16 yards and Burks converted the two-point play. Later, McDonald escaped from 31 yards and Brown notched the two points to put them back up 30-24. The Indians mounted a response, but Michael Magee's interception in the end zone killed the threat. Magee simply ran the clock afterwards.

The Trojans led in first downs (16-11) and rushing (262-178) while the Indians led in the air (94-24). Hubbard rushed for 117 yards. Funchess had 9 solo tackles and 4 assists to go along with a sack.

GAME 13: MAGEE (11-1) vs PURVIS (10-1)
MAGEE 12 PURVIS 6
November 20, 1998

Magee (3rd in 3A) now faced a familiar face in Purvis (5th in 3A). The previous season, Magee had beaten Purvis 14-7 in the South State finals. This game would prove to be everything sportswriters, coaches and fans thought it would be with the margin of victory even smaller than that of the previous year. Halftime was a precarious 6-0 in favor of Magee thanks to Hubbard's 5-yard run.

Perry Tisdale changed that in the 3rd quarter with his 20th touchdown on the season from 34 yards. In the final frame, Traxler's hurry of Purvis punter Tom Graham put Magee at their 23-yard line. Brown then *"rolled to his left and threw"* to Traxler for the 20-yard deciding score. The defense held strong the last few minutes and Magee was once more advancing. First downs were even (10-10) and the other stats were just as close. Rushing went to Magee (142-140) while passing went to Purvis (56-45). Pace and Michael Magee led tacklers with 6 solo and 5 assists each. Dampier had 2 sacks, Funchess added another, and Griffith picked off a pass.

"We're really thrilled to get back in the South Mississippi championship game. I don't think anybody really expected us to be there this year, considering the caliber of people we lost. This was a tough game tonight. Purvis has an outstanding football team and we just happened to come out on top. The defense played exceptionally well. Other than one big play, we bent some but we never did break. Our kids played well".

GAME 14: MAGEE (12-1) vs FOREST (11-1)
MAGEE 30 FOREST 22
November 27, 1998

The 36th meeting between the Bearcats and the Trojans would not be for divisional honors any longer. Now, they were fighting to see who would make the final two in state 3A competition. After an opening loss to Pearl, and such a tight game against Purvis, many thought that this team could not come close to coming this far. But it would get better for Trojan players, coaches and fans.

An opening interception by the Cats' Brent Odom was immediately fumbled back with Travis Stringer recovering. Then, they drove 78 yards to the end zone in 10 plays with Chatman rushing in from 8 yards and Brown counting two points on the conversion. Forest didn't quit; instead driving the other way with Walter Franklin finishing from 2 yards to make it 8-6. In the 2nd quarter, they took the lead when Marcus Lee darted in from 57 yards and Mario Thomas converting the two-point play.

A long Chatman kick return set up Brown's strike to Traxler from 30 yards and Shivers converted. Now 15-14 at halftime, the Cats fumbled the kickoff and Darius Cox fell on the loose pigskin. Eight minutes later, Magee finished the 60-yard march when Brown hit Traxler from a yard away. Shivers' kick made it 22-14. Magee promptly fumbled a Cat punt and Lyfatoriest Young got the ball at the 41. Mario Thomas made the most of it with a 10-yard run and Franklin's two-pointer tied the game 22-22.

With 3:26 left, Brown found Chatman *"in his right flat and Chatman broke a tackle at the 3 to score on a 14-yard pass play covering 55 yards"*. Hubbard's two-point conversion meant the end of scoring. A Cat fumble on the kick was recovered by Magee to seal it. Brown rushed for 111 yards and Traxler pulled in 163 yard in receiving. Magee led all the way around: first downs (16-7), rushing (245-95) and passing (224-9). Funchess led tacklers with 10 solo while Darius Cox (9) and Pace (8) were close behind.

Said Coach Jack French, *"We just made too many mistakes and you can't do that against Magee. They are a good ball club"*. Added Kinslow, *"It was back and forth, back and forth. This is what high school football is all about. These two teams just went after each other. Forest has a very good football team. These Trojans never gave up. I am very proud of them"*.

GAME 15: MAGEE (13-1) vs AMORY (14-0)
MAGEE 18 AMORY 35
December 5, 1998: VETERANS MEMORIAL STADIUM; JACKSON

Another trip to the state championship and another first-time opponent awaited the Trojans. Amory, under legendary Coach Bobby Hall, had held the top spot in 3A the entire season. And they had 2 titles in the last 4 years. *"When you think of high school football in Mississippi, there are few teams you think of immediately. Magee is one of them and I think it's similar with us. Both schools have rich and storied traditions"*. Said Kinslow, *"We're going to have to play well. Amory is 14-0 and they are good. We can play with them. They are good, but we are not in awe of them. We've got to keep them from getting the ball because they can score a lot of points. If we keep going three-and-out, it'll be a long day"*. The Clarion-Ledger though Amory best 21-14.

There were 10,881 *"frenzied football fans"* in 80-degree weather at Veterans Memorial Stadium to see which of the two powerhouse teams would claim the title. Amory's first drive ended with Steve Griffin's 6-yard run and David Mooneyham's PAT. Magee came right back with a 76-yard drive and Brown 4-yarder. But, the two-point conversion failed and kept it 7-6. In the 2nd quarter, Amory went 56 yards with Mooneyham pulling in a 25-yard throw from Will Hall. Late in the frame, Magee moved to the Amory 24 but their pass was picked off to keep intermission 14-6.

Amory started to pull ahead in the 3rd quarter with Clifton Moore's 30-yard escape and Mooneyham conversion followed by Hall's pass to Mooneyham lateraled to Deshaun Fields and taken 41 yards to paydirt. Mooneyham also added the point-after. Magee did not quit; instead driving 78 yards with Brown finding McDonald from 17 yards. Amory responded with a 37-yard Fields run and Mooneyham PAT to make it 35-12. The last score came from the Trojans when they moved 80 yards with Chatman running *"straight up the middle"* from 43 yards for the finale.

The champions led in rushing (302-228) while Magee held first downs (20-16) and passing (100-54). The Magee Courier agreed, with some exceptions in yardage. Brown led Trojan rushers with 93 yards while Hubbard had 74 yards. *"We knew we had to keep Amory's offense off the field. They kept Brown off-balance all day. I think our kids played gallantly. Nobody gave us a chance to be here. It was very satisfying for us to make it this far. I told the kids before the game that whatever happens, don't forget what we have accomplished this season"*.

1999 (11-3)

As was common, realignment in MHSAA meant new opponents for the Trojans. For example, long-time foe Forest was now in the division and picked 1st in the grouping. Larry Kinslow's Trojans were picked 2nd in 7-3A and 5th in overall 3A after three-straight amazing seasons. Magee had 15 lettermen back, including 5 offensive starters and 4 on defense. *"When we take the field, we must be ready to play every down. Folks will be looking at us and try to slip up on us. We have got to play good from the start"*.

GAME 1: MAGEE (0-0) @ COLUMBIA (0-0)
MAGEE 0 COLUMBIA 6
August 27, 1999

Columbia had always proven to be a tough opponent for the Trojans. Since 1977, the series between the teams sat 4-4. The Wildcats had posted a 12-3 campaign the previous season that ended in the 4A title game. Said Kinslow of Coach Joey Porter's team, *"They will be extremely tough. They have a lot of good position people coming back from an excellent team last year"*.

The Magee mentor was accurate in his estimation of the Cats. The battle at Gardner Stadium of South State Champions was a defensive struggle. Magee managed trips to the Columbia 8, 25 and 7-yard lines in the first quarter but could capitalize on none of the opportunities. The only tally of the contest came in the 3rd frame when Darrell Abram hit Antoiuine Brown for a 76-yard touchdown. Magee was in a giving mood the entire night, fumbling 7 times, throwing an interception, and committing 80 yards in second half penalties.

Columbia outgained Magee 239-183 in total yardage. Said Porter, *"Magee's defense was really good. Our offense played real good, but we're still inexperienced"*.

GAME 2: MAGEE (0-1) @ LAWRENCE COUNTY (1-0)
MAGEE 12 LAWRENCE COUNTY 29
September 3, 1999

The schedule would get no easier as Coach Danny Adams' Cougars awaited the Trojans for their very first tussle. They were now 4th in overall 4A, had gone 10-2 the previous year with 22 seniors on the team. Said Kinslow, *"That tells me they are tough at all positions"*. Added Adams, *"Magee's a great football school. That's the kind of people we want to bring in here. We want to be able to play with the Magees of the world"*. The Clarion-Ledger picked Lawrence County 21-14.

After a 25-minute weather delay, LCHS was able to secure the first score on Lorenzo Townsend's 35-yard FG. The Trojans marched right back down the field and recorded a touchdown on Mitch Mangum's 17-yard pass to Corey Payne. The 6-3 lead would not hold long. A 2nd quarter fumble by Magee set up Michael Loving's 2-yard plunge and Townsend's PAT. Again Magee fumbled to Jermaine Maye and Townsend turned it a few plays later into a 16-yard score. Halftime was 16-6.

The Cougars had the only points of the 3rd quarter via Loving's 4-yard dive and Townsend kick. Townsend's last came in the 4th quarter from 26 yards while Magee managed just one more response. Brian Hayes' 38-yard pass to Willis Hobbs put them at the 2-yard line from where Cedric Crosby plunged into the end zone. LCHS led in total yardage 364-194. Said Adams, *"Magee played in the last two 3A title games and won it in '97. They've been where we'd love to go. Any win against a program of that caliber is a good win"*.

GAME 3: MAGEE (0-2) vs BILOXI (1-1)
MAGEE 25 BILOXI 7
September 10, 1999

It had been since 1982 that a Magee team started the season 0-3. In order to avoid matching that feat, they would have to now focus on Coach Mike Battle's Gulf Coast squad. Magee had beaten them two years in a row, but the Indians had finished a lowly 2-8 that previous season.

A Biloxi fumble toward the end of the opening frame set up Crosby's 2-yard scoring dive. James Pittman recovered another loose football and A.J. Holloway made the most of the gift from a yard out. In the 3rd quarter, Chatman increased the lead with a 20-yard run to make it 18-0. Biloxi secured their only points afterwards when Bernard Vinson *"ran straight up the middle"* from 18 yards would and Brandon Moore converted. Holloway finished things in the final stanza with a 40-yard dash to paydirt and Chatman knocked home the extra point.

Chatman led rushers with 114 yards. A host of defensive players played admirably for the Trojans, while Nick Williams, Louis Hull and LaCarlos Winn recorded sacks. Hull and Darius Cox also had interceptions.

GAME 4: MAGEE (1-2) vs HEIDELBERG (2-1)
MAGEE 55 HEIDELBERG 6
September 17, 1999

Things looked easier for this week in Simpson County as the Oilers came to town. Coach Larry McGill's team finished 3-8 the previous season and were slotted 4th in 7-3A for the coming year. In seven tilts between the two teams since 1986, Magee had yet to drop a contest. Only the opening frame was close.

An early fumble recovery led to Josh Warren's 12-yard run and the first of 7 Williams extra points. Heidelberg managed their only score thereafter when Perry Buxton hit Gabriel Ferguson from 25 yards. The Clarion-Ledger called it a Bridges pass to Shaw. The Trojans then began to score at will; putting up a pair before halftime. Holloway ran in from 11 yards for the first and from 5 yards for the last. Magee bested that mark with three scores in the 3rd quarter. Hayes hit Holloway from 5 yards, Tony Floyd picked off a pass and turned it into a 50-yard pick-six, and Slovakia Griffith did the same thing for 60 yards.

Now in the final quarter, Mangum hit Michael Stubbs for a 70-yard touchdown. With reserves in play, Eric Floyd dashed in from 32 yards to finish scoring. Holloway led rushers with 93 markers while Magee threw for 101 yards on the night. The defense allowed 9 Oiler first downs.

GAME 5: MAGEE (2-2) @ PRENTISS (1-3)
MAGEE 46 PRENTISS 0
September 24, 1999

Though Magee would now be on the road, it was to face a Bulldog team that finished 1-9 the previous year. Coach Alvin Gray's squad was projected no better this year, picked last in 7-3A. Their last game against Forest ended 48-0.

The first three quarters was a barrage of Trojan scoring. Prentiss fumbled the opening kick to set up Mangum's 21-yard pass to Payne. Myricks Cole then forced a fumble to Ty Green; leading to Holloway's 5-yarder and 12-0 lead. In the 2nd quarter, Crosby broke free for a 33-yard score. Then, Roderick Nelson picked off a pass and Hobbs finished things from 3 yards away. An errant Dog punt snap and ensuing fumble allowed Griffith the easy recovery for yet another score. Three Williams kicks made halftime 33-0.

It took only as long as the kickoff to record another touchdown, as Mario Weathersby took the ball 86 yards to the end zone. Finally, Hobbs dove in from 5 yards away and Williams iced the evening. Magee put up 354 offensive yards with Crosby rushing for 101 of them. Hobbs pitched in with 85 more. The defense held Prentiss to 67 yards of output and forced 6 fumbles.

GAME 6: MAGEE (3-2) vs COLLINS (4-1)
MAGEE 46 COLLINS 12
October 1, 1999: HOMECOMING

Things would get harder for Homecoming as Coach Bruce Merchant's Tigers came to town. They had been picked 3rd in the division after an 8-3 season but were already 4-1 thus far. Their only loss had come the week before to Forest 33-12. Among those in attendance at this affair was *"quite a presence"* of Forest observers scouting their upcoming opponent. The Clarion-Ledger felt Magee better 24-14.

An opening-kick fumble by Magee gave Collins a golden opportunity. But the solid defense held the advance at the 8-yard line. Hobbs turned that stand into a 66-yard dash to daylight for a 6-0 lead. In the 2nd quarter, Chatman dodged in from 3 yards and Hobbs converted the two points. Shortly before intermission, a snap over the Cat punter's head was recovered by Williams for another touchdown and 26-0 lead. Magee continued the pressure in the 3rd with Nelson's 31-yard pick-six off of Kentrael Groudy, but the Cats got on the board afterwards when John Holloway found the end zone from 2 yards.

Hobbs finished the quarter with a 12-yard run and, with a pair of Williams extra points, it was now 40-6. Collins found paydirt again on a 27-yard Shannon Lockhart escape for what would be their final score. Later, a jarring hit on their QB forced a fumble to Jonathan Varnes. He picked up the pigskin and raced 40 yards to the end zone. Collins led in first downs (18-14) and passing (116-61) while Magee held the ground (237-139). Hobbs rushed for 117 yards.

"I thought we played pretty well with a lot of intensity. We didn't make a lot of mistakes. I was surprised. If you'd told me we'd score 46 points on Collins, I'd have said you were crazy". Said Merchant, *"Magee just whipped the stew out of us. They wanted it and they took it. They came ready to play. They got after it, and that was it in a nutshell"*.

GAME 7: MAGEE (4-2) @ FOREST (4-1)
MAGEE 12 FOREST 0
October 8, 1999

The biggest game of the year was now at hand in Scott County. Coach Jack French's Bearcats went 11-2 the previous year and were now top-ranked in 3A polling. Magee sat 5th in the same poll. *"Forest will be a tremendous challenge for us. They're a very big, physical team. It should be a good one"*. The winner of this tilt held the definite advantage in claiming the 7-3A crown at year's end.

The rainy game lived up to its billing, with mistakes being the deciding factor in the outcome. Magee's first touchdown came after a *"vicious hit"* forced one fumble. Chatman took advantage of the gift with his 2-yard plunge to make it 6-0. Forest threatened before halftime, but their 44-yard scoring pass play between Mario Thomas and Michael Wells was called back for illegal motion. Either Winn or Cole recovered a 3rd quarter fumble to allow Hobbs a later 24-yard scoring dash and the final points of the night. Williams' sack in the final frame and a later interception *"put the lid on the game"*.

Magee led in first downs (11-7), rushing (125-102) and passing (60-16). Forest lost 5 of their 7 fumbles on the night while Magee coughed up only one to the Cats. *"This was just two good football teams that played hard and with a couple of breaks could have gone either way. This was a tremendous challenge for us to be able to come in here and get some things done"*. For his efforts, Kinslow was voted Clarion-Ledger Coach of the Week. Added French, *"Magee came to play and they played extremely well. They have a fine program and believe in what they're doing ..."*

GAME 8: MAGEE (5-2) vs NEWTON (3-4)
MAGEE 57 NEWTON 15
October 15, 1999

Magee was now tops in 7-3A and up to 4th overall in 3A voting. Next on the calendar was the Newton squad. Magee had run up against teams from Newton County twice in the past. In 1932, a Newton team took home a win while Magee redeemed themselves in 1961.

The opening quarter was a scoring frenzy for the Trojans, as was the last. Newton fumbled on their second possession to Hull at midfield. Hobbs "*blasted off left tackle*" from 2 yards for the touchdown and Mangum provided the two-pointer. They then went 64 yards with Chatman doing the honors from 3 yards and Williams converting his first of 5 PATs. Hobbs' 13-yard scoring run was followed by a bad Newton snap resulting in a safety after the punter kicked the ball out of the end zone.

A Newton interception by Moses Evans led a few plays later to Lonnie Jones' 1-yard plunge and Josh Thoms' PAT. But Williams came back with his own interception of Ladarrian Blaylock and raced 65 yards to paydirt. Halftime now sat 30-7. Reserves taking the field held the game scoreless in the 3rd quarter, but Magee exploded in the final frame. After Blaylock hit Thomas from 10 yards for their last tally, Chatman started the barrage with a 2-yard run. Then, Griffith returned a fumble 30 yards for a touchdown, Darius Cox recorded a 30-yard pick-six, and finally Michael Paul Meadows recovered yet another Newton fumble and took it 40 yards to the end zone.

The game ended tied for 6th all-time in points-scored for a Magee football team. Nick Williams was named a Clarion-Ledger Top Performer.

GAME 9: MAGEE (6-2) vs McLAURIN (5-3)
MAGEE 55 McLAURIN 6
October 22, 1999

Another new face was at hand at Trojan Field in the form of the team picked 5th in 7-3A. The opponent was in store for more offensive, defensive, and special teams' fireworks from Magee. That started with a safety when Magee tackled Chad Sebren in the end zone. Hobbs added a 21-yarder and Holloway did the same later from a yard away. Williams converted on the first score to make it a quick 15-0.

McLaurin's only threat thus far was spoiled when Williams blocked a 33-yard Jay Eklund FG attempt. Then, Chatman dove in from a yard, Joey Warren added a 37-yard pick-six, and Hayes hit Craig from 28 yards for another. With Williams kicks, it was 36-0. Substitutes took over for the second half and Sebren managed a 1-yard sneak for the score. Griffith blocked their PAT. The Trojans responded with a 72-yard drive with Chatman getting in from the 24-yard line. They recovered a kickoff fumble and Warren found the end zone from 18 yards. Tomario Weathersby did the same from 35 yards for the last tally.

Magee now had another 7-3A championship in hand. Chatman led rushers with 90 yards while Williams led tacklers with 9 solo. The Trojan defense held McLaurin to just 140 yards of total offense on the evening.

GAME 10: MAGEE (7-2) @ RALEIGH (5-4)
MAGEE 32 RALEIGH 19
October 29, 1999

Raleigh, under former Trojan assistant coach Terrell Luckey, was vastly improved from their 2-9 season. Picked 4th in the division, they now had a winning record toward the end of the year. While Magee would not put up another 55-point performance, it still ended in their favor.

The Trojans went 74 yards in seven minutes and 14 plays for their first tally. That came on Mangum's 8-yard pass to Craig to make it 6-0. The Lions moved 80 yards in response with Keller hitting Milo Epting from 18 yards and Goodwin providing the go-ahead PAT. Surprisingly, they moved 77 yards on their next touch with the two players hooking up from 44 yards. Magee was now down 13-6. Before halftime, a horrid punt put Magee in striking distance and Crosby finished the gift from a yard out to make it 13-12 at intermission.

A Lion fumble by Bobby Keyes in the 3rd set up Hobbs' 17-yard run and Magnum hit Chatman for the two points. Cox then picked off a Raleigh pass by Keller and Hobbs again found daylight from 7 yards to make it 26-13. Raleigh came back with an 84-yard Barry Haynes dash, but Chatman took the ensuing kick 97 yards for a touchdown. However, a flag brought it back for clipping. With 8:21 left, Tate McAlpin found a loose Lion football and took it 30 yards to the end zone for what would be the finale. Chatman rushed for 110 yards while Eric Floyd and Cole led tacklers with 8 solo and 3 assists each.

GAME 11: MAGEE (8-2) @ MENDENHALL (6-4)
MAGEE 21 MENDENHALL 2
November 5, 1999

Rival Mendenhall had a first-year coach in Andy Stevens. The Tigers went 4-7 the year before but now had 22 lettermen back. Of those, 6 were offensive starters while 5 came back from the defensive side of the football. Mendy was assured of a playoff berth as runners-up in 5-4A and had suffered two of their losses only to power teams Lawrence County and South Pike. With Magee now 2nd in 3A overall, The Clarion-Ledger picked the Trojans 31-20.

After an opening fumble by the Tigers, Magee moved 56 yards with Holloway getting in for the final 2 yards and Williams converting. In the 2nd, Holloway dove in from a yard and Williams increased the lead to 14-0 at halftime. Both defenses stood tall for the scoreless 3rd quarter, but each found points in the final one. A low Trojan snap gave Mendenhall a safety, but Magee marched 87 yards with Chatman *"bolting around his own left end and (speeding) 53 yards down the sidelines to the Tiger 20"*. Hobbs finished the effort from 3 yards and Williams knocked home the PAT.

Magee led in first downs (18-6) and rushing (278-83) while Mendy held the air by two yards (11-9). Stats vary depending on the source. Chatman led rushers with 104 while Holloway added another 88. James Pittman's 8 tackles was best for Magee while Warren added 6 of his own. *"They were shutting us down on the outside, so we looked to go inside a little more than usual. We were able to move the ball and eat up a lot of clock on those* drives".

GAME 12: MAGEE (9-2) vs TYLERTOWN (8-2)
MAGEE 7 TYLERTOWN 5
November 12, 1999

The Chiefs under coach Walter Denton were coming into the playoffs after a win over West Marion. Now, they faced the top team in 3A voting. Said Kinslow, *"When you get to the four-game playoffs, anything can happen. We're a young team with only two senior starters. Right now, our defense is playing extremely well"*. The two teams had played before. Tylertown beat Magee in 1942 before losing the rematch a year later. But Magee came back with five-straight wins between 1959-1963.

The game would be as tight as they come, with The Magee Courier noting that the Trojans *"dodged a bullet"*. The only touchdown of the night came from Magee with :06 left in the 2nd quarter when reserve QB Hayes hit Craig from 28 yards. After a celebration penalty, Williams *"calmly stepped up and booted the 35-yard extra point"*. A strong Chief drive to start the 3rd quarter got to the Trojan 4 before Griffith picked off a Jeremy Clement pass to kill the threat.

Tylertown again moved steadily on their next possession and finished drive with John McBeth's 30-yard FG. Now in the final frame, they drove again deep in Magee territory. But their opportunity was nullified at the Trojan 10 on downs. However, Holloway was *"dropped at his own goal line with the referee awarding the Chiefs a safety"* with 4:32 remaining. Rem Ginn was credited with the tackle. It wouldn't be enough as the defense stood tall for the last threat. The Magee Courier made special mention of LaCarlos Winn by saying that he *"probably played the best game of the season"*.

Tylertown had a pair of touchdowns called back. The first was a 52-yard Angelo Magee punt return while a QB sneak was also flagged. Said Denton, *"Sometimes the best team doesn't always win. Our kids played their hearts out"*. The Tylertown Times said that overall yardage favored the Chiefs 285-80.

GAME 13: MAGEE (10-2) @ NEWTON COUNTY (11-0)
MAGEE 14 NEWTON COUNTY 7
November 19, 1999

Not to be confused with Newton, the Cougars of Newton County were undefeated thus far. Their last game had resulted in a 21-0 win over Amite County. Their QB (Corey Amis) was 4th in 3A with 14 touchdown passes. It was to be another nail-biter for Trojan fans in attendance.

Magee struck first in the 2nd quarter on Holloway's bulldozing run to paydirt from 4 yards and Williams' PAT. The Cougars came right back with an 80-yard march ending on Cedric Cotton's 9-yard dash and David McConnell's PAT. The Trojans may have added some insurance just before halftime at the 10-yard line, but the effort failed. After a scoreless 3rd quarter, Magee inserted the dagger when Griffith picked off an Amis pass and took it to the 17-yard line. Crosby ran for 14 yards and then, after a penalty, Hobbs *"cut up field"* for the touchdown. Newton County made a valiant effort afterwards by moving to the Trojan 13, but the defense held to give Magee the win.

Chatman rushed for 81 yards while Holloway pitched in another 52 yards. First downs (14-12) and passing (52-44) went to Newton County while Magee held the ground 193-166.

GAME 14: MAGEE (11-2) vs FOREST (10-2)
MAGEE 18 FOREST 53
November 26, 1999

The rematch against Forest was at hand but now in Simpson County. On October 8th, Forest had fumbled their way into a loss against the Trojans and fans were hoping that the result of this tilt would be the same. This one was for the South Mississippi 3A title. Forest had just beaten Wilkinson County 38-8 and sat 2nd in overall 3A behind Magee. Those eight points were the only ones they had allowed thus far in the playoffs. The two teams had been in the same situation the year before, but Magee was best then by a 30-22 final.

The first half was a slugfest between two teams with phenomenal high school football histories. Magee was up first in the opening frame on Holloway's 1-yarder. The Bearcats responded with a pair of scores. The first on a 38-yard Titus White run and David Turner PAT and the last on Marcus Lee's 4-yard dive. In the 2nd quarter, Hayes hit Hobbs from 33 yards to cut into the lead 13-12. Forest responded with a 29-yard strike from Mario Thomas to Daryl Slaughter, but Chatman changed things with an ensuing 93-yard kick return to make halftime 19-18.

The remainder of the game was totally in the hands of the visitors. Pete McBride escaped from 7 yards, a fumble to Corey Hayes led to McBride's 4-yard run, another fumble (or B.J. Jones interception) resulted in Lee's 22-yard scamper, Lee did it again from 5 yards and then Stephen Goodlow picked up another fumble and took it 20 yards for the touchdown. Turner's kick was true. First downs (14-6) and rushing (346-89) were dominated by Forest. Passing (41 to -8) was held by Magee. The Trojans had no first downs and only 22 yards of offense in the second half.

At season's end, Slovakia Griffith earned a MHSAA First Team 3A nod for their All-Defensive Team. All 7-3 honors also went to him, Josh Chatman, Willis Hobbs, Myricks Cole, Joey Warren, Eric Floyd, Nick Williams, Tate McAlpin and A.J. Holloway. Forest beat Shannon 36-23 to claim the 3A title.

2000

2000 Team (13-2): 3A State Champions

2000 (13-2) 3A STATE CHAMPIONS

Third-year Coach Larry Kinslow brought 17 starters and 24 lettermen back to his 7-3A Trojans. Voters had them picked 2nd in 3A to start the season. Shannon held the top spot. *"We could have a pretty good team if we stay healthy. On offense we should be fairly strong with most of last year's starters returning. On defense, we have good team speed and run to the ball well; although we have a lack of depth at certain spots. We have some players that may have to play on both sides of the ball"*.

GAME 1: MAGEE (0-0) vs COLUMBIA (0-0)
MAGEE 8 COLUMBIA 14
August 25, 2000

Magee had lost 3 season openers in 5 years and now they played a team against whom the Trojans held just a 6-5 advantage since 1973. Coach Joey Porter's Cats had finished 9-2 the previous season and brought back 17 starters. *"Our goal is to get back to the playoffs. We've got a good football team but it will be tough ... We've got to hit on all cylinders"*. Said Kinslow, *"They have an outstanding team returning"*.

Like other recent games, the contest was stalled by a severe thunderstorm. Lighting went out in front of 3,500 fans in Simpson County to delay the start of the season. When Columbia finally took the field, they hit the board in 13 plays when Anoiuine Brown *"busted into the end zone from one yard out"*. Brown then threw to Joseph Paige to make it 8-0. The Wildcats increased the lead in the next quarter on another 1-yard Brown run to make it 14-0. Magee's only points came before halftime when A.J. Holloway dashed 65 yards for the touchdown and Willis Hobbs notched the two-pointer.

The rest of the game, with *"tired and weary (teams) on a wet, steamy football field"* turned into a defensive struggle with neither finding the end zone. Magee had chances but a drive to the Cat 30 and 35 yard lines, as well as a Boyce Varnes fumble recovery, went for naught. Said Porter, *"Magee is a very solid ball club and that's why we scheduled them for the first game. This is a good measuring stick for our club"*.

GAME 2: MAGEE (0-1) vs LAWRENCE COUNTY (0-1)
MAGEE 34 LAWRENCE COUNTY 25
September 1, 2000

The only other meeting between the teams came the year before when Lawrence County defeated the Trojans. In a tight contest, this one went to Magee. It didn't start that way as Jerry Smith took the opening touch 77 yards to the end zone and John Eley booted the PAT. A few minutes later, the Trojans finished a 69-yard drive when Holloway burst through from 9 yards and Brian Hayes snuck in for the two-pointer. Back came LCHS with a 69-yard move ending in Jeremy Graves' (or Eley's) 1-yard dive to make it 13-8.

But the Trojans had a few more left in them before halftime. They went 72 yards with Hayes finding Mario Craig from the 5-yard line and Hayes again converting. Then, they recorded a safety on a Smith tackle. With less than a minute left, Hayes and Craig hooked up from 40 yards and Hayes' two-point keeper made halftime 26-13. Now in the 4th quarter, Magee drove 94 yards with Holloway gaining purchase from the 9-yard line. Hayes converted yet again and it was 34-13.

The Cougars kept going with a 1-yard dive by Smith and his ensuing 7-yard run with 1:04 remaining. The last touchdown was set up by Eskia Rhodes' fumble recovery. First downs (19-12) and passing (63-12) went to Magee. Rushing was even at 264 yards each. Holloway, with 176 rushing yards, was voted the Pacesetter Stores Player of the Week for his efforts. Tony Floyd and Paul Overby each had 6 tackles while Brian Robinson added 5 more. Said Coach Danny Adams, *"The best team won the football game"*.

GAME 3: MAGEE (1-1) @ BILOXI (0-2)
MAGEE 6 BILOXI 31
September 8, 2000

The sixth all-time game against the Indians would be perhaps the most disappointing. Magee had lost to Biloxi in 1948 and 1949 but had rallied to win the last 3 games over the same span of years. It would be a poorly-attended game, albeit on the road, with The Magee Courier calling it *"the smallest crowd in the history of Magee High School"*.

An opening squib kick by Brandon Moore was recovered by David Blaine at the Magee 36. One play later, Rophyel Howell hit Josh Leonard for a touchdown and Moore made it a quick 7-0. They moved 78 yards in the next quarter with Leonard running from 14 yards and Moore again converting. Before intermission, that lead grew when Moore hit a 35-yard FG to make it 17-0. The 4th quarter was no better for the Trojans. Martinez Lowe's 1-yarder and Moore kick made it 24-0. Darius Cox returned the kick 50 yards but Magee could not capitalize.

On their next possession, Hayes hit Holloway from the 8-yard line for their only tally. Biloxi still added another score and, with just :08 remaining, Chris Mason dove in and Moore converted.

GAME 4: MAGEE (1-2) @ HEIDELBERG (1-2)
MAGEE 40 HEIDELBERG 0
September 15, 2000

Magee couldn't have picked a better team for their 800th all-time football game. Not only were the Oilers 1-2, but they had not defeated the Trojans in any of the eight previous encounters. On this night, the offense came to life.

Hobbs' 25-yard run for a touchdown was followed by Holloway's two-pointer and later 14-yard reception to make it 14-0. In the 2nd quarter, Josh Warren blocked a punt for a safety. Weathersby found the end zone from 15 yards, Hobbs notched the two-point conversion, and Crosby added another and a two-pointer before intermission. Now 24-0, Magee put up one score in the 3rd quarter when Holloway dove in from a yard away and Hobbs ran in the conversion. The reserves came in afterwards and held the Oilers scoreless for the remainder.

Holloway led rushers with 106 yards, Hobbs ran for 83 more, Varnes led tacklers with 8 solo and Jamie McIntyre pitched in 7 more. Tony Floyd picked off two Heidelberg passes. Magee led in first downs (19-5), rushing (268-68) and passing (53-1). Magee had one throw intercepted and lost a fumble along the way.

GAME 5: MAGEE (2-2) vs PRENTISS (0-4)
MAGEE 48 PRENTISS 20
September 22, 2000

New head coach Artis Mark had 47 players on his team but thus far sat winless. Their last game had been a beat-down by Forest 48-6. Said Mark before the season, "*This is one of the strongest districts in the state with Forest going to the State Championship and Magee making it to South State*". Things would get no better for the Bulldogs in Simpson County, but at least better than the 46-0 final from the previous year's meeting.

An opening 1-yard touchdown run from Hayes and a Holloway two-pointer was quickly forgotten as Jermaine Bryant hooked up with Dearon Myers for a 74-yard response to make it 8-6. Hobbs punched back with a 51-yard dash and Warren's two-point play ended the quarter 16-6. The Trojans exploded before halftime with Hayes 19-yard scamper, Holloway's 23-yarder, Hobbs' two-point play, Floyd's 25-yard fumble return for a touchdown, and Crosby's 27-yard dart put intermission 42-6

Crosby added an 87-yard dash in the 3rd quarter before Michael Lofton put Prentiss on the board from 20 yards and Frankie Ward converted for two points. Lofton did it again with 2:10 remaining to finish out scoring. Magee led in first downs (15-10) and rushing (353-124) while Prentiss held the air 73-40. Crosby led rushers with 133 yards. Willis had 92 yards and Holloway 75 yards. Cole had 9 solo tackles and 2 assists.

The week after the contest, it was announced that recent player Zanyon Dampier had passed away due to injuries from a car-train collision. The Magee Courier said, "*Everyone remembers Zanyon as a huge lad with a huge heart. He was a very likeable young man who always had a smile everywhere except the football field. He was truly a great kid…*"

GAME 6: MAGEE (3-2) @ COLLINS (5-0)
MAGEE 30 COLLINS 7
September 29, 2000

There was, perhaps, no hotter team by kickoff than Bruce Merchant's Tigers. They finished 9-2 the previous year and were now undefeated. Said he before the season, "*Everybody in our division will be chasing Magee and Forest. We've got good speed and good strength, though*". The Hattiesburg American picked Magee 19-14 and said, "*Expect a barn-burner when Magee travels to Collins, which is hot off a one-point (28-27) upset of long-time tormenter Forest. Collins is a great team, but it has lived so long in Magee's shadow that it may be unable to see the light".* The Clarion-Ledger called it 21-20 for Collins.

Magee was quick to set the tone on the road with a pair of touchdowns in the initial quarter. Hobbs took the opening kick 76 yards to the end zone and Hayes hit Michael Stubbs from the 7 for the next tally. Holloway's two-point conversion put the scoreboard at 14-0. Collins attempted to cut into the lead with a drive to the Magee 5 but could get no further. They finally got going in the 3rd quarter when Voncarie Owen escaped for 78 yards and then took it later from 9 yards. Ronald Mickel's PAT made it 14-7. But the Trojans finished in fine fashion with two more touchdowns.

After recovering a Tiger fumble, Hayes snuck in from a yard away and added the two-points. Then, Hayes kept for 6 yards and a touchdown to ice the game. First downs (13-9), rushing (144-108) and passing (48-10) favored the Trojans. Both teams lost a pair of fumbles. Holloway rushed for 93 yards with numerous defensive players recording at least 8 tackles. Said Merchant, *"We just didn't get the job done. Poor field position and our kicking game hurt us".*

GAME 7: MAGEE (4-2) vs FOREST (3-2)
MAGEE 26 FOREST 13
October 6, 2000

It was rematch time in Magee against the team that ended the chase for the 1999 state title. The defending 3A champs had now dropped 2 games by kickoff to give the Trojans hope. For the Cats, it was do-or-die as a loss pretty much closed the coffin on divisional honors. The Clarion-Ledger picked Magee 21-17.

Hobbs started things with a 51-yard drive-capping run from 9 yards out and Williams converted. Forest responded with a 55-yard procession and Mario Thomas 1-yard dive. Magee would then turn on the jets with 19 unanswered points. Hayes found Stubbs from 12 yards, Holloway moved in from 3 yards and Cox recovered a Bearcat fumble to set up Hobbs' 7-yard effort. Forest had the only other score of the night. That came in the 3rd quarter after a number of Trojan fumbles. Pete McBride took advantage of one for the 33-yard escape and Thomas knocked home the PAT.

First downs (23-7) and rushing (363-98) were lopsided in favor of the Trojans. Forest, however, led by two yards in passing (30-28). Hobbs, a Clarion-Ledger Top Performer, led rushers with 224 yards while Holloway pitched in 84 yards. Magee had one more lost fumble (5-4) than the Cats and had an interception to boot. *"We moved the ball well except for when we turned it over. I don't think we had a letdown after getting a big lead, but Forest was just making us fumble".*

Said Coach Jack French, *"You can't spot a good team like Magee with that kind of cushion. We've played them enough times to know that. We were able to get some turnovers in the second half, but messed ourselves up with our own mistakes".*

GAME 8: MAGEE (5-2) @ NEWTON (3-4)
MAGEE 43 NEWTON 0
October 13, 2000

Newton sat under .500 thus far and would give Magee a bit of a breather after rigorous games against both Collins and Forest. They made the most of it at E.L. Morgan Field, with The Newton Record calling it *"the good, the bad and the ugly".*

The home team's onside kick was recovered, but their ensuing 27-yard FG attempt by Sam Thames *"was a dud".* Magee put up a score in the frame on an 80-yard drive finalized by a 3-yard Hobbs run. Craig then recovered a fumbled snap on the PAT and raced the other way for two points. Magee added two more touchdowns in the 2nd quarter when Hayes recorded a 12-yard keeper, Magee blocked a punt, Hayes scrambled 36 yards to paydirt, and Williams converted on both extra points.

In the 3rd quarter, Warren raced 23 yards to the end zone and the combination of Varnes and Lofton sacked the Newton QB in the end zone for a safety. Finally, Varnes crossed the stripe from 5 yards and the game was over. First downs (18-7), rushing (336-133) and passing (65-26) went to Magee with Hayes rushing for 65 markers.

GAME 9: MAGEE (6-2) @ McLAURIN (0-8)
MAGEE 47 McLAURIN 0
October 20, 2000

The game would be almost a mirror image of the previous one against the Big Blue of Newton. And, it would be similar to their only other contest the year before where Magee drubbed McLaurin 55-6. In an astounding display of scoring, the Trojans put up a jaw-dropping 33 points in the opening quarter alone.

Hobbs took the football on the 3rd play of the game 45 yards to the end zone. Craig then returned a punt 50 yards for a score, Holloway moved in from the 6-yard line, Crosby recovered a fumble to set up Hobbs' 10-yard streak and Hayes hit Crosby from 72 yards for yet another touchdown. Williams added three more points via PATs. They mercifully ended the massacre in the 2nd quarter with just a pair of scores. Teddy Robinson found Justin Burgess for a 26-yard tally and Warren *"did a tightrope job down the sidelines"* for 46 yards for the last. McLaurin lost 7 of their 8 fumbles on the night.

GAME 10: MAGEE (7-2) vs RALEIGH (4-5)
MAGEE 40 RALEIGH 0
October 27, 2000

With one game played between the teams in 1938 and 7 more since 1987, it had been Magee with wins in each tilt. They had held Forest to just a 19-13 final the week before and could theoretically claim a second-place 7-3A position with a win. It was not to be.

On the game's first play, Hayes hit Craig for a 62-yard bomb to make it a quick 6-0. After Crosby recovered a Lion fumble, Holloway dashed in from 3 yards and, four plays later, Warren blocked a Raleigh punt. Hobbs *"picked a hole and ran in from four yards"* to make it an 18-0 runaway. In the 2nd quarter, Crosby found his second fumble and Warren dodged in from 10 yards. Craig's two-pointer put halftime 26-0. In the 3rd quarter, Hobbs got in again; this time from 3 yards and Williams converted. Finally, in the final stanza, Joey Smith fell on a loose football. Crosby ended a 74-yard march from 12 yards and Williams knocked home the PAT.

First downs (15-7), rushing (251-106) and passing (149 to -3) all went to Magee. Tony Floyd led tacklers with 11 and Varnes added a sack. Raleigh suffered 5 fumbles in the game.

GAME 11: MAGEE (8-2) vs MENDENHALL (7-3)
MAGEE 21 MENDENHALL 20
November 3, 2000

Coach Andy Stevens was anticipating a better season than the 6-6 campaign of 1999. Boasting of 18 returning starters, he said *"If we stay healthy, we'll win several games this year. Returning the offensive line, plus our QB and wide receivers will be a big plus for us"*. His prognostication was accurate at the Tigers were now 7-3 and coming off of a win over Northeast Lauderdale 43-14. It was no surprise that this edition of The Simpson County Super Bowl would be one of the closest ones in the long history.

Unlike past games, it was the Trojan opponent setting the tone early. On their first drive, the Tigers went 88 yards in 7 plays and finished things with Julius Roberson's 12-yard scamper to make it 6-0. Magee mustered a response in the next quarter with two touchdowns to take the lead. Holloway's 1-yarder and Hobbs' 69-yarder were matched with Williams extra points and halftime stood in favor of the Trojans 14-6. They increased that lead in the 3rd quarter when Hayes topped an 80-yard drive with his 1-yard sneak and Hobbs ran in for the two points.

The final quarter, however, would be worth the price of admission. Howard Overby picked off a Hayes throw to set up a James Hobbs 1-yard plunge and his two-point play to make it 21-14. With under 4:00 remaining, Magee went for it on 4th down but came up short. Now with 2:32 left, Roderick Bridges found paydirt from a yard away to make it 21-20. Deciding to go for the win, James Hobbs *"took the snap and ran to his right on the option play. He pitched the ball as he was hit and the pitch man never got the football"*. Magee recovered and ran the clock for the rivalry win and a year of bragging rights.

First downs (16-14), rushing (375-183) and passing (53-49) favored the Trojans. *"I told the guys to watch the option. That's their best play and I thought they were coming with it. I didn't think we could stop them"*. Added Stevens, *"I'd go for two every time right there. I want the win, but that's my luck. I guess I don't live right"*.

GAME 12: MAGEE (9-2) vs VELMA JACKSON (8-3)
MAGEE 42 VELMA JACKSON 0
November 10, 2000

In 1997, the Trojans were matched up with Velma Jackson in the playoffs. Magee effectively handled them then 34-8. Coach Willie Young's squad was a preseason favorite in 5-3A but suffered a late loss to Newton County to send them to Magee for the opening round. This marked their 5th consecutive playoff appearance.

The game was, for all purposes, over at halftime. In the opening frame, Holloway got in from 2 yards, Hobbs added 2 points, Warren found the end zone from 4 yards and Hayes notched the two-pointer. In the next, it was Holloway from 29 yards, Hull pulled a 30-yard pick-six, Hayes and Craig hooked up from 48 yards to put the ball at the 1-yard line, and Hobbs burst through for the score. Warren's two-pointer made it a commanding 36-0. The last score came in the 3rd when Crosby *"crashed through the Falcon's defense and scored on a 17-yard run"*.

Magee dominated in stats much like they did in scoring. First downs (22-2), rushing (306-71) and passing (120-11) were gaudy. Warren was the leading ball-carrier with 121 yards. Said Young, *"We didn't show up. We didn't do a thing. It's like the kids said this is as far as we want to go. We didn't play ball at all. We couldn't stop them or run on them. I can take a butt-whipping, but not like that"*.

GAME 13: MAGEE (10-2) vs WILKINSON COUNTY (9-1)
MAGEE 32 WILKINSON COUNTY 18
November 17, 2000

Of 111 different teams that had taken the field against Magee in their 75-year history, Wilkinson County had not been one of them. This inaugural battle against the Wildcats from Woodville would be similar to many other contests the Trojans had during the year. They opened quickly to effectively put the game away and then coasted to victory.

It was 16-0 after a quarter. Floyd's interception allowed Hobbs a 13-yard score and Holloway a two-point play. They then went 61-yards via Hayes' 37-yard strike to Craig and Holloway's second conversion. Hobbs increased the lead with a 63-yard dash to paydirt, Holloway ran it in, Hayes found Stubbs from 12 yards with no time left and Hobbs provided the conversion. The halftime scoreboard read 32-0. The Cats put up 6 of their points in the 3rd quarter on a Carl Cage 1-yard dive.

In the final quarter, they added two more. The first came on a 70-yard march capped by Peter Lollis' 3-yard burst. Then, after an onside kick, Travis Dent hit DeMario Russ from 10 yards. Magee led in first downs (17-14) and rushing (312-64) while the Cats led in the air 134-63. Hobbs, a Clarion-Ledger Top Performer, rushed for 125 yards. Holloway added another 83 yards. Floyd's 11 tackles and interception led the defense. Boyce Varnes had 8 tackles while Jonathan Varnes added 7 more.

GAME 14: MAGEE (11-2) @ NEWTON COUNTY (10-2)
MAGEE 14 NEWTON COUNTY 13
November 24, 2000

Exactly like the 1999 season, Magee would have to beat Newton County in order to have a chance to play for the state title. That year, the Trojans squeezed out a tight 14-7 win for the opportunity. This one would be even closer in Decatur at East Central Community College.

Magee opened scoring in the 1st quarter via Holloway's 1-yard dive. Down 6-0 in the next quarter, Newton County went to work on a *"muddy and slippery field"*. Germaine Smith's 4-yard run and David McConnell's PAT gave them the 7-6 lead. With 1:01 left, Magee turned it over and the Cougars used it with McConnell's 31-yard FG to make halftime 10-6. A deep drive in the 3rd by the Trojans went for naught, and they fumbled it yet again in the final frame to Newton County. McConnell again turned the gift into a 25-yard FG to pad the advantage.

With time running out, *"a funny thing happened to the Cougars on the way to the celebration"*. Hayes, under pressure, could find no receiver and simply took off running. His journey ended at the 2-yard line. With 1:16 left, Holloway burst in from 2 yards to make it 13-12. Deciding on the win, the ball went to Hobbs for the conversion. He was *"stopped short of the goal line and fumbled the football into the end zone where an unidentified Trojan (Alex Floyd)"* recovered for the two-points.

Surprisingly, first downs (12-11), rushing (183-96) and passing (62-24) all went to Magee. Hayes rushed for 80 yards but it was Holloway (70 yards on the ground) named as a

Clarion-Ledger Top Performer. *"Newton County ... played their hearts out. They're a well-coached team and they play hard. We're just very fortunate to get away with a win. It's a shame one of us had to lose"*.

GAME 15: MAGEE (12-2) vs RIPLEY (13-1)
MAGEE 42 RIPLEY 14
December 2, 2000: MISSISSIPPI MEMORIAL STADIUM; JACKSON

Another first-time opponent awaited, and it would be for everything that the Trojans had been working towards since the August practices in the Mississippi heat. Now, they played in front of 6,000 fans in the cold on their 811th football game since that first one in October of 1926. The Clarion-Ledger though Ripley best by a close 21-20 score.

Ripley's first mistake was costly, as a bad snap over Brandon Roberson's head put Magee at the 16-yard line. Hobbs went to work four plays later from the 6-yard line and Williams gave the Trojans a 7-0 lead. But Ripley and fantastic running back Vashon Pearson would not be denied. They answered with Pearson's 13-yard run and Luciano Perez's extra point. They took the lead afterwards on Brandon Roberson's 34-yard connection with Jimmy Brooks and Perez put it 14-7. It would be all the Trojans would allow.

In the 2nd quarter, they capped a 51-yard drive on a pass from that distance between Hayes and Craig. Williams, picking up a bad snap, raced in for the two points. Still, they had a few more scores in them before intermission. Hobbs capped an 82-yard drive with his 1-yard dive, Cox picked off a Roberson throw and Hobbs burst *"up the middle"* for a 57-yard jaunt to the 6-yard line. Hayes then hit Stubbs for the touchdown and Williams converted for the 28-14 halftime lead.

The final points of the game came in the 3rd quarter. The first was after a drive of 65 yards found Hobbs in the end zone from 28 yards away. The next, after a fumble recovery, came from Holloway on a 24-yarder. Williams knocked home both extra points. *"The remainder of the game was defensive struggle with neither team able to mount a scoring drive of any type"*. Stats vary widely. One report had Magee leading in rushing (372-209) and Ripley in first downs (18-14) and passing (111-57). Another had Magee ahead in first downs (21-13), rushing (483-186) and passing (196-115).

Hobbs, a Clarion-Ledger Top Performer, ran for 203 (Magee Courier) or 171 (Clarion-Ledger) yards. Holloway was close behind with 143 markers. Joseph Brown led with 10 solo tackles and 2 assists while Brian Robinson was one behind. Said Ripley Coach Terry Allen, *"They made plays when they had to and we didn't respond. We had our chances"*.

"It's just a good feeling. I can't find the words to describe what it feels like to finally win a state championship. It is a wonderful feeling to see the players rewarded for a job well done. Our guys played hard the entire game. We came up here to win it all and we did just that. Our kids battled the whole game and never quit until the final horn. People counted us out when we were 1-2 ... but these kids wouldn't give up. They scrap and claw and give everything they have. They deserved this moment and earned the right to be state champions".

The Mississippi Association of Coaches voted Kinslow Coach of the Year. Additionally, Tony Floyd made their First Team 3A list. Willis Hobbs made the Second Team list. Floyd also made The Clarion-Ledger All-State list. All-Division honors went to Hobbs (MVP), Floyd (Defensive Back MVP), A.J. Holloway, Alex Floyd, James May, Brian Hayes, Myricks Cole, Mario Craig and Darius Cox. Honorable Mentions included Michael Stubbs, Cedric Crosby, Johnathan Varnes, Brian Robinson, Deondra King, Nick Williams, and Josh Warren.

Magee High School Football Accomplishments
1926-2000

1933	Middle Mississipppi Runner-Up
1939	Class A Middle Mississippi Runner-Up
1946	Middle Missisippi Champions
1947	Veterans Bowl
1951	Class A Champions
1957	Gas Bowl Champions
1959	Oil Bowl (Tie)
1960	Little Dixie and State Champions
1961	Mississippi Bowl Champions
1962	Little Dixie Champions
1963	Little Dixie Champions
1964	Little Dixie Champions
1965	Little Dixie Champions
1966	Little Dixie South Champions
1967	Little Dixie Champions
1969	Little Dixie South Champions
1971	Little Dixie Champions
1975	Little Dixie South Champions
1976	Mississippi Bowl
1977	Southern Athletic Champions
1978	Little Dixie North Champions
1982	Division 6A Champions
1984	3A State Champions
1985	3A State Runner-Up
1986	Southern Athletic Champions
1989	3A State Champions
1991	Division 5-4A Champions
1992	Division 5-4A Champions
1993	4A State Runner-Up
1995	Division 4-4A Champions
1996	Division 4-4A Champions
1997	3A State Champions
1998	3A State Runner-Up
1999	Division 7-3A Champions
2000	3A State Champions

Undefeated Seasons: 1960, 1923, 1963, 1965, 1989

All-Time Magee Football Head Coaches

(Unknown) Carr	1927
R.T. Walker	1928-1930
Heber Ladner	1931
Claude Mangum	1932
Hobart Stowers	1933-1934
A.D. Ott	1935-1936
Brad White	1937-1939
David Holland	1940
Ira Wilson	1941
B.L. Kisner	1942-1948
Jim Carballo	1949-1953
Prentiss Irving	1954
Bucky McElroy	1954
Jack Bailey	1955-1957
Charlie Callaway	1958-1961
John Williams	1962-1963
Malcolm Nesmith	1964-1968
Troy Greer	1969-1973
Jerry Sullivan	1974-1978
John Mangum	1979-1980
Johnny Woitt	1981
David Bradley	1982-1987
Lum Wright, Jr.	1988-1990
Johnny Mills	1991
Perry Wheat	1992-1994
Danny Cowart	1995-1997
Larry Kinslow	1998-2000

All-Time Magee Football Assistant Coaches

Includes Only Coaches Found; Years May Not Be Fully-Inclusive

Bass	David	1990	Mangum	John	1973-1978
Berch	Dennis	1983-1984	Mangum	Todd	1992-1994
Berry	Dale	1982-1984	McElroy	William	1954
Berry	Mickey	1991	McIntyre	Randy	1991-95; 1999-00
Blair	Willard	1976-1977	McLaughlin	J.F.	1949
Bounds	Mickey	1990	McLemore	Lonnie	1986-1987
Carter	Zaus	1996-1997	Nesmith	Malcolm	1962-1963
Clark	Bob	1955-1957	Pierce	Eddie	1988-1989
Cochren	Shane	2000	Ponder	Mike	1960
Dearing	George	1967	Reddoch	Mark	1982-1984
Everett	Bob	1975-1980	Risher	Gary	1982
Everett	Orland	1957-59; 1963-72	Saul	Richard	1979
Everett	Raymond	1953-1954	Schneider	Edward	1998-1999
Foster	Royce	1972-75; 1985-86	Shearer	Hugh	1967
Gordon	Emmett	1950	Shepard	David	1998-1999
Hardy	Paul	1997-2000	Shepard	Lewis	2000
Hawkins	C.B.	1964-1966	Smith	Mike	1976-1979
Huffman	George "Bo"	1996-1999	Smith	Terry	1990
Hutchinson	Jerry	1961	Sullivan	Jerry	1968-1972
Jaynes	Ernest	1970-1987	Taylor	Jerry	1959-1960
Jordan	Collier	1958	Walker	A.L.	1946-1947
Keeton	Charlie	1978-1981	Weems	Chip	1987
Kinslow	Larry	1996-1997	Wendt	Dick	1996
Luckey	Terrell	1987-1990; 2000	White	Tim	1988-1995
Lyons	Ken	1995	Willard	Blair	1973
Mangum	Bob	1974	Wilson	Ira	1940
Mangum	Jimmy	1980-1987			

Partial List of All-Time Magee Football Managers

Includes Only Those Found; Years Not Fully-Inclusive

Alexander	Junior	1946
Allen	Billy	1943
Allen	Pat	1946
Allen	Winky	1947
Anderson	James	2000
Ashley	Herman	1948
Badeaux	Mack	1970-1973
Barron	Chaun	1983
Bass	Marcus	1986
Bishop	Hamilton	1975
Bishop	Kelly	1947
Blackledge	Tommy	1979
Bradley	David	1983-1984
Brewer	Bobby	1956
Brewer	Larry	1957
Bullock	Tony	1986
Butler	Jeff	1972-1974
Camper	Patrick	1978
Cockrell	Bobby	1964
Cook	Robert	1989-1990
Dabbs	Paul David	1942
Dampeer	Karrell	1986
Dickey	Steve	1969
Douglas	John	1974-1975
Duckworth	Billy	1959-1961
Duckworth	Billy Mac	1974
Duckworth	Junior	1939
Dunn	David	1971
Fortenberry	Larry	1970
Fortenberry	Paul Lee	1968
Frost	Horace	1948
Fulcher	Kevin	1979
Funchess	Victor	1992
Graham	John	1992
Greer	Kyle	1973

Greer	Troy	1968
Griffith	Donnie	1975
Hankins	Josh	2000
Harris	Dwayne	1967
Hayes	Brian	1993
Hayes	Michael	1982-1983
Hayes	Michael	1986
Hooker	unk	1956
Hoover	Robert	1982-1984
Hopkins	Glen	1972
Hubbard	Marcus	1998
Hubbard	Roosevelt	1982
Hughes	Andy	1971-1973
Jaynes	Ronnie	1971
Johnson	David	1984
Johnson	Tomone	1992
Jones	John D.	1957
Kelly	Jonathan	1986
Layton	Ronnie	1964
Lee	Jarrod	1989-1990
Little	Jeff	1975
Logan	Josh	1998-2000
Lott	Steve	1974
Lott	Steve	1984
Maddox	John C.	1955
Mangum	Chris	1979
Mangum	Edgar	1993
Mangum	John	1979
Mangum	John	1980
Mangum	Kris	1980
McDonald	Emmanuel	1986
McInnis	Jamie	1993
McKinley	Allen	1993
McNair	Gary	1967
Middleton	Michael	1963

Millis	Carey	1998
Milton	Arthur	1972-1973
Monk	Ladd	1984
Myers	Marcus	1993
Nowell	Mark	1979-1982
Odom	Gene	1945-1947
Owens	Jerry	1981
Padgett	Paul	1974
Puckett	Toxey	1942
Reed	Glenn	1983-1984
Reed	Patrick	1980, 1982
Reid, Jr	Lee	1951
Roberts	Kelly	1956
Sharble	Napoleon	1983
Sims	Roosevelt	1982-1983
Smith	Benny	1957
Smith	Derek	1997
Spangler	Allen	1978-1979
Steele	Shane	1997
Steele	Shane	1998
Stewart	Terry	1981
Sullivan	John	1969-1970
Swain	Justin	1990

Taylor	James	1956
Thames	Billy	1962
Thames	Charlie	1954
Traxler	Novak	1993
Tuggle	Buddy	1951-1955
Turner	Elden	1974-1975
Walker	Otto	1945-1946
Wallace	Chris	1986
Warren	Jimmy	1954
Weathersby	Jason	1992-1993
Webber	Hayden	1939
West	Lee	1957
Wheat	Tim	1992-1993
Wilkinson	David	1975
Williams	Dyron	1982
Williamson	Davie	1978-1979
Williamson	Thomas	1981
Windham	Jimmy	1961-1962
Windham	Mike	1963
Womack	Raymon	1983-1984
Wright	Bert	1989-1990
Wright	Tony	1989-1990
Yelverton	David	1956

Magee Homecoming Queens

1928	Ruby McKee
1938	Josephine Burnham
1943	Erma Lee Stubbs
1945	Ann Ryan
1946	Mary Joyce Stephens
1947	Charlene Tullos
1948	Mary George Watkins
1949	Adva Jean Runnels
1954	Mary Frances Giggs
1955	Ella Mary Brown
1956	Betty Ann Gravis
1957	Betty Ann Gravis
1958	Kay Coats
1959	Ann Puckett
1960	Ann McIntosh
1961	Betty Dennis
1962	Jane Mangum
1963	Linda Dickey
1964	Becky Hughes
1965	Becky Berry
1966	Kay Kees
1967	Sue Dickey
1968	Sandra Anderson
1969	Gale Walker
1970	Jan Herring
1971	Sallye Williamson
1972	Janet Earles
1973	Lynn Ates

1974	Angie Nichols
1975	Cathy Monahan
1976	Glenda Keys
1977	Kaye Barrette
1978	Cathy Monahan
1979	Cindy Thompson
1980	Jackie Keys
1981	Susan Ramsay
1982	Allyson Allen
1983	Lorianne Tullos
1984	Carol Jones
1985	Demetria Kirk
1986	Shanna Craft
1987	Kathy Dampeer
1988	Yvette Herrington
1989	Jennifer Runnels
1990	Alise Blackwell
1991	Kristy Earles
1992	Angie Eavenson
1993	Jada Kirk
1994	Chrisanna Brown
1995	Lasondra Hayes
1996	Alicia Davis
1997	Patrice Durr
1998	Tanya Patterson
1999	Arlisha Griffin
2000	Rebecca Brown

Apologies to 1929-37; 1939-42; 1944; 1950-53

Magee High School Football Cheerleaders

Adcox	Ashley	19951998
Adcox	Michele	1985-1988
Barnes	Laura Lyn	1999-2000
Benton	Belba	1949
Benton	Tiffany	1990
Blackwell	Alise	1987-1988
Books	Brenda	1965
Booth	Joe	1963
Boswell	Neil	1932
Brandon	Jessica	1997-2000
Brooks	Brenda	1964, 1966
Brooks	Huree	1938
Brooks	Karen	1970-1972
Brooks	Tawesia	1966-1968
Brown	Averie	1995
Brown	Chrisanna	1992-1994
Brown	Ella Mary	1954-1955
Buchanan	Tracy	1985
Burnham	Josephine	1938
Butler	Cindy	1980, 1982
Butler	Gayle	1980
Carroll	Marie	1969-1970
Carter	Kathryn	1948
Caughman	Nancy	1954-1956
Chatman	Anita	1978-1980
Chatman	Sherry	1981-1982
Clyde	Kristi	1989, 1992
Cockrell	Phil	1985
Cole	Jan	1984-1987
Collins	Cheryl	1976-1978
Cook	Cookie	1961-1962
Cook	Morgan	1999
Courtney	Hilarie	1994-1997
Craft	Brandy	1991-1993
Creel	Paige	1991-1993
Dickey	Lynda	1960-1963
Dickey	Sue	1965-1967
Dickson	Lynn	1985-1988
Dixey	Linda	1961
Duckworth	Judy	1968-1970
Earles	Angela	1978-1980
Earles	Kristy	1988-1991
Eubanks	Ashley	2000
Evans	Wanda	1966, 1968
Everett	Sue	1962-1965
Fagan	Ann	1961-1963
Garner	Brenda	1965
Garner	Carolyn	1954-1955
Harris	Joell	1982
Garner	Leslie	1984
Garner	Maxie	1963-1964
Garner	Paula	1985-1986
Gordy	Kami	1988, 1990-91
Gosa	Patricia	1969

Grace	Linda Jo	1963
Gray	Cherie	1998-2000
Green	Vickie	1975
Griffith	Peggy	1959-1962
Grimes	Mary	1938
Hancock	Jessica	1997-2000
Hansbrough	Casey	1994-1996
Herring	Jan	1970
Herrington	Denise	1984-1987
Herrington	Stephanie	1983-1985
Herrington	Yvette	1985-1988
Holloway	Tanya	1978-1980
Hughes	Becky	1963-1964
Hughes	Rebecca	1961-1962
Jaynes	Kashondra	1999
Johnson	A.J.	1981-1982
Johnson	Mandi	2000
Johnson	Maxine	1960-1961
Jones	Bobby	1995-1996
Jones	Bonnie Jean	1946
Jones	Sarah	1998-1999
Kees	Jane	1969-1970
Keith	Pam	1976
Kennedy	Kathy	1978
Keys	Glenda	1974-1976
King	Kayla	2000
Kirk	Demetria	1982-1983
Knight	Jena	1987-1990
Kreel	Paige	1990
Leach	Donna	1968-1969
Leach	Sherry	1967
Lee	Audarshia	1993
Lewis	Leslie	1999-2000
Little	Morgan	1999
Mach	Jennifer	1998-2000
Maddox	April	1982-1985
Maddox	Pam	1974
Magee	Amanda	1981, 1983-84
Magee	Gussie	1932
Magee	Patsy	1967-1968
Magee	Suzanne	1986
Magnum	Aylisa	1978-1979
Mangum	Barbara	1964
Mangum	Jane	1960-1962
Mangum	Jenny	1992-1994
Mangum	Valerie	1966
Marsh	Jessica	1992-1994
Martiniere	Ashley	1996-1997
Mason	Grace	1958-1961
Mathis	Shelly	1984
May	Buffy	1981-1984
May	Rita	1964-1965
McAlpin	Deborah	1966
McAlpin	Lynda	1959-1960

McCallum	Jane	1964, 1966
McCollum	Markeela	1998, 2000
McCoy	Tracy	1992-1994
McDonald	Sharon	1974-1976
McInnis	Angela	1978
McInnis	Sheila	1975-1977
McInnis	Sherry	1978-1979
McIntosh	Ann	1958-1960
McIntosh	Geraldine	1955-1958
McIntosh	Lynn	1965
McLaurin	Hope	1981-1982
McNair	John	1957-1959
McNair	Jolyn	1967-1969
McRaney	John	1958-1959
Meador	Ashley	1989-1992
Mitchell	Mims	1938
Mitchell	Vanessa	1994
Monahan	Cathy	1974-1975
Morris	Demethous	1978-1981
Myers	Becky Jo	1949
Myers	Patricia	1954
Nichols	Angie	1972-1974
Nichols	Georgia Faye	1954-1955
Nichols	Patti	1971-1972
Pace	Holly	2000
Padgett	Patty	1971-1973
Paige	Stephanie	1999-2000
Patterson	Tanya	1995-1998
Pearson	Miranda	1993
Pittman	Tabatha	1983
Pope	Dorothy	1945-1947
Prince	Paige	1990-1991
Pruitt	Doris	1945
Puckett	Ann	1955-1959
Puckett	Polly	1942-1943
Rankin	Janet	1976-1977
Rankin	Josephine	1981-1982
Rankin	Sue	1972, 1974
Rankin	Tracy	1981-1983
Reed	Carol	1989-1992
Ridgley	Malissa	1991
Risher	Jan	1981
Roberts	Helen Temple	1947-1948
Roberts	Mattie Rachel	1947
Roberts	Vicki	1977
Robinson	Emma	1979
Robinson	Suzy	1965-1967
Rowan	Martha Ann	1942-1943
Runnels	Adva J.	1949
Runnels	Jennifer	1986-1989
Runnels	Katherine	1945
Runnels	Roshanna	1986
Runnels	Shannon	1983-1985
Ryan	Ann	1945-1947
Sams	Kim	1976-1977
Sarafield	Debra	1970-1971
Sawyer	Kim	1971-1973
Shows	Leslie	1996-1999
Shows	Tanya	1989
Sibley	Sunnie	1998-1999
Sims	Monica	1986-1989
Skinner	Dallas	1995
Skinner	Dallas	1996
Slater	Becky	1973-1975
Smith	Aimee	1989-1992
Smith	Chassity	1993
Smith	Freddie	1971
Smith	Murlene	1954-1958
Smith	Sue	1968
Smith	Zan	1969
Stennett	Betsye	1973
Stephens	Mary Joyce	1946
Stringer	Jane	1967-1969
Stubbs	Betty	1955-1957
Stubbs	Erma Lee	1942
Stubbs	Staci	1977-1979
Styron	Jessica	1994-1996
Sullivan	Jessica	1996-1999
Sykes	Melinda	1977-1978
Thompson	Cinda	1967
Thompson	Keisha	1995, 1997
Tullos	Charlene	1948
Tutor	Amanda	1997
Walker	Bobbie	1955-1956
Walker	Dena	1984
Walker	Doug	1983
Walker	Fay	1957
Walker	Jane	1942
Walker	Patti	1981-1983
Warren	Ashley	1993-1995
Warren	Brandi	1998-2000
Warren	Carey	1997-1998
Warren	Courtney	1990-1993
Warren	Jena	1999-2000
Warren	Tammy	1979-1981
Watkins	Mary George	1947-1948
Welch	Dana	1996-1999
Welch	Deidra	1999-2000
Welch	DeShea	1994-1997
West	Dianne	1971-1972
West	Evie	1971
Wheat	Karen	1994
White	Jenny	1995-1996
Williamson	Anthony	2000
Williamson	Sallye	1970-1971
Williamson	Sandra	1975-1977
Winstead	Nancy	1949
Womack	Jean	1962-1964
Womack	Krysti	1987-1989
Worrell	Jennifer	1993-1995
Yates	Kathy	1973-1975
Yates	Robin	1972-1973
Zaborski	Kristen	1997

A Partial List Of Magee High School Football Players

Abel	Duke	1984
Adcox	Charles	1968-1970
Adcox	Jerrell	1984-1986
Adcox	Jimmy	1971-1973
Adcox	Rudolph	1948
Ainsworth	D.C.	1932-1936
Ainsworth	Dick	1954-1955
Ainsworth	J.W.	1951-1953
Ainsworth	Kenny	1962
Ainsworth	Randall	1972
Ainsworth	Ray	1951
Ainsworth	Ronnie	1963-1965
Akers	Chuck	1966-1967
Akers	Freddie	1955-1957
Akers	Tommy	1993-1995
Alexander	James	1936-1937
Allen	Ben	1936-1937
Allen	Billy	1943-1947
Allen	Charles	1951
Allen	Chuckie	1988-1989
Allen	Cyril	1933-1934
Allen	Fred	1934
Allen	Jimmy	1948
Allen	Jock	1963-1965
Allen	Joe	1953-1954
Allen	Marcus	1991-1993
Allen	Pat	1944-1947
Allen	Preston	1935-1936
Allen	Ruel	1928-1931
Allen	S.	1935
Allen	Ted	1954-1957
Allen	Tommy	1974
Allen	Truman	1932-1934
Allen	Unknown	1939
Allen	Van	1935; 1937
Allen	Winky	1948-1950
Amesbury	George	1999
Anderson	Benny	1975-1977
Anderson	James	1950
Anderson	Lance	2000
Anderson	Sammy	1949-1952
Anderson	Wendell	1977
Andrews	Gene	1951
Andrews	James	1951-1953
Arnold	Paul	1977-1979
Arnold	Roy	1973-1975
Ashley	Danny	1964-1965
Ashley	Herman	1948
Ates	James	1960-1961
Ates	Maurice	1943
Ates	Unknown	1945
Ates	Vernon	1943
Axton	Charles	1957; 1960
Badeaux	Mack	1974

Bailey	Grayson	1948-1949
Baldwin	Brooks	2000
Baldwin	Charles	1971-1973
Baldwin	John Kent	1956
Banks	Allen	1975-1976
Barnard	Brandon	1999
Barnard	Brian	2000
Barnard	James	1956-1957
Barnard	Jerry	1973-1974
Barnard	Jimmy Dale	1972
Barnard	Phil	1972-1973
Barnes	Joe	1954-1957
Barnes	Julius	1995-1997
Barnes	Robbie	1977-1978
Barnes	Robert	1955-1958
Barnett	Unknown	1931
Barr	Donald	1961
Barr	Guy	1955-1959
Barr	James	1976-1977
Barr	Jamie	1999-2000
Barr	John Pat	1977
Barr	Mike	1968-1969
Barr	Pat	1953-1955
Barrett	Buddy	1955
Barrett	Donald	1966-1968
Barrett	J.D.	1944-1947
Barrett	Jeff	1990-1991
Barrett	Johnny	1969-1970
Barron	Chaun	1985-1988
Barron	Chris	2000
Barron	Eddie	1980-1982
Barron	Estus	1984-1986
Bass	Garfield	1979
Bass	Marcus	1988-1990
Baughn	Jerry	1954
Beatty	Don	1964-1966
Belding	Rudolph	1942-1943
Bell	James	1942-1945
Bell	Phillip	1940-1942
Benefield	Mike	1963-1965
Benson	Efron	1979-1981
Benton	Clyde	1938-1940
Berch	Creston	1984-1986
Berry	Dale	1972-1974
Berry	Dexter	1984-1985
Berry	Hal	1973-1975
Berry	Mickey	1989-1991
Bishop	Bill	1945; 1947-49
Bishop	Billy	1970-1972
Bishop	Hamilton	1975
Bishop	Henry	1944-1947
Bishop	Junior	1944-1948
Bishop	Kelly	1948-1951
Bishop	Kenneth	1957

Bishop	W.E.	1946-1948
Blackledge	Carl	1935-1936
Blackledge	Tommy	1983
Blackwell	Bud	1940-1941
Blackwell	Glendale	1998
Blackwell	Jonathan	1998
Blackwell	Terrance	1991
Blackwell	Theron	1937-1940
Blair	Billy	1964
Blair	Calvin	1970-1972
Blair	Joseph	1997-1998
Blair	Unknown	1940
Blakeney	Randy	1971
Boles	Andy	1991-1993
Boles	Charles	1988
Boone	Billy	1960-1961
Booth	George	1963
Booth	Gerald	1969
Bourne	Harold	1936
Bourne	Unknown	1933
Bowen	Marcus	1986
Boyanton	Thomas	1988
Boyles	Doug	1991-1993
Bradford	Lewis	1933-1935
Bradley	Dalton	1984-1986
Bradley	David	1985
Bratcher	Josh	1999-2000
Brewer	James	1944
Brewer	Larry	1961-1962
Brewer	Paul	1964-1965
Brewer	Red	1943
Brinson	James	1980; 1982
Brinson	Ray	1990-1992
Brister	Unknown	1930; 1932; 1935
Brooks	Hobart	1940-1941
Brooks	Lloyd	1938-1939
Brooks	Ronnie	1960
Brown	Edmund	1982-1983
Brown	Emmett	1950-1951
Brown	Joseph	1998-2000
Brown	L.H.	1957
Brown	Michael	1987
Brown	Patrick	1978-1980
Brown	Ralph	1970-1971
Brown	Thomas	1996-1998
Brown	Tim	1995-1997
Brown	Willie	1998-1999
Bruce	Mike	1991
Bryant	Stanley	1962
Bryant	Travis	1954-1956
Buffington	Bobby	1941-1944
Buffington	Scott	1944-1948
Buffington	Unknown	1932
Bulger	Stanley	1961-1962
Bullard	Kelvin	1979-1980
Bullock	James	1992-1993

Bullock	Tony	1988-1990
Burch	Kylie	1943
Burgess	Justin	2000
Burgess	Vince	1982-1984
Burnham	Dick	1926
Burnham	Tommy	1947-1948
Burnham	Unknown	1931-1932
Burnham	Vic	1951
Burns	"Wormy"	1930
Burns	John W.	1935-1936
Burns	Unknown	1933
Busby	D.	1950
Busby	John Ray	1947-1949
Butler	Bobby	1956
Butler	Jerry	1956
Butler	Jimmy	1948
Butler	Mike	1965-1967
Byars	Larry	1981
Cahee	Avery	1974-1976
Cahee	Larry	1980
Calder	Brian	1953
Calhoun	Carlon	1938-1940
Calhoun	Mike	1978
Canoy	Dick	1953-1954
Canoy	Durwood	1956
Canoy	Leon	1954-1957
Canoy	Lowery	1961-1963
Canoy	Stanley	1968
Carmichael	Craig	1978
Carmichael	Mike	1961-1963
Carmichael	Terry	1980-1981
Carr	Archie	1940
Carr	Charles	1940-1941
Carr	T.	1940
Carroll	Jimmy	1955
Carroll	Randall	1978
Carter	Bill	1968-1970
Carter	John	1966-1967
Carter	Lamar	1963-1965
Caughman	Bill	1950-1953
Channell	Jim	1992
Chatman	George	1981
Chatman	Josh	1997-1999
Chatman	Ronnie	1979-1980
Chestnut	Kaine	1993-1995
Clark	Jeremy	1993-1995
Clements	Tony	1991-1993
Cockrell	Chris	1992-1994
Cockrell	David	1988-1990
Cockrell	James	1969
Cockrell	James	1988-1989
Cockrell	Jimmie	1950
Cockrell	Justin	1990-1992
Cockrell	Randy	1964
Cockrell	Ronnie	1965-1967
Cockrell	Steve	1972-1974

Cole	Cory	1992-1994
Cole	Jason	1995
Cole	Luper	1928-1929
Cole	Myricks	1998-2000
Cole	Nick	1984; 1986
Coleman	Grover	1965-1967
Collins	Darryl	1986-1988
Collins	Taraki	1995-1997
Colson	Ivan	1980
Cone	Harold	1953-1954
Cone	Zeno	1962
Cook	Lawrence	1983-1984
Cook	Randy	1978-1979
Cook	Robert	1992-1993
Cooper	Charles	1976-1978
Cooper	Garland	1968-1969
Cooper	Lee	1977; 1979
Counts	Tarvey	1988
Cowan	Trey	1999
Coward	Chris	1991
Cowart	Donald	1961-1963
Cox	Darius	1998-2000
Cox	Doug	1984-1986
Craft	Curtis	1979-1981
Craft	David	1992-1993
Craft	Donald	1961
Craft	Eugene	1957
Craft	Jackie	1975-1976
Craft	James	1984
Craft	Jeff	1977-1979
Craft	Jerry	1966-1968
Craft	Michael	1996
Craft	Monique	1985-1987
Craft	Murl	1946-1947
Craft	Thad	1983
Craig	Mario	1998-2000
Creel	Larry	1963-1965
Creel	Peyton	1993
Creel	Rex	1972-1973
Creel	Steve	1964-1966
Crockwell	Jimmy	1951
Crosby	Cedrick	1999-2000
Curtis	Bob	1988-1990
Dale	Roland	1941-1944
Dampeer	Karrell	1989-1991
Dampier	Edward	1970
Dampier	Zanyon	1996-1998
Davis	Hal	1929
Davis	Jack	1955-1958
Davis	James	1985-1987
Davis	Randolph	1974-1975
Davis	Wendell	1991
Dearing	George	1967
DeJong	Billie	1949-1950
Dickerson	Roy Lee	1983-1984
Dickey	Eddie	1967-1969
Dillon	Bobby	1978-1980
Dilmore	Danny	1975
Dixon	James	1970-1971
Dixon	Robert	1979-1981
Drone	Shane	1996-1998
Duckworth	Clifton	1937-1939
Duckworth	David	1970; 1972
Duckworth	Junior	1940-1942
Duckworth	Unknown	1931-1933
Duhon	Ronnie	1966
Dukes	Stanley	1967-1968
Dunn	Bruce	1970-1971
Dunn	David	1972-1973
Durr	Adrian	1996-1997
Durr	Bruce	1980
Durr	Cedric	1990
Durr	Dante	1995-1996
Durr	James	1979
Durr	Jamie	1974
Durr	Paul	1978
Durr	Sedrick	1988-1989
Dykes	Parker	1957
East	Jason	1988
Easterling	Charles	1973-1975
Easterling	Chris	1991-1993
Easterling	Corey	1994
Easterling	Darron	1982-1984
Easterwood	Jeff	1983
Edmonson	Ben	1957
Edmonson	Richard	1953-1955
Edwards	David	1975; 1977
Edwards	Scott	1986-1987
Ellison	Paul	1963-1964
Eubanks	Alan	1995
Evans	Bobby	1964-1966
Everett	Billy	1949-1951
Everett	Billy Mack	1960-1961
Everett	Bob	1966-1968
Everett	Bob	1991
Everett	Gene	1963
Everett	H	1930-1932
Everett	Harold	1960
Everett	Jack	1977-1978
Everett	Jeff	1975-1977
Everett	Judene	1943
Everett	Ralph	1947-1950
Everett	Tim	1967-1969
Everett	Tommy	1942-1944
Everett	Unknown	1938
Everett	W	1931-1932
Field	Joe	1926
Field	Teeny	1936
Floyd	Alex	1998-2000
Floyd	Anthony	1994-1995

Floyd	Charles	1975
Floyd	Charles	1995
Floyd	Eric	1997-1999
Floyd	Marcus	1994-1996
Floyd	Nicky	1975-1977
Floyd	Tony	1998-2000
Floyd	Unknown	1933
Forest	Tony	1982-1983
Forrest	Richard	1984-1986
Fortenberry	Chris	1985-1986
Fortenberry	Donald	1977-1978
Fortenberry	George E.	1955-1958
Fortenberry	James Earl	1955
Fortenberry	Joe	1967-1968
Fortenberry	Paul	1968
Fortenberry	Scott	1988
Fortenberry	Toby	1957
Fortenberry	Unknown	1947
Foster	Royce	1964-1965
Franks	Willie	1995-1997
Frost	Horace	1949
Funchess	Chaucer	1985-1988
Funchess	Ricky	1996-1998
Gales	Shawn	1991; 1993
Gardner	Dan	1955
Garner	A.J.	1940-1941
Garner	Bennie	1949-1952
Garner	David	1985-1988
Garner	Donald	1961-1962
Garner	Fred	1948-1949
Garner	Herbert	1941
Garner	Jerry	1957; 1960-61
Garner	Randy	1974-1976
Garner	Ronnie	1962; 1965-67
Garner	Terreal	1961-1962
Garner	Unknown	1937-1938
Garner	Wayne	1961-1963
Garrett	Gary	1954
Gaskin	Stan	1971
Gaskin	Steve	1969
Gibson	Byron	1989-1991
Gill	Unknown	1940
Glass	Unknown	1940
Glisson	Kenny	1962
Gordon	Evan	1999
Gordon	Preston	1935-1938
Gordy	Kyle	1985-1988
Gore	Johnny	1969
Grace	Jerry	1957-1958
Graham	Patrick	1978
Gray	Kenny	1973-1975
Gray	Tommy	1960
Gray	Tony	1978; 1980
Grayson	Chad	1992-1994
Green	Amie	1956-1959
Green	Amie	1985-1988
Green	Donald	1981-1983
Green	Greg	1978-1980
Green	Johnny	1955-1957
Green	Keith	1981-1983
Green	Michael	1982-1984
Green	Ronnie	1957
Green	Terry	1973-1974
Green	Tim	1977-1978
Green	Ty	1997; 1999
Greer	Billy	1961
Gregory	Johnny	1974-1976
Griffith	Bill	1974-1976
Griffith	James	1969
Griffith	John	1963
Griffith	Julius	1995-1997
Griffith	Justin	1995-1997
Griffith	Milton	1957-1960
Griffith	Slovakia	1997-1999
Grubbs	Darrel	1977
Grubbs	Emmit	1999-2000
Grubbs	Grafton	1950-1953
Grubbs	Greg	1980
Grubbs	Herbert	1950
Grubbs	James	1995-1997
Grubbs	Johnny	1961-1963
Grubbs	Junior	1942
Grubbs	Keith	1972
Grubbs	Mark	1977-1978
Grubbs	Mike	1977
Grubbs	Wayne	1982-1983
Hall	Brelon	1954
Hall	Bruce	1969
Hall	Buddie	1974
Hall	Greg	1966
Hall	Jerry	1956-1958
Hall	Jerry	1960-1961
Hall	Jimmy	1980
Hall	Keith	1982-1984
Hall	Lee	1970-1971
Hall	Robert	1954
Hall	Thomas	1942
Ham	David	1979
Hamilton	Bobby	1973-1975
Hamm	Robert	1951-1952
Hampton	Rodney	1980-1981
Hancock	Gerry	1979-1980
Hankins	Johnathan	2000
Hankins	Johnny	1974-1976
Hankins	Junior	1954-1955
Hansbrough	Bobby	1971-1972
Hansbrough	Freddy	1973-1975
Harris	DeWayne	1969
Harris	Jimmy	1969
Hart	Lee	1974

Hart	Ted	1971-1974
Harvey	Eldwyn	1990-1992
Harvey	Wayne	1962
Hayes	Andre	1993-1995
Hayes	Brian	1998-2000
Hayes	Curtis	1989-1991
Hayes	Dewon	1990
Hayes	Marcus	1988-1989
Hayes	Michael	1984
Hemby	Joey	1978
Henry	John	1942
Heriard	David	1974-1976
Heriard	Tony	1971
Herrington	Bernie	1969-1970
Herrington	Bobby	1948-1950
Herrington	Cecil	1943-1947
Herrington	David	1974-1975
Herrington	Frank	1966-1968
Herrington	Gary	1971-1973
Herrington	Harold	1951
Herrington	Jackie	1951-1953
Herrington	Jerry	1957
Herrington	Kelly	1943-1947
Herrington	Kelly	1963-1965
Herrington	Kenny	1966-1967
Herrington	Lowery	1955-1957
Herrington	Mike	1973-1975
Herrington	Olis	1937-1939
Herrington	Pat	1975-1977
Herrington	Ronnie	1968-1969
Herrington	Ted	1954-1957
Herrington	Unknown	1940
Hester	Belton	1938-1939
Hester	Lamar	1941-42; 1945
Hester	Unknown	1940
Hicks	Robert	1983-1984
Higdon	Chris	1990-1991
Hill	Fred	1998
Hinton	Phil	1969
Hobbs	Willie	1977-1978
Hobbs	Willis	1998-2000
Holbrook	Charles	1957-1958
Holbrook	Chip	1983-1985
Holbrook	Manley	1955-1957
Holbrook	Rob	1985-1987
Holder	Willis	1936-1937
Holloway	A.J.	1999-2000
Holloway	George	1986
Holloway	Jameryl	1985; 1987
Holloway	Monte	1992
Holloway	Scottye	1977-1978
Holloway	Sheppard	1971
Holloway	Terry	1982-1984
Holloway	Tyrone	1993-1994
Holmes	Earl	1940-1942

Holmes	Lowell	1935-1936
Holt	Lance	1992
Hopkins	David	1970-1972
Horn	Carroll	195-1959
Horn	Edgar	1936
Horn	L.G.	1936
Horn	Paul	1946-1948
Horn	Unknown	1933-1935
Horton	Joey	1964-1965
Hosey	Byron	1975-1977
Hosey	Dane	1989-1991
Hosey	John	1981-1983
Howell	Jerry	1978
Hubbard	Billy	1983-1985
Hubbard	Bruisha	1996-1998
Hubbard	David	1993-1995
Hubbard	Dennis	1978
Hubbard	Gene	1951
Hubbard	Jerry	1986
Hubbard	Michael	1983
Hubbard	Montario	1971
Hubbard	Reginald	1975-1977
Hudson	Richard	1979-1980
Hudson	Unknown	1934-1935
Hughes	Chad	1982
Hughes	Joey	1969-1972
Hughes	Mickey	1961-1963
Hughes	Paul	1937-1939
Hughes	Paul	1963-1965
Hughes	Travis	1942-1943
Hull	Brian	2000
Hull	Louis	1998-2000
Hunter	Unknown	1940
Ingram	Jamie	1997-1998
Irvin	Unknown	1930
Jackson	Keith	1974-1976
Jackson	Kevin	1987-1989
Jackson	Tony	1989-1991
Jaynes	Eric	19851986
Jaynes	Erndaryl	1980-1983
Johnson	Buddy	1964
Johnson	Charles	1992-1994
Johnson	Chris	1989-1991
Johnson	James	1995
Johnson	Kevin	1989
Johnson	Maurice	1991-1992
Johnson	Sam	1937-1938
Johnson	Tomone	1994-1996
Johnson	Unknown	1945
Jones	Austin "Tubby"	1928-1930
Jones	Cedrick	1998
Jones	Demetrius	1992
Jones	Doug	1961-1962
Jones	Jeff	1986
Jones	Jimmy	1993-1995

Jones	John D.	1953-1956
Jones	Julio	1978
Jones	Mack	1984
Jones	Paul	1937
Jones	W.C.	1940
Jordan	Stanley	1975-1977
Keeler	John	1969
Kees	"Dedie"	1930
Kees	Clarence (C.J.)	1928-1932
Kees	Robert	1930-1933
Kees	Wiley	1928
Keith	Mike	1974-1976
Keith	Ricky	1982
Kelly	Johnny	1979-1981
Kelly	Mike	1985-1986
Kemp	Bobby	1986
Kemp	David	1990-1991
Kemp	Willie	1983-1985
Kennedy	Billy	1946-1948
Kennedy	Brian	1989-1992
Kennedy	David	1956-1959
Kennedy	Fred	1932-1934
Kennedy	James	1954
Kennedy	James	1981
Kennedy	Jimmie	1962
Kennedy	Nuel Gene	1954-1955
Kennedy	Paul	1951
Kennedy	Steve	1965-1967
Kennedy	Unknown	1929
Kennedy	W.D.	1946-1947
Kennedy	Waylon	1988
Keys	George	1998
Keys	Jerry	1982-1984
Kidd	Derrick	1982
King	Deondra	1999-2000
King	Douglas	1987
King	Dwayne	1983-1985
King	James	1995-1996
King	Jerry	1984-85; 1987
King	Kelvin	1983
King	Terrance	1994-1996
Kinslow	Raynold	1996-1997
Knauss	Tommy	1956
Lack	Allen	1970
Ladner	Wendell	1941
Landrum	Robert	1962-1964
Lane	Evan	1944-1945
Lane	Rick	1966-1968
Lang	Homer	1957; 1960
Lang	Robert	1957-1959
Langston	Bruce	1978
Langston	Chris	1995-1997
Langston	Kelvin	1978-1979
Langston	Kenneth	1979-1980
Langston	Wallace	1980; 1982
Layton	Chris	1990-1992
Layton	Glen	1944-1945
Layton	Maurice	1946-1947
Layton	Ronnie	1963
Lee	Edgar	1993
Lee	Edison	1995-1997
Lee	Fredrick	1971-1974
Lee	John	1986-1988
Leggett	Lonnie	1992
Lewis	Kevin	1988
Lewis	Lynn	1969
Little	Charles	1962
Little	Danny	1970; 1972
Little	Edward	1988-1989
Little	James	1953-1954
Little	Jerry	1973
Little	Jerry	1979
Little	Thomas	1988-1989
Little	Unknown	1926
Lockett	Joe Willie	1986
Lockett	John	1986; 1988
Lockett	Willie	1985
Lockhart	Edward	1981-1983
Lockhart	Michael	1979
Lofton	Bernard	1975-1977
Lofton	Billy	1973-1975
Lofton	Billy	2000
Lofton	Jimmy	1974
Lofton	Mitch	1948-1951
Lofton	Shawn	1989
Logan	Juan	1986; 1988
Logan	Steven	1985
Logan	Terrance	1995-1997
Lomax	Darrell	1986-1988
Long	Joe	1953
Longino	Santonio	1997
Luckey	Terral	1980-1982
Luke	Dwayne	1981-1983
Lytle	Matt	1949
Maddox	Allen	1974-1976
Maddox	Charles Ray	1949
Maddox	Doyle	1962-1964
Maddox	Gene	1955-1956
Maddox	John	1949
Maddox	John Cullen	1956-1960
Maddox	Keith	1978
Maddox	Larry	1969-1971
Maddox	Mike	1971-1973
Maddox	Preston	1973-1975
Maddox	Ricky	1975-1977
Maddox	Roger	1974-1976
Maddox	Unknown	1940
Maddox	Unknown	1947
Magee	Billy	1946
Magee	Byron	1995-1997

Magee	Carl	1968
Magee	Charlie	1985-1986
Magee	Dick	1957
Magee	Donald	1970-1972
Magee	Harvey	1977-1979
Magee	Hugh	1969
Magee	James Robert	1957-1959
Magee	Maurice	1991
Magee	Michael	1996-1998
Magee	Robert	1927-1928
Magee	Shane	1990-1991
Magee	Wayne	1982-1984
Magee	Willie	1990-1991
Malloy	Dewayne	1981
Malloy	Donnie	1983-1985
Malloy	Dwayne	1980; 1982
Malloy	Kevin	1987
Mangum	Alan	1986
Mangum	Bobby	1942-43; 1945
Mangum	C.	1945
Mangum	James	1993-1995
Mangum	Jerry	1954-1957
Mangum	Jim	1948
Mangum	Jimmy	1951
Mangum	Jimmy	1972-1974
Mangum	Joe	1953-1957
Mangum	John	1955-1960
Mangum	John	1983-1985
Mangum	Kris	1989-1991
Mangum	Leo	1935-1936
Mangum	Mayo	1946-1948
Mangum	Mitch	1998-1999
Mangum	Steve	1963-1965
Mangum	Ted	1960-1962
Mangum	Unknown	1931
Mangum	Unknown	1947
Mangum	W.R.	1938-1940
Mangum	Willie	1954
Manning	Tommy	1981-1982
Marbury	Curtis	1979-1980
Marbury	Mark	1977-1979
Martin	Mike	1969-1971
Martin	W.T.	1943
Mason	Newton	1957
Matte	Nathan	1994
May	Buster	1943-1947
May	David	1963-1964
May	Dennon	1955-1958
May	Durwood	1942
May	Eugene	1973-1974
May	Gary	1973-1974
May	Henry	1941-1942
May	James	1982-1984
May	James	1998-2000
May	Robert	1955-1960
May	Russ	1984; 1986
May	Travis	1988-1989
May	Unknown	1932-1933
May	Will	1990-1991
May	Willis	1961
McAlpin	Art	1980
McAlpin	B.J.	1984-1986
McAlpin	Boyd	1951-1952
McAlpin	Daniel	1955-1959
McAlpin	Earnest	1962-1964
McAlpin	Jack	1961-1963
McAlpin	Jake	1941
McAlpin	Jeff	1946-1948
McAlpin	Jim	1964-1966
McAlpin	John	1949-1951
McAlpin	L.J.	1940; 1942
McAlpin	Mike	1974-1976
McAlpin	Tate	1997-1999
McAlpin	Tom	1940
McAlpin	Tom	1963-1965
McAlpin	Tom	1990-1992
McAlpin	Tyler	1993-1995
McAlpin	Unknown	1939
McCallum	Hugh	1981-1983
McCallum	Paul	1961-1963
McCallum	Steve	1978-1979
McCallum	Walter	1957; 1960
McCallum	Walter	1978-1980
McCarty	Johnny	1961-1963
McCarty	Ronnie	1961-1963
McCollum	Alfred	1978-1980
McCollum	Louis	1980; 1982
McCollum	Marcus	2000
McCollum	Steve	1980
McCollum	Willie	1975-1977
McDonald	Havard	1980-1982
McDonald	Jeff	1979-1981
McDonald	Kedric	1996-1998
McDonald	Larry	1974-1976
McDonald	Lee	1988
McFarland	Unknown	1935
McGlaston	Stanley	1979
McGuire	Jerry	1990-1992
McInnis	Scott	1961
McIntyre	Jamie	2000
McKee	Randy	1935-1936
McKenzie	Butch	1967-1969
McKinley	Allen	1991
McLaurin	Arthur	1996
McLaurin	Kendrick	1999-2000
McLean	David	1988-1999
McMillan	Terry	1960-1963
McMillan	Tony	1965; 1967
McNair	Bill	1930-1932
McNair	Chris	1986

McNair	Hudson	1942
McNair	Jerry	1970-1971
McNair	Joe	1943-1947
McNair	Ronnie	1964
McNair	Unknown	1926
McRaney	Unknown	1930
McVey	Buster	1966
McWilliams	Dwight	1971-1973
McWilliams	Marty	1987-1989
McWilliams	Mike	1986
McWilliams	Terry	1977-1979
Meador	Joe	1962
Meador	Tommy	1966-1968
Meadors	Jerry	1983
Meadows	Charles	1955-1960
Meadows	Gene	1955
Meadows	Joe	1961
Meadows	Michael	1998-1999
Meadows	Randy	1985-86; 1988
Medina	Thomas	1998
Medlock	Billy	1961
Medlock	Gary	1965
Medlock	Mickey	1960
Melton	Joe	1996
Millis	Shea	1997-1999
Milton	Jarius	1992-1994
Milton	Lavell	1997
Mitchell	John Mac	1954-1955
Mitchell	Larry	1950-1953
Mize	Charles	1948-1950
Mize	John H.	1950
Monk	Chris	1985-1988
Monk	Ladd	1985
Morris	Charles Ray	1955
Mowdy	Thomas	1995-1996
Munn	James	1954-1955
Munn	Marion	1954
Myers	"Lazy"	1930
Myers	Bob	1947-1949
Myers	Bobby	1957; 1960
Myers	Clifton	1926-1927
Myers	Durwood	1937-1938
Myers	Jerry	1955-1958
Myers	Marcus	1994-1996
Myers	Truett	1942
Myers	Unknown	1935
Neely	Buford	1933-1934
Neely	Unknown	1929-1932
Neely	Wyck	1964-1966
Nelson	Ed	1979-1980
Nelson	Leon	1996-1998
Nelson	Roderick	1998-2000
Newsom	Billy Ray	1991-1992
Nichols	Gary	1967; 1969
Nichols	Herschell	1948
Nichols	Paul	1995
Nix	Nary	1950
Norris	Wesley	1992-1994
Nowell	Jimbo	1981-1983
Odom	Buck	1943-1947
Osby	Mike	1990-1991
Overby	E.J.	1971
Overby	Paul	1998-2000
Overby	Virgil	1971-1973
Owens	Edward	1997
Owens	Lamond	1990
Pace	Hugh	1997-1998
Pace	Randy	1988-1989
Padgett	Delmos	1947
Padgett	Ural	1951
Parham	Randy	1971
Parham	Scotty	1973-1974
Parham	Steve	1971-1972
Parish	James	1971-1973
Parker	G.O.	1935-1938
Parker	Gary	1964-1966
Parker	Rufus	1936
Patrick	Fernando	1995-1996
Patrick	Fred	1993-1995
Patrick	Pete	1970
Patterson	Brad	1992
Patterson	David	1983-1985
Patterson	Mark	1989; 1991
Patterson	Wardell	1997
Payne	Corey	1997-1999
Payne	Gerald	1994-1996
Pearson	Edwin	1957-1959
Peden	David	1977-1978
Pellegrin	Sean	1986
Pendergrass	Orell	1942-1943
Phillips	Sammy	1984-1986
Pittman	James	1997-1999
Pittman	Jeremy	1995-1996
Pittman	Michael	1983-1985
Polk	James	1928
Pope	Charles Ray	1949-1953
Pope	James	1946-1948
Price	Bennie	1951-1953
Prince	Billy	1948-1949
Prince	Charlie	1962
Prince	Randy	1961
Pruitt	Vernon	1966
Puckett	D.C.	1943
Puckett	Elden	1952
Puckett	Norman	1926-1928
Puckett	Ralph "Ferd"	1928-1929
Puckett	Toxey	1943
Purvis	Gerard	2000
Purvis	Glendale	1946-1949
Puys	Unknown	1929

Quick	Danny	1978-1980	Runnels	Terry	1961-1962
Quick	Randy	1980	Rushing	Greg	1974
Rainer	Jerry	1974	Russell	Brian	1978-1980
Rainey	Unknown	1937-1940	Russell	Danny	1973-1974
Rankin	Delvin	1985-1988	Russell	Darrell	1986
Rankin	Jason	1989; 1991	Russell	Don	1971-1972
Rankin	Jason	1996-1998	Russell	Harold	1984-1987
Rankin	Jimmy	1955	Russell	Jake	1969-1971
Rankin	Lavoyd	1947-1950	Russell	Ken	1991
Rankin	Michael	1994	Russell	Mark	1974-1975
Rankin	Scott	1978-1980	Russell	Pete	1944-1947
Rankin	Steve	1971-1973	Russell	Scott	1982
Rankin	Terry	1972-1974	Salters	Glenn	1955
Ready	Ronnie	1975	Sanders	Joe	1943-1945
Reed	Clifton	1957-1960	Sanders	Josh	1991-1993
Reed	George	1954	Sanders	Kenny	1977
Reed	Ray	1957-1959	Sanders	Unknown	1933
Reed	Ray	1960-1962	Sanford	Marty	1971
Reed	Steve	1975	Sartin	Bennett	1974
Reeves	Scott	1988	Saucier	Al	1955
Rhodes	Unknown	1935	Schaub	David	1982
Rice	Daniel	1985-1988	Schaub	Stephen	1978
Ricks	Tim	2000	Scoggins	Sammy	1966
Rigsby	Roy	1988-1990	Sharble	Napoleon	1985-1988
Roberts	Billy	1961-1963	Sharpe	Billy	1957
Roberts	Bob	1970-1972	Shaw	Eddie	1991-1993
Roberts	Chris	1981	Shaw	Harold	1991-1993
Roberts	Daryll	1975	Shelby	Bertelle	1989
Roberts	James	1966	Shivers	Bill	1996-1998
Roberts	Kelly	1960-1963	Shivers	Unknown	1940
Roberts	Larry	1955-1956	Shoemaker	Bobby	1977-1978
Roberts	Larry	1959-1961	Shoemaker	Gordon	1948-1951
Roberts	Ray	1944-1947	Shoemaker	Hollis	1954-1955
Roberts	Stewart	1969	Shows	Jared	1995
Robertson	Billy	1969-1971	Simmons	Johnny	1956-1957
Robertson	Jason	1996-1997	Sims	Deshaun	1990-1992
Robinson	Brian	1999-2000	Smith	Billy	1943-1947
Robinson	C.	1940	Smith	Billy	1954-1955
Robinson	George	1955-1959	Smith	Bruce	1968-1970
Robinson	Hugh	1959	Smith	Casey	1996
Robinson	J.L.	1973-1974	Smith	Danny	1984-1985
Robinson	Kenneth	1939	Smith	Donald	1979-1981
Robinson	Kenny	1961	Smith	Douglas	1971
Robinson	Leon	1939	Smith	Eric	1995-1997
Robinson	Owen	1928-1931	Smith	Fordie	1964
Robinson	Red	1940	Smith	Frank	1980-1982
Robinson	Teddy	2000	Smith	Freddie	1969
Robinson	Tracy	1980-1982	Smith	Glenn	1972
Rogers	Fred	1981-1983	Smith	Greg	1989-1991
Rogers	Henry	1977	Smith	Henry	1965
Ross	Marcus	1989	Smith	Hiram	1951
Roster	Royce	1966	Smith	J. Mike	1969-1970
Runnells	A.J.	1955	Smith	J.C.	1977-1978
Runnells	L.J.	1953-1955	Smith	James	1962
Runnels	Junior	1944-45; 1948	Smith	Jimmy	1950-1951

Smith	Joe Harold	1975-1977
Smith	Joey	2000
Smith	Kindle	1975
Smith	Kirby	1981-1982
Smith	Lowery	1956
Smith	Mark	1980; 1982
Smith	Melvin	1973-1975
Smith	Mike S.	1968-1971
Smith	Pat	1960-1963
Smith	Randy	1977
Smith	Ronald	1981
Smith	Ronnie	1954
Smith	Shelton	1971
Smith	Steve	1978-1980
Smith	Tommy	1991-1993
Smith	Tony	1987-1989
Smith	Truvillion	1988-1990
Smith	Unknown	1929
Sobczek	Dennis	1992-1993
Sodon	Unknown	1932; 1938
Spencer	John	1953-1954
St. Amant	Ronnie	1980-1981
Stapleton	Freddie	1986
Stapleton	Tyrone	1980-1981
Steele	Bruce	1968-1970
Steele	Lynn	1967-1969
Stephens	Billy Henry	1954-1956
Stephens	James	1946-1947
Stephens	Joe	1973-1975
Stephens	Oscar	1955-1956
Stewart	Harrell	1965-1967
Stewart	Lannie	1966-1968
Stewart	Mike	1969-1971
Strickland	Ricky	1971-1973
Stringer	Nathan	1949-1951
Stringer	Travis	1996-1998
Stringer	Unknown	1933; 1938
Stroud	Unknown	1926-1927
Stuard	Hilton	1942
Stuard	Jimmy	1969-1971
Stubbs	Barry	1980
Stubbs	Billy Earl	1940-1945
Stubbs	Frank	1954-1956
Stubbs	Hugh Jack	1956-1959
Stubbs	Jackie	1953-1956
Stubbs	John Henry	1941
Stubbs	Larry	1982
Stubbs	Lazar	1983; 1985
Stubbs	Lincoln	1933-1935
Stubbs	Mack	1954
Stubbs	Michael	1998-2000
Stubbs	Odell	1941-1943
Stubbs	Ricky	1982
Stubbs	Robert Lee	1940-1941
Stubbs	Sparkey	1951
Stubbs	Terrell	1966
Stubbs	Unknown	1930-1932
Stubbs	Unknown	1939
Sturm	Jerry	1966-1968
Styron	Al	1973-1975
Styron	Gary	1967
Styron	Jonathan	1967-1969
Styron	Jonathan	1996-1998
Sullivan	Brooks	1977-1999
Sullivan	Geoffrey	1977-1979
Sullivan	James	1962
Sullivan	Jerry	1951-1954
Sullivan	Jimmy	1964-1966
Sullivan	Jimmy Charles	1948-1949
Sullivan	John	1970
Sullivan	Mike	1965; 1968-70
Sullivan	Richard	1980-1982
Sullivan	Seth	1997-1998
Swain	Corey	1992-1993
Switzer	Curtis	1954-1957
Talbert	Larry	1961
Talley	Quincy	1985-1987
Tatum	Michael	1984
Tatum	Morice	1992-1994
Tatum	Thomas	1985-1986
Tatum	Tony	1987-1988
Taylor	Alton "Tang"	1928-1930
Taylor	Billy	1962
Taylor	Bobby	1951-1952
Taylor	Joel	1999
Taylor	Mike	1965-1967
Tedford	David	1962-1964
Terry	Unknown	1934-1935
Thames	Bobby	1928-1932
Thames	Charles	1970-1971
Thames	Charlie	1954
Thames	Jerry	1966; 1968
Thames	Timmy	1978
Thomas	Fred	1993-1995
Thompson	Danny	1973-1975
Thompson	Jory	1969-1971
Thornton	Calvin	1997
Thornton	Ellis	1970
Thornton	Malcolm	1935-1936
Thornton	Unknown	1933
Thurman	Emanuel	1997-1999
Thurman	Eric	1996
Thurman	Samuel	1997-1999
Tindall	Clem	1943
Tindall	Geo Taylor	1942-1944
Tindall	Jack	1930-1932
Tindall	Jimmy	1954-1955
Tolbert	Larry	1962-1963
Tracy	Barry	1975
Traxler	Etoya	1993-1995

Traxler	Novack	1997-1998
Tuggle	Jimmy	1946-1950
Tuggle	Robert	1999-2000
Tuggle	Thomas	1957
Tuggle	Tommy	1960-1961
Tullos	Dan	1951-1956
Tullos	Daryll	1978
Tullos	G.C.	1942-1943
Tullos	G.J.	1949-1951
Tullos	Jerome	1948
Tullos	Lavelle	1943-1944
Tullos	Robert May	1926-1929
Tullos	Tommy	1986
Tullos	Vernon	1944-1947
Turner	Aundrial	1994-1996
Turner	Charles	1953-1954
Turner	Dana	1990-1992
Turner	Garfield	1977-1979
Turner	Kirby	1977-1978
Turner	Myron	1982
Tutor	Terry	1972-1973
Varner	James E.	1950-1951
Varner	Mike	1969-1971
Varnes	Boyce	2000
Varnes	Jonathan	1998-2000
Vining	Blake	1996
Vinson	James	1936
Vinson	Unknown	1932
Wade	Frank	1973-1975
Wade	Zack	2000
Waldrop	Kelsie	1964
Waldrop	Unknown	1926
Walker	Brent	1997
Walker	Cecil	1954-1955
Walker	Chad	1991-1992
Walker	Clifton	1980-1982
Walker	Clint	1984
Walker	E.	1938
Walker	Emmanual	1993
Walker	Ernie	1960
Walker	Everett	1933
Walker	Mark	1990-1991
Walker	Otto	1946-1949
Walker	Paul	1962
Walker	Rayvon	1954
Walker	Roger	1970-1971
Walker	Tommy	1960-1961
Walker	Unknown	1939
Wallace	Budgie	1955-1957
Wallace	Chris	1989-1990
Wallace	Scott	1985-1986
Wallace	Wayne	1954
Walters	Buddy	1942-44; 1946-47
Walters	Earl	1926-1929
Walters	Mike	1966-1968

Walters	Ray	1956-1959
Ward	Maurice	1938-1940
Ware	Charlie	1932-1935
Ware	David	1969
Ware	George	1945-1947
Ware	Jackie	1951
Ware	James	1965
Ware	Jimmy	1949-1953
Ware	Paul	1971-1973
Warren	David	1991
Warren	Donal	1997
Warren	Jason	1997-1999
Warren	Joe	1977
Warren	Joe David	1983
Warren	Joey	1997; 1999
Warren	Josh	1998-2000
Warren	Michael	1986-1987
Warren	Neal	1990-1992
Warren	Thomas	1973-1974
Warren	Timmy	1994-1995
Washington	Kenny	1992-1994
Waters	Brandon	1999
Watkins	Unknown	1926
Weathersby	David	1977
Weathersby	Jason	1996-1998
Weathersby	Mark	1984-1986
Weathersby	Scott	1985; 1988
Weathersby	Tomario	1998; 2000
Welch	Bill	1979-1981
Welch	Bob	1981; 1983
Welch	Danny	1970-1971
Welch	Dick	1950-1951
Welch	Donny	1990-1992
Welch	Royce	1955-1958
Wells	Jimmy	1957; 1960
Wells	Johnny	1960-1963
West	Chris	1990-1991
West	John	1972
West	Joseph	1973-1975
West	Lee	1958-1961
West	Steve	1971
Westmoreland	Mickey	1957
Whatley	James	1955-1957
Wheat	Billy	1969-1971
White	Daniel	1943
White	Jamie	1991-1992
White	Jim Henry	1947-1951
White	W.D.	1943
Williams	Brent	1989
Williams	David	1991-1993
Williams	James	1979-1980
Williams	Jerry Todd	1979
Williams	Jhointea	1996
Williams	Justin	2000
Williams	Kelvin	1978-1980

Williams	Nick	1998-2000
Williams	Ronnie	1978-1979
Williams	Tremayne	1991-1993
Williams	Willie	1982-1984
Williamson	David	1973-1975
Williamson	Eugene	1986-1988
Williamson	Jeremy	1997-1998
Williamson	Jerome	1978-1979
Williamson	Phillip	1985-1986
Williamson	Ralph	1981
Williamson	Steve	1985-1986
Williamson	Tim	1981-1982
Willis	John	1988-1990
Willis	Steven	1991-1993
Winborne	Gilbert	1953-1955
Winborne	Harold	1947-1948
Windham	James	1966-1968
Windham	Leo	1954-1957
Winn	Charles	1974-1975
Winn	Jerry	1971-1972
Winn	LaCarlos	1997-1999
Winstead	Buddy	1943-1944
Winstead	Otho	1931-1933
Winters	Dennis	1966
Womack	Billy	1960-1962
Womack	Calvin	1984-1985
Womack	Donald	1960-1962
Womack	Dwayne	1985-1988
Womack	Fred	1959-1961
Womack	Freddie	1957
Womack	Henry	1957
Womack	James	1982-1983
Womack	Jim	1948-1949
Womack	Johnny	1954
Womack	Ritchie	1988
Womack	Spencer	1994
Womack	Unknown	1938-1940
Womack	Walter	1974-1975
Wright	Jeff	1982
Wright	Tim	1983-1984
Wyatt	Gail	1985
Wyatt	Jay	1988-1989
Yates	Dwayne	1966-1968
Yates	Glen	1963-1965
Yates	James	1964
Yates	Jason	1989-1991
Yates	Junior	1960-1961
Yates	Kenneth	1954
Yates	Robert	1946-1948
Yates	Ronnie	1972-1974
Yelverton	C.A.	1949
Yelverton	James	1955
Yelverton	Jewel	1928-1929
Yelverton	Kenneth	1956-1957
Yelverton	Unknown	1932